Teacher Companion

MyMaths
for Key Stage 3

3B

Powered by **MyMaths**.co.uk

OXFORD
UNIVERSITY PRESS

OXFORD
UNIVERSITY PRESS

Great Clarendon Street, Oxford, OX2 6DP, United Kingdom

Oxford University Press is a department of the University of Oxford.
It furthers the University's objective of excellence in research, scholarship,
and education by publishing worldwide. Oxford is a registered trade mark of
Oxford University Press in the UK and in certain other countries.

© Oxford University Press 2014

The moral rights of the author have been asserted

First published in 2014

All rights reserved. No part of this publication may be reproduced,
stored in a retrieval system, or transmitted, in any form or by any means,
without the prior permission in writing of Oxford University Press,
or as expressly permitted by law, or under terms agreed with the appropriate
reprographics rights organization. Enquiries concerning reproduction
outside the scope of the above should be sent to the Rights Department,
Oxford University Press, at the address above.

You must not circulate this book in any other binding or cover
and you must impose this same condition on any acquirer

British Library Cataloguing in Publication Data
Data available

978-0-19-830469-2

10 9 8 7 6 5 4 3 2 1

Paper used in the production of this book is a natural, recyclable product made
from wood grown in sustainable forests. The manufacturing process conforms
to the environmental regulations of the country of origin.

Printed in Great Britain by Bell and Bain Ltd., Glasgow

Acknowledgements

The editors would like to thank Gwen Wood, Katie Wood and Ian Bettison
for their excellent work on this book.

Contents

Number

1 Whole numbers and decimals
- Introduction 2
- 1a Powers of 10 4
- 1b Rounding 6
- 1c Factors, multiples and primes 8
- 1d Estimating and approximating ... 10
- MySummary/MyReview 12
- MyPractice 14

Geometry

2 Measures, perimeter and area
- Introduction 16
- 2a Measures 1 18
- 2b Measures 2 20
- 2c Area of a 2D shape 22
- 2d Circumference of a circle 24
- 2e Area of a circle 26
- 2f Compound measures 28
- MySummary/MyReview 30
- MyPractice 32

Algebra

3 Expressions and formulae
- Introduction 34
- 3a Factors in algebra 36
- 3b Algebraic fractions 38
- 3c Formulae in context 40
- 3d Rearranging formulae 42
- 3e Deriving and graphing formulae ... 44
- MySummary/MyReview 46
- MyPractice 48

- **CS1** Why do bikes have gears? 50

Number

4 Fractions, decimals and percentages
- Introduction 52
- 4a Adding and subtracting fractions ... 54
- 4b Multiplying fractions 56
- 4c Dividing by fractions 58
- 4d Decimals and fractions 60
- 4e Percentage change 62
- 4f Percentage problems 64
- 4g Financial maths 1: Repeated percentage change ... 66
- MySummary/MyReview 68
- MyPractice 70

- MyAssessment 1 72

Geometry

5 Angles
- Introduction 74
- 5a Angle properties of a triangle 76
- 5b Angle properties of a quadrilateral ... 78
- 5c Angle properties of a polygon 1 ... 80
- 5d Angle properties of a polygon 2 ... 82
- 5e Congruent shapes 84
- MySummary/MyReview 86
- MyPractice 88

Algebra

6 Graphs
- Introduction 90
- 6a Tables of values 92
- 6b Drawing straight-line graphs 94
- 6c Gradient of a straight-line graph ... 96
- 6d y-intercept of a straight-line graph ... 98
- 6e The equation $y = mx + c$ 100
- 6f Equations given implicitly 102
- 6g Real-life graphs 104
- 6h Distance-time graphs 106
- 6i Time series 108
- MySummary/MyReview 110
- MyPractice 112

- **CS2** Jewellery business 114

Number

7 Decimal calculations
- Introduction 116
- 7a Adding and subtracting decimals ... 118
- 7b Multiplying decimals 120
- 7c Dividing decimals 122
- 7d Using a calculator 124
- 7e Interpreting the calculator display ... 126
- MySummary/MyReview 128
- MyPractice 130

Statistics

8 Statistics
- Introduction 132
- 8a Planning a project 134
- 8b Data collection 136
- 8c Frequency tables 138
- 8d Statistical diagrams 1 140
- 8e Statistical diagrams 2 142
- 8f Calculating averages 144
- 8g Interpreting graphs 146
- 8h Correlation 148
- 8i Averages from grouped data ... 150
- 8j Comparing distributions 152
- 8k Communicating the results of an enquiry 154
- MySummary/MyReview 156
- MyPractice 158

- MyAssessment 2 160

Geometry

9 Transformations and scale
- Introduction 162
- 9a Transformations 164
- 9b Enlargements 166
- 9c Combinations of transformations 168
- 9d Maps and scale drawings 170
- 9e Bearings 172
- MySummary/MyReview 174
- MyPractice 176

CS3 Climate change 178

Algebra

10 Equations
- Introduction 180
- 10a Solving equations 182
- 10b Equations with brackets 184
- 10c Unknowns on both sides 186
- 10d Constructing equations 188
- 10e Trial and improvement 190
- MySummary/MyReview 192
- MyPractice 194

Number

11 Powers and roots
- Introduction 196
- 11a Square roots and cube roots 198
- 11b Indices 200
- 11c Indices and surds 202
- 11d Standard form for large numbers 204
- 11e Standard form for small numbers 206
- MySummary/MyReview 208
- MyPractice 210

Geometry

12 Constructions and Pythagoras
- Introduction 212
- 12a Constructing a triangle 1 214
- 12b Constructing a triangle 2 216
- 12c Loci and constructions 218
- 12d Pythagoras' theorem 1 220
- 12e Pythagoras' theorem 2 222
- MySummary/MyReview 224
- MyPractice 226

CS4 Garden design 228

MyAssessment 3 230

Functional

17 Everyday maths
- Introduction 310
- 17a The AfriLinks project 312
- 17b Building the schoolhouse 314
- 17c Laying the path 316
- 17d The basketball court 318
- 17e The school garden 320

Algebra

13 Sequences
- Introduction 232
- 13a Sequences and terms 234
- 13b Position-to-term rules 236
- 13c The general term 238
- 13d Real-life sequences 240
- 13e Recursive sequences 242
- MySummary/MyReview 244
- MyPractice 246

Geometry

14 3D shapes
- Introduction 248
- 14a 3D shapes 250
- 14b Plans and elevations 252
- 14c Symmetry of a 3D shape 254
- 14d Surface area of a prism 256
- 14e Volume of a prism 258
- MySummary/MyReview 260
- MyPractice 262

CS5 The Golden Rectangle 264

Ratio

15 Ratio and proportion
- Introduction 266
- 15a Direct proportion 268
- 15b Comparing proportions 270
- 15c Ratio 272
- 15d Uses of ratio 274
- 15e Ratio and proportion problems 276
- 15f Proportional reasoning 278
- 15g Financial maths 2: Living on a budget 280
- MySummary/MyReview 282
- MyPractice 284

Statistics

16 Probability
- Introduction 286
- 16a Prediction and uncertainty 288
- 16b Mutually exclusive events 290
- 16c Calculating probabilities 292
- 16d The outcomes of two trials 294
- 16e Experimental probability 296
- 16f Comparing theoretical and experimental probabilities 298
- 16g Venn diagrams 300
- MySummary/MyReview 302
- MyPractice 304

CS6 Crime scene investigation 306

MyAssessment 4 308

Homework book answers .... on CD-ROM

Scheme of Work .... on CD-ROM

About this book

This Teacher Companion is part of the MyMaths for Key Stage 3 series which has been specially written for the new National Curriculum for Key Stage 3 Mathematics in England. It accompanies Student Book **3B** and is designed to help you have the greatest impact on the learning experience of middle ability students towards the end of their Key Stage 3 studies.

The author team collectively bring a wealth of classroom experience to the Teacher Companion making it easy for you to plan and deliver lessons with confidence.

The structure of this book closely follows the content of the student book so that it is easy to find the information and resources you need. These include for each

Lesson: objectives; a list of resources – including MyMaths 4-digit codes; a starter, teaching notes, plenary and alternative approach; simplification and extension ideas; an exercise commentary and full answers; the key ideas and checkpoint questions to test them; and a summary of the key literacy issues.

Chapter: National Curriculum objectives; any assumed prior knowledge; notes supporting the Student Book introduction and starter problem; the associated MyMaths and InvisiPen resources – including those offering extra support to weaker students; questions to test understanding; and how the material is developed and used.

The accompanying CD-ROM makes all the lesson plans available as Word files, so that you can customize them to suit your students' needs. Also on the CD are full sets of answers for Homework Book **3B**.

The integrated solution

This teacher guide is part of a set of resources designed to support you and your students with a fully integrated package of resources.

Online Testbank
A complete suite of assessment tests: Good to Go, formative (including feedback), auto-marked and print based.

MyMaths
Direct links to the ever popular site's lessons and auto-marked homeworks.

Online Student Book
Digital versions of the student books for home and classroom use.

Homework Book
Handy, pocket-sized books, tailored to the content of each student book lesson.

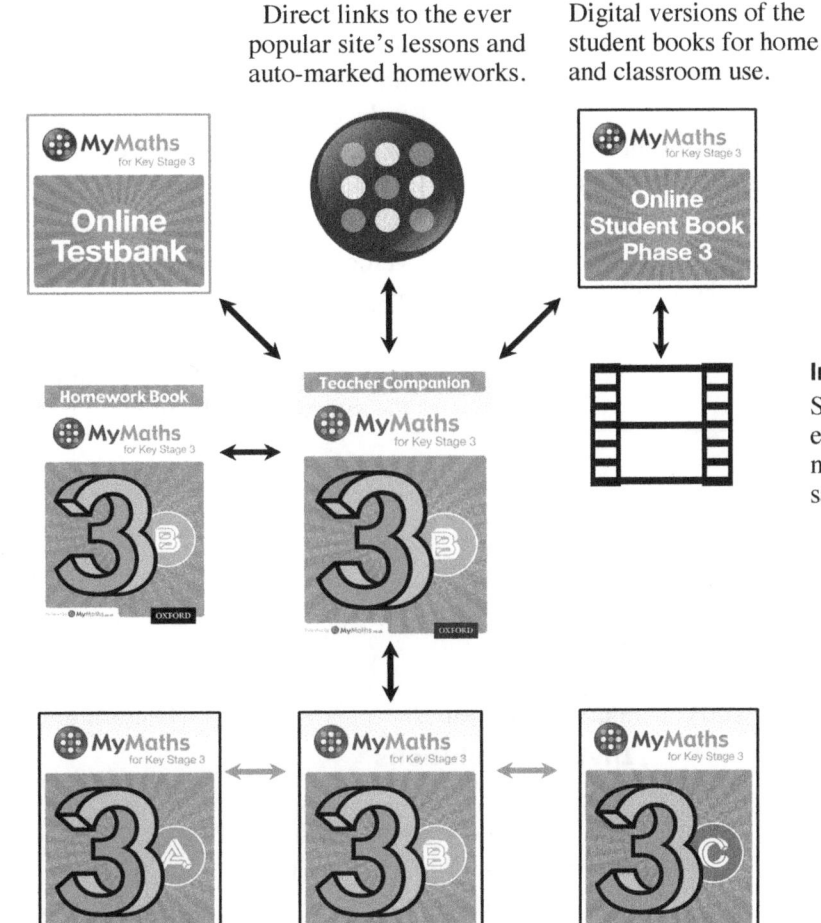

InvisiPen solutions
Student friendly videos explaining just what is needed to solve a sample problem.

Student Book
The three books in a phase are organized to cover topics in the same order but at three ability levels.

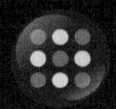

1 Whole numbers and decimals

Learning outcomes

N3 Use the concepts and vocabulary of prime numbers, factors (or divisors), multiples, common factors, common multiples, highest common factor, lowest common multiple, prime factorisation, including using product notation and the unique factorisation property (L6)

N13 Round numbers and measures to an appropriate degree of accuracy [for example, to a number of decimal places or significant figures] (L7)

N14 Use approximation through rounding to estimate answers and calculate possible resulting errors expressed using inequality notation a < x ≤ b (L7)

Introduction

The chapter starts by looking at multiplying and dividing by powers of ten and simplifying expressions involving powers of ten. The next section covers rounding to the nearest 10, 100, 100 or a number of decimal places. Factors, multiples and primes, including prime factorisation are covered in section three before the final section on estimating and approximating the answers to calculations.

The introduction discusses the need for accuracy in certain jobs. It discusses the accuracy required from navigators and engineers to successfully land the Mars Exploration Rover in the right place when the spacecraft had travelled such a long distance but also the need for accuracy in jobs such as doctors and nurses who administer drugs and other treatments. Getting the dosage of powerful drugs wrong, even by a few milligrams could have catastrophic effects on the health of the patient.

It is supposed that if the designers of the channel tunnel had been out by as much as half a millimetre in their plans, then the two halves of tunnel would have missed meeting up in the middle when they were dug from opposite sides of the English Channel!

Prior knowledge

Students should already know how to…
- Use basic rules of indices
- Order decimals
- Multiply and divide by powers of ten

Starter problem

The starter problem considers an equation for the trajectory of a missile. While the derivation of such a formula is way beyond the scope of Key Stage 3 mathematics and the formula involves unfamiliar functions such as sine and cosine, it can still provide a useful discussion as to the inter-relatedness of the variables.

Students should be able to determine that the *maximum* range of the missile for each velocity is achieved when launching at 45°. This should also enable them to quickly determine that if the particular launch speed has a larger maximum range than this, the range can be reduced to the required 100 metres by either increasing or decreasing the angle of launch.

For a fixed angle of launch, the range is proportional to the launch speed so therefore we can adjust the velocity of the missile to achieve the required range.

These sorts of ideas are used by the artillery divisions of the armed forces during combat and therefore they require skilled mathematicians and engineers to ensure the success of their operations.

Resources

MyMaths
Decimal places	1001	Significant figures	1005	Factors and primes	1032

Online assessment
InvisiPen solutions

Chapter test	3B–1	Rounding		112
Formative test	3B–1	Multiply and divide by powers of 10		114
Summative test	3B–1	Estimating and approximating		135
		Multiples and factors	171	HCF and LCM	172
		Primes and prime factors	173	Powers of 10	182

Topic scheme

Teaching time = 4 lessons/2 weeks

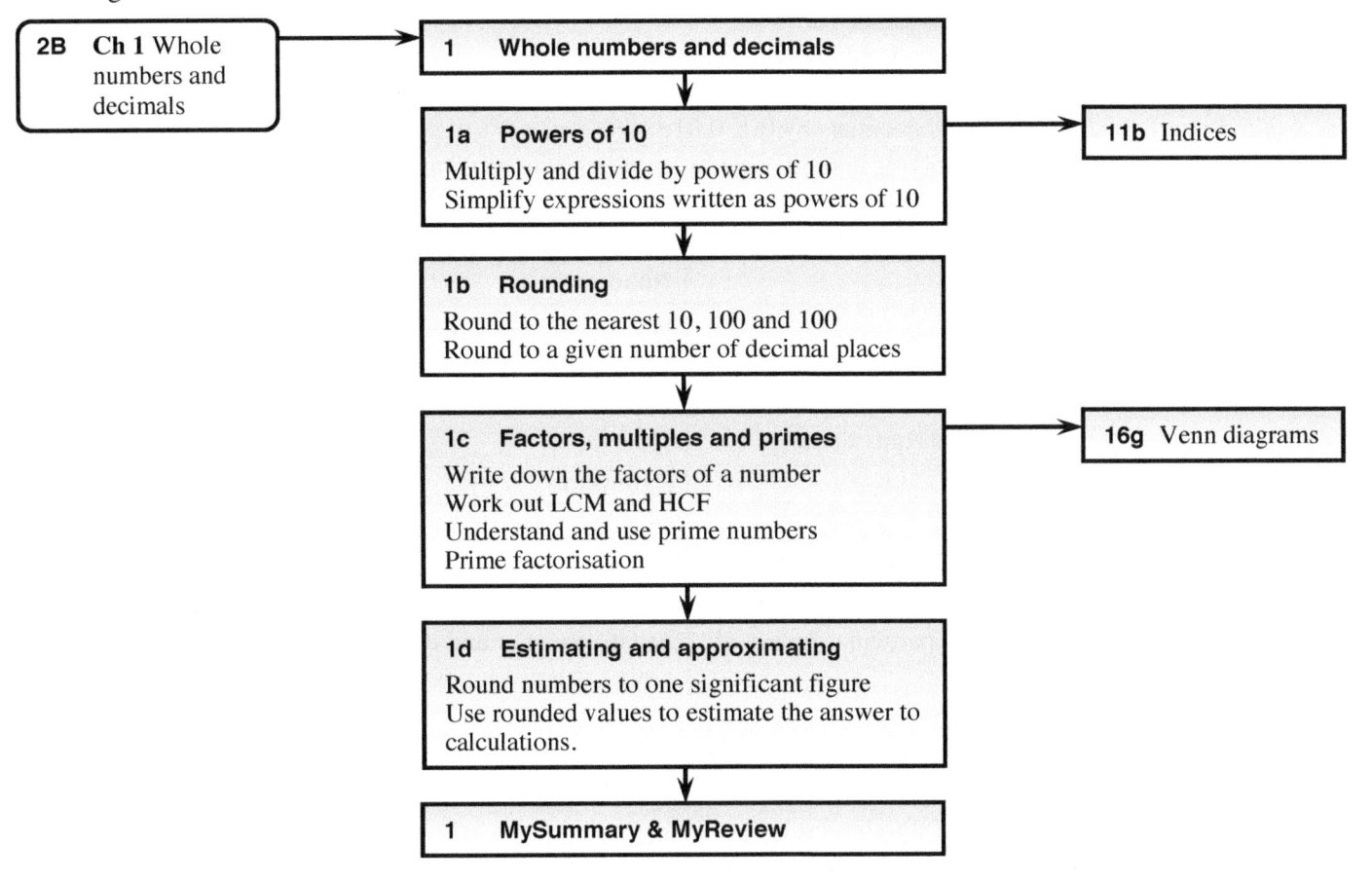

```
2B  Ch 1 Whole  ──►  1   Whole numbers and decimals
    numbers and
    decimals
                         │
                         ▼
                     1a  Powers of 10                              ──►  11b  Indices
                         Multiply and divide by powers of 10
                         Simplify expressions written as powers of 10
                         │
                         ▼
                     1b  Rounding
                         Round to the nearest 10, 100 and 100
                         Round to a given number of decimal places
                         │
                         ▼
                     1c  Factors, multiples and primes             ──►  16g  Venn diagrams
                         Write down the factors of a number
                         Work out LCM and HCF
                         Understand and use prime numbers
                         Prime factorisation
                         │
                         ▼
                     1d  Estimating and approximating
                         Round numbers to one significant figure
                         Use rounded values to estimate the answer to
                         calculations.
                         │
                         ▼
                     1   MySummary & MyReview
```

Differentiation

Student book 3A 2 – 19

Multiply and divide by powers of 10
Round integers and decimals to the nearest 1, 10, 100, 1000 and a given number of decimal places
Order of operations
Factors, multiples and primes including prime factors, HCF and LCM
Order decimals

Student book 3B 2 – 15

Multiply and divide by powers of 10
Round numbers to a given place, including decimal places and significant figures
Work with factors and multiples, LCM, HCF and prime factors
Estimate the answer to calculations by rounding

Student book 3C 2 – 15

Round numbers to a given number of significant figures
Work out and calculate with upper and lower bounds
Use numbers written in index form

1a Powers of 10

Objectives

- Know and use the index laws for multiplication and division of positive integer powers (L6)
- Extend knowledge of integer powers of 10 (L6)
- Recognise the equivalence of 0.1, $\frac{1}{10}$ and 10^{-1} (L6)
- Multiply and divide by any integer power of 10 (L6)
- Multiply and divide integers and decimals by 0.1, 0.01 (L6)
- Understand the effects of multiplying and dividing by numbers between 0 and 1 (L7)
- Express numbers in standard index form (L7)
- Convert between ordinary and standard index form representations (L7)

Key ideas	Resources
1 Consolidating and strengthening the concept of place value and using powers of 10 to facilitate mental calculations 2 Having a sense of multiplicative equivalence	Multiply decimals by 10 and 100 (1013) Mini whiteboards

Simplification	Extension
Some students struggle with the concept of multiplying and dividing by 10, 100, *etc*. Encourage these students to draw place value diagrams for each question, clearly showing how the digits move for a particular power of 10. As the students move on to equivalent calculations it may be necessary to use some simple examples such as $2 \div 0.1$ to convince them that this equivalent calculation method works. It is useful to represent the calculation on the number line, so that the students can see that 20 lots of 0.1 make 2.	The more able students should concentrate on working with powers, looking at examples involving both multiplication and division, examples that result in a negative power and examples that involve raising a power to a given power.

Literacy	Links
Speaking maths sentences in different but equivalent ways: e.g...× 0.5, half of, or ÷ 2, how many halves in, extended to × 0.1 and so on. The notation conventions conveying concepts of power with indices. Make use of the opportunity to revisit prefixes such as kilo, centi, and so on. This might include use of the relatively recent term googolplex, its meaning and its history.	The Egyptians used seven different symbols to represent different powers of ten. To write a number, each symbol was written down as many times as was necessary. For example, the symbol for ten would be written down three times to represent the number thirty. There is more information about Egyptian Hieroglyphics and a conversion tool to write numbers in hieroglyphics at http://library.thinkquest.org/16325/e-hie.html

Alternative approach

Start by exploring the students perceptions of size changes following multiplying or dividing by powers of 10. Using the 'millionaire' game referenced in the resources might be a good introduction. Further exploration can be be tackled using a list of operations such as × 100; ÷ 10; × 1, which students then simply identify if the result is higher or lower than the start, using cards or mini whiteboards. This can be extended later to explore the effects of, for example, × 0.1 or ÷ 0.01, in order to make connectionsto the multiplicative equivalents.

Checkpoint

Work out 7.9×0.01	(0.079)
Work out $46 \div 0.1$	(460)
Work out 4.8×10^4	(48,000)

Number Whole numbers and decimals

Starter – The question is...

Challenge students to find as many different questions as they can in four minutes with an answer of 0.05.

Can be differentiated by the choice of answer.

Teaching notes

Make use of students' prior learning here, possibly using early questions in the **exercise** as a whole-class mini whiteboard activity to gauge student understanding.

The most likely areas requiring consolidation are multiplication and division by tenths and hundredths, and the rules for combining indices.

There are opportunities here to build connections between number operations using mathematical reasoning; for example, dividing by a number like 10 is the same as multiplying by its reciprocal ($\frac{1}{10}$ or 0.1). Incorporating 'higher' or 'lower' responses using mini whiteboards will help to strengthen these connections.

Plenary

Use examples similar to those in questions **3** and **6** of the exercise as a mini whiteboard activity to identify whether any problems persist in understanding.

Exercise commentary

Question 2 – Students should be encouraged to rewrite each question with an equivalent calculation, that is, 37 × 0.1 should be written as 37 ÷ 10 and then proceed as in question **1**.

Question 3 – A good question for class discussion to clarify any misconceptions.

Question 4 – Students will quickly articulate the connection between the power of 10 and the number of places moved by the digits. Ensure that they talk about moving the digits and not moving the decimal point.

Question 5 – Watch out for part **h** where students will need to think of 10 as 10^1

Question 6 – This question is best set out as a spider diagram, to encourage students to see the effect of the changing powers of 10. More able students could be asked to work out the answer to a related division such as 795.6 ÷ 34.

Question 7 – This is a good activity to do before question **4**. Students may find it more difficult to articulate what happens when they divide a number by a negative power of 10.

Answers

1	a	300	b	1.6	c	12000	d	0.037
	e	18	f	1320	g	0.75	h	930
2	a	3.7	b	7800	c	0.51	d	93
	e	830	f	4.8	g	0.0054	h	4.83
3	a	100	b	0.01	c	10	d	0.1
	e	0.01	f	0.001	g	0.1	h	1000
4	a	2700	b	56 000	c	130 000	d	62 000
	e	4 100 000	f	270	g	3600	h	14 000
	i	170 000						
5	a	10^4	b	10^2	c	10^7	d	10^3
	e	10^5	f	10^3	g	10^4	h	10^6
	i	10^4						

6 a i 795.6   ii 7.956   iii 79.56
  b Students' answers

7 a Students' answers
  b Yes, move digits to the right instead
  c Yes, move in the opposite direction to positive powers

Powers of 10

1b Rounding

Objectives

- Round positive numbers to any given power of 10 (L5)
- Round decimals to the nearest whole number or to one or two decimal places (L5)
- Use rounding to make estimates and to give solutions to problems (L6)

Key ideas	Resources
1 Rounding correctly to up to 2 decimal places 2 Applying rounding skills when estimating a result of a problem	Decimal places (1001)

Simplification	Extension
Students may need to recap with simple whole number examples to be rounded to the nearest 10, 100 and 1000, for example, 'round 46 to the nearest 10' and 'round 378 to the nearest 100'. The drawing of a line after the degree of accuracy required helps some students to focus on the correct digit to determine whether a number should be rounded up or down. For example, round 4.97 to 1 decimal place 4.9|7 Problems occur because it rounds to 5.0 and not 4.10 ('four point ten') – students may benefit from using a number line marked in divisions of 0.1 to show that '4.9 and a bit' rounded up is 5.0.	Students could estimate the answer to two-stage problems that require multiplication and division. Students could be introduced to significant figures as a consistent method for rounding numbers of different sizes. Students can begin to explore the ideas of maximums and minimums for any given value.

Literacy	Links
Check the understanding of the notation = and ≈ . Share/explore awareness that these signs are not always used consistently or accurately in general media and explore what is being communicated when a number is recorded. The notion of recording accuracy and its impossibility appeals to many students.	The Earth takes about 365.2422 days to make one complete revolution around the sun. To reduce the error in rounding the year to 365 days, the Gregorian calendar adds an extra day every four years (except for those years divisible by 100 unless also divisible by 400) to keep the calendar aligned with the seasons. The calendar is still inaccurate by 1 day in every 3236 years. There is more information about the Gregorian calendar at http://jonathan.rawle.org/hyperpedia/calendar.php

Alternative approach

Explore perceptions of number values and extend to widen the idea that any value is recorded approximately, so when noting a length is say 5 cm what actually might it be? Explore the largest and smallest values possible. Compare two value: say 6.5 and 6.50. what is the same about them and what is different. Use the ideas generated to establish the fine lines of rounding, using various number lines to represent values as appropriate.

Effects of rounding in calculations can be explored, initially in simple cases, then extending to multi-stage problems where anomalies can arise and be discussed.

Checkpoint

Round 456.83 to the nearest 10	(460)
Round 3.7812 to two decimal places	(3.78)
Round 1206.265 to (a) the nearest hundred, and (b) two decimal places	(1210, 1206.27)

Number Whole numbers and decimals

Starter – Matching form

Ask students to find the pairs in the following numbers.

3.1×10^3,   30100, 3.1×10^5,   310,
3.01×10^4,   30.1,   3100, 3.01×10^0,
310000,   3.01, 3.1×10^2, 3.01×10^1

Can be extended by including red herrings.

Teaching notes

The two emphases in this spread are on the technique of rounding to a specific degree of accuracy and on the process of using rounded numbers to make estimates in calculations.

The second requires quite different mathematical thinking to the first, so it is worth spending time talking through the need for having a ballpark idea of the size of the answer to a problem before using a calculator to work it out exactly (so that if any error in entry occurs it may be obvious because the answer is of the wrong order). For example, when $24 \div (2 \times 3)$ is entered without brackets it will give 36 rather than 4 as the answer. Looking at a similar problem such as $\frac{614.5}{87 \times 11.3}$ will help motivate the technique, and allow you to explore why rounding to 1 sf is all that is required when estimating.

Plenary

Ask students to work in pairs to think of real-life estimation problems: how many times will their heart beat or how much money will they earn in their lifetimes. Feedback the best suggestions from each pair to the whole class.

Exercise commentary

Question 2 – In part **d** the answers are 9 (nearest whole number) and 9.0 (1dp). The notion of the degree of accuracy expressed will need to be explained and makes a good link to question **5**.

Question 3 – Students need to be encouraged to round the answers to calculations to a stated degree of accuracy. Emphasise the need for rounding in other branches of mathematics and in real life.

Question 5 – Students are invited to work out the answers by estimating, rather than calculating. Emphasise that for questions of this type, we do not need an *exact* answer.

Question 6 – A slightly challenging question with no direct references in the text. Emphasise that a rounded number could lie anywhere ± half unit of accuracy stated. This could be a useful plenary or discussion point.

Answers

1. a i 3000   ii 3100   iii 3110
   b i 6000   ii 5700   iii 5680
   c i 10 000 ii 9800   iii 9840
   d i 4000   ii 4000   iii 3990
   e i 13 000 ii 13 200 iii 13 180
   f i 26 000 ii 26 400 iii 26 390
   g i 4000   ii 3600   iii 3590
   h i 2000   ii 2000   iii 1970
2. a i 4   ii 4.4   iii 4.36
   b i 6   ii 6.3   iii 6.28
   c i 7   ii 7.4   iii 7.42
   d i 9   ii 9.0   iii 9.03
   e i 3   ii 3.4   iii 3.40
   f i 18   ii 17.6   iii 17.64
   g i 128   ii 128.4 iii 128.43
   h i 1   ii 0.7   iii 0.71
3. a 0.33   b 0.31   c 1.86   d 0.27
   e 0.88   f 4.90   g 0.62   h 1.42
4. a i 300   ii 325   iii 325.2
   b i 800   ii 845   iii 845.4
   c i 100   ii 139   iii 138.7
   d i 600   ii 625   iii 625.5
   e i 1000   ii 974   iii 974.1
   f i 700   ii 652   iii 652.0
   g i 100   ii 150   iii 150.0
   h i 1000   ii 1000   iii 1000.0
5. a Women $30 \times 60 = 1800$ kg, Men $20 \times 80 = 1600$ kg
   b $(50 \div 0.25 =)$ 200 days
6. a 5.5 m and 6.5 m   b 1.75 m and 1.85 m
   c 1150 kg and 1250 kg
7. a $450\,000 \div 25 = 18\,000$ lengths
   b $18\,000 \div 60 = 300$ hours

Rounding

1c Factors, multiples and primes

Objectives

- Use multiples, factors, common factors, highest common factors, lowest common multiples and primes (L5)
- Find the prime factor decomposition of a number, e.g. $8000 = 26 \times 53$ (L5)
- Use squares, positive and negative square roots, cubes and cube roots, and index notation for small positive integer powers (L6)
- Use the prime factor decomposition of a number (L6)
- Use index notation for integer powers (L6)
- Use index notation for integer powers and simple instances of the index laws (L6)

Key ideas	Resources
1 A prime number has only two factors; 1 and the number itself 2 Venn diagrams can be used to work out the LCM and HCF of two numbers	Factors and primes (1032) Mini whiteboards

Simplification	Extension
Students are quickly comfortable with the notion of 'factor pairs' leading to factors of a number. The notion of 'multiple' should be associated with 'multiplication tables'. In this way, the meanings of 'factor' and 'multiple' should not become confused. Display a number, say 12, and ask students to write factors (and later, multiples) on their mini whiteboards. It will then be clear whether their thinking is correct.	Students can draw a Venn diagram (of three interlocking circles) and insert the factors of three numbers, such as 12, 20 and 28. Then give a more challenging trio of numbers.

Literacy	Links
The key vocabulary here should be familiar to students but the links to reasoning and understanding may not be as strong. Use the opportunity to explore definitions fully and also to explore students perceptions of these words in other contexts, such as in science as well as every day life.	Encrypting credit card information relies on the difficulty of finding the prime factors of large numbers. Encryption companies have to keep up with new methods for factorising numbers and until 2007, the company RSA offered prizes worth thousands of pounds to anyone who managed to find the two prime factors of certain given numbers. Some of the numbers have never been factorised. There is more information about the RSA Factoring Challenge at http://en.wikipedia.org/wiki/RSA_Factoring_Challenge

Alternative approach

The concepts covered here are likely to be familiar with most students, so it is possible to re visit these key ideas by taking an investigatory approach to problems involving primes, factors, etc. such as the escaping prisoners, or expressing primes as a power of 2 ±1. Sources of such problems and puzzles can be found at www.nrich.org.uk

The key learning ideas can be drawn out from the students' work.

Checkpoint

Write the number 1540 as a product of its prime factors	($2^2 \times 5 \times 7 \times 11$)
What is the highest common factor of 140 and 220?	(20)
What is the lowest common multiple of 36 and 42?	(252)

Number   Whole numbers and decimals

Starter – Codewords

Explain these code rules to the students:

Write a 16 letter message, for example, HOMEWORK TONIGHT? in four rows of four letters.

Read down the columns to make the code, for example, HWTGOOOHMRNTEKI?

Ask students to reverse the procedure to decode the following:

MEISAMCFTASUHTIN
(mathematics is fun)
WERCRYOOIOWDTUNE
(write your own code)

Teaching notes

To link with students' prior knowledge, ask them to work in pairs to write a definition of a prime number and to explain why one is not a prime number. (There is a unique prime factor representation of every integer providing one is not prime). Explore why two must be the only even prime in a whole class discussion. Use mini whiteboards to identify factors of large numbers and strategies for working through a factor tree (10, 2, 5 are immediately obvious as factors, and 3 can be tested by the sum of digits). Look at the end result of different factor trees, for example starting 360 as 60 and 6.

Plenary

Display the answers to question **5** in a table, showing the values of A and B, the HCF and LCM and the product of the two numbers, that is, AB. Ask students to discuss in pairs, using the Venn diagrams they constructed, why the product of AB should also be the product of the HCF and LCM.

Exercise commentary

Question 6 – This question requires the students to work backwards from the concepts of HCF and LCM to work out one of the original numbers. This is likely to be challenging for many but can be extended with further examples for able students.

Answers

1.
   a $1 \times 15, 3 \times 5,$ 1, 3, 5, 15
   b $1 \times 20, 2 \times 10, 4 \times 5,$ 1, 2, 4, 5, 10, 20
   c $1 \times 24, 2 \times 12, 3 \times 8, 4 \times 6,$
      1, 2, 3, 4, 6, 8, 12, 24
   d $1 \times 25, 5 \times 5$
      1, 5, 25
   e $1 \times 30, 2 \times 15, 3 \times 10, 5 \times 6$
      1, 2, 3, 5, 6, 10, 15, 30
   f $1 \times 36, 2 \times 18, 3 \times 12, 4 \times 9, 6 \times 6$
      1, 2, 3, 4, 6, 9, 12, 18, 36
   g $1 \times 60, 2 \times 30, 3 \times 20, 4 \times 15, 5 \times 12, 6 \times 10$
      1, 2, 3, 4, 5, 6, 10, 12, 15, 20, 30, 60
   h $1 \times 100, 2 \times 50, 4 \times 25, 5 \times 20, 10 \times 10$
      1, 2, 4, 5, 10, 20, 25, 50, 100

2. a 8 b i 4 ii 4 iii 8
3. a 60 b i 40 ii 45 iii 42
4. a 2, 3, 5, 7, 11, 13, 17
   b i $2^3 \times 3 \times 5$ ii $2^4 \times 3$
      iii $2^3 \times 3^2$ iv $2^3 \times 5^2$
      v $2^2 \times 3 \times 5^2$ vi $2^4 \times 3^2$
      vii $2^3 \times 5^3$ viii $2^4 \times 3^2 \times 5$
      ix $2^3 \times 3^3$ x $2^3 \times 3^3 \times 5$

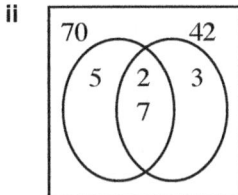

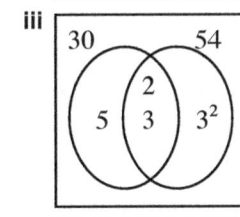

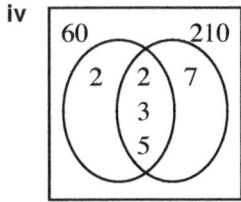

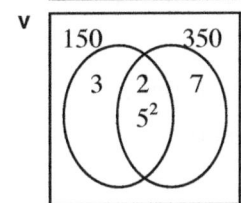

5. a i [Venn diagram: 40, 110; 2^2, 2, 5, 11]
      ii [Venn diagram: 70, 42; 5, 2, 3, 7]
      iii [Venn diagram: 30, 54; 5, 2, 3, 3^2]
      iv [Venn diagram: 60, 210; 2, 2, 7, 3, 5]
      v [Venn diagram: 150, 350; 3, 2, 7, 5^2]
      vi [Venn diagram: 90, 84; 3, 2, 2, 7, 5, 3]

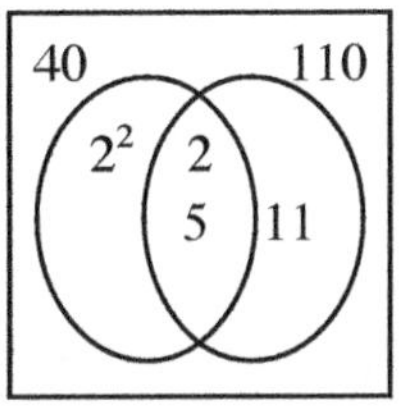

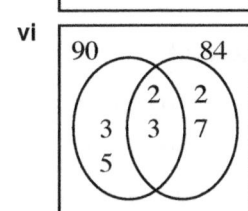

   b i 10, 440 ii 14, 210
      iii 6, 270 iv 30, 420
      v 50, 1050 vi 6, 1260

6. N = 105
7. a 4, 9, 16, 25, 36, 49, All are square numbers
   b 1, 2, 3, 4, 5, 6, 10, 12, 15, 20, 30, 60; 90

Factors, multiples and primes

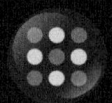

1d Estimating and approximating

Objectives

- Use rounding to make estimates and to give solutions to problems to an appropriate degree of accuracy (L6)
- Round to a given number of significant figures (L7)
- Use significant figures to approximate answers when multiplying or dividing large numbers (L7)
- Make and justify estimates and approximations of calculations by rounding numbers to one significant figure and multiplying or dividing mentally (L7)

Key ideas	Resources
1 Rounding to at least one significant figure 2 Apply effectively in order to estimate calculations	Significant figures (1005) Mini whiteboards

Simplification	Extension
Students will need to practise rounding to the nearest 100, 10, 1, 1 dp and 2 dp which they have covered previously in spread 1b. Practising some very easy approximations such as 2.8 × 5.1 might be useful before working on question 2.	Students could be asked to round numbers to different numbers of significant figures. Students could extend question 5 by looking at debt: they could identify other items they pay for in different time periods, for example, their dinner money each week, their spending on sweets each day, the amount they spend on presents each year, *etc.*, and be introduced to the idea of budgeting (financial planning). There are several websites which help people to work out their monthly and weekly expenditure.

Literacy	Links
Both the terms approximation and estimation are worth discussing with students – what they understand by the terms; what the difference is between them; how the context alters the nature of approximation, and so on.	Ask the class to estimate their ages to the nearest year, nearest day and nearest second. There is an accurate age calculator online at http://www.onlineconversion.com/howold.htm How accurate are the estimates?

Alternative approach

Begin by asking students to examine two values such as 5.0 and 5.00. Ask them to come up with something that is the same about them and something that is different. Establish similarity as both values are '5 or about 5'- estimation-, the differences will begin to extend the different level of approximation each has, perhaps by examining possible range of values for each. Display a hidden value of four digits each covered (2294) miles. Explore this value with the students as the length of the longest river in Europe (Volga, in Russia). In order to establish a good estimation, which of the digits should be uncovered? Would this give a result to the nearest thousand, and so on, in order to establish significant figures – one, two, and three. Rehearse significant figure finding using mini whiteboards with the students. Include questions which explore possible values for a number given to one or two significant figures. Apply to estimation, stressing one s.f. as key in order to make mental work efficient, as students will still tend to be concerned about accuracy levels.

Checkpoint

Round 256.87 to one significant figure	(300)
Round 0.486 to one significant figure	(0.5)
Estimate an answer for 3746 × 0.83	(4000 × 1 = 4000)

Starter – Farmer Jones

Farmer Jones has some hens and pigs. There are the same number of hens' legs as there are pigs' legs. There are 27 heads altogether (excluding Farmer Jones). Ask students to give the ratio of pigs to hens (1 : 2). How many hens are there? (18). What fraction of the animals are pigs? ($\frac{1}{3}$)

Teaching notes

Numbers are all around us, and many very large numbers arise from modest unit amounts being multiplied by large numbers of people, or time periods, *etc*. It is an important part of functional skills to be able to make sense of such situations without having to make exact calculations. To introduce the work in this spread, ask students to work in pairs to estimate how many times their heart has beaten so far (for a 14-year-old, with an average heart-rate of 80 beats per minute over the lifetime, it is around 600 million), or how much it would cost the government to give teachers in schools a 5% rise in pay (there are about 400 000 teachers in schools in England, with an average salary of about £35 000, giving a cost of about £700 million annually).

Emphasise the need to communicate clearly what is being calculated at each stage in problems such as question **4**.

Plenary

Working in pairs, students devise their own estimation problems. They should then discuss what they think the answer is and how they arrived at the answer.

Exercise commentary

Question 1 – Students should be encouraged to identify the place value of the first significant figure for each number. This should help them to round each number appropriately.

Question 2 – Remind students to round each number to 1 significant figure for their approximations.

Question 3 and **4** – Students could provide their own data for these questions or invent similar problems of their own. This could provide the basis of an interesting homework activity. Question **4** in particular requires higher level processing skills to identify the relevant information for each part.

Question 5 – An activity that would readily lend itself to using a spreadsheet. Students could also explore the rounding function provided in the spreadsheet.

Answers

1. a 100 b 2000 c 90 d 20 000
   e 5 f 0.4 g 100 h 20
2. a $200 \times 30 = 6000$ b $30 \div 5 = 6$
   c $3000 \times 0.7 = 2100$ d $200 \times 10 = 2000$
   e $20 \times 200 \div 10 = 400$ f $0.3 \times 1000 \div 6 = 50$
3. a $4000 \div 50 = 80$ b $2 \times 70 + 1 \times 80 = 220$ m
4. a $900 \div 200 = 4.5$ miles
   b $40000 \div 900 = 44.4 = £40$ per mile
   c $900 \times 7 = 6300$ minutes = 105 hours = 4 days and 9 hours
5. Approximate guide for answers

Item	Daily Cost	Weekly cost	Monthly cost	Yearly Cost
TV Licence	£0.25	£2	£10	£139.50
Mobile phone	£0.66	£5	£24.99	£250
Food shopping	£10	£88.95	£360	£4500
Newspaper	£0.85	£7	£30	£300
Total	£12	£104	£420	£5200

Estimating and approximating

1 Whole numbers and decimals – MySummary

Key outcomes	Quick check
Multiply and divide numbers by powers of 10.　　L6	Calculate a 36×0.1 (3.6)　　b $7.3 \div 0.01$ (730)　　c $0.483 \div 0.1$ (4.83)
Use index notation for integer powers.　　L6	Simplify a $10^3 \times 10^4$ (10^7) b $10^5 \div 10^3$ (10^2) c $10^8 \div 10$ (10^7)
Round numbers to decimal places and significant figures.　　L6	Round the following numbers as indicated a 3.47 (1 d.p.) (3.5) b 56.09 (1 s.f.) (60) c 0.32185 (3 d.p.) (0.322)
Use prime factors to find the HCF and LCM of pairs of numbers.　　L7	Find the HCF and LCM of a 16 and 20 (4, 80) b 12 and 50 (2, 300) c 17 and 11 (1, 187)
Use rounding to make estimates.　　L7	Estimate the answer to a 310.4×19.8 ($300 \times 20 = 6000$) b $1984 \div 9.979$ ($2000 \div 10 = 200$)

MyMaths extra support

Lesson/online homework			Description
Rounding to 10, 100	1003	L4	Rounding numbers to the nearest 10, 100 and 1000
Multiplying by 10, 100	1027	L4	Methods for multiplying by powers of 10
Multiples	1035	L4	How can we test for divisibility? What is the lowest common multiple?

MyReview

1 MySummary

Check out
You should now be able to ...

	Test it Questions
✓ Multiply and divide numbers by powers of 10.	1
✓ Use index notation for integer powers.	2 – 3
✓ Round numbers to decimal places and significant figures.	4 – 5
✓ Use prime factors to find the HCF and LCM of pairs of numbers.	6 – 7
✓ Use rounding to make estimates.	8 – 9

Language	Meaning	Example
Index/indices	The index tells you how many times a number is multiplied by itself.	$5^3 = 5 \times 5 \times 5$
Significant figures (sf)	The first non-zero figures in a number.	The first two significant figures in 456.7 are 4 (400) and 5 (50).
Rounding	You can round numbers to a given number of sf.	456.7 rounded to 2 sf is 460
Estimate	Use rounding to approximate an answer.	$\frac{3.4 + 2.1}{1.9} \approx \frac{3 + 2}{2} = \frac{5}{2} = 2.5$
Factor	A number which divides exactly into another number.	1, 3, 9 and 27 are all factors of 27. $27 = 1 \times 27 = 3 \times 9$
Multiple	A multiple of a number appears in its times table.	6, 12, 18, 24... are all multiples of 6. $6 = 1 \times 6$, $12 = 2 \times 6$, $18 = 3 \times 6$, $24 = 4 \times 6$
Prime	A prime number has only two factors, the number itself and 1.	2, 3, 5, 7, 11, 13, 17... are all primes. 1 is not a prime number
HCF (Highest common factor)	The highest number that is a factor of two or more numbers.	The HCF of 24 and 40 is 8.
LCM (Lowest common multiple)	The lowest number that is a multiple of two or more numbers.	The LCM of 24 and 40 is 120.

12 Number Whole numbers and decimals

1 MyReview

1 Calculate
 a 0.76×0.1 b $45.1 \div 0.01$
 c 15.2×100 d 0.92×1000
 e 216.8×0.01 f $0.36 \div 0.1$

2 Each of these numbers have been written in standard form. Work out the size of each number.
 a 7.2×10^3 b 8.29×10^6
 c 4.1×10^{-2} d 30.8×10^{-5}

3 Simplify leaving your answer as a single power of the number.
 a $10^4 \times 10^3$ b $10^2 \times 10^5$
 c $10^7 \times 10^9$ d $10^5 \div 10^4$
 e $10^6 \div 10^3$ f $10^{10} \div 10^6$

4 Round 271.0985 to the nearest
 a 100   b 10
 c whole number   d 1dp
 e 2dp   f 3dp

5 Round each of these numbers to 1 sf.
 a 462   b 25945
 c 6.28   d 0.29
 e 0.094   f 0.98

6 Write these numbers as products of their prime factors.
 a 2376   b 546   c 680

What next?

Score	
0 – 4	Your knowledge of this topic is still developing. To improve look at Formative test: 3B-1; MyMaths: 1001, 1005, 1013 and 1032
5 – 7	You are gaining a secure knowledge of this topic. To improve look at InvisiPen: 112, 114, 135, 171, 172, 173 and 182
8 – 9	You have mastered this topic. Well done, you are ready to progress!

7 a Complete the Venn diagram to show the prime factors of 180 and of 240. 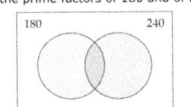
  b Use your Venn diagram to find the HCF of 180 and 240.
  c Use your Venn diagram to find the LCM of 180 and 240.

8 Estimate the answer to each calculation without using a calculator.
 a 39×21
 b $18.9 \div 5.1$
 c $8870 \div 295$
 d $413 \times (153 + 641)$
 e $(0.473 + 0.509) \times 0.92$
 f $\frac{0.708 \times 451}{4.71}$

9 One bottle of water costs £0.84, One bottle of cola costs £1.48.
 a Estimate the cost of 19 bottles of water.
 b Rita wants to buy 36 bottles of cola. She has £60 to spend. Use an estimate to decide if Rita can buy the cola.

MyMaths.co.uk   13

Question commentary

Questions 1, 2 – Students can think of multiplying by a negative power of 10 as dividing by the positive power

Question 3 – Students will sometimes multiply the base numbers to give 100 instead of 10 in their solutions.

Question 4 – Part e is likely to cause the most issues here

Question 5 – In e some students may mistakenly round to 0.1

Question 6 – Students should first draw factor trees to find the prime factors then should write their answers using index form

Question 7 – Students should write out each number as a product of its prime factors first, $180 = 2^2 \times 3^2 \times 5$, $240 = 2^4 \times 3 \times 5$. To find the HCF they multiply the numbers in the intersection ($2^2 \times 3 \times 5$). To find the LCM they multiply all the numbers in the diagram ($3 \times 5 \times 2^2 \times 3 \times 2^2$)

Question 8 – Students should round all numbers to 1 sig. fig. first **a** 40, 21 **b** 20, 5 **c** 9000, 300 **d** 400, 200, 600 **e** 0.5, 0.5, 0.9 **f** 0.7, 500, 5

Question 9 – Emphasise that exact answers to the calculations are not required and that students should work to one significant figure where possible

Answers

1 a 0.076   b 4510   c 1520   d 920
  e 2.168   f 3.6
2 a 7200   b 8 290 000   c 0.041   d 0.000308
3 a 10^7 b 10^7 c 10^{16} d 10^1
  e 10^3 f 10^4
4 a 300   b 270   c 271   d 271.1
  e 271.10   f 271.099
5 a 500   b 30000   c 6   d 0.3
  e 0.09   f 1
6 a $2^3 \times 3^3 \times 11$
  b $2 \times 3 \times 7 \times 13$
  c $2^3 \times 5 \times 17$
7 a (Venn diagram: 180 ∩ 240 contains 2², 5; 180 only contains 3, 3; 240 only contains 2², 2²... shown with 3 in intersection with 2² and 5, outside 180 side: 3, outside 240 side: 2²)   b 60   c 720
8 a 800   b 4   c 30   d 320 000
  e 0.9   f 70
9 a $19 \times 0.84 \approx 20 \times 0.8 = £16$
  b $£1.48 \times 36 \approx £1.50 \times 40 \approx £60$
  This is an overestimate, £60 will be enough.

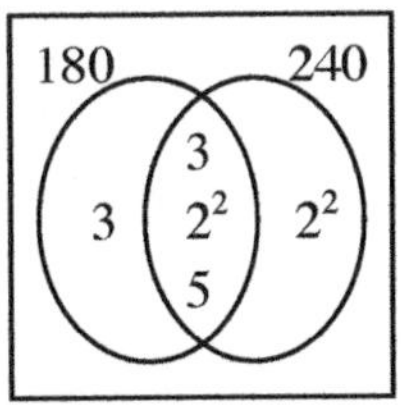

MySummary/MyReview 13

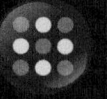

1 MyPractice

1a

1 Calculate

a $46 \div 10$
b 3.8×100
c $29.7 \div \frac{1}{10}$
d $0.16 \div 10$
e $13.02 \times \frac{1}{10}$
f 0.27×0.1
g 22.68×0.01
h $33.6 \div 0.1$
i $58.13 \div 0.01$

2 Each of these numbers have been written in standard form.
Work out the value of these numbers.

a 5×10^2
b 2.7×10^3
c 7.62×10^2
d 1.04×10^5
e 3.72×10^3
f 4.11×10^6
g 8.361×10^7

3 Calculate:

a 1.7×0.01
b 0.01×43
c 10000×1.2
d $8 \div \frac{1}{1000}$
e 9×0.001
f $23 \times \frac{1}{1000}$
g $3.7 \div 0.001$
h $0.025 \div 0.01$
i 0.07×0.01

1b

4 Round each number to the nearest

i 10
ii whole number
iii to 1dp
iv to 2dp

a 43.181
b 9.951
c 129.333
d 12.0999
e 98.985
f 26.007
g 144.236
h 11.777
i 101.101
j 12.6002
k 909.909
l 14.999

1c

5 a Use this table to find the HCF of 18 and 30.

Number	Factors
18	
30	

b Find the HCF of 20 and 45.
c Find the HCF of 72 and 80.

6 a Use this table to find the LCM of 8 and 10.

Number	Multiples
8	
10	

b Find the LCM of 6 and 9.
c Find the LCM of 15 and 25.

7 Use factor trees and prime factors to find

a the HCF of
  i 60 and 260
  ii 210 and 270
b the LCM of
  i 12 and 20
  ii 60 and 126

1d

8 Round all of the numbers in each calculation to 1 or 2 significant figures.
Then work out an estimate for each calculation.

a 503×31
b $15.16 \div 2.97$
c 5673×0.388
d $\frac{19.3 \times 415}{11.4}$
e $\frac{0.482 \times 317}{4.9}$
f $\frac{38.2 \times 6.39}{0.783}$

9 Work out an estimate for this problem.
Show all the numbers you have rounded and the calculations you have worked out.

Debbie is trying to save money.
She spends £4.89 on a coffee and a sandwich each working day.
Her friend suggests that she could save some money by making a sandwich and bringing a flask of coffee from home.
Making her own sandwiches and flask of coffee costs £1.08 per day.
Debbie works 5 days a week for 46 weeks of the year. How much money could she save each year if she takes her friend's advice?

10 When a toilet flushes it use 9.24 litres of water.

a If a toilet is flushed 17 times a day, **approximately** how much water is used
  i per day
  ii per week
  iii per month
  iv per year
  v per lifetime of a person?
b The volume of water in Lake Windermere is about 330 000 000 m³.
Approximately how long would it take to flush the volume of the lake down the toilet? (1 m³ = 1000 litres)

Question commentary

Questions 1 to 3 – Students should remember the rules for shifting the digits in the number when multiplying and dividing by powers of 10.

Question 4 – Each number should be rounded to each level of accuracy. Students may need help understanding the way that the numbers are represented in parts **d** and **l**.

Questions 5 to 7 – Venn diagrams could be used to help with **question 7**.

Question 8 – Emphasise that exact answers are not required and that students should round the numbers in a way that makes the calculations easy to do in their heads.

Questions 9 and **10** – These problem-solving questions will require students to think carefully and plan their approach from analysing the information given. Literacy may be an issue for some and guidance may be given to get the students started.

Answers

1. a 4.6 b 380 c 297 d 0.016
   e 1.302 f 0.027 g 0.2268 h 336
   i 5813
2. a 500 b 2700 c 762 d 104 000
   e 3720 f 4 110 000 g 83 610 000
3. a 0.017 b 0.43 c 12000 d 8000
   e 0.009 f 0.023 g 3700 h 2.5
   i 0.0007
4. a i 40   ii 43   iii 43.2   iv 43.18
   b i 10   ii 10   iii 10.0   iv 9.95
   c i 130 ii 129   iii 129.3 iv 129.33
   d i 10   ii 12   iii 12.1   iv 12.10
   e i 100 ii 99   iii 99.0   iv 98.99
   f i 30   ii 26   iii 26.0   iv 26.01
   g i 140 ii 144   iii 144.2 iv 144.24
   h i 10   ii 12   iii 11.8   iv 11.78
   i i 100 ii 101   iii 101.1 iv 101.10
   j i 10   ii 13   iii 12.6   iv 12.60
   k i 910 ii 910   iii 909.9 iv 909.91
   l i 10   ii 15   iii 15.0   iv 15.00
5. a 18: 1, 18, 2, 9, 3, 6
      30: 1, 30, 2, 15, 3, 10, 5, 6
      HCF = 6
   b 5   c 8
6. a 8: 8, 16, 24, 32, 40, 48
      10: 10, 20, 30, 40, 50, 60
      LCM = 40
   b 18   c 75
7. a i $60 = 2^2 \times 3 \times 5$ $260 = 2^2 \times 5 \times 13$
         HCF = $2^2 \times 5 = 20$
      ii $210 = 2 \times 3 \times 5 \times 7$ $270 = 2 \times 3^3 \times 5$
         HCF = $2 \times 3 \times 5 = 30$
   b i $12 = 2^2 \times 3$ $20 = 2^2 \times 5$
         LCM = $2^2 \times 3 \times 5 = 60$
      ii $60 = 2^2 \times 3 \times 5$ $126 = 2 \times 3^2 \times 7$
         LCM = $2^2 \times 3^2 \times 5 \times 7 = 1260$
8. a $500 \times 30 = 15\ 000$ b $15 \div 3 = 5$
   c $6000 \times 0.4 = 2400$ d $20 \times 400 \div 10 = 800$
   e $0.5 \times 300 \div 5 = 30$ f $40 \times 6 \div 0.8 = 300$
9. $(5 - 1) \times 5 \times 50 = £1000$
10. a i $10 \times 17 = 170$ litres
       ii $170 \times 7 = 1200$ litres
       iii $170 \times 30 = 5100$ litres
       iv $170 \times 365 = 62\ 000$ litres
       v $62\ 000 \times 100 = 6\ 200\ 000$ litres
    b $330\ 000\ 000\ 000 \div 62\ 000 = 5\ 300\ 000$ years

MyPractice

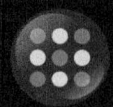

2 Measures, perimeter and area

Learning outcomes

G1 Derive and apply formulae to calculate and solve problems involving: perimeter and area of triangles, parallelograms, trapezia, volume of cuboids (including cubes) and other prisms (including cylinders) (L6)

G2 Calculate and solve problems involving: perimeters of 2D shapes (including circles), areas of circles and composite shapes (L6)

R10 Use compound units such as speed, unit pricing and density to solve problems (L7)

N12 Use standard units of mass, length, time, money and other measures, including with decimal quantities (L6/7)

Introduction

The chapter starts by looking at converting between metric units of length, capacity and mass before covering similar content involving imperial units. Areas of 2D shapes including compound shapes are covered before sections on the circumference and area of a circle. The final section covers compound measures including speed, density and pressure.

The introduction discusses Usain Bolt and his world record 100 metre time. It compares his time to that of some of the fastest land animals and points out that his average (or even top) speed is nothing compared to these creatures. It is interesting to note that his 200 metre world record was completed at almost the same average speed (10.42 m/s as opposed to 10.44 m/s). Michael Johnson's 400 metre world record of 43.18 seconds implies an average speed of 9.26 m/s which over a much longer distance is still pretty fast!

Students could be invited to work out the average speed of some other athletic world records. A table of these records can be found at:

http://www.iaaf.org/records/by-category/world-records

Prior knowledge

Students should already know how to…
- Calculate the perimeter and area of simple 2D shapes
- Find the volume of a cuboid
- Multiply and divide by powers of 10

Starter problem

The starter problem actually requires students to have completed the work on circumference and area of a circle (sections 2e and 2f). Knowledge that a tangent to a circle and its radius are at 90° might also be useful.

In working out the perimeter of the band, students might notice that the band touches each circle for one third of its circumference and so the total of touching band is equal to one complete circumference. The three lengths of band that do not touch the circles are actually equal to two times the radius each so we need to add on six times the radius in total.

$2 \times \pi \times 10 + 6 \times 10 = 20\pi + 60 \approx 122.8$ cm

The area is more difficult to find. We have to break the enclosed area down into three components: three one third circles on each corner, three rectangles down each side (vertices at the centre of each circle and where the tangents meet the circles) and an equilateral triangle in the middle (vertices at the centre of each circle). The three one third circles add up to a complete circle area. Calculating the area of the triangle without knowledge of trigonometry is not possible so this might be given to the students: 173.2 cm².

$\pi \times 10^2 + 10 \times 20 \times 3 + 173.2 \approx 1087$ cm²

Resources

MyMaths

Metric conversion	1061	Area of circles	1083	Circumference of a circle	1088
Converting measures	1091	Area of a parallelogram	1108	Speed	1121
Area of a trapezium	1128	Imperial measures	1191	Density	1246

Online assessment

Chapter test	3B–2
Formative test	3B–2
Summative test	3B–2

InvisiPen solutions

Area of shapes made from rectangles	311		
Area of a triangle	314	Area of a parallelogram	315
Composite shapes	316	Metric measures	332
Metric and imperial measures			333
Compound measures	335	Circumference of a circle	351
Area of a circle	352	Composite shapes circles	353

Topic scheme

Teaching time = 6 lessons/2 weeks

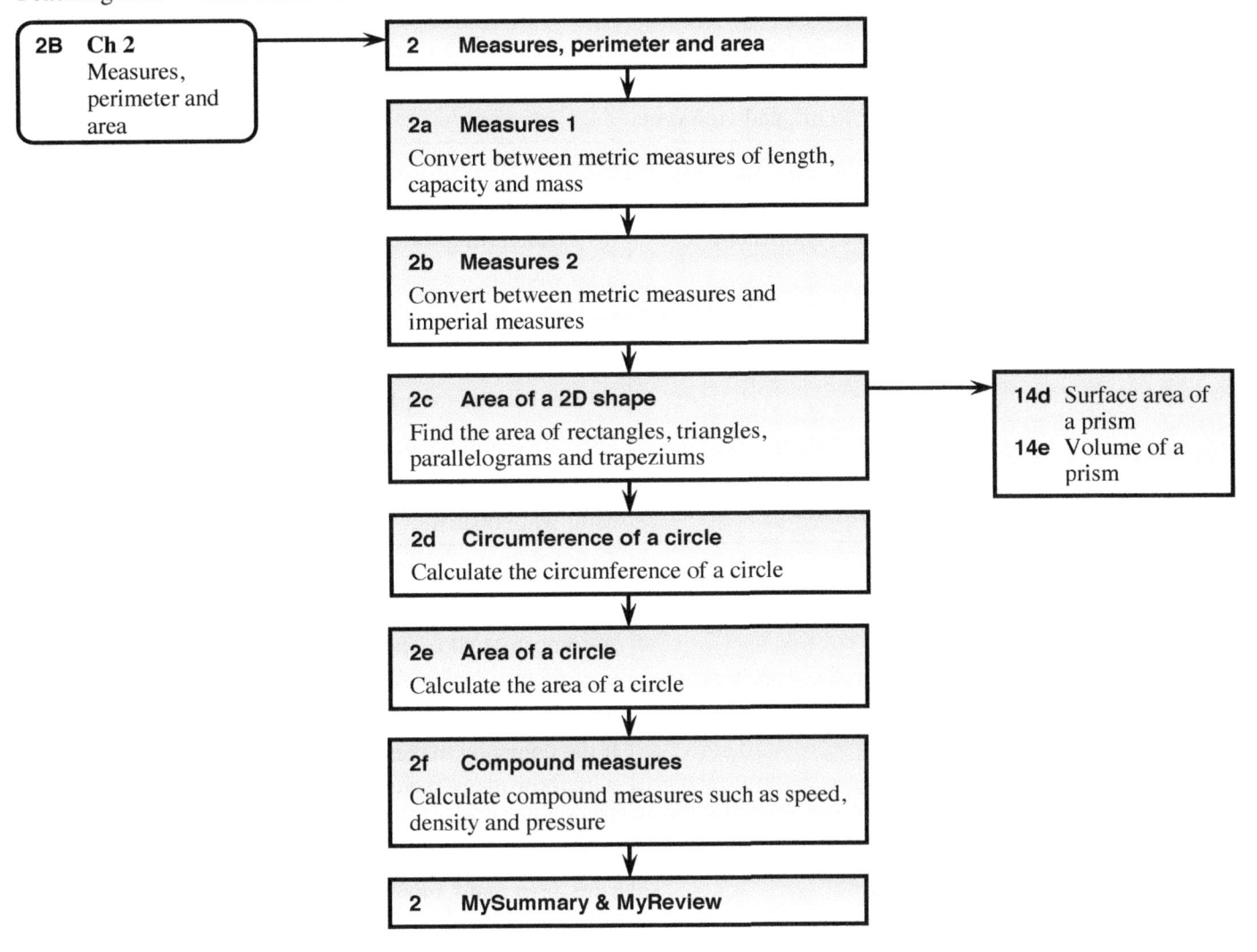

- **2B Ch 2** Measures, perimeter and area
  → **2 Measures, perimeter and area**
    - **2a Measures 1** — Convert between metric measures of length, capacity and mass
    - **2b Measures 2** — Convert between metric measures and imperial measures
    - **2c Area of a 2D shape** — Find the area of rectangles, triangles, parallelograms and trapeziums
      → **14d** Surface area of a prism
        14e Volume of a prism
    - **2d Circumference of a circle** — Calculate the circumference of a circle
    - **2e Area of a circle** — Calculate the area of a circle
    - **2f Compound measures** — Calculate compound measures such as speed, density and pressure
    - **2 MySummary & MyReview**

Differentiation

Student book 3A 20 – 37	Student book 3B 16 – 33	Student book 3C 16 – 29
Convert between metric and metric and imperial units Calculate the areas of simple 2D shapes including triangles and parallelograms Find the circumference of a circle	Covert between metric units and between metric and imperial units Calculate the area of 2D shapes including compound shapes Find the circumference and area of a circle Work with compound measures	Convert between units of measure Understand dimension Calculate lengths and areas of 2D shapes Work with compound measures

Introduction 17

2a Measures 1

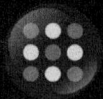

Objectives

- Choose and use units of measurement to measure, estimate, calculate and solve problems in a range of contexts (L5)
- Solve problems involving measurements in a variety of contexts (L6)
- Convert between area measures (e.g. mm^2 to cm^2, cm^2 to m^2, and vice versa) and between volume measures (e.g. mm^3 to cm^3, cm^3 to m^3, and vice versa) (L6)

Key ideas	Resources
1 Understand and use units of measure apporpriately 2 Confidently convert measures into equivalent metric versions.	Metric conversion (1061) Converting measures (1091) 1 kg weight Ruler Drink can Square centimetre grid One centimetre cube Sheets of A4 paper Mini whiteboards

Simplification	Extension
Pair students and invite them to discuss how to do each conversion. Allow students to use a calculator and if necessary say whether a conversion requires a multiplication or a division.	Pose this question to the students. A company makes models out of wire. Each model uses 45 cm of wire. What is the greatest number of models that can be made from 50 metres of wire? If the company makes a larger model, using 65 cm of wire, how many fewer models can be made from 50 metres of wire? If the company makes a smaller model, using 30 cm of wire, how many more models can be made from 50 metres of wire?

Literacy	Links
Check measures vocabulary as well as categories – capacity/volume; area and length. Include mass versus weight, making link with appropriate curricular areas and general usage of terms. Remin students of the basic prefixes and their numerical meanings: milli (1/1000), centi (1/100) and kilo (1000).	There is a table listing countries of the world by area at http://en.wikipedia.org/wiki/List_of_countries_and_outlying_territories_by_area Which is the smallest country in the World? (Vatican City) Which country has the longest coastline in the World? (Canada)

Alternative approach

Begin with a card sort activity in pairs, preparing cards which include the headings capacity, length and area as well as a number of different values which include units. Check and discuss the results. Remind students of some rough estimates such as a bag of sugar weighs 1 kg. Using mini whiteboards ask students to sketch a length of about 10 cm, an area of about 1 cm^2 and to estimate the weight of their maths text book. Compare answers in pairs, then discuss and share with whole group. Check equivalent measures, by asking students to write a value such as 3 km in metres and so on, again using mini whiteboards. Consolidate the work and pose a challenge for student pairs: what is the same and what is different about the two measures 0.5 km and 0.50 km.

Checkpoint

A large jug of squash is prepared and contains 2 litres.
If each plastic cup needs to hold 25 cl, how many cups will this jug fill? (8)

Starter – Estimate

Ask students to estimate in cm the lengths and/or widths of objects in the room. Then ask students to convert the measurements to mm or m.

Can be extended by asking for imperial equivalents or estimated areas in mm^2, cm^2 or m^2.

Teaching notes

Students often find it difficult to remember the conversions of units of area and volume and that they are very different to the conversions for length and mass. A practical activity may help them form a concrete representation which will help them to remember the rules. Drawing a $1\ m^2$ area divided into one cm squares is very time consuming, but drawing a square 10 cm by 10 cm and counting that there are 100 small squares in it allows a discussion of how many there would be in the square metre.

It also allows a discussion of how many cubic centimetres there would be in a block 10 cm high (10 layers thick), and then in a full cubic metre.

Plenary

Ask students to work in pairs to estimate how many litres of water they think there is in a bath, and in a swimming pool (they will need to estimate dimensions first). Use whole-class feedback to compare estimates and discuss strategies used by different pairs.

Exercise commentary

Question 1 – Allow students access to a 1 kg weight, a ruler, a can of drink, a $1\ cm^2$ grid and a $1\ cm^3$ cube to make reference to.

Question 2 – This is based on the example. It uses the conversion information given in the hint boxes. Students should multiply if a bigger numerical answer is required and to divide if a smaller numerical answer is required. Encourage students to work out the answers without using a calculator.

Question 3 – A hectare is $100\ m \times 100\ m = 10\ 000\ m^2$.

Question 4 – Some students may need to be reminded of the formula for the volume of a cuboid.

Question 5 – Students may need a sheet of A4 paper for this activity. They will need to round off some of the answers. For example, $297 \div 2 = 149$ to the nearest integer. This activity is suitable for paired work.

Answers

1.
   a 100 g b $1\ m^2$ c 50 cm d 33 cl
   e 600 km f 900 kg g $1400\ cm^3$
2.
   a 4.8 m b $450\ mm^2$
   c 0.5 ha d $4\ m^3$
   e 0.75 litres f $80\ 000\ cm^2$
   g 750 g h 0.65 km
   i $500\ 000\ cm^3$ j 0.75 t
3. a $4500\ m^2$ b 0.45 ha
4. a $252\ 000\ cm^3$ b 252 litres
5.

Size	Measurements
A1	840 mm × 594 mm
A2	594 mm × 420 mm
A3	420 mm × 297 mm
A4	297 mm × 210 mm
A5	210 mm × 149 mm
A6	149 mm × 105 mm
A7	105 mm × 75 mm
A8	75 mm × 53 mm

Measures 1

2b Measures 2

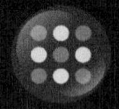

Objectives
- Know rough metric equivalents of imperial measures in common use, such as miles, pounds (lbs) and pints (L5)

Key ideas	Resources
1. Have a knowledge and awareness of size linking common metric and imperial units 2. Be able to use approximate conversion factors to convert between metric and imperial units	Imperial measures (1191) Mini whiteboards Pint container Litre container Ruler

Simplification

To help with the conversions in questions **2** and **4** students could be given them in a structured format. For example, in question **2a**

Imperial measurement	Metric unit	Known fact	Metric measurement
6 oz	gram	1 oz = 30 g	

To further simplify inform students whether the question is a multiplication or division.

Extension

Students should find their height and weight in both metric and imperial units. This could be extended to group work if appropriate.

Alternatively ask students to investigate other units of measurements, for example, what is a stade, cubit, fathom, light year, US gallon, carat, hundred weight, *etc.*?

Literacy

The key imperial vocabulary should be checked: miles, pounds, pints, and also gallons, inches, feet and yards. Some historical background may be useful here, as well as referring to older members of student's family – can they tell the students about these common measures? The common notation for these can be shared and linked with visual clues. It can be useful to have a list of common conversion factors in a student diary. If this is used in your school, make sure that students refer to it during these lessons.

Links

British shoe sizes are based on a unit of length called the barleycorn, equivalent to one-third of an inch. Children's shoe sizes start at size 0 which is equivalent to 4 in. Sizes then increase by one barleycorn each time, so size 13 is 13 barleycorns longer than size 0, or $8\frac{1}{3}$ in. The next size up is adult size 1 which is one barleycorn larger. There is more about shoe sizes at http://www.internationalshoesizes.com/uk-shoe-sizes.htm

Alternative approach

Check with students to see if they know or have heard of some of the rough equivalents. Use visual and/or real examples to help students remember these, for example a bag of sugar, 1 kg, 2.2 lbs; middle joint of thumb, 1 inch, 2.5 cm; a man's height, 6 ft, 1.8 m; and so on. Students may be given the task of preparing a crib sheet for themselves to assist this work. Draw attention to sources of conversion factors that can be found online or in reference books, and note that these tend to be more accurate conversion factors – one or two may be used to compare the results to make the point more explicitly.

Checkpoint

The distance between London and Paris is 343 km. The distance between London and Edinburgh is 332 miles. Which is furthest away and by how much? (Edinburgh is further from London by 119 miles or 191 km)

Starter – Metric match

Ask students to find pairs in the following:

30 000 m², 120 cl, 0.45 t, 300 000 m², 4.5 kg, 0.3 km², 120 ml, 3 ha, 12 cl, 450 kg, 1.2 litres, 4500 g.

(Solution: 30 000 m² = 3 ha; 120 cl = 1.2 litres; 0.45 t = 450 kg; 4.5 kg = 4500 g; 300 000 m² = 0.3 km²; 120 ml = 12 cl)

Can be extended by including extra quantities as red herrings and asking students to make up matches for them.

Teaching notes

Ask students to name imperial and metric units of measurement for length, capacity and mass, and discuss which of them they ever actually use.

Ask them to estimate some lengths in the classroom (a book height, table width, room length) in both metric and imperial units. If you can find some containers, ask students to estimate some capacities as well.

Working with different systems in daily life means that it is important for students to be comfortable in moving between the two measurement scales. All our road signs give distances in miles, but most other measurements of lengths are now metric.

Plenary

Use a mini whiteboard activity where you display a measurement in one system and the students give an equivalent approximation in the other system. This will help you to identify any students who do not have reasonable fluency in moving between the two systems.

Exercise commentary

Students will need a calculator for this exercise.

Question 1 – Allows a comparison between metric and imperial units. It may be helpful to have examples of standard measurements, for example, a pint, a litre, a ruler.

Questions 2 and **3** – These are based on the example and use the given conversion information. Encourage students to check whether their answers are realistic and to use 'known' measurements as benchmarks.

Question 4 – Students should round their answers to the nearest mile.

Question 5 – This is suitable for group work and exploration on the internet.

Answers

1. a   1 mile, 1 mile ≈ 1.6 km   b   1 kg, 1 kg ≈ 2.2 lb
   c   1 inch, 1 inch ≈ 2.5 cm   d   1 litre, 1 pint ≈ 0.6 litre
   e   1 ounce, 1 oz ≈ 30 g
2. a   180 g   b   4.8 m   c   45000 ml   d   219 cm
   e   42.5 kg   f   0.9 m   g   75.2 km   h   2700 ml
3. a   15 oz   b   4 in   c   15 pints   d   8 gallons
   e   3 feet   f   68 in   g   7.7 lb   h   0.25 pints
4.
   Calais
288	Cherbourg		
537	576	Grenoble	
181	221	354	Paris

5. a   Give him a centimetre and he will take a metre
   b   You can't get a litre into a centilitre pot
   c   A miss is as good as a kilometre
   d   I wouldn't touch it with a ten-metre barge pole
   e   A gram of prevention is worth a kilogram of cure

Measures 2

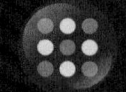

2c Area of a 2D shape

Objectives		
• Derive and use formulae for the area of a triangle, parallelogram and trapezium		(L6)
• Calculate areas of compound shapes		(L6)

Key ideas	Resources	
1 To understand the nature of area formulae	Area of a parallelogram	(1108)
2 Know and use area formula for triangle, parallelogram and trapezium	Square grid paper	

Simplification	Extension
For question **1**, supply squared grid paper as an aid to making accurate copies of the diagrams. If necessary, supply drawings with one or more of the shapes already divided into rectangles and possibly also with missing dimensions filled in. For question **6**, provide the students with templates of the two right-angled triangles and the square. The shapes could also have 1 cm grid lines on them.	Ask students to investigate the following. The perimeter of a rectangle is 24 cm. Find the values of the length and the width that gives the greatest area. Extend this problem to rectangles with different perimeters.

Literacy	Links
Check vocabulary and spelling of parallelogram and trapezium, including recognition of these shapes in a variety of forms. Maintain verbal descriptions of the formula before using algebraic or generalised forms in order to communicate the reasoning clearly. Include perimeter and check the differences to area in terms of both definition and units.	Tile-making died out after the dissolution of the monasteries in the sixteenth century but was revived by the Victorians. The Victorians used many geometric shapes including the trapezium and the parallelogram to produce stunning designs for floors in both grand buildings, such as Windsor Castle and the Houses of Parliament, and in ordinary houses. There are examples of original and reproduction Victorian floor designs at http://www.europeanheritage.com/victorian_floor_tiles.asp and at http://www.londonvictorianmosaicrestoration.co.uk/welcome.html

Alternative approach

Begin with a compound shape made up of 2 rectangles (e.g. 1c) for students to find the area. Encourage working in pairs on this problem using a mini whiteboard. Share results and discuss approaches – the two basic ways of dividing into two rectangles and adding, or finding the extended rectangle's area and subtracting. Check units, and lead into prompting students to give formulae for rectangular area and triangular area. Pose a further problem using a parallelogram – but do not lead students towards an approach. Discuss their offered results and strategies – removing and shifting a triangle from one side to the other of the shape is likely to be more popular than dividing into two triangles. Evolve with the students a formula resulting from their approaches. Tackle a trapezuium in the same way.

Checkpoint

A triangle has area 60 cm^2. If the base is 20 cm, what is the height? (6 cm)

A parallelogram has base 5 cm and perpendicular height 15 cm. Find the area. (75 cm^2)

A trapezium has parallel sides of length 4 cm and 10 cm.
If the perpendicular distance between them is 6 cm, what is the area? (42 cm^2)

Starter – True or false?

Give statements and ask students if they are true or false. For example

4 in ≈ 10 cm	(True)
5 km > 5 miles	(False)
1 gallon ≈ 6000 ml	(False, should be 4500 ml)
11 lb ≈ 5 kg	(True) *etc*

Teaching notes

Many students have some difficulty in putting together the geometrical ideas and the application of relatively simple algebra. It may be worthwhile to revise simple manipulation, using letters commonly used in geometrical formulae but less commonly used when just working with algebra. Expansion of simple brackets, factorization, substitution and solving simple equations are all used in the next two spreads.

Emphasise the importance of drawing sketches when breaking composite shapes into component parts and of labelling the sides carefully. Many mistakes are made by not correctly identifying the dimensions.

Plenary

Display some composite shapes similar to those in question **1**, with sketches to show the component parts, some correctly labelled and others with some incorrect dimensions. Ask students to check the diagrams and find and correct any mistakes.

Exercise commentary

Encourage students to give the correct units in their answers.

Question 1 – Students should draw the extra lines on their diagrams to create the rectangles.

Question 2 – Students can estimate the length and width as $\sqrt{192} \approx 14$ and proceeding to test nearby (integer) possibilities. Alternatively suggest looking at factors: $192 = 2^6 \times 3$.

Question 3 – Some students will not realise the significance of the shape being a triangle and not a rectangle. Ensure that students check their answers for **b** by calculating the area of each triangle.

Question 4 – This is based on the example. In part **b**, students cannot find the area of the rhombus with a single calculation. They could, for example, find the area of triangle ADB, and then multiply the answer by two.

Question 5 – Here, the orientation of the box given is not going to give the best answer. Encourage students to think about the different ways the box can be placed before proceeding to work out the best way (the 5 by 4 cm face should be placed in the tray, giving 24 boxes in total).

Question 6 – Students can cut out accurate drawings of the shapes, if necessary.

Answers

1. **a** 125 cm²   **b** 78 m²   **c** 48 cm²
2. **a** 12 cm   **b** 56 cm
3. **a** $b = 4$ cm   **b** $b = 6$ cm
   c $b = 9.6$ cm
4. **a** 80 cm²   **b** 160 cm²   **c** 90 cm²
5. 24
6. Triangle: Perimeter = 12 cm, Area = 6 cm²
   Square: Perimeter = 16 cm, Area = 16 cm²
   a 22 cm, 28 cm²   **b** 24 cm, 28 cm²
   c 24 cm, 28 cm²
   Area of rectangle = $4 \times 7 = 28$ cm²
   Area of parallelogram = $4 \times 7 = 28$ cm²
   Area of trapezium = $\frac{1}{2} \times (4 + 10) \times 4 = 28$ cm²

Area of a 2D shape

2d Circumference of a circle

Objectives		
• Know the definition of a circle and the names of its parts		(L5)
• Know and use the formulae for the circumference of a circle		(L6)

Key ideas	Resources
1 Identify some key features of a circle and their terms 2 Be able to find the circumference of a circle.	Circumference of a circle (1088) IWB set up with circles to support the estimation exercises

Simplification	Extension
In question **1** parts **c** and **d**, give students the diameters only: $d = 9$ cm and $d = 18$ m respectively. In question **4**, tell students the proportion of the circumference that is required.	Pose this question to the students. The diameter of a large circular table is 4.5 metres. Decide how many people can sit around the table.

Literacy	Links
Circumference is frequently related to 'perimeter', but this can be unhelpful for students when finding perimeter of compounds shapes which include circle parts. Explicitly tackle both words, their similarities and their differences. Matching vocabulary cards/paper to circle diagrams with arrows will help students to nail the meaning of the words. This can include parts mentioned in the next section and be completed as one task.	A surveyor's wheel is used to measure distances. The radius is chosen so that the circumference of the wheel is an exact length such as a metre or a yard. As the wheel is rolled along the ground, a mechanical device attached to the wheel counts the revolutions and so measures the distance. There are pictures of surveyors' wheels at http://laserlengthmeasurement.com

Alternative approach

An alternative way to estimate circumference is to begin by considering how far the diameter would stretch onto the circumferemnce. By getting students to estimate this on a variety of different sized circles, all sharing a common end of a diameter will produce a rough graph showing the scale of the circumference, or that k ≈ 3. Prepare this on an interatice whiteboard so that students can mark their estimates and graphing can be added to the diagrams. It is also possible to use string to measure circumferences approximately and explore the approximate scale factor needed to achieve the circumference from the diameter as in **q7**, but the level of approximation to π will need to be fully discussed. Students frequently confuse this formula and that of the circle's area, so it is worth asking them to devise rhymes or songs to help them remember each appropriately.

Checkpoint

The radius of a circle is 4 cm. Estimate the length of the circumference.   ($2 \times 4 \times 3 = 24$ cm)

A circle has a circumference of about 120 cm. Estimate what the length of the radius would be.   (20 cm)

Geometry and measures   Measures, perimeter and area

Starter – Puzzling shapes

A rectangle and a triangle both have an area of 18 cm². The length of the rectangle is one and a half times the base of the triangle. The width of the rectangle is one-third the perpendicular height of the triangle. Ask students to find the measurements of both shapes.
(9 cm, 2 cm; 6 cm, 6 cm)

Hint: Try factors of 18.

Can be extended by asking students to make up a similar puzzle of their own.

Teaching notes

Students often struggle with why the circumference should be in the form that it is. In the diagram below, the distance around the square is $4d$ but the distance around the circle is less than that because you cut corners. The distance around the circle must be greater than $2d$ since you go over and back, but not in a straight line. This gives upper and lower limits for the distance around the circle and students will normally guess it is closer to $4d$ than to $2d$.

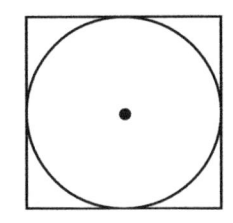

Making the picture larger and smaller and discussing what happens to the ratio between the circumference and the side of the square (the diameter) will lead to $C = kd$ with the value of k around 3.

The hexagon in question **6** allows a closer estimate of the value of pi.

Plenary

Pi day is on March 14th each year and there are many websites showing activities for Pi day which you could use to illustrate the history or the usefulness of this strange number. Pi has been calculated to over 1 trillion digits now.

Exercise commentary

Encourage students to check their answers using $\pi = 3$. Remind students that circumference is a measure of length with units, for example, cm.

Question 1 – This is based on the example. Emphasise that parts **a** and **b** use diameter, whereas **c** and **d** use radius.

Question 2 – Remind students that the circumference is required.

Question 3 – Part **b** requires students to carry out a follow-on calculation from their answer to part **a**. They will also need to convert the 1km distance to cm if they leave their answer to part **a** in that unit.

Question 4 – Remind students to include the straight edges in their calculations. Some students may calculate the circumference of the whole circle, rather than the required part circle.

Question 5 – Asks for the reverse process to find the diameter given the circumference.

Question 5 – Remind students that the six triangles in the diagram are equilateral. Ask, what can you say about the value of π? (> 3).

Question 7 – Students can extend the activity by using an extra column, C ÷ D, which should give them a value for π.

Answers

1   a   25.12 cm   b   62.8 cm
    c   28.26 cm   d   56.52 cm
2   423.9 m
3   a   219.8 cm   b   455 rotations
4   a   10.28 cm   b   39.27 cm   c   10.065 m
5   11.5 cm
6   a   i   30 cm   ii   31.4 cm
    b   Each arc between the touching points is bigger than the straight line between them.
7   Students' answers

Circumference of a circle

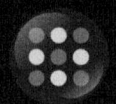

2e Area of a circle

Objectives		
• Know the definition of a circle and the names of its parts		(L5)
• Know and use the formulae for the circumference and area of a circle		(L6)

Key ideas	Resources	
1 Identify some key features of a circle and their terms 2 Be able to find the area of a circle	Area of circles Spare drawing equipment Dictionaries	(1083)

Simplification	Extension
In question 2, tell students that the radius is 1.75 m. In question 3, tell students the proportion of the whole circle that is required.	Students can extend question 5 by calculating the area of the square that circumscribes the circle.

Literacy	Links
See Literacy in previous section, 2d. Check correct use of units, and stress the comparison between circumference and area in terms of the units.	Bring in some dictionaries for the class to use. Many words ending in -us have the plural -i, for instance cactus (cacti). Can the class find any other examples? (Examples are crocus, terminus, gladiolus, nucleus, fungus). However the rule does not hold true for all words ending in –us. What are the plurals of circus, omnibus and chorus?

Alternative approach
An alternative way of establishing the formula for the area of a circle as shown in the student book, can be used as a practical student activity, with support to establish the appropriate lengths and therefore the formula. This can also be set up on an interactive whiteboard, with a greater number of sectors used hence a closer approximation to a rectangle visually. Again encourage students to devise rhyms or a song to help them remember each formula – deal with both in this section. Finally, pose a challenge by asking students to consider a circle with a segment cut off it. Does this mean that the area and the preimeter of the new shape will be smaller?

Checkpoint	
A circle has a diameter of 10 cm. Roughly, what would its area be?	($3 \times 25 = 75$ cm^2)
A circle has area 48 cm^2. Roughly, what is the radius of the circle?	($48 \div 3 = 16$, $\sqrt{16} = 4$ cm)

Starter – Jumble

Write a list of anagrams on the board and ask students to unscramble them and then make up their own. Possible anagrams are

ICECCREMENURF DREAMIET CAR GETHIH
ABSE TERMPERIE PEASH IDIAR
INCLUDEPREPAR RICCEL

(circumference, diameter, arc, height, base, perimeter, shape, radii, perpendicular, circle)

Teaching notes

As with the discussion of the circumference in the previous spread, students can be encouraged to discover that the area of a circle is proportional to r^2 (with the constant around 3) fairly simply and quickly. In the diagram below the outer square has area $4r^2$ and the inner square is exactly half that or $2r^2$.

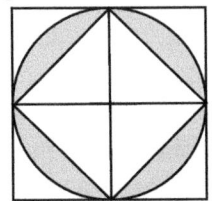

As before, making the picture smaller or larger is convincing that the circle area is always the same proportion. That is, $A = kr^2$, with the constant k around 3.

That k is the same constant as before can be established by splitting a circle into a large number of narrow triangles, each of approximate height r and total base $2\pi r$, so that total area $A \approx \frac{1}{2} \times 2\pi r \times r = \pi r^2$.

Plenary

Show the calculation of the area of a circle as $\pi \times r$ then squaring the answer. Ask students to check if the sum is right and to correct any mistake. Ask students to explain the mistake. Emphasise the need for the correct order of operations here.

Exercise commentary

Encourage students to check their answers using $\pi = 3$ and emphasise that $r^2 = r \times r$.

Remind students that area is measured in squares, for example, square centimetres (cm^2).

Question 1 – This is based on part **a** of the example.

Question 2 – This is based on part **b** of the example.

Question 3 – This question leads students through the process of finding the area of sectors of circles. Depending on the method used, students can check their answers. For example, part **c** + part **d** = part **a**.

Question 4 – This is suitable for paired work if completed practically. If students rearrange the coloured shapes, each question consists of two semicircles, one of each colour.

Question 5 – The area of the square cannot be found in one calculation. Students will first have to find the area of the triangles.

Question 6 – Students first need to work forwards to find the first area and then backwards to find the second radius.

Question 7 – This question leads onto the principle of value for money. There are several possible answers (and justifications thereof) for part **c**.

Answers

1. a $314\ cm^2$ b $1256\ cm^2$
   c $254.34\ cm^2$ d $19.625\ cm^2$
2. $9.61625\ cm^2$
3. a $113.04\ cm^2$ b $56.52\ cm^2$
   c $28.26\ cm^2$ d $84.78\ cm^2$
4. a $100.48\ cm^2$; $100.48\ cm^2$
   b $100.48\ cm^2$; $100.48\ cm^2$
   c $100.48\ cm^2$; $100.48\ cm^2$
5. a $50\ cm^2$ b $78.5\ cm^2$ c $28.5\ cm^2$
6. 12 cm, radius is doubled
7. a Small: $379.94\ cm^2$
      Large: $803.84\ cm^2$
   b Large pizza, bigger area per pound
   c 27 cm diameter, £7
      As it gives a smaller pizza than the large, but at a better value than the small one

Area of a circle

2f Compound measures

Objectives
- Use compound units such as speed, unit pricing and density to solve problems (L7)

Key ideas
1. Work out speed, distance or time using a formula
2. Work with density and pressure

Resources
Speed (1121)
Density (1246)
Calculators

Simplification
Omit questions that are not in standard units, for example question **1** parts **d, f** and **l**.

Provide students with the conversions from m/s to km/h ($\div 1000 \times 3600$) (question **4** part **b**) and from mph to km/h ($\times 1.6$) (question **5** part **a**).

Questions **6** and **7** can be omitted.

Extension
Additional questions could be given where it is the time to be calculated:

For example, calculate the time taken to travel

a 640 km at 40 km/h (16 hours)

b 8500 m at 1.7 km/h (5 hours)

Students could also be asked to investigate the history of the land speed record (question **5**) or look at other songs which contain references to distances or speeds (question **7**).

Literacy
Students may be meeting some of the language for the first time, e.g. density or pressure so these words can be defined.

Ensure correct units are used for calculated values.

Links
There are clear links to science here. Many of the students may have encountered the concept of compound measure in science lessons and a cross-curricular link can be developed.

There are also obvious links to real-world situations as outlined in the exercise (particularly questions **3** to **5**).

Alternative approach
An alternative way of helping the students to work out exactly which 'version' of the formulae should be used to calculate the specified unknown is to take each of the compound measure triangles and employ a 'cover-up' method. For example, with the speed, distance, time triangle, if I want to find the distance, I cover up the D in the triangle and this leaves me with S and T side-by-side, hence 'multiply'. If instead I want to find T, I cover this over and it leaves D and S on top of each other, hence 'divide'.

Checkpoint
a Work out the speed of a snail, in metres per minute, which travels 12 cm every hour. (0.002)

b A block of lead has mass 2.5 kg and volume 220 cm^3. What is the density of the lead? (11.36g/cm^3)

Geometry and measures   Measures, perimeter and area

Starter – Quick-fire mental quiz

Since much of the exercise is to do with multiplying and dividing, try a quick-fire mental arithmetic quiz with the students. They could use mini-whiteboards to show their answers quickly and for easy checking.

Questions could those include such as

200 × 4

150 ÷ 3

and be very quick for the students to work out.

Teaching notes

The principle of speed is something that students should have some knowledge of. Emphasise that speed is the *rate* at which something covers a specified distance and is measured in units *distance/time* such as m/s or km/h. Some basic examples can be given to the students where the units are straightforward and reference can be made to the formula triangle and the various rearrangements for finding alternative unknowns.

A parallel can be drawn between speed and the other two compound measures covered in the section: density and pressure. Both of these are also *rates* and a link can be made to science. A similar approach using formulae triangles can be shown to the students.

Plenary

Which is faster? A cheetah which runs at an average speed of 26 m/s or a car travelling at 58 mph? (The cheetah, with an equivalent speed of 58.5 mph)

Exercise commentary

Question 1 – Check that the students are working in standard units such as km/h or m/s and not km/min or m/min. For part **l**, they will need to convert the time into the correct units first (seconds).

Question 2 – Once the calculations are completed in part **a**, the comparison can be made directly (calculators may be allowed).

Question 3 – Reference can be made to the pressure formula triangle here.

Question 4 – Students may need help working out the conversion from m/s to km/h (see simplification).

Question 5 – Students could be asked to convert the speed of sound into alternative units as an extension activity.

Question 6 – In part **a**, students will first need to calculate the volume of the cube of cork (= 1000cm^3) and in part **b** may need reminding that there are 1000cm^3 in a litre of water.

Question 7 – Students may need to successively calculate miles per day, miles per month, etc. and a calculator will be very useful in this regard.

Answers

1 a 50 km/h   b 70 km/h   c 40 mph   d 60 km/h
   e 3000 m/s f 4.8 km/h g 75 km   h 140 km
   i 175 km   j 600 m   k 550 m   l 3600 m
2 a Kathy: 4 m/s
      Jayne: 3.2 m/s
   b Kathy ran faster
3 No, pressure is only 3 000 000 N/m^2
4 a 72.3 m/s   b 260 km/h
5 a 1230 km/h   b Yes he did
6 a 250 g   b 1000 g
7 38 years

Compound measures

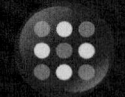

2 Measures, perimeter and area – MySummary

Key outcomes	Quick check
Convert between metric units. L5	Convert: **a** 3cm to mm (30) **b** 400m to km (0.4) **c** 2300ml to litres (2.3)
Convert between metric and imperial units. L5	Convert: **a** 510g to ounces (17) **b** 110 miles to km (176) **c** 12 gallons to litres (54)
Calculate the area of a 2D shape. L6	Find the areas of the following shapes: **a** A triangle with base 5cm and height 8cm (20cm^2) **b** A parallelogram with base 3cm and perpendicular height 6cm (18cm^2) **c** A trapezuim with parallel sides 6cm and 10cm. The perpendicular distance between them is 5cm. (40cm^2)
Calculate the circumference and area of a circle. L6	Calculate the area and circumference of each circle, given the radius: **a** $r = 5$cm (78.5cm^2, 31.4cm) **b** $r = 8$cm (201cm^2, 50.2cm)
Recognise and use compound measures. L7	Find the following speeds, in m/s: **a** 40 metres in 8 seconds (5 m/s) **b** 1.8km in 3 minutes (10 m/s)

⊕ MyMaths extra support

Lesson/online homework	Description
Area of rectangles 1084 L4	Area is a measure of how many squares fit inside a 2D shape.
Area of a triangle 1129 L6	Formula for the area of a triangle. The area of a triangle relies on its base and height.

MyReview

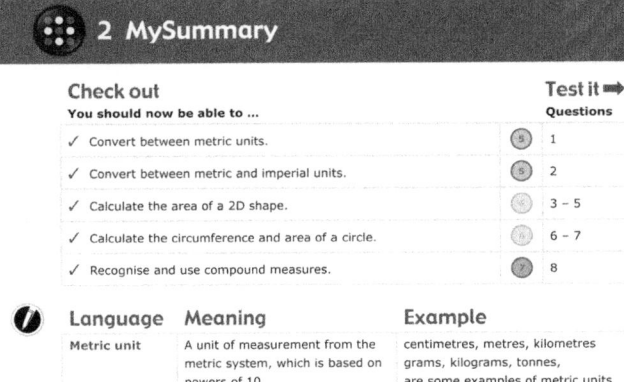

2 MySummary

Check out
You should now be able to ...

	Test it → Questions
✓ Convert between metric units.	(5) 1
✓ Convert between metric and imperial units.	(5) 2
✓ Calculate the area of a 2D shape.	(6) 3 – 5
✓ Calculate the circumference and area of a circle.	(6) 6 – 7
✓ Recognise and use compound measures.	(7) 8

Language	Meaning	Example
Metric unit	A unit of measurement from the metric system, which is based on powers of 10.	centimetres, metres, kilometres grams, kilograms, tonnes, are some examples of metric units
Imperial unit	A unit of measurement from the older imperial system.	inches, feet, yards, miles ounces, pounds, stone, tons are some examples of imperial units
Area	The space inside a 2D shape.	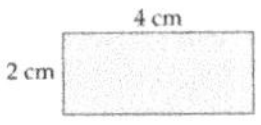 The area of the rectangle is 8 cm²
Circumference	The distance around a circle.	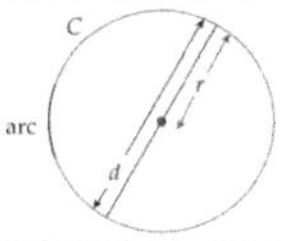
Diameter	The distance across a circle, through the centre.	
Radius	The distance from the centre of a circle to the circumference.	
Speed	A measure of the rate at which distance is covered.	The speed of sound travelling through air is roughly 343 metres per second.

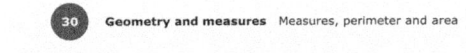

Geometry and measures — Measures, perimeter and area

2 MyReview

1. Convert between these metric measurements.
   a. 4.9 m to mm
   b. 87 cl to litres
   c. 0.47 kg to g
   d. 0.9 cm² to mm²
   e. 3 m² to cm²
   f. 3 l in cm³

2. Convert these imperial measurements to metric.
   a. 3 pints to litres
   b. 24 lb to kg
   c. 90 miles to km
   d. 39 inches to m

3. Calculate the area of this shape. State the units of your answer.

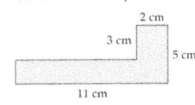

4. The area of a right-angled triangle is 16 cm². The base is 4 cm in length. What is the height of the triangle?

5. Calculate the area of the trapezium. State the units of your answer.

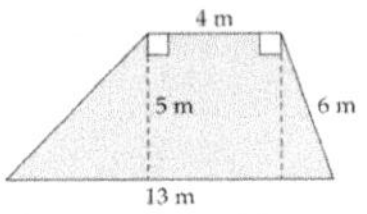

6. Calculate
   a. the area
   b. the circumference of the circle. 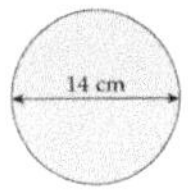
   Give your answers to 1 dp.

7. The diagram shows a quarter of a circle with radius 14 cm. Calculate
   a. the area
   b. the perimeter. 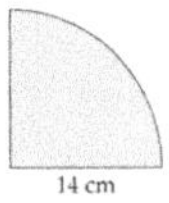
   Give your answers to 1 dp.

8. a. A car travels 30 miles in 45 minutes. Calculate the car's average speed in miles per hour.
   b. A 2 centimetre cube of lead has a mass of 90.7 grams. Calculate the density of lead in g/cm³.

What next?

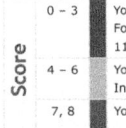

Score	
0 – 3	Your knowledge of this topic is still developing. To improve look at Formative test: 3B-2; MyMaths: 1061, 1083, 1088, 1091, 1108, 1121, 1128, 1191 and 1246
4 – 6	You are gaining a secure knowledge of this topic. To improve look at InvisiPen: 313, 314, 315, 316, 332, 333, 335, 351, 352 and 353
7, 8	You have mastered this topic. Well done, you are ready to progress!

MyMaths.co.uk

Question commentary

Question 1 – Parts **d**, **e** and **f** are most likely to cause problems.

Question 2 – Students need to learn the approximate conversions between metric and imperial units as given in **2b**.

Question 3 – Students can split the shape into 11×2 and 3×2 rectangles or 5×2 and 9×2 rectangles.

Question 4 – A common mistake is to halve the area when it should be doubled (giving 1) or to do neither (giving 4).

Question 5 – The formula for the area of a trapezium does not necessarily need to be memorized but students need to know how to apply it and be able to identify trapeziums. If they use the diagonal length (6) instead of the height (5) in their calculation they will get an incorrect answer of 51 m².

Questions 6 and 7 – Use $\pi = 3.14$ or the π button on a calculator; students will need to find the radius first in question **6**. A possible error in question **7** is to divide 14 by 4 before working out the area (giving 38.5). For the perimeter of **7b** the curved part is 21.98 cm, students must remember to add the two lengths of 14 cm.

Question 8 – Students must make sure they are working in the correct units in both parts.

Answers

1. a. 4900 mm   b. 0.87 l   c. 470 g   d. 90 mm²
   e. 30 000 cm²   f. 3000 cm³
2. a. 1.8 l   b. 10.9 kg   c. 144 km   d. 0.975 m
3. 28 cm²
4. 8 cm
5. 42.5 m²
6. a. 153.9 cm²   b. 44.0 cm
7. a. 283.5 cm²   b. 50.0 cm
8. a. 40 mph   b. 11.3375 g/cm³

MySummary/MyReview

2 MyPractice

2a

1 Choose the most sensible estimate for these quantities.
 a the capacity of a medicine bottle   20 ml   200 ml   2 litres
 b the length of a badminton court   13.4 cm   13.4 m   13.4 km
 c the mass of a person   6 kg   60 kg   600 kg
 d the area of a window   1 mm²   1 cm²   1 m²
 e the volume of a tennis ball   14 cm³   140 cm³   1400 cm³

2 How many square millimetres are there in one square centimetre?
 Sketch a diagram to show your working.

3 Convert these metric measurements to the units in brackets.
 a 67 mm (cm)   b 850 g (kg)
 c 8 m³ (cm³)   d 1 km (mm)
 e 400 g (kg)   f 7.5 ha (m²)
 g 3.5 m (mm)   h 75000 cl (litres)
 i 5 m² (cm²)   j 18 tonnes (kg)

2b

4 Convert these imperial measurements to the metric units in brackets using approximations.
 a 2.5 oz (g)   b 7 pints (ml)
 c 12 in (cm)   d 40 in (cm)
 e 154 lb (kg)   f 35 miles (km)
 g 8.5 pints (litres) h 2.5 gallons (ml)

5 Convert these metric measurements to the imperial units in brackets using approximations.
 a 160 cm (in)   b 3.9 litres (pints)
 c 84 km (miles)   d 48 kg (lb)
 e 45 g (oz)   f 49.5 litres (gallons)
 g 8.4 m (feet)   h 2100 ml (pints)

2c

6 The area of the rectangle and the triangle are the same.
 Calculate the value of h.

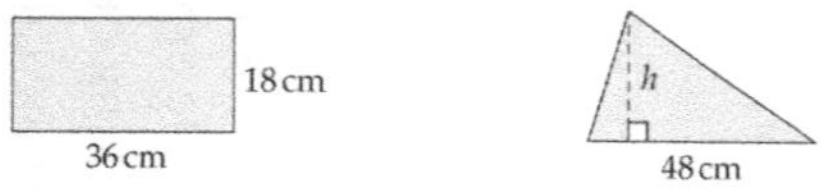

7 Calculate the areas of these shapes.
 State the units of your answers.
 a 16 mm   b 7.5 cm, 8 cm, 11.5 cm   c 6.5 m, 18 m

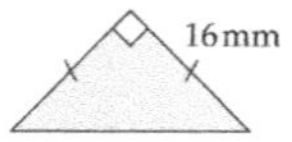

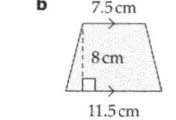

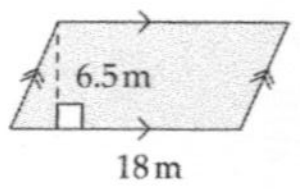

2d

8 Calculate the circumferences of these circles.
 Use $\pi = 3.14$. 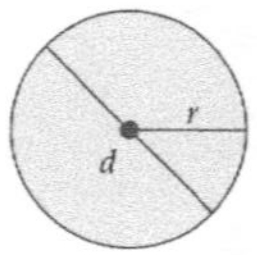
 a $r = 6$ cm
 b $r = 8.5$ m
 c $d = 15$ cm
 d $d = 11$ cm
 e $r = 2.75$ m

9 A coin with a diameter of 25 mm is rolled along a table.
 Calculate
 a the circumference
 b the distance travelled in metres during 20 complete rotations.
 Use $\pi = 3.14$.

2e

10 Calculate the areas of these circles.
 Use $\pi = 3.14$. 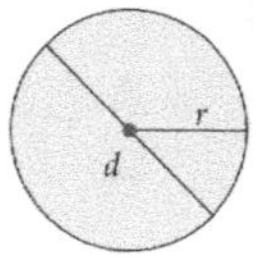
 a $r = 7$ cm
 b $r = 3.5$ m
 c $r = 9.5$ cm
 d $d = 11$ cm
 e $d = 25$ cm

11 A circumcircle is drawn round a regular hexagon.
 The hexagon has a perimeter of 36 cm.
 Calculate the area of the circle.
 Use $\pi = 3.14$.

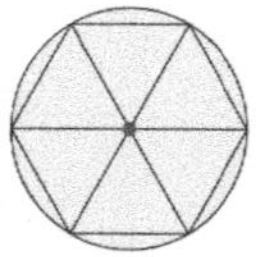

Question commentary

Questions 1, 2 and **3** – Students should be able to deduce the correct estimates in question **1** by comparison to other things. Questions **2** and **3** require recall of conversions.

Questions 4 and **5** – Students should be able to recall approximate conversions from imperial to metric units.

Questions 6 and **7** – Students will need to recall formulae for the area of 2D shapes. The trapezium formula (for question **7b**) could be given.

Questions 8 to **11** – Make sure that students work correctly with either radius or diameter as given. Questions **9** and **11** are more problem-solving in nature and some guidance may be required.

Answers

1. a 200 ml b 13.4 m c 60 kg d 1 m^2
   e 140 cm^3
2. 100 mm^2 = 1 cm^2
3. a 6.7 cm b 0.85 kg
   c 8 000 000 cm^3 d 1 000 000 mm
   e 0.4 kg f 75 000 m^2
   g 3500 mm h 750 litres
   i 50 000 cm^2 j 18 000 kg
4. a 75 g b 4200 ml c 30 cm d 100 cm
   e 70 kg f 56 km g 5.1 litres h 11 250 ml
5. a 64 in b 6.5 pints c 52.5 miles d 105.6 lb
   e 1.5 oz f 11 gallons g 28 feet h 3.5 pints
6. 27 cm
7. a 128 mm^2 b 76 cm^2 c 117 m^2
8. a 37.68 cm b 53.38 m c 47.1 cm d 34.54 cm
   e 17.27 cm
9. a 78.5 mm b 1570 mm
10. a 153.86 cm^2 b 38.465 m^2
    c 283.385 cm^2 d 94.985 cm^2
    e 490.625 cm^2
11. 113.04 cm^2

MyPractice

3 Expressions and formulae

Learning outcomes

A1 Use and interpret algebraic notation, including:
- ab in place of $a \times b$
- a^2 in place of $a \times a$, a^3 in place of $a \times a \times a$; a^2b in place of $a \times a \times b$
- a/b in place of $a \div b$
- $3y$ in place of $y + y + y$ and $3 \times y$
- coefficients written as fractions rather than as decimals
- brackets (L7)

A2 Substitute numerical values into formulae and expressions, including scientific formulae (L7)

A3 Understand and use the concepts and vocabulary of expressions, equations, inequalities, terms and factors (L7)

A4 Simplify and manipulate algebraic expressions to maintain equivalence by:
- collecting like terms
- taking out common factors
- multiplying a single term over a bracket (L7)

A5 Understand and use standard mathematical formulae; rearrange formulae to change the subject (L7)

A6 Model situations or procedures by translating them into algebraic expressions or formulae and by using graphs (L6)

Introduction

The chapter starts by looking at algebraic factorisation and simplifying algebraic fractions before moving on to formulae in context, including substitution into formulae. Rearranging formulae is covered before the final section on deriving formulae and graphing formulae.

The introduction discusses two very famous equations from the history of mathematics: Newton's formula for gravitation and Einstein's equation $E = mc^2$. Both of these incredibly important scientists and mathematicians led the way in their respective fields and most of modern mathematics and physics is based on the work of one or the other of them. Newton worked with small-scale mechanics and the motion of bodies relative to each other whereas Einstein is more famous for his laws of relativity which apply on a cosmological scale. Biographies of Newton and Einstein can be found at:

http://www-history.mcs.st-andrews.ac.uk/Biographies/Newton.html

http://www-history.mcs.st-andrews.ac.uk/Biographies/Einstein.html

Prior knowledge

Students should already know how to...
- Write down and substitute into simple algebraic expressions
- Expand single brackets and collect like terms

Starter problem

The starter problem is an investigation into 'L' numbers, formed by joining five cells on a standard number square to form a 3 by 3 'L' shape. In the example, the 'L' based on square 35 is shown and students are asked to come up with a formula connecting this base number with the sum of the cells.

If we take the base number to be x, we can write the two cells to the left as $x - 1$ and $x - 2$. The numbers on the rows above are similarly $x - 12$ and $x - 22$. If we sum these terms algebraically, we get $5x - 37$ as the expression for the total of all the numbers in the 'L'.

For the base number 35, this gives a sum of:

$5 \times 35 - 37 = 138$ which agrees with the arithmetic sum given in the example.

Students could be directed to investigate the sums numerically, or to dive straight into the algebra, depending on their ability and previous knowledge.

Resources

MyMaths

Factorising linear	1155	Rearranging 1	1171	Simplifying 2	1178
Substitution 2	1186				

Online assessment

Chapter test	3B-3
Formative test	3B-3
Summative test	3B-3

InvisiPen solutions

Algebraic fractions			223
Find unknown when it's not the subject			241
Creating a formula	252	Substitution	254
Further substitution			255
Changing the subject of a formula			256

34 Algebra Expressions and formulae

Topic scheme

Teaching time = 5 lessons/2 weeks

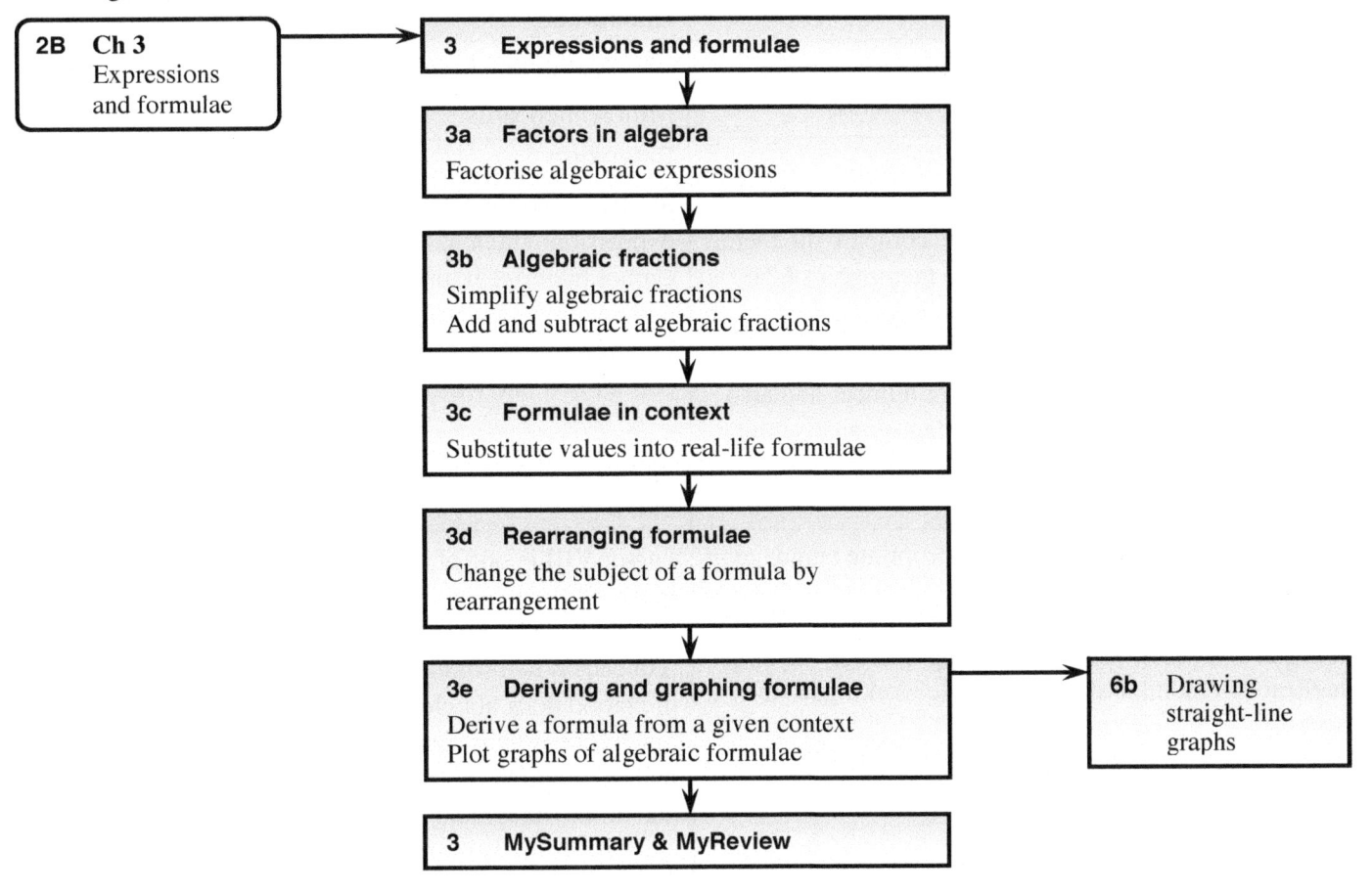

2B	Ch 3 Expressions and formulae

→ **3 Expressions and formulae**

↓

3a Factors in algebra
Factorise algebraic expressions

↓

3b Algebraic fractions
Simplify algebraic fractions
Add and subtract algebraic fractions

↓

3c Formulae in context
Substitute values into real-life formulae

↓

3d Rearranging formulae
Change the subject of a formula by rearrangement

↓

3e Deriving and graphing formulae → **6b Drawing straight-line graphs**
Derive a formula from a given context
Plot graphs of algebraic formulae

↓

3 MySummary & MyReview

Differentiation

Student book 3A   38 – 51
Simplifying expressions
Using brackets
Formulae
Writing algebraic expressions from context

Student book 3B   34 – 49
Factorise expressions
Simplify algebraic fractions
Add and subtract algebraic fractions
Substitute into formulae in context
Rearranging formulae
Deriving formulae
Graphing formulae

Student book 3C   30 – 51
Index laws
Multiplying linear expressions
Factorising expressions
Identities
Formulae in context
Rearranging formulae

Introduction   **35**

3a Factors in algebra

Objectives	
• Simplify or transform algebraic expressions by taking out single-term common factors (L6)	
Key ideas	**Resources**
1 Recognising that algebra is generalised number 2 Manipulate and rearrange algebraic terms	Factorising Linear (1155) Mini whiteboards
Simplification	**Extension**
Factors of numbers should be found before moving into algebraic factors. For example, compare the factor pairs of 6 (1 × 6 and 2 × 3) and the factor pair of $3x$ (3 and x), before looking for factors which are common to $3x$ and 6. Factorising $3x + 6$ follows naturally. Cuisenaire rods can be used both for number and also for general expressions to help students visualise the process.	Students, working in pairs, can offer each other an expression which has to be factorised. If the partner cannot factorise it, the expression is returned to the author for the answer. A balance has to be struck between finding an expression which challenges the partner and one which the creator can factorise.
Literacy	**Links**
Check that students can use the appropriate language in the contexct of algebra, recognising terms and expressions. Check that students can read algebraic terms and expressions with meaning. Include the term highest common factor (HCF) while working in this section.	Factor VIII is one of the blood proteins and is needed to form blood clots. Haemophilia A is a genetic disorder where the level of factor VIII in the blood is reduced. When someone with haemophilia is injured, the blood does not clot and so bleeding carries on for much longer than normal. Haemophilia mainly affects males, although the gene is inherited from the mother and all the daughters of a haemophiliac will be carriers. There is more about haemophilia at http://www.sciencemuseum.org.uk/exhibitions/genes/212.asp
Alternative approach	

Begin by rehearsing equivalent spider diagrams with centres of both terms and expressions, such as $5xy$; $3x^2$; $6x + 4y$, and so on. Relate terms such as $5xy$ to area of rectangles and consider possible ways of of representing this term. Extend this to include an expression with brackets such as $6(2x + 8)$, and examine the various area representations possible. Make sure that students are clear that all the versions are equivalent, then go on to compare them and ask them in pairs to decide which version would they they consider 'the best' and why. Share the results with the whole group, making sure that the students continue to treat every version of equal value. Which version is the 'best' tends to be reliant on what context or purpose is required. The term factorised can be related to the results, together with which expression is fully factorised, i.e. using the HCF. Include and link area representation to the use of grids in multiplication. When students are consolidating these skills, allow the use of mini whiteboards for visual support by using grid/area sketches.

Checkpoint

Factorise $6x + 12$. $(6(x + 2))$

Factorise completely $8x^2 - 2x$. $(2x(4x - 1))$

Two consecutive numbers are multiplied together.
Record an expression for this result in as many different ways as possible . $(x(x+1); x^2 + x;$ or equivalent)

Algebra   Expressions and formulae

Starter – Index bingo

Ask students to draw a 3 × 3 grid and enter nine numbers representing indices between 1 and 20. Give questions involving indices, for example, $2^4 \times 2^5$. If a student has the index of the answer, 9 in this example, in their grid they cross it out. The winner is the first student to cross out all their nine numbers.

Teaching notes

Students often question why they have to be able to factorise as well as expand brackets. Show them a £5 note, five £1 coins, four £1 coins and ten 10p coins and ask which they would prefer, and why. This can help to demonstrate that expressions can be equivalent but one form may be more useful than another in some circumstances (a £5 note is easier to carry, the £1 coins may be more useful when a shop has little change, and the 10p coins may be needed if you want to use a vending machine).

It is useful to point out that in factorising an expression such as $40x + 24y$, an answer of $2(20x + 12y)$ or $4(10x + 6y)$ is not 'wrong' but is not what is required, the full factorisation is $8(5x + 3y)$.

Plenary

Use a mini whiteboard activity to confirm that students are able to factorise simple expressions confidently and fluently.

Exercise commentary

Questions 1 and **2** – Question **1** asks students to spot the common factor, whereas question **2** requires students to use the common factor to factorise the expressions. Question **2** has numerical factors only.

Question 3 – This question extends to factors which are algebraic. There are no numeric factors in this question. Students should note that, for example, x can be written as $1 \times x$.

Question 4 – This question brings together the work of questions **2** and **3**; each part requires a common numeric and algebraic factor to be found.

Question 5 – The four parts of this question are designed to make students think carefully.

Question 6 – Students need to realise that the factors they find can represent the length and width of the rectangle and that there are several possibilities (even discounting fractions).

Question 7 – Students will see that the addition leads, by collecting like terms, to a common factor of 3.

Question 8 – Question **7** provides a lead-in to this question.

Answers

1. a 2 b 3 c 5 d 4
   e 2 f 3 g 2 h 5
2. a $2(x-4)$ b $3(y+3)$ c $4(x-3)$ d $5(m+6)$
   e $3(3n+2)$ f $2(3x-5)$ g $5(3y+5)$ h $2(4z-5)$
   i $3(2-3x)$ j $2(9+2x)$ k $5(5-2x)$ l $4(3-x)$
   m $4(3x-2)$ n $5(2x+1)$ o $3(2x+1)$ p $7(x-2)$
3. a $x(x+5)$ b $y(y+7)$ c $z(z-3)$ d $p(4+p)$
   e $x(x+5y)$ f $a(a-2b)$ g $t(t+3s)$ h $z(6y-z)$
   i $y(8+y)$ j $y(8x+y)$ k $z(3z+1)$ l $x(5x-1)$
   m $x(x^2+5)$ n $x^2(x-2)$ o $z(z^2-z+3)$
   p $y(2+y-y^2)$
4. a $2x(x+3y)$ b $3x(3x+y)$
   c $2y(y-4z)$ d $3p(2p+q)$
   e $4q(q-2p)$ f $2z(3z+4y)$
   g $3y(3x+2z)$ h $2b(2a-3c)$
   i $2n(3m+4p)$ j $2x(2x-3)$
   k $2x(3x-2)$ l $2x(3x-1)$
   m $3x(3x+y)$ n $4z(3+2z)$
   o $3z(3z-1)$ p $2y(y^2+2)$
5. a $2z(4z^2-3)$ b $2z^2(4z-3)$
   c $4z(2z^2+1)$ d $4z^2(2z+1)$
6. Possible lengths and widths are 3 and $x^2 + 2x$, $3x$ and $x + 2$, x and $3x + 6$, etc.
7. a $x+1, x+2$ b $T = 3x + 3$
   c $T = 3(x+1)$, therefore T is a multiple of 3
8. a $T = x^2 + x = x(x+1)$ b x and $x + 1$

Factors in algebra

3b Algebraic fractions

Objectives	
• Add simple algebraic fractions	(L7)

Key ideas	Resources	
1 Recognising that algebra is generalised number 2 Manipulate and add simple algebraic fractions	Simplifying 2 Dictionaries Mini whiteboards	(1178)

Simplification	Extension
Even students who struggle with numerical fractions can, in some instances, find algebraic fractions easier because the factors of numerator and denominator are more explicit. Addition and subtraction of fractions are likely to be more difficult and time should be spent on gaining a secure understanding of question **3** before attempting question **4**.	Students work in pairs and each partner separately devises an incorrect simplification as in question **6** of the exercise. Students exchange their working and each has to find and correct the other's mistake.

Literacy	Links
Use fractional vocabulary in context, particularly numerator and denominator, as these will not be new terms, but students may not readily use them in their own language. Encourage them to do so. Also encourage them to say terms meaningfully, for example '3x over 2' or 'half of 3x' and so on.	Bring in some dictionaries for the class to use. The word *fraction* comes from the Latin *fractio*, meaning 'to break'. How many other words can the class find beginning or ending with *fract-*? What is the connection between these words and 'to break'?

Alternative approach
Use an equivalent spider diagram to begin, including centre expressions such as $6x + 8$, $8x \div 3$, $8ab \div 2b$, $6n^2 \div 3n$, and so on. Students can offer their alternatives using mini whiteboards. Address any misconceptions that arise. Questions 1 and 2 of the exercise can be completed using mini whiteboards. Extend by asking some simple verbal questions of add/subtract algebraic fractions with the same denominator, e.g 'two fifths of x add one fifth of x'. Now ask student pairs to consider possible equivalents where the fractions do not share the same denominator. Share the results.

Checkpoint	
Simplify $3xy/6x$	($y/2$)
Write an expression for two thirds of m added to a fifth of n.	$((10m + 3n)/15)$

Algebra   Expressions and formulae

Starter – Guess my number

Give clues for students to solve. For example

It is even. It is both a square and a cube. It has two digits. (64)

It is a prime number. It is greater than five cubed but less than twelve squared. The first digit and last digit are the same. (131) *etc*.

Teaching notes

When working with arithmetic fractions, the expressions become simpler because the numbers contract when the fractions are added or subtracted (after taking common denominators).

This does not normally happen with algebraic fractions and students will need reassurance that their method is correct when they reach problems such as question **5**.

Plenary

Ask students to work in pairs to set each other problems similar to those in question **5**.

Exercise commentary

Question 1 – This question only has one factor to cancel in each part.

Question 2 – There is more than one factor to cancel in each part.

Question 3 – The additions and subtractions are straightforward as the denominators are the same in each part.

Question 4 – Students need to first find equivalent fractions to give the fractions common denominators before they can add or subtract.

Question 5 – As in question **4**, common denominators are needed first. The additions and subtractions, however, do not simplify and give two-term expressions in the numerators (except in parts **d** and **g**).

Question 6 – These are common errors and could usefully be discussed with the whole class.

Answers

1 a $\frac{x}{3}$ b $\frac{y}{3}$ c $\frac{3z}{4}$ d $\frac{b}{5}$

 e $\frac{v}{4}$ f $\frac{3q}{p}$ g $\frac{2m}{n}$ h $\frac{4}{5y}$

2 a $\frac{y}{4}$ b $\frac{n}{3}$ c $\frac{2ab}{25}$ d $\frac{2y}{3x}$

 e $\frac{p}{2r}$ f $2t$ g $\frac{x}{y}$ h $\frac{a}{bc}$

 i $\frac{m}{2}$ j $\frac{2z}{3y}$ k $\frac{2hk}{3}$ l $\frac{3y}{2z}$

3 a $\frac{5x}{7}$ b $\frac{3x+2y}{7}$ c $\frac{5a}{9}$ d $\frac{4a+b}{9}$

 e $\frac{s}{5}$ f $\frac{4s-3t}{5}$ g $\frac{6y}{11}$ h $\frac{9y-3z}{11}$

4 a $\frac{5x}{6}$ b $\frac{8y}{15}$ c $\frac{13z}{10}$ d $\frac{11x}{15}$

 e $\frac{23a}{21}$ f $\frac{c}{10}$ g $\frac{41m}{24}$ h $\frac{5x}{8}$

 i $\frac{7y}{12}$ j $\frac{p}{12}$ k $\frac{29q}{20}$ l $\frac{5s}{24}$

5 a $\frac{8x+3y}{12}$ b $\frac{25c-6d}{10}$ c $\frac{4e+7f}{14}$ d $\frac{9x}{10}$

 e $\frac{12p-15q}{20}$ f $\frac{25y+12z}{20}$ g $\frac{z}{4}$ h $\frac{x-6y}{8}$

 i $\frac{10y+3z}{12}$ j $\frac{16a-15}{18}$ k $\frac{3p+5}{10}$ l $\frac{8x-3}{12}$

6 In both cases, the pupil merely adds the numerators and denominators. He does not find the lowest common denominator and convert into equivalent fractions.

 a $\frac{5}{6}$ b $\frac{3x+2y}{6}$

Algebraic fractions

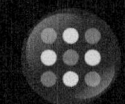

3c Formulae in context

Objectives	
• Use formulae from mathematics and other subjects	(L7)
• Substitute numbers into expressions and formulae	(L7)
• Derive a formula and, in simple cases, change its subject	(L7)

Key ideas	Resources
1 Recognise and understand the nature of a formula in order to apply to a problem 2 Use a formula in order to find unknown values.	Substitution 2 (1186) Mini whiteboards

Simplification	Extension
This exercise is essentially for revision and further practice. Students can be given a formula as a class and given a substitution. They can use their mini-white boards to show the first line of working only, where the numerical value replaces the variable. Having shown and discussed (and, if necessary, corrected) their mini-white boards, they can then work out and show their final answers.	Students use the formula of question **8** to find the kinetic energy E of a car of mass 1000 kg at different speeds and then draw a graph of E against v. They can repeat for cars of different masses. Why are the graphs not straight?

Literacy	Links
Use the words term and expression as well as revisiting the difference between equation and formula. This difference can be challenging for students, so try to use their own descriptions for similarities and differences, drawing attention to specific cases of equality and general cases of equality. Emphasise the importance of answers in context when using to find values, by using appropriate units and/or descriptions.	The first electric light bulb was constructed in 1860 by Sir Joseph Swan in the UK using a carbon paper filament which burned up very quickly. The idea was developed by Thomas Edison in the USA who, in 1879, used a carbonized cotton filament to produce a bulb that stayed lit for almost 40 hours. He eventually produced a bulb that could glow for over 1500 hours. There is a timeline for the development of the light bulb at: inventors.about.com/library/inventors/bllight2.htm

Alternative approach

Begin by presenting the students with a collection of terms, expressions, formulae and equations and ask them to group them. Encourage students to work in pairs on this, sharing their thoughts. This can be done as a prepared card sort or by using mini whiteboards from a class display. Ask students to explain how they distinguish between a formula and an equation, tackling some of the misconceptions as they occur, while recognising that the clues used may still be helpful for them. For example 'formulae have capital letters', 'there is only one letter in an equation', and so on. Use this discussion to emphasise specific versus general equality.

Checkpoint

Find the value of this expression: $3A + 2B$ when $A = 7$ and $B = -1$ (23)

Find the value of this expression: $4x^3 - 2x$ when $x = 0.2$. (-0.368)

Starter – Algebraic products

Draw a 4 × 4 table on the board to form 16 cells.

Label the rows with the terms $2x^3, xy, x^4, z$.
Label the columns with the terms $x^2, xy, y^3, 3x^5$.

Ask students to fill in each cell of the table by multiplying the row and column terms together. For example, the top row would read: $2x^5, 2x^4y, 2x^3y^3, 6x^8$.

Can be differentiated by the choice of terms.

Teaching notes

This spread is an opportunity to show students the power of mathematics in summarising the behaviour of many things in the world around us, by expressing the dependency on other quantities (variables) in a formula.

Emphasise that fluency and accuracy in manipulation of formulae will mean that students can concentrate on the context and the interpretation more fully and the maths will make more sense.

Plenary

Ask students to work in pairs to write down as many formulae as they can recall from mathematics, science or other subjects. Pool the list, with explanations of what the formula describes and create a poster for the classroom display. Students can add new formulae to the poster through the year.

Exercise commentary

The exercise uses formulae, of slightly increasing complexity, in many different contexts. Students could be challenged to not use their calculators for some of the questions.

Question 1 – It should be mentioned that this formula works only if you withdraw the interest each year and do not add it to the original investment (non-compound, or simple interest).

Question 2 – This formula works only while the string remains 'within its elastic limit'. If stretched too much, the string will not return to its original shape.

Question 3 – The voltage drop V is the total of the drop, E, across the meter and the drop across the resistor.

Question 4 – Students should be familiar with pie charts but may not know this formula.

Question 5 – The energy of the car due to its motion is called its 'kinetic energy'.

Questions 6 to 8 – These require numerical rearrangement of the formulae. Students should substitute, simplify where possible and then treat the formulae as equations. Part **b** of question **8** is more demanding.

Question 9 – BMI is an interesting concept used in the medical world. Emphasise that the formula provided here is for adults, not students at school.

Answers

1 a £10   b £60
2 a 4   b 20
3 a 30   b 40
4 a 120   b 270
5 a 45   b 320
6 a 24   b 12
7 a 8   b 30
8 a 6   b 4
9 Severely underweight <16.5   Normal 18.5 – 25
   Obese class I   30 – 35   Obese class II 35 – 40
   Obese class III >40

Formulae in context

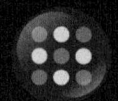

3d Rearranging formulae

Objectives

- Use formulae from mathematics and other subjects (L7)
- Substitute numbers into expressions and formulae (L7)
- Derive a formula and, in simple cases, change its subject (L7)

Key ideas	Resources
1 Recognise and understand the nature of a formula in order to apply to a problem 2 Rearrange formula and equations	Rearranging 1 (1171) Mini whiteboards

Simplification	Extension
If students struggle to perform the algebraic rearrangement, an alternative method is to substitute known numeric values, simplify where possible, and then treat the result as an equation.	Students should know of Albert Einstein and may have heard of his formula $E = mc^2$, where the speed of light, $c = 3 \times 10^8$ metres per second. Students can work out E in Joules when 1 kilogram of mass is changed into energy. They can compare their answer with the energy released (5×10^7 Joules) when 1 kg of petrol is burned.

Literacy	Links
Use the words term and expression as well as revisiting the difference between equation and formula. This difference can be challenging for students, so try to use their own descriptions for similarities and differences, drawing attention to specific cases of equality and general cases of equality. Emphasise the importance of answers in context when using to find values, by using appropriate units and/or descriptions	Hooke's Law describes the way that elastic materials and springs behave when they are stretched by a load. It was discovered by the English scientist Robert Hooke who lived from 1635 to 1703. Steel obeys Hooke's Law so it is very important when designing bridges and other steel structures. It can also be used to calculate the length of cord necessary for a successful bungee jump!

Alternative approach

Begin with a simple reminder of writing expressions/equations in response to verbal descriptions, for example I'm thinking of a value which I then add 6 to and double.....if the answer is....Students should use mini whiteboards to record expressions and equations. Concentrate on the recording and the order of operations with the students, rather than an answer to a specific case, but use the answer to illustrate the importance of correct order interpretation. Extend to presenting a simple formula and asking students to identify the separate operations in order. This can be recorded as a flow chart or function machine, for illustrative purposes. Extend to a formula such as that given in the example in this section and ask students to identify what happens to one of the specific variables. Use this to demonstrate how a formula may be rearranged for a particular subject, applying inverses in the correct order.

Checkpoint

Make x the subject in this formula: $y = 3x - 1$ $(x = (y + 1)/3)$

The formula $F = 9C/5 + 32$ demonstrate the link between Fahrenheit and Celsius temperature.
Make C the subject of this formula. $(C = 5(F - 32)/9)$

Algebra   Expressions and formulae

Starter – Connections

If $C = -2, D = 3, E = 5$ and $F = 6$, ask students to write down as many equations as they can in four minutes. For example $CF = -4D$, $DE = D - CF$.

Can be differentiated by the choice of values for C, D, E and F.

Teaching notes

As with factorising, students often grumble about why they need to be able to rearrange formulae. A formula summarises the relationship between a number of variables but often the variable you are interested in finding is not the subject of the formula. Rearranging the formula once allows immediate calculation of the variable of interest from substitution rather than having to solve an equation every time.

Plenary

On the board display $V = \pi r^2 h$ so $r = \dfrac{V}{\pi r h}$

Ask students why this is insufficient as a formula to find r.

Exercise commentary

Questions 1 to 5 – These require only simple algebraic rearrangement, as the required variable is readily available. Part **b** in each case requires students to use the rearranged formula to find the missing value.

Question 6 and **7** – These are a little more complicated.

Questions 8, 9, 10 and **12** – These may, for some students, be easier solved by the alternative approach suggested above.

Questions 11 and **13** – These involve using a square root.

Question 14 – Newton gave his name to many laws and formulae, for example, his law of gravity and his laws of motion. The Internet will give other examples.

Answers

1 a $t = \dfrac{s}{v}$ b   5

2 a $R = \dfrac{V}{I}$ b   6

3 a $W = \dfrac{D}{K}$ b   6

4 a $u = v - at$ b   24

5 a $E = V - RI$ b   8

6 a $I = (V - E)/R$ b   -6

7 a $m = \text{BMI}h^2$ b   2400

8 a $m = \dfrac{2E}{V^2}$ b   6

9 a $h = \dfrac{3V}{lb}$ b   6

10 a $R = \dfrac{P}{i^2 t}$ b   3

11   $I = \sqrt{\dfrac{E}{R}}$

12   $L = \dfrac{P - 2W}{2}$

13   $r = \sqrt{\dfrac{V}{\pi h}}$

14   In mathematics Newton did significant work on the binomial theorem, calculus and series expansions. In science he did significant work in optics, the laws of motion, gravitation and celestial mechanics.

Rearranging formulae

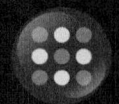

3e Deriving and graphing formulae

Objectives
- Use formulae from mathematics and other subjects (L7)
- Substitute numbers into expressions and formulae (L7)
- Derive a formula and, in simple cases, change its subject (L7)

Key ideas
1. Apply reasoning skills in order to derive a formula for a simple situation
2. Recognise the generality of a formula and plot specific values in order to view trends or changes

Resources
Pyramids (NRICH): http://nrich.maths.org/488

Derive a formula for the area of any kite (NRICH): http://nrich.maths.org/1780

AP rectangles (NRICH): http://nrich.maths.org/729

Simplification
Revise calculating compound areas with numeric sides, using the idea of adding (or subtracting) the areas of two rectangles. This approach is then developed using algebra into the areas of question 1. The usual progression applies: formula → table of values → coordinates → graph, except in this exercise the students have to derive their own formulae from the contexts.

Extension
Students can devise simple formulae for metric-imperial conversions, such as inches to centimetres. They can also make currency converters for (say) euros to pounds sterling. All these conversions can be drawn as graphs.

Literacy
Use the opportunity of graphing in this section in order to help nail the differences between equations and formulae.

Being precise with the recording of reasoning is important, with students recognising the need to communicate clearly and accurately. This includes defining their use of any general terms, such as 'let x be the number of cm long', and so on.

Links
Prices for tickets for upcoming concerts and events can be found at
http://www.ticketmaster.co.uk/ or at
http://www.seetickets.com

A booking fee per ticket and/or a transaction fee are usually charged in addition to the face value of the ticket. Choose an event and select a ticket category. How much would it cost to book one, two, three or four tickets in this category? Can the class derive a formula to calculate the cost of buying tickets?

Alternative approach
Using pyramid puzzles such as those referenced from NRICH can be used to introduce recording and developing expressions. Paired work deriving formulae such as that of a kite (NRICH) can be used to discuss some finer points of recording reasoning. Students are likely to use a range of different letters to represent height or length; have they made it clear which is which? Does the final formula always look the same? Are formulae equivalent? AP rectangles explores when a rectangle's area is numerically equal to its perimeter. Graphing length against width of these will demonstrate links in a visual way, providing further material for discussion.

Checkpoint
A rectangle measures $x + 2$ cm by x cm. Write down a formula for the area A cm^2. $(A = x(x + 2))$

When cooking roast beef, the suggested cooking time is 20 minutes per 100 grams plus 30 minutes. Write a formula for the total cooking time T in terms of the mass of the beef joint m kg. $(T = 200m + 30)$

Algebra Expressions and formulae

Starter – I think of a number

I think of a number. I halve it and subtract two, then multiply the answer by six. I get the same answer if I double my number and subtract five. What is my number? (7)

Encourage students to construct an equation to solve the problem.

Teaching notes

One of the most common difficulties for students in deriving formulae is that they often do not define their variables precisely and end up using the same symbol to mean more than one thing in a problem, for example where there are two radii. Encourage students to define variables either in a clear diagram or in words.

Plenary

Ask students to work in pairs to consider whether there are a limited range of values for which x makes sense in the problems of question **1** (Part **b** needs $x < 3$ and part **d** needs $x > 3$, otherwise any non-negative value for x makes sense).

Exercise commentary

Question 1 – Parts **a** and **b** demonstrate the two basic methods. Part **a** requires the addition of two areas and part **b** is best calculated by subtracting two areas.

Question 2 – After finding a formula (as in question 1), this question requires the student to use it and graph the results.

Question 3 – In this question, the formula is given by means of a function machine (or flow diagram). Data is generated and the results plotted as in question **2**.

Question 4 – This question requires students to find the formula before using it and plotting a graph of the results.

Question 5 – This is a more challenging formula. Students will have used the Celsius scale in science lessons and should have heard of the Fahrenheit scale, for example on national weather forecasts. They could ask their older relatives which temperature scale they prefer!

Answers

1 **a** $A = 15 + 2x$ **b** $A = 15 - 2x$
   c $A = 5x + 6$ **d** $A = 6x - 12$
   e $A = 4x + 10$ **f** $A = 6x + 12$

2 **a** $A = 40 + 3x$
   b

x (cm)	2	4	6	8	10
A (cm^2)	46	52	58	64	70

   c Straight-line graph drawn through (2, 46) and (10, 70)

3 **a** $n = 50x + 20$
   b

x (kg)	6	8	10	12
n (min)	320	420	520	620

Straight-line graph drawn through (6, 320) and (12, 620)

4 **a** $n = 80 - x$
   b

x (age)	10	20	30	40	50	60	70
n (years)	70	60	50	40	30	20	10

Straight-line graph through (10, 70) and (70, 10)

5

°C	60	30	0	-30	-60
°F	140	86	32	-22	-76

Straight-line graph through (60, 140) and (-60, -76)
−40° C = −40° F

Deriving and graphing formulae

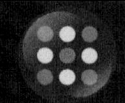

3 Expressions and formulae – MySummary

Key outcomes	Quick check
Factorise expressions using brackets. L7	Factorise a $3 + 6x$ $(3(1 + 2x))$ b $5x^2 + 10x$ $(5x(x + 2))$ c $4xy + 2xz$ $(2x(2y + z))$
Simplify algebraic expressions. L7	Simplify a $3x/6$ $(x/2)$ b $4xyz/2y$ $(2xz)$ c $3x/4 + 4x/3$ $(25x/12)$
Substitute values in formulae to find unknown variables. L7	$V = 3A + b$ a Find V when $A = 4$ and $b = 7$ (19) b Find A when $V = 16$ and $b = 1$ (5)
Change the subject of a formula. L7	$a = m + n^2$ a Make m the subject ($m = a - n^2$) b Make n the subject ($n = \sqrt{(a - m)}$)
Derive and graph formulae. L6	A rectangle measures $3x + 2$ cm by $x - 1$ cm a Write down a formula for the perimeter, P. ($P = 4x + 1$) b Write down a formular for the area, A. ($A = (3x + 2)(x - 1)$)

MyMaths extra support

Lesson/online homework			Description
Rules and formulae	1158	L5	Using letters to represent unknown numbers in simple formulae
Simplifying 1	1179	L5	Expressions such as $a+a+a+b+b$ can be simplified to $2a + 3b$
Substitution 1	1187	L5	Substituting into formulae with one variable
Single brackets	1247	L5	Expanding single brackets such as $3(3x - 2)$

Algebra Expressions and formulae

MyReview

3 MySummary

Check out
You should now be able to ...

	Test it ➡ Questions
✓ Factorise algebraic expressions.	1 – 2
✓ Simplify algebraic expressions.	3 – 4
✓ Substitute values in formulae to find unknown variables.	5
✓ Change the subject of a formula.	6 – 7
✓ Derive and graph formulae.	8 – 9

Language	Meaning	Example
Algebraic fractions	Fractions containing algebraic expressions.	$\frac{5x+2y}{xy}$, $\frac{2z}{5}$ and $\frac{3}{a+b}$ are all algebraic fractions
Change the subject	Rearrange a formula so that a different variable is 'on its own'.	$v = \frac{b^2}{k}$ rearranged to make b the subject gives $b = \sqrt{vk}$
Derive	Construct a formula from information given.	The cost C pence of n chocolate bars each costing 35p is $C = 35n$
Expand	Multiply a bracket out.	$3(2x + 4y) = 6x + 12y$
Factorise	The reverse of expanding a bracket by taking out common factors.	$6x + 12y = 6(x + 2y)$
Formula (plural formulae)	A rule linking two or more variables.	The formula for finding the circumference of a circle is $A = \pi d$
Substitute	Replace variables with numerical values.	Substitute $a = 4$ in $a^2 − 2a$ gives $16 − 8 = 8$

3 MyReview

1 Factorise these expressions.
  a $15x − 3$ b $8a + 24b$
  c $24pq + 48p$ d $21 − 28v$

2 Factorise these expressions.
  a $x^2 + 8x$ b $3x^2 + 9xy$
  c $z^3 + 3z^2 − z$ d $16y^3 − 12y^2$

3 Simplify
  a $\frac{6rs}{3s}$ b $\frac{pq^2}{5q}$
  c $\frac{12a^2b}{4a}$ d $\frac{33x^2y}{44xy^2z}$

4 Add or subtract these fractions.
  a $\frac{x}{6} + \frac{2x}{6}$ b $\frac{3a}{14} − \frac{a}{7}$
  c $\frac{2y}{3} + \frac{y}{8}$ d $\frac{5b}{6} − \frac{3b}{8}$

5 A formula for distance travelled is given by
  $s = ut + \frac{1}{2}at^2$
  Use this formula to find the value of s when
  $u = 30$, $a = −4$, $t = 3$

6 Make x the subject of each formula.
  a $x − 3b = 2a$
  b $8 + 2x = y − 7$
  c $3x^2 + 4y = 5z$

7 a Make v the subject of $E = \frac{mv^2}{2}$
  b Find v when $m = 7$, $E = 200$
  c Find m when $E = 100$ and $v = −3$

8 a Derive a formula for the area, A, of this trapezium.

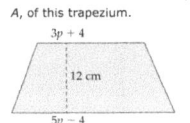

  b If the area of the trapezium is 306 cm², what is the value of p?

9 a Find a formula for the shaded area, A, of this shape.

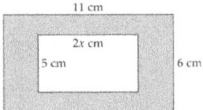

  b Copy and complete the table of values.

x(cm)	1	2	3	4	5	6
A(cm²)						

  c Draw a graph of A against x.

What next?

Score	
0 – 4	Your knowledge of this topic is still developing. To improve look at Formative test: 3B-3; MyMaths: 1155, 1171, 1178 and 1186
5 – 7	You are gaining a secure knowledge of this topic. To improve look at InvisiPen: 215, 223, 241, 252, 254, 255, 256 and 273
8, 9	You have mastered this topic. Well done, you are ready to progress!

Question commentary

Questions 1 and 2 – Encourage students to think about the HCF of the terms, the second term in the bracket of question **1a** sometimes causes confusion.

Questions 3 and 4 – It is often useful to recap dealing with non-algebraic fractions and emphasize the similarities with algebraic fractions. Answers should be fully simplified.

Question 5 – This formula is for displacement (s) where u = initial velocity, a = constant acceleration and t = time.

Question 6 – Students sometimes try to square-root everything too early in part **c**. They should first make x^2 the subject then the final step is the square root.

Question 7 – In part **c**, students can rearrange the formula again to make m the subject ($m = \frac{2E}{v^2}$) or they can substitute for E and v then solve the equation. Either way they must take care with the negative value of v.

Question 8 – Students need to simplify $3p + 4 + 5p − 4$ to $8p$ then multiply by 6. For **b** they must solve the equation $48p = 306$.

Question 9 – Students need to know that 'A against x' means that A is on the y-axis.

Answers

1 a $3(5x − 1)$ b $8(a + 3b)$ c $24p(q + 2)$
  d $7(3 − 4v)$

2 a $x(x + 8)$ b $3x(x + 3y)$
  c $z(z^2 + 3z − 1)$ d $4y^2(4y − 3)$

3 a $2r$ b $\frac{pq}{5}$ c $3ab$
  d $\frac{3x}{4yz}$

4 a $\frac{x}{2}$ b $\frac{a}{14}$ c $\frac{19y}{21}$
  d $\frac{5b}{24}$

5 12

6 a $x = 2a + 3b$ b $x = \frac{y-15}{2}$
  c $x = \sqrt{\frac{5z-4y}{3}}$

7 a $v = \sqrt{\frac{2E}{m}}$ b 7.56   c 22.2

8 a $A = 48p$ b 6.375 cm

9 a $A = 66 − 10x$
  b
x (cm)	1	2	3	4	5	6
A (cm²)	56	46	36	26	16	6

  c See master Answers file for graph

MySummary/MyReview

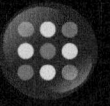

3 MyPractice

1 Factorise these expressions.

a $4x - 20$
b $5y + 15$
c $6b + 18$
d $7m - 35$
e $4 - 6z$
f $8p - 6$
g $12b + 16$
h $20 - 15q$
i $x^2 + 6x$
j $3y + y^2$
k $u^2 - 4u$
l $9f - f^2$

2 Factorise these expressions. Look for two common factors.

a $3xy + 6xz$
b $9pq + 3pr$
c $6x^2 - 4x$
d $8y^2 + 2yz$
e $6ab - 3a^2$
f $5xy + x^2y$
g $4g^2 - 18fg$
h $2m^2n - 11mn$
i $8r^2s - 13rs^2$

3 Find equivalent fractions by cancelling.

a $\frac{3x}{6}$
b $\frac{2y}{8}$
c $\frac{4t}{16}$
d $\frac{9m}{18}$
e $\frac{6z}{10}$
f $\frac{mn}{3n}$
g $\frac{15r}{20}$
h $\frac{5ab}{6b}$
i $\frac{3xy}{6y}$
j $\frac{2yz}{8z}$
k $\frac{16pq}{20p}$
l $\frac{15mn}{24n}$
m $\frac{4a^2}{8a}$
n $\frac{4b^3}{6b}$
o $\frac{10x^2}{12x}$
p $\frac{24p^3}{32p}$
q $\frac{s^2t^3}{s^3t}$
r $\frac{x^3y}{x^2y}$
s $\frac{9ab^2}{6b}$
t $\frac{3y^2z}{6y^2z^2}$
u $\frac{20m^2n}{28m^2n^2}$

4 Add or subtract these fractions.

a $\frac{x}{5} + \frac{2x}{5}$
b $\frac{2y}{7} + \frac{3y}{7}$
c $\frac{5a}{9} + \frac{2a}{9}$
d $\frac{2x}{3} + \frac{y}{3}$
e $\frac{7v}{9} - \frac{5v}{9}$
f $\frac{3m}{10} - \frac{n}{10}$
g $\frac{z}{2} + \frac{z}{4}$
h $\frac{3a}{8} + \frac{a}{4}$
i $\frac{4t}{5} + \frac{s}{10}$
j $\frac{5c}{9} - \frac{c}{3}$
k $\frac{9x}{10} - \frac{3x}{5}$
l $\frac{11a}{12} - \frac{5b}{6}$
m $\frac{z}{2} + \frac{3z}{3}$
n $\frac{2a}{3} + \frac{a}{5}$
o $\frac{3p}{8} + \frac{p}{6}$
p $\frac{4x}{5} - \frac{3x}{4}$
q $\frac{2y}{5} - \frac{3y}{10}$
r $\frac{7a}{8} - \frac{5a}{6}$

5 I cycle for x hours and walk for y hours.
The total distance travelled, D miles, is given by the formula $D = 12x + 2y$.

a Find D when $x = 4$ and $y = 3$.
b Find x when $D = 46$ and $y = 2$.

6 The speed, S, of water pouring from a tank is given by
$S = \frac{rt}{2h}$.

a Find S when $r = 10$, $t = 6$ and $h = 15$.
b Find t when $S = 24$, $r = 36$ and $h = 3$.

7 a Make t the subject of the formula $v = u + at$.
b Find t when $v = 30$, $u = 18$ and $a = 2$.

8 a Make w the subject of the formula $P = 2l + 2w$.
b Find w when $P = 50$ and $l = 6$.

9 a Make n the subject of the formula $C = \frac{2n}{3}$.
b Find n when $C = 30$.

10 I buy one packet of nails for 30 pence and x boxes of screws at 50 pence per box.

1 packet x boxes

a Write a formula for the total cost, C, of the nails and screws.
b Find the value of C when $x = 2, 4, 6, 8$ and 10 and draw a graph of C against x.
c Find the value of x when $C = 680$.

Question commentary

Questions 1 and **2** – Students have lots of practice questions here for this skill.

Question 3 – Students again have lots of practice questions for this skill. They should be discouraged also from writing 'over 1' in part **r**.

Question 4 – Remind students to use a common denominator where necessary and simplify the resulting numerator.

Question 5 and **6** – Students have the choice here of rearranging the formulae first before substituting, or solving an equation for part **b** of each question.

Questions 7 to **9** – The questions require students to rearrange the formulae before using the rearrangement to solve the substitution.

Question 10 – Students are directed to first find the formula and then graph it using a table of values. Note there is only one variable since the purchase is for a single packet of nails. As an extension, students could be asked to write a formula for the purchase when it is for *y* packets of nails.

Answers

1. a $4(x-5)$ b $5(y+3)$ c $6(b+3)$ d $7(m-5)$ e $2(2-3z)$ f $2(4p-3)$ g $4(3b+4)$ h $5(4-3q)$ i $x(x+6)$ j $y(3+y)$ k $u(u-4)$ l $f(9-f)$

2. a $3x(y+2z)$ b $3p(3q+r)$ c $2x(3x-2)$ d $2y(4y+z)$ e $3a(2b-a)$ f $xy(5+x)$ g $2g(2g-9f)$ h $mn(2m-11)$ i $rs(8r-13s)$

3. a $\frac{x}{2}$ b $\frac{y}{4}$ c $\frac{t}{4}$ d $\frac{m}{2}$ e $\frac{3z}{5}$ f $\frac{m}{3}$ g $\frac{3r}{4}$ h $\frac{5a}{6}$ i $\frac{x}{2}$ j $\frac{y}{4}$ k $\frac{4q}{5}$ l $\frac{5m}{8}$ m $\frac{a}{2}$ n $\frac{2b^2}{3}$ o $\frac{5x}{6}$ p $\frac{3p^2}{4}$ q $\frac{t^2}{s}$ r x s $\frac{3ab}{2}$ t $\frac{1}{2z}$ u $\frac{5}{7n}$

4. a $\frac{3x}{5}$ b $\frac{5y}{7}$ c $\frac{7a}{9}$ d $\frac{2x+y}{3}$ e $\frac{2y}{9}$ f $\frac{3m-n}{10}$ g $\frac{3z}{4}$ h $\frac{5a}{8}$ i $\frac{8t+s}{10}$ j $\frac{2c}{9}$ k $\frac{3x}{10}$ l $\frac{11a-10b}{12}$ m $\frac{3z}{2}$ n $\frac{13a}{15}$ o $\frac{13p}{24}$ p $\frac{x}{20}$ q $\frac{y}{10}$ r $\frac{a}{24}$

5. a 54 miles b 3.5 hours
6. a 2 b 4
7. a $t = \frac{v-u}{a}$ b 6
8. a $w = \frac{P-2l}{2}$ b 19
9. a $n = \frac{3C}{2}$ b 45
10. a $C = 30 + 50x$

   b

x	2	4	6	8	10
C	130	230	330	430	530

   Straight-line graph drawn through (2, 130) and (10, 530)

   c $x = 13$

MyPractice 49

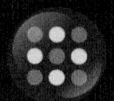

Case Study 1: Why do bikes have gears?

Related lessons		Resources	
Area of a 2D shape	2c	Circumference of a circle	(1088)
Formulae in context	3c	Substitution 1	(1187)
Rounding	1b	Significant figures	(1005)
Circumference of a circle	2d	Catalogues or magazines showing detail of bike sprockets and gears	
		Lego gears	

Simplification	Extension
The first two tasks link directly into the work in **2d** and should be reasonably straightforward for all students. Calculators will help. The ratios considered in task **3** should also be simple to calculate. It is in tasks **4** and **5** where the main opportunities for simplification arise.	Students could work out the speed ranges for the gears of their own or a friend's bike.
	Students could also work out different speed ranges for different sized front sprockets other than the two given in the case study.
The initial table is quite straightforward for students to complete if they have the answer to part **a** of task **4** but the calculations of speed in task **5** are both labour-intensive and require conversions. These conversions could be given to the students and/or the task simplified by taking a single value for the number of turns of the pedal, for example 50 turns. Parts **c** and **d** of task **5** could be omitted altogether.	An interesting video clip which covers the principles of mechanical advantage and other things to do with gears can be found at http://www.sciencekids.co.nz/videos/physics/gears.html. Students could be asked to write about other things that they find out from watching the clip.

Links

Students who are particularly interested can see a range of information related to power and efficiency when cycling at http://users.frii.com/katana/biketext.html and a detailed consideration of gearing at http://www.phred.org/~alex/kenkifer/www.kenkifer.com/bikepages/touring/gears.htm

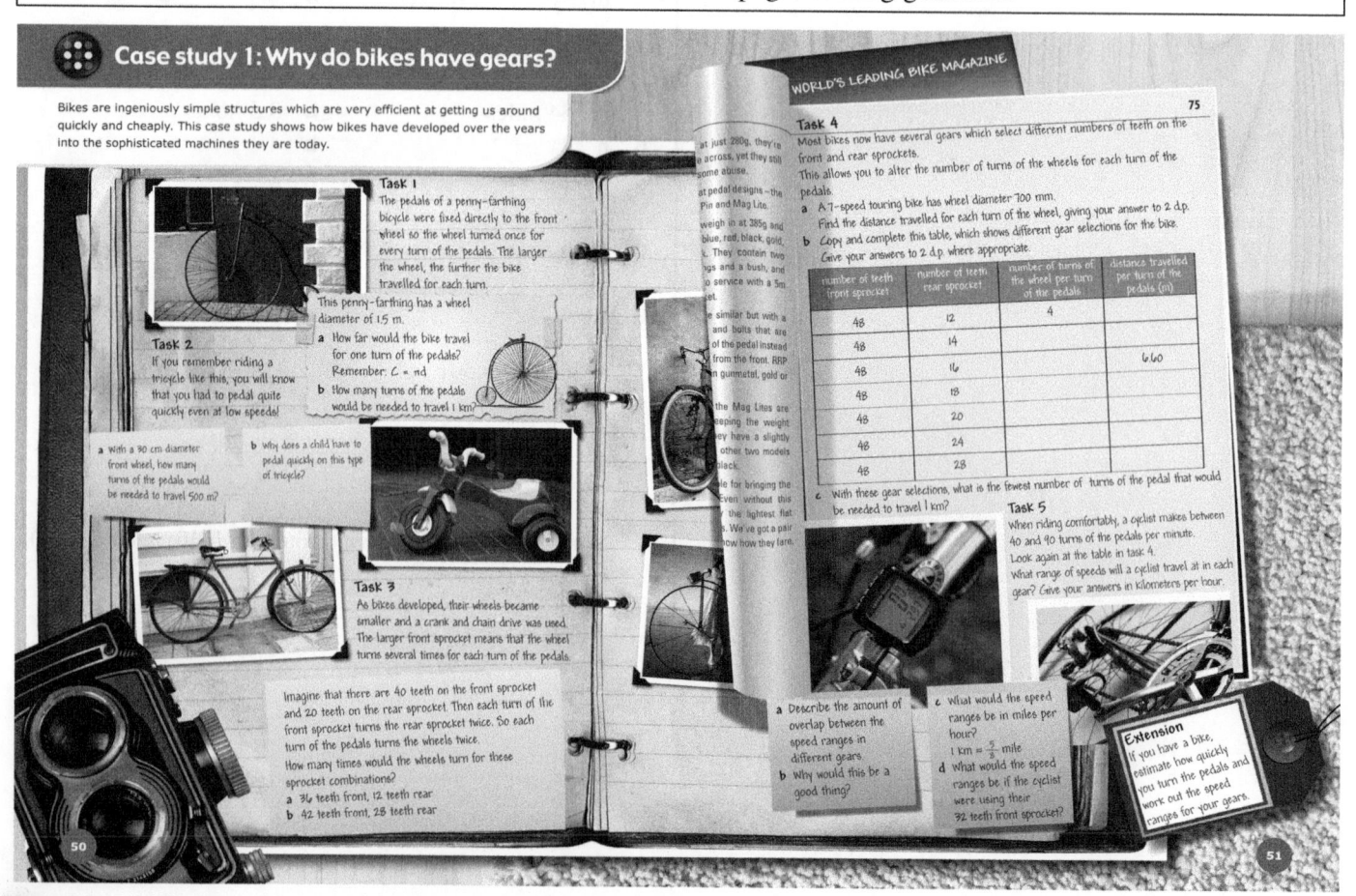

Case Study

Teaching notes

This case study starts from a historical point of view with the penny farthing bicycle which, as its pedals were fixed directly to the front wheel, needed a large front wheel in order to reach a reasonable speed. The gearing of a penny farthing was described as the diameter of the wheel (in inches). A fairly normal diameter would be 60 inches. Bike enthusiasts still sometimes refer to the gearing of a bike in inches. A '60 inch gear' means a gear that will make the bike travel the same distance for one turn of the pedals as a penny farthing would with a 60 inch diameter wheel.

Talk to the students about any bicycles they might own. Ask them about the types of bikes they have and whether they have several gears (most touring, racing and mountain bikes) or just a single gear (BMX bikes).

Task 1

Look at the penny farthing and point out that it has no chain; the pedals are fitted directly to the front wheel. Look also at the picture of the tricycle which also has its pedals attached directly to the front wheel. Students may have had something similar when they were young. Explain that the size of the wheel determines how far the penny farthing travels for each turn of the pedals and ask, how would you work out how far it travels for one turn of the pedals?

Task 2

Then look together at the bicycle at the bottom of the page. Discuss how the chain and sprockets mean that the wheel doesn't turn at the same rate as the pedals; as the front sprocket is larger, the wheel makes several turns for each turn of the pedals. Some students might find that hard to follow. Using examples with 'easy' numbers such as 40 teeth on the front sprocket and 20 on the rear might help. You could try explaining that each turn of the front sprocket moves 40 links of the chain and 40 links of the chain will turn the rear sprocket twice.

Task 3

Give students a few minutes to work with a partner through the questions about the bike before looking at the yellow post it note at the bottom of the page, asking how will you work out the speed of the bike? Hear ideas and establish that you need to know how far the bike travels for one turn of the pedals and that the gearing means that for each turn of the pedals the bike moves forward by an amount based on the ratio of the gears and the circumference of the wheels.

Task 4

Look at the right hand page and talk about the use of gears, asking when and how they use any gears they have on their bike. Talk about the way you can use gears to keep your pedalling rate reasonably constant at different speeds so that it stays within an efficient range.

Look together at the table and ensure that students understand its contents. Discuss how to work out the missing figures from the information given, noting that the sprocket sizes can be used to find the number of times the wheel turns for every turn of the pedals and that the wheel size can then help them find the distance travelled.

Task 5

Look at the questions about the speed ranges that would be achieved for the given rates of turning the pedals. Make sure that students understand what is being described. Then ask them to work out the speed ranges for each gear. If students work as a group for this they can spread the workload between them.

Answers

1. **a** 4.71 m   **b** 212 turns
2. **a** 529 turns
   b The pedals are fixed directly to the wheel, which is small so it doesn't travel far for each turn.
3. **a** 3   **b** 1.5
4. **a** 2.20 m
   b 4, 8.80; 3.43, 7.54; 3, 6.60; 2.67, 5.86; 2.4, 5.28; 2, 4.40; 1.71, 3.77
   c 113.64 turns
5. 21.11 – 47.50; 18.10 – 40.72; 15.83 – 35.63; 14.07 – 31.67; 12.67 – 28.50; 10.56 – 23.75; 9.05 – 20.36
   a Students' comments.
   b Students' comments; highest and lowest gears don't overlap.
   c 13.19 – 29.69; 11.31 – 25.45; 9.90 – 22.27; 8.80 –19.79; 7.92 – 17.81; 6.60 – 14.84; 5.65 – 12.72
   d 14.07 – 31.67 / 8.79 – 19.79; 12.06 – 27.14 / 7.54 – 16.96; 10.56 – 23.75 / 6.60 – 14.84; 9.38 – 21.11 / 5.86 – 13.19; 8.44 – 19.00 / 5.23 – 11.88; 7.04 – 15.83 / 4.40 – 9.90; 6.03 – 13.57/3.77 – 8.48

Why do bikes have gears?

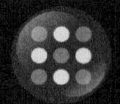

4 Fractions, decimals and percentages

Learning outcomes

N2 Order positive and negative integers, decimals and fractions; use the number line as a model for ordering of the real numbers; use the symbols $=, \neq, <, >, \leq, \geq$ (L7)

N4 Use the 4 operations, including formal written methods, applied to integers, decimals, proper and improper fractions, and mixed numbers, all both positive and negative (L7)

N9 Work interchangeably with terminating decimals and their corresponding fractions (such as 3.5 and 7/2 or 0.375 and 3/8 (L7)

N10 Define percentage as 'number of parts per hundred', interpret percentages and percentage changes as a fraction or a decimal, interpret these multiplicatively, express 1 quantity as a percentage of another, compare 2 quantities using percentages, and work with percentages greater than 100% (L7)

N11 Interpret fractions and percentages as operators (L7)

SP2 Develop their use of formal mathematical knowledge to interpret and solve problems, including in financial mathematics (L8)

Introduction

The chapter starts by looking at adding, subtracting, multiplying and dividing fractions before a section on converting between decimals and fractions, including ordering decimals and fractions. Percentages of and percentage change are covered before a section on percentage problems. The final section covers the application of repeated percentage change to financial problems such as investments and depreciation.

The introduction discusses the nature of fractals. Fractals occur in nature but can also be generated by computer using simple interative formulae on a special kind of number called a complex number:

http://www.mathsisfun.com/numbers/complex-numbers.html

Fractals were first developed by Benoit Mandelbrot in the 1960s and since then they have become an important branch of mathematics. The notion of 'self-similarity' has been applied to practical problems such as 'How long is the coastline of Britain?' and they are also used extensively in computer graphics to generate environments for games.

Prior knowledge

Students should already know how to…
- Find equivalent fractions
- Find simple percentages of amounts
- Convert between fractions, decimals and percentages
- Find the HCF and LCM of two numbers

Starter problem

The starter problem looks at a basic principle of fractal generation – where the original shape is copied and repeated at a smaller scale and this repeated again and again.

The first square is split into four similar squares and the top right square shaded (one quarter is shaded). Now each of the three non-shaded squares is cut into four similar squares and the top right shaded again. The remaining, already shaded, square is left alone.

Now three sixteenths plus the original quarter is shaded giving us seven sixteenths shaded in total. If the pattern is repeated, we will get 9/32 additional shading which when added to the 7/16 we have already gives us 23/32 of the original square now shaded. This pattern can obviously be repeated again and again. Students could be asked to investigate the sequence formed by the fraction shaded for each iteration.

Resources

MyMaths

Fractions to decimals	1016	Adding subtracting fractions	1017	Dividing fractions	1040
Multiplying fractions	1047	Percentage change 1	1060	Percentage change 2	1073
Change as a percentage	1302				

Online assessment

Chapter test	3B–4
Formative test	3B–4
Summative test	3B–4

InvisiPen solutions

Multiplying by fractions	143	Dividing by fractions	144
Adding and subtracting fractions			145
Percentage increase and decrease			152
Calculating a percentage change			153
Repeated percentage change			155
Fractions and decimals	161	Ratio and proportion	193

Topic scheme

Teaching time = 7 lessons/3 weeks

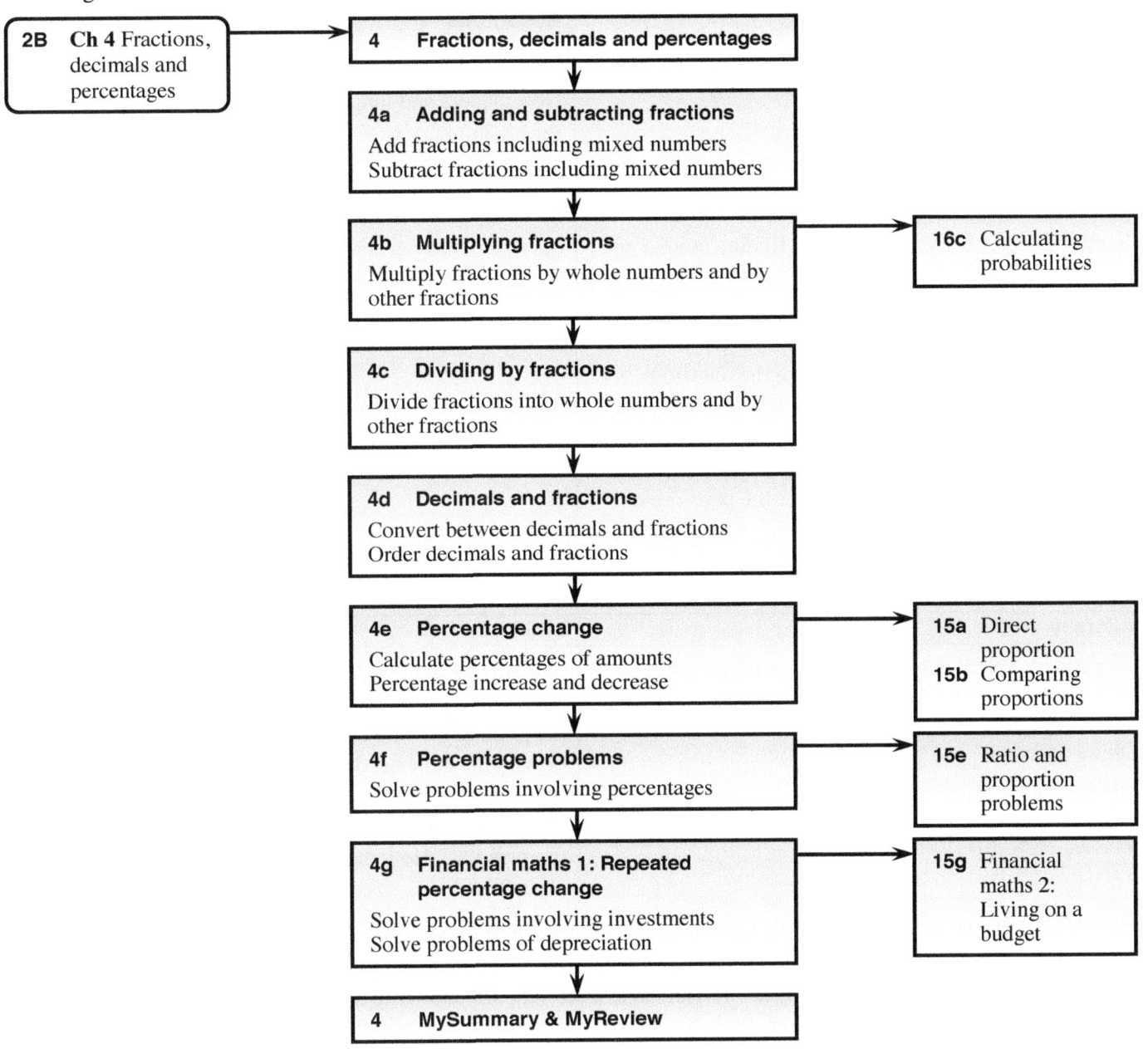

- **2B Ch 4** Fractions, decimals and percentages →
  - **4** Fractions, decimals and percentages
    - **4a Adding and subtracting fractions**
      - Add fractions including mixed numbers
      - Subtract fractions including mixed numbers
    - **4b Multiplying fractions**
      - Multiply fractions by whole numbers and by other fractions → **16c** Calculating probabilities
    - **4c Dividing by fractions**
      - Divide fractions into whole numbers and by other fractions
    - **4d Decimals and fractions**
      - Convert between decimals and fractions
      - Order decimals and fractions
    - **4e Percentage change**
      - Calculate percentages of amounts
      - Percentage increase and decrease → **15a** Direct proportion / **15b** Comparing proportions
    - **4f Percentage problems**
      - Solve problems involving percentages → **15e** Ratio and proportion problems
    - **4g Financial maths 1: Repeated percentage change**
      - Solve problems involving investments
      - Solve problems of depreciation → **15g** Financial maths 2: Living on a budget
    - **4** MySummary & MyReview

Differentiation

Student book 3A   54 – 75
Add and subtract fractions
Multiply and divide fractions
Convert between fractions and decimals
Find fractions and percentages of amounts
Solve percentage problems
Repeated percentage change

Student book 3B   52 – 71
Add and subtract fractions and mixed numbers
Multiply and divide by fractions
Convert between fractions and decimals
Order fractions and decimals
Percentage of and percentage increase and decrease
Solve percentage problems
Repeated percentage change

Student book 3C   54 – 69
Calculate with fractions
Recurring decimals and reciprocals
Percentage increase and decrease
Reverse percentage change
Solve percentage problems

Introduction

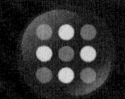

4a Adding and subtracting fractions

Objectives	
• Use efficient methods to add, subtract, multiply and divide fractions	(L7)

Key ideas	Resources	
1 Recognise & use equivalent fractions in the context of addition and subtraction 2 Add and subtract fractions accurately	Adding Subtracting fractions Newspapers and magazines Mini whiteboards	(1017)

Simplification	Extension
Students struggling with addition/subtraction of fractions need plenty of practice in finding equivalent fractions and in understanding that fractions can only be added or subtracted when they have the same denominator. Students may find it helpful to make the questions more visual. In question **2e** try asking the students to draw two identical rectangles and shading one-fifth of the first and one half of the second. Emphasise that it is difficult to add the fractions because the parts are of different sizes. Now demonstrate further dividing each rectangle so that there are 10 parts in each and explain that it is now easy to add the parts together.	More able students could practice more involved questions such as adding or subtracting three or more fractions written as mixed numbers, or they could make up questions of their own such as finding the perimeters of real objects measured in inches.

Literacy	Links
Revisit equivalent addition and subtraction language with students. Encourage students to read fractions with meaning, for example 'three quarters' rather than 'three over four'.	Bring in some newspapers or magazines. Fractions are often used in advertising to express the proportion of the population who claim to prefer a particular brand or who have the need for a particular product. Examples are '1 in 4 people over the age of 40 have high cholesterol' or '8 out of 10 owners said their cat preferred …' How many examples of fractions can the class find?

Alternative approach
Using mini whiteboards with students in pairs, ask them to write as many equivalent fractions as they can to the fraction 2/5. Now ask them, working as individuals to start with 3/8 and write a sequence adding 3/8 every time as fast as possible in a given short time, say 30 seconds. What is the largest value reached? Did all the students give the simplest answers with no top-heavy fractions? Repeat, but this time with these points being applied for 1 minute. Recap the principles of addition and subtraction with fractions and consolidate.

Checkpoint	
Work out $\frac{3}{4} + \frac{1}{7}$	($\frac{25}{28}$)
Work out $\frac{2}{5} - \frac{1}{4}$	($\frac{3}{20}$)
Work out $1\frac{1}{3} + 2\frac{1}{2}$	($3\frac{5}{6}$)

Number Fractions, decimals and percentages

Starter – Factors and multiples

Write the following list on the board:
3, 7, 15, 16, 18, 21, 24, 60.
Ask questions, for example,

Which two numbers have a highest common factor of 8? (16 and 24)

The HCF of which two numbers is 12? (24 and 60)

Which two numbers have a lowest common multiple of 21? (3 and 7) *etc.*

Teaching notes

Pre-requisites for being able to add fractions include being able to identify common denominators (preferably the lowest common denominator) and to find equivalent fractions. Taking some time to review and practice these components will be helpful as competency in these two skills will allow students to focus on the other processes of adding and subtracting fractions.

Changing between mixed numbers and improper fractions also requires some practice.

A common mistake is to add both the denominators and the numerators (it leads immediately to an absurdity if you do the same with subtraction).

Looking at $\frac{1}{2} + \frac{1}{2}$ will usually convince students that the method is wrong because it gives an answer of when the fraction is simplified, and they know $\frac{1}{2}$ the answer should be 1.

Plenary

Provide a number of examples with different characteristics, for example one denominator being a factor of the other, use of mixed numbers or fractions less than 1, subtraction and addition of the same pair of numbers. Ask students to work in pairs to identify the differences in the methods required between pairs of examples. Take class feedback and discuss.

Exercise commentary

Question 1 – Revises work on equivalent fractions.

Question 2 – In parts **e-h** the two denominators are co-prime.

Question 3 – All the questions have denominators with a common factor so encourage students to choose the *lowest* common denominator rather than simply multiplying the two denominators together.

Question 4 – Students need to first change each fraction into an improper fraction (see second example). Ask students how to change between mixed numbers and improper fractions and vice versa.

Questions 5 and **6** – These are applications of the skills covered in this section and students may need guidance extracting the information from the text.

Question 7 – This is a great opportunity for linking to Egyptian history. Also for group work by asking groups of students to investigate writing different fractions in 'Egyptian' form. The students' work would make good display material – they could even investigate how to write their answers in hieroglyphics.

Answers

1 a 5   b 20   c 28   d 42
2 a $\frac{4}{5}$ b $\frac{1}{3}$ c $1\frac{4}{13}$ d $1\frac{3}{5}$
   e $\frac{7}{10}$ f $\frac{11}{12}$ g $\frac{1}{24}$ h $\frac{16}{21}$
3 a $\frac{9}{10}$ b $\frac{1}{12}$ c $\frac{1}{4}$ d $1\frac{5}{24}$
   e $\frac{35}{72}$ f $\frac{37}{60}$ g $\frac{1}{16}$ h $\frac{43}{48}$
4 a $3\frac{1}{4}$ b $\frac{5}{8}$ c $3\frac{1}{15}$ d $\frac{4}{5}$
   e $4\frac{13}{30}$ f $4\frac{3}{20}$ g $1\frac{1}{40}$ h $3\frac{2}{21}$
5 a $\frac{9}{40}$
   b $\frac{101}{105}$ He has not completed the race.
6 $16\frac{3}{10}$ cm
7 a $\frac{1}{2}+\frac{1}{8}$ $\frac{1}{2}+\frac{1}{5}$ $\frac{1}{2}+\frac{1}{12}$
   b Student's Answers
   c Student's Answers

Adding and subtracting fractions

4b Multiplying fractions

Objectives	
• Calculate fractions of quantities (fraction answers)	(L6)
• Multiply and divide an integer by a fraction	(L6)
• Cancel common factors before multiplying or dividing	(L6)
• Use efficient methods to add, subtract, multiply and divide fractions	(L7)

Key ideas	Resources
1 Recognise that finding a fraction of a value is equivalent to multiplying 2 Multiply a fraction by another fraction	Multiplying fractions (1047) Dice Scientific calculators Mini whiteboards

Simplification

Students struggling with multiplication of fractions by integers could benefit from illustrating the problems on a number line. Students could be encouraged to draw the first examples in question **1** on a number line before being asked for a quicker method of working out the answer, that is, multiplying the numerator by the integer.

The ideas can be made more practical for some students by using real-life examples such as three packets of flour each weighing $\frac{3}{4}$ kg. This should help students to visualise the size of answer to expect.

Extension

Students could be asked to draw a diagram to illustrate a multiplication of a fraction by a fraction starting with a straightforward example such as $\frac{2}{3}$ of $\frac{3}{4}$

three quarters   two thirds of three quarters

The more able students should be taught to cancel down fractions before they are multiplied together. Confident students could be given examples written as mixed numbers.

Literacy

Revisit multiplication equivalent language. Encourage students to read questions out loud, rearranging and using equivalent language in order to convey conceptual thinking. For example: **q1** – $3 \times \frac{1}{7}$ read as 'one seventh of three' or 'three sevenths of 1, etc.

Links

The Romans used words to describe fractions as parts of the whole. In calculations, they used fractions based on the *as*, a unit of weight. As there were twelve *unciae* in an *as*, *uncia* came to mean one-twelfth of anything. *Unciae* were added to make halves, thirds and quarters. *Semis* was six *unciae* or one-half. There is more information about Roman fractions at http://ancienthistory.about.com/od/romannumerals/p/RomanFractions.htm

Alternative approach

Recap repeated addition of fractions such as ¾ and equate to ¾ of 6 for example. Encourage students to use mental strategies in order to find answers where possible. Challenge students to solve harder problems using mini whiteboards and explore the approaches and strategies applied. Draw out the key principles, consolidate and extend to fractions of a fraction, again using mental strategies supported by visual images such as those given in Extension. Students should also be encouraged to use the fraction buttons on a calculator, and may apply this to support and confirm written and/or mental strategies.

Checkpoint

Find $\frac{2}{5}$ of 250 km.	(100 km)
Find $\frac{7}{8}$ of 43 kg.	($37\frac{5}{8}$ kg)
Find $\frac{4}{5}$ of $\frac{2}{3}$.	($\frac{8}{15}$)

Number   Fractions, decimals and percentages

Starter – Make one

Ask students to draw four boxes representing the numerators and denominators of two fractions. Throw a dice four times. After each throw, ask students to place the score in one of their boxes. Students then add their two fractions together and score a point if the sum is one.

Can be extended by increasing the number of boxes or by changing the target value.

Teaching notes

Cancelling fractions accurately is a key skill in multiplying fractions, so some practice will be helpful. Encourage students to look for larger factors which can be cancelled but emphasise that cancelling small factors that are easy to spot such as 2, 3, 5 will reduce both the denominator and the numerator and any more common factors will be easier to see. However, they need to look after simplifying once to check whether any further cancelling is possible.

The rules for multiplying fractions differ from those for addition / subtraction and students are prone to mix and match parts of the two techniques. In particular, they will sometimes convert to equivalent fractions with a common denominator. If they continue correctly by multiplying both denominators and the numerators they will get the right answer, but will normally have to do much more work in cancelling than is necessary.

Plenary

Review the rules for addition / subtraction and for multiplication of fractions. Ask students to work in pairs to set mixed technique problems for their partner to solve.

Exercise commentary

Question 1 – Revision of writing an improper fraction as a mixed number may be necessary; remind students to cancel down fractions to simplest form.

Question 2 – Encourage students to give some answers in sensible units, for example, $2\frac{11}{12}$ feet as 2 feet 11 inches (part **f**).

Question 3 – Ask students to explain their strategies for solving these kinds of questions such as 'doing the opposite of finding half of something, which is multiplying by two'.

Question 4 – A calculator question so encourage the students to estimate the size of answer they expect.

Question 5 – Many of these questions can be simplified by cancelling down before performing the multiplication.

Question 6 – Ask the students if there is a quicker way to work out the answers which does not involve subtracting the reduction.

Question 7 – This is about recognising that a fraction of a fraction is a multiplication.

Answers

1	a $\frac{3}{7}$	b $\frac{6}{7}$	c $\frac{12}{13}$	d $7\frac{1}{5}$
	e $10\frac{2}{3}$	f $12\frac{1}{2}$	g 21	h $8\frac{4}{7}$
2	a $6\frac{2}{5}$ cm	b $8\frac{1}{7}$ kg	c 18 m	d $13\frac{1}{3}$ mins
	e 35 kg	f $2\frac{11}{12}$ feet	g $10\frac{2}{11}$ tonnes	
	h $22\frac{1}{2}$ km			
3	a 90	b 20	c 3	d 3
4	a 53.6 km	b £233.33	c 11.43 km	d 103.13 m
	e 15.38 kg	f 25 g	g 272.73 ml	h 56.25°
5	a $\frac{8}{15}$	b $\frac{5}{8}$	c $\frac{1}{14}$	d $\frac{1}{4}$
	e $\frac{5}{14}$	f $\frac{1}{4}$	g $\frac{1}{6}$	h $\frac{5}{26}$
6	a £10.80	b £16 071.43		
7	a £24			

7 b Multiply the fractions together and then multiply by the amount OR write all the fractions and amount as multiplication and cancel the common factors
   c i £6
     ii 30 kg

Multiplying fractions

4c Dividing by fractions

Objectives

- Multiply and divide an integer by a fraction (L6)
- Cancel common factors before multiplying or dividing (L6)
- Interpret division as a multiplicative inverse (L6)
- Use efficient methods to add, subtract, multiply and divide fractions (L7)

Key ideas	Resources
1 Recognise that repeated subtraction of a fraction is equivalent to dividing by that fraction 2 Recognise that dividing by a fraction is equivalent to multiplying by its reciprocal 3 Divide a fraction by another fraction	Dividing fractions (1040) Mini whiteboards Scientific calculators

Simplification

Students struggling with division by a fraction will benefit from illustrating the problems on a number line. Students could be encouraged to draw the first examples in question **1** on a number line for example $2 \div 1/4$

Then ask for a quicker method of working out the answer, that is, multiplying by the inverted fraction.

The ideas will need to be made more practical for some students by using real-life examples such as how many $\frac{3}{4}$ kg of flour are there in three kilograms? Relating these examples to those used in the previous spread will help students link the work with multiplication.

Extension

Students should be encouraged to cancel down common factors before they divide or multiply fractions.

More able students could be asked questions involving division of a mixed number by another mixed number.

Literacy

The term reciprocal needs to be introduced through modelling and active learning techniques with mini whiteboards – thus what is the reciprocal of....; and so on.

Continue to encourage students to read calculations with meaning and equivalent vocabulary, thus $2 \div \frac{1}{3}$ might become 'how many thirds are there in 2?'

Links

American cookery books usually list dry ingredients in terms of fractions of cups, teaspoons and tablespoons. Cups and spoons measure ingredients by volume rather than by weight. The weight of a cup of each ingredient will vary according to the density of the ingredient. To find out about US cooking measures and conversions see: www.miketodd.net/encyc/cooking.htm

Alternative approach

Begin with simple verbal divisions of integers by a unit fraction, with students using mini whiteboards for responses. Now model some of the verbal questions used in a written form and encourage students to spot the equivalent statement using multiplication. Introduce the term reciprocal and externd as appropriate for the students needs, differentiating appropriately. Again explore the use of the fractions button on the calculator and encourage students to check both their mental and written approaches.

Checkpoint

Find out how many $\frac{2}{5}$ there are in 8. (20)

Divide $\frac{7}{8}$ by $\frac{3}{4}$. ($1\frac{1}{6}$)

Starter – Two-fifths

Ask students questions involving two-fifths, for example,

What is double two-fifths?
What is two-fifths multiplied by six?
Subtract two-fifths from seven-tenths.
What is two-fifths squared?
What is two-fifths of 15?

Encourage students to give their answers in the simplest form

Teaching notes

Working with the multiplicative inverse of fractions (reciprocals) is new to students so identifying them from a fraction is a useful activity before using them to perform divisions.

Some students may have difficulty in understanding that the inverse of $\frac{1}{3}$ is $\frac{3}{1}$ and that this is the same as 3, even though they understand that the inverse of $\frac{2}{5}$ is $\frac{5}{2}$. Practising a variety of examples should help identify any students with this difficulty.

Plenary

Ask students to work in pairs to set mixed technique problems for their partner to solve, using any of addition, subtraction, multiplication or division.

Exercise commentary

Question 1 and **2** – These can be illustrated on number lines to aid understanding. In part **f** of question **1** you may need to explain how there can be fifths in a half. A diagram with the whole divided into ten pieces should help.

Question 3 – Encourage students to leave answers as whole numbers, not improper fractions.

Question 4 – Students may need to revise changing improper fractions into mixed numbers; encourage students to cancel the fractions before multiplying.

Question 5 – Encourage students to cancel the fractions before multiplying; the answers can be written as mixed numbers.

Question 6 – Students may need to revise changing mixed numbers into improper fractions.

Question 7 – The fractional part of the answer needs to be interpreted in the context of the question.

Question 8 – This is a good introductory activity for students to see the connection between dividing by a fraction and multiplying by the inverted fraction.

Answers

1	a	10	b	12	c	32	d	2
	e	3	f	2.5				
2	a	8	b	10	c	12	d	15
	e	20	f	60	g	56	h	21
3	a	4	b	6	c	10	d	16
	e	12	f	10	g	21	h	24
4	a	$6\frac{2}{3}$	b	$8\frac{3}{4}$	c	$7\frac{1}{2}$	d	$18\frac{2}{3}$
	e	$2\frac{4}{7}$	f	$8\frac{3}{4}$	g	$26\frac{2}{3}$	h	$14\frac{1}{7}$
5	a	$1\frac{1}{8}$	b	$\frac{5}{6}$	c	$\frac{5}{7}$	d	$2\frac{1}{2}$
	e	$1\frac{13}{14}$	f	$\frac{2}{3}$	g	$\frac{2}{5}$	h	$\frac{4}{5}$
6	a	2	b	4	c	4	d	$\frac{25}{8}$
7	a	14	b	12				

8 a i 3, 6, 9, 12, 15, 18
   ii 4, 8, 12, 16, 20, 24
   iii 5, 10, 15, 20, 25, 30
  b Students' answers: $\div \frac{1}{n} = \times n$
  c Students' answers: $\div \frac{2}{n} = \times \frac{n}{2}$

Dividing by fractions

4d Decimals and fractions

Objectives

- Recognise that a recurring decimal is a fraction (L6)
- Use division to convert a fraction to a decimal (L6)
- Order fractions by writing them with a common denominator or by converting them to decimals (L6)

Key ideas	Resources
1 Be able to write a fraction as a decimal 2 Be able to write a rational decimal as a fraction	Fractions to decimals (1016) Mini whiteboards Decimal number line Scientific calculators.

Simplification	Extension
Students may need to revise work on equivalent fractions in order to cancel down fractions and to rewrite fractions as equivalent fractions with a denominator that is a power of 10. Encourage students to break down the process into smaller steps, for example to cancel down $\frac{25}{100}$, keep dividing numerator and denominator by five; to change $\frac{11}{25}$ into a fraction out of 100 keep multiplying numerator and denominator by two, *etc*.	Students could recap on work on percentages by expressing each of their decimal answers as percentages. More able students could be introduced to a method for converting a recurring decimal into a fraction.

Literacy	Links
Stress and encourage students to use equivalent values not only of decimals and fractions, but also percentage.	π is an irrational number which means that the decimal does not terminate or recur but instead goes on for ever. π has been calculated to over one trillion decimals places without any pattern emerging. In 2005, a Japanese man called Akira Haraguchi, 59, managed to recite π to 83,431 decimal places from memory. The first million digits of π can be found at http://newton.ex.ac.uk/research/qsystems/collabs/pi/

Alternative approach

By modelling the simple statement 50% = ½ = 0.5, encourage students to write as many common equivalents as they can in a short space of time. Show and share with the whole group, exposing any misconceptions if they arise. Now repeat the activity by ask students to find some less well known equivalent statements, working in pairs to support each other and giving them a little more thinking time. Explore some of the strategies offered by students and recap or expand as required. Include or introduce the use of a calculator, including the fraction button, and perhaps also the % key in order to strengthen the equivalence connections.

Checkpoint

Write these values in order starting with the smallest value: $\frac{3}{7}$; 0.54; $\frac{5}{9}$; 0.49; 47%; $\frac{1}{2}$.

($\frac{3}{7}$, 47%, 0.49, $\frac{1}{2}$, 0.54, $\frac{5}{9}$)

Starter – True or false

Give statements and ask whether they are true or false. For example,

438.4 is 438.0 to nearest whole number
(False, should be 438)

$2.5 \times 10^4 \times 4 = 10^5$ (True)

39000 is 39×10^3 written in standard form
(False, should be 3.9×10^4)

0.56×10^{13} is a large number written in standard form
(False, should be 5.6×10^{12}) *etc*.

Teaching notes

Review prior learning and associated vocabulary: numerator, denominator, terminating and recurring decimals, equivalent fractions, cancelling.

It may be helpful to use a whole-class mini whiteboard activity on basic manipulation of fractions and decimals to gauge student understanding and fluency in manipulation.

Plenary

Discuss with the class whether a fraction must always produce a recurring (or terminating) decimal. Using simple denominators, such as 7, show that the decimal must repeat in no more than 10-digit blocks. This can lead to 2-digit denominators repeating in no more than 100-digit blocks, and so to understanding that any fraction must terminate or repeat.

Exercise commentary

Question 1 – The answers to parts **g** to **j** are greater than one and produce mixed numbers.

Question 2 – In parts **h**, **i** and **j** the denominators are not obvious factors of 100. Students will need to simplify these fractions (where appropriate) before writing as fractions with a denominator that is a power of 10.

Question 3 – Students could use a calculator or short division.

Question 6 – A good question for paired discussion. Students should try their own strategies to identify fractions smaller than $\frac{1}{12}$.

Question 7 – Students need to show the conversion between fraction and decimal in their explanation.

Question 8 – A decimal number line would be useful here. Challenge students to keep finding more decimal numbers between any two answers given, for example 'find another decimal that lies between 0.5 and 0.6'.

Question 9 – Students could be encouraged to use a spreadsheet.

Answers

1 a $\frac{3}{5}$ b $\frac{12}{25}$ c $\frac{1}{4}$ d $\frac{37}{50}$
   e $\frac{1}{8}$ f $\frac{117}{200}$ g $\frac{3}{2}$ h $\frac{21}{20}$
   i $\frac{9}{4}$ j $\frac{39}{25}$

2 a 0.7   b 0.65   c 0.44   d 0.46
   e 1.24   f 1.2   g 1.35   h 0.425
   i 0.75   j 0.8

3 a 0.69   b 0.22   c 0.27   d 0.86
   e 1.17   f 0.58   g 1.29   h 0.73
   i 0.62   j 1.10

4 a <   b <   c >   d >
   e <   f >   g <   h >

5 a $\frac{2}{7}, 0.33, \frac{4}{11}, 0.4$ b $\frac{1}{5}, \frac{3}{11}, 0.2929, 0.3$
   c $\frac{6}{7}, \frac{7}{8}, \frac{8}{9}, \frac{9}{10}$

6 a Yes, $\frac{1}{12} - \frac{1}{16} > 0$ b No, $\frac{1}{12} - \frac{1}{8} < 0$
   c No, $\frac{3}{24} = \frac{1}{8}$ d No, $\frac{1}{4} = \frac{3}{12}$
   e Yes, $\frac{1}{12} - \frac{4}{50} > 0$

7 a Jameela has £0.75   b Farah uses 1.8 kg of flour

8 0.5, 0.6, 0.7

9 $\frac{11}{17}$

Decimals and fractions

4e Percentage change

Objectives
- Calculate percentages and find the outcome of a given percentage increase or decrease   (L6)
- Solve problems involving percentage changes   (L6)

Key ideas	Resources
1 Finding percentage increases and decreases 2 Use multiplicative relationships or scaling when finding increases and decreases	Percentage change 1 (1060) Mini whiteboards

Simplification	Extension
At the most basic level, students should be given lots of practice at finding percentages using mental methods, particularly focusing upon finding 10% and 1%. This allows all other percentages to be calculated. Students should be introduced to converting between percentages and decimals (by recognition) and be given opportunities to use a calculator to multiply the decimal by the amount.	Give students questions which involve repeated percentage increases/decreases, for example, compound interest problems. Students could be encouraged to use a spreadsheet and calculate the effect of say interest on a bank account over an extended period of time such as 30 years…50 years…100 years *etc*.

Literacy	Links
Continue to encourage the equivalent language using decimals, fractions and percentage. Recognise equivalent vocabulary referring to either increase or decrease, identifying this accurately within written problems.	National tables of GCSE and A-level results are published each year. The tables list the percentage of candidates at each school who passed five or more GCSEs at grades A* to C. Choose a school in the tables at http://www.education.gov.uk/schools/performance/ Has the percentage increased or decreased for the chosen school over the last four years?

Alternative approach

Begin with a task examining multiplicatives and their results with students indicating simply if the answer is higher or lower (increase/decrease). Use mini whiteboards, thumbs up/down or higher/lower cards here. Use a mix of multipliers in terms of fractions, decimals and percentage, such as × 1.5; ¾, 60%, 115%, 2 ½. Challenge students with a percentage increase problem for work on mini whiteboards and compare approaches. Most are likely to have employed a two stage approach of finding the percent and adding. Introduce the one stage scaling or mulitplier equivalent of the problem if this has not arisen from any student approaches. Examine equivalent multipliers for a variety of percentage changes, agfain encouraging students to use mini whiteboards, before applying to any word problems.

Checkpoint

What multiplier would you use to: increase £30 by 15%?   (×1.15; £34.50)

decrease £30 by 15%?   (× 0.85; £25.50)

Number   Fractions, decimals and percentages

Starter – Fraction challenge

Ask students to find as many fractions as they can between one-third and one-half in a given time, for example, two minutes. Discuss strategies used by the students.

Can be differentiated by the choice of fractions.

Teaching notes

The worked examples illustrate a number of approaches which students should discuss to support learning.

A review of the equivalence between percentages, fractions and decimal forms, and some practice in finding equivalent values in other forms should help to develop fluency and confidence in the component skills students will need to use in this unit.

Working with percentage change is an important component of functional mathematics, so linking to real-life problems will support this.

Plenary

Ask students to work in pairs to ask questions involving percentage changes in real-life situations for their partner to solve. Students can compare the method they used for each problem and discuss any different approaches.

Exercise commentary

Question 1 – Students should be encouraged to use all three methods for finding a percentage of an amount rather than an over-reliance on a particular method.

Questions 2 and **3** – Initially, students should be encouraged to find the reduction or increase and subtract/add to the original amount. Students successful at this method should be encouraged to try to represent the calculation using a single multiplier (this requires an understanding of the decimal equivalent method). Question **3** is applied in context so some students may need help extracting the information from the text.

Question 4 – This question examines students understanding of using the decimal multiplier and would make a good plenary.

Question 5 – This activity provides a good opportunity for students to practice using a decimal multiplier.

Answers

1 a £12   b 157.5 kg   c 7.15 m   d $4.32
   e 118.75 cm f £24.65   g 7.68 MB   h 32.67 kg

2 a £92   b £68   c 24.42 km   d 46.4 kg
   e 33.6 m   f 48.91 cm   g £263.25   h 334.88 kJ
   i 34.08 kB   j £3191.50

3 a £29.75   b £31.36   c 192 g   d £1.55

4 a 1.3×40 b 0.3×40 c 0.7×40 d 1.03×40
   e 0.03×40 f 0.97×40

5 a The price increase is 10% of £20 = £2. The price reduction is 10% of £22 = £2.20.
     Therefore the January sale price is less
   b Students' answers

Percentage change

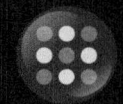

4f Percentage problems

Objectives
- Use proportional reasoning to solve problems (L6)
- Choosing the correct numbers to take as 100%, or as a whole (L6)
- Solve problems involving percentage changes (L6)

Key ideas	Resources
1 Correctly unpick word problems involving percentage 2 Apply proportional knowledge effectively in order to solve a problem	Percentage as a change (1302) Dice Newspapers KS3 Percentages (NRICH): nrich.maths.org/5567

Simplification	Extension
Students will need to revise previous work on finding the percentage of an amount (4e). Once they are comfortable with calculating a percentage of an amount, tackle only percentage increase questions and make sure they are confident with these before moving on to decreases.	Ask students to calculate the interior angles of regular polygons by calculating the angle at the centre first and then calculating the base angles in the isosceles triangles. Students should compare the results with their answers from question **2**.

Literacy	Links
Working with worded problems will support students when strategies such as read out loud; identifying, underlining or highlighting key vocabulary; translating into appropriate mathematics sentences. Continue to encourage use of equivalent proportional language.	Students should practise questions involving use of the single decimal multiplier for percentage change. More able students should attempt questions involving repeated percentage change such as compound interest and reverse percentage problems.

Alternative approach
Recap with some rehearsal work on multipliers as in last section, before modelling tackling a word problem with the whole group. Encourage students to work in pairs, using the modelled strategies for unpicking each problem and solving. Further examples of problems can be found at NRICH as referenced or from past SATs papers.

Checkpoint
A jar of jam is usually 550 grams but a limited edition jar is offered at 15% extra free.
What is the mass of the limited edition? (632.5 g)

A shop offers clothing at a sale price of 20% off.
If a shirt cost £32 before the sale, what was the sale price? (£25.60)

Number Fractions, decimals and percentages

Starter – Dice challenge

Throw three dice at least twenty times. After each throw, ask students to make one number between 1 and 20 inclusive, using all three dice scores and any operations. The winner is the first student to make all the numbers.

Alternatively, the winner is the student to make the most numbers in a given number of throws.

Teaching notes

Review the basic skills of calculating percentages of a quantity and the equivalence of fractions, percentages and decimals before starting to work with problems in context.

Many students have weak literacy skills and will work mainly with word problems in this spread. Emphasise the need to identify the key information, and encourage students to use the worked examples as templates for communicating the processes involved in solving problems.

Plenary

Bring in a newspaper, or several newspapers, and give some pages to each pair of students. Ask students to find as many uses of percentages as they can in their pages. Feedback to the whole class how often percentages appear, emphasising the importance of being able to work accurately and confidently with them. This has strong links with functional mathematics.

Exercise commentary

Question 1 – This question does not relate directly to the examples in the text but encourages students to work out two percentage calculations and compare the results.

Question 2 and **3** – Students should compare their answers by writing them as percentages (proportions). They will need to use a calculator.

Question 4 – A good opportunity for students to compare their methods by working in pairs or through class discussion.

Question 5 and **6** – Students may wish to use the method of calculating the increase or decrease and adding or subtracting from the total. In question **5** part **a** encourage students to work out 115% of 240g and compare with finding 15% of 240g.

Question 7 – Students have to combine the two key teaching ideas from this section and will need to be clear about what the question is asking them. Some students will think the answer is just 15%.

Question 8 – A challenging question that is ideal for paired work. Students should be encouraged to make up the prices of, say, 10 items in the shop first and then work out the sale prices after both price reductions.

Answers

1. English 16 500
   Maths 20 880
   4380 students
2. Kane family: 6.4%
   Walton family: 8.5%
   The Walton family spent more.
3. Jack: 6.5%
   Deidre: 6%
   Jack received 6.5% interest
4. A 7.5 g per 1p
   B 7.66 g per 1p
   B
5. a 276 g   b £24.60
6. a 472.5 cm   b 427.5 cm
7. 13.04%
8. a 0.88   b $1 - 0.88^2 = 0.2256$

Percentage problems

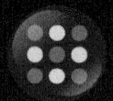

4g Financial maths 1: Repeated percentage change

Objectives
- Interpret percentages as operators (L7)
- Develop their use of formal mathematical knowledge to interpret and solve problems, including in financial mathematics (L8)

Key ideas	Resources
1 Compound interest and depreciation 2 Investments, savings and loans	Percentage change 2 (1073) Calculators

Simplification	Extension
Students who struggle to work with a single multiplier raised to a power could be encouraged to tabulate the changes year on year. So for example in question **2**, £8000 × 1.07 = £8560 and then £8560 × 1.07 = £9159.20. This approach does not work efficiently for a large number of years. Hence questions **4a** and **5** can be omitted. Question **4b** is complicated to work through and can also be omitted.	Students could investigate how the value of savings under a compound interest scheme differs from the value under a simple interest scheme. Do the values diverge from each other, or does the gap stay the same? A spreadsheet can again be used to help with this investigation. They could also graph the relative values for a given amount saved.

Literacy	Links
Financial literacy: Words like 'interest' and 'depreciation' may be new to the students and will need careful explanation.	There is a wealth of information on financial products and services available to the students. They could investigate actual savings and loan rates by visiting a local bank or going on the internet. Links to the 'credit crunch' and the banking crisis over the last five years can also be developed.

Alternative approach
While the use of multipliers is by far the simplest method for solving problems of this type, an alternative approach (for a small number of time periods) is by systematically calculating the interest earned, adding it to the principal and repeating. Students should get used to the repetitive nature of the calculations and be able to tabulate the outcomes at each stage. An example table might look something like this:

Year	Start amount	Interest	Finish amount
1			
2			
3			
4			

Checkpoint
£7000 is invested at 8% per year interest. How much is it worth after three years? (£8817.98)

A car costs £12 500 new and depreciates at a rate of 12% per year. How much is it worth after four years?
(£7496.19)

Number Fractions, decimals and percentages

Starter – Find the multiplier

Following on from work in **4e** and **4f**, students could be asked to find the multiplier for different percentage changes. This could be by calculating the percentage change and converting it to a multiplier or by trial and improvement. Some example questions:

What is the multiplier that turns 400 into 480? (1.2)

What is the multiplier that turns 72 into 90? (1.25)

What is the multiplier that turns 650 into 585? (0.9)

Teaching notes

When introducing the concept of compound interest emphasise that the interest earned in the first year is added to the *principal* amount so this is the new principal for the second year, etc. This leads on to the concept of repeated multiplication with the multiplier raised to the appropriate power (the number of *periods* of time, usually years). Depreciation can likewise be introduced by emphasising that it is the same as compound interest but a decrease (hence the multiplier is less than one). Further examples similar to the ones in the book or question **2** can be used as appropriate to illustrate the key ideas.

Plenary

John invests £3000 at a rate of interest of 4% per year. Alison invests £2500 at a rate of interest of 8% per year. How long will it take Alison to have more money than John? (5 years)

Exercise commentary

Question 1 – Students should not be working out the value of each multiplier, merely writing it in index form.

Question 2 – These questions mirror those in the worked examples.

Question 3 – Further examples similar to the worked examples but given in a table.

Question 4 – Part **a** is a good example of trial and improvement to get the right answer. $85,000 \times 1.06^n$ for various n can be input into a calculator or spreadsheet. Part **b** is more complicated since there is a repayment element to take into account. Tabulation of the monthly balance may be necessary.

Question 5 – Part **b** can be done in isolation using the methods outlined in the examples but otherwise this question requires access to a spreadsheet.

Answers

1. a 1.04   b 1.04^4 c 1.05^5 d 0.92^6
   e 0.99^{20} f 0.5^{20}

2. a £9159.20   b £7369.50

3. Car: £19706.75
   House: £145800
   TV: £128.23
   Savings: £17073.57

4. a 43 years   b 35 months

5. a Students' answers   b £386 268.36
   c Graph from (1, 90 000) to (25, 386 268), smooth curve showing exponential growth.
   d Students' answers
   e Students' answers; > £7100 works

Financial maths 1: Repeated percentage change

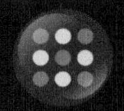

4 Fractions, decimals and percentages – MySummary

Key outcomes		Quick check
Add and subtract fractions	L6	Calculate these and give your answer in its simplest form **a** $\frac{5}{6}-\frac{1}{2}$ $(\frac{1}{3})$ **b** $\frac{7}{9}+\frac{1}{3}$ $(1\frac{1}{9})$ **c** $2\frac{1}{4}-1\frac{2}{3}$ $(\frac{7}{12})$
Multiply and divide fractions.	L6	Calculate the following and give your answer in its simplest form **a** $\frac{3}{8} \times \frac{4}{5}$ $(\frac{3}{10})$ **b** $\frac{2}{3} \div \frac{3}{5}$ $(1\frac{1}{9})$ **c** $1\frac{1}{2} \times 2\frac{1}{3}$ $(3\frac{1}{2})$
Convert between decimals and fractions.	L6	Write these fractions as decimals **a** $\frac{9}{25}$ (0.36) **b** $\frac{7}{5}$ (1.4) **c** $\frac{53}{20}$ (2.6)
Calculate percentage changes.	L6	**a** Increase £12 by 20% (£14.40) **b** Decrease 850 grams by 5% (807.5 g)
Solve problems involving percentages.	L7	A computer is offered for sale at 30% off. If it cost £540 originally, what is the sale price? (£378)

MyMaths extra support

Lesson/online homework			Description
Frac Dec Perc 1	1029	L4	Converting well-known fractions, decimals and percentages
Percentages of amounts 1	1030	L4	How to find 10%, 25% and 75% of whole numbers
Equivalent fractions	1042	L5	How to recognise fractions with the same value

MyReview

4 MySummary

Check out
You should now be able to ...

✓ Add and subtract fractions.
✓ Multiply and divide fractions.
✓ Convert between decimals and fractions.
✓ Calculate percentage changes.
✓ Solve problems involving percentages.

Test it ➡
Questions

1 – 2
3 – 5
6
7 – 10
11

Language	Meaning	Example
Numerator	The top number in a fraction.	In the fraction $\frac{4}{5}$, the numerator is 4.
Denominator	The bottom number in a fraction.	In the fraction $\frac{4}{5}$ the denominator is 5.
Simplify a fraction	Divide the numerator and denominator by common factors.	$\frac{30}{33}$ simplifies to $\frac{10}{11}$.
Mixed number	A number that is made of a whole number part and a fraction part.	$4\frac{2}{3}$ is a mixed number.
Proportion	A numerical comparison of the size of a part with the size of the whole.	If 4 out of 5 people in a room are girls, then the proportion that are girls is $\frac{4}{5}$.
Percentage	The numerator of a proportion out of 100.	$\frac{4}{5} = \frac{80}{100} = 80\%$
Recurring decimal	A decimal with an infinite number of repeating digits.	$\frac{1}{3} = 0.33333... = 0.\overline{3}$
Terminating decimal	A decimal with a finite number of digits.	$\frac{3}{5} = 0.6$
Improper fraction	A fraction whose numerator is greater than its denominator.	$\frac{11}{8}$ is an improper fraction.

4 MyReview

1 Calculate these and give your answer as a fraction in its simplest form.
   a $\frac{3}{8} + \frac{5}{32}$ b $\frac{9}{15} - \frac{3}{20}$
   c $\frac{1}{4} + \frac{2}{7}$ d $\frac{19}{21} - \frac{5}{28}$

2 Calculate these, write your answers as improper fractions.
   a $2\frac{3}{4} + 1\frac{1}{7}$ b $5\frac{1}{9} - 3\frac{5}{6}$
   c $4\frac{1}{6} + 2\frac{1}{8}$ d $3\frac{3}{4} - 1\frac{5}{6}$

3 Calculate these, give your answer to 2 dp.
   a $\frac{3}{11}$ of £60   b $\frac{4}{9}$ of 40 kg
   c $1\frac{1}{3}$ of 11 m   d $2\frac{2}{7}$ of 250 ml

4 Calculate these using a mental or written method, and simplify your answers.
   a $12 \times \frac{3}{21}$ b $15 \times \frac{7}{20}$
   c $\frac{2}{11} \times \frac{9}{20}$ d $\frac{9}{10} \times \frac{5}{21}$

5 Calculate and simplify your answers.
   a $18 \div \frac{27}{28}$ b $\frac{2}{7} \div \frac{3}{14}$

6 Change these fractions into decimals without using a calculator.
   a $\frac{3}{20}$ b $\frac{7}{35}$
   c $\frac{11}{10}$ d $\frac{9}{40}$

7 Calculate these percentage changes.
   a Increase 80 by 15%
   b Decrease 240 by 38%

8 Jamie was paid £900 a month. His pay was increased by 3.2%. How much is he paid now?

9 An antique vase increases in value from £770 to £890. What is the percentage increase?

10 A laptop is reduced in price from £750 to £680. What is the percentage reduction?

11 The table shows the number of students in each class and what percentage passed their maths test.

Class	A	B	C
Students	24	20	28
% pass	54%	70%	43%

Which class had the most students passing the test?

What next?

Score	
0 – 4	Your knowledge of this topic is still developing. To improve look at Formative test: 3B-4; MyMaths: 1016, 1017, 1040, 1047, 1060, 1073 and 1302
5 – 9	You are gaining a secure knowledge of this topic. To improve look at InvisiPen: 143, 144, 145, 152, 153, 155, 161 and 193
10, 11	You have mastered this topic. Well done, you are ready to progress!

Question commentary

Question 1 – Students should look for the LCM of the two denominators.

Question 2 – Students should write as improper fractions first.

Question 3 – Calculators will be required for this question. Check students are rounding correctly.

Question 4 – Encourage students to write the 12 and the 15 as 'over 1' and cancel down first if they can.

Question 5 – Encourage students to cancel down first, where possible.

Question 7 – Encourage students to use a decimal multiplier (**a** 1.15, **b** 0.62).

Question 8 – Increasing by 32% instead of 3.2% would give incorrect answer of £1188.

Question 9 – Dividing the difference by 890 instead of 770 would give 13%.

Question 10 – Dividing the difference by 680 instead of 750 would give 10%.

Question 11 – The number of students are:
   A 13, **B** 14, **C** 12.

Answers

1 a $\frac{17}{32}$ b $\frac{9}{20}$ c $\frac{15}{28}$ d $\frac{61}{84}$

2 a $\frac{109}{28}$ b $\frac{23}{18}$ c $\frac{151}{24}$ d $\frac{23}{12}$

3 a £16.36   b 17.78 kg   c 14.67 m   d 571.43 ml

4 a $\frac{12}{7}$ b $\frac{21}{4}$ c $\frac{9}{110}$ d $\frac{3}{14}$

5 a $\frac{56}{3}$ b $\frac{4}{3}$

6 a 0.15   b 0.2   c 1.1   d 0.225

7 a 92   b 148.8

8 £928.80

9 15.6%

10 9.3%

11 B

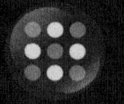

4 MyPractice

1 Work out these.
Give each answer as a fraction in its simplest form.

a $\frac{2}{7} + \frac{5}{14}$ b $\frac{1}{2} + \frac{1}{8}$ c $\frac{4}{9} - \frac{1}{3}$ d $\frac{5}{6} + \frac{3}{8}$

e $\frac{2}{12} + \frac{2}{5}$ f $\frac{7}{12} - \frac{1}{3}$ g $\frac{4}{21} + \frac{9}{14}$ h $\frac{11}{12} - \frac{3}{4}$

2 Work out these.
Give your answer as a fraction in its simplest form and as a mixed number where appropriate.

a $\frac{7}{12} + \frac{11}{18}$ b $\frac{2}{15} + \frac{7}{20}$ c $\frac{13}{15} - \frac{7}{10}$ d $\frac{1}{12} + \frac{5}{16}$

e $\frac{4}{21} + \frac{4}{15}$ f $\frac{13}{16} - \frac{3}{4}$ g $\frac{19}{30} + \frac{5}{18}$ h $\frac{17}{40} - \frac{3}{16}$

3 Work out these.
Give each answer as a fraction in its simplest form and as a mixed number where appropriate.

a $\frac{3}{5}$ of 15cm   b $\frac{3}{8}$ of 13kg   c $\frac{2}{3}$ of £51   d $\frac{5}{12}$ of 40sec

e $\frac{3}{10}$ of $70   f $\frac{7}{12}$ of 15m   g $\frac{3}{5}$ of 240ml   h $\frac{3}{4}$ of 50km

4 Work out these. Use cancelling to simplify your answers where possible.

a $\frac{3}{4} \times \frac{8}{9}$ b $\frac{2}{3} \times \frac{6}{7}$ c $\frac{5}{8} \times \frac{7}{10}$ d $\frac{2}{7} \times \frac{7}{12}$

e $\frac{3}{8} \times \frac{12}{21}$ f $\frac{9}{10} \times \frac{5}{6}$ g $\frac{3}{4} \times \frac{6}{7}$ h $\frac{8}{15} \times \frac{25}{32}$

5 Work out these.
Give each answer as a mixed number in its simplest form.

a $3 \div \frac{2}{3}$ b $4 \div \frac{3}{5}$ c $8 \div \frac{3}{5}$ d $9 \div \frac{6}{7}$

e $4 \div \frac{8}{9}$ f $5 \div \frac{10}{11}$ g $12 \div \frac{3}{5}$ h $6 \div \frac{4}{11}$

6 Calculate these.

a $\frac{2}{5} \div \frac{3}{4}$ b $\frac{3}{4} \div \frac{5}{7}$ c $\frac{4}{9} \div \frac{2}{5}$ d $\frac{1}{6} \div \frac{1}{5}$

e $\frac{5}{8} \div \frac{3}{4}$ f $\frac{7}{9} \div \frac{5}{6}$ g $\frac{7}{12} \div \frac{3}{4}$ h $\frac{8}{15} \div \frac{16}{21}$

7 Write these decimals as fractions in their simplest form.

a 0.8   b 0.76   c 0.75   d 0.77   e 0.875

f 0.325   g 1.4   h 1.35   i 3.75   j 2.16

8 Change these fractions into decimals using an appropriate method.
Give your answers to 2dp where appropriate.

a $\frac{13}{20}$ b $\frac{9}{16}$ c $\frac{5}{11}$ d $\frac{8}{15}$ e $\frac{7}{10}$

f $\frac{12}{15}$ g $\frac{17}{23}$ h $\frac{11}{22}$ i $\frac{14}{21}$ j $\frac{21}{30}$

9
a A mobile phone normally costs £75.
In a sale the price is reduced by 20%. What is the sale price of the mobile?

b Last year Archie earned £240 a week.
At the start of this year, the manager increased Archie's wage by 18%.
What is Archie's new wage?

10 Basil's salary last year was £32 600.
He had to pay £8234 in tax.
Mohinder's salary last year was £44 321.
He had to pay £12765 in tax.
Who had to pay the higher percentage of their salary in tax?

11 Here are two offers.

Offer A   400g pack of biscuits at 90p
Offer B   400g pack + 15% extra at £1.02

Which offer is the better value for money?
Explain your reasoning.

12
a A bag of crisps normally weighs 150g.
This week the weight of the bag is increased by 22%.
What is the new weight?

b A pair of trousers normally costs £76.
In a sale all the prices are reduced by 35%.
What is the sale price of the trousers?

Number   Fractions, decimals and percentages

Question commentary

Questions 1 and 2 – Encourage students to look for the lowest common denominator in each question.

Questions 3 and 4 – Students should give their answers to question **3** in the correct units. Encourage them to cancel down first before multiplying.

Questions 5 and 6 – Whole numbers could be written as 'over 1' to turn the calculations in question **5** into fraction divisions. Encourage cancelling down first throughout.

Question 7 – Parts **g** to **j** will give mixed numbers. Emphasise the need for simplest forms.

Question 8 – Calculators will be required for many of these questions. Some are simpler than they look however, and students could be asked to check whether the fractions cancel first (parts **f**, **h**, **i** and **j**).

Question 9 – Encourage the use of a single multiplier in this question.

Questions 10 to 12 – Problem solving using percentages may be made easier by allowing a calculator and encourage students to use efficient methods and write down their reasoning carefully.

Answers

1. a $\frac{9}{14}$ b $\frac{5}{8}$ c $\frac{1}{9}$ d $1\frac{5}{24}$
   e $\frac{17}{30}$ f $\frac{1}{4}$ g $\frac{5}{6}$ h $\frac{1}{6}$

2. a $1\frac{7}{36}$ b $\frac{29}{60}$ c $\frac{1}{6}$ d $\frac{19}{48}$
   e $\frac{16}{35}$ f $\frac{1}{16}$ g $\frac{41}{45}$ h $\frac{19}{80}$

3. a 9 cm b $4\frac{7}{8}$ kg c £34 d $16\frac{2}{3}$ s
   e $21 f $8\frac{3}{4}$ m g 144 ml h $37\frac{1}{2}$ km

4. a $\frac{2}{3}$ b $\frac{4}{7}$ c $\frac{7}{16}$ d $\frac{1}{6}$
   e $\frac{3}{14}$ f $\frac{3}{4}$ g $\frac{9}{14}$ h $\frac{5}{12}$

5. a $4\frac{1}{2}$ b $6\frac{2}{3}$ c $13\frac{1}{3}$ d $10\frac{1}{2}$
   e $4\frac{1}{2}$ f $5\frac{1}{2}$ g 20 h $16\frac{1}{2}$

6. a $\frac{8}{15}$ b $1\frac{1}{20}$ c $1\frac{1}{9}$ d $\frac{5}{6}$
   e $\frac{5}{6}$ f $\frac{14}{15}$ g $\frac{7}{9}$ h $\frac{7}{10}$

7. a $\frac{4}{5}$ b $\frac{19}{25}$ c $\frac{3}{4}$ d $\frac{77}{100}$
   e $\frac{7}{8}$ f $\frac{13}{40}$ g $1\frac{2}{5}$ h $1\frac{7}{20}$
   i $3\frac{3}{4}$ j $2\frac{4}{25}$

8. a 0.65 b 0.56 c 0.45 d 0.53
   e 0.7 f 0.8 g 0.74 h 0.5
   i 0.67 j 0.7

9. a £60 b £283.20

10. Basil: 25.26% Mohinder: 28.80% (Higher)

11. A 4.44g per p B 4.51g per p (better value)

12. a 183 g b £49.40

MyPractice

MyAssessment 1

These questions will test you on your knowledge of the topics in chapters 1 to 4. They give you practice in the questions that you may see in your GCSE exams. There are 95 marks in total.

1. Calculate
   a 3.4×10^3 (1 mark)
   b $0.34 \div 0.1$ (1 mark)
   c 3.4×0.01 (1 mark)
   d $10^6 \times 10^4$ (1 mark)
   e $10^6 \div 10^4$ (1 mark)
   f $10^2 \times 10^6 \div 10^4$ (1 mark)

2. Round each of these to the accuracy indicated in brackets.
   a 5278 (nearest 10) (1 mark)
   b 0.8965 (2dp) (1 mark)
   c 1235.6 (nearest 100) (1 mark)
   d 4.6135 (1dp) (1 mark)
   e 86422 (nearest 1000) (1 mark)
   f 0.873 (1sf) (1 mark)
   g 5278 (1sf) (1 mark)

3. Find the HCF and LCM of 136 and 96 using a Venn diagram. (4 marks)

4. Work out an estimate for each calculation. Check your answer using a calculator. Giving your answers to 1 dp.
   a $67.5 \div 3.72$ (2 marks)
   b 712×11.5 (2 marks)
   c $\dfrac{13.9 \times 451}{7.3}$ (2 marks)
   d $\dfrac{0.837 \times 825}{9.4}$ (2 marks)

5. Convert these measurements into the units indicated in brackets. Give your answer to an appropriate degree of accuracy.
   a 62 miles (km) (1 mark)
   b 428ml (pints) (2 marks)
   c 3000 m² (hectares) (1 mark)
   d 17oz (grams) (1 mark)

6. A single sheet of A4 paper is 29.7cm by 21.0cm. A0 paper is 16 times larger. Work out the area of A0 paper and give your answer in square metres to 1dp. (3 marks)

7. Atoms can be modelled as solid spheres and one of the simplest cell structures is shown.
   a Calculate the area of the square cell. (2 marks)
   b Calculate the total area of the circular atoms inside the square. (3 marks)
   c Hence determine the area of the free space inside the cell. (1 mark)

8. The diameter of a racing bicycle wheel is 70cm. In a local cycle race distances of up to 40 miles are regularly run. Work out how many revolutions a bicycle wheel makes in order to complete the race. (4 marks)

9. The Devonshire Dome in Buxton is the second largest circular dome in the UK with a diameter of 44.2m. Work out the circumference of this dome. (2 marks)

10. Factorise these expressions.
    a $9x + 15$ (1 mark)
    b $y^2 - 4y$ (1 mark)
    c $6m^2 + 3m$ (1 mark)
    d $4u^3 + 8u^2$ (1 mark)

11. Add or subtract these fractions and simplify where possible.
    a $\dfrac{3x}{4} - \dfrac{2x}{3}$ (2 marks)
    b $\dfrac{4y}{7} + \dfrac{y}{3}$ (2 marks)

12. The energy E stored in a capacitor is given by $\frac{1}{2}CV^2$.
    a Find E when $C = 3$ and $V = 20$. (2 marks)
    b Find E when $C = 400$ and $V = 3$. (2 marks)

13. The force of an object that is moving in a circle is $F = \dfrac{mv^2}{r}$.
    a Find F when $v = 12$, $r = 4$ and $m = 8$. (2 marks)
    b Rearrange the formula to make v the subject. (3 marks)
    c Find v when $F = 500$, $r = 2$ and $m = 5$. (2 marks)

14. Derive formulae for the shaded areas A in each of these diagrams.
    a (2 marks)
    b (3 marks)

15. a A small passport-sized photograph measures $4\frac{3}{8}$cm by $2\frac{2}{3}$cm.
    i What is the perimeter of the photograph? (3 marks)
    ii What is the area of the photograph? (3 marks)
    b It is being trimmed to size by cutting off $\frac{1}{2}$cm from the length and width. What are the new dimensions of the photograph? (3 marks)

16. Calculate these divisions.
    a $2\frac{3}{4} \div \frac{2}{3}$ (2 marks)
    b $5\frac{4}{7} \div \frac{3}{5}$ (3 marks)

17. In a recent test Sarah scored $\frac{26}{40}$ in Maths, $\frac{38}{50}$ in Biology and $\frac{45}{60}$ in Chemistry.
    a Write these results in terms of decimals without using a calculator. (3 marks)
    b Write these decimals as percentages. (1 mark)

18. a Increase 550ml by 16%. (2 marks)
    b Decrease £28.50 by 8%. (2 marks)

19. a The number of people joining a gymnasium increased from 128 to 165. What is the percentage increase? (2 marks)
    b A house bought ten years ago for £275000 has increased in value by 4%. How much is the house currently worth? (2 marks)

Mark scheme

Question 1 – 6 marks
a   1   3400   b   1   3.4
c   1   0.034   d   1 10^{10}
e   1 10^2 f   1 10^4

Question 2 – 7 marks
a   1   5280   b   1   0.90
c   1   1200   d   1   4.6
e   1   86 000   f   1   0.9
g   1   5000

Question 3 – 4 marks
     4   HCF = 8; LCM = 1632

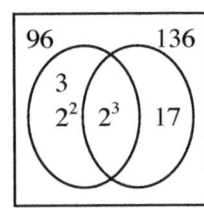

Venn diagram: 96 and 136 labels outside; inside left circle: 3, 2^2; intersection: 2^3; inside right circle: 17.

Question 4 – 8 marks
a   2   20, 18.1   b   2   7000, 8195.1
c   2   600, 858.7   d   2   80, 73.5

Question 5 – 5 marks
a   1   99km; accept 99.2km or 100km
b   2   0.7 pints; accept 0.71 pints
c   1   0.3 ha; 3000/10 000 for 1 mark
d   1   510g; accept 500g

Question 6 – 3 marks
     3   $1.0m^2$; $0.9979m^2$ earns 2 marks; $0.06237m^2$ for 1 mark

Question 7 – 6 marks
a   2   17.6 square units; accept 17.64 square units
b   3   13.9 square units; accept 13.85 square units; 1 mark for $r = 2.1$ units seen; 1 mark for πr^2 seen
c   1   3.7 square units; accept 3.79 square units

Question 8 – 4 marks
     4   29 117 revolutions; 1 mark for 2.198m seen; 1 mark for 64 000km seen;

Question 9 – 2 marks
     2   139m; accept 138.9m; $44.2 \times \pi$ seen for 1 mark

Question 10 – 5 marks
a   1 $3(x + 5)$ b   1 $y(y - 4)$
c   1 $3m(2m + 1)$ d   2 $4u^2(u + 2)$

Question 11 – 4 marks
a   2 $\frac{x}{12}$; 1 mark for $(9x - 8x)/12$
b   2 $\frac{19y}{21}$; 1 mark for $(12y + 7y)/21$

Question 12 – 4 marks
a   2 $E = 600$; 1 mark for 400 seen
b   2 $E = 1800$; 1 mark for 9 seen

Question 13 – 7 marks
a   2   288   b   3 $v = \sqrt{((F \times r)/m)}$
c   2   14.1; accept $\sqrt{200}$;

Question 14 – 5 marks
a   2 $A = 45 - 3x$; 1 mark for area $3 \times x$ seen;
b   3 $A = 66 - 3x$ or $A = 66 - \frac{1}{2}(6x)$; 2 marks for triangle area $\frac{1}{2} \times x \times 6$ seen;

Question 15 – 9 marks
a i   3 $\frac{169}{12} = 14\frac{1}{12}$ cm; working must be shown
   ii   3 $\frac{35}{3} = 11\frac{2}{3}$ cm^2; working shown
b   3 $3\frac{7}{8}$ by $2\frac{1}{6}$; working shown for both parts

Question 16 – 4 marks
a   2 $\frac{33}{8} = 4\frac{1}{8}$; working must be shown for 2 marks
b   2 $\frac{65}{7} = 9\frac{2}{7}$; working must be shown for 2 marks

Question 17 – 4 marks
a   3   0.65 (maths), 0.76 (biology), 0.75 (chemistry); working must be seen
b   1   65%, 76%, 75%

Question 18 – 4 marks
a   2   638ml; 1.15 seen for 1 mark
b   2   £26.22; 0.92 seen for 1 mark

Question 19 – 4 marks
a   2   29%; accept 28.9%; 37/128 seen for 1 mark
b   2   £286 000; 1.04 seen for 1 mark

5 Angles

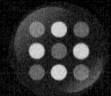

Learning outcomes

G5 Describe, sketch and draw using conventional terms and notations: points, lines, parallel lines, perpendicular lines, right angles, regular polygons, and other polygons that are reflectively and rotationally symmetric (L6)

G6 Use the standard conventions for labelling the sides and angles of triangle ABC, and know and use the criteria for congruence of triangles (L6)

G7 Derive and illustrate properties of triangles, quadrilaterals, circles, and other plane figures [for example, equal lengths and angles] using appropriate language and technologies (L6)

G10 Apply the properties of angles at a point, angles at a point on a straight line, vertically opposite angles (L6)

G12 Derive and use the sum of angles in a triangle and use it to deduce the angle sum in any polygon, and to derive properties of regular polygons (L6)

G13 Apply angle facts, triangle congruence, similarity and properties of quadrilaterals to derive results about angles and sides, including Pythagoras' Theorem, and use known results to obtain simple proofs (L6)

Introduction	Prior knowledge
The chapter starts by looking at the angle properties of triangles and in parallel lines before reviewing quadrilaterals and the angles within. Two sections covering polygons follow this before the final spread which covers congruent shapes. It looks at simple rules for congruence and students have to identify congruent shapes.	Students should already know how to… • Calculate missing angles using simple rules • Identify and name 2D shapes
	Starter problem
The introduction discusses the need for accurate measurement of, and estimation of, angles in real life. It also talks about the different types of angle measure used. The commonly used degrees measure which children learn about from an early age stems from ancient times when geometers were trying to tackle things like measuring distances and angles of places on the globe and in the cosmos. The French attempt to decimalise angles came at a time when every other unit of measure was being turned into metric units (the metre, for example, was devised in France and there are still examples of the 'original' metre dotted around Paris). Grads are still used today in things like artillery targeting, but this was one area where the change to a metric system was largely resisted!	The starter problem is an investigation into tessellations using regular polygons. Students should be familiar with a standard 'tile' tessellation using squares and are invited to investigate which other regular polygons tessellate. By working out the internal angles of the regular polygons, they will be able to see that just two further polygons tessellate on their own: the equilateral triangle and regular hexagon. When it comes to tessellations involving more than one regular polygon (so-called semi-regular tessellations) it might be nice to provide the students with shapes to play about with. They will find some quite quickly but might need to be guided into working out possible combinations before trying them. The following website gives all of the examples and also more detailed information on tessellation: http://www.mathsisfun.com/geometry/tessellation.html

Resources

MyMaths

Angle reasoning	1080	Angle sums	1082	Congruent triangles	1148
Sum of angles in a polygon	1320				

Online assessment   **InvisiPen solutions**

Chapter test	3B–5	Congruent shapes	317	Calculating angles	342
Formative test	3B–5	Types of triangles and angles			343
Summative test	3B–5	Properties of quadrilaterals and angles			344
		Angles and parallel lines	345	Polygon angles	346

Topic scheme

Teaching time = 5 lessons/2 weeks

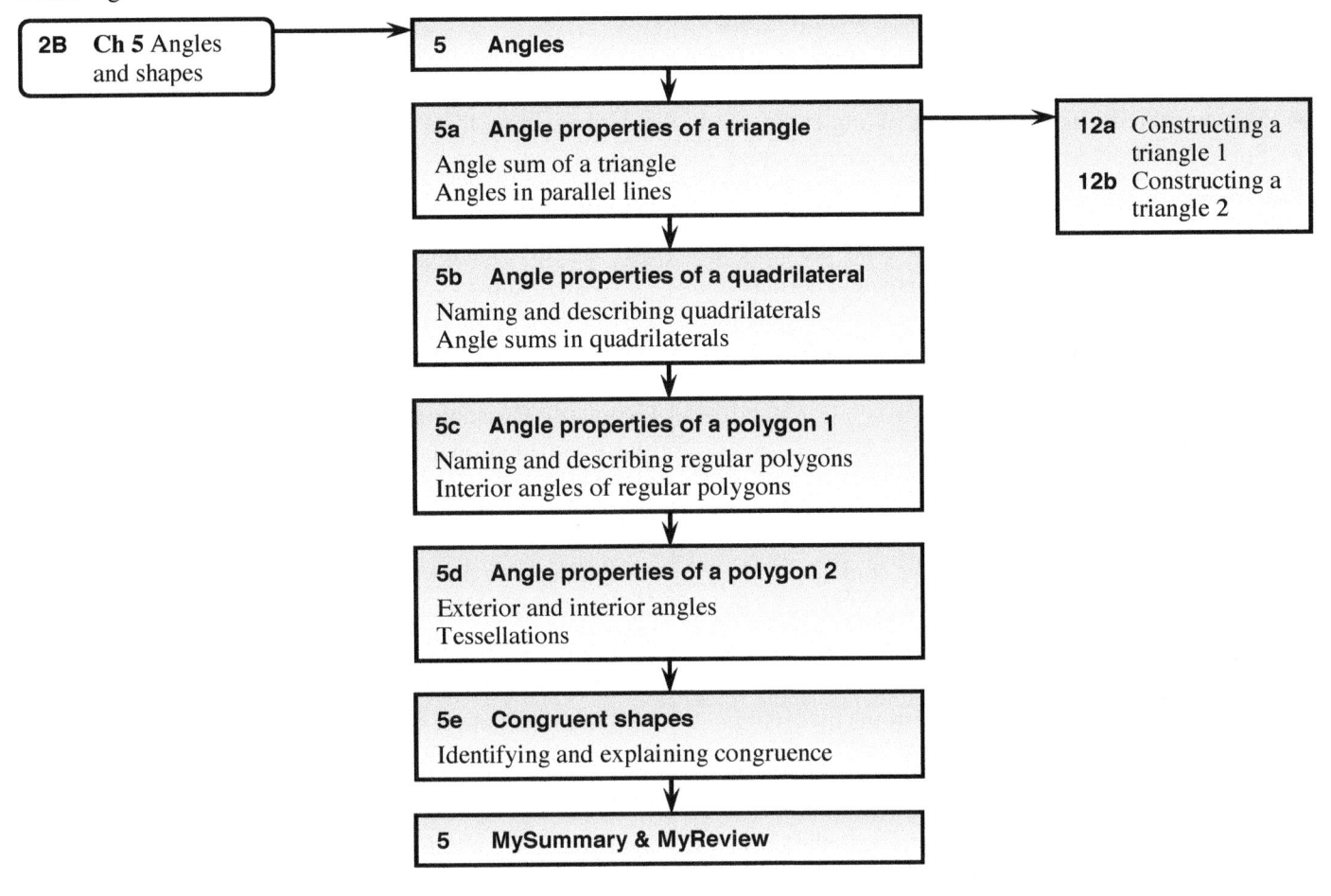

2B Ch 5 Angles and shapes

5 Angles

5a Angle properties of a triangle
Angle sum of a triangle
Angles in parallel lines

12a Constructing a triangle 1
12b Constructing a triangle 2

5b Angle properties of a quadrilateral
Naming and describing quadrilaterals
Angle sums in quadrilaterals

5c Angle properties of a polygon 1
Naming and describing regular polygons
Interior angles of regular polygons

5d Angle properties of a polygon 2
Exterior and interior angles
Tessellations

5e Congruent shapes
Identifying and explaining congruence

5 MySummary & MyReview

Differentiation

Student book 3A 78 – 93
Angles in parallel lines
Angles and properties of a triangle
Angles and properties of a quadrilateral

Student book 3B 74 – 89
Angle properties of triangles
Angles in parallel lines
Properties of quadrilaterals
Angles in quadrilaterals
Interior and exterior angles in regular polygons
Properties of congruent shapes

Student book 3C 72 – 87
Angle problems
Angles in a polygon
Properties of a circle
Arcs and sectors
Properties of congruent shapes

Introduction 75

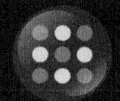

5a Angle properties of a triangle

Objectives	
• Identify alternate angles and corresponding angles	(L6)
• Understand a proof that the angle sum of a triangle is 180°	(L6)
• Understand a proof that the exterior angle of a triangle is equal to the sum of the two interior opposite angles	(L6)
• Solve problems using properties of angles, of parallel and intersecting lines	(L6)
• Solve problems using properties of triangles and other polygons	(L6)

Key ideas	Resources	
1 Be able to identify and name correctly the three key groups of angles – vertically opposite, alternate and corresponding angles 2 To use knowledge of simple line, angle and triangle properties in order to establish further information from a diagram	Angle reasoning Angle sums Mini whiteboards Tracing paper Geometric Reasoning Y9 minipack (DfES): http://www.nationalstemcentre.org.uk/elibrary/resource/4983/year-nine-geometrical-reasoning-mini-pack	(1080) (1082)

Simplification	Extension
As preparation for this exercise, give students questions involving • the recognition of acute and obtuse angles and the values each could take. • finding the missing angle in questions involving angles on a straight line and in a triangle.	Ask students to draw tessellations each using a different quadrilateral, using successive rotations about the midpoint of a side. Students should indicate the alternate angles in the tessellation. Will the tessellation work for a concave quadrilateral? What about other polygons?

Literacy	Links
It is essential to fully cover both the vocabulary and the diagramatic conventions throughout this chapter. Include conventional notation for marking equal sides, equal angels and parallel lines. Cover labeling as well, including the correct use of lower case letters for scalar quantities and upper case for vertices of shapes. Ensure that students are aware that visual clues should not be relied on for making assumptions; that it is essential to know if, for example, lines are parallel.	Canberra, the capital of Australia, contains the Parliamentary triangle. The city was planned by the American architect Walter Burley Griffin after winning a competition in 1911. He placed Parliament House (representing government) at one vertex, the Defence Headquarters (representing the military) at the second and City Hill (representing the civilian part of Canberra) at the third vertex of a giant equilateral triangle. There is more information about the Parliamentary triangle at http://www.library.act.gov.au/reflectionscd/REFLECT/actv/td3/td3.htm

Alternative approach

Use some visualisation exercises in order to remind or explore the nature of two intersecting lines, two parallel lines with one intersecting line and extending the sides of a triangle. Example prompts for such can be found in the Y9 Geometric Reasoning minipack referenced in Resources. Follow this up by checking with sketches of the visual images using mini whiteboards. The problems in the exercise can be completed in pairs by the students, encouraging them to explain verbally to each other why or how a value is found. More able pairs can be encouraged to try to record these reasoning in a short form

Checkpoint

Two angles in a triangle are 54° and 72°. What is the third angle? (54°)

Angle x is equal to 63°. What is the value of the angle alternate to x? (63°)

Starter – Make 180

Give questions, for example

The largest angle in an isosceles triangle is 108°, what are the sizes of the other angles? (36°, 36°)

Two angles in a scalene triangle are 47° and 26°, what is the size of the third angle? (107°)

If one angle in an isosceles triangle is 44°, what sizes are the other angles? (44° and 92° or 68° and 68°)

Teaching notes

In questions involving parallel lines, there are usually a number of equal angles and it is relatively easy to identify them by inspection. However, many students assume that lines are parallel, or that angles are equal, because they appear so, even when this is not known. Encourage students to check what is actually given, and give some indication (for example, the Z shape) of their reasoning when they make a deduction of the size of another angle.

When solving problems, students need to be able to recall all the possible facts which might give them another angle. Before starting the exercise, use a mini whiteboard activity to help establish how well they know triangle and parallel line facts.

Plenary

Show some solutions to problems similar to those in question **4** but containing errors (angles equal when they should add to 180°, reasons as Z angle when it should be F angle, *etc*.). Ask students to identify and correct any mistakes.

Exercise commentary

Questions 1 and **2** – Check that students know the properties of different types of triangles.

Questions 3 and **4** – Students should always first decide whether the required answer is an acute or an obtuse angle. Students can superimpose the Z and F shapes on their diagrams to help decide which angles are equal and whether the angles are alternate or corresponding.

Questions 5 and **6** – Ask students to list each step together with an explanation so that they have a proof of the angle sum in a triangle and encourage discussion over the equivalence of the two methods.

Question 7 – Tracing paper could be used to rotate the triangles. The tessellation will consist of three sets of parallel lines.

Answers

1. a 90°, right-angled   b 32°, isosceles
    c 60°, equilateral   d 35°, scalene
    e 90°, right-angled isosceles
    f 18°, isosceles
2. a $a = 39°$ b $b = 134°$ c $c = 84°, d = 78°$
3. a $a = 47°$, alternate angles are equal
    b $b = 113°$, corresponding angles are equal
    c $c = 110°$, alternate angles are equal
       $d = 110°$, corresponding angles are equal or vertically opposite angles are equal
    d $e = 125°$, angles on a straight line add to 180°, then alternate angles are equal
       $f = 55°$, vertically opposite angles are equal, then corresponding angles are equal
4. a $a = 64°, b = 116°, c = 48°, d = 132°, e = 68°$
    b $p = 65°, q = 115°, r = 80°, s = 100°, t = 35°$
5. $p = b$, corresponding angles
    $q = a$, alternate angles
6. Both answers use corresponding or alternate angles to show three angles on a straight line being equal to the three angles inside the triangle. They are different ways of showing the same thing.
7. Tessellation using triangles showing alternate angles and corresponding angles.

Angle properties of a triangle

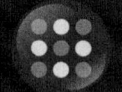

5b Angle properties of a quadrilateral

Objectives	
• Identify all the symmetries of 2D shapes	(L5)
• Solve problems using properties of angles, of parallel and intersecting lines	(L6)
• Solve problems using properties of triangles and other polygons	(L6)
• Understand a proof that the angle sum of a quadrilateral is 360°	(L6)

Key ideas	Resources
1 Be able to identify and name correctly groups of quadrilaterals and their properties 2 To use knowledge of line, angle and quadrilateral properties in order to establish further information from a diagram	Mini whiteboards Isometric grid paper Paper quadrilaterals Tracing paper Squares of paper A map of Italy

Simplification	Extension
To help gain familiarity with the various quadrilaterals and their properties, ask students to name the quadrilaterals in question **1** using their angle and side properties. Then ask them to find the missing angle in a quadrilateral, given three angles as in the example. To make question **2** a more practical activity, provide the students with paper copies of the eight different types of quadrilateral that can be rotated and folded.	Ask students to draw different types of quadrilaterals on isometric grid paper and to calculate the interior angles of each quadrilateral. What do they sum to? Does it make a difference if the quadrilateral is convex? What is the sum of the angles in an irregular pentagon? Allow students to work in pairs.

Literacy	Links
Revise the technical vocabulary covered in this section, being careful to make sure that students are exposed to particular naming as well as group naming, thus a square is a rectangle with a further property; a rectangle is a parallelolgram, an arrowhead is kite, and so on. Recap the conventional notation for indicating equality of angles and sides as well as parallels.	Bring in some atlases for the class to use. A quadrilateral is also a military term used to describe an area defended by four fortresses supporting each other. The most famous quadrilateral is the Quadrilatero comprising the four fortified towns of Mantua, Peschiera, Verona and Legnago in northern Italy. The area was important during the wars in Italy in 1848. There is a map showing the Quadrilatero at http://commons.wikimedia.org/wiki/File:QuadrilateroAustriaco.png Can the class find this area on the map of Italy in the atlas?

Alternative approach
Begin with visualisations which extend those of the previous section to include examining pairs of parallels which intersect and extending the sides of a parallelogram. Examples of these can also be found in the Y9 Geometric reasoning mini pack. Again check the visual images with sketchs on mini whiteboards. Again tackle some selected questions from the exercies in student pairs where the students explain verbally how and why they can find any missing angles. Ask pupils in pairs to try to reason why any quadrilateral interior anlges must total 360°. Share the results or ideas gathered here with the whole group, being prepared to take two alternative approaches: either splitting into two triangles, or using exterior angles totalling 360°, and angles on a straight line total 180°, if it arises.

Checkpoint	
Three of the angles of a quadrilateral are 70°, 44° and 124°. Find the fourth angle.	(122°)
One angle of an isosceles trapezium is 64°. Find, with reasoning, its other interior angles.	(64°; 116°; 116°)

Geometry and measures Angles

Starter – How many triangles?

Draw an equilateral triangle on the board. Divide each side into quarters. Draw three lines parallel to each side connecting the quarter marks to form 16 small triangles. Ask students how many triangles? (27)

If necessary, discuss the different-sized triangles in the diagram.

Teaching notes

Students often draw quadrilaterals which are special cases of the shape they have been told to use – such as drawing a parallelogram or a kite which looks like a rhombus. A review of the properties of the different quadrilaterals will be helpful.

Students often confuse rotational symmetry and lines of symmetry and may insist that a parallelogram has line symmetry. A practical activity where the parallelogram (or other shapes) can be folded along any possible line of symmetry will help them to identify whether or not the 'two halves' map directly onto each other and will often help them to construct a practical mental model for identifying line symmetry.

Plenary

As a mini whiteboard activity, show a variety of shapes and sizes of quadrilateral. Ask students to identify all the types of quadrilateral each example satisfies (so a rhombus is also a parallelogram, a kite, a trapezium and an isosceles trapezium). Ask students to write all eight names at the beginning and then put ticks against their choices in each case to make the activity manageable in terms of time.

Exercise commentary

Question 1 – The angles can be found using the quadrilaterals' symmetries and the sum of the angles. Ask students to explain their reasoning.

Question 2 – This question is suitable for discussion in pairs or groups.

Question 3 – Alternate angle properties are used.

Question 4 – Would using equilateral triangles make a difference?

Question 5 – Rotate the parallelogram through 180° about the centre using tracing paper.

Question 6 – This is a practical activity, using a square of paper, which is suitable for paired work.
When finding the interior angles of the kite, it is recommended to mark the values of the angles on the paper, in particular angles that are equal.

Question 7 – Students could be directed to find the angle sum of the four triangles and then deduct from this the sum of the angles at a point.

Answers

1   a $a = 126°, b = c = 54°$, isosceles trapezium
    b $d = e = 80°$, kite
    c $f = h = 69°, g = 111°$, rhombus

2   Square goes in (4, 4), rectangle and rhombus go in (2, 2), parallelogram goes in (0, 2), trapezium goes in (0, 1), isosceles trapezium, kite and arrowhead go in (1, 1)

3   a $a = 32°, b = 38°$
    b $a = 27°, b = 40°, c = 113°, d = 86°$

4   Kite, Rhombus and Parallelogram

5   The parallelogram fits exactly onto itself after a rotation of 180° and so the opposite angles are equal.

6   Kite. 45°, 90°, 112.5°, 112.5°

7   Sum of all the angles of the 4 triangles is 720° (4 × 180°) and so the sum of the quadrilateral is 720° – sum of angles around P. Hence, angles in quadrilateral sum to 360°. Yes, sum of interior angles in a pentagon is 540°

Angle properties of a quadrilateral

5c Angle properties of a polygon 1

Objectives

- Solve problems using properties of triangles and other polygons (L6)
- Explain why inscribed regular polygons can be constructed by equal divisions of a circle (L6)
- Explain how to find, calculate and use the sums of the interior and exterior angles of quadrilaterals, pentagons and hexagons (L6)
- Explain how to find, calculate and use the interior and exterior angles of regular polygons (L6)

Key ideas	Resources
1 Be familiar with and apply the properties of regular polygons, for example when constrcting the shape. 2 To use knowledge of line, angle and polygon properties in order to establish further information from a diagram	Tracing paper Spare drawing instruments

Simplification	Extension
Before doing question **1** it may help to find the order of rotational symmetry and any lines of symmetry for simpler shapes. In preparation for questions **2, 3** and **4** ask students to find the missing angle, when given three or more angles at a point. Then to find the value of one angle if three, four, five, *etc.* equal angles meet at a point.	Ask students to construct other inscribed regular polygons by first calculating the angle at the centre and then marking the vertices of the polygon on the circumference of a circle. For example, for a regular octagon 360° ÷ 8 = 45° and so mark points at 0°, 45°, 90°, 135°, *etc*. Will drawing a similar star like shape result in a smaller version of the original regular polygon?

Literacy	Links
Recap or check vocabulary, all of which should be familiar to the students.	The UK uses two heptagonal (seven-sided) coins, the 50 pence and 20 pence pieces. The sides of the coins are curved rather than straight lines so that the coins have the same diameter everywhere and the resulting shape is called an Equilateral Curve Heptagon. The shape means that the coins will roll smoothly and can be used in vending machines. There are pictures of other polygonal and other unusually shaped coins at http://www.fleur-de-coin.com/articles/unusualcoins.asp and at http://www.bezalelcoins.com/BezalelCoins/Pages/worldcoins/World_Shape.htm

Alternative approach

Prepare a card sort where examples of some polygons, quadrilaterals and others can be grouped into regular and irregular polygons by student pairs. Ask students to establish what makes a polygon regular, making sure that just one of the properties is insufficient. The card sort will provide a way of checking other polygon vocabulary, for example by asking students how many hexagons are in the group, which are regular, and so on. Ask the students how they would use a circle to help them draw a regular 5 sided shape. They can use a mini whiteboard to sketch possible ideas. Share and discuss with the whole group. **Q5** can then be set as a construction for all the students. More able may have just a written description of the diagram, while others may use a diagram to follow. Can they name the star-shape formed?

Checkpoint

Find the sum of the interior angles of an octagon. (1080°)

Each of the interior angles of a regular polygon is 160°. How many sides does it have? (18)

Starter – Angle bingo

Ask students to draw a 3 × 3 grid and enter nine multiples of 5 between 30 and 125. Give questions, for example,

A right-angled triangle has an angle of 55°, what is the smallest angle? (35°)

What is the angle between the diagonals of a kite? (90°)

The smallest angle in a parallelogram is 65°, what is the largest angle? (115°)

The winner is the first to cross out their nine numbers.

Teaching notes

There is a difference between the lines of symmetry for regular polygons with an odd number of sides (where each line joins a vertex to the midpoint of the opposite side) and an even number of sides (where opposite vertices are joined and midpoints of opposite sides) but in both cases there are the same number of lines as sides. Explore at least a couple of examples of each type of polygon so students are convinced that it will always work for any regular polygon.

Labelling the vertices often helps students to identify clearly that there will be n different positions that the regular polygon will map onto when rotated.

Plenary

Show an isosceles triangle, a rectangle, and a rhombus. Ask students to discuss in pairs whether or not they are regular polygons, and, if not, to give reasons why not.

Exercise commentary

Question 1 – Students who can see only one vertical line of symmetry should be encouraged to rotate the diagram to find the other lines of symmetry. Cutting out and folding the shapes reinforces the lines of symmetry. Tracing paper can be used to find the order of rotation symmetry of the regular polygons.

Questions 2, 3 and 4 – are based on the second example, using the angle sum at the centre and isosceles triangle properties.

Question 5 – Students can show the smaller pentagon is regular by measuring both the angles and the lengths. This can be extended to calculating the angles in the smaller pentagon, but you must give the students some initial information. The three angles at each vertex of the larger pentagon are all 36°. This means the interior angle of a regular pentagon is $3 \times 36° = 108°$.

Question 6 – Students will need to calculate the interior angles of the regular hexagon and octagon before using the angle rule for angles at a point.

Answers

1. **a** 3, 4, 5, 6 and 8 lines respectively
   b equilateral triangle 3   square 4
   regular pentagon 5   regular hexagon 6
   regular octagon 8

2. **a** 60°   **b** 120°   **c** 720°

3. **a** $a = 120°, b = 30°, c = 30°, d = 60°$
   b $a = 90°, b = 45°, c = 45°, d = 90°$

4. **a** $a = 36°$ **b** $b = 72°$ **c** 144°   **d** 1440°

5. **a,b** Student's constructions
   c The five interior angles of the smaller polygon are all 108°

6. 105°

Angle properties of a polygon 1

5d Angle properties of a polygon 2

Objectives	
• Solve problems using properties of triangles and other polygons	(L6)
• Explain how to find, calculate and use the sums of the interior and exterior angles of quadrilaterals, pentagons and hexagons	(L6)
• Explain how to find, calculate and use the interior and exterior angles of regular polygons	(L6)

Key ideas	Resources
1 Be familiar with the terms and connections of interior and exterior angles 2 To use line, angle and polygon properties in order to establish further information from a diagram	Sum of angles in a polygon (1320) Equilateral triangles, squares, pentagons, hexagons and octagons Copies of the question 2 table

Simplification	Extension
It will help kinesthetic learners if they are provided with copies of the shapes in question 1 and question 3 in order to experiment and get a feel for possible tessellations. To enable students to focus on the calculations, provide copies of the table needed for question 2. Allow the students to work in pairs.	Ask students to calculate the interior angles of regular polygons by calculating the angle at the centre first and then calculating the base angles in the isosceles triangles. Students should compare the results with their answers from question 2.

Literacy	Links
Recap or check vocabulary, all of which should be familiar to the students. The most challenging here will be that of exterior angle, as students often remember the outsideness, but not the extended side and which angle is referred to, so check this carefully and precisely.	Honey bees build hexagonal cells from wax to form a honeycomb which they use to store nectar, make honey, and raise larvae. For thousands of years, mathematicians tried to prove that the hexagonal shape provides the maximum amount of space to store the honey using the least amount of beeswax. The idea became known as the Honeycomb Conjecture and was finally proved by Professor Thomas Hales in 1999. He showed that the best way to divide a surface into regions of equal area with the least total perimeter is a hexagonal grid.

Alternative approach
Illustrating that exterior angles always add to 360° is best modelled by students walking around shapes marked out on the ground. Make sure that a mix of both regular and irregular polygons are used for this, otherwise students tend to believe it is only true of regular polygons. An alternative is to use a pencil or ruler turning and following the sides and angles, but this will need modelling for the students initially.

Checkpoint	
Calculate the exterior angles of a regular dodecagon.	(30°)
Each one of the exterior angles of a regular polygon is 12°. How many sides does it have?	(30)

Starter – Jumble

Write a list of anagrams on the board and ask students to unscramble. Possible anagrams are
ROADWHARE, EQUARTIALLARD, TIEK, FRICENOTEL, MOBSHUR, MERYMYST, ZEPMITURA, LAPOLMARGERAL
(arrowhead, quadrilateral, kite, reflection, rhombus, symmetry, trapezium, parallelogram)

Can be extended by asking students to make up their own anagrams or a shape word search.

Teaching notes

Introduce the idea that the exterior angles of a polygon always add to 360° with a practical demonstration. Ask a student to walk in a circle and ask the class what angle the student has turned through. Repeat with the student walking in a series of straight lines, returning to the same point and facing the same way (start the journey at the midpoint of a side rather than at a vertex for clarity). Ask the class what angle the student turned through each time.

Many students, especially kinesthetic learners, struggle with the abstract arguments about which regular polygons will tessellate. Offer a short practical activity with a number of equilateral triangles, squares, pentagons, hexagons and octagons. Asking students to try to make them tessellate will often help them remember which do, and why the others do not.

Plenary

Islamic architecture and art feature many beautiful patterns which are built up using geometrical shapes repeatedly in different orientations (although they are not straightforward tessellations). MC Escher also produced art using interlocking shapes. Examples can be found at www.mcescher.com where the symmetry gallery provides some wonderful examples of tessellations of unusual shapes. Identifying translational, reflective and rotational symmetries can provide a focus for a discussion.

Exercise commentary

Questions 1 and **2** – are based on the initial text in the student book.

Question 3 – This extends the example to other regular polygons.

Question 4 – $a = 108°$ is the important necessary information required to start this question. Ask students to explain the reasoning behind their calculations; did some students calculate the angles in a different order; are some ways quicker than others?

Question 5 – Some students will need guidance with this question. It reverses the process of the preceding questions, by giving the exterior angle rather than the number of sides of the regular polygon.

Question 6 – This is suitable for discussion between pairs of students. Initially students could use specific regular polygons to verify the statement.

Question 7 – The sum of the interior angles of an octagon will be required.

Answers

1   a   120°   b   90°   c   72°   d   60°

2

Number of sides	Sum of the exterior angles	Each exterior angle	Each interior angle
3	360°	120°	60°
4	360°	90°	90°
5	360°	72°	108°
6	360°	60°	120°
7	360°	51 3/7°	128 4/7°
8	360°	45°	135°
9	360°	40°	140°
10	360°	36°	144°

3   a $3 \times 120° = 360°$, angles at a point add up to 360°
    b $4 \times 90° = 360°$, angles at a point add up to 360°
    c $6 \times 60° = 360°$, angles at a point add up to 360°

4   $a = 108°, b = 36°, c = 36°, d = 108°, e = 36°, f = 36°,$
    $g = 36°, h = 72°, i = 72°$

5   15 sides

6   The angle at the centre is calculated by dividing 360° by the number of sides.
    The exterior angle is calculated by dividing 360° by the number of sides.

7   Maximum of 3 right angles, which is the same for all other polygons with 5 or more sides.

Angle properties of a polygon 2

5e Congruent shapes

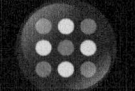

Objectives		
• Know that if two 2D shapes are congruent, corresponding sides and angles are equal		(L6)
• Understand congruence and explore similarity		(L6)

Key ideas	Resources
1 To further develop the concept of congruence and similarity 2 To apply this knowledge in order to find further information about a diagram or shape.	Congruent triangles (1148) Tracing paper Isometric paper Y9 Proportional reasoning (DfES) resources: http://www.nationalstemcentre.org.uk/elibrary/resource/4982/year-nine-proportional-reasoning-mini-pack

Simplification	Extension
As preparation for the exercise, give students questions requiring simple recognition of congruent shapes. For example, see *My Maths for KS3* Book **2B**, Exercise **5f**. Provide tracing paper so that students can copy one shape and then test to see if it will exactly overlay a second. Be aware that this relies on any diagrams being 'drawn to scale'.	Ask students to find ten different ways to divide a 4 × 4 square grid into two congruent shapes. This task is suitable for paired or group work.

Literacy	Links
Revisit both of the terms congruent and similar in order to check the concepts of each, the similarities and the differences. Check that the term corresponding is fully understood – linking back to corresponding angles which slide into position from parallel lines.	Many puzzles use the properties of congruent shapes. There is a Tangrami Square puzzle using congruent triangles at http://www.cyffredin.co.uk/Tangrami.htm

Alternative approach

Ask students in pairs to establish what is the same and what is different between shapes that are congruent and shapes that are similar. This will help to establish how much previous coverage has remained with the students and form the basis of refreshing this knowledge. Follow this up with a recognition exercise such as Cat Faces – a resource sheet given in the Y9 PR minipack resources. Again students can tackle this in pairs and be encouraged to use rulers and or tracing paper to identify sets of congruent and sets of similar shapes. Challenge students to consider the following questions in pairs: are all squares/rectangles/equilateral triangles/isosceles trapezium congruent or similar? Share and explore the explanations given to these responses.

Checkpoint

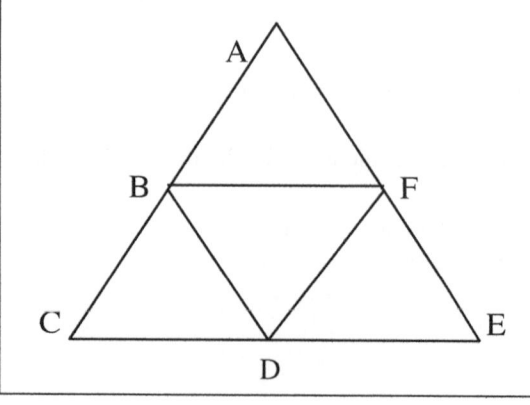

Identify any three congruent triangles, and a pair of similar triangles.

(Any three from ABF, BCD, FDE, BDF; and any of these together with ACE)

Geometry and measures   Angles

Starter – Name the shape

Ask students to take the following letters and rearrange them to spell a shape. First from arrowhead, the last from square, sixth from pentagon, first from rhombus, sixth from parallelogram, first from trapezium, second from kite, sixth from scalene. (Triangle)

Can be extended by giving clues to each shape, for example, the first letter from a quadrilateral with a reflex angle.

Teaching notes

Explain to students that congruent means that the shapes are exactly the same shape and size but that they can look quite different because they can be rotated and reflected.

Discuss strategies for testing whether or not shapes are congruent, such as identifying a longest side, the largest angle *etc.* and that labelling corresponding points in the two diagrams as they are identified helps keep track of what has been covered.

Plenary

Draw the eight quadrilaterals shown in **5b** and draw in the diagonals for each (discuss what happens for the arrowhead: only one internal diagonal since the shape is concave). Ask students to work in pairs to find as many congruent pairs of triangles as they can, and to find whether any of the shapes have more than two congruent triangles. (You can allow students to use triangles created by only one diagonal, or restrict the activity to only the small triangles).

Exercise commentary

Questions 1 and 2 – These can be made easier by rotating one of the shapes through 180° to allow a direct comparison.

Question 3 – The order of the letters to describe each congruent triangle is important. Ask students to explain why this is significant.

Question 4 – Students may need to reflect triangle D to check for congruency.

Question 5 – Guide students to use alternate angles to find the equal angles.

Question 6 – The missing sides can be found by comparing corresponding sides.

Question 7 – The isometric paper must be orientated correctly to copy the shape. This task is suitable for grouped work.

Answers

1. **a** $p = 55°, q = 55°, r = 70°$
   b AC = 8 cm, BC = 8 cm

2. $a = 50°, b = 130°, c = 95°, d = 85°$

3. **a** BXC **b** BAC **c** BDC

4. **a** $a = 55°, b = 45°, c = 80°, d = 80°$
   b B and C

5. Alternate angles and angle sum of a triangle

6. Corresponding angles and sides are equal
   $x = 4.7$cm $y = 7.1$cm

7. **a** Chop it half down the middle and across the middle
   b Students' own answers

Congruent shapes

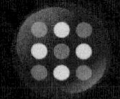

5 Angles – MySummary

Key outcomes	Quick check
Know and use angle facts for triangles and parallel lines. L6	Find the missing angle in these triangles a 70°, 81° (29°) b 110°, 36° (34°)
Know and use properties of quadrilaterals and regular polygons. L6	a A quadrilateral has three angles of 70°, 83° and 94°. What is the missing angle? (113°) b A parallelogram has two angles equal to 40° and 140°. What are the other two angles? (40° and 140°)
Calculate interior and exterior angles of polygons. L6	a What is the sum of the interior angles of a regular heptagon? (900°) b A regular polygon has exterior angles of 10°. How many sides does it have? (36)
Use congruence. L7	Show how you can divide a regular pentagon into five congruent triangles.

MyMaths extra support

Lesson/online homework			Description
Interior Exterior angles	1100	L6	Interior and exterior angles of polygons
Lines and Quadrilaterals	1102	L4	Parallel and perpedicular lines. Properties of quadrilateral
Angles in parallel lines	1109	L6	Alternate angles, supplementary angles and corresponding angles in parallel lines
Angle proofs	1141	L6	Formal proofs of angle theorems such as angles in a triangle, quadrilateral and exterior angles.

MyReview

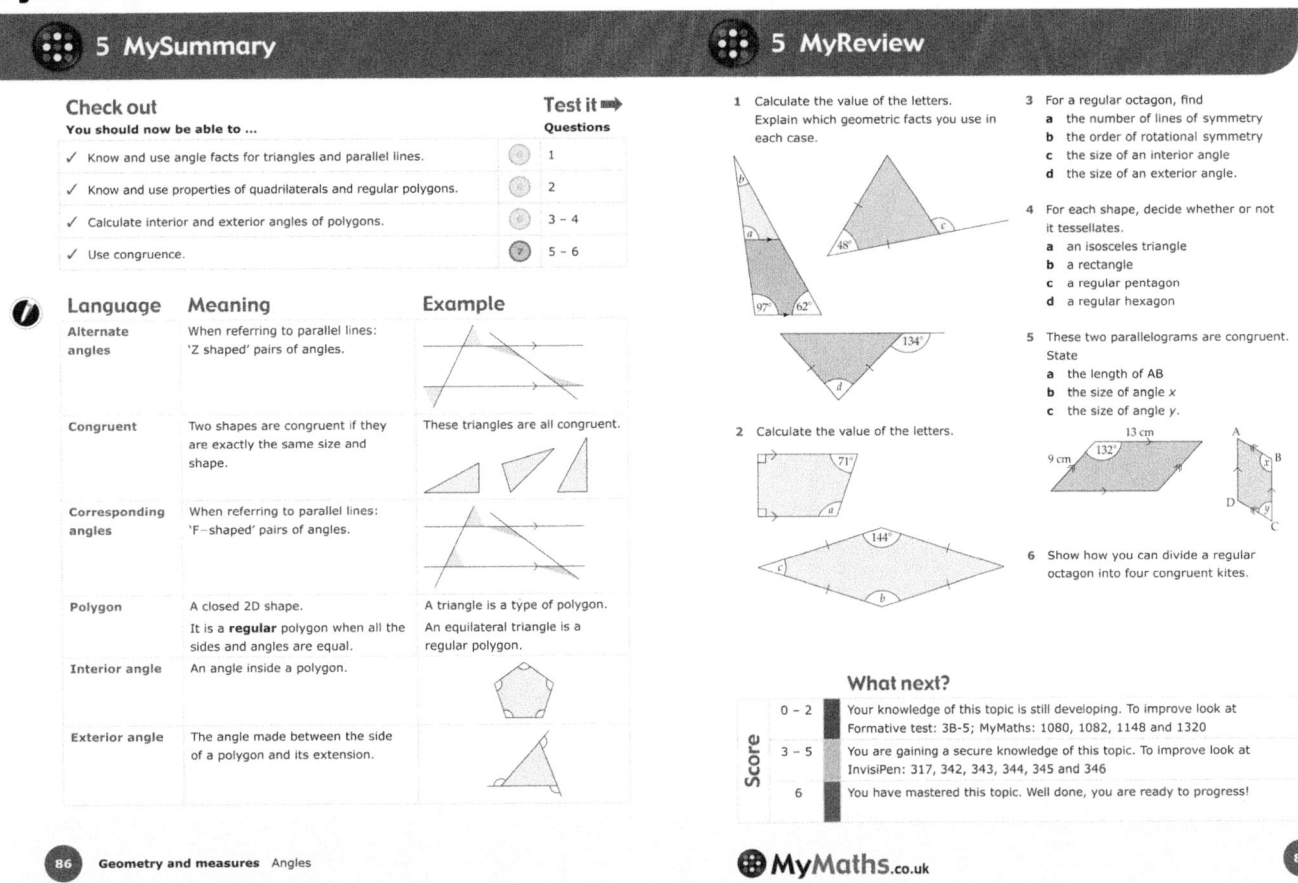

5 MySummary

Check out
You should now be able to ...

	Test it → Questions
✓ Know and use angle facts for triangles and parallel lines.	1
✓ Know and use properties of quadrilaterals and regular polygons.	2
✓ Calculate interior and exterior angles of polygons.	3 – 4
✓ Use congruence.	5 – 6

Language	Meaning	Example
Alternate angles	When referring to parallel lines: 'Z shaped' pairs of angles.	
Congruent	Two shapes are congruent if they are exactly the same size and shape.	These triangles are all congruent.
Corresponding angles	When referring to parallel lines: 'F–shaped' pairs of angles.	
Polygon	A closed 2D shape. It is a **regular** polygon when all the sides and angles are equal.	A triangle is a type of polygon. An equilateral triangle is a regular polygon.
Interior angle	An angle inside a polygon.	
Exterior angle	The angle made between the side of a polygon and its extension.	

Geometry and measures Angles

5 MyReview

1 Calculate the value of the letters. Explain which geometric facts you use in each case.

2 Calculate the value of the letters.

3 For a regular octagon, find
 a the number of lines of symmetry
 b the order of rotational symmetry
 c the size of an interior angle
 d the size of an exterior angle.

4 For each shape, decide whether or not it tessellates.
 a an isosceles triangle
 b a rectangle
 c a regular pentagon
 d a regular hexagon

5 These two parallelograms are congruent. State
 a the length of AB
 b the size of angle x
 c the size of angle y.

6 Show how you can divide a regular octagon into four congruent kites.

What next?

Score	
0 – 2	Your knowledge of this topic is still developing. To improve look at Formative test: 3B-5; MyMaths: 1080, 1082, 1148 and 1320
3 – 5	You are gaining a secure knowledge of this topic. To improve look at InvisiPen: 317, 342, 343, 344, 345 and 346
6	You have mastered this topic. Well done, you are ready to progress!

MyMaths.co.uk

Question commentary

Question 1 – The important thing here is the reason for each answer, particularly for the question involving parallel lines. Some of the angles can be worked out using different geometric facts.

Question 2 – Students should also know what the quadrilaterals are called.

Question 3 – Students should use the fact that the octagon can be split into 6 triangles giving a total angle sum of 6 × 180 = 1080, so ÷ 8 since a regular octagon.

Question 4 – You could discuss with students why all triangles will tessellate. They should be able to explain why a regular pentagon does not tessellate since its interior angles are each 108° which is not a factor of 360°, whereas for a regular hexagon they are 120° so it does tessellate.

Question 5 – Students could label the original parallelogram ABCD if this helps. They also need angle rules from **5b**.

Question 6 – This can be done using prepared paper templates of diagrams. Can the octagon be split into other congruent shapes?

Answers

1 $a = 97°$, corresponding angles are equal
   $b = 21°$, angles in a triangle add to 180°
   $c = 114°$, other two angles are 66° since its isosceles, angles in a straight line add to 180°
   $d = 88°$, angles at top of triangle are both 46° (angles straight line, isosceles triangle)

2 $a = 109°$, $b = 144°$, $c = 36°$

3 a 8   b 8   c 135°   d 45°

4 a Yes   b Yes   c No   d Yes

5 a 9cm   b 132°   c 48°

6 Check students' drawings

MySummary/MyReview

5 MyPractice

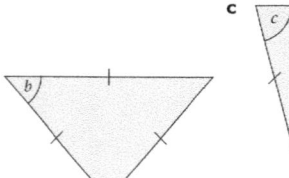

1 Calculate the values of the unknown angles.

a [diagram: triangle with 116° and angle a]
b [diagram: symmetric figure with angles c, e, f, d, g and 108°]
c [diagram: parallel lines with angles p, q, r, 61° and 70°]

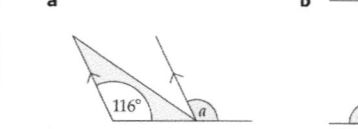

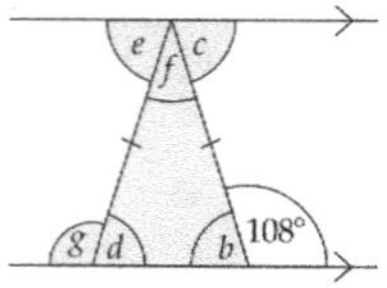

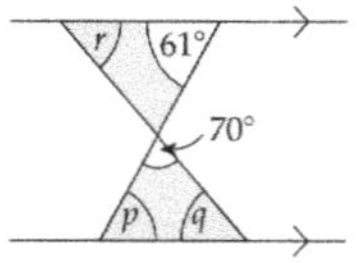

2 Calculate the angles marked with letters.

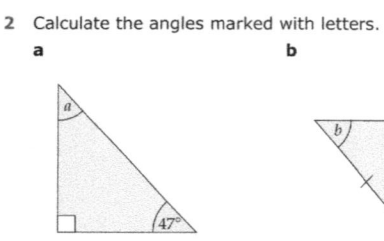

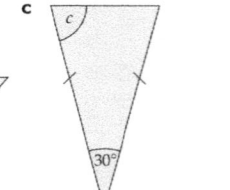

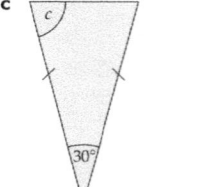

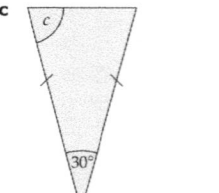

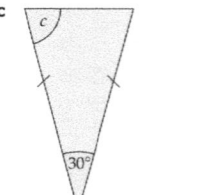

a [right triangle with 47° and angle a]
b [isosceles triangle with angle b]
c [isosceles triangle with 30° and angle c]

3 Find the missing angles and give the mathematical name of each quadrilateral.

a Angles 90°, 90°, ☐, ☐
   Rotation symmetry of order 2

b Angles 18°, 18°, 90°, ☐
   1 line of reflection symmetry

c Angles 45°, 135°, ☐, ☐
   Rotation symmetry of order 2

d Angles 36°, 36°, ☐, ☐
   2 lines of reflection symmetry

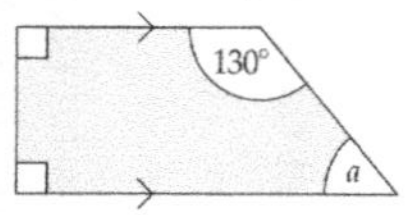

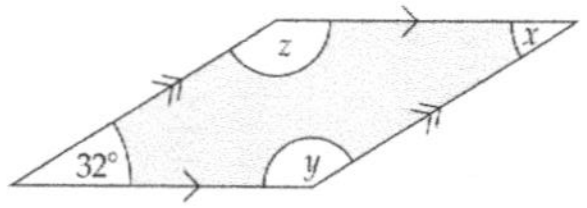

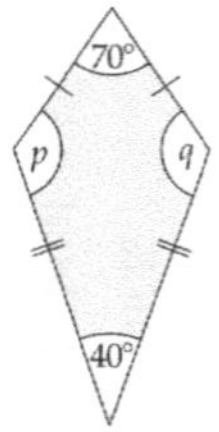

4 Calculate the angles marked with letters.

a [right triangle with 130° and angle a]
b [triangle with 32° and angles x, y, z]
c [kite with 70°, 40°, p, q]

5 The diagram shows a regular nonagon.
   a Calculate the values of a, b and c.
   b Hence find the interior angle of a regular nonagon.

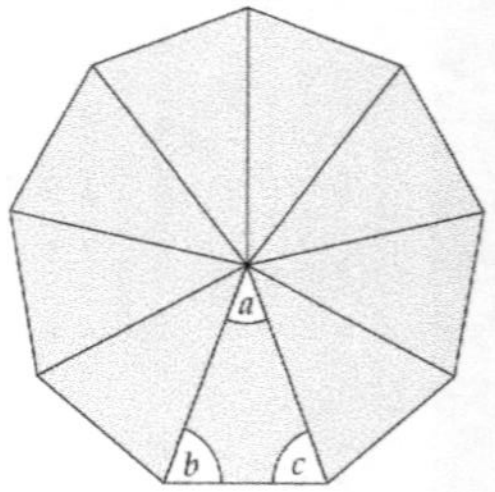

6 An inscribed polygon is one whose vertices all lie on a circle.
   a Draw a circle with radius 5 cm
   b Construct the inscribed regular decagon.

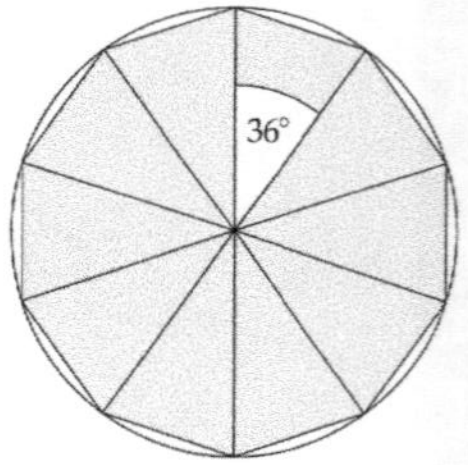

7 ABCD is a kite.
   Which triangle is congruent to
   a ADX   b ADC   c DXC?

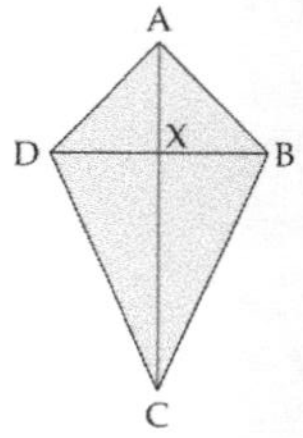

8 a Tessellate eight congruent trapezia on a copy of this grid.
   b Draw the lines of reflection symmetry on your completed grid.

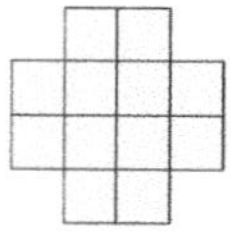

Geometry and measures   Angles

Question commentary

Questions 1 and **2** – Students should recognize that parallel lines are involved and start by identifying pairs of alternate and corresponding angles.

Questions 3 and **4** – Students must recall quadrilateral facts and use angle rules.

Question 5 – Students should be able to work out angle *a* by using angles at a point before recognising that the triangles are all isosceles.

Question 6 – Students will need to use a protractor accurately for this question.

Questions 7 and **8** – Encourage students to provide reasons for their choice in question **7**.

Answers

1. a $a = 116°$
   b $b = 72°, c = 72°, d = 72°, e = 72°, f = 36°, g = 108°$
   c $p = 61°, q = 49°, r = 49°$

2. a 43°   b 60°   c 75°

3. a 90°, 90°, square
   b 234°, arrowhead
   c 45°, 135°, rhombus or parallelogram
   d 144°, 144°, rhombus

4. a $a = 50°$
   b $x = 32°, y = z = 148°$
   c $p = q = 125°$

5. a $a = 40°, b = c = 70°$
   b 140°

6. Check students' drawings

7. a ABX   b ABC   c BXC

8. Check students' drawings

MyPractice

6 Graphs

Learning outcomes

A6 Model situations or procedures by translating them into algebraic expressions or formulae and by using graphs (L6)

A9 Recognise, sketch and produce graphs of linear and quadratic functions of 1 variable with appropriate scaling, using equations in x and y and the Cartesian plane (L6)

A10 Interpret mathematical relationships both algebraically and graphically (L6)

A11 Reduce a given linear equation in two variables to the standard form $y = mx + c$; calculate and interpret gradients and intercepts of graphs of such linear equations numerically, graphically and algebraically (L6)

A12 Use linear and quadratic graphs to estimate values of y for given values of x and vice versa and to find approximate solutions of simultaneous linear equations (L6)

A13 Find approximate solutions to contextual problems from given graphs of a variety of functions, including piece-wise linear, exponential and reciprocal graphs (L6)

Introduction	Prior knowledge
The chapter starts by plotting straight-line graphs using a table of values before moving onto more general work on straight-line graphs. Gradient, y-intercept and then the full equation of a straight-line are then covered before a section on equations given implicitly. General real-life graphs, distance-time graphs and time series graphs are covered in the last three sections. The introduction discusses the importance of graphs in helping us to make sense of the masses of data that we are presented with every day. The wide variety of graphs available allows us to represent many different types of data and other functions but we must be aware that graphs can often be misleading. In fact, there is a specific topic in the GCSE Statistics curriculum which looks at misleading graphs! Some examples of graphs of this type can be found at: http://www.khanacademy.org/student-res/college-arithmetic/interpret-data-brushups/v/misleading-line-graphs	Students should already know how to… • Substitute numbers into formulae • Plot coordinates in all four quadrants
	Starter problem
	The starter problem gives the students six examples of functions and asks them to plot each one. If the students plot them on separate sets of axes, they will need to make sure they use the same scaling on the axes for all. Basic observation will tell them that the first two have the same slope (gradient), likewise the fourth and fifth. The first and fourth both go through +3 on the y-axis while the second and the fifth both go through -3. The sixth graph turns out the be perpendicular to the first two (at right angles) while the third graph is a quadratic curve. Students could be invited to come up with their own examples which have something in common with one or more of the functions as an extension activity.

Resources

MyMaths

Conversion graphs	1059	$y = mx + c$	1153	Real life graphs	1184
Gradients	1312	Distance time graphs	1322		

Online assessment

		InvisiPen solutions			
Chapter test	3B–6	Plotting straight lines from tables			262
Formative test	3B–6	Gradients	263	Understanding $y = mx + c$	265
Summative test	3B–6	Quadratic sequences	273	Cubic graphs	274
		Real-life graphs	275		

Topic scheme

Teaching time = 9 lessons/3 weeks

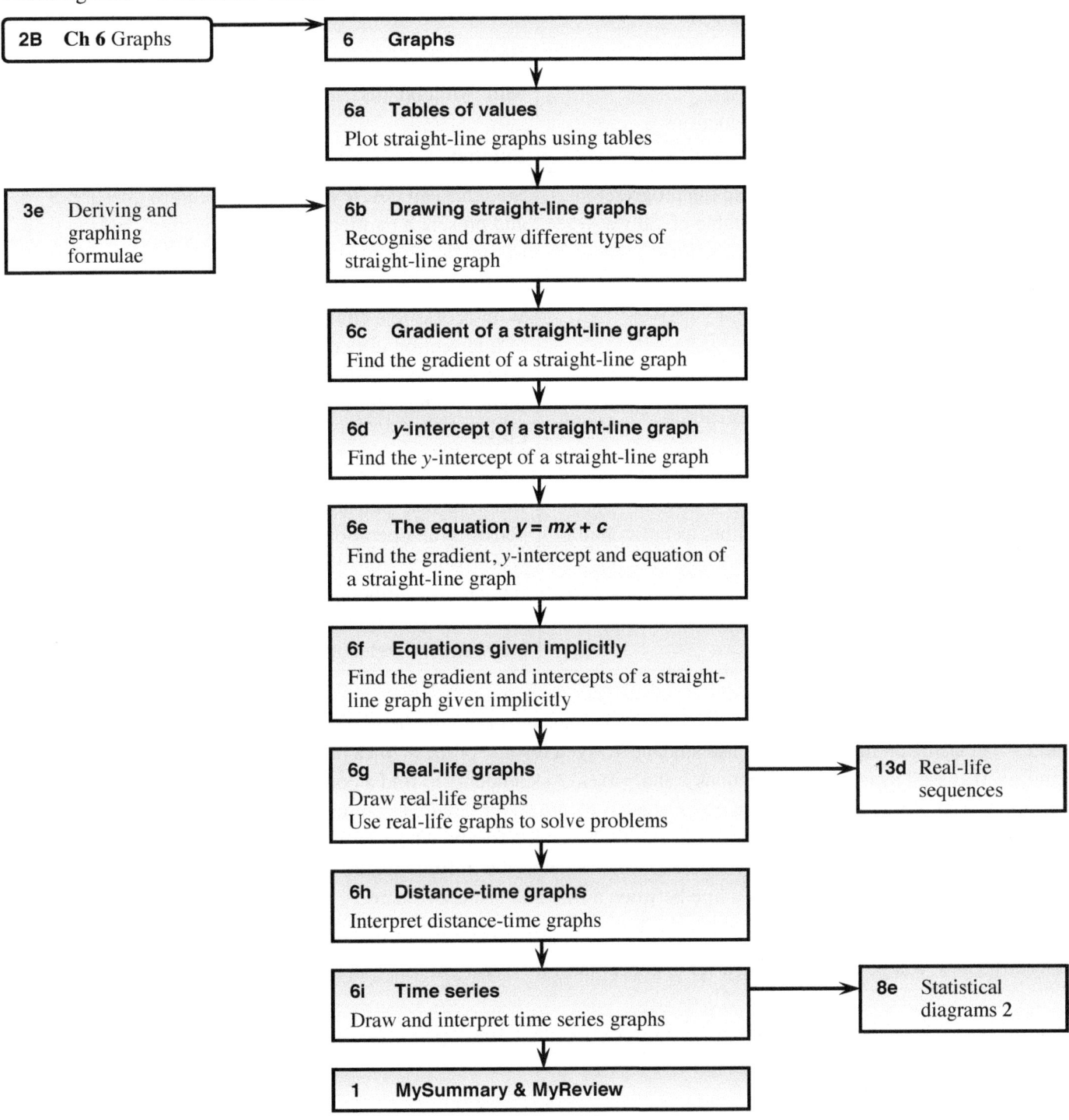

```
[2B  Ch 6 Graphs] ──────► [6   Graphs]
                              │
                              ▼
                          [6a  Tables of values
                               Plot straight-line graphs using tables]
                              │
                              ▼
[3e  Deriving and      ──►[6b  Drawing straight-line graphs
     graphing               Recognise and draw different types of
     formulae]              straight-line graph]
                              │
                              ▼
                          [6c  Gradient of a straight-line graph
                               Find the gradient of a straight-line graph]
                              │
                              ▼
                          [6d  y-intercept of a straight-line graph
                               Find the y-intercept of a straight-line graph]
                              │
                              ▼
                          [6e  The equation y = mx + c
                               Find the gradient, y-intercept and equation of
                               a straight-line graph]
                              │
                              ▼
                          [6f  Equations given implicitly
                               Find the gradient and intercepts of a straight-
                               line graph given implicitly]
                              │
                              ▼
                          [6g  Real-life graphs           ────► [13d Real-life
                               Draw real-life graphs                sequences]
                               Use real-life graphs to solve problems]
                              │
                              ▼
                          [6h  Distance-time graphs
                               Interpret distance-time graphs]
                              │
                              ▼
                          [6i  Time series                ────► [8e  Statistical
                               Draw and interpret time series graphs]    diagrams 2]
                              │
                              ▼
                          [1   MySummary & MyReview]
```

Differentiation

Student book 3A 94 – 113
Horizontal and vertical lines
Plotting straight-line graphs from tables of values
Drawing and using straight-line graphs
Interpreting real-life graphs and time series graphs

Student book 3B 90 – 113
Recognise and draw straight-line graphs
Find the gradient, y-intercept and equation of a straight-line graph, including those defined implicitly
Draw, understand and use real-life graphs, distance-time graphs and time series graphs

Student book 3C 88 – 113
Gradient of a straight-line
Graphs of linear functions
Parallel and perpendicular lines
Recognise and draw quadratic and cubic graphs
Draw, understand and use real-life graphs, distance-time graphs and time series graphs
Exponential and reciprocal graphs

Introduction

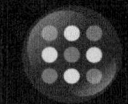

6a Tables of values

Objectives

- Generate points in all four quadrants and plot the graphs of linear functions, where y is given explicitly in terms of x, on paper and using ICT (L6)

Key ideas	Resources
1 Plot and graph linear functions 2 Recognise some simple linear functions	Mini whiteboards

Simplification	Extension
As previously, students should grasp the progression: function machine (or equation) → table of values → coordinates → graph. Students can use their mini whiteboards to offer values for the inputs to a function machine. Function machines should be used before attempting equations.	Students can devise a problem similar to question **5** and present a partner with three equations, asking them to find the triangle and calculate its area. The two sets of answers can then be compared. With access to a computer, students can find the point of intersection of two lines of their own choosing and grapple with the situation where the coordinates of the point of intersection are not integers.

Literacy	Links
Encourage students to read each equation with meaning as this will help them apply it and find values. Tables of values can be recorded either as horizontal or vertical tables, thus: $x \mid y$	The word 'function' comes from the Latin word *fungi* which means 'perform', so a function machine performs an operation on the input number. The word was first used in mathematics by the mathematician Leibnitz (or Leibniz) in the seventeenth century. There is more about Leibnitz at http://en.wikipedia.org/wiki/Gottfried_Leibniz

Alternative approach

Remind students of previous work with linear functions, encouraging them to name some lines in the form $x = c$ and $y = c$. Using an imaginary grid ask students to sketch some of these lines in the air, including the lines $x = 0$ and $y = 0$ as well as referring to them as x and y axes. Ask students to find a coordinate of a point which lies on a different type of linear function, e.g. $y = x$; $y = x + 6$, and so on. Students can use mini whiteboards to offer coordinates, which can then be plotted onto an IWB version for the whole group to view. As samples are added, can any mistakes be spotted? How? Address points such as the inifinite nature of the linear function in order to encourage styudents not to restrict a line between a first and last coordinate.

Checkpoint

Describe how you go about finding a set of coordinates for a straight line graph, such as $y = 3x - 1$.

(Responses should include allocating some values for x, and finding the appropriate y results).

Starter – 357

Challenge students to make the number 4 using only the digits 3, 5 and 7 in as many ways as possible in four minutes. Possible solutions are
7 – 3, (7 + 5) ÷ 3, (5 + 3) ÷ (5 – 3),
(5 × 3 – 7) ÷ (5 – 3), (7 × 3 – 5) ÷ (7 – 3),
(7 × 5 – 3) ÷ (5 + 3).

Teaching notes

There are strong links between representations such as functions, equations, tables of values and graphs. Encourage students to make explicit in their own minds the relationships between them, and to be comfortable moving between them.

While two points are sufficient to draw a straight line, encourage students to use at least three in a table of values as a check.

If students are weak at algebra it may be helpful to review basic substitution into expressions before starting to create tables of values that then have to be used to do something else.

Plenary

Ask students to work in pairs, one chooses an expression and the other creates a table of values.

Exercise commentary

Question 1 – This question reinforces the links between a function machine, a table of values and a graph.

Question 2 – The function machine of question 1 is replaced by an equation. The links are now between the equation, the table of values and the graph.

Question 3 – A simple substitution of the x-values determines whether the point has a suitable y-coordinate.

Question 6 – This provides a contextual application and a graph which needs to be interpreted.

Answers

1

x	0	1	2	3
y	-2	1	4	7

Straight-line graph from (0, -2) to (3, 7)
$y = 3x - 2$

2 a

x	0	1	2	3	4
y	2	3	4	5	6

Straight-line graph from (0, 2) to (4, 6)

b

x	0	1	2	3	4
y	-2	-1	0	1	2

Straight-line graph from (0, -2) to (4, 2)

c

x	0	1	2	3	4
y	3	5	7	9	11

Straight-line graph from (0, 3) to (4, 11)

d

x	0	1	2	3	4
y	-2	0	2	4	6

Straight-line graph from (0, -2) to (4, 6)

e

x	0	1	2	3	4
y	10	9	8	7	6

Straight-line graph from (0, 10) to (4, 6)

f

x	0	1	2	3	4
y	4	3	2	1	0

Straight-line graph from (0, 4) to (4, 0)

3   **a** Yes   **b** Yes   **c** No   **d** No
4   **a** 4   **b** 1   **c** 2   **d** 5
    e 3
5 height = 3 units, area = 27 square units
6

x	1	2	3	4	5
C	7	9	11	13	15

    a 3 ½ hours   **b** 8 hours
7 Graphs intersect at (16, 44)

Tables of values   **93**

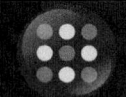

6b Drawing straight-line graphs

Objectives	
• Recognise that equations of the form $y = mx + c$ correspond to straight-line graphs (L6)	

Key ideas	Resources
1 Recognise functions that are linear 2 Plot and graph linear functions	Mini whiteboards Computers with a graphing facility such as Geogebra, Geometer's SketchPad, Autograph or Cabri

Simplification	Extension
Present lines, one at a time, which are parallel to either axis or with slope. Students use their mini whiteboards to write the equation of any line parallel to an axis or just write the word 'sloping'. There is likely to be some confusion with lines parallel to axes as students often write (say) $x = 3$ for the line $y = 3$.	Ask students to draw their own rectangles using lines of the form $x = \pm a$. and $y = \pm b$. A partner draws the rectangles from the equations and finds the areas, checking the results with the first student. Triangles can be used for increased difficulty.

Literacy	Links
Introduce students to vocabulary that will help them compare linear functions both in graph form and in equation form, thus using and encouraging student use of the terms constant, coefficient, slope or gradient, intercept.	Dogs have a much shorter lifespan than humans. Convert 'dog years' to 'human years' using the conversion tool at http://www.onlineconversion.com/dogyears.htm Would the resulting graph be a straight line? If not, why not? It is a popular misconception that dogs age 7 years for each calendar year. In reality, dogs age much more quickly during the first two years of life and subsequent aging depends on size and breed.

Alternative approach
Begin with some sample completed tables of values, explaining that one of these is not a linear function. Use say $y = x^2$ for the non linear function. Ask students to work in pairs to decide which is non-linear, and why. Discuss the results, drawing attention to the regularity of differences in the linear table of values, which indicates the constant slope of a line. If computers are available, the students can be set up to explore linear functions for themselves. Use the opportunity to check and widen knowledge and use of graphing software. The students may then continue to use computers in the following three sections, to explore the nature of linear functions.

Checkpoint
Are the following lines horizontal, vertical or diagonal?

$y = 2x$ (Diagonal)

$y = 3$ (Horizontal)

$y = 3x - 1$ (Diagonal)

$x = -4$ (Vertical)

Algebra   Graphs

Starter – Algebraic sums

Draw a 4 × 4 table on the board to form 16 cells.

Label the rows with the terms: $7x, 2y, -3x, y$

Label the columns with the terms: $2x, -3x, 4y, -2y$

Ask students to fill in each cell of the table by adding the row and column terms together. For example, the top row would read $9x$, $4x$, $7x + 4y$, $7x - 2y$.

Can be differentiated by the choice of terms.

Teaching notes

Many students find it confusing that x (which is across) = constant gives a vertical line, so a good starting point is to ask students to give you points where $x = 3$, and plot them on a grid; asking for 'different types' of points if you don't get negative or fractional y.

Once there are a number of points plotted, ask students what they think all the points which have $x = 3$ will have in common and then what the line $x = 3$ should look like. It is non-trivial for students to go from $x = 3$ as the solution to simple equations to it being the equation of a straight line in two variables.

While two points are sufficient to draw a straight line, encourage students to use at least three as a check and to think what the line should look like before starting to plot the graph (is it horizontal, vertical or oblique?).

Plenary

Use a mini whiteboard activity to check that students are able to identify correctly when a line should be horizontal, vertical or oblique from the form of the equation.

Exercise commentary

Question 1 – Simply asks students to recognise the three types of equations in graphical form.

Question 2 – Requires students to use their knowledge to draw rectangles and to find their areas.

Question 3 – Practises the opposite skills – finding a line's equation from its position on the axes. The diagonals are horizontal and vertical.

Question 4 – Practises plotting points and drawing graphs of straight lines. The task is extended to finding a point of intersection.

Question 5 – Similar to question **4** but extends the task to finding the area of a triangle.

Answers

1. **P** $x = 2$ **Q** $y = x + 3$ **R** $x = 5$ **S** $y = 4$
   T $y = 2$
2. **a** **i** Vertical lines through $x = 3$ and $x = 5$, horizontal lines through $y = 4$ and $y = 6$
      ii 4 units^2
   b **i** Vertical lines through $x = 4$ and $x = 5$, horizontal lines through $y = 1$ and $y = 4$
      ii 3 units^2
   c **i** Vertical lines through $x = 1$ and $x = 6$, horizontal lines through $y = 3$ and $y = 5$
      ii 10 units^2
3. **a-d**   **i** Check students' drawings
   a **ii** $x = 3, y = 4$ **b** **ii** $x = 4, y = -2$
   c **ii** $x = -2, y = -3$ **d** **ii** $x = -4, y = 3$
4. See master Answer file for this question
5. **a** Vertices at (0, 2), (2, 4) and (4, 2)   4 units^2
   b Vertices at (2, 5), (2, 2) and (3.5, 3.5)   2.25 units^2
   c Vertices at (6, 2), (6, 5) and (4, 4)   3 units^2

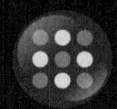

6c Gradient of a straight-line graph

Objectives		
• Recognise that equations of the form $y = mx + c$ correspond to straight-line graphs		(L6)
• Find the gradient of lines given by equations of the form $y = mx + c$, given values for m and c		(L6)

Key ideas	Resources
1 Plot and graph linear functions 2 Recognise the effects of changing the coefficient of x in terms of its graph	Gradients (1312) Mini whiteboards Computers with a graphing facility such as Geogebra, GSP or Autograph

Simplification	Extension
Present lines, one at a time, which have non-zero integer gradients and with staircases of triangles drawn on them. Students use their mini whiteboards to give the gradients, both positive and negative. Once confident, students can be presented with lines of zero gradient and can discuss what gradient a line such as $x = 5$ might have.	Students can be challenged to draw a line which has one gradient at one point and a different gradient at another point. They will realise that the line must be partly straight and partly curved (or totally curved). If such a line rises and then falls, ask them what is special about the gradient where it stops rising and begins to fall.

Literacy	Links
Continue to refer to the specific features- constant, coefficient, gradient, intercept - that will help students compare linear functions both in graph form and in equation form.	The steepest road in the world is thought to be Baldwin Street in Dunedin, New Zealand which has a gradient of 1 in 2.86 or 35%. The road was laid according to plans drawn up by planners in the UK who were unaware of the steep hills in the area. There are pictures of Baldwin Street at http://en.wikipedia.org/wiki/Baldwin_Street,_Dunedin

Alternative approach
Begin with some rehearsal of common lines parallel to x axis and y axis, with students drawing 'in the air'. Allow students to continue to investigate the effects of changing one variable in a linear equation and the effects on the resulting graphs. Encourage students to form hypotheses and to test these. Note that students may find exploring the effects of a changing constant more easy initially, then move on to exploring the effects of changing the coefficient of x. Allowing investgatory time in this section and the next should help them establish a familiarity and confidence with both effects.

Checkpoint
What is the difference between these functions: $y = 2x + 5$ and $y = 4x + 5$? How does this difference affect the graphs of each? (Responses indicate recognisiton that the coefficient of x reflects the slope of the line – the larger coefficient producing steeper lines)
What is the gradient of the line $y = -2x + 7$? (-2)

Algebra Graphs

Starter – Missing coordinates

Give students an equation of a line and either an x-coordinate or a y-coordinate and ask them to find the missing coordinate. For example

$y = 2x - 7$ (-1,) (,7) (-5,) (1.5,) (,-1)

Solutions: (-1, -9) (7, 7) (-5, -17) (1.5, -4) (3, -1)

Can be differentiated by the choice of equation and coordinates

Teaching notes

Start with a discussion of the properties of a straight line – that it is always 'heading in the same direction' wherever you are on the line. This is a justification for the gradient being a way that you can identify the direction of a straight line using a single number. This will tie into later work with parallel lines.

Explore what happens when the line is made more steep or less steep, what happens to the gradient? What difference is there when the line is sloping down? Steepness is related to the size of the gradient, whether it is rising (positive gradient) or falling (negative gradient).

Plenary

Use a mini whiteboard activity to check that students are able to identify facts correctly about the gradient of lines, whether they slope up or down, which of a pair will be steeper *etc.* from the equations.

Exercise commentary

Question 1 - Simply requires students to count the size of the steps on the diagram. Notice that coordinate axes are not needed to find a gradient.

Question 2 – This is similar to question **1** after students have drawn the lines on a grid.

Questions 3 and **4** – These reinforce the fact that the multiplier of x in $y = f(x)$ gives the gradient of the straight line.

Question 5 – This can be used to confirm that the multiplier of x in the equation of the line gives the gradient of the graph.

Question 6 – Gives a physical meaning to the gradient as the 'rate of increase in temperature'.

Question 7 – This activity explores how lines are affected by different values of the gradient. The meaning of zero gradient and infinite gradient can be explored.

Answers

1 A 3, B 2, C 1, D -2, E ½, F -1, G 0

2 a 2 b 3 c ½ d 0
   e -1 f -2

3 a 5 b 4 c 1 d ½
   e -6 f -3

4 a 8 b -8 c -8 d -4
   e -1 f $-\frac{1}{2}$

5

x	0	2	4	6
$y = 2x - 1$	-1	3	7	11
$y = \frac{x}{2} + 3$	3	4	5	6

gradient = 2, gradient = 1/2

6 Straight-line graph drawn through (0, 2) and (5, 17)
   3° C per minute

7 c The line is horizontal because the gradient is zero.
   d The line looks almost vertical because the gradient is a large number.

Gradient of a straight-line graph

6d *y*-intercept of a straight-line graph

Objectives		
• Recognise that equations of the form $y = mx + c$ correspond to straight-line graphs		(L6)
• Find the gradient of lines given by equations of the form $y = mx + c$, given values for m and c		(L6)

Key ideas	Resources
1 Plot and graph linear functions 2 Recognise the effects of changing the constant in terms of the resulting graph	$y = mx + c$ (1153) Mini whiteboards Computers with a graphing facility such as Geogebra, GSP or Cabri

Simplification	Extension
The intercept of a straight line is an easy concept. Present students with straight lines and ask students to use their mini whiteboards to show the intercept and, later, as revision, the gradient of each line. A discussion about the intercept of a line passing through the origin is useful as students may say that there is no intercept rather than that the intercept is zero.	Ask students to work in pairs. One student says 'I'm drawing a graph of a line with an intercept on the *y*-axis of (something) and a gradient of (something)'. Both students draw a line unseen by the other and then compare their results. Fractional gradients can be introduced for mutual challenge.

Literacy	Links
Continue to refer to the specific features- constant, coefficient, slope, intercept - that will help students compare linear functions both in graph form and in equation form.	Graphical calculators are calculators that can plot and display graphs, and also are usually programmable. The first graphical calculator was produced in 1985. There is an online graphical calculator at http://www.coolmath.com/graphit/

Alternative approach
Extend investigatory time with computers and graphing software as given in the alterrnative approach of **6c**. Bear in mind that if students have been allowed to choose their own order of investigation, the intercept may have produced their first results or hypotheses.

Checkpoint
What is the difference between these functions: $y = 2x - 3$ and $y = 2x + 5$? How does this difference affect the graphs of each?(Responses indicate recognition that the constant reflects the intercept of the line with the *y* axis.) What is coordinate of the *y*-intercept for the graph of $y = 3x - 7$?   (0, -7)

Starter – Coordinate bingo

Ask students to draw a 3 × 3 grid and enter nine numbers between 1 and 20 inclusive. Write the equation $y = 2x + 3$ on the board. Give values for the x coordinate (between -1 and 8.5 inclusive). Students cross out the y coordinate if it is in their grid. The winner is the first student to cross out all nine numbers.

Can be differentiated by the choice of equation.

Teaching notes

There are many ways to think about the role of c in the graph of $y = mx + c$. It is important that students grasp both the idea that all lines with the same m have the same gradient, and so are parallel to one another, and the idea that the value of c moves all points up or down by the same amount, and in particular moves the origin by that amount to where the line cuts the y-axis, the intercept. This is a good opportunity for student dialogue: to explain to one another all that they can say about a pair of equations without actually drawing the detail.

For example, $y = 2x + 1$ and $y = 2x - 3$ are parallel, the first is always 4 units above the second, the first has intercept at 1 and the second at -3.

Similarly, $y = 3x + 2$ and $y = x + 2$ meet at the y-axis because they share the same intercept (0, 2) and they both slope up from right to left with the first line being steeper.

Plenary

Use a mini whiteboard activity to check that students are able to identify facts about the intercept correctly from the equations, especially equations which require some manipulation before they can be written in the form $y = mx + c$.

Exercise commentary

Question 1 – The answers are simply read off the y-axis.

Question 2 – This question is similar to question **1**, after students have drawn lines on axes.

Questions 3 and **4** – These do not require graphs. Intercepts are found directly from the equations.

Question 5 – This question confirms that the intercept taken from the equation matches the intercept read from the graph.

Question 6 – This gives the meaning of the intercept as the initial value of the voltage.

Question 7 – This activity confirms that all graphs in each family are parallel to each other but with different intercepts.

Answers

1   A 2, B 3, C 0, D -1

2   a   3   b   2   c   -2   d   0
     e   -3   f   -4 ½

3   a   6   b   1   c   -5   d   -2
     e   0   f   1

4   a   5   b   3   c   3   d   6
     e   9   f   8

5

x	-2	0	2	4	6
$y = 2x - 3$	-7	-3	1	5	9
$y = 1/2\, x + 3$	2	3	4	5	6

y intercepts are -3 and 3

6   a   Straight-line graph drawn through (0, 2) and (4, 18)
     b $V = 2$

7   The second set of graphs will have the same y-intercepts as before but each graph will be steeper because the gradient has increased from 2 to 3.

y-intercept of a straight-line graph

6e The equation $y = mx + c$

Objectives	
• Recognise that equations of the form $y = mx + c$ correspond to straight-line graphs	(L6)
• Find the gradient of lines given by equations of the form $y = mx + c$, given values for m and c	(L6)
• Understand that equations in the form $y = mx + c$ represent a straight line and that m is the gradient and c is the value of the y-intercept	(L6)

Key ideas	Resources
1 Be able to identify both gradient and intercept from either equation or graph forms of liniear functions 2 Use this knowledge in order to plot or provide further detail about a function	$y = mx + c$ (1153) Mini whiteboards Computers with a graphing facility such as Geogebra, GSP or Cabri Interpreting functions and graphs A7 from SU Box: http://www.nationalstemcentre.org.uk/elibrary/resourc e/2006/interpreting-functions-graphs-and-tables-a7

Simplification	Extension
The teacher could present students with straight lines and ask students to use their mini whiteboards to show, first, the intercept and, second, the gradient of each line. If the students can see the expression $y = \Box x + \Box$, they use their mini whiteboards to insert their values of m and c and write the equation. Initially, both m and c are positive. Later, use examples where c is negative before giving examples where m is negative.	Question **6** of the exercise can become a whole-class activity where many equations are written on cards and in sight of the class. Suggestions are made, with reasons, as to which 'family' each card belongs.

Literacy	Links
Continue to refer to the specific features- constant, coefficient, gradient, intercept - that will help students compare linear functions both in graph form and in equation form.	Algebra is the universal language of mathematics. The equation of a straight-line graph $y = mx + c$ is used around the world, however, not all countries use the same letters for the y-intercept and the gradient. In US textbooks the equation is usually written $y = mx + b$, in Austria it is written $y = kx + d$, in the Netherlands it is usually written $y = ax + b$, in Russia it is written $y = kx + b$, in Sweden it is written $y = kx + m$ while in Uruguay it can be written as $y = mx + n$.

Alternative approach
The students may be encouraged to continue with computer research initially, for instance by using their knowledge of linear functions in order to form a linear design or 'tartan'. Alternatively, students may work in pairs with card sorts pairing a linear graph with its equation. Resources for similar activities may be found from the Unit A7 of the Standards Unit Box referenced in Resources. Students may also be encouraged to 'draw graphs in the air' with their hands in response to some equations, as well as write on mini whiteboards a possible equation for a linear function from a given graph.

Checkpoint
I want to draw a linear function which is parallel to $y = 3x + 4$, but which is 5 units below it. What function would I need to plot? $\hspace{2cm} (y = 3x - 1)$

Starter – Rectangles

Ask students to write down four equations that, if plotted on a graph, will make a rectangle with an area of 15 cm². Challenge students to find different possibilities. Possible solutions are

$x = 0$ $y = 0$ $x = 5$ $y = 3$,
$x = 1$ $y = 2$ $x = -2$ $y = -3$,
$x = -1$ $y = 8$ $x = -2$ $y = -7$.

Teaching notes

Finding the equation of a line through two given points requires calculation of the gradient and either reading off the intercept from a graph or calculating the constant by substitution. If students struggle with algebra it may be worth concentrating separately on these two components before starting problems where they have to do both to find the equation of the line.

Emphasise the importance of m as the coefficient of x and c as the constant, rather than the first and second numbers in the equation, as falling graphs will often be written as $y = 4 - 3x$ or similar.

Plenary

Use a mini whiteboard activity to check that students are able to correctly identify the important features of a graph correctly from its equation and that they can write examples of equations with particular properties, for example sloping upwards, going through the point (1, 3) or with intercept at -4, *etc*.

Exercise commentary

Question 1 – Students have to pick out the values of m and c from the equations.

Question 2 – The values of m and c are now taken from the graphs of the lines.

Question 3 – This question, in effect, combines questions **1** and **2**. Students use the graphs to find m and c and then use their values to write the equations.

Question 4 – This question presents slightly different variations of the equation $y = mx + c$.

Question 5 – This contextual question builds up to showing that the speed of the train is given by the gradient of the straight line on the distance-time graph.

Question 6 – This task reinforces what the exercise has practised. The computer activity confirms the students' answers.

1

Equation	$y = 3x + 1$	$y = 4x - 5$	$y = 0.5x + 2$	$y = 4 - 2x$
Gradient	3	4	½	-2
y-intercept	1	-5	2	4

2   A a 2   b 3   c $y = 2x + 3$
    B a 3   b -2   c $y = 3x - 2$
    C a ½   b -2   c $y = \frac{1}{2}x - 2$
    D a -2   b 4   c $y = -2x + 4$
    E a $-\frac{1}{2}$ b 5   c $y = -\frac{1}{2}x + 5$

3

	Gradient	y intercept	Equation
A	1	3	$y = x + 3$
B	2	1	$y = 2x + 1$
C	-1	5	$y = -x + 5$
D	3	-2	$y = 3x - 2$
E	-0.5	-1	$y = -½ x - 1$
F	0	-4	$y = -4$

4

	Gradient	y intercept
a	6	-4
b	7	2
c	4	-2
d	-4	9
e	-0.5	7
f	-1	3

5   **a-c** Straight-line graph from (0, 10) to (5, 20)
    d 2 km/min

6   **a** $y = 3x - 1$ is parallel to $y = 3x + 4$
       $y = 4 - 2x$ is parallel to $y = 1 - 2x$
    b $y = 2x + 1$ has the same y intercept as $y = 1 - 2x$
       $y = 4 - 2x$ has the same y intercept as $y = 3x + 4$

The equation $y = mx + c$

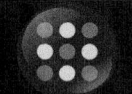

6f Equations given implicitly

Objectives

- Generate points and plot graphs of linear functions, where y is given implicitly in terms of x (e.g. $ay + bx = 0$, $y + bx + c = 0$), on paper and using ICT (L6)

Key ideas	Resources
1 Recognise linear functions in equivalent forms 2 Find and plot coordinates of implicit linear functions	Mini whiteboards

Simplification	Extension
As an introduction, keep the coefficients of the equation positive, so that students are not troubled with negative intercepts. When explaining the substitution of $x = 0$ and then $y = 0$, use your hand to cover up the zero term in the equation so that students see the two remaining non-zero terms. This ploy avoids the formal written form of the substitution.	Students can explore what the graph in question **5** (and then question **6**) looks like if the purchaser is prepared to spend *less than* £24. The graph is then $2x + 4y < 24$. Students need to keep in mind that x and y can only take integer values.

Literacy	Links
The term implicit function will be new to students, but they should be familiar with equivalent versions of maths sentencing, given sufficient reference and practice.	A seismograph is used to detect vibrations caused by shock waves moving through the Earth caused by earthquake activity. The graphical record of the vibrations is called a seismogram. Seismograms from stations around the World can be viewed at http://rev.seis.sc.edu/ and there is an animation of a seismogram at http://www.yenka.com/freecontent/attachment.action?quick=9w&att=704

Alternative approach

Students will have met graphs of the form $x + y = k$ in Y8 work. Begin by displaying an example of such a graph, e.g. $x + y = 7$. Ask students to work in pairs in order to establish an equation for the line. This may produce different but equivalent versions depending whether students have examined coordinates and established the 'sum to 7' relationship, or if they have worked with intercept and slope. Check and gather the equivalents that arise, adding or encouraging other versions where appropriate. Use the examples to identify the implicit versions of the function as well as the explicit function, $y = mx + c$ Use equivalent spider diagrams to explore other functions expressed in equivalent versions. The second example in the section will provide a good starting point here. Encourage students to also consider equivalent versions of m that might result from such an equation,. For example in the second example $m = \frac{3}{2}$ or $\frac{6}{4}$ or $\frac{1.5}{1}$ etc. - all of which produce the correct gradient. Refer students to work previously addressed in chapter 3 on rearranging equations and formulae.

Checkpoint

A linear function is given as $3x - 4y = 6$.
Find the gradient and the coordinates of the intercept of the line with the y-axis.

($m = \frac{3}{4}$; $c = -\frac{6}{4}$ so coordinate $(0, -1.5)$)

Algebra   Graphs

Starter – What is my line?

Give clues to straight-line equations. Possible clues are

My gradient is the square root of 25. My y-intercept is -2.   ($y = 5x - 2$)

My gradient is one-third of 21. My y-intercept is one-quarter of 6. ($y = 7x + 1.5$)

I am parallel to $y = 13 - 8x$. My y-intercept is 6.5. ($y = 6.5 - 8x$) *etc*.

Teaching notes

Many students struggle with implicit equations because they do not realise why different forms of equation are used at different times, for example, in ensuring that the equation does not contain fractions, or in preparation for solving simultaneous equations.

If students sometimes struggle with algebra, it may be worth reviewing substitution and looking at simple rearrangements of equations without linking these initially to graphs. Then go on to use the techniques in the context of graphs.

Plenary

Ask students to work in pairs to challenge each other to produce equations with specific gradients and intercepts.

Exercise commentary

Question 1 – All intercepts are positive and students should not be troubled with negative values.

Question 2 – Some intercepts are negatives, hence the need for axes that extend into negative values.

Question 3 – Only positive intercepts are required and the gradient of the graphs can then be found.

Question 4 – This is a more challenging question, with students needing to take care with their use of signs.

Question 5 – This practical application has the added feature of needing only integer values of *x* and *y* when the final answers are being found.

Question 6 – This question is similar to question **5** but has far less structured support.

Answers

1. a (0, 4), (6, 0)   b (0, 5), (2, 0)
   c (0, 3), (5, 0)   d (0, 4), (3, 0)
   e (0, 3), ($4\frac{1}{2}$, 0)   f (0, 2), (6, 0)

2. a (0, -2), (4, 0)   b (0, -6), (5, 0)
   c (0, -3), (-4, 0)

3. a (0, 8), (4, 0), -2   b (0, 6), (2, 0), -3
   c (0, 2), (4, 0), -0.5

4. a 3   b 3   c -0.5   d 1
   e $\frac{1}{2}$ f -2

5. a Straight-line graph from (0, 6) to (12, 0)
   b (0, 6), (2, 5), (4, 4), (6, 3), (8, 2), (10, 1), (12, 0)
   c 4

6. $4x + 8y = 84$
   Straight-line graph from (0, 10.5) to (21, 0)
   (1, 10), (3, 9), (5, 8), (7, 7), (9, 6), (11, 5), (13, 4), (15, 3), (17, 2), (19, 1), (21, 0)
   7 Coxes and 7 Bramleys

6g Real-life graphs

Objectives

- Construct functions arising from real-life problems and plot their corresponding graphs (L6)

Key ideas	Resources
1 Find values and plot linear graphs from a variety of contexts	Conversion graphs (1059) Matching graphs and scenarios: http://www.nationalstemcentre.org.uk/elibrary/resource/6658/matching-graphs-and-scenarios

Simplification	Extension
Students may, by now, be quite confident with the progression: equation → table of values → coordinates → graph. However, in question 1, students will more readily accept that the angle sum of a triangle gives $y + 2x = 180$ rather than formally writing $y = 180 - 2x$. They should be encouraged to work out the value of y for a given x mentally, without any confusing algebra. Provide weaker students with pre-prepared axes where appropriate.	Question 5 can be extended to other perimeters. How will changing the perimeter change the graph? Will a different perimeter give a different shape for a maximum area? Can students see a pattern so that they can compute the maximum area directly from the perimeter?

Literacy	Links
Liaise with work done in science, here. Experimental results are frequently graphed in science, as scatter graphs, but are intended for use in exploring relationships between two variables. There is a subtle difference here, but it is worth discussing with colleagues and students. Communicating the context of any values established within a problem here will need emphasising. Students should use correct units and/or appropriate descriptions in solutions.	UK law requires lorries and coaches to have a tachograph fitted to record the speed of the vehicle and whether it is moving or stationary. A mechanical tachograph has a marker which writes on a circular rotating disc of paper. As the speed of the vehicle increases, the marker moves out from the centre of the disc. The resulting trace can be used to check the driver's speed and hours worked. There is an image of a completed tachograph chart at http://www.transportoffice.gov.uk/crt/vehicledrivers/drivershoursandtachographs/tachographchartdiagram.htm

Alternative approach

Matching graphs to scenarios will remind students of work covered previously and rehearse the nature of graphing various situations. Students can then go on to work on and plot examples from the exercise. Working in pairs to compare and check results with the aim for each to improve the quality of responses will help to focus on the context of each problem and how the solution is conveyed in writing.

Checkpoint

A taxi company charges £2.20 plus 40 pence per mile.
Write down a formula for the total cost C in terms of the number of miles m. ($C = 2.2 + 0.4m$)
Plot a graph of C against m for journeys up to 10 miles.

Starter – Coordinates

For each of the following lines, ask students to give three pairs of coordinates that lie on the line.
$2y = 6x - 5$, $3x = 8 - y$, $9x - 3y = 8$

Ask students if any of the lines are parallel, encouraging students to justify their responses.

Can be extended by challenging students to think outside the first quadrant.

Teaching notes

The key processes in algebra in this spread focus on interpretation and evaluation and are important elements of functional skills in mathematics. Emphasise the need for clear communication, in everyday language, when providing answers to problems such as these.

Showing how the graphs are used in solving the problem, by showing arrows from one axis to the graph and then to the other axis, is a good habit to encourage in the students.

Plenary

The constant terms in the equations in the examples can be explained as the wait time and a fee. Ask students work in pairs to provide explanations for the constant terms in the equations for questions **2** and **3** and to explain why there is not a constant in the equation in question **4**. Use whole-class feedback for students to share good use of language in these contexts.

Exercise commentary

Question 1 – The angle sum of 180° provides a readily understood equation in x and y.

Question 2 – Students should be used to the progression shown here: equation, to table of values, to graph, to interpretation of graph.

Questions 3 and 4 – Both provide the same progression in different contexts. Question **4** makes the further point that not all graphs are straight and the x^2 indicates a non-linear graph.

Question 5 – The equation of the line, namely $x + y = 12$, can be found by inspection of a table of values or, more formally, by finding the gradient and intercept of the graph. A second table of values which gives the area of different sized rectangles can be constructed to find the maximum.

Answers

1 a

x	10	20	30	40	60	80	90
y	160	140	120	100	60	20	0

b i It is a right angled triangle.
ii The triangle does not close; it forms three sides of an infinite rectangle.

2 a

x, miles	50	100	200	300
C, £	21	22	24	26

Straight-line graph from (0, 620) to (300, 26)

b £25

3 a

x, km	0	100	200	400	600	800
y, litres	40	35	30	20	10	0

Straight-line graph from (0, 40) to (800, 0)

b 40 litres **c** 800 km

4 a

t, sec	1	2	3	4	5
x, metres	5	20	45	90	125

Quadratic graph from (0, 0) to (5, 125)

b the symbol for squared **c** 101 metres

5 a Straight-line graph from (0, 12) to (12, 0)
b $x + y = 12$ **c** $x = 6$ m, $y = 6$ m, square

Real-life graphs

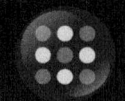

6h Distance-time graphs

Objectives	
• Interpret graphs arising from real situations, e.g. time series graphs	(L6)
• Interpret and explore combining measures into rates of change in everyday contexts (e.g. km per hour, pence per metre)	(L6)

Key ideas	Resources
1 Interpret information conveyed by a D-T graph correctly 2 Use reasoning in order to infer further information from D-T graphs	Distance time graphs (1322) Interpreting distance-time graphs(MARS): http://map.mathshell.org/materials/lessons.php?taskid=208

Simplification	Extension
Some students may have an initial misunderstanding that the shape of the graph is the shape of the road on which the journey takes place. It is worthwhile having pupils describe the 'story' of the journey by looking at various graphs. For example, a story might be 'you leave home, travel for 10 minutes, have a rest for 5 minutes, then continue for another 15 minutes.......'.	In pairs, students could share their answers to question 5 of the exercise and ask their partner to describe the journey home. A development would be for one of the pair to describe a journey in words and the other to draw a graph of the journey as it is being described.

Literacy	Links
Communicating a scenario, to match clues from a graph gives students the opportunity to speak to an audience, and recognise the importance of clarity, together with appropriate levels of detail.	Helium gas is lighter than air and so balloons filled with helium rise into the air. Balloons filled with hydrogen would be lighter still but hydrogen is flammable and could cause the balloon could explode. Helium occurs naturally in the air and is also found underground with natural gas deposits. There is more about how helium balloons work at http://science.howstuffworks.com/helium2.htm and pictures of the hydrogen-filled Hindenburg airship, which exploded in 1937 at http://www.nlhs.com/tragedy.htm

Alternative approach

By way of an introduction use a D-T graph with no scaled axes other than distance, time. Ask pupils to come up with a 'story' that is described by the graph. Share some of the results, drawing attention to different interpretation of what units might be represented by the scales in each scenario. Address any misconceptions that might arise. Further examples and resources, including card sorts, may be found on the MARS site as referenced.

Checkpoint

Jennifer cycled 30 km in two and a half hours. What was her average speed? (12 km/h)

John rode on his motorbike for 120 km at an average speed of 50 km/h. For how long did he ride? (2.4 hours)

Algebra Graphs

Starter – True or false?

Give students equations with values for the gradient or y intercept and ask whether the statements are true or false. Possible equations and values are

$x - 4y = 8$ has a y intercept of -2   (True)

$2y + 7x - 1 = 0$ has a gradient of 3.5   (False, should be -3.5)

$2x + 3y = 6$ has a y intercept of -2   (False, should be 2)

$3y - x = 2$ has a gradient of $\frac{1}{3}$ (True) *etc*.

Teaching notes

Many students find it hard to relate these graphs with what is happening in the physical context, especially the ideas of the lines sloping down. Asking students to walk through some different distance-time graphs can help to give them a concrete association between the shape of the graph and actual motion. Use two students, one starting before the other and the second walking quicker to catch up to help to clarify the role of the gradient of the graph as the speed of the motion and a reinforcement of why a horizontal line has gradient zero.

Plenary

The graphs here are all formed from straight line segments, that is, constant speed in each period. Ask students to work in pairs to draw what they think a graph of a car moving away from traffic lights would actually look like - as a practical introduction to the use of curved graphs at a later stage.

Exercise commentary

Questions 1 and 2 – These questions do not involve speed but require students to interpret distances and times. In particular, students should understand that a horizontal section of a graph indicates constant distance and being at rest.

Question 3 – This simple matching task is an easy introduction to how gradient gives speed on a distance-time graph.

Question 4 – This question requires a deeper interpretation of a graph, involving two movements in opposite directions.

Question 5 – This task is made more worthwhile if students are asked to explain their graph and give numerical details.

Answers

1   **a** 200 m   **b** 4 min   **c** 2 min   **d** 100 m
     e 8 min   **f** 12 min

2   **a** 2   **b** 2 min   **c** 300 m   **d** 2 min

3   **a** Y   **b** Z   **c** X

4   **a** Shara, 1 hour   **b** 2.5 hours
     c 50 km, 10 km/h   **d** 10 km/h

5   Students' answers

Distance-time graphs

6i Time series

Objectives	
• Interpret graphs arising from real situations, e.g. time series graphs	(L6)

Key ideas	Resources
1 Recognise information being communicated by time series graphs 2 Use time series graphs to estimate values, infer and suggest results.	Real life graphs (1184) Graph drawing software Creating a time-series graph (EXCEL): http://www.youtube.com/watch?v=_CRRWnkbyfA

Simplification	Extension
Some students may need help to understand the motion of 'a trend'. The teacher could present different jagged-line graphs of different variables against time and have students decide and describe any trends. Questions **1** and **2** require students to know how to calculate a mean; a brief reminder may be needed.	There are an infinite number of prime numbers and various prizes are offered to anyone who discovers a prime number larger than those already known. A prime number with 13 million digits was discovered in August 2008. There is a time-series graph showing the number of digits in the largest known prime number at http://primes.utm.edu/notes/by_year.html

Literacy	Links
It is important to discuss the nature of continuity of data with the students. Prompt students to estimate values between as well as on clearly marked points; can this be done realisitcally? Would the values have meaning? Use and explore the words extrapolate, as well as trend. Use the opportunities for students to speak about their findings to an audience of other classmates or wider, in order to strengthen communication and reasoning skills.	Honey bees build hexagonal cells from wax to form a honeycomb which they use to store nectar, make honey, and raise larvae. For thousands of years, mathematicians tried to prove that the hexagonal shape provides the maximum amount of space to store the honey using the least amount of beeswax. The idea became known as the Honeycomb Conjecture and was finally proved by Professor Thomas Hales in 1999. He showed that the best way to divide a surface into regions of equal area with the least total perimeter is a hexagonal grid. There is more information about honeycomb at http://en.wikipedia.org/wiki/Honeycomb

Alternative approach
A video such as that of creating a time-series graph on rainfall may be used to introduce this lesson. It will serve also as a reminder to previous work on these graphs. Other sources of data for graph construction, by hand or computer, may be found from other curricular areas such as PE or geography. These sources are likley to provide inferences which may stimulate lively discussion.

Checkpoint	
A company made profits of £5000, £4000, £4200 and £3600 in four consecutive months. What was the average profit made?	(£4200)
Describe the trend in profits during this period.	(Falling)

Starter – Trapezium equations

Draw a trapezium on the board. Ask students to suggest a possible equation for each of the four sides. If available, check responses with a graphical package. Can be extended by changing the orientation of the trapezium.

Teaching notes

In practical terms, graphs showing change over time are amongst the most commonly used, so understanding how to interpret them is a very important part of functional skills in mathematics. Thinking about 'rates of change' can be a very helpful way for students to think about the slope of the graph. For example, a hot cup of tea will cool down over time, so the graph is falling, but the rate of cooling will slow down as its temperature drops, so the graph will start to level off.

The key to this is using the context of the problem in describing what is happening, so talking about cooling rather than 'the graph falling'. There are opportunities here for students to work together in pairs to produce good descriptions, in everyday language, of what is happening in a graph.

Plenary

Ask students to work in pairs to construct a real-life graph for their partner to describe.

Exercise commentary

Questions 1 and **2** – Both questions use the first worked example as a model. In question **2**, students provide their own graphs from the table.

Questions 3 and **4** – These provide a different style of question. Students have to interpret graphs from their shape with little or no numerical data. Answers will involve written explanations which can be further explored orally.

Question 5 – The shapes of the graphs are more important than any detailed numerical labelling of axes. The explanations are as important as the graphs themselves.

Answers

1 a

Week	1	2	3	4	5
No. of births	8	6	7	9	6

  b 2 and 5   c 7.2

  d Flat – no trend can be seen

2 a Check students' graphs

  b 5   c 12   d Falling

3 a Y   b W   c Z   d X

4 No oil is used for a time, then about half the oil is used in 'one go'. Some oil is now returned to the bottle. Later, all the remaining oil is used and the bottle is then empty.

5 Students' answers.
   a Instant drop (tax loss) followed by 'exponential fall off' (loses fraction of value each year).
   b Initially zero (warranty) followed by 'exponential rise' (growing number of repairs which are more significant as car ages).
   c Several possibilities.

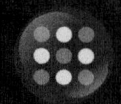

6 Graphs – MySummary

Key outcomes	Quick check
Use a table of values to draw a straight-line graph. L6	Using a table of values with x from 0 to 3, draw a graph for the equation $y = 2x + 1$. (Coordinates are (0, 1), (1, 3), (2, 5) and (3, 7))
Recognise the equations of simple straight-line graphs. L6	**a** Is the graph $y = -4$ a horizontal or vertical line? (Horizontal) **b** Write down the coordinate of the point of intersection of the lines $y = 4$ and $x = 3$. (3, 4)
Relate gradient and y-intercept to the general equation $y = mx + c$. L6	Find the gradient and intercept of these lines **a** $y = 3x - 7$ ($m = 3$, $c = -7$) **b** $2x + 4y = 7$ ($m = -\frac{1}{2}$, $c = 1.75$)
Draw and interpret real-life graphs. L6	Joanna travels by bus and by train. She travels 6 miles by bus at an average speed of 24 miles per hour. Her train journey is 30 miles and the train travels at an average speed of 40 miles per hour. Draw a graph of her journey (axes should be labelled in minutes and miles). How long did it take? (Graphs should be straight line segments between (0, 0) and (15, 6) and between (15, 6) and (60, 36). Her journey took one hour)

MyMaths extra support

Lesson/online homework			Description
Interior Exterior angles	1100	L6	Interior and exterior angles of polygons
Lines and Quadrilaterals	1102	L4	Parallel and perpedicular lines. Properties of quadrilateral
Angles in parallel lines	1109	L6	Alternate angles, supplementary angles and corresponding angles in parallel lines
Angle proofs	1141	L6	Formal proofs of angle theorems such as angles in a triangle, quadrilateral and exterior angles.

Algebra Graphs

MyReview

6 MySummary

Check out
You should now be able to ...

	Test it ➡ Questions
✓ Use a table of values to draw a straight-line graph.	1
✓ Recognise the equations of simple straight-line graphs.	2 – 4
✓ Relate gradient and y-intercept to the general equation $y = mx + c$.	5 – 6
✓ Draw and interpret real-life graphs.	7 – 9

Language	Meaning	Example
Equation	A statement of mathematical equality.	$y = 2x + 1$
Table of values	A table giving the coordinates of the points on a given line.	x: 0, 1, 2, 3 / y: 1, 3, 5, 7
Constant	A number in an expression or equation. It does not change.	$y = 2x + 1$, 1 is a constant
Gradient	A number that describes the steepness of a line defined as $\frac{\text{change in } y}{\text{change in } x}$.	A line through (0, 0) and (4, 2) has gradient $\frac{2-0}{4-0} = \frac{2}{4} = \frac{1}{2}$.
Intercept	The point at which a line crosses an axis.	The line $y = 2x + 1$ has a y-intercept (0, 1).

6 MyReview

1 For the equation $y = 12 - 4x$
  a copy and complete the table

x	1	2	3
y			

  b plot the graph of the equation
  c on the same axes draw the graph of $y = \frac{1}{2}x + 3$
  d find the coordinates of the point where the lines intersect.

2 Does the line $y = 11 - 3x$ pass through the point (2, 5)?

3 Find the equations of each of these straight lines.

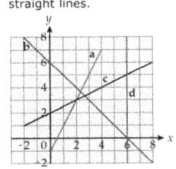

4 Where does the graph of $4x + 3y = 24$ intersect the coordinate axes?

5 Find the gradients of the straight lines with these equations.
  a $y = \frac{x}{2} - 4$ b $y = -7(3 - 2x)$

6 Find the y-intercepts of the straight lines with these equations.
  a $y = 11 - 7x$ b $y = 5x$

7 a Calculate the area of this triangle when $x = 4$ cm. 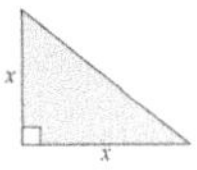
  b Copy and complete the table of values to show A for different values of x.

x	1	2	3	4	5	6	7
A							

  c Draw a graph of your results.

8 Kate leaves her school which is 6 km from her home at 15:10. She takes 40 minutes to walk 4 km towards her home. She stops at her friend's house for 30 minutes. She cycles the rest of the way home at a speed of 12 km per hour.
Draw this journey on a distance-time graph.

9 The money in Geoff's bank account on Monday morning each week for a month is shown on the time-series graph.

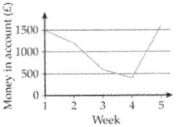

During which week do you think
  a Geoff was paid
  b Geoff had to pay his rent?

What next?

Score	
0 – 4	Your knowledge of this topic is still developing. To improve look at Formative test: 3B-6; MyMaths: 1059, 1153, 1184, 1312 and 1322
5 – 7	You are gaining a secure knowledge of this topic. To improve look at InvisiPen: 262, 263, 264, 265, 273, 274, 275 and 276
8, 9	You have mastered this topic. Well done, you are ready to progress!

Question commentary

Question 1 – Students may need to draw a table of values for part **c**.
Question 2 – Substitute $x = 2$ into the equation, does it give 5?
Question 3 – Students should read the gradient and y-intercept from the graph for parts **a** to **c** before recognising the special case in part **d**.
Question 4 – Students are not expected to rearrange the equation or draw the graph. They just need to set $x = 0$ to find the y-intercept and vice-versa.
Question 5 – Students should identify the value of m in $y = mx + c$.
Question 6 – Students are not expected to rearrange the equation or draw the graph. They just need to set $x = 0$ to find the y-intercept.
Question 7 – Points on the graph should be joined with a smooth line.
Question 8 – It would be best to make the y-axis 'distance from home' but 'distance from school' would also work (graph would be 'upside-down').
Question 9 – Students may choose the week after the correct answer if they do not notice that the graph shows the amount on a Monday.

Answers

1 a (1, 8), (2, 4) and (3, 0)
  b Straight-line graph through these points
  c Straight-line graph through (1, 3.5) and (3, 4.5)
  d (2, 4)

2 Yes

3 a $y = 2x - 1$ b $y = 6 - x$ c $y = \frac{1}{2}x + 2$ d $x = 6$

4 (0, 8), (6, 0)

5 a $\frac{1}{2}$ b 14

6 a 11   b 0

7 a $\frac{1}{2}x^2$, Area = 8 cm²
  b

x	1	2	3	4	5	6	7
A	0.5	2	4.5	8	12.5	18	24.5

  Quadratic graph through (0, 0) and (7, 24.5)

9 a Week 4   b Week 2

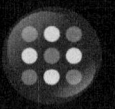

6 MyPractice

1 Copy and complete this table for each of the equations.
Draw the graph of each equation on appropriate axes.

x	0	2	4	6
y				

a $y = 2x - 3$ b $y = 9 - x$ c $y = 10 - 2x$

2 Match the equations in the box with lines A, B, C or D.

$y = x + 6$ $y = 6 - x$ $x = 3$ $y = 3$

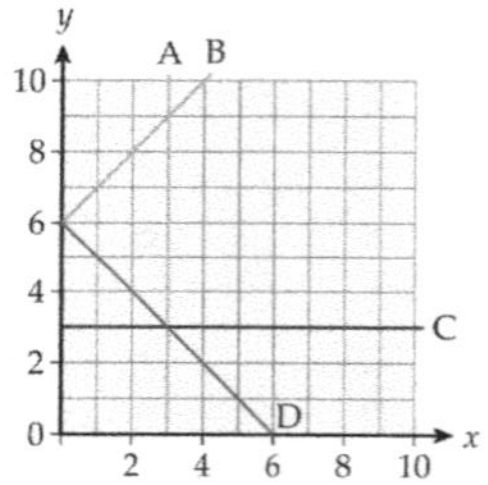

3 Draw and label axes from 0 to 6. Plot each pair of points and join them with a straight line. Find the gradient of each line.
a (1, 2) and (3, 6)   b (3, 5) and (6, 2)   c (0, 1) and (4, 3)

4 Find the y-intercepts of the lines A to C in the graph.

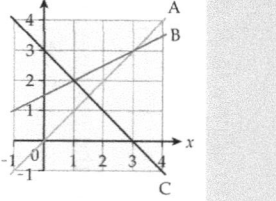

5 Find the gradient and the y-intercept of the straight lines with these equations. Do not draw any graphs.
a $y = 5x - 2$ b $y = \frac{1}{2}x + 9$
c $y = -3x + 4$ d $y = 6 - 2x$

6 For the straight lines P, Q, R and S, find
a the gradient   b the y-intercept   c the equation.

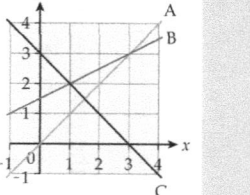

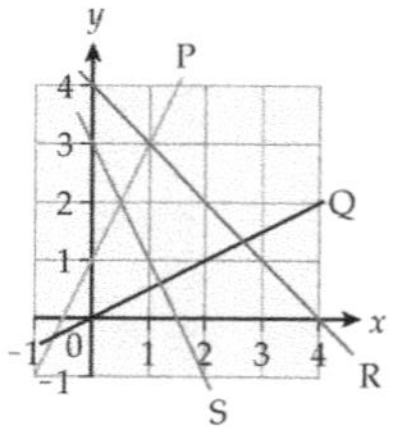

7 Find the points where these lines cut the x-axis and y-axis.
Draw their graphs on axes labelled from -6 to 6.
Use your graphs to find the gradient of each line.
a $2x + y = 6$ b $2x + 4y = 12$ c $2x - 2y = 9$

8 A car has a full tank of petrol. It uses p litres. It can now travel a further distance of d km before it needs more petrol.
a If $d = 800 - 20p$, copy and complete this table and draw a graph of your results on a copy of these axes.

p	0	10	20	30	40
d					

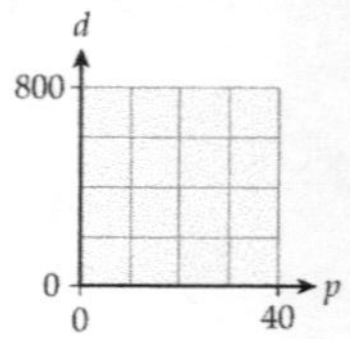

b What is the furthest distance the car can go on a full tank?
c How many litres does a full tank hold?
d What is the gradient of the graph?
What does the gradient tell you about the fuel consumption?

9 The graph shows the distance travelled by a railway truck over a period of 40 seconds.
Find its speed during
a the first 10 seconds
b the next 10 seconds
c the last stage of its journey.

10 These four graphs show changes over time t.
Match the graphs to these descriptions of the variable, y.
a The distance travelled by a train moving at a steady speed
b The temperature of a cup of coffee left undrunk
c The outdoor temperature on a cloudy day
d The amount of pocket money still to be spent during a holiday.

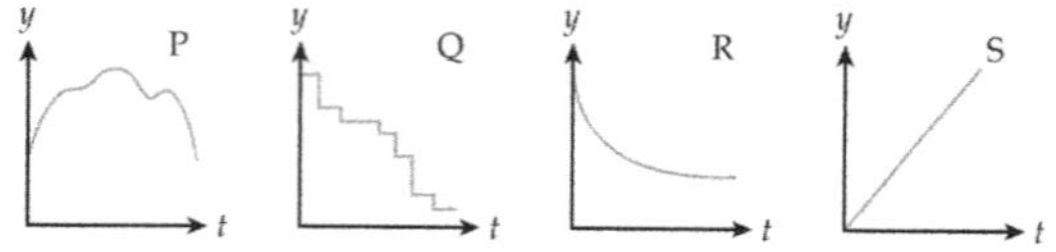

Algebra Graphs

Question commentary

Question 1 – Students should draw up tables of values for each graph. They could be plotted on the same set of axes.

Question 2 – This is a matching exercise. Students may get the horizontal and vertical lines mixed up.

Question 3 – Gradients can be found by reading from the lines the students have drawn.

Question 4, 5 and 6 – Students should simply read from the graphs or from the equations given.

Question 7 – Students must first draw the graphs and then they can read from them to identify m.

Question 8 – This question is in context and links a practical situation to the work in this chapter.

Question 9 – Students may need reminding that speed equals distance divided by time.

Question 10 – Students should be encouraged to explain their reasoning in this question.

Answers

1

x	0	2	4	6
a $y = 2x - 3$	-3	1	5	9
b $y = 9 - x$	9	7	5	3
c $y = 10 - 2x$	10	6	2	-2

2   A $x = 3$ B $y = x + 6$ C $y = 3$ D $y = 6 - x$

3   a   2   b   -1   c   ½

4   A   0   B   1.5   C   3

5   a   Gradient = 5   Intercept = -2
    b   Gradient = $\frac{1}{2}$ Intercept = 9
    c   Gradient = -3   Intercept = 4
    d   Gradient = -2   Intercept = 6

6   P   a   2   b   1   c $y = 2x + 1$
    Q   a $\frac{1}{2}$ b   0   c $y = \frac{1}{2}x$
    R   a   -1   b   4   c $y = 4 - x$
    S   a   -2   b   3   c $y = 3 - 2x$

7   a   (0, 6), (3, 0), gradient = -2
    b   (0, 3), (6, 0), gradient = $-\frac{1}{2}$
    c $(0, 4\frac{1}{2})$, $(4\frac{1}{2}, 0)$, gradient = 1

8   a

p	0	10	20	30	40
d	800	600	400	200	0

      Straight-line graph through (0, 800) and (40, 0)
    b   800 km   c   40 litres
    d   -20, the fuel consumption is 20 km per litre.

9   a   2 m/s   b   0   c   1.5 m/s

10   a   S   b   R   c   P   d   Q

MyPractice

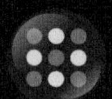

Case Study 2: Jewellery business

Related lessons		Resources	
Adding and subtracting decimals	7a	Order of operations	(1167)
Multiplying decimals	7b	Multiply two decimals	(1011)
Dividing decimals	7c	String; beads; padded envelopes	
Using a calculator	7d	Postal rate leaflets; scales	

Simplification	Extension
The bulk purchasing elements could be ignored and the beads and thread just priced by the unit. Likewise, the online auction costings can be simplified to include just a listing fee or a selling fee. Alternatively, ask the students to work out the number of beads that can fit on each piece of jewellery first and then price up the beads for each necklace and bracelet before working out how many they can make per metre of the thread/cord.	Students could consider diversifying their range. They would need to research the cost of materials, either from catalogues that you provide or from online suppliers. Students could be encouraged to find other suppliers in order to compare costs and secure the best deal. Students could also repeat the whole process for a different product of their choosing, maybe in response to the question, what business would you try if you could?

Links
One example of an online supplier is http://www.the-beadshop.co.uk/ For Royal mail postage costs see http://sg.royalmail.com/portal/rm/PriceFinder?catId=23500532&gear=pricingcalc

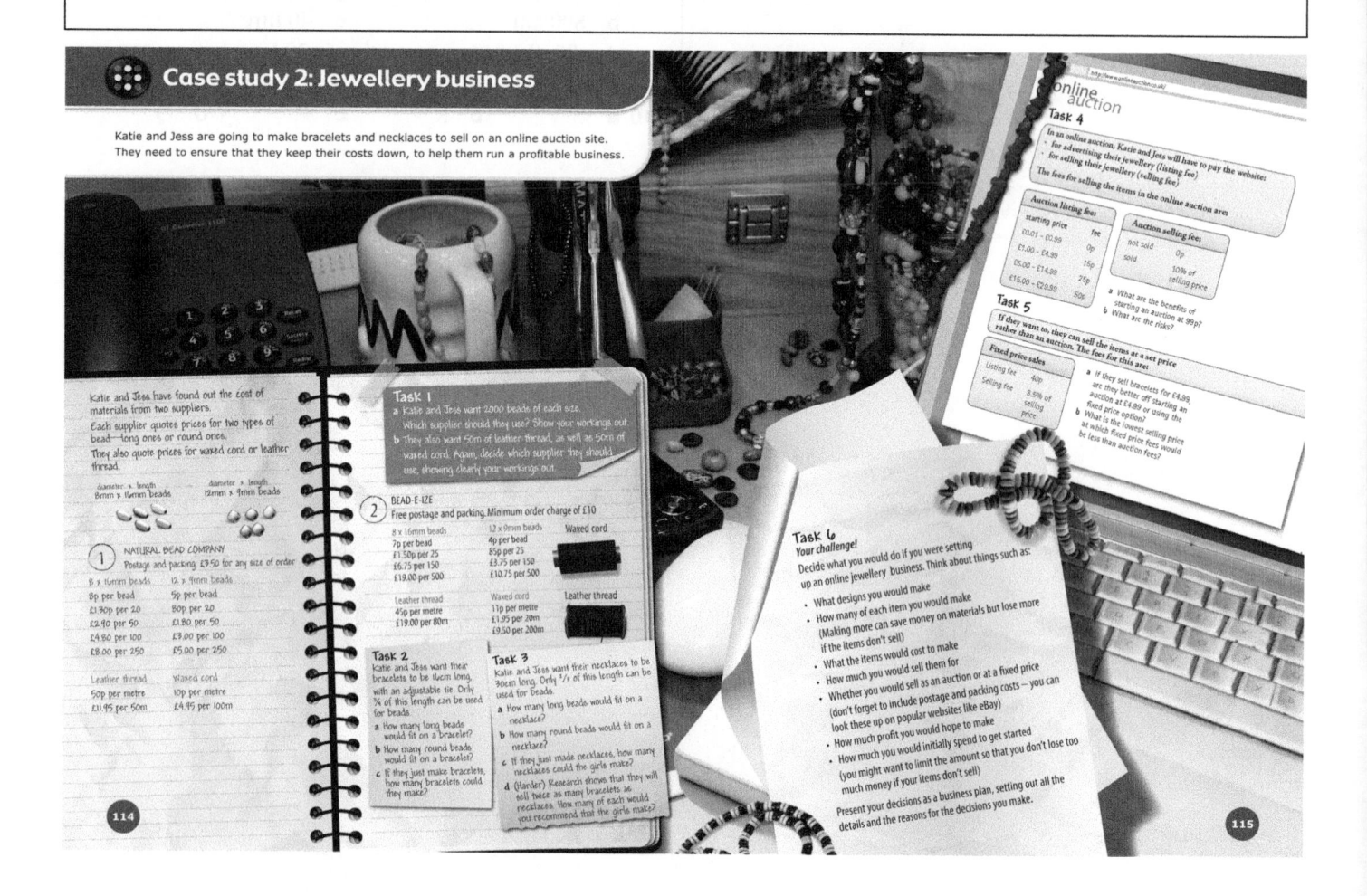

Case Study

Teaching notes

Start with a general discussion about buying on-line. Have you or your family ever bought or sold anything by online auction? Ask students who have experience of this to describe what it involves.

Read through the start of the case study to see that two friends are setting up a small business selling bracelets and necklaces through an online auction site. Discuss how, before they can start selling, they will need to buy in supplies to make their bracelets and necklaces, so will be spending some money at the outset. What would they need to think about when deciding what materials to buy? Hear students' suggestions and discuss how the group will want to make sure that they don't lose a lot of money, so will need to think about how much to spend and what profit they are likely to make.

Tasks 1, 2 and 3

Make sure the students are clear that there are two possible suppliers and then give them time, working with a partner, to tackle the questions relating to the beads.

Tasks 4 and 5

Move on to the right hand page to consider the costs involved in the auction. Make sure that students understand the charges involved: a charge for putting an item on sale (the listing fee) and a commission charged if the item sells (selling fee). Also point out that there is a choice of two ways of selling: either using an auction where people bid against one another, steadily raising the price or as a fixed price sale, where the seller sets the price they want and any buyer will pay that price. Give students time to answer the questions about the auction. They could create a spreadsheet to find out at what price fixed price fees become less than auction fees.

Task 6

Finally the students should work with their partner to produce a detailed business plan that they think should provide a profit. It should contain reasons for their decisions and an estimate of the costing involved and predicted income, including an estimate of the number they will need to sell to break even. They should also give examples of ideas that they rejected along the way, explaining why they rejected them. When complete, it would be interesting for the students to compare their decisions.

Answers to Tasks

1 a, b

		NBC	B-e-l
2000	8 × 16	£64.00	£76.00
	12 × 9	£40.00	£43.00
	P & P	£3.50	free
	Total	£107.50	£119.00
	50m leather thread	£11.95	£22.50
	50m waxed cord	£5.00	£5.00
	Grand total	£124.45	£146.50

2 a 7.5 long beads (so 7 actual beads)
 b 13 round beads
 c 312

3 a 12.5 long beads (so 12 actual beads)
 b 22 round beads
 c 166

4 Students' answers: for – no listing fee, may tempt buyers; against – could sell for 99p.

5 a By auction (15 + 50 = 65p < 40 + 42 = 82p)
 b Fees coincide at £10, so lowest theoretical price is £10.01 However if prices are rounded to nearest penny, then £10.35 (127.975 p fixed price < 128.5 p auction).

6 Students' answers

Jewellery business

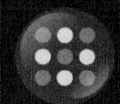

7 Decimal calculations

Learning outcomes

N1 Understand and use place value for decimals, measures and integers of any size (L6)
N4 Use the 4 operations, including formal written methods, applied to integers, decimals, proper and improper fractions, and mixed numbers, all both positive and negative (L6)
N5 Use conventional notation for the priority of operations, including brackets, powers, roots and reciprocals (L6)
N15 Use a calculator and other technologies to calculate results accurately and then interpret them appropriately (L6/7)

Introduction

The chapter starts by looking at mental and written methods for adding and subtracting decimals before looking at similar methods for multiplying and dividing decimals. Efficient use of a calculator (including the appropriate order of operations) is covered before the final section on interpreting the calculator display.

The introduction discusses the use of the binary number system in computing. By converting numbers into binary, computers can recognise the on/off state of the various electronic switches and understand the numbers. They can then perform arithmetic using logic gates.

As of July 2013, the fastest computer has been developed in China and can work out over 33,000 trillion calculations per second. This number is getting so difficult to represent using our standard language of large numbers so computer scientists have invented another number to represent 1,000 trillion – the 'Petaflop'. 33,000 trillion is therefore 33 petaflops. In reality, the 'flop' part stands for floating point operation which is the standard type of calculation carried out by a computer processor.

http://www.petaflop.info/

Students could be invited to investigate other large numbers such as the google or the googaplex.

Prior knowledge

Students should already know how to…
- Multiply and divide by powers of ten
- Round numbers
- Carry out simple calculations
- Use the correct order of operations

Starter problem

The starter problem is a classic refresh of the 'four fours' problem. This task is to make all of the numbers from one to twenty using just the four digit 4s and a combination of brackets and standard operations.

Repeating this task on a broken calculator allows more flexibility since numbers such as 44 and 444 can be formed and there are also other functions available such as squared, square root and other powers. In addition, we are not restricted to just four 4s.

There should be lots of variety in this investigation since there are almost limitless ways of calculating each number. You could restrict some of the operations, the number of fours to be used, the use of brackets or putting more than one four together to make a longer number.

The task could also be extended by varying the target numbers, the available number keys on the calculator or by getting students to challenge each other to make, say 68 with just the 5 key available… A competition could even be arranged!

Resources

MyMaths

Add and subtract decimals	1007	Divide decimals by whole numbers	1008
Multiply decimals by whole numbers	1010	Multiply two decimals	1011
Order of operations	1167		

Online assessment

Chapter test	3B-7
Formative test	3B-7
Summative test	3B-7

InvisiPen solutions

Calculator methods	128	Solving calculation probs	129
Adding and subtracting decimals			131
Multiplying and dividing decimals, mental methods			132
Written methods multiplying decimals			133
Written methods dividing decimals			134

Topic scheme

Teaching time = 5 lessons/2 weeks

2B Ch 7 Mental calculations

→ **7 Decimal calculations**

7a Adding and subtracting decimals
Add and subtract decimals using mental methods
Add and subtract decimals using written methods

7b Multiplying decimals
Multiply decimals using mental methods
Multiply decimals using written methods

7c Dividing decimals
Divide decimals using mental methods
Divide decimals using written methods

7d Using a calculator
Use a calculator efficiently
Calculate using correct order of operations

7e Interpreting the calculator display
Calculate with decimal remainders
Interpret the remainder and covert to units

1 MySummary & MyReview

Differentiation

Student book 3A   116 – 133
Addition and subtraction
Mental and written methods for multiplication and division
Estimating and approximating
Use a calculator efficiently

Student book 3B   116 – 131
Add, subtract, multiply and divide decimals using efficient mental and written methods
Use a calculator efficiently, including the correct order of operations
Interpret the calculator display

Student book 3C   116 – 129
Order of operations
Calculating with decimals
Use a calculator efficiently, including the correct order of operations
Interpret the calculator display

Introduction

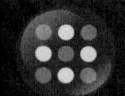

7a Adding and subtracting decimals

Objectives

- Use known facts to derive unknown facts (L6)
- Extend mental methods of calculation, working with decimals, fractions, percentages, factors, powers and roots (L6)
- Solve problems mentally (L6)
- Use efficient written methods to add and subtract integers and decimals of any size (L6)

Key ideas	Resources
1 Extending complements of 10 to support mental calculations with decimals 2 Adding and subtracting decimals effectively and efficiently	Add and subtract decimals (1007) Mini whiteboards

Simplification	Extension
Students may need to revise work on whole-number addition and subtraction using number lines. Encourage students to draw number lines to support their working out, and to count up and down these lines.	Students could practise adding larger numbers to smaller numbers, for example, 4325.15 + 38.176 + 0.0027. However, at this stage these students can add and subtract confidently so it would be more meaningful for them to solve practical problems which use decimals in context.

Literacy	Links
Check equivalent language of addition and subtraction with students. While a variety of strategies supporting student mental approaches are important to share, the terminology of each is not required.	In chemistry, an addition reaction is a reaction where one molecule adds on to another. When two or more identical molecules undergo an addition reaction, a long chain molecule with repeating links is formed called a polymer. Many polymers occur naturally including proteins, cotton and natural rubber but polymers are also made synthetically including most plastics. There is an animation illustrating addition polymerisation at http://www.tvo.org/iqm/plastic/animations.html#

Alternative approach

Reheasrse complements to ten with students by asking them for decimal additions in order to make up a whole number, such as 3.4 would require 0.6; 13.8 requires 0.2 using mini whiteboards. Extend to complements of 100 for two decimal places. Ask students to work in pairs in order to discuss and share mental approaches used for any of the questions from **q1** or **2**. Share and discuss some of the approaches suggested by students. Repeat this task but this time focus on more challenging questions for sharing written approaches.

Checkpoint

Find the results of: 231.57 + 53.07 (284.64)
786.6 − 185.04 (601.56)

Number Decimal calculations

Starter – Order!

Write the following list of fractions on the board.

$\frac{13}{40}, \frac{1}{3}, \frac{7}{20}, \frac{5}{16}, \frac{3}{10}, \frac{3}{8}, \frac{17}{50}, \frac{8}{25}$

Ask students to put them in order from lowest to highest value.

($\frac{3}{10}, \frac{5}{16}, \frac{8}{25}, \frac{13}{40}, \frac{1}{3}, \frac{17}{50}, \frac{7}{20}, \frac{3}{8}$)

Can be differentiated by the choice of fractions.

Teaching notes

Use an initial discussion to assess students' prior knowledge of place values in whole numbers and then in decimals. Comparisons of decimals such as 9.3 and 9.03; 12.4 and 8.37; 0.06 and 0.048 will help to show the security of their prior knowledge.

Confidence and fluency in calculating mentally and with written methods is crucial to developing mathematical skills, so it is important that the basic understanding of the methods shown in the examples is secure.

Plenary

Ask students work in pairs to make up both mental and written calculations for their partner to do, using whatever level of difficulty they are comfortable with but aiming to extend one another.

Exercise commentary

Question 1 – Students should decide whether they are using a partitioning or compensation method for each question. They will need to be encouraged to write this down.

Question 2 – Some students will need to use written methods for these questions. This is acceptable at this level of difficulty.

Question 3 – Students will need to recognise the link to inverse operations here.

Questions 4 and 5 – Encourage students to use a written method as shown in the example, clearly lining up the decimal points and adding extra zeros as appropriate. Students should use two separate written calculations for the questions involving mixed operations.

Question 6 – A more light-hearted question which could encourage students to make up some questions of their own.

Question 7 – A good activity for paired work – very challenging but will provide lots of practice.

Answers

1	a	14.4	b	8.5	c	18.3	d	19.5
	e	7.7	f	8.4	g	11.2	h	4.45
2	a	22.2	b	9.47	c	13.25	d	16.15
	e	10.5	f	1.96	g	-2.65	h	19.2
3	a	1.85	b	16.2	c	5.7	d	23.05
4	a	629.9	b	400.42	c	81.05	d	75.6
	e	385.26	f	349.33				
5	a	650.23	b	353.78	c	14.6	d	662.949
	e	296.2	f	1490.76	g	63.5	h	306.74

6 a i 656.8 kg ii 70.357 kg
   iii 1713.8 kg iv 854.36 kg
 b 61.2 kg

7 a 12.75 + 7.85 + 6.4 + 3.9
 b 6.4, 12.75 and 7.85
 c 12.75 + 7.85 + 6.4 − 4.56 − 5.6 − 3.9
 d 12.75 + 7.85 − 6.4 − 4.56 − 5.6 − 3.9; 0.14

Adding and subtracting decimals

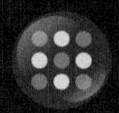

7b Multiplying decimals

Objectives

- Use known facts to derive unknown facts (L6)
- Extend mental methods of calculation, working with decimals, fractions, percentages, factors, powers and roots (L6)
- Solve problems mentally (L6)
- Multiply by decimals (L6)

Key ideas

1 Understanding and applying place value to support mental calculations with decimals
2 Multiplying decimals effectively and efficiently

Resources

Multiply decimals by whole numbers (1010)
Mini whiteboards

Simplification

Students may need to use a simpler method such as the grid method for multiplying pairs of whole numbers. For example the calculation 17 × 52 could be set out as

×	50 (5 × 10)	2
10	10 × 50 = 500	10 × 2 = 20
7	7 × 50 = 350	7 × 2 = 14

500
350
20
+14
884

Extension

Students could practise more real-life problems involving three-digit by three-digit decimal multiplications.

More able students could attempt to multiply smaller numbers together for example 0.0632 × 0.047, which will test the understanding of the place value of their answers.

Literacy

Check equivalent vocabulary of multiplication with students.

Use and compare the language clues given in the word problems indicating 'multipy'.

Links

Pyramid selling is an illegal scam that operates like a chain letter. People are asked to invest money and are then rewarded for recruiting more people to join the scheme. If an investor recruits ten friends who each recruit ten (different) friends and so on, after eight generations there have to be one hundred million recruits, more than the population of the UK! All the schemes eventually run out of recruits and then everyone loses their money. There is more about pyramid selling at
http://www.consumerdirect.gov.uk/watch_out/scams/pyramids-chains/

Alternative approach

Model an example of a related facts spider diagram with a centre of 72 × 7 = 504. Add legs showing for example 72 × 0.7 = 50.4; 7.2 × 7 = 50.4; 7.2 × 0.07 = 0.504; and so on. Encourage students to offer suggestions using mini whiteboards and address any misconcpetions that arise. Students can repeat this task in pairs using a different multiplication statement. Students may apply this to **q1** of the exercise. Encourage students to use a written approach to a more challenging problem using mini whiteboards, then discuss and share their approaches before consolidating.

Checkpoint

Calculate: 72.6 × 0.2 (14.52)
34.8 × 3.6 (125.28)

Number Decimal calculations

Starter – Sums and products

Challenge students to find two numbers
- with a sum of 1.3 and a product of 0.36 (0.4, 0.9)
- with a sum of 1.3 and a product of 0.42 (0.6, 0.7)
- with a sum of 1.3 and a product of 0.4   (0.5, 0.8)
- with a sum of 1.3 and a product of 0.22 (0.2, 1.1)

Can be differentiated by the choice of decimals

Teaching notes

The processes in this spread require accuracy in identifying factors and in multiplying integers correctly. Starting with a whole-class mini whiteboard activity to gauge student competencies in these basic skills will allow you to build from their current level.

Students should keep a note of how many decimal places there were in the original numbers to be multiplied, and so how many there need to be in the answer. This will help students to remember that they need to do something after completing the integer multiplication.

Plenary

Ask students work in pairs to make up both mental and written calculations for their partner to do, using whatever level of difficulty they are comfortable with, but aiming to extend one another.

Exercise commentary

Question 1 – Weaker students will need to revisit the work on mental methods for whole numbers.

Question 2 – Encourage students to use the standard method and to estimate the size of their answers as a check.

Question 3 – Students can work out each of these using a mental or written method. This is an opportunity for paired work, encouraging students to discuss the different methods they use.

Question 4 – This provides a good opportunity to link to previous learning on powers of 10 (see **1a**).

Question 5 – Once students are confident with the whole number multiplication part of each question, the important skill to learn is to write the answers with the decimal point in the correct place. Linking to the previous work on powers of 10 and emphasising the need to estimate are useful ways to support their learning.

Question 6 – Three practical applications of the skills learned in this section.

Question 7 – This could be a useful activity to precede the work on multiplying decimals and could replace the time spent on question **2**.

Answers

1	a	19.84	b	0.17	c	4.32	d	0.135
	e	31.5	f	1.8	g	83.7	h	1.66

2	a	884	b	3526	c	1890	d	2492
	e	3432	f	8125	g	16512	h	19536

3	a	88.2	b	2.8	c	21.6	d	350.9
	e	94.3	f	4.235	g	58.8	h	83.64

4 a i 38.92   ii 3.892
     iii 389200 iv 389.2
  b Students' answers

5	a	20.65	b	27.12	c	80.6	d	143.1
	e	6.3	f	16.12	g	156.94	h	241.3
	i	141.21	j	225.72	k	576.15	l	62.64
	m	72.24	n	13.395	o	5.852	p	33.012

6 a £14.10   b 12.304 rounded to £12.30
  c i £5.60 ii £292

7 a 13328   b $3 \times 4 \times 5 \times 6 \times 7 = 2520$
  c $753 \times 64 = 48192$ d Students' answers

7c Dividing decimals

Objectives

- Use known facts to derive unknown facts (L6)
- Extend mental methods of calculation, working with decimals, fractions, percentages, factors, powers and roots (L6)
- Solve problems mentally (L6)
- Divide by decimals by transforming to division by an integer (L6)
- Understand the effects of multiplying and dividing by numbers between 0 and 1 (L7)

Key ideas	Resources
1 Understanding and applying place value to support mental calculations with decimals 2 Dividing decimals effectively and efficiently	Divide decimals by whole numbers (1008) Dice Mini whiteboards

Simplification	Extension
Weaker students may need plenty of practice at dividing smaller whole numbers by smaller integers, for example, $45 \div 3$ and $65 \div 5$. This will help students use the 'chunking' method. Encourage students to write down some parts of the times table for each divisor. For example, in question **1a** it would be useful to write down $10 \times 6 = 60$ and $5 \times 6 = 30$, *etc*.	Students could practise more real-life problems similar to question **6** involving selecting the information necessary to first form a division calculation and then to solve it. More able students could attempt to divide smaller decimals by larger decimals $0.0735 \div 0.68$.

Literacy	Links
Check equivalent vocabulary of division with students. Use and compare the language clues given in the word problems indicating 'divide'. Include different written forms of division such as 35/3 as well as $35 \div 3$. Where a division results in a remainder, share/remind students of all three approaches to recording such a result – as a remainder, as a fraction or as a decimal.	Human cells divide in two ways. Cells not involved in reproduction divide by a process called mitosis to produce cells identical to the original cell. Reproductive cells divide by a process called meiosis to form gametes which contain half the number of chromosomes of the original cell. There is more about mitosis and meiosis at http://www.pbs.org/wgbh/nova/miracle/divide.html and an interactive activity at http://www.biologyinmotion.com/cell_division/index.html

Alternative approach

Model an example of equivalent division spider diagram with a centre of say $390 \div 15 = 26$. Add legs showing for example $3900 \div 150$; $39 \div 1.5$, $78 \div 3$; and so on. Encourage students to offer suggestions using mini whiteboards and address any misconcpetions that arise. Students can repeat this task in pairs using a different division statement. Students may apply this to **q1** of the exercise having found the results first. Encourage students to use a written approach to a division using mini whiteboards, then discuss and share their approaches before consolidating and extending appropriately. When students have a reasonable level of confidence challenge them to consider the statement 'division makes a value smaller'. Discuss in pairs whether the statements is always/sometimes/never true and use examples to justify any decisions made.

Checkpoint

Find $375 \div 0.3$ (1250)

Find $577 \div 6.5$ ($88 \text{ r } 5$; 88.77; $88\frac{10}{13}$)

Number Decimal calculations

Starter – Make the most

Ask students to draw six boxes in a line and then enter a multiplication sign into one of the intermediate boxes. Throw a dice five times. After each throw, ask the students to enter the score into one of the remaining boxes. Students then multiply the two resulting numbers together. Highest result wins.

Can be differentiated by the number of boxes or by restricting the position of the operator.

Teaching notes

The processes in this spread require accuracy in dividing integers correctly. Some students have difficulty in dividing by single digit numbers, in performing other simple mental calculations and in using long division.

Revision of these basic processes, possibly starting with a whole-class mini whiteboard activity to gauge student competencies, will allow more secure progression for the students.

Plenary

The strategies for multiplying and dividing using factors and partitioning are similar but have important differences. In the first examples, when 15 is factored into 5 × 3 for division, you have to divide by both 5 and 3; when partitioning for multiplication you can use either number but in division it must be the dividend (388) that is partitioned and not the divisor (12). Review and summarise the similarities and differences between the processes with the class.

Exercise commentary

Question 1 – No remainders.

Question 2 – Students might need to break down some of the divisions using the partitioning method into three steps, for example, in part **h**, 700 ÷ 12 could be written as 600 ÷ 12 + 60 ÷ 12 + 40 ÷ 12 = 50 + 5 + 3 R4 = 58 R4.

Question 3 – Remind students to work to two decimal places if they want to give an answer rounded to 1dp.

Question 4 – Watch out for the answers to parts **j** and **l** where the answers are bigger than the dividend. This makes a good link to question **6** on dividing by numbers less than one.

Question 5 – Here students have to construct the division calculations by selecting the appropriate pieces of information from that given in each part of the question. This skill is worth highlighting to the students.

Question 6 – Students could use a calculator if time is short but otherwise it provides plenty of meaningful practice of division and multiplication of decimals.

Answers

1	a 17	b 13	c 16	d 23
	e 42	f 24	g 41	h 23
	i 23	j 31	k 22	l 21

2	a 20 R 10	b 23 R 1	c 25	d 33 R 5
	e 30 R 15	f 12 R 2	g 13	h 58 R 4
	i 38	j 44	k 24	l 32

3	a 2.4	b 6.4	c 2.7	d 5.4
	e 6.9	f 21.7	g 14.1	h 24.1
	i 6.1	j 5.4	k 4.4	l 2.1

4	a 220	b 340	c 340	d 170
	e 135.1	f 232	g 335.7	h 230
	i 124.5	j 461.4	k 224.8	l 1070

5 a 10.3 m/s   b 15.9 km
  c i £3.20   ii 0.95 kg

6 a i 504   ii 288   iii 257.14   iv 450
   Multiplying by numbers larger than one and dividing by numbers less than one makes the answer bigger.
  b Students' answers

Dividing decimals

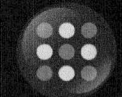

7d Using a calculator

Objectives

- Consolidate use of the rules of arithmetic and inverse operations (L6)
- Understand the order of precedence of operations, including powers (L6)
- Use the function keys for powers, roots and fractions (L6)
- Use brackets and the memory (L6)
- Use the constant, π and sign change keys (L7)
- Knowing not to round during intermediate steps of a calculation (L7)

Key ideas	Resources
1 Understand and apply the order of operations 2 Interpret calculation sentences correctly and carry out the calculation. 3 Use a calculator efficiently and effectively	Order of operations (1167)

Simplification	Extension
Begin with simple examples that involve multiplication, division, addition and subtraction only and let students check their answers using a scientific calculator. Introduce examples using brackets and explain that brackets are used when we need to do the operations in a different order to that prescribed by BIDMAS, so brackets always come first.	Students could extend question **5** to larger numbers than 10 or invent similar problems to those found in question **4**. The best use and development of calculator skills will always be in the context of solving problems where it is appropriate to use a calculator, for example percentage problems, checking answers, *etc*. Students could extend question **4** by playing the Countdown game on a computer and writing their solutions using the correct order of operations.

Literacy	Links
Writing and reading calculation sentences in order to give meaning and correct interpretation of operational order should be explicitly addressed.	Early calculators were large and bulky. The first slimline pocket calculator was invented by Sir Clive Sinclair in 1972. Sinclair went on to introduce the UK's first digital wristwatch, the first pocket TV, and his latest invention is the folding A-bike. There is more about Sinclair's inventions at http://www.nvg.ntnu.no/sinclair/

Alternative approach

Challenge pairs of students to decide whether the statement $4 \times 3^2 = (4 \times 3)^2$ is true or not, being prepared to justify the decision. A further statement: $-3^2 = -(3^2) = (-3)^2$ may also be discussed and calculators used to help explore any equivalence or not. Ask students to explain calculator entries for questions such as those in **2** onwards before tackling them, thus exposing any misconceptions that may arise. Ask students to consider why it is *not* a good idea to carry out a calculation sentence with a calculator, recording steps/answers on route to the final result in pairs. Open and share these results and the conclusions, thus tackling efficiency of calculator use and also the dangers of rounding before a final result.

Checkpoint

Find the answer to: $\{4.5^2 + (7.5 - 0.46)\}^2$ (744.7441)

Starter – Estimate

Write decimal numbers on the board, for example, 3.2, 14.81, 5.9, 7.06, 27.9, 79.4, 69.4, 11.8. Ask questions.

Which two numbers have a product close to 90? (3.2, 27.9)

Which number has a square root close to 9? (79.4)

What calculation has an answer close to 2? (14.81 ÷ 7.06)

Which two numbers have a product close to 490? (69.4, 7.06) *etc*.

$a \div b = 2.023255814$. a and b each represent a two-digit number. Challenge students to find them! ($a = 87, b = 43$)

If necessary give hints, for example, a is greater than nine squared.

Teaching notes

Emphasise the importance of estimating the size of answers to complex calculations before entering them in the calculator, so any error involving orders of operation are more-easily identified.

When students are unsure of the key sequence, encourage them to write down the same sum but with simpler numbers, which they can calculate themselves mentally, and see if a key sequence produces the same answer. For example $\frac{7.3+19.2^2}{\sqrt{8.71-3.06}}$ and $\frac{5+3^2}{\sqrt{9-5}}$ require the same key sequence for the operations but the second can be done without a calculator, so checking the sequence.

Plenary

Invite feedback from students as to which problems and key sequences they found most difficult in the exercises, and encourage suggestions (for example, where using extra brackets might help) from other students.

Ask students to work in pairs to set questions with different numbers of intermediate stages, to investigate how great the error can be if values are rounded each time

Exercise commentary

Question 1 – A good activity for students to work in pairs. Encourage students to try to convince their partners that they are correct.

Question 2 – Students need to 'see' the hidden brackets indicated by the division, and should be advised to rewrite the calculation as a bracketed division as in the first example.

Question 3 – It might be necessary to revise work on rounding answers to two decimal places.

Question 4 – A good problem-solving activity which is ideal as a paired activity. Students could explain to the rest of the class any strategies they have used to find the answer.

Question 5 – This problem could be extended for numbers past 10 and might be a challenge that can be revisited with some classes or become a useful homework activity. Students could also try alternative numbers such as four 3s.

Answers

1 a i X   iii $(5 + 3)^2 \times 2$
   b i Y   iii $10 + 3^2 - 1$
   c i Y   iii $(8 - 5)^2$
   d i X   iii $-(5)^2 + 8$
   e i Y   iii $160 \div (8 \times 5) + (2 \times 3)^2$
   f i X   iii $(2 \times 3^2) \div (2 \times 3)$

2 a 14.4   b 14   c 1.7

3 a 0.60   b 21.97   c 11.15

4 a $\frac{\sqrt{2+34}}{6} + 5 = 6$ b $\frac{2^4 \times 5 \times 3}{4 \times 6} = 10$

5 a $1 = 4/4 \times 4/4$ $2 = 4/4 + 4/4$
      $3 = (4 + 4 + 4)/4$ $4 = \sqrt{4} \times \sqrt{4} \times 4/4$
      $5 = \sqrt{4} \times \sqrt{4} + 4/4$ $6 = (4 + 4)/4 + 4$
      $7 = 4 + 4 - 4/4$ $8 = 4 \times 4/4 + 4$
      $9 = 4 + 4 + 4/4$ $10 = (4 + 4/4) \times \sqrt{4}$

   b Students' answers

Using a calculator

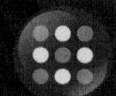

7e Interpreting the calculator display

Objectives	
• Enter numbers and interpret the display in different contexts (extend to negative numbers, fractions, time)	(L5)
• Make and justify estimates and approximations of calculations	(L7)

Key ideas	Resources
1 Maintain a sense of the context of a problem and its results or solutions. 2 Use a calculator effectively and efficiently	Calculator problems from NRICH: http://nrich.maths.org/public/leg.php?code=5028

Simplification	Extension
Weaker students will need to have division calculations set in contextual problems such as slicing up pizzas. These are more visual and easier to interpret for whole number and fractional remainders. For example, pizzas are cut into six slices. Jake eats 19 slices. How many pizzas does he eat? It is easy to interpret the remainder of one as either one piece or $\frac{1}{6}$ of a whole pizza.	Students would benefit from more practice at converting decimal remainders into whole number remainders. They could be encouraged to make up their own questions which involve units of time and share these with the rest of the class

Literacy	Links
Revisit the strategies that help students interpret word problems effectively including identifying key vocabulary and information by underlineing or highlighting. Make sure that students include the appropriate units or descriptions relevant to each context of any problems both verbally and in writing.	The display used in a calculator is made up of liquid crystal sandwiched between layers of glass. The molecules in a liquid crystal are more ordered than in a normal liquid and can be aligned precisely by an electric current. When a current passes through a segment on the display, it becomes opaque and forms part of the digit to be displayed. There is an explanation of how calculators work at http://www.explainthatstuff.com/calculators.html

Alternative approach

Encourage students to ask themselves whether any answer makes sense, by modelling a problem and discussing the sense of a result. Students can support each other by working in pairs and asking themselves the same question, covering sensible estimation as well as interpretation of calculator results. Further calculator problems can be used from the NRICH pages referenced where stage 3 and 4 problems are likely to be appropriate. More able students may even try a stage 5 problem.

Checkpoint

When a whole number is divided by 34, the result is 15.88235294.

What is the value of that whole number and what is the remainder? (540; remainder is 30)

126 Number Decimal calculations

Starter – One, two, three, four

Ask students to make as many numbers up to 20 as they can by using all the digits 1, 2, 3, 4 and any operations for each number. For example,
$(4 - 1) \times 3 + 2 = 11$

Can be extended by challenging students to make each number keeping the digits 1, 2, 3 and 4 in numerical order, for example, $(1 + 2) \div 3 + \sqrt{4} = 3$

Teaching notes

Sometimes students view the calculator as magic rather than as a tool which needs careful use and thought in its application. The worked examples illustrate some of the contexts such as money or time where a little thought is required to produce answers which are appropriate to the context.

In some of the problems, a division has to be rounded up to the next whole number. Students are often poor at communication when solving problems in real contexts and here there is an opportunity to encourage them to communicate – to offer brief reasons why rounding up is appropriate.

Plenary

Ask students to work in pairs to identify any contexts from the exercise where rounding had to be up to the next integer rather than to the nearest whole number. Take feedback from the whole class and ask if they can think of any other situations where they would have to do the same thing.

Exercise commentary

Question 1 – A question to practise estimation skills. Ensure that students estimate their answers when using a calculator.

Question 2 – A good opportunity for a class discussion to emphasise that context is important to interpretation of the remainder.

Questions 3 and 4 – These questions are about choosing the correct form for writing the remainder. If a calculator is used then the conversion of the decimal remainder to a whole number remainder becomes important in some cases.

Question 5 – These questions focus on the conversion of a decimal remainder to a whole number remainder.

Question 6 – An activity that can easily be extended into 'have you lived longer than a 10 million seconds?'; 'could you live to be a million hours?' etc.

Answers

1. a 1444 $40 \times 40 = 1600$
   b 288.9 $130 \div 0.5 = 260$

2. a £4.29   b 4 R 2   c $\frac{30}{7}$

3. a 24 m 58 cm   b 64 min 36 sec
   c 43 m 15 cm 5 mm

4. a 13   b $12\frac{11}{12}$

5. a 5 jars, 1 kg sugar   b 5

6. 3 years, 8 weeks, 6 days, 9 hours, 46 mins and 39 secs

Interpreting the calculator display

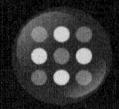

7 Decimal calculations – MySummary

Key outcomes	Quick check
Consolidate mental and written strategies for addition and subtraction of decimals. L6	Work out **a** 4.36 + 7.21 (11.57) **b** 32.58 – 21.47 (11.11) **c** 7.2 + 6.5 – 2.8 (10.9)
Consolidate mental and written strategies for multiplication and division of decimals. L6	Work out **a** 13.2 × 6 (79.2) **b** 1.8 × 6.3 (11.34) **c** 78 ÷ 0.3 (260)
Know and use the correct order of operations. L6	Work out **a** $3^2 + 9 \times 4$ (45) **b** $4(2 + 7) - 5^2$ (11) **c** $13 - 7 \times 8 + 2 \times 3$ (-37)
Use the function keys on a calculator and interpret the calculator display. L7	Work out how many days there are in 778 hours? Give your answer in days and hours. (32 days, 25 hours)

MyMaths extra support

Lesson/online homework			Description
Estimating Inro	1002	L4	Use rounding to estimate answer to simple calculations
Division chunking	1021	L4	Division by chunking and subtracting numbers
Long division	1041	L5	Long division using written methods
Mixed sums all numbers	1345	L4	Adding and subtracting with numbers of different sizes

MyReview

7 MySummary

Check out
You should now be able to ...

	Test it → Questions
✓ Consolidate mental and written strategies for addition and subtraction of decimals.	1 – 2
✓ Consolidate mental and written strategies for multiplication and division of decimals.	3 – 6
✓ Know and use the correct order of operations.	7
✓ Use the function keys on a calculator and interpret the calculator display.	8 – 9

Language	Meaning	Example
Partitioning	Splitting a number into parts to make a mental calculation easier.	$5.7 \cdot 6.6 = 5.7 \cdot 6 \cdot 0.6$
Factor	Factors of a number divide into it exactly.	The factors of 6 are 1, 2, 3 and 6
Divisor	The number you divide by.	In $10 \div 5 = 2$, 5 is the divisor
Order of operations	A standard order of doing operations in a calculation: **B** brackets **I** powers/indices **D** division **M** multiplication **A** addition **S** subtraction.	$3 + (4^2 - 7 \times 2)$ $= 3 + (16 - 14)$ $= 5$
Rounding errors	Errors that occur by rounding an intermediate answer in a calculation.	
Remainder	The number left after a division.	$26 \div 5 = 5$ remainder 1
Estimate	Work out an approximate answer.	An estimate of £7.56 shared between 9 people would be: $8 \div 10 = 0.8$ or 80p.

Number Decimal calculations

Question commentary

Question 1 – In parts **c** and **d** students should do two separate calculations.

Question 2 – Students need to extract the information from the question and set out two separate calculations.

Questions 3 to **6** – Long and short multiplication and division can be used along with informal mental methods where appropriate. Ensure students are giving their answers in an appropriate form.

Question 7 – Ensure students take account of 'hidden' brackets (parts **b** and **d**).

Questions 8 and **9** – Writing the remainder in the correct form is important in these questions.

7 MyReview

1. Work out these without using a calculator.
    a. $0.383 + 5.48 + 89.1$
    b. $103.2 + 25.11 + 1.57$
    c. $9.56 - 0.892 + 0.09$
    d. $44.42 - 0.147 - 0.0319$

2. Three adults in a lift have a combined weight of 195.4 kg.
    The weights of two of the adults are 65.03 kg and 77 kg. What is the weight of the third adult?

3. Work these out using a written method.
    a. 3.1×4.5
    b. 0.4×57.4
    c. 31.8×0.28
    d. 816×1.58

4. Carrots cost 1.32 per kg and come in 750 g bags. What is the cost of six bags?

5. Work out these, give your answer with a remainder.
    a. $39 \div 7$
    b. $437 \div 8$
    c. $699 \div 9$
    d. $626 \div 12$

6. Work out these, give your answer to 1 dp where appropriate.
    a. $836 \div 3.8$
    b. $741 \div 3.5$
    c. $509 \div 0.8$
    d. $767 \div 1.9$

7. Calculate these, giving your answer to 2 dp where appropriate.
    a. $(47 - 2^5) \times 3$
    b. $\dfrac{\sqrt{130 + 2 \times 9}}{25 - 17.1}$
    c. $14 \times (7.3 - 2.4)^3$
    d. $\dfrac{(8.1 - 9.9)^2}{\sqrt{19.3 + 7.8}}$

8. Convert these measurements.
    a. 2095 cm to m and cm
    b. 1678 s to minutes and seconds
    c. 5243 mm to m, cm and mm
    d. 49088 minutes to weeks, days, hours and minutes

9. Terrence has eight 1.35 l bottles of orange juice. He fills 250 ml glasses with the juice.
    a. How many glasses can he fill completely?
    b. How much orange juice is left over?

What next?

Score	
0 – 4	Your knowledge of this topic is still developing. To improve look at Formative test: 3B-7; MyMaths: 1007, 1008, 1010, 1011 and 1167
5 – 7	You are gaining a secure knowledge of this topic. To improve look at InvisiPen: 128, 129, 131, 132, 133 and 134
8 – 9	You have mastered this topic. Well done, you are ready to progress!

MyMaths.co.uk

Answers

1. a 94.963 b 129.88 c 8.758 d 44.2411
2. 53.37 kg
3. a 13.95 b 22.96 c 8.904 d 1289.28
4. £5.94
5. a 5 R 4 b 54 R 5 c 77 R 6 d 52 R 2
6. a 220 b 211.7 c 636.3 d 403.7
7. a 45 b 1.54 c 1647.09 d 0.62
8. a 20 m, 95 cm b 27 min, 58 s
    c 5 m, 24 cm, 3 mm
    d 4 weeks, 6 days, 2 hours, 8 min
9. a 43 b 50 ml

7 MyPractice

7a

1 Work out these calculations using a written method.

a 452.7 + 86.6
b 753.68 + 67
c 82.65 + 58.4
d 939.8 − 45.9
e 687.1 − 72.46
f 852.17 − 690.4

2 Work out these calculations using an appropriate method.

a 4.27 + 475.6 + 3
b 26.4 + 894.2 + 58.72
c 65.7 + 831.4 − 82.3
d 4567.4 + 68.74 − 23.8
e 364.3 − 73 − 54.4
f 42.4 + 526.4 − 74.69

7b

3 Work out these products using a written method. Remember to do a mental estimate first.

a 6 × 3.97
b 4 × 6.58
c 24 × 4.8
d 43 × 5.7
e 38 × 0.75
f 44 × 0.48
g 53 × 6.97
h 32 × 18.3
i 35 × 7.87
j 61 × 4.26
k 73 × 2.78
l 7.4 × 13.6
m 6.7 × 14.2
n 6.3 × 8.25
o 7.2 × 1.66
p 4.7 × 6.86

4 Nigella buys 3.2 kg of olives.
The olives cost £4.78 per kilogram.
How much do the olives cost Nigella?

7c

5 Work out these divisions using an appropriate method.
Give your answer to 1 dp where appropriate.

a 756 ÷ 4.2
b 756 ÷ 3.8
c 756 ÷ 2.1
d 754 ÷ 5.8
e 754 ÷ 5.9
f 754 ÷ 6
g 414 ÷ 1.8
h 414 ÷ 1.9
i 414 ÷ 2
j 386 ÷ 0.6
k 386 ÷ 0.5
l 406 ÷ 0.7

6 Boris runs 60 m in 5.9 seconds.

a What is his speed in metres per second?
b How long would it take Boris to run 100 m at this speed?

How many metres does he travel in each second?

7d

7 Calculate these giving your answer to 1 dp where appropriate.

a $\dfrac{(5+6)^3}{\sqrt{35}+41}$
b $\dfrac{(4+3^2)(2-5)^2}{(18-3)^2}$
c $\dfrac{(12-3.5)^2 \sqrt{28-4.5}}{(7-2.5)^2}$

8 Calculate these giving your answer to 2 dp where appropriate.

a $\left(\dfrac{4}{15}+\dfrac{5}{3}\right)^2$
b $\sqrt{45-4.8^2+13.2}$
c $14 \times (2.4 - 0.63)^3$

7e

9 Calculate these divisions using your calculator. Give the answer in the form specified.

a 48 kg ÷ 9   (a decimal to 2 dp)
b 48 sheep ÷ 9 (a whole number remainder)
c 48 pizzas ÷ 9 (a fraction)

10 Convert these measurements to the units in brackets

a 3867 seconds (into minutes and seconds)
b 4126.7 m   (into km, m and cm)
c 3675 ml   (into litres and ml)
d 7395 minutes (into days, hours and minutes)

11 Use your calculator to solve these problems.

a Sezer has 110.5 hours of music downloaded on her computer.
She accidentally deletes 80.15 hours of her music (luckily she has a back-up)!
How much music does Sezer have remaining on her computer?
Give your answer
  i in hours and minutes
  ii in minutes.
b Véronique puts carpet in her bedroom.
The bedroom is rectangular with length 4.23 m and width 3.6 m.
The carpet cost £6.79 per m² and can only be bought by the square metre.
  i Calculate the floor area of the bedroom.
  ii Calculate the cost of the carpet that is needed to cover the floor.

Question commentary

Questions 1 and **2** – Ensure students line up decimal points and also do two separate calculations where appropriate (question **2**, parts **c** to **f**).

Questions 3 and **4** – Lots of practice before an applied question.

Questions 5 and **6** – Lots of practice before an applied question again.

Questions 7 and **8** – Remind students to check for 'hidden' brackets in division calculations and to round answers appropriately. Estimation of the size of the final answer should also be emphasised.

Questions 9 to **11** – Ensure students give the remainders in the appropriate form. In question **11**, students will need to extract the required information from the text and select the appropriate calculation(s).

Answers

1. a 539.3   b 820.68   c 141.05   d 893.9
   e 614.64   f 161.77

2. a 482.87   b 979.32   c 814.8   d 4612.34
   e 236.9   f 494.11

3. a 23.82   b 26.32   c 115.2   d 245.1
   e 28.5   f 21.12   g 369.41   h 585.6
   i 275.45   j 259.86   k 202.94   l 100.64
   m 95.14   n 51.975   o 11.952   p 32.242

4. £15.30

5. a 180   b 198.9   c 360   d 130
   e 127.8   f 125.7   g 230   h 217.9
   i 207   j 643.3   k 772   l 580

6. a 10.17 m/s   b 9.83 seconds

7. a 152.7   b 0.52   c 17.3

8. a 3.74   b 5.93   c 77.63

9. a 5.33 kg b 5 R 3   c $5\frac{1}{3}$

10. a 64 mins 27 secs   b 4 km 126 m 70 cm
    c 3 litres 675ml   d 5 days 3 hours 15 mins

11. a i 30 hours, 21 mins   ii 1821 mins
    b i 15.228 m^2 iii £135.80

MyPractice

8 Statistics

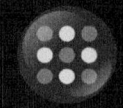

Learning outcomes	
S1	Describe, interpret and compare observed distributions of a single variable through: appropriate graphical representation involving discrete, continuous and grouped data; and appropriate measures of central tendency (mean, mode, median) and spread (range, consideration of outliers) (L6)
S2	Construct and interpret appropriate tables, charts, and diagrams, including frequency tables, bar charts, pie charts, and pictograms for categorical data, and vertical line (or bar) charts for ungrouped and grouped numerical data (L6/7)
S3	Describe simple mathematical relationships between 2 variables (bivariate data) in observational and experimental contexts and illustrate using scatter graphs (L7)

Introduction	Prior knowledge
The chapter starts by looking at how we plan a statistical project and then moves on to methods of data collection. Types of data are covered here also. Drawing up frequency tables, statistical diagrams and the calculation of averages are all covered before a section on interpreting statistical diagrams. Correlation is covered in section 8h before a section on averages from grouped data. The final two sections are on comparing distributions and communicating the findings from a statistical enquiry.	Students should already know how to… • Find the mean, median, mode and range of simple data sets • Construct simple statistical diagrams
	Starter problem
The introduction discusses the spurious use of statistics by politicians and advertisers to support their policies or products. In fact the majority of 'statistical' claims made in newspapers and in advertisements are based on very little supportive data and evidence. Small sample sizes, hidden alternative results and a lack of controlled conditions allow the claims to be made but we should always take time to consider the nature of these claims.	The starter problem is about correlation. If we consider the possible reasons for such a claim, such as 'taller people have longer legs', 'taller people have a bigger stride', etc. we can see where such a hypothesis might come from. The students are invited to investigate the truth of this statement and can therefore set up a practical investigation. Heights can be measured in class and the jumping part can also take part in class or outdoors as appropriate. A standing jump is probably the easiest to control since running speed is obviously a factor in the distance someone can jump (just look at the speed the long and triple jumpers get to on the runway in an athletics event).
More rigorous statistical testing takes place over longer periods of time with large, unbiased samples and a high degree of control over the conditions. Medical testing, for example, uses what are called 'control groups' of people who think they are getting the drug on trial but are in fact getting a placebo.	You can also use an investigation like this to discuss data collection methods, the validity of the sample and how we might process the results in order to prevent false or dubious conclusions being reached.

Resources

MyMaths
Frequency tables and bar charts			1193	Mean and mode	1200
Mean of grouped data 1	1201	Median and range	1203	Drawing pie charts	1207
Scatter graphs	1213	Two-way tables	1214	Types of data	1248
Questionnaires	1249				

Online assessment
Chapter test	3B–8	Organising data	411	Collecting data	413
Formative test	3B–8	Planning an enquiry	414	Pictograms	421
Summative test	3B–8	Bar charts	422	Pie charts	423
		Line graphs data	424	Histograms	426
		Scatter graphs	427	Averages of a list	441
		Averages from tables	442	Averages of a list	443
		Interpreting graphs	444	Averages from tables	446
		Averages from tables	447	Writing statistical reports	448

InvisiPen solutions

Topic scheme

Teaching time = 11 lessons/4 weeks

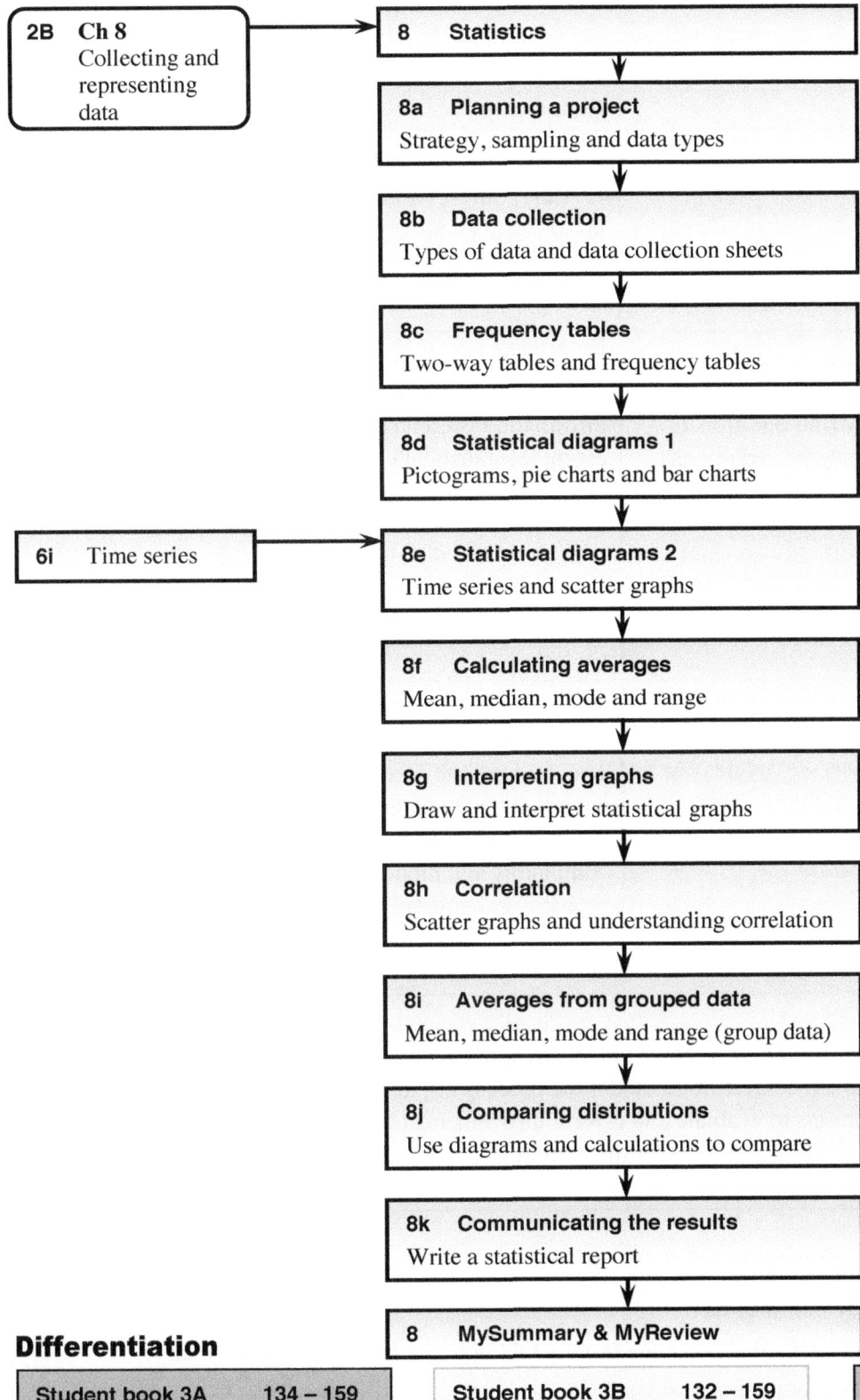

- **2B Ch 8** Collecting and representing data → **8 Statistics**
  - **8a Planning a project** — Strategy, sampling and data types
  - **8b Data collection** — Types of data and data collection sheets
  - **8c Frequency tables** — Two-way tables and frequency tables
  - **8d Statistical diagrams 1** — Pictograms, pie charts and bar charts
  - **6i Time series** → **8e Statistical diagrams 2** — Time series and scatter graphs
  - **8f Calculating averages** — Mean, median, mode and range
  - **8g Interpreting graphs** — Draw and interpret statistical graphs
  - **8h Correlation** — Scatter graphs and understanding correlation
  - **8i Averages from grouped data** — Mean, median, mode and range (group data)
  - **8j Comparing distributions** — Use diagrams and calculations to compare
  - **8k Communicating the results** — Write a statistical report
  - **8 MySummary & MyReview**

Differentiation

Student book 3A 134 – 159	Student book 3B 132 – 159	Student book 3C 130 – 155
Planning projects and collecting data	Planning projects and collecting data	Planning projects and collecting data
Two-way tables, statistical diagrams and the interpretation thereof	Two-way tables, statistical diagrams and the interpretation thereof	Statistical diagrams and the interpretation thereof
Scatter diagrams and correlation	Scatter diagrams and correlation	Scatter diagrams and correlation
Averages and range	Averages and range	Averages and range
Writing statistical reports	Writing statistical reports	Cumulative frequency and box plots

Introduction 133

8a Planning a project

Objectives

- Discuss how different sets of data relate to the problem (L6)
- Identify possible primary or secondary sources (L6)
- Determine the sample size and most appropriate degree of accuracy (L6)
- Suggest a problem to explore using statistical methods, frame questions and raise conjectures (L7)

Key ideas	Resources
1 Understand the importance of the planning stage 2 Recognise and use accurately the vocabulary of data	Types of data (1248) Five Hypotheses and data: Unit M1, from http://www.nationalstemcentre.org.uk/elibrary/resource/4980/year-eight-handling-data-mini-pack

Simplification	Extension
Writing good, measurable hypotheses can be challenging and some students may find question **1** difficult. A group work approach may be useful - ask pairs of students to suggest improvements to the conjectures given, and then exchange these with another pair. As a group of four, read, evaluate and suggest improvements to the conjectures from each pair.	Ask students to identify examples of statistical information presented in published materials - for example, statistical claims in advertisements. What claims are being made? How precise are the claims? What statistics are being used, and how were they collected? Are the claims justified?

Literacy	Links
Knowing, understanding and using the vocabulary given on p.134 is key in this section. Check by using matching activities, group collections of examples as well as evaluation activities of the appropriateness in a variety of contexts.	In the UK, the content of advertisements is regulated by The Advertising Standards Authority (The ASA). The ASA makes sure that advertisers follow the advertising standards codes so that advertisements are not misleading, harmful or offensive. It investigates complaints and monitors advertisements, sales promotions or direct marketing in all kinds of media. There is more information about the ASA at http://www.asa.org.uk/asa/

Alternative approach

Introductory activites focused on the literacy will help students to apply accurate vocabulary and reasoning in both this and later lessons. Use Carla's conjecture to model the process of planning with the whole class. Students may then work in small groups to evaluate and offer improvements on other conjecture or hypotheses such as those given in the resources. Group feedback of their findings can then progress to consideration of data accuracy and relevance.

Checkpoint

Are the following primary or secondary data?

a Asking your classmates how many pets they have. (Primary)

b Looking up the times of the 100m race winners for the last six Olympic games. (Secondary)

Are the following categorical, discrete or continuous data?

a The number of brothers and sisters your classmates have. (Discrete)

b The heights of the trees in the school grounds. (Continuous)

c The colours of the cars passing the school gates. (Categorical)

Starter – Today's number is… 4.9

Ask questions based on 4.9. For example

What is double 4.9? (9.8)
Give the fourth multiple of 4.9? (19.6)
What is 10% of 4.9? (0.49)
Subtract 4.9 from 17. (12.1) *etc*

Teaching notes

Discuss the differences between primary and secondary data, and the advantages and disadvantages of using each. Secondary data may be hard to find to answer the particular question in which you are interested but collecting enough data yourself to get reliable answers also may be difficult.

Conjectures need to be a specific statement about the question of interest. Ask students to produce different conjectures relating to the same investigation. For the example shown 'height does not make any difference in how well people do in the long jump' is an alternative conjecture.

Thinking about what data is to be collected, and how it is to be recorded, are key aspects of planning a project which are often left until too late in the process.

Plenary

Many students find writing about maths difficult. It is worth having a class discussion about the discursive answers needed for the questions in this exercise so that students can discuss how to construct good responses with their peers.

Exercise commentary

Question 1 – Discuss the importance of clear, measurable hypotheses.

Question 2 – Invite students to explain their choices of data sources to the class before asking them to write this down in a sentence.

Question 3 – Emphasises the idea that measurements should be as precise as necessary but no more.

Question 4 – Ask students to design an experiment to test this claim. Refer to the sample sizes now shown on some television advertisements.

Answers

1 All of these statements are too vague to test, and should be made more precise. For example:
   a Average winning times in this year's track events will be lower than last year.
   b Runners have better average times on a dry track than a wet one.
   c Year 11 pupils have faster average times in track events than Year 7 pupils.
2 Students' answers.
3 Jason is correct that measuring to the nearest millimetre will be too time-consuming and difficult, but measuring to the nearest 10cm will probably be too imprecise. Measuring to the nearest centimetre will probably be a good compromise.
4 The claim may be fair, but you would want to find out what evidence there was to support it. The company could carry out an experiment to test the claim – perhaps offering a sample of cats a choice of food, and recording how many cats choose Kitty Cuisine.

8b Data collection

Objectives

- Design a survey or experiment to capture the necessary data from one or more sources (L6)
- Design, trial and if necessary refine data collection sheets (L6)

Key ideas	Resources
1 Understand and use the vocabulary of data collections 2 Evalaute and design data collections	Questionnaires (1249) Just What is a Sample? Do we need to ask everyone? http://www.censusatschool.org.uk/resources/data-handling Evaluating questionnaires: http://www.bbc.co.uk/bitesize/quiz/q84750849

Simplification	Extension
Some students may need to spend more time on questions **1** and **2**, which deal with some of the common issues in designing and improving data collection sheets. For example, students could work in groups to test the improved questionnaire that they design in question **2**, perhaps further refining the design after collecting a small set of data.	Students who make good progress with this work could be encouraged to look at how spreadsheets can be used to collate sets of data collected in a survey. For example, they could be asked to design a spreadsheet to show the results of the survey from question **1**. Some features that could be incorporated include data formats (for example, date, number, general, *etc*.), data validation (for example, cell must contain 'M' or 'F') and filtering and sorting (For example, show women's responses only, or sort data by journey length). This could lead into spreadsheet-based approaches to the charts and summary statistics covered later.

Literacy	Links
Test the vocabulary in this section and include the terms census and sampling, discussing which may be more appropriate in different contexts.	The UK Census is held every ten years but the information collected cannot be released to the general public until one hundred years later. Past census information is invaluable for research into family and social history. The 1921 census will be released in 2021 but then no more until 2051. No Census was held in 1941 due to the Second World War and all the records from the 1931 Census were destroyed in a fire in 1942. The 1901 census can be searched at http://www.ukcensusonline.com/free-search.php

Alternative approach

Ask students to work in pairs to discuss the relevance of each section in Carla's data sheet – e.g. is the name relevant to her survey? Why might it be useful to include on the sheet? And so on. CensusAtSchool resources can be used with pairs of students emphasise the difference between census and sampling. Evaluation of questionnaires such as those in ex. 8b can be followed up with paired responses to the quiz given in BBC Bitesize as given in the resources

Checkpoint

Criticise the following potential survey question:

   'How much money do you spend on lunch?'

Suggest an alternative. (Responses may include adding a timeframe (e.g. 'each day') and adding response boxes)

Statistics and probability   Statistics

Starter – Four in a line

Ask students to draw a 5 × 5 grid and enter the numbers 10 to 34 in any order.
Ask students questions, for example:

What is the mean average of 15, 29 and 43? (29)

The smallest value is 9 and the largest value is 22. What is the range? (13)

The mean of four numbers is 2.5.
What is the total? (10)

Winner is the first student to cross out four in a line.

Teaching notes

Students can be confused because lengths, heights, areas, *etc.* are actually continuous measurements even though the data is listed as 165 cm or 166 cm, making it look very much like discrete data. It is worth making some actual measurements with the class to draw out the process, using rounding before reporting the measurement.

The experience of filling out a questionnaire about themselves provides a valuable insight for students into the process of collecting data and it need not take a long time. Examples designed for school students can be found at http://www.censusatschool.org.uk

Plenary

If students completed one of the CensusAtSchool questionnaires, use it to discuss what questions could be investigated, and how the data collected would be used to answer those questions.

Exercise commentary

Question 1 – Students should use one line of data for each respondent and provide categories for gender, travel mode, distance and duration.

Question 2 – This could form the basis of a class discussion before getting students to write down their answers.

Question 3 – Use a two-way entry table, breaking down data by gender and vehicle type.

Question 4 – The first diagram is useful where a continuous range of responses is possible, for example, rating a recipe.

Question 5 – The overriding consideration is to obtain a reliable set of results. A long questionnaire may not be completed, and questions that are complicated or imprecise may be omitted or answered randomly. Respondents may be more likely to answer a difficult question at the end of a survey, when they have already invested time in the previous answers.

Answers

1 Students' answers

2 a The 'age' and 'television' questions are imprecise and subjective. The final question has overlapping categories (1-2 and 2-3) and a category (0) that isn't needed at all.
  b Students' answers

3 a The data collection sheet should be organised as a two-way table, so that each tally mark records both the gender of the driver and their type of vehicle.
  b Students' answers

4 Students' answers

5 Students' answers

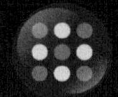

8c Frequency tables

Objectives

- Construct tables for gathering large discrete and continuous sets of raw data, choosing suitable class intervals (L6)
- Design and use two-way tables (L6)

Key ideas	Resources
1 Accurately and efficiently sort raw data into a table 2 Choose and use suuitable class intervals for continuous data	Frequency tables and bar charts (1193) Two way tables (1214) Copies of data sets Frequency tables quiz: http://www.mangahigh.com/en-gb/maths_games/data/representing_data/use_frequency_tables

Simplification	Extension
Providing a copy of the data sets on a separate sheet of paper will allow students to cross off values as they are entered into tally charts. This will help some students to ensure that values are not omitted or repeated.	Some students could investigate the effects of grouping continuous data in different ways. For example, the data in question 4 could be organised in groups of 'width' 5 kg or 10 kg; an appropriate choice depends on the spread of the data and the number of values.

Literacy	Links
Check and confirm use of previously met vocabulary. Ensure that students fully understand notation that is in the form of $A \leq h < B$	The largest shoe size in the world was that of Robert Pershing Wadlow, the world's tallest man, who died in 1940. His American shoe size was 37, about UK size 36 (47 cm long) and he was 2.27m (8ft 11.1in) tall. Robert Wadlow worked as a spokesperson for a shoe company and one of the benefits of his job was that he was supplied with free shoes. There is a picture of one of Robert Wadlow's shoes at http://www.roadsideamerica.com/tip/10147

Alternative approach

It is worth modelling/recapping how students should read a list of data completely just once, tallying appropriately into groups rather than searching for items within in each group separately. It may help to do this in pairs with one reading and the other tallying, then swapping over and checking. Challenge the students to decide on how many groups it is sensible to aim for when organising large data sets. This can be done electronically, showing the same set of data expressed into different groupings. The students will be able to see how an appropirate choice can affect the usefulness of such a data set, and draw conclusions about a sensible number of groups. A simple quiz on frequency tables from MangaHigh in resources may be used to consolidate the knowledge of less confident students.

Checkpoint

Read out the following list of data. Ask students to draw up a suitable data collection table. Then read the list again and ask them to complete it.

Number of peas in a pod: 8, 7, 6, 3, 8, 6, 7, 4, 7, 8, 5, 6, 4, 7, 8, 5

Starter – True or false?

Give statements and ask students if they are true or false. For example,

   The artistes' names at a concert are discrete data. (False, should be categorical)
   The track lengths on CDs are continuous data. (True)
   The sizes of sweatshirts in a store are discrete data. (True) *etc*.

Teaching notes

Transferring data from a list into a frequency table requires a little care and students should be prepared to work methodically through the data list. Although it appears to be more work, using a tally chart to do the transfer is as quick as counting the frequency of each value, or each interval, and is much more reliable.

Values at the boundaries of intervals are most likely to be incorrectly assigned. The choice of the endpoints can help to make this easier. If intervals are in 10s then 160 – 169, 170 – 179, *etc.* are much easier to use accurately than 161 – 170, 171 – 180, *etc*.

The spread gives students experience in summarising data by creating frequency tables and two-way tables. When students use data already presented in summary form they often have little feel for what the data actually represents. The plenary activity may help them visualise the data from a table.

Plenary

Students work in pairs, where one student produces two frequency tables, one for discrete data and one for grouped continuous data. The other student has to produce a list of values which match the frequency tables (there will only be one possible list for the discrete but many for the grouped data). A maximum total frequency of around 15 will mean this should not take too long. Then reverse the roles.

Exercise commentary

Question 1 – A two-way table will have boys/girls and basketball/hockey as the two headings.

Question 2 – A combined tally and frequency table (as shown in the example) can be used in this question.

Question 3 – Students may need to be reminded about the use of the inequality signs.

Question 4 – Students need to design their own class intervals. This can be done in various ways. Ask what are the advantages of having more or fewer intervals: ease of compilation versus level of detail.

Question 5 – The table here will need to show grouped continuous data for the heights, and discrete data for the shoe sizes.

Answers

1

	Boys	Girls
Hockey	4	8
Basketball	11	7

2

Shoe size	Tally	Frequency
4	||||-|||	8
5	||||- ||||-||	12
6	||||- ||||-||||-||	17
7	||||- ||||-|||	13
8	||||-||	7
9					3

3

Height, h cm	Frequency
$155 \leq h < 160$	2
$160 \leq h < 165$	9
$165 \leq h < 170$	10
$170 \leq h < 175$	4
$175 \leq h < 180$	4
$180 \leq h < 185$	3

4

Weight, w kg	Frequency
$40 \leq w < 50$	2
$50 \leq w < 60$	13
$60 \leq w < 70$	10
$70 \leq w < 80$	6
$80 \leq w < 90$	1

5 See master Answers file

Frequency tables

8d Statistical diagrams 1

Objectives

- Construct graphical representations, on paper and using ICT, and identify which are most useful in the context of the problem. Include
  - pie charts for categorical data,
  - bar charts and frequency diagrams for discrete and continuous data (L6)
- Select, construct and modify, on paper and using ICT, suitable graphical representations to progress an enquiry and identify key features present in the data (L6)

Key ideas	Resources
1 Revisiting types of statistical diagrams and their key features 2 Evaluating strengths and weaknesses of these diagrams to inform decision making	Drawing pie charts (1207) Mini whiteboards Newspaper articles containing graphs Data Unit Library (Show Me OM3; Mixed Charts M3.3): http://www.nationalstemcentre.org.uk/elibrary/resource/4980/year-eight-handling-data-mini-pack

Simplification	Extension
Students may need additional practice in the calculations, measurements and constructions involved in drawing pie charts. Encourage estimation to check results. For example, if 14 out of 29 pupils had green eyes, the corresponding angle on a pie chart should be a little less than 180° because 14 is a little less than half of 29.	Students should be able to produce all of the chart types in the exercise, using a spreadsheet or data-handling package. They should note any variations in terminology; for example, a 'vertical bar chart' may be referred to as a 'column chart'.

Literacy	Links
Visual communcation and its interpretation is an important feature of mathematical literacy and the evaluative skills of students should be called upon frequently through this section as well as the next. It may also be worth referring to HISTOGRAM as an example, where a histogram (with equal group widths) is equivalent to a frequency table.	Florence Nightingale was the first woman to become a Fellow of the Royal Statistical Society. On her return from the Crimean War, she realised that many of the deaths had been due to poor sanitation and that the hospitals needed reform. She wrote a report for Queen Victoria showing the statistics using charts and diagrams, including variations of the modern pie chart and so became the first person to use statistical charts to persuade people of the need for change. There is a picture of one of these charts at http://commons.wikimedia.org/wiki/File:Nightingale-mortality.jpg

Alternative approach

Paired students can be required to compile a list of the many statistical diagrams they know, together with one or two key features of each using mini whiteboards. These results can be shared with the whole group as an introduction or starter. Equivalent bar chart and pie chart interpretatioin of the same sets of data is a useful activity to promote comparison and evaluation among the students, examples and reources can be found in the OM3 section Show Me. Further work with Mixed Charts from the same reference can be undertaken by pairs of students for further consolidation work.

Checkpoint

Ask students to complete a pie and/or bar chart for the following data:

Eye colour of students in 9X: Blue 13, Green 10, Brown 6, Hazel 1 (Pie chart sectors are 156°, 120°, 72°, 12°)

Starter – Two-way table

Draw a two-way table on the board. Label the rows Girls, Boys and label the columns Football, Swimming, Tennis. Enter numbers, top row 3, 4, 8 and bottom row 7, 5, 5. Ask questions, for example,

What proportion of students preferred swimming? ($\frac{9}{32}$)

What percentage of students favouring football are girls? (30%)

Discuss any assumptions made.

Teaching notes

Different types of statistical diagram are more effective than others at displaying particular features of the data. Draw a bar chart and show the pie chart for the first example and ask students which is easier to use to tell whether there is more brown or blue (the bar chart), and to tell what proportion is green (the pie chart). The pictogram is a type of bar chart, which takes a much longer time to draw, but is visually more interesting.

When students calculate angles for a pie chart where the total frequency is not a factor of 360, their angles may not add up to 360 after rounding. Remind them how difficult it is to draw angles of, say, 83° exactly and that visually it will not make an important difference if it should have been 82° or 84°.

Plenary

Bring in newspaper stories where these types of graphs appear and ask students to decide which are most effective in communicating the data.

Exercise commentary

Question 1 – Some students may need reminding how to interpret a pictogram, in particular the half car.

Question 2 – The total frequency is 46.

Question 3 – This could also be drawn as a time-series graph.

Question 4 – This is continuous data - as in the final example on the facing page.

Question 5 – The bar chart is quite easy to draw, while the pie chart angles need to be calculated as in the example. The bar chart makes it easy to compare subjects to each other; the pie chart shows how each subject compares to the whole.

Answers

Exercise 8d

1   Three bars, lengths 50, 30 and 35.

2   Angles 141°, 63°, 86° and 70°
    Silver/grey is the most popular

3   Check bar heights as per table
    Average max temp increases from Jan to Aug, and then decreases again until Dec

4   Bars touching, heights of 2, 19, 24 and 9.

5   a   Check bar heights as per table
    b   Angles 70°, 93°, 81°, 70° and 46°
        Students' answers

Statistical diagrams 1

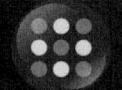

8e Statistical diagrams 2

Objectives

- Construct graphical representations, on paper and using ICT, and identify which are most useful in the context of the problem. Include
  - simple scatter graphs. (L6)
- Select, construct and modify, on paper and using ICT, suitable graphical representations to progress an enquiry and identify key features present in the data. Include
  - line graphs for time series
  - scatter graphs to develop further understanding of correlation (L6)

Key ideas	Resources
1 Further practice with evaluating statistical diagrams 2 Further practice with constructing time series graphs and scatter graphs	Rulers Tape measure Time series graphs from a variety of sources Data Unit Library (Reports M3.5): http://www.nationalstemcentre.org.uk/elibrary/resource/4980/year-eight-handling-data-mini-pack

Simplification	Extension
Check that students understand how to construct a correct scale for each axis in a time-series or scatter graph. The data in questions 1 and 2 are regularly spaced; ask how irregular data (for example, values for 1989, 1992, 1997, 2001) would be plotted.	Time-series graphs are commonly used to show trends in data. Students could be asked to review examples from a variety of sources, and to comment on any interesting features; for example, use of scales or extrapolation beyond the data provided.

Literacy	Links
Continue to emphasise that visual communcation and its interpretation is an important feature of mathematical literacy. Verbal explanation of any trends spotted can be refined into written versions by drafting and sharing in student pairs.	Austin is the capital city of the state of Texas. The area was originally settled in the 1830s as a small village called Waterloo. There is a brief history of Austin at http://www.ci.austin.tx.us/library/ahc/briefhistory.htm Can students match historical events with the growth in population shown in the time-series graph in the student book?

Alternative approach

A group exercise with 3 or 4 students where aspects of two statistical survey reports are mixed up will help to focus attention on key features. A source for such an activity is Reports as referenced. The sections will need to printed and cut so that each group has a complete mixed collection for sorting. This task can be extended by asking the groups to suggest improvements to each report once sorted and checked. Exercise 8e provides further consolidation in diagram construction.

Checkpoint

Plot a time series graph for the following data on ice cream sales:

Month	Jan	Feb	Mar	Apr	May	June	July	Aug	Sept	Oct	Nov	Dec
Sales £	450	400	500	560	670	890	950	900	780	600	400	350

Describe the trend. (Rises as the months get hotter, then falls again)

Starter – Hands

Ask students to measure their hand span (tip of thumb to tip of little finger). Record the smallest and largest measurements on the board and ask students to suggest ways of grouping the data. For example, $16 \leq h < 18$, $18 \leq h < 20$, $20 \leq h < 22$, $22 \leq h < 24$, where h is hand span in cm.

Can be extended by measuring the heights of the shortest and tallest students in the class or by asking students to measure their foot lengths.

Teaching notes

Time-series graphs are a particular form of scatter graph, where the *x* axis variable is time. The process for plotting values is the same, but often it makes sense to join up plotted points in a time-series graph to show estimates of intermediate values. The interpretation of time-series will use the language of time, often describing trends, where the descriptions of scatter graphs will be different. In the second example the graph shows that programmers with more experience tend to earn higher salaries.

Encourage students to work in pairs to improve the language they use to describe statistical graphs. Students often write better descriptions if given the opportunity to describe and discuss the graphs first. The experience may help them to write better descriptions in the future.

Plenary

The Office for National Statistics website regularly produces a bulletin on Social Trends, which can be obtained at http://www.statistics.gov.uk/default.asp It has time-series graphs on many different aspects of life in the UK today. Display a selection of graphs and ask the students to discuss in pairs or small groups how they would best describe the data. Take feedback from different groups to share best practice (many of the graphs have some commentary with them on the website).

Exercise commentary

Questions 1 and **2** – Likely problems include drawing consistent scales, and deciding on the values for each axis.

Question 3 – Note that this is a scatter diagram; the axes should be labelled 'maths mark' and 'science mark'. Discuss the nature of the correlation.

Question 4 – Students need to use the first table of data to produce a time-series chart showing changes in median height by age; the second table is then used to plot the ages and heights of four boys on the same chart.

Answers

1. Check students' answers
   Over the years, the percentage of year 9 students achieving level 5 or above increased

2. Check students' answers
   The percentage of smokers fell from just over 50% (men) and 40% (women) in 1974 to about 25% for both men and women in 2002. The rate of decrease has slowed down.

3. Check students' answers
   In general student's scores in maths and science are similar

4. a Check students' answers
   b Check students' answers
   Ben is above the median height for his age by about 25 cm, whilst Neil is below the median height for his age by about 20 cm.

Statistical diagrams 2

8f Calculating averages

Objectives
- Calculate statistics and select those most appropriate to the problem or which address the questions posed (L7)

Key ideas	Resources
1 Revisiting calculating mean, median and mode 2 Evaluating the appropriateness of each in a variety of contexts	Mean and mode (1200) Median and range (1203) Mini whiteboards Data Unit Library (Photos M3.4): http://www.nationalstemcentre.org.uk/elibrary/resource/4980/year-eight-handling-data-mini-pack Standard Unit Box S4 Understanding Mean median,mode: http://www.nationalstemcentre.org.uk/elibrary/collection/493/mostly-statistics-materials

Simplification	Extension
Question 1 includes examples where there are odd and even numbers of data values - students need to know how to find the median in each case. Question 2 could be used as an opportunity to discuss which of the averages is more appropriate, emphasising the idea of the average as a value representative of a whole set of data.	Ask students to make up sets of numbers where one or more average would not be a typical value for the whole set of data. For example, is it possible to have a set of values where the median is not representative of the data?

Literacy	Links
Explore the general perceptions of the word average in society and whether this is fair or accurate. It is also worth reminding students of RANGE as well, how to find it and its effect on interpreting an average.	Different jobs attract different rates of pay, but individual employers also set salary levels according to experience and skills. This means that salaries for the same job can vary from company to company and even within the same company. The calculator at http://jobs.guardian.co.uk/careers/200261/ gives the median salary range for many different jobs in the local region.

Alternative approach
Introduce the lesson with mini whiteboard exercises in repsonse to questions such as 'Give me three (four..) numbers which have a (mean/median/mode) of 5'; 'now a different set of three'. After a recap on the calculation of each it is worth exploring the effects of changes within a data set and the influence this has on an average. This can be particularly effective if recent topical data sets are used, but some can be found Unit Library Photos as referenced where individuals may be considered to have 'joined or left' the group and the effect on a mean or median weght/height/age etc. Matching data to averages provides good comparative discussion between students. Sources for this may be found in the Standards Unit box as refrerence.

Checkpoint
Work out the mean, median and mode of this set of data:

7, 8, 10, 12, 10, 12, 6, 8, 7, 8, 10, 10, 9   (Mean: 9, Median: 9, Mode: 10)

Statistics and probability   Statistics

Starter – Line graph

Draw a varying line graph on the board but do not label or number the axes. Ask students to suggest what the graph might represent, for example, a journey to school. Emphasise the importance of Scales, Title, Axes Labels (and a Key) – STALK

Can be extended by repeating with other types of chart.

Teaching notes

Students often have difficulty in remembering which average is which. Ask students how they remember,

mOde: is the mOst common term; it is the only one which can be used for none numerical data

medIan: is the mIddle term

mean: is the hardest one to calculate.

Work through a simple example, similar to those in question 1, to remind students how to find these statistics. Discuss how to calculate the averages if the data is presented in a (discrete) frequency table. Start by discussing what the data would look like in a list as this is a form where students should be familiar with the calculation. Then show how the equivalent calculation is done if the data is placed in a frequency table.

A useful discussion can be had over which average is most representative of a data set. Pathological cases can be used to highlight the issues,

0, 0, 47, 48, 49, 50, – unrepresentative mode

0, 0, 4, 5, 9, 9 – ill-defined mode

1, 2, 3, 4, 5, 100 – unrepresentative mean

0, 1, 2, 98, 99, 100 – no representative average

Each case must be considered separately.

Plenary

Students work in pairs to discuss the following questions. Take whole-class feedback and discuss any differences in their responses.

Eight people all have different amounts of money. The one with the most money is given another £2. What difference will this make to the mode, the median and the mean? If the £2 had been given to the person with the least money, would there be any difference in your answers?

Exercise commentary

Question 1 – Part **e** needs care when ordering negatives for the median and has two modes.

Question 2 – In part **b**, the key idea is to find an average that is typical of the data values.

Question 3 – Here the table could equally well be replaced by a list of the numbers of words.

Question 4 – Emphasise the difference between this frequency table here and the table in question 3. It may be helpful to replace the table by a list of numbers, 14, 14,..., 14 (8 times), 15, 15, etc. so that it is easier to grasp the meaning of the table and as a means of checking answers.

Question 5 – As a first step the data could be copied into a frequency table. For the mean, calculate the total number of points awarded, and divide by the total number of competitors.

Answers

1. a 6.8, 7, 5
   b 11.5, 9, 9
   c 5.125, 5, two modes: 5 and 8
   d 1.6, 1.6, no mode
   e 0.714, 0, two modes: 0 and 4

2. mean = £50.75, median = £10, mode = £5
   The mean is much larger than all except one of the values. The mode is the smallest value in the data. The median is the most representative of the data as a whole. Therefore, use the median in this case.

3. a Mode is 133
      Mean is 122
      Median is 130.5
   b No, the mean is not as it includes the first page which has far fewer words than any other page.
   c 129
   d The median, as the value is not skewed by the low number of words on the first page

4. a mode = 15 years
   b median = 15 years
   c mean = total of ages ÷ number of people
      = (14 × 8 + 15 × 11 + 16 × 4) ÷ (8 + 11 + 4)
      = 341 ÷ 23 = 14.83 years

5. mode = 0, median = 2, mean = 2

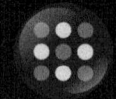

8g Interpreting graphs

Objectives
- Interpret graphs and diagrams and make inferences to support or cast doubt on initial conjectures (L7)

Key ideas	Resources
1 Evaluating statistical diagrams 2 Justifying conclusions drawn from a statistical diagram	Mini whiteboards Standard Unit Box S6 Interpreting Frequency Graphs: http://www.nationalstemcentre.org.uk/elibrary/collection/493/mostly-statistics-materials

Simplification	Extension
Some students may benefit from working carefully through question 1 only. This will provide reinforcement in drawing and interpreting a range of statistical diagrams.	Students who complete the exercise successfully can be challenged to produce a set of proportional pie charts for the data in question 1.

Literacy	Links
In order to strengthen written communication – justifying evaluative comments – Students should work in pairs then share with another pair in order to clarify thoughts before drafting and redrafting written responses.	Rivers flow from higher to lower ground. The speed of a river depends on the gradient of the river channel, the roughness of the river bed and tides. As a river nears the sea, an incoming tide causes the river to slow down and, in some cases, can even cause it to flow in the opposite direction. More information about factors that affect the speed of rivers can be found at http://www.swgfl.org.uk/rivers/River%20Speed.htm

Alternative approach
A simple card matching activity could introduce this session, for instance using frequency charts Set A and statements Set B from the S6 materials of the Standards Unit referenced. With the whole group choose two sets of comparative data in diagram form and ask pairs of students to record on mini whiteboards one/two things that are the SAME about the diagrams and one/two things that are DIFFERENT. Drawing conclusions as a result may prove more accessible for students. Secondary data of relevant and local issues can provide good sources of comparative information for discussion e.g. road casualties of under 16s in term time or vacation time, or morning versus evening. Another good source of data for comparison as a pair and share activity can be past exam questions, both GCSE and KS3 SATs papers. This type of activity should be followed up with paired evaluation of written response as well in order to help raise the quality of the work.

Checkpoint
A quick check of the learning in this section is difficult. Students could be presented with real-life examples of misleading graphs (taken from the internet, newspapers, magazines, etc.) or they could be asked to draw examples of their own from made-up data.

Starter – Prime calculations

Ask students to make the numbers one to twenty using exactly two prime numbers for each one. For example, 3 − 2, 19 − 17, 5 − 2, 11 − 7, 3 + 2, 3 × 2, ...

Can be extended by asking students to make the numbers using three prime numbers. Can they make any even number using just two primes?
(the Goldbach conjecture)

Teaching notes

Use a classroom discussion to agree what information can be extracted from bar charts and line graphs and any ways that graphs can be misleading (vertical scale not starting at 0, unequal intervals, *etc*.)

This may be the first time that students have seen this type of combined graph where two different vertical scales are used, in which case a discussion about how to read the graph, and the role of the key, will be important.

The red dot for January is beside the left vertical axis (at 32) but this is the rainfall scale, not temperature.

The rainfall bar for October is greater than twice the height of the bar for September but the truncated vertical axis is misleading (the values are 51 and 34).

The average maximum daily temperature in July is 21, but on many days the maximum will be lower than this; most days it will be lower for at least part of the day.

Plenary

Working in pairs, ask students to make three true statements about the data in the climate example. Students exchange statements with another pair to check that the statements are true. You may be able to find other examples of this type of graph in newspapers to use as an alternative.

Exercise commentary

Question 1 – This question stresses the importance of reading the data as well as comparing diagrams and provides a further opportunity to compare alternative statistical representations.

Question 2 – This question focuses on the idea that there could be more than one pattern underlying a regularly-spaced sample of data points.

Question 3 – This question explores the idea of misleading representations in statistical diagrams.

Answers

1. a. Act B won.
   b. We cannot be sure, but it may be that Act D was from France, and Act C from Croatia.
   c. Bar heights of 8.1, 1.1, 0.8 and 0.8
   d. A: Angles 249°, 28°, 55°, 28°
      B: Angles 321°, 10°, 19°, 10°
      C: Angles 261°, 25°, 12°, 62°
      D: Angles 223°, 87°, 37°, 12°
   e. Various answers possible
2. a. Check students' answers
   b. i By using a trend line for the even hours speeds, which start out halving every two hours.
      ii Various possible answers.
3. y-axis starts at 407,000

8h Correlation

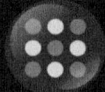

Objectives

- Select, construct and modify, on paper and using ICT, suitable graphical representations to progress an enquiry and identify key features present in the data. Include scatter graphs to develop further understanding of correlation (L6)
- Gather data from specified secondary sources, including printed tables and lists, and ICT-based sources, including the internet (L6)
- Have a basic understanding of correlation (L7)
- Appreciate that correlation is a measure of the strength of association between two variables (L7)
- Distinguish between positive, negative and zero correlation, using lines of best fit (L7)

Key ideas	Resources
1 Revisit and strengthen the key features of correlation 2 Using correlation knowledge in context to strengthen conjectures and conclusions	Scatter graphs (1213) Dice Set up IWB or large squared paper with axes so that height (vertical axis) is true height above floor, and length (horizontal axis) is in actual centimetres. Excel axis

Simplification	Extension
Question **2** uses smaller numbers than question **3** and does not use decimals. Students may need support in setting up the axes for the scatter graph correctly; a suitable choice would be 0 – 200 for the burglaries axis, and 0 – 50 for car thefts. Students could also be encouraged to use suitably labelled interrupted axes, perhaps 80 – 200 and 20 – 50.	Question **4** provides ample opportunity for students to take this work further. Encourage them to investigate the relationships between other variables (the link provides many suitable sets of data at), using a spreadsheet or graph-plotting package to generate the scatter graphs

Literacy	Links
Refresh the appropriate vocabulary, making sure that it is used contextually, e.g. stating 'positive correlation' may earn one mark but adding that 'taller people tend to weigh more' gains a further mark. The terms may include adjectives such as strong or weak to add more detail. Make sure that students are clear that correlation in this section refers to linear relationships, so having no correlation does not necessarily mean that the variables do not influence each other – simply that there is no apparent *linear* one.	The British Crime Survey measures the amount of crime experienced in England and Wales. It differs from police records because it includes crimes that have not been reported to the police. The survey aims to collect data from around 1000 members of the public in each of the 20 Police Force areas. Since January 2009, the survey has included young people aged 11 – 15. British Crime Survey: http://www.statistics.gov.uk/ssd/surveys/british_crime_survey.asp

Alternative approach

As an introduction students can mark each other up against a class height versus armspan graph, lining themselves up against the vertical axis of a class grid (see Resources). Any adults within the class should also take part. The results will quickly produce a scatter graph with a positive correlation, and thus can provide the basis for discussional recap. If computer/laptop access is available, it is useful to have saved sets of secondary data for the group to explore using the scatter diagram facilities with Chart Wizard, refining results and drawing conclusions.

Checkpoint

Describe the possible correlation in these situations:

a Sales of ice cream and temperature. (Positive)

b Age of car and resale value. (Negative)

c The mark achieved in a mathematics test and mark achieved in a physics test (Positive?)

Starter – Three dice

Throw three dice. Ask students to use the scores to generate a multiple of two, a multiple of three, a multiple of four ... For example, using scores of 1, 5 and 4

    1 + 5 – 4 (multiple of two)
    5 + 4 × 1 (multiple of three)
    4 + 5 – 1 (multiple of four)
    54 + 1 (multiple of five) *etc.*

Teaching notes

Students met the idea of the gradient of a straight line in **6c**. Use a classroom discussion to review the main ideas, including that a positive gradient means the line slopes up (from left to right) and a negative gradient means that the line slopes down.

Use the scatter diagrams to introduce the ideas of positive and negative correlation and to explain what zero correlation means. Take the opportunity to highlight the difference between the steepness of the line of best fit for a set of data and how closely to a straight line the points lie (the idea of the strength of the correlation).

Plenary

Give the students a list of related variables, for example height, weight, age, shoe size, score in last maths exam, distance from school, number of brothers or sisters, *etc.* and ask them to write lists of pairs they would expect to show positive, negative and no correlation. Take whole-class feedback to see whether students agree.

Exercise commentary

Question 1 – Reviews the ideas of positive and negative correlation. This could be incorporated into a class discussion.

Questions 2 and **3** – Examples involving positive and negative correlation, respectively. In question **3**, explain that GDP is gross domestic product; see question **4**.

Question 4 – Students can be encouraged to test their hypothesis, using data from the internet.

Answers

1   **a** Zero   **b** Positive   **c** Negative   **d** Positive
     e Positive
2   **a** Check students' diagrams
     b There is a positive correlation between the two variables.
3   **a** Check students' diagrams
     b There is a negative correlation between the two variables.
4   You might expect there to be a positive correlation between GDP per head and life expectancy – the richer a country, the longer the life expectancy of its inhabitants. How does this compare to the actual situation shown by the data?

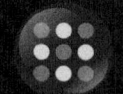

8i Averages from grouped data

Objectives

- Calculate statistics and select those most appropriate to the problem or which address the questions posed (L7)

Key ideas	Resources
1. Understanding how to deal with finding averages from grouped data 2. Recognising that the averages thus found are 'good estixmates'.	Mean of grouped data 1 (1201) Averages from grouped data (summative ppt): http://www.tes.co.uk/ResourceDetail.aspx?storyCode=6341039 Access to EXCEL

Simplification	Extension
Students who find the use of grouped data difficult could start with an even simpler example - perhaps using categories such as 1 – 2, 3 – 4, and so on. It is then worth emphasising the idea that if we do not have the original data, we have to base calculations on the assumption that all of the data points in each category are at the mid-point; we do not know how many of the values in the first category were 1's and how many were 2's, so we assume that they were all 1.5.	Students who complete this work quickly could go on to calculate summary statistics for other sets of grouped discrete and continuous data, perhaps obtained from the internet.

Literacy	Links
While students will be familiar with the averages vocabulary by now, the term *modal class* or *modal value* may confuse some. Address the difference between the versions re noun or adjective. Include the addition of the term estimate and its implications. Encourage students to discuss averages in their contextual terms appropriate to each problem	The UK Government recommends eating at least 5 portions (400 g) of fruit and vegetables each day to reduce the risk of diseases such as heart disease, stroke, and cancer. Purchases of fruit and vegetables in the UK since 1990 in grams per person per week are shown at https://statistics.defra.gov.uk/esg/indicators/h7_data.htm What is the mean of the number of portions of fruit eaten each week in the UK? How does this compare with the mean in 1990?

Alternative approach

Pick up any comments made during the session linked to **8f** if the aspects/problems of grouped data were discussed with the students. A summative development of the key points in powerpoint form from TES resources as referenced may be used. If access to computers is available, pairs of students may work alternately using Excel facilities, or calculator. Excel may be used with students in order to set up a spreadsheet for the calculations, or to explore the functions provided. It may also be used to stimulate comparison between and discussion of the differences in exact averages and estimated averages.

Checkpoint

Work out the mode and an estimate of the mean from this grouped frequency table:

Number of peas	Frequency
1-3	6
4-6	14
7-9	10

(Modal class: 4-6, Mean: 5.4)

Starter – Pizza puzzle

A pizza is cut into four unequal slices. The second slice is twice the size of the first slice. The third is three times the size of the second. The fourth is half the size of the third. What is the angle of each sector? (30°, 60°, 180°, 90°)

Can be extended by asking students to make up their own pizza puzzle.

Teaching notes

Students often forget exactly what the meaning is of grouped frequency tables. A quick construction of a table through a tally chart will help to review this. Ask for suggestions for possible values for the three students' scores in the first group to ensure that the class knows what the data table means.

Discuss the largest and smallest possible totals for the group in the first interval (0 and 12) and ask for suggestions for a value that would be sensible to use as a 'guess' (estimate) for the total of the group. Show how the same value could be calculated as midpoint times frequency.

Discuss how the total number of students in the group (31) could have been calculated if the total had not been given explicitly in the question.

Plenary

The maximum possible error in the estimate of the mean in this example is two. Ask students what would need to happen for the estimate to be two out (all the values have to be at the lower or upper end of each interval) and discuss the size of error they might expect using real data.

Exercise commentary

Question 1 – This question is very similar to the example provided on the facing page.

Questions 2 and 3 – Two further applications of the same techniques to further sets of grouped discrete data.

Question 4 – Here students compare the summary statistics obtained from grouped continuous data with those calculated from the ungrouped raw data.

Answers

1. **a** 15 **b** 0 – 4 **c** 6.33; 14.
2. **a** 59
   b We do not know the individual data values.
   c 20 – 29
   d We know the frequency for each class - the modal class is simply the class with the highest frequency.
   e 27
   f 20 – 29
3. **a** 33 **b** 50 – 74 **c** 46.85; 99
4. **a**

Length, cm	Frequency
100 – 109	3
110 – 119	9
120 – 129	12
130 – 139	7

   b 121.9 **c** 122.3
   d The estimate is close to the exact value.

Averages from grouped data

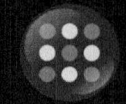

8j Comparing distributions

Objectives
• Compare two or more distributions and make inferences, using the shape of the distributions (L7)

Key ideas	Resources
1 Comparing and writing comments about two or more distributions 2 Revisiting stem-and-leaf diagrams and their use for comparison	Introduction to "the standard score" at https://statistics.laerd.com/statistical-guides/standard-score.php

Simplification	Extension
The use of frequency *polygon*s is new and some students may need to be shown how the data values are plotted; with the key idea that the same horizontal coordinate is used for the points in each pair of values. In question **2**, a 'pair of frequency diagrams' could involve some sort of stacking or overlapping bar charts or drawing a pair of frequency diagrams. Some students may need to discuss possible approaches before proceeding to draw the diagram. In question **3** some students may need to be supported in producing the stem-and-leaf diagram required, although this should be used as an opportunity to revise this topic rather than calculating the required statistics directly from the raw data provided.	The questions in the exercise suggest the statistics that should be calculated. Ask students to make a suitable choice from these in order to compare the distributions. For students who complete this work well, a suitable next step would be to compare two distributions without such guidance. For example, ask students to compare the distribution of house sizes for the two streets shown in the table. | Number of bedrooms	1	2	3	4	5
---	---	---	---	---	---
Duke Road	8	7	2	0	0
Duchess Place	0	1	3	12	6	 Students who attempt question **3** can go on to produce *frequency polygons* for the data sets provided by joining the mid-points of the tops of the bars of the frequency diagram. They should also be encouraged to write a paragraph, using suitable summary statistics, to compare the two distributions.

Literacy	Links
The term frequency polygon is not used in this section but may be worth referring to with reference to the overall shapes resulting from two distributions, thus in comparison. Verbalising comparisons followed by drafting comments should encouraged of pairs of students, swapping with another pair for evaluation and improvement.	Many different organisations including the government, the pharmaceutical industry, manufacturing industries, research facilities and the NHS employ statisticians to analyse and interpret data. Statisticians provide information and advice to help the government, the press or the wider population make decisions. There is information about becoming a statistician at - http://www.rss.org.uk/careers

Alternative approach
This session may be introduced with an examples of 2 distributions frequency diagram form and with the same data expressed in back-to-back stem-and-leaf diagram form. This will assist students in both revisiting terms and also in an introduction to the term frequency polygon. Pairs of students may be encouraged to discuss and note on mini whiteboards one or two similarities and one or two differences bewteen the two distributions. Question 4 of the exercise may be tackled by pairs of students as a short, 15+ minute project, allowing each pair to discuss and decide their own methodology.

Starter – Four numbers

Give students one or more averages and a range and ask what the four numbers might be. For example
  Mean = 14, median = 12, range = 18 (Possible solution: 7, 11, 13, 25)
  Mean = 7, median = 5.5, range = 23 (Possible solution: -3, 0, 11, 20)
  etc.

Teaching notes

Use a classroom discussion to agree the features of a frequency diagram and the information that can be extracted from it. Ask students to discuss in small groups what comparisons they would expect to be able to make easily if two frequency *polygons* were drawn on the same diagram for related datasets. Take whole class feedback. The range and the modes can be compared very easily, and it is often easy to see which distribution has the larger average, either median or mean. If the larger average is not immediately obvious, then it is likely that the averages of the two groups are quite similar.

In the example, because the total number of traps in the two locations are the same it is easy to conclude that more insects are trapped at location A than at B without making any detailed calculations. The fact that the green polygon is higher for larger number of insects allows you to say this with certainty.

Plenary

Display a set of axes showing 'ages' (11 to 18) on the horizontal axis and 'average number of hours sleep' (0 to 9) on the vertical axis. Ask students to work in pairs to draw what they think the frequency polygons would look like for boys and girls. Students then exchange graphs with another pair and explain why they drew the graphs as they did.

Exercise commentary

Question 1 – Students compare data shown as a comparative bar chart, and redraw as a pair of frequency polygons.

Question 2 – Students draw different statistical diagrams for the same set of data, and compare representations.

Question 3 – This question revises stem-and-leaf diagrams for finding median and range, and uses these to compare distributions.

Question 4 – Here students compare two sets of continuous data. A careful choice of calculation and/or diagrammatical representation will be needed.

Answers

1   a   Various answers possible
    b   Check students' diagrams
2   a   9A: Angles 216°, 60°, 48° 36°
        9B: Angles 120°, 192°, 48°
    b   Check students' diagrams
    c   In 9A most students achieve grade A whilst in 9B most students achieve grade B. The range of grades achieved is greater in class 9A than 9B.
    d   various answers possible.

3   a

Group B		Group A
9 7 6 5 5 5 5 4 4 3 3 3 3	10	
9 8 5 4 2 0	20	
6 6 6 4 3 3 2 1	30	5
6 5 3 1	40	1 2 5 6 7 7
9 8 6 4 4 3 2 1 0	50	0 0 2 2 4 6 8 8
2 1	60	0 0 0 2 3 3 4 6 6 8 8
	70	1 3 4 4 4 5
	80	1 2 2 3 4 7
	90	0 0 2 4

Key   50 | 5   means 55 marks

   b   Group A: median = 63.5, range = 59
       Group B: median = 32.5, range = 49
   c   Scores for group A were generally higher (but more varied) than those for group B.
   d   It is impossible to reach this conclusion from the data given. For example, Group A might have been given more time to do the test, access to dictionaries, etc

4   Draw up a tally chart, notice that Carla has a much greater range of values compared to Dan's consistent data. Consequently, Carla has the tallest and smallest dandelions in her field.

Comparing distributions

8k Communicating the results of an enquiry

Objectives

- Review interpretations and results of a statistical enquiry on the basis of discussions (L6)
- Communicate these interpretations and results using selected tables, graphs and diagrams (L6)
- Gather data from specified secondary sources, including printed tables and lists, and ICT-based sources, including the internet (L6)

Key ideas	Resources
1 Bringing the results of a statistical survey together in order to make and support conclusions 2 Seeing a statistical survey as a whole, with all its stages playing important parts of the whole.	Computer access

Simplification	Extension
The first two questions involve straightforward calculations based on the supplied data. Some students may need further guided examples of this sort - for example, finding the median life expectancy in G8 countries.	As explained in question **7**, students who complete the questions in the exercise should be encouraged to download further data (perhaps for additional countries or more data for the countries in the example) in order to investigate further questions.

Literacy	Links
This whole section is about communicating effectively using data and strategies to strengthen arguments. Group discussion, drafting and presentation of conclusions could be an opportunity for students to assess each other as well.	The G8 is a group of eight of the World's industrialised countries: Canada, France, Germany, Italy, Japan, Russia, the United Kingdom, and the United States. The Heads of State of these countries meet every year to discuss economic and political issues that affect the World. The European Union is also represented in the G8, but it can not host or chair any of the meetings. There is more about the G8 at http://news.bbc.co.uk/1/hi/world/americas/country_profiles/3777557.stm

Alternative approach

After discussing the data given on page 154, establishing that all the students understand the meaning of each column, its source and reality, students could be grouped into 3s or 4s in order to tackle one of the questions from this lesson fully as a mini project with results communicated as a report for TV or a newspaper article. The questions can either be selelcted for each group, differentiating appropriately or some student choice allowed. Student groups may wish to use computer facilities both for processing data and for any presentation. Allow time for the group presentations. Suggest time frames for the session with reminders during the session.

Checkpoint

What are the four key stages of the data handling cycle? (Responses should be along the line of 'formulate the hypothesis/plan', 'collect data', 'analyse data' and 'draw conclusions'.)

Starter – Jumble

Write a list of anagrams on the board and ask students to unscramble them and then make up their own. Possible anagrams are
RENTCAROOLI, MEATIEST, STREECID, NUTTIBIRDIOS, DENMAI, PARSED, USCOUNTION, TASTICITSS
(correlation, estimate, discrete, distribution, median, spread, continuous, statistics)

Teaching notes

GDP (Gross Domestic product) per capita is the total value of all the goods and services produce in a country in one year divided by the population of the country. Ask students to work in pairs to write down at least six other statistics which they think would be useful in investigating links between health and poverty in different countries. Students exchange their list with another pair and discuss why they chose their particular set of measurements.

Take whole-class feedback and discuss how this data would be collected in different countries and how reliable they would expect the data to be.

Plenary

Many national statistical offices are moving away from statistics such as GDP as measures of how well a society is doing. Ask the students to discuss in small groups what they feel would be appropriate things to include as measures of a good society today (may include aspects of health, education, crime, use of renewable energy sources, ...)
www.oecd.org/oecdworldforum gives more information and ideas.

Exercise commentary

Questions 1 and **2** – Straightforward calculations of summary statistics for groups of data.

Questions 3 and **4** – Investigating correlation using scatter diagrams.

Questions 5 and **6** – These are more open-ended investigations of features of the data set.

Question 7 – This can be used as extension material and/or a homework task.

Answers

1

Group	G8	SAM	SSA
Median income ($)	32 760	7 755	1 320

2

Group	G8	SAM	SSA
Median doctors per 1000	2.90	1.18	0.04

3 For incomes below $15 000, there is a moderate, positive correlation: the higher the average income the higher the life expectancy. For incomes over $15 000, there is no correlation.

4 There is a strong, negative correlation: the higher the adult mortality rate the lower the life expectancy.

5

Group	G8	SAM	SSA
Median population growth (%)	0.30	1.20	2.55

For incomes below $15 000, there is a moderate, negative correlation: the higher the average income the lower the population growth. For incomes above $15 000, there is a moderate, positive correlation: the higher the average income the higher the population growth (immigration?).

6 Various possible answers. In general if poor you can expect not to live as long and to have more children.

7 Students' answers

Communicating the results of an enquiry

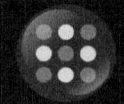

8 Statistics – MySummary

Key outcomes	Quick check
Organise data into frequency tables. L6	Put the following data into a frequency table: 13, 15, 12, 11, 10, 13, 13, 14, 12, 13, 14, 12, 10, 11, 13 (Table should have 10 – 2, 11 – 2, 12 – 3, 13 – 5, 14 – 2, 15 – 1)
Interpret statistical diagrams. L6	A pie chart has sectors 135°, 45°, 30° and 150°. If there are 24 items represented, how many are in each sector? (9, 3, 2, 10)
Plot and analyse time-series graphs. L6	Plot a time series graph for the following data: <table><tr><td>Year</td><td>2010</td><td>2011</td><td>2012</td><td>2013</td><td>2014</td></tr><tr><td>Sales (£million)</td><td>1200</td><td>1400</td><td>1450</td><td>1500</td><td>1600</td></tr></table> Analyse the trend. (Increasing)
Estimate averages from grouped tables. L6	Estimate the mean from this frequency table: <table><tr><td>Marks</td><td>10-12</td><td>13-15</td><td>16-18</td><td>19-21</td><td>22-24</td></tr><tr><td>No of students</td><td>4</td><td>5</td><td>7</td><td>3</td><td>1</td></tr></table> (15.8)
Make comparisons between sets of data. L6	Draw two frequency diagrams for these set of data: <table><tr><td>Scores</td><td>3</td><td>4</td><td>5</td><td>6</td><td>7</td></tr><tr><td>Boys</td><td>10</td><td>14</td><td>12</td><td>9</td><td>4</td></tr><tr><td>Girls</td><td>3</td><td>8</td><td>16</td><td>15</td><td>7</td></tr></table> Compare the set of data. (Girls scored more highly than boys)

MyMaths extra support

Lesson/online homework			Description
All averages	1192	L5	Use the three types of average to compare two data sets
Grouping data	1196	L6	Choosing intervals to group data and writing intervals as quantities. Includes drawing frequency graphs.
Pictograms and bar charts	1205	L3	Planning and drawing pictograms and bar charts as well as reading information from charts
Reading pie charts	1206	L5	Solving problems by reading information from a pie chart
Sampling	1212	L7	How do we take a stratified random sample from a population?
Stem and leaf	1215	L7	Finding mean and range from a stem and leaf diagram, and using them to compare sets of data

Statistics and probability   Statistics

MyReview

8 MySummary

Check out
You should now be able to ...

	Test it → Questions
✓ Organise data into frequency tables.	1 – 2
✓ Interpret statistical diagrams.	3
✓ Plot and analyse time-series graphs.	4
✓ Estimate averages from grouped tables.	5 – 6
✓ Make comparisons between sets of data.	7

Language	Meaning	Example
Categorical data	Data that can be described in words and may not have any numerical values.	Hair colour and gender are examples of categorical data.
Discrete data	Data that can only take certain values.	Number of people in a classroom and shoe size are examples of discrete data.
Continuous data	Data that can take any value in a range.	Height and weight are examples of continuous data.
Average	One number that represents a set of numbers.	Mean, median and mode are different types of averages.
Correlation	A relationship between two variables, such as number of ice creams sold and temperature.	There is a positive correlation between the number of ice creams sold and the temperature. As the temperature increases, so does the number of ice creams sold.
Mean	An average value found by adding the data and dividing by the number of data items.	9, 9, 9, 15, 2, 3, 5 This mean is: $\frac{9+9+9+15+2+3+5}{7} = \frac{49}{7} = 7$
Median	The middle value in order of size.	2, 3, 5, ⑨, 9, 9, 15 The median is 9.
Mode	The value that occurs most often	The mode is 9.
Range	The difference between the largest and smallest data values.	15 – 2 = 13 The range is 13.

8 MyReview

1. Phil is going to record how many of each type of bird he sees in the morning, afternoon and evening). The birds he thinks he will see are chaffinch, sparrow, starling and wood pigeon. Design a data-collection sheet for him to use.

2. The weights of 3 month old babies were recorded (kg).
   5.8 5.7 4.9 6.1 6.7 5.4
   5.0 4.5 6.2 6.2 7.2 7.4
   6.8 4.9 5.5 5.8
   Construct a frequency table for this data.

3. The pie chart shows the flavours of ice cream sold. 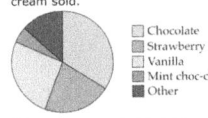

   ☐ Chocolate
   ☐ Strawberry
   ☐ Vanilla
   ☐ Mint choc-chip
   ■ Other

   38 people were asked in total.
   How many preferred each flavour?

4. The graph shows the approximate population of a town over 60 years.

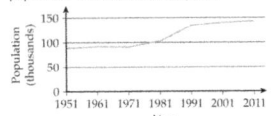

5.

4. a Describe the trend.
   b A large factory employing thousands of people opened in the town. In which ten-year period do you think this happened?

5. The table shows the class sizes in a school.

Size	26	27	28	29	30
Frequency	1	2	1	2	6

   Find
   a the mode   b the mean (to 1 dp)
   c the median   d the range.

6. A group of students recorded how many pieces of homework they were set in a week.

Homework	0-4	5-9	10-14	15-19
Frequency	2	12	13	6

   a Estimate the range.
   b Find the modal class.
   c Estimate the mean (1 dp).
   d Estimate the median.

7. The score of boys and girls in a spelling test was recorded.

Score	0	1	2	3	4	5
Boys	1	4	7	8	3	2
Girls	0	2	13	8	1	1

   a Draw frequency diagrams on the same axes for the boys and the girls.
   b Compare these sets of data.

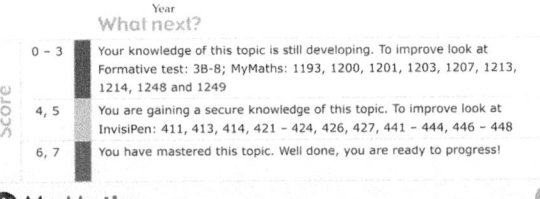

What next?

Score	
0 – 3	Your knowledge of this topic is still developing. To improve look at Formative test: 3B-8; MyMaths: 1193, 1200, 1201, 1203, 1207, 1213, 1214, 1248 and 1249
4, 5	You are gaining a secure knowledge of this topic. To improve look at InvisiPen: 411, 413, 414, 421 – 424, 426, 427, 441 – 444, 446 – 448
6, 7	You have mastered this topic. Well done, you are ready to progress!

Question commentary

Question 1 – Students often confuse data collection sheets with questionnaires. They could include an 'other' column.

Question 2 – Students could group in 1kg classes, but 0.5kg classes preserve more detailed information.

Question 3 – Students should first measure the angles to the nearest degree: choc 123°, strawb 76°, van 95°, mint 19°, other 47°, they will need to round their answers.

Question 4 – There is a sharp rise in population in this decade.

Question 5 – There are 12 classes and total number of students is 347. Median is between 6th (29) and 7th (30).

Question 6 – The estimated range is the biggest possible difference so 19 – 0. Students may need to copy the table and add columns for midpoint (2, 7, 12, 17) and frequency × midpoint (4, 84, 156, 102). A common error is to ÷ 4, not the total (33), leading to an unrealistic answer of 86.5. Median is the 17th value so in 10-14 class, to be more precise it is 3 values into the class so $\frac{3}{13}$ through the class.

Question 7 – Two comments are needed here.

Answers

1.

Time	Chaffinch	Sparrow	Starling	Wood Pigeon
Morning				
Afternoon				
Evening				

2.

Weight, w	Frequency
4.5 ≤ w < 5	3
5 ≤ w < 5.5	2
5.5 ≤ w < 6	4
6 ≤ w < 6.5	3
6.5 ≤ w < 7	2
7 ≤ w < 7.5	2

3. Chocolate 13   Strawberry 8   Vanilla 10
   Mint choc-chip 2   Other 5

4. a Increasing   b 1981-1991
5. a 30   b 28.9   c 29.5   d 4
6. a 0   b 10-14   c 10.5   d 10.9
7. b For example, mode for boys higher than girls, boys have bigger range.

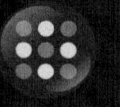

8 MyPractice

1 Students in class 9B were given a choice of topics for a statistics project.
For each of the topics, suggest one conjecture that could be made and tested.
  a Healthy lifestyles   **b** Travel to school   **c** Leisure and recreation

2 This question was included in a questionnaire.

> How much television do you watch?

  a Explain why the answers to this question might not be easy to analyse.
  b Write a better version of this question.

3 Jack measures the heights, in cm, of 40 seedlings in an experiment.

13.5	13.6	13.7	12.9	14.0	13.6	13.2	12.6	13.5	13.8
13.2	13.7	13.7	13.2	13.1	13.1	14.2	13.2	13.8	13.2
14.5	13.7	13.9	13.8	14.4	13.9	13.5	13.3	13.0	13.4
13.5	14.1	13.5	13.5	13.7	12.9	14.0	13.6	14.1	12.7

Construct a frequency table for this set of data.

4 This table shows the sports options chosen by students in class 9Y.

Option	Football	Hockey	Rounders	Tennis
Frequency	9	11	7	4

Draw   **a** a bar chart   **b** a pie chart for this set of data.

5 The table shows the growth of the population of New York City.

Year	1800	1850	1900	1950	2000
Population (thousands)	79	696	3437	7891	8008

Draw a time-series graph for this set of data.

6 This frequency table shows the number of points awarded to competitors in an athletics competition.

Points	0	1	2	3	4	5
Frequency	13	28	41	39	21	7

Find the mean, median and mode of this set of data.

7 This chart shows the number of sofas sold one weekend in three different branches of a furniture store.
  a Explain why this chart is misleading.
  b Draw a new version of the chart to give a fairer impression of the data.

8 Students on a PE course did a fitness test at the beginning of the course and repeated the same test at the end.

Student	A	B	C	D	E	F	G	H	I	J
Test 1	24	37	16	23	29	42	31	22	21	29
Test 2	39	42	34	35	30	44	40	33	35	39

  a Plot a scatter graph for this set of data.
  b What does the graph tell you about the course?

9 This frequency table shows the number of points awarded to competitors in a skating competition.

Points	1	2	3	4	5
Frequency	2	9	18	12	3

  a Find the range of this set of data.
  b Find the mean, median and mode of the number of points awarded.

10 The table shows the number of parking tickets issued to vehicles parked on two streets each day during one week.

Day	Mon	Tue	Wed	Thu	Fri	Sat	Sun
King Street	8	7	6	6	3	8	0
Queen Street	4	3	5	2	4	11	0

  a Find the mean, median, mode and range of the number of tickets issued each day in each street.
  b Use the statistics you calculated in part **a** to compare the two distributions.

11 Gather information similar to that shown in the table on page 152 for a selection of countries in Asia. Investigate any link between health and poverty in these countries, and report your findings.

Question commentary

Question 1 – This is very open-ended but encourage students to choose conjectures that are easily tested.

Question 2 – A common GCSE-style question on criticising survey questions.

Question 3 – A careful choice of class interval is required.

Question 4 – Angles will need to be rounded for the pie chart..

Question 5 – The scaling of the population axis will be tricky here.

Question 6 – Check students are not dividing by six for the mean.

Question 7 – Students should start their frequency axis at zero for part **b**.

Question 8 – Students could be encouraged to start their axis scales at a sensible point other than zero. For example, 15 for test 1.

Question 9 – Check students are not dividing by five for the mean.

Question 10 – Two comments, one to do with average and one to do with spread, are required for part **b**.

Question 11 – This question requires research and lends itself to a homework task.

Answers

1. Students' answers
2. The responses to the question could be very varied – some people might answer 'hardly any', and others might answer 'it depends what's on'. A better approach would be to present some numerical options for people to choose from.
3.

Height, h cm	Frequency
$12.5 \leq h < 13.0$	4
$13.0 \leq h < 13.5$	10
$13.5 \leq h < 14.0$	19
$14.0 \leq h < 14.5$	6
$14.5 \leq h < 15.0$	1

4. Correctly drawn charts
5. Correctly drawn graph
6. mean = 2.32, median = 2, mode = 2
7.
   a. The fact that the vertical scale does not start at zero exaggerates the differences between the sales figures.
   b. A better version will have the vertical scale starting at zero.
8.
   a. Check students' diagrams
   b. There is a moderate, positive correlation between test 1 and test 2.
   The scores of all the students improved, but the course works better for unfit students than for initially fit students
9.
   a. 4
   b. Mean = 3.1 , median = 3, mode = 3.
10.
    a. King Street: mean = 5.4, median = 6, two modes (6 and 8), range = 8.
    Queen Street: mean = 4.1, median = 4, mode = 4, range = 11.
    b. On average less parking tickets are issued on Queen Street but the there is more variation in the number issued on King Street
11. Students' answers

MyPractice

MyAssessment 2

These questions will test you on your knowledge of the topics in chapters 5 to 8.
They give you practice in the questions that you may see in your GCSE exams.
There are 85 marks in total.

1 Calculate the values of
  a angles p and q and $(p + q)$ (2 marks)
  b angle r. (1 mark)

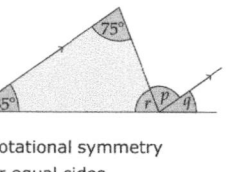

2 Name the quadrilateral that has these properties:: Rotational symmetry of order 2, two lines of reflection symmetry and four equal sides (2 marks)

3 **a** Calculate the angles marked with letters. (3 marks)
  b Determine $a + b + c + d$ and state what property it shows. (2 marks)

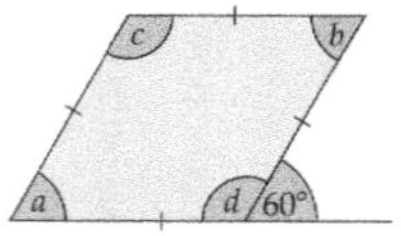

4 This is a regular nonagon. Calculate
  a the angle at the centre a (2 marks)
  b the angle marked b in the isosceles triangle (2 marks)
  c the interior and exterior angles of a regular nonagon (3 marks)
  d the sum of all the interior and exterior angles of a regular nonagon. (4 marks)

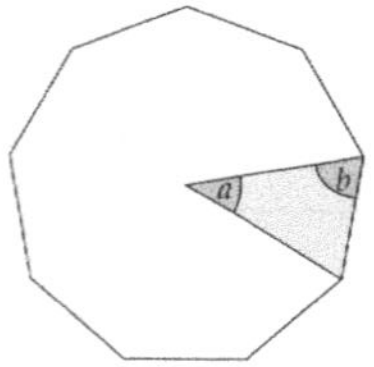

5 The diagonals of two pentagons joined together are drawn to form a set of triangles.
  a Which triangles are congruent to triangle A? (give your reasons) (2 marks)
  b Which triangles are congruent to triangle B? (give your reasons) (2 marks)

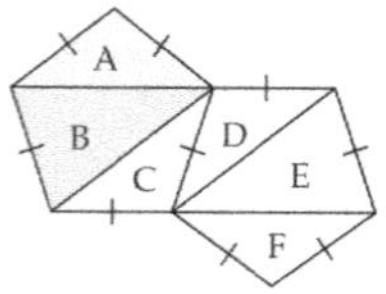

6 **a** On square grid paper draw an x-axis from -3 to $+4$ and a y-axis between ± 10. (2 marks)
  b Copy and complete this table of values for the equations $y = 2x + 2$ and $y = 4x - 2$ (4 marks)

x	-2	-1	0	1	2	3
$y = 2x + 2$						
$y = 4x - 4$						

  c What is the gradient of the graph $y = 4x - 2$? (1 mark)
  d What is the y-intercept of the equation $y = 2x + 2$? (1 mark)
  e Plot both graphs and give the coordinate point where both lines meet. (4 marks)

7 **a** Find the gradient and the y-intercept of the straight lines with these equations. Do not draw any of the graphs.
    i $y = -2x - 5$ (2 marks)   **ii** $2y = -10 - 4x$ (2 marks)
    iii $y = \frac{2}{3}x + 6$ (2 marks)   **iv** $12 + 9x = 3y$ (2 marks)
  b Rewrite each of these equations in the form $ax + by = c$ (5 marks)

8 Work out these using an appropriate method.
  a $7.49 + 87.12 - 34.5$ (1 mark)   **b** $2391 - 678.9 + 38.48$ (2 marks)
  c 76×13.95 (2 marks)   **d** $738 \div 6.3$ (3 marks)

9 **a** Convert 63 400 seconds into hours minutes and seconds. (3 marks)
  b Calculate these expressions giving your answer to 1 dp.
    i $\dfrac{(9 - 2^3)\sqrt{(65 - 27)}}{(3 + 3^2)}$ (3 marks)   **ii** $\dfrac{(-6)^2 + (-2^3)}{(-3^4)}$ (3 marks)

10 The amounts of money collected during a schools' charity week were
£2.34 £1.98 £2.89 £3.03 £0.95 £1.64 £3.32 £1.12 £1.78 £2.18
£3.15 £0.78 £1.98 £1.76 £2.36 £2.71 £1.73 £0.90 £3.16 £2.07
  a Construct a frequency table using class intervals
$£0 \leq m < £0.50$, $£0.50 \leq m < £1.00$, …. (4 marks)
  b Draw a bar chart to represent this information. (4 marks)
  c What was the mean amount of money collected per form group? (3 marks)

11 This table shows the journey time to work for 50 people. The times are recorded to the nearest minute

Time (minutes)	1-5	6-10	11-15	16-20	21-25	26-30	31-35	36-40
Number of people (f)	3	7	5	11	14	5	2	3

  a For this data, estimate
    i the mean (3 marks)   **ii** the median (2 marks)
    iii the mode (1 mark)   **iv** the range for the data. (1 mark)
  b What conclusions can you draw about the journey to work? (2 marks)

MyMaths.co.uk

Mark scheme

Question 1 – 3 marks
a 2 $p = 75°$, $q = 35°$ and $p + q = 110°$
b 1 $r = 70°$

Question 2 – 2 marks
   2 rhombus; 1 mark for kite

Question 3 – 5 marks
a 3 $a = 60°$, $b = 60°$, $c = 120°$, $d = 120°$
b 2 $360°$; internal angles of a quadrilateral add up to $360°$

Question 4 – 11 marks
a 2 $40°$; 1 mark if 360/9 seen
b 2 $70°$; 1 mark if $180° - 40°$ seen
c 3 interior angle $140°$, exterior angle $40°$; mark for $70° + 70°$ seen
d 2 sum of exterior = $360°$; 40×9 seen 1 mark;
   2 sum of interior = $1260°$; 140×9 seen 1 mark

Question 5 – 4 marks
a 2 A is congruent to C, D, F
      2 sides equal and included angle
b 2 B is congruent to E
      2 diagonals equal and included angle

Question 6 – 12 marks
a 2 Correct axes drawn and labeled
b 4 Table correct; -2, 0, 2, 4, 6, 8 and -10, -6, -2, 2 6, 10; -1 mark each error/omission
c 1 4
d 1 +2
e 4 Both graphs plotted correctly; straight lines drawn (ruled); (2, 6)

Question 7 – 13 marks
a i   2 gradient -2, intercept -5
  ii 2 gradient -2, intercept -5
  iii 2 gradient $\frac{2}{3}$, intercept +6
  iv 2 gradient 3, intercept +4
b i   1 $2x + y = -5$ ii 1 $4x + 2y = -10$
  iii 2 $2x - 3y = -18$ iv 1 $9x - 3y = -12$

Question 8 – 6 marks
a 1 60.11; method seen for two marks
b 1 1750.58; method seen for two marks
c 2 1060.2; method seen for 2 marks
d 2 117.14; method seen for two marks

Question 9 – 9 marks
a   3 17 hours 36 minutes 40 seconds
b i 3 0.51; 1 mark awarded for each part
  ii 3 -0.35; 1 mark awarded for each part

Question 10 – 10 marks
a 4 Correct class intervals used; tally chart and frequencies 0, 3, 1, 6, 4, 2, 4; total checked
b 4 Correct bar chart drawn; axes labeled; no gaps
c 3 £2.09; total £41.83 seen for 1 mark

Question 11 – 9 marks
a i   3 19 minutes; accept 19.4 minutes; 1 mark for mid-interval values seen; 1 mark for 970 seen;
  ii 2 16 – 20 minutes; median is mid-way between 25th-26th seen for 1 mark
  iii 1 21 – 25 minutes
  iv 1 39 minutes
b   2 the majority of people take between 16 – 25 minutes to get to work

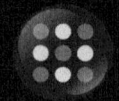

9 Transformations and scale

Learning outcomes
G3 Draw and measure line segments and angles in geometric figures, including interpreting scale drawings (L7)
G8 Identify properties of, and describe the results of, translations, rotations and reflections applied to given figures (L6)
G9 Identify and construct congruent triangles, and construct similar shapes by enlargement, with and without coordinate grids (L6)

Introduction	Prior knowledge
The chapter starts by looking at rotations, reflections and translations before covering enlargements. Combinations of transformations and the notion of congruence are then covered. Sections on maps and scale drawing and bearings complete the chapter.	Students should already know how to… • Perform simple transformations including enlargement • Convert between metric units • Measure angles using a protractor
	Starter problem
The introduction discusses how 15th century artists started to use the concept of perspective to draw three-dimensional objects to scale and develop a sense of depth in their pictures. Before this time, perspective was largely ignored and most paintings looked 'flat'. A history of, and some excellent examples of, perspectival paintings can be found at: http://www.op-art.co.uk/history/perspective/ The link to the concept of enlargement using ray lines can be made explicit to the students or they could be directed to investigate these themselves, as in the starter problem.	The starter problem asks the students to investigate the perspective in the picture given. Basically, if the object is half the height (measured in the picture) but on the same lines of perspective, it should be half the distance from the vanishing point. As a cross-curricular link and an exercise in constructing neat diagrams, students could be instructed to complete their own perspective drawings using a motif and the concepts covered in the section on enlargements. Having a single vanishing point and motifs either side of the point, they can create a 3D-looking diagram in quite quick time.

Resources

MyMaths

Bearings	1086	Enlarging shapes	1099	Map scales	1103
Reflecting shapes	1113	Rotating shapes	1115	Scale drawing	1117
All transformations	1125	Translating shapes	1127		

Online assessment			InvisiPen solutions		
Chapter test	3B–9		Reflection	362	Translation	363
Formative test	3B–9		Rotation	364	Enlargements	366
Summative test	3B–9		Describing a combination of transformations			368
			Scale drawings	372	Bearings	374

162 Geometry and measures — Transformations and scale

Topic scheme

Teaching time = 5 lessons/2 weeks

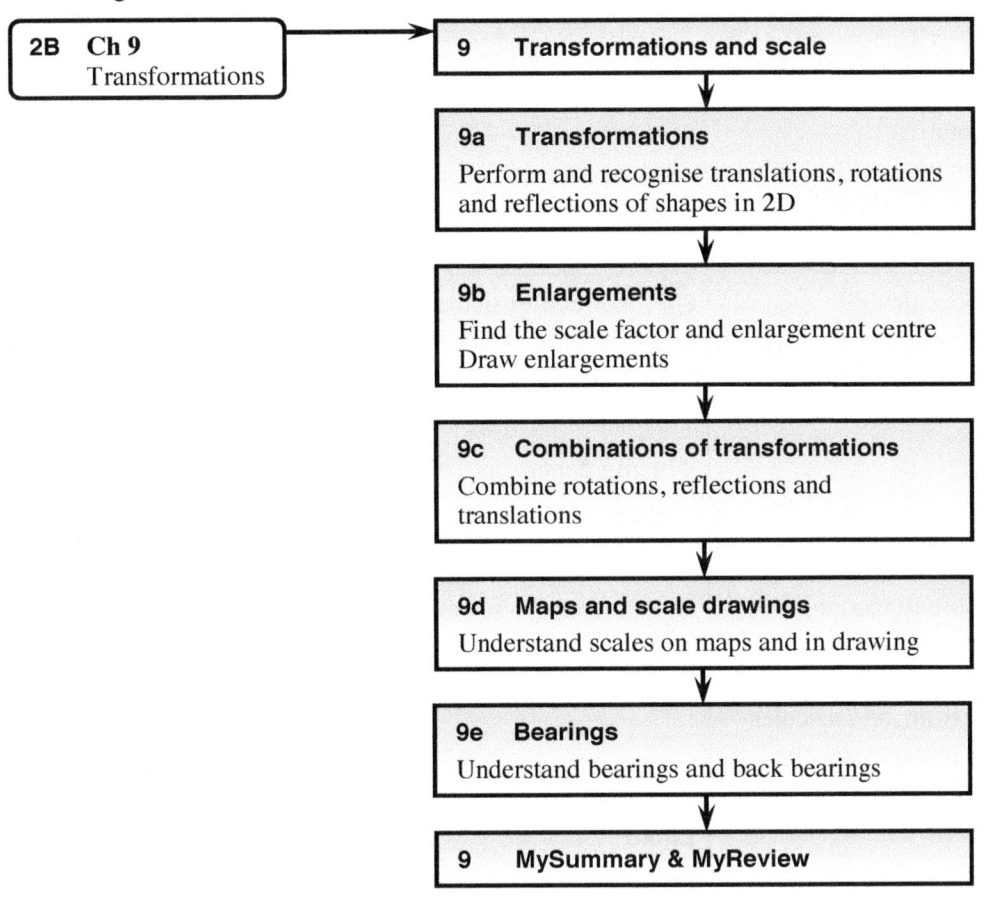

2B Ch 9
Transformations

9 Transformations and scale

9a Transformations
Perform and recognise translations, rotations and reflections of shapes in 2D

9b Enlargements
Find the scale factor and enlargement centre
Draw enlargements

9c Combinations of transformations
Combine rotations, reflections and translations

9d Maps and scale drawings
Understand scales on maps and in drawing

9e Bearings
Understand bearings and back bearings

9 MySummary & MyReview

Differentiation

Student book 3A   162 – 181
Rotation and reflection symmetry
Reflection, rotations and translations
Enlargements using a scale factor with and without a centre of enlargement
Scale drawings

Student book 3B   162 – 177
Rotations, reflections and translations, including combinations thereof
Enlargements using a scale factor and centre of enlargement
Map scales and scale drawings
Bearings

Student book 3C   158 – 173
Transformations and combinations of transformations
Enlargements using a scale factor and centre of enlargement
Map scales and scale drawings
Enlargements and similar shapes

Introduction

9a Transformations

Objectives

- Recognise that translations, rotations and reflections preserve length and angle, and map objects on to congruent images (L6)
- Use the coordinate grid to solve problems involving translations, rotations, reflections and enlargements (L6)
- Use any point as the centre of rotation (L6)
- Measure the angle of rotation, using fractions of a turn or degrees (L6)
- Use congruence to show that translations, rotations and reflections preserve length and angle (L7)

Key ideas	Resources
1 Identify fully and transform shapes using translation, reflections and rotation 2 Explore the key features and effects of each on a shape both geometrically, and resulting positions.	Reflecting shapes (1113) Rotating shapes (1115) Translating shapes (1127) Geometry software Tracing paper Square grid paper

Simplification	Extension
In question **1**, students need to be able to recognise the types of quadrilaterals and know their associated properties. Ask students to draw a square, a rectangle, a rhombus, a parallelogram, a trapezium, an isosceles trapezium, a kite and an arrowhead and to mark the equal sides and equal angles. See **5b** for guidance.	Ask students to investigate the coordinates of a shape after rotations of 90°, 180°, 270° about (0, 0). They could start with the triangle in question 5.

Literacy	Links
Revise the key vocabulary, all of which should be familiar with the students. Encourage students to identify that resulting images are congruent. Encourage the use of correct vocabulary and detail from the students.	Cross stitch is a traditional form of embroidery in which cross-shaped stitches of the same size but different colours are used to create a picture. The fabric used usually has an even weave so it has a regular number of threads per centimetre. The designs are usually drawn on squared-paper and then stitched on the cloth by counting threads. There is a website devoted to creating designs using mathematical transformations at http://mathstitch.com/

Alternative approach

Ask students to work in pairs and to come up with the key features of each of the three transformations in terms of what remains unchanged, and what is changed, using mini whiteboards. Share and discuss the results fully, establishing the detail in each case. If students have access to computers, they may further investigate each transformation with a view to trying to predict resulting image coordinates. For reflection suggest that they first explore reflection in each axis and its effects, then examine mirror lines which are parallel to either axis. For rotation, students should consider the changes from a centre at the origin firstly. Differentiate the levels of challenge appropriately for the ability of each pair. Encourage each pair to summarise their findings in, say, a poster form.

Checkpoint

A triangle has coordinates at (2, 1), (4, 1) and (4, 5). State the coordinates of the triangle after a reflection in the line $y = 0$ (the x axis).   (2, -1), (4, -1) and (4, -5)

Starter – Number rotations

Using digits from 0, 0, 1, 1, 6, 8, 8, 8, 9, what is the highest number that can be made that reads the same when turned upside down? (981080186) What is the highest multiple of four? (809181608) What is the highest multiple of nine? (810018)

Teaching notes

The teaching of transformations can be greatly enhanced by the use of dynamic geometry to show the process, especially by showing construction marks, such as the circles tracing the path of a vertex being rotated or the vector in a translation. The immediate association between moving the centre of rotation and the effect on the image can be a powerful learning tool.

Students often struggle with drawing a reflection when the mirror line goes through the shape and particularly when the mirror line is not vertical or horizontal. Encourage them to turn the paper round so that the mirror line is horizontal or vertical before reflecting the shape as this will often help.

Plenary

Ask students to work in pairs to discuss the three translations in question **2**. A to C is the sum of the other two. Why should this be? Will it always work?

Exercise commentary

Tracing paper could be used for the rotations.

Questions 1 and **3** – Encourage students to look at the side lengths and the interior angles of the resulting quadrilaterals to explain their reasoning.

Question 2 – Students need to consider the translation of one vertex of the trapezium to its corresponding vertex in the image.

Question 4 – Encourage students to reflect each vertex in turn to find the position of the image.

Question 5 – This question is based on the example: using tracing paper and trial-and-improvement to find the centre of rotation.

Question 6 – Each transformation gives a different symmetrical pattern. Students can extend the activity by describing the symmetry for each pattern or by starting with a different tile of their choice.

Answers

1 a Rectangle, two pairs of equal sides and four right angles
   b Parallelogram, two pairs of equal sides and no right angles
   c Rhombus, four equal sides and no right angles
   d Rectangle, two pairs of equal sides and two right angles
   e Rhombus, four equal sides and no right angles

2 a 3 right   1 up
   b 1 left   4 down
   c 2 right   3 down

3 a, b Vertices at (0, 2), (1, 0), (0, -2) and (-1, 0)
   c Rhombus, four equal sides and no right angles

4 a Vertices at (1, -3), (2, -1), (1, 2) and (-1, -2)
   b Vertices at (-1, 3), (-2, 1), (-1, -2) and (1, 2)

5 a Check students' drawings
   b (1, 0), 90° clockwise

6 Check students' drawings

Transformations

9b Enlargements

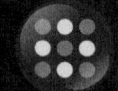

Objectives	
• Enlarge 2D shapes, given a centre of enlargement and a positive integer scale factor, on paper and using ICT	(L6)
• Identify the scale factor of an enlargement as the ratio of the lengths of any two corresponding line segments	(L6)
• Recognise that enlargements preserve angle but not length, and understand the implications of enlargement for perimeter	(L6)
• Use the coordinate grid to solve problems involving translations, rotations, reflections and enlargements	(L6)

Key ideas	Resources	
1 Recognise and describe fully: enlargement 2 Be able to follow appropriate information in order to draw an enlargement	Enlarging shapes Geometry software Isometric paper Square grid paper	(1099)

Simplification	Extension
As preparation for this exercise, students should enlarge shapes on square grid paper without a centre of enlargement. Encourage students to check their answers by considering the lengths of all the corresponding sides of the shapes, (image length = scale factor × object length).	Ask students to find the scale factor and centre of enlargement that would map the image back to the original object. They may also consider negative or fractional scale factors. This is suitable for pairs of students.

Literacy	Links
The vocabulary will be familiar to the students but confidence in its accurate use will need to be developed by encouraging oral descriptive sentences which include the appropriate detail. Maintain reference to *congruent* and *similar*. Link enlargement with proportional reasoning vocabulary and multiplicative relationships/scale factor.	File sizes for images captured using a digital camera are usually too big to email or to post on a website, so the images have to be resized. Digital images are made up of pixels, one pixel being the smallest picture element. To resize an image, the resolution of the picture is changed so that it is displayed using fewer pixels. The more pixels that are used to represent an image, the more closely the image will resemble the original. There are examples of resized images at http://www.shrinkpictures.com/examples.php

Alternative approach

It may help to provide students with a small group of card cut outs of similar shapes, such as those torn from a square of A4 paper, halved, halved again and so on. Students may then work in pairs or threes to identify the similar shapes (squares and rectangles) followed by arranging them in order to find centre of enlargement, as well as establish a scale factor. Rulers or lengths of string/ribbon will help to line up corresponding vertices. This will help students to transfer the skills onto drawn versions. Modelling with two images and encouraging students to estimate rough position of centre will also help. Further exploration using dynamic geometry software can follow, allowing for quicker recognition of results of changes in each variable.

Checkpoint

A rectangle measures 5cm by 4cm. It is enlarged so that the new rectangle has one side of length 20cm. What are the two possible scale factors of enlargement? Find the length of the other side of the enlargement in both cases.
(scale factor 4, other side = 16cm; scale factor 5, other side = 25cm)

Geometry and measures   Transformations and scale

Starter – Triangular polyminos

Ask students to find shapes made from equilateral triangles, touching edge to edge, with exactly one line of symmetry or two, three, six,... lines of symmetry. What is the order of rotational symmetry of each of their shapes? Can they find a shape with four lines of symmetry? Why not? Provide isometric paper if necessary.

Teaching notes

Again, the use of dynamic geometry with construction lines allows the process of enlargements to be explored very effectively in a relatively short time. Changing the scale factor while keeping the centre fixed shows that both the size and the position of the image vary. Keep the scale factor constant but move the centre around to show the effect on position.

The same technique can also show that joining corresponding vertices in shape and image and finding the intersection of these lines will find the centre of the enlargement.

Plenary

Show a shape and ask students to discuss in pairs what centre and scale factor will give an image completely inside the original (centre inside shape and SF < 1). Other tasks would be for it to enclose the original, for it to be completely separate from the original, specifying larger or smaller, *etc*.

Exercise commentary

Question 1 – Encourage students to draw lines through the corresponding vertices of the shapes so that the centre of enlargement can be found.

Question 2 – This is based on the example. Ensure that students always measure distances from the centre of enlargement.

Question 3 – In part **d**, would the same result hold for a different centre of enlargement?

Question 4 – Students may need guidance to realise that the measurement of 12cm could be the length or the width.

Question 5 – Pairs of students could extend this activity by finding similar problems using different letters.

Answers

1 **a** 3, (-2, 3)   **b** 3, (-3, 0)   **c** 2, (3, 0)

2 **a** Check students' drawings
   b Check students' drawings
   c Check students' drawings

3 **a, b** Check students' drawings
   c (4, 8), (6, 2), (2, 4)
   d Each digit is multiplied by two to get the image

4 **a** 4, 6   **b** 8 cm, 18 cm

5 **a** Check students' drawings
   b Check students' drawings

Enlargements

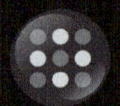

9c Combinations of transformations

Objectives

- Recognise that translations, rotations and reflections preserve length and angle, and map objects on to congruent images (L6)
- Explore and compare mathematical representations of combinations of translations, rotations and reflections of 2D shapes, on paper and using ICT (L6)
- Use the coordinate grid to solve problems involving translations, rotations, reflections and enlargements (L6)
- Transform 2D shapes by combinations of translations, rotations and reflections, on paper and using ICT (L6)
- Use any point as the centre of rotation (L6)
- Measure the angle of rotation, using fractions of a turn or degrees (L6)
- Use congruence to show that translations, rotations and reflections preserve length and angle (L7)

Key ideas	Resources
1 Investigating combinations of transformations and the resulting effects. 2 Carry out accurately a combination of transformations following given directions.	All transformations (1125) Geometry software A pair of mirrors Tracing paper

Simplification	Extension
Students who have difficulty with question **1a** should look at question **3** on spread **9a** for guidance. In order to make question **3** more concrete, give students an actual shape drawn on a square grid.	Ask students to investigate whether two transformations are commutative, that is, does the order of two transformations matter? For example, use a) reflection in the *y*-axis and b) clockwise rotation of 90° about (0, 0). Ensure that students use a non-symmetrical shape as the object.

Literacy	Links
Maintain use of key descriptive vocabulary. Introduce/revise vector notation for describing translations making the clear distinction between ppint coordinate notation (scalar) and movement notation (vector).	The first Ferris wheel was designed by George Ferris in 1893 for the World's Fair in Chicago. A Ferris wheel rotates around a central axis but the individual gondolas rotate by gravity in the opposite direction around their own axes of rotation. As a result, the gondolas and the people inside are translated around the edge of a large circle and do not rotate at all. There is a picture of the first Ferris wheel at http://www.hydeparkhistory.org/newsletter.html

Alternative approach

If students have access to computers with dynamic geometry software, they should be encouraged to investigate certain transformation combinations for themselves. Structure to help student decisions by suggesting examining firstly two from the same group, e.g. one translation followed by another; then a simple combination of any two. Does order make a difference? Can a combination be described by one transformation? Is it predicatable? Allow sufficient time to discuss result findings and share with whole group.

Checkpoint

A triangle has coordinates (2, 0), (3, 1) and (4, 7). Write down the coordinates of the triangle after success reflections in first the *x*-axis and second the *y*-axis. (-2, 0), (-3, -1) and (-4, -7)

Geometry and measures Transformations and scale

Starter – Congruent or similar?

Ask students to plot (or imagine) a triangle with vertices at (1, 5), (2, 5) and (1, 7). Challenge students to give the vertices of a congruent triangle, a similar triangle and a triangle that is neither congruent nor similar. If available, check responses with a graphical package.

Teaching notes

Use a pair of mirrors to create a series of images as reflections stretching infinitely into both mirrors as this can make the ideas presented more concrete than just pencil and paper or electronic activities can. Looking at the images of a symmetrical object (a rectangular box for example) and one which is not (a book with writing visible or a student's head for example) will help identify which of the sequence of images are just translations of the original and which are reflections.

Students often expect that two transformations of the same type will give another of the same (as translations do), so look carefully at the second example where two reflections combine to give a rotation.

Plenary

Sometimes the order in which two transformations are carried out is important because they give the image in different places. Ask students to reverse the order of the transformations in the two examples. The order does not matter in the first but gives an anti-clockwise rotation about (0, 0) in the second.

Exercise commentary

Tracing paper could be used for rotations.

Question 1 – In part **b**, encourage students to look at the side-lengths and the interior angles of the quadrilateral to explain their reasoning.

Question 2 – Students could draw their own shape and image if they cannot state the answer.

Question 3 – This question is based on the second example.

Question 4 – The orientation of shapes A and B should suggest that the transformation is a rotation. Similarly for shapes B and C.

Question 5 – Students must use the midpoint of the sides for the centres of rotation.

Answers

1   a   Rhombus
     b   Four equal sides and no right angles

2   Translation of 1 right, 2 down

3   a   Coordinates at (1, 1), (1, 3) and (2, 3)
     b   Coordinates at (1, -1), (1, -3) and (2, -3)
     c   Clockwise rotation of 90° about (0, 0)

4   a   Translation of 3 right, 1 up
     b   Anticlockwise rotation of 90° about (4, 3) followed by a clockwise rotation of 90° about (6, 2)

5   Students' tessellations

Combinations of transformations

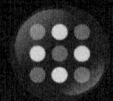

9d Maps and scale drawings

Objectives	
• Use and interpret maps and scale drawings in the context of mathematics and other subjects (L6)	

Key ideas	Resources
1 Interpret accurately scale information on diagrams 2 Solve contextual problems involving use of scale	Map scales (1103) Scale drawing (1117) World atlas Understanding scale: mapzone.ordnancesurvey.co.uk/mapzone/PagesHomeworkHelp/docs/mapabilityunderstandingscale.pdf Scale drawing of a worm: www.naturewatch.ca/english/wormwatch/resources/drawing.html

Simplification	Extension
In question **4**, give students the length, height and width of the lorry in cm.	Students can repeat question **4** using a scale of their choice or repeat for the height and length of other animals. Alternatively students can make an accurate scale drawing of the classroom or rooms in their home.

Literacy	Links
Further link the vocabulary of transformations to that of proportional reasoning. Include the ratio notation and in its form 1 : *n* (see Ch 15) and link to scale factor. Liaise with other curricular areas in order to use current examples that will be familiar to the students in other school contexts; e.g. science, geography, art.	The Angel of the North is a steel sculpture which overlooks the A1 at Gateshead on Tyneside. The sculpture was unveiled in 1988 and was designed by Antony Gormley. It stands 20 m tall and has a wingspan of 54 m. The 1 : 16 scale model originally used for fundraising for the statue was the first item ever to be valued at £1 million on the BBC television programme Antiques Roadshow in 2008. There is more information about the Angel of the North at http://www.icons.org.uk/theicons/collection/angel

Alternative approach
Display a simple scale, 1:50, and orally ask students to use mini whiteboards in order to give actual distances in response to given measurements and vice versa. Check correct use of units, and also challenge students with appropriate changes in units. Other visual sources can be used such as that of the earth worm – see reference in Resources . how would this scale be written in 1: *n* form? Use wherever possible real contexts for practice, including actual ordnance survey maps. A simple reference to scales found on these and their interpretation can be found at the site.referenced in Resources.

Checkpoint
On a Landplan map of a new town, a park length measures 2cm. The scale of a Landplan map is 1:10 000. How long is the actual park in the new town? (200m)

Starter – Growing triangles

Ask students to plot (or imagine) a triangle with vertices at (0, 2), (2, 2) and (1, 4). Ask students to multiply the coordinates by two. What transformation has taken place? How does this compare with a triangle having vertices at (0, 2), (4, 2) and (2, 6)?

Can be extended by further changing the centre of enlargement.

Teaching notes

To work comfortably with the ideas in this unit, students need to have fluency and accuracy in simple ratio calculations and in conversions between units. Distances on maps will be measured in centimetres but on the ground, normally, the distances will be measured in kilometres, or sometimes metres.

Revision of these basic competencies and emphasising their importance in real-life contexts is a good starting point for the work in this spread.

Plenary

Discuss appropriate scales for maps. Why are they not all the same? Borrow an atlas from the geography departments and look at maps of parts of the UK, countries such as Portugal, maps of Africa or Australia shown on one page and World maps. Compare with a street map of a town.

Exercise commentary

Emphasise that all the calculations in this exercise are either a multiplication or a division.

Questions 1, 2 and **3** – The questions use the scale in the form '1 cm represents X'. Emphasise to students that this means that 1 cm on the map or scale drawing is the same as X in real life.

Question 4 – Remind students who are unable to understand the ratio 1 : 20, that the scale model distances are 20 times smaller than real-life distances, the real-life distances are 20 times larger than the scale model distances and that 1 cm represents 20 cm.

Question 5 – Use similar reminders as in question **4**, for students who cannot understand the ratio 1 : 100.

Answers

1. **a**   **i**   40 km   **ii**   75 km   **iii**   32.5 km   **iv**   17 km
         v   15 km
       b   **i**   3 cm   **ii**   12 cm   **iii**   25 cm   **iv**   2.5 cm
         v   0.5 cm

2. 22.5 m

3. **a**   Student's scale drawing   **b**   87.5 m

4. 82.5 cm, 22 cm, 12.5 cm

5. Student's scale drawing
   15 cm, 14 cm; 6 cm, 3 cm; 5 cm, 2 cm; 1.6 cm, 3.5 cm

Maps and scale drawings

9e Bearings

Objectives	
• Use bearings to specify direction	(L5)

Key ideas	Resources	
1 Understand the key features of bearings 2 Be able to follow and construct bearing instructions	Bearings	(1086)
	Spare protractors	
	Compass Bearings: http://mapzone.ordnancesurvey.co.uk/mapzone/Pages HomeworkHelp/docs/mapabilitycompassbearings.pdf	
	A few orienteering compasses	
	Tube Map Challenge: http://www.tes.co.uk/teaching-resource/Bearings-Tube-Map-Challenge-6315703/	

Simplification	Extension
In order to practice the correct use of a protractor, give students acute, obtuse and reflex angles to measure and draw. Orientate the angles to be measured so that the angles can be measured from the vertical in a clockwise direction. Insist that the students draw the angles in a similar way.	Challenge students to create shapes, for example regular polygons, using sets of points as in question **3**.

Literacy	Links
Check that students are clear about the conventions of both recording and measuring bearings, particularly that every section of a journey is referenced from North, regardless of the last leg direction.	True north is the direction of the Geographic North Pole, where all lines of longitude converge. The angular difference between true north and magnetic north is called the magnetic declination and is often shown on maps. In the UK at the moment, magnetic north lies between 3° (in SE England) and 7° (in NW Scotland) west of Grid North. However, the Magnetic North Pole is currently moving northwest at a rate of around 40 km per year so this difference will change in time. Using a compass to find true north is explained at http://www.scoutingresources.org.uk/compass/compass_magvar.html

Alternative approach

As a reheasal and revision exercise get students to stand and turn referenced to the front of the room as North, following bearing conventions. Emphasise both the clockwise direction and three figure recording of bearings. Simple key aspects can be found on the Ordnance Survey resources as referenced. The Tube Map Challenge (TES) provides a good source of activity which consolidates bearings and scale, also referenced in Resources. Make use of student interest in orienteering or D of E activities, where these skills are also likely to be put into practice. Perhaps one or two students can explain how an orienteering compass is used with a map.

Checkpoint

If a journey requires travelling on a bearing of 125°, what bearing would be required for the return journey?

(305°)

Starter – Angle estimation

Draw a mixture of acute, obtuse and reflex angles on the board. Ask students to estimate the size of each angle in degrees before measuring them. Use a scoring system, for example, 10 points for an exact answer, 5 points if the answer is within 10 degrees and 2 points if within 15 degrees.

Teaching notes

Emphasise the real-life application of this work and the importance of precision in giving directions for navigation, especially where rescue operations are concerned.

Review the correct use of protractors and ensure students have the correct equipment they need. Encourage students to draw rough sketches showing the known information in a problem before they start to construct a scale drawing.

Plenary

A radio distress signal gave a bearing as 13 with interference on the signal before the one and after the three. Ask students to discuss in pairs what possible three-figure bearings could have been given.

If the message had given 85, what three-figure bearings might have been intended?

Exercise commentary

Questions 1, 2 and **3** – Require measurement of angles using a protractor. The measurements are easier with a 360° protractor. It is essential that the protractor is positioned correctly so that the angles are measured from north and in a clockwise direction.

Question 4 – This is based on the example and uses alternate angle properties to calculate the back bearings.

Question 5 – Students will need to draw a vertical line to act as the north direction at the Finish point, in order to complete the question. Refer students back to **9d** for help with scale drawings.

Answers

1   a 030°   b 050°   c 080°   d 120°
    e 150°   f 180°   g 220°   h 260°
    i 290°   j 330°

2   a-e Check students' diagrams

3   a Square, four lines of symmetry
    b Rhombus, two lines of symmetry

4   a 055°   b 235°   c 120°   d 300°

5   a Students' scale drawings
    b 9.0 sea miles, 086°
    c 266°

Bearings

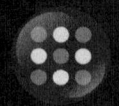

9 Transformations and scale – MySummary

Key outcomes	Quick check
Reflect, rotate and translate 2D shapes. L6	a Write down the vector which translates point (3, 2) to (7, -1) ((4, -3)) b Write down the coordinates of the triangle whose vertices are located at (-2, -3), (-1, -4) and (-1, -1) *after* a 180° rotation. ((2, 3), (1, 4) and (1, 1))
Enlarge a 2D shape using a given centre of enlargement. L6	A triangle has vertices at (1, 2), (3, 2) and (3, 5). Enlarge the triangle by sclae factor 2 using (0, 0) as the centre. (New vertices at (2, 4), (6, 4) and (6, 10))
Use maps and scale drawings. L6	A map has a scale of 1cm to 2km. How far, on the map, are the following distances? a 22km (11cm) b 15km (7.5cm) c 4.5km (2.25cm)
Use bearings to specify direction. L6	The bearing of B from A is 048°. What is the bearing of A from B? (228°)

MyMaths extra support

Lesson/online homework	Description
Lines of symmetry 1114 L4	Understanding reflective symmetry and recognizing symmetrical shapes

MyReview

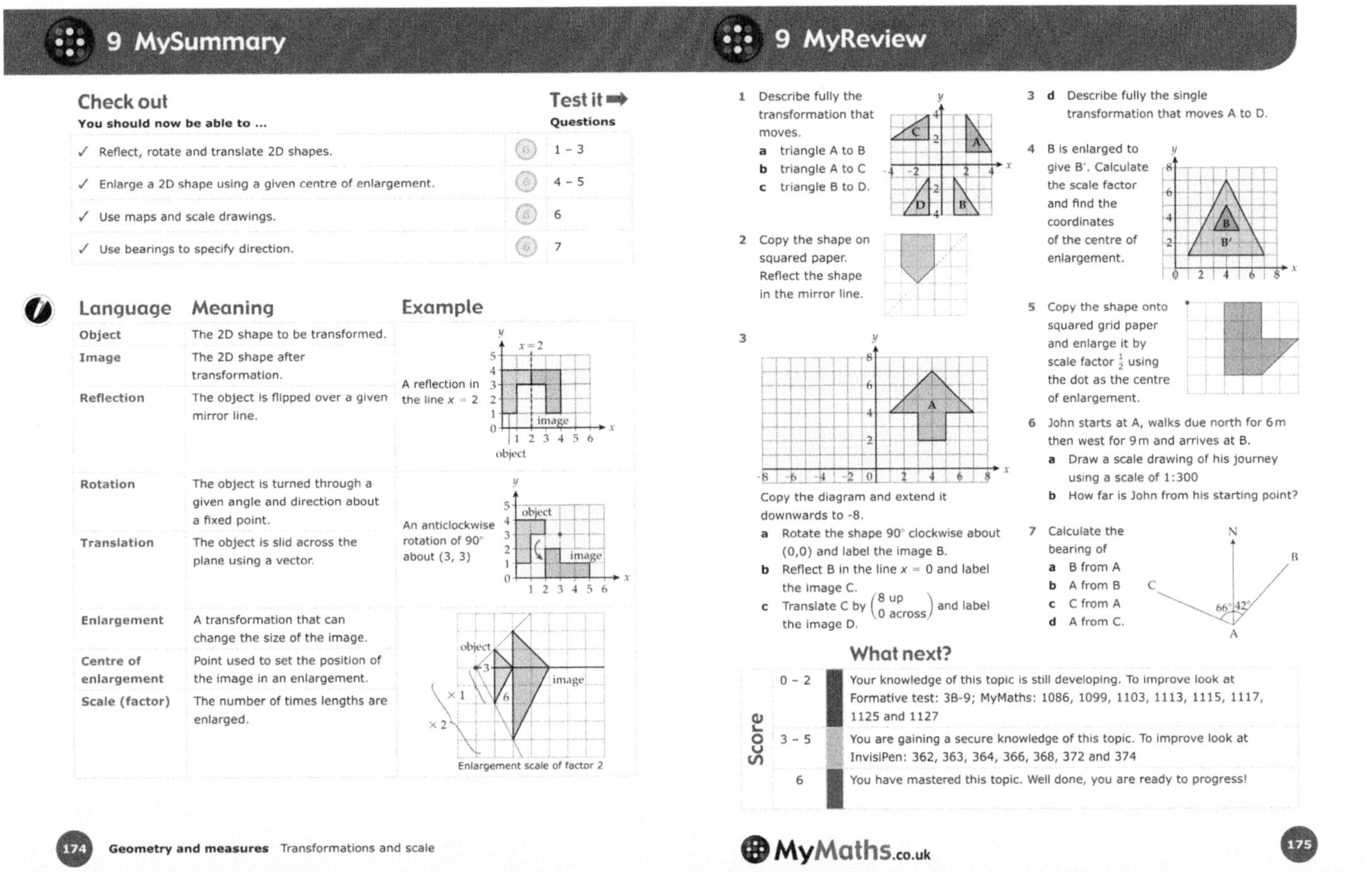

9 MySummary

Check out
You should now be able to ...

Test it ➡
Questions

- ✓ Reflect, rotate and translate 2D shapes. — 1 – 3
- ✓ Enlarge a 2D shape using a given centre of enlargement. — 4 – 5
- ✓ Use maps and scale drawings. — 6
- ✓ Use bearings to specify direction. — 7

Language	Meaning	Example
Object	The 2D shape to be transformed.	
Image	The 2D shape after transformation.	A reflection in the line $x = 2$
Reflection	The object is flipped over a given mirror line.	
Rotation	The object is turned through a given angle and direction about a fixed point.	An anticlockwise rotation of 90° about (3, 3)
Translation	The object is slid across the plane using a vector.	
Enlargement	A transformation that can change the size of the image.	Enlargement scale of factor 2
Centre of enlargement	Point used to set the position of the image in an enlargement.	
Scale (factor)	The number of times lengths are enlarged.	

Geometry and measures Transformations and scale

9 MyReview

1. Describe fully the transformation that moves.
   a triangle A to B
   b triangle A to C
   c triangle B to D.

2. Copy the shape on squared paper. Reflect the shape in the mirror line.

3. Copy the diagram and extend it downwards to -8.
   a Rotate the shape 90° clockwise about (0,0) and label the image B.
   b Reflect B in the line $x = 0$ and label the image C.
   c Translate C by $\binom{8 \text{ up}}{0 \text{ across}}$ and label the image D.
   d Describe fully the single transformation that moves A to D.

4. B is enlarged to give B'. Calculate the scale factor and find the coordinates of the centre of enlargement.

5. Copy the shape onto squared grid paper and enlarge it by scale factor $\frac{1}{2}$ using the dot as the centre of enlargement.

6. John starts at A, walks due north for 6 m then west for 9 m and arrives at B.
   a Draw a scale drawing of his journey using a scale of 1:300
   b How far is John from his starting point?

7. Calculate the bearing of
   a B from A
   b A from B
   c C from A
   d A from C.

What next?

Score	
0 – 2	Your knowledge of this topic is still developing. To improve look at Formative test: 3B-9; MyMaths: 1086, 1099, 1103, 1113, 1115, 1117, 1125 and 1127
3 – 5	You are gaining a secure knowledge of this topic. To improve look at InvisiPen: 362, 363, 364, 366, 368, 372 and 374
6	You have mastered this topic. Well done, you are ready to progress!

MyMaths.co.uk

Question commentary

Question 1 – For each question students must state the type of transformation and describe it fully. Students can use tracing paper to help with the rotation in **b**.

Question 2 – Students should check their mirror line is a line of symmetry of the finished diagram.

Question 3 – Students sometimes confuse the lines $x = 0$ and $y = 0$.

Question 4 – Students should draw lines through the corresponding vertices of the object and the image to see where they cross for the centre of enlargement.

Question 5 – Suggest students start with one vertex, e.g. top left, the distance in the object is 2 squares from the dot so in the image it will be 1 square from the dot. Now draw the whole image with all the side lengths halved from the original.

Question 6 – For part **b**, students should get 3.6cm for the length in the scale drawing. The answer should be given to no more than 1 decimal place given the inaccuracy of measurement.

Question 7 – The phrases e.g. 'B from A' confuse some students. They may measure anticlockwise giving incorrect answers 066° for **c** and 246° for **d**. Their bearings must have 3 digits.

Answers

1.
   a Translation of 1 unit left and 5 units down
   b Rotation of 90° anti-clockwise about (0, 0)
   c Reflection in the y-axis

2. Check students' drawing

3.
   a Coordinates at (2, -3), (2, -5), (4, -5), (4, -7), (7, -4), (4, -1) and (4, -3)
   b Coordinates at (-2, -3), (-2, -5), (-4, -5), (-4, -7), (-7, -4), (-4, -1) and (-4, -3)
   c Coordinates at (-2, 5), (-2, 3), (-4, 3), (-4, 1), (-7, 4), (-4, 7) and (-4, 5)
   d Anti-clockwise rotation of 90° about (0, 0)

4. Scale factor 3, centre (4, 4)

6. b 10.8 m

7. a 042°   b 222°   c 294°   d 114°

9 MyPractice

1 A shape is rotated three times through a right angle about the point O.
Write the mathematical name of the shape formed by the object and its images when the rotated shape is

 a a right-angled isosceles triangle

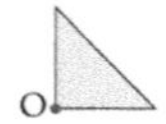

 b a square.

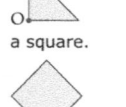

2 a Draw an enlargement of the grey trapezium by scale factor 2.

 b Show how four congruent grey trapeziums tessellate to make the image.

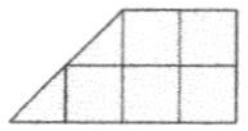

3 Draw coordinate axes from 0 to 10 on square grid paper.
Plot and join the points (2, 1), (3, 2), (3, 3) and (2, 4) to form a quadrilateral.

 a What is the mathematical name of the quadrilateral?

 b Enlarge the quadrilateral by scale factor 3 using (0, 1) as the centre of enlargement.

 c Write the coordinates of the vertices of the enlargement.

4 Two mirrors M_1 and M_2 are 4 units apart.

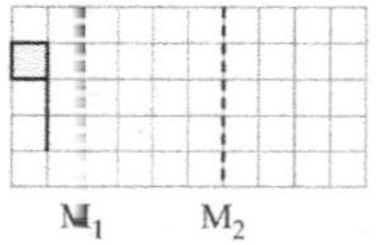

 a Reflect the green flag in the mirror M_1.
 Label the image I_1.

 b Draw the reflection of I_1 using the mirror M_2.
 Label the image I_2.

 c Describe the single transformation that maps the green flag to I_2.

5 The scale on a map is 1 : 25 000.

 a Calculate the real-life distance represented by
 i 7 cm **ii** 8.5 cm **iii** 4.5 cm **iv** 24 cm.

 b Calculate the distance on the map for these real-life distances.
 i 1200 m **ii** 850 m **iii** 8 km **iv** 4.5 km.

6 The diagram shows the positions of four trees drawn to scale.
Calculate the real-life distances between these trees.

 a Ash to Beech

 b Ash to Cherry

 c Ash to Oak

 d Beech to Cherry

 e Beech to Oak

 f Cherry to Oak

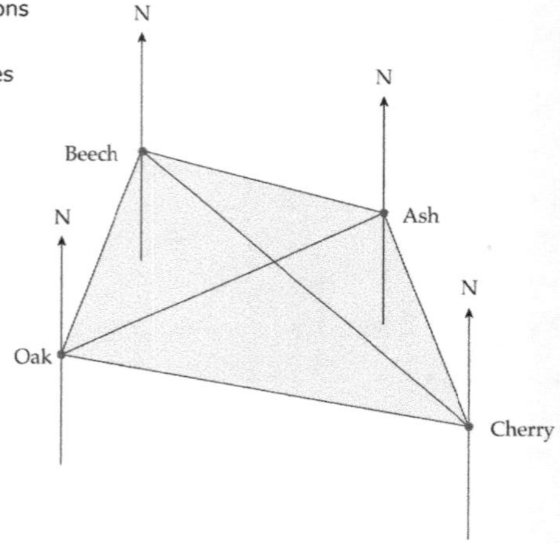

Scale: 1 cm represents 0.5 km

7 Use the diagram in question **6**.
Measure the bearing of

 a Ash from Oak

 b Beech from Oak

 c Beech from Ash

 d Cherry from Ash

 e Oak from Ash

 f Cherry from Beech

 g Oak from Beech

 h Ash from Beech

 i Ash from Cherry

 j Beech from Cherry.

Question commentary

Question 1 – Encourage students to look at the geometrical properties of the completed quadrilateral. Tracing paper could be used.

Questions 2 and **3** – Students should be encouraged to draw ray lines from the centre of enlargement in question **3**.

Question 4 – Students should recognise that successive reflections lead to a translation.

Questions 5 and **6** – Students should be encouraged to work in sensible units for question **5**. In question **6**, students must measure carefully before using the scale given. Again, check they are using sensible units for their answers.

Question 7 – Ensure bearings are given using three figures and that they are all measured clockwise from North.

Answers

1. **a** Square **b** Square
2. **a** Check students' drawings
   b Check students' drawings
3. **a** Isosceles trapezium **b** Students' diagrams
   c (6, 1), (9, 4), (9, 7), (6, 10)
4. **a, b** Check students' diagrams
   c Translation of 8 right 0 up
5. **a** **i** 1750 m **ii** 2125 m **iii** 1125 m **iv** 6 km
   b **i** 4.8 cm **ii** 3.4 cm **iii** 32 cm **iv** 18 cm
6. **a** 2 km **b** 1.8 km **c** 2.8 km **d** 3.45 km
   e 1.75 km **f** 3.35 km
7. **a** 065° **b** 020° **c** 285° **d** 160°
   e 245° **f** 130° **g** 200° **h** 105°
   i 340° **j** 310°

MyPractice

Case Study 3: Climate change

Related lessons		Resources	
Percentage change	4e	Percentage change	(1060)
Percentage problems	4f	Change as a percentage	(1302)
Real-life graphs	6g	Conversion graphs	(1059)
Time series	6i	Real life graphs	(1184)
Statistical diagrams 1	8d	Drawing pie charts	(1207)
Statistical diagrams 2	8e	Mean and mode	(1200)
Calculating averages	8f	Median and range	(1203)
Interpreting graphs	8g	Literature on global warming	

Simplification

Often students are vague with their justifications in data tasks like this. A writing frame could be used for tasks **3a**, **4c** and **4d** to help students structure their answers.

Making sensible predictions is often difficult and in this repect students may need guidance on how to approach task **2c**.

The values given in the table in task **4** can be rounded to the nearest whole number to make it easier for the students to calculate the ranges and means.

Extension

Ask if two sets of data are really sufficient to draw conclusions. Discuss how one or both of the years chosen might have freak temperatures, maybe having a particularly warm summer or cold winter. Looking at the data, do they think this is the case? Establish that you could compare other pairs of years that are 100 years apart, such as 1907 and 2007.

Students could also research information about carbon footprints, maybe using one of the online calculators to measure their own footprint.

Links

New Scientist magazine has lots of interesting articles on climate change on their website: http://www.newscientist.com/topic/climate-change

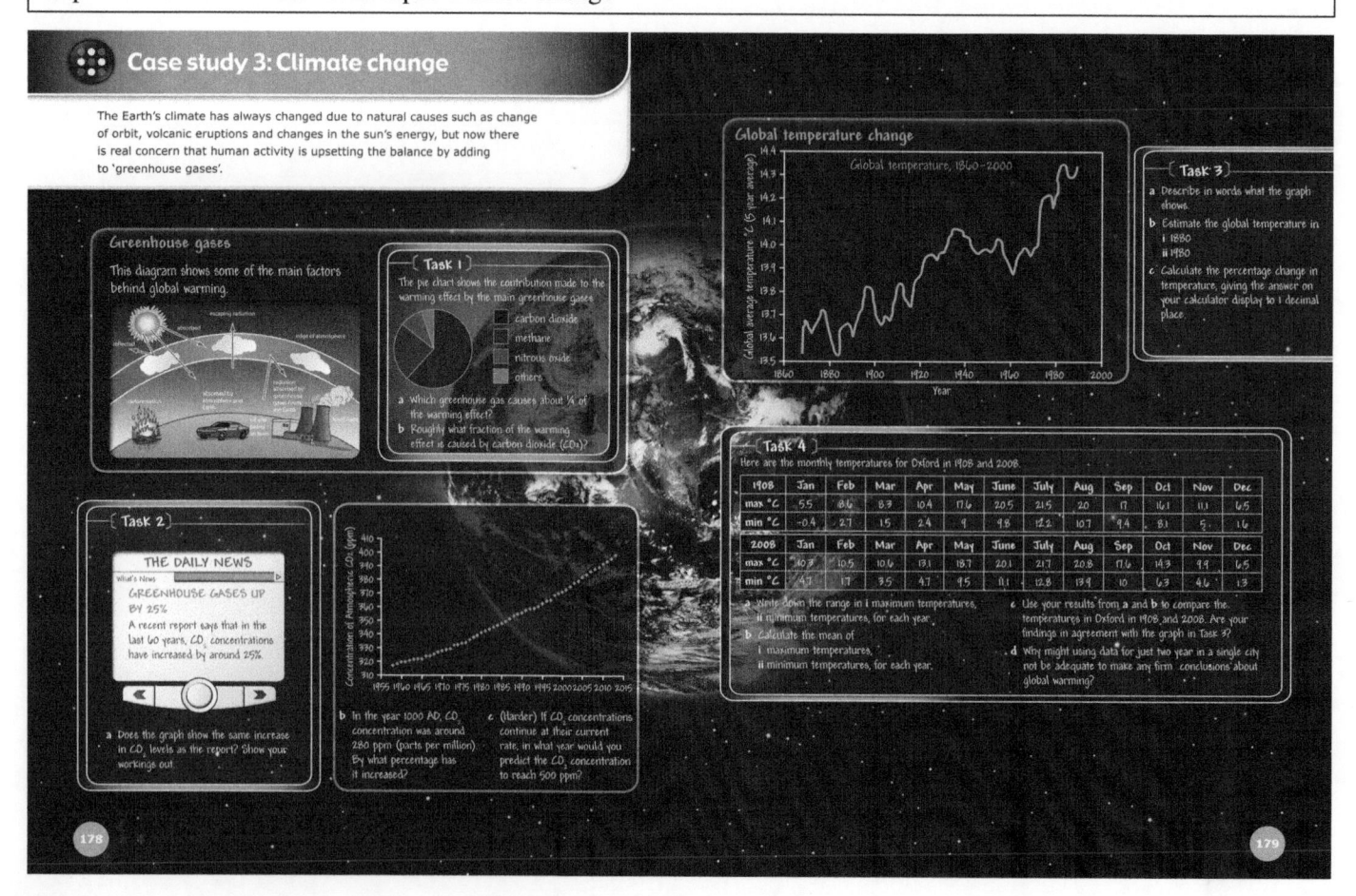

Teaching notes

This case study provides a limited amount of information about greenhouse gases and temperatures, leaving students to draw their own conclusions from the data.

Discuss how the greenhouse effect is needed to keep the Earth at a habitable temperature. Use the diagram to talk about the main processes involved:

– Most of the energy that the Earth receives from the Sun is in the form of visible light.

– Some of the energy is directly absorbed by the atmosphere and some is reflected off the top of the atmosphere, but as the atmosphere is fairly transparent to visible light, most of the energy passes through the atmosphere.

– The heat absorbed by the Earth warms it up. The warmed Earth radiates heat back to the atmosphere, but this time in the infrared range rather than as visible light.

– The infrared energy radiated from the Earth does not pass through the atmosphere. Instead, the energy is absorbed by the atmosphere, heating it up.

– The warmed atmosphere then radiates some of its heat back to Earth and some of it out into space.

A balance of heat gains and heat losses maintains the Earth at a habitable temperature. Ensure that students realise that the greenhouse effect is not a bad thing. Without it, Earth would be too cold to sustain life. Much reporting of climate change makes it sound as if the greenhouse effect is in some way bad, rather than the problem being that the balance of heat gains and losses could be changing.

Task 1

Look at the pie chart and establish that carbon dioxide has the greatest effect on warming. Then look at the report describing how CO_2 levels have risen. Introduce the idea of human activity altering the levels of greenhouse gases. Ask questions such as; what things do you know about that increase the CO_2 levels in the atmosphere?

Task 2

Give students a few minutes to work on the questions relating to the report and CO_2 levels graph before asking: if CO_2 levels have increased, what is likely to have happened to temperatures? Hear students' thoughts. Establish that it is likely that temperatures will have risen as CO_2 has the greatest warming effect of the greenhouse gases.

Task 3

Look at the global temperatures graph and ask; what does the vertical axis show? What do you think is happening with the temperature? Some may mention that temperatures went down steadily for several years beginning about 1915, despite greater industrial activity and increasing motorised transport at the time.

Task 4

Looking quickly at the data, do you think there has been much change in Oxford's temperatures in the past 100 years? They could argue that temperatures have increased, giving reasons such as Jan 2008 being much warmer than Jan 1908. They could argue that temperatures haven't changed very much, giving reasons such as July in both years being very similar and December in both years being very similar.

What could we do with the data to get a better idea of any changes? Talk about their answers and decide as a class whether you think there is any change in Oxford temperatures and whether this mirrors the change in global temperatures.

Answers

1 a Methane   b $\frac{5}{8}$ or 60%

2 a Yes, there was about a 30% increase.
   b 43%
   c Students' own answers but somewhere in the region of 2115.

3 a There is a general upward trend. Temperatures appear to be rising.
   b i 13.6°C   ii 14.2°C
   c 4.4%

4 a i 1908: 16°C, 2008: 15.2°C
       ii 1908: 12.6°C, 2008: 12.6°C
   b i 1908: 13.59 °C, 2008: 14.51 °C
       ii 1908: 6.00°C, 2008: 7.01 °C
   c Students' opinions: generally yes, both have increased.
   d Students' opinions: The two years could be 'freak' years and looking at more pairs across more cities would improve reliability.

Climate change

10 Equations

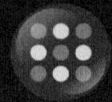

Learning outcomes

A2 Substitute numerical values into formulae and expressions, including scientific formulae (L7)

A3 Understand and use the concepts and vocabulary of expressions, equations, inequalities, terms and factors (L7)

A4 Simplify and manipulate algebraic expressions to maintain equivalence by:
- collecting like terms
- taking out common factors
- multiplying a single term over a bracket (L7)

A6 Model situations or procedures by translating them into algebraic expressions or formulae and by using graphs (L7)

A7 Use algebraic methods to solve linear equations in 1 variable (including all forms that require rearrangement) (L7)

Introduction

The chapter starts by looking at simple two-step equations before moving on the solve equations with brackets and then equations where the unknown is on both sides. Constructing equations from a given context (and solving them) is covered in the next section before the final section which covers solving equations by trial and improvement.

The introduction discusses the widespread use of equations in everyday, scientific contexts. The use of equations and mathematical formulae is an essential part of any scientific research and modelling. In fact Eric Temple Bell wrote a book in 1931 entitled 'The Queen of the Sciences' in which the importance of mathematics in a scientific context was discussed. He followed this up with the sequel 'The Handmaiden of the Sciences' in 1937. This book rather looked at mathematics as a tool which is used by scientists rather than as a fundamental underpinning that is necessary for science to even exist. Whatever your view, there is no doubt that the examples given in the introduction are all important cases for the scientific fields mentioned. Further examples can be given as part of the discussion of these ideas as required.

Prior knowledge

Students should already know how to...
- Use operations and inverse operations to work out arithmetic problems
- Simplify by collecting like terms and expanding brackets

Starter problem

The starter problem is an example of a pair of simultaneous equations. While the algebraic or graphical solution of simultaneous equations is outside the scope of the chapter, students can still be given time to consider informal methods of solution such as trial and improvement or blind guess work.

Algebraically, if we let x be the height of the Gelbhaus pod and y be the height of the Blauhaus pod, we get:

$$4x + 2y = 16$$
and $$2x + 4y = 17$$

If we solve these using a standard method, we get that $x = 2.5$ metres and $y = 3$ metres. Students should be able to come up with these 'neat' answers by an informal method.

Resources

MyMaths

Trial and improvement	1057	Simple equations	1154	Factorising quadratics 1	1157
Solving equations	1182				

Online assessment

Chapter test	3B–10
Formative test	3B–10
Summative test	3B–10

InvisiPen solutions

Expanding brackets	214	Making equations	231
One-step equations	234	Two-step equations	235
Equations with brackets	236	Unknowns on both sides	237
Solving equations with fractions			242

Topic scheme

Teaching time = 5 lessons/2 weeks

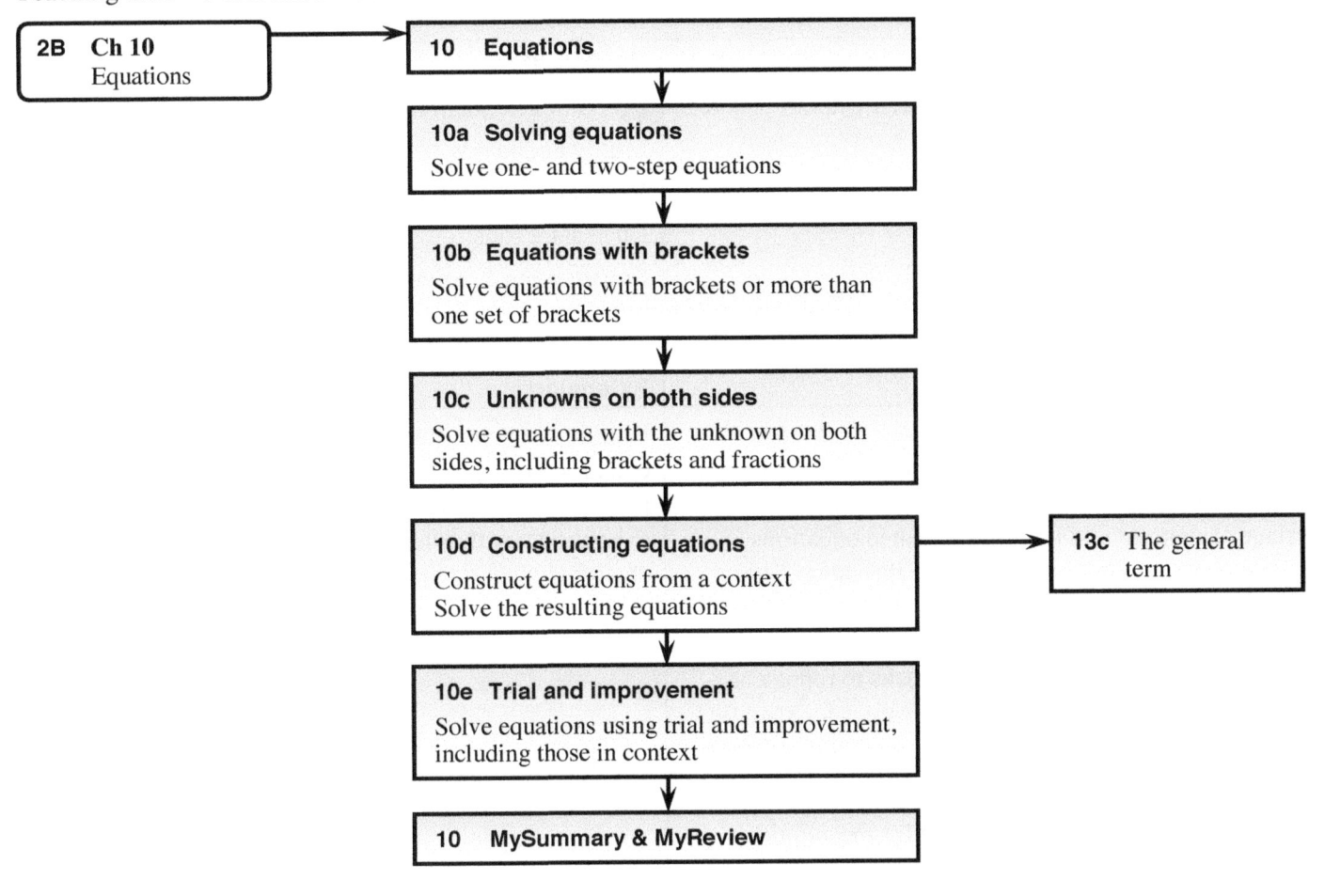

```
2B  Ch 10
    Equations
```
→
10 Equations

↓

10a Solving equations
Solve one- and two-step equations

↓

10b Equations with brackets
Solve equations with brackets or more than one set of brackets

↓

10c Unknowns on both sides
Solve equations with the unknown on both sides, including brackets and fractions

↓

10d Constructing equations
Construct equations from a context
Solve the resulting equations   →   **13c The general term**

↓

10e Trial and improvement
Solve equations using trial and improvement, including those in context

↓

10 MySummary & MyReview

Differentiation

Student book 3A   184 – 199
Equality and inequality
Solving simple equations
Solve equations by balancing
Write down and solve equations given in context

Student book 3B   180 – 195
Solve one- and two- step equations
Solve equations involving brackets
Solve equations with the unknown on both sides
Construct equations from contexts and solve them
Solve equations using trial and improvement

Student book 3C   176 – 195
Consolidation of linear equations
Forming and solving pairs of simultaneous equations
Solving simultaneous equations graphically
Solving inequalities
Solving equations using trial and improvement

Introduction

10a Solving equations

Objectives	
• Construct and solve linear equations with integer coefficients (with and without brackets, negative signs anywhere in the equation, positive or negative solution) (L6)	

Key ideas	Resources
1 Solving two-stage linear equations without brackets	Simple equations (1154) Mini whiteboards Vertical and horizontal number lines Cuisenaire rods Constructing & solving Linear Equations -Y9 Booklet: http://www.nationalstemcentre.org.uk/elibrary/resource/4633/constructing-and-solving-linear-equations

Simplification	Extension
Refer to question **1**. It cannot be overstated that a secure understanding and use of the four basic inverse operations is needed before students can tackle two-stage 'balances' and more complicated equations. Encourage students to write one of the sides of an equation in different ways on order to help identify similar terms, and maintain visual support by using number lines and/or Cuisenaire blocks to represent unknown values. Keep to positive values for specific unknown values until a student shows full confidence.	Working in pairs, students can offer each other an equation of their own invention, mindful that, if their partner cannot solve it, then it returns to them for them to solve. They thus have to strike a balance between challenging their partner but not beyond what they themselves can do.

Literacy	Links
Maintain an emphasis on 'reading for meaning' in order to secure the concept of equality. Encourage students to use different but equivalent expressions, including changing order e.g. $2x + 5 = 7$; $7 = 5 + 2x$; $5 + 2x = 7$ and so on. Encourage students to check that their recording conserves the equality concept of the = symbol.	The first equation ever written with an equals sign appeared in a book by Robert Recorde in 1557. He was a physician and a mathematician and taught mathematics at Cambridge. More info at: http://www.bbc.co.uk/wales/southwest/halloffame/innovators/robertrecorde.shtml

Alternative approach

Use an equivalent spider diagram as a starter with a centre equation such as $3x + 4 = 19$. Students may offer alternative equivalent versions using mini whiteboards, and examples chosen from those offered to add to a class display. Encourage a variety of equivalents by asking for 'simpler' versions or 'complex' versions as well as 'different' ones. Versions that demonstrate equality of term(s) on each side of the equation should be used to strengthen 'balancing' or 'inverse' intuitively, e.g. $3x + 4 = 15 + 4$ which can lead easily to $3x = 15$ and so on. Support this by modelling using a number line thus:

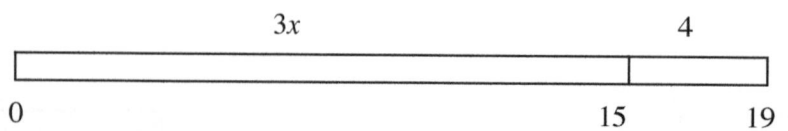

```
              3x                    4
    |─────────────────────|──────|
    0                    15     19
```

Where an equation has a negative solution, avoid using number lines for modelling. When working with any examples for consolidation, encourage students to choose an approach of their own preference rather than a stated procedure. Different approaches can be shared with the whole group together with discussions about approach preferences and efficiency.

Checkpoint

Solve the equation $3p - 7 = -13$. ($p = -2$)

Solve the equation $2x - 9 = 15$. ($x = 12$)

Starter – Make fifteen

Write $a = -2$, $b = -3$, $c = 5$ on the board.

Ask students for expressions that have a value of 15, for example, $-bc$, $4c + a + b$

Can be differentiated by the choice of target number or values of the variables.

Teaching notes

Students often know the answer intuitively to equations similar to those in the first example. Revision of harder single operation equations, such as $x + 7 = 3$ and $3x = 8$ (where the answers are not positive integers), can be useful to emphasise the need for care and attention to detail when using the balance method.

Many students are poor at communicating what they do on paper in solving equations. Shorthand annotations such as (+3) or (÷5) beside each new line can be very valuable in developing this skill.

Plenary

Students can check a sample of their solutions to the questions in this exercise by substituting back into the original equation. This builds experience of checking by substitution and is a good habit to cultivate.

Exercise commentary

Question 1 – Use mini whiteboards to check that students are confident in using inverse operations. Oral work beyond the nine equations of question **1** may be needed for students to be secure in choosing the correct inverse operation before moving on to the two-stage balances and equations of questions **2** and **3**.

Question 2 – The balances illustrate the inverse operations of 'subtract' and 'divide'. For example, we subtract to 'get rid of' or 'undo' what has been added to the balance.

Question 3 – These two-stage equations all require students to add/subtract before dividing. In parts **i** to **l** remind students that a balance works either way round. The first fractional answer appears in part **g**.

Question 4 – A number line visible to the whole class is useful here. In part **b**, subtracting 6 from both sides has students finding the 2 on the number line and counting down 6 steps to reach -4.

Question 5 – A testing set of equations. Students meet 'multiplying both sides' for the first time in part **d**. The order of the two operations also needs care. Parts **d** to **g** may be worthy of a class discussion.

Question 6 – Constructing the equation is straightforward but given that it has xs on both sides students will need to go back to thinking of the equation as a balance.

Question 7 – Part **a** needs like-terms collecting first.

Answers

1	a	5	b	13	c	1	d	5
	e	20	f	5	g	6	h	8
	i	-3						
2	a	4	b	1½				
3	a	7	b	8	c	5	d	9
	e	3	f	0	g	1½	h	5½
	i	2¼	j	5	k	-1½	l	-½
4	a	7	b	-2	c	-2	d	3
	e	5	f	-1	g	½	h	-1½
	i	-2	j	-1	k	-4	l	-2¼
5	a	0	b	8½	c	2½	d	10
	e	13	f	12	g	9	h	$2\frac{2}{3}$
	i	-2	j	-2	k	-4	l	1

6   $x = 6$

7   a $x = 5$, area = 75 cm²   b $y = 4$

Solving equations

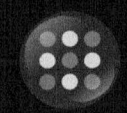

10b Equations with brackets

Objectives

- Construct and solve linear equations with integer coefficients (with and without brackets, negative signs anywhere in the equation, positive or negative solution) (L6)

Key ideas	Resources
1 Solving linear equations which include brackets	Simple equations (1154) Mini whiteboards Bags Blank cards Vertical and horizontal number lines (See also Y9 booklet referenced in 10a)

Simplification	Extension
Have two or three bags with identical contents, the contents being cards on which are written expressions or numbers (such as, a *3x* card and a 5 card in each of two bags). The contents of the bags can then be emptied out and 'like terms' physically collected (to get *6x + 10* in the above example). The written expression mirrors what is seen physically.	Students, working in pairs, can each tell a 'story' which the other of the pair has to write algebraically. (They can use the wording of the second example or question **6** as a model). The student who writes the algebra then hands the equation back to the story-teller for the story-teller to solve.

Literacy	Links
Continue to encourage reading equations with meaning, e.g. 'two lots of..' rather that 2(....) and so on. Maintain attention on the correct use of the = symbol in any steps that students record.	There are four types of brackets in use in the English language. The word 'bracket' usually refers to round brackets or parentheses ( ) which are used for explanations. Square brackets [ ] are just called brackets in the US and are used for comments or corrections. Braces or curly brackets { } are used to link two lines together and are also used in computing and music. Angle brackets < > are used around highlighted phrases.

Alternative approach

The students should be familiar with expanding brackets, but a reminder can serve as a useful starter: use an equivalent spider diagram with an expression such as $3(2x + 4)$ as the centre. Encourage students to think about the solving approaches when reading any initial equation. Encourage students to recognise that it is not always necessary to expand brackets when solving such equations. For example, all the equations in **2** may be solved without expanding brackets if students recognise the equivalence of, e.g. 'halving' **2a** to give $3x + 2 = 8$; doubling **2f**, and so on. Students may need to build greater confidence with manipulating expressions either using further equivalent spider diagrams or examples such as 9A.1a. found in referenced Y9 booklet.

Checkpoint

Solve $3(x - 7) = 15$ $\hfill (x = 12)$

Solve $5(b + 1) - 4(b - 1) = 0$ $\hfill (b = -9)$

Starter – Connections

If $x = 4$, $y = -3$ and $z = 7$, ask students for rules connecting x, y and z, for example, $2x + y = z - 2$. Encourage students to use all three variables in their rules.

This can be differentiated by the choice of values for the variables.

Teaching notes

Students sometimes find the process of solving equations with brackets quite daunting because there are a lot of steps. One way to emphasise the separation of 'tasks' within the process is to solve two or three equations from the stage where the brackets have been removed and terms collected – on the bottom of the board. Write the equation with brackets at the top of the board, and work through the simplification.

An alternative approach is to ask students just to remove brackets and collect like terms, without solving, until they are comfortable with this process. They can then go back and solve these equations and then progress to solving equations in one continuous process.

Plenary

Use a mini whiteboard activity to confirm that students are confident with each stage of the process (expand brackets, collect like terms, solve).

Exercise commentary

Question 1 – The diagrams remind students to think of balances. They also offer a visual method for students to see the total number of xs and the numeric totals.

Question 2 – The words '2 lots of' or '2 bags of' are useful to help explain the multiplication by 2 when the 2 is 'outside' a bracket.

Question 3 – This question does not require the multiplication of two negative numbers (see question 5). A number line could be useful to help any simplification.

Question 4 – Care with negative numbers is needed and, again, reference to a number line would be useful.

Question 5 – Confidence with multiplication of directed numbers (including two negative numbers) is needed.

Question 6 – Understanding how the algebra builds up towards an equation is as important as being able to solve the resulting equation. A class discussion could be valuable here.

Answers

1. a 5 b 5

2. a 2 b 2 c 4 d 8
   e 2 f 5 g 1 h 2
   i 5

3. a 2 b 1 c 0 d 3
   e 2 f 3 g $1\frac{5}{6}$ h 0

4. a 3 b -1 c 3 d -1
   e -2 f -3 g 4 h -3
   i 0 j 1

5. a 2 b 1 c 3 d 5
   e 1 f 2 g 4 h 2
   i -2 j -4

6. $3(x - 5) - 5 = 13$ $x = 11$
   Grandma's gift is £12

Equations with brackets

10c Unknowns on both sides

Objectives
- Construct and solve linear equations with integer coefficients (with and without brackets, negative signs anywhere in the equation, positive or negative solution) (L6)

Key ideas	Resources
1 Solving linear equations with unknowns on both sides 2 Solving linear equations involving fractions	Solving equations (1182) Small blank cards Number lines

Simplification	Extension
Continue to practice equivalent expressions in order to make the 'balancing' approach more visual. Use also the number line approach, but here do not use equations with negative solutions.	Students can invent other triangle puzzles similar to the one in the exercise. They can extend the puzzles to quadrilaterals. Each puzzle is given to a partner to solve.

Literacy	Links
Maintain attention on the correct use of the = symbol in any steps that students record while also encouraging 'reading with meaning' – this time with an emphasis on, e.g. 'half', 'third' and so on, to encourage inverse operation consideration.	Equations are used in chemistry as a form of shorthand to describe the changes that occur during a chemical reaction. The substances reacting (reactants) are shown on the left hand side of the equation with an arrow pointing to the chemicals formed (products) on the right. The equation must account for every atom that is used so there must be the same number of atoms of each element on each side of the equation. There is more information about chemical equations at http://www.chemtutor.com/react.htm

Alternative approach
Use equivalent spider diagrams as in the previous sections. Students are likely to recognise equivalent statements that help in solving more confidently with practice, thus suggesting, e.g. $5x + 3x + 2 = 3x + 10 + 2$, which readily becomes $5x = 10$, and so on. This can also be supported by representations of each side on a number line for comparision. Similarly, for the first example an equivalent of $7x - 1 = 6x + 9$ may result, followed by $6x + x - 1 = 6x + 10 - 1$; and so on.

Checkpoint
Solve the equation $2x - 5 = 7x + 10$ ($x = -3$)

Solve the equation $6 + x = 4(x - 3)$ ($x = 6$)

Starter – Identities

Ask students to match up identities from the following (there are some red herrings).

$\frac{1}{5}(30x-5)$, $5(3x+2)$, $4(3x-7)$,

$3(2x-4)+2(3x-3)$, $14-3(5-2x)$, $3(6x-5)$,

$7(2x-3)-(2x+7)$, $\frac{1}{4}(12x-8)$,

$2(6x-9)$, $\frac{1}{3}(9x-6)$

Can be extended by asking students for possible identities for the left over expressions, $5(3x+2)$ and $3(6x-5)$

Teaching notes

Review solving equations in the form $ax = b$. Using values of a and b which give integer and fractional solutions, include both fractions less than 1, improper fractions which should be converted into mixed numbers, and values of a and b which give negative solutions.

As with brackets in the last spread, it may be helpful to separate out the stage of multiplying through to remove fractions in the starting equation into an activity of its own until students are confident.

At the end of a calculation students should be encouraged to check their solution by back substitution.

Plenary

As a consolidation exercise, use three 'solved' equations which contain errors in the solutions (in multiplying to remove the fractions, in collecting like terms, and in the division stage). Ask students to work in pairs to find the errors and correct the solutions.

Exercise commentary

Question 1 – All parts have more xs on the left than on the right. So 'collecting the xs on the left' is straightforward.

Question 2 – These equations practise adding or subtracting xs to both sides to 'get rid of' all xs from the RHS.

Question 3 – These equations practise multiplying both sides (to eliminate a fraction). Students need to know that there are two ways of writing a fraction of an expression – parts **h** and **i** are identical.

Question 4 – These equations practise all that has gone before.

Question 5 – Ask students to check their answers by relating the values they get to the original problems.

Question 6 – Circle A leads to expressions in circles B and C. An equation can then be written for the bottom side of the triangle.

Answers

1	a	5	b	3½	c	1½	d	$2\frac{1}{3}$
	e	3	f	2	g	1¼	h	3½
	i	1¼	j	2½				

2	a	5	b	3	c	3	d	2
	e	2½	f	1¼	g	0	h	2
	i	1	j	2½				

3	a	2½	b	10	c	1	d	2
	e	4½	f	1.5	g	3	h	2
	i	2						

4	a	7	b	10	c	1	d	3
	e	5	f	$3\frac{1}{5}$				

5   a   13   b   £30

6   B $14-x$, C $21-x$
     $(14-x)+(21-x)=27$
     $x = 4$

Unknowns on both sides

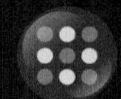

10d Constructing equations

Objectives

- Construct and solve linear equations with integer coefficients (with and without brackets, negative signs anywhere in the equation, positive or negative solution) (L6)
- Use formulae from mathematics and other subjects (L7)
- Derive a formula (L7)

Key ideas	Resources
1 Interpret and represent a problem using algebra 2 Use an algebraic approach to solve problems	Mini whiteboards Creating algebraic expressions: http://nrich.maths.org/8469

Simplification	Extension
'Think of a number' problems are a straightforward lead-in to this exercise. As the teacher says the words, students should write a further step on their mini whiteboards. For example, the teacher says 'I'm thinking of a number' and the students write 'x'; the teacher continues 'I multiply it by 3' and the students write a 3 to get '$3x$' ….. etc. The equation thus builds up. Students then solve the equation individually and show their answers for class discussion.	Ask students to make their own Start to Finish diagrams as in the puzzle of the exercise. The diagrams must have two routes, but the routes can be more complex. Each diagram is given to a partner to solve and then returned to the creator for checking.

Literacy	Links
Check sense and accuracy of mathematical sentences. Where problems do not give a suggested algebraic unknown, show students that they will need to state their approach simply; e.g. 'let m be the length of the rod in cm'.	Navigational satellites move continuously in orbit around the Earth and use solar panels for power. Engineers use complex equations to calculate each satellite's future position and to orientate the solar panels to capture the most energy from the sun. Info on the Navstar Block II navigation satellite at www.spacetoday.org/Satellites/GPS.html

Alternative approach

Model a simple geometric problem: e.g. find the perimeter of a rectangle which is $3x$ long and $x + 4$ wide. Encourage students to give you as many different versions of the expression for the perimeter as possible, using mini whiteboards, thus consolidating equivalence. Discuss which expression the students consider the 'simplest' and why? Give a value for the perimeter and ask students to find x. Check correctness then explore how they solved it, for instance, which expression (or not) did they use, and why. Continue to practice with some given unknown values, but extend by including general problems/puzzles such as those given at NRICH as referenced.

Checkpoint

Construct an expression for the area of a rectangle where its length is 3 times its width.
If its perimeter is 24 cm what would its area be?   ($A = 3x^2$; $x = 3$ so area = 27cm^2)

Starter – Jumble

Write a list of anagrams on the board and ask students to unscramble them and then make up their own. Possible anagrams are

VEGINATE PANDEX TIDYNITE STUBUTIEST
FUNNICOT RENXPOISES RALFMOU
OREOPAINT REVISEN ANOQUITE

(negative, expand, identity, substitute, function, expression, formula, operation, inverse, equation)

Teaching notes

This unit supports the development of links between areas of mathematics such as geometry and measures and algebra, and students gain experience in using formulae in real-life situations.

Weak literacy skills are an obstacle for many students. Emphasise the need to identify key information in word problems and to write down equations and expressions clearly, with an indication as to where they come from.

Students can work in pairs, to explain their understanding of the problem first, and then their reasoning in solving. This may help to develop confidence amongst the weaker students.

Plenary

As a consolidation exercise, provide some 'solved' problems involving equations which contain errors in the solutions (incorrect equation, wrong simplification, incorrect solution). Ask students to work in pairs to find the errors and correct the solutions.

Exercise commentary

Question 1 – Students' knowledge of angle facts leads into writing simple equations.

Question 2 – Similarly, students' understanding of perimeter and area leads to equations.

Question 3 – This question is similar to the worked example about Hassim on the previous page.

Questions 4, 5 and 6 – Students need to read the questions carefully. The English is precisely written to convey accurate meaning. Pair students with weaker language skills together.

Question 7 – The two routes provide expressions of equal value.

Answers

1   a   55°   b   35°   c   50°   d   30°

2   a   5 cm   b   4 cm   c   2½ cm   d   5 cm
     e   7 cm   f   2 cm

3   a $3x + 5 = 4x$, $x = 5$
     b $2x + 7 = ½(x + 29)$, $x = 5$

4   a $x = 5$ m,   b   area = 50 m²

5   £20

6   £60

7    $6\frac{1}{2}$

Constructing equations

10e Trial and improvement

Objectives	
• Use ICT to estimate square roots and cube roots	(L6)
• Use systematic trial and improvement methods and ICT tools to find approximate solutions to equations such as $x^2 + x = 20$	(L6)

Key ideas	Resources	
1 Understanding the nature of trialling an estimation and making appropriate adjustments 2 Finding approximate solutions to equations through trialling.	Trial and improvement Mini whiteboards Scientific calculators Computer spreadsheet software	(1057)

Simplification	Extension
As in the discussion, the initial equations should have only integer solutions. The next stage is to use equations with solutions which have exactly one decimal place – for example, $x^2 + x = 48.75$ has the solution 6.5. Students will not encounter difficulty with having 48.75 in the equation and will gain confidence in finding a solution in decimal form.	Students should invent a problem of the style in question **5** of the exercise and know the solution to it. They then write it in words as if in a textbook, they can present it to a partner who has to solve it. The two solutions should then compared, any differences resolved and agreement reached on why on why one set of trials might have lead to a faster solution.

Literacy	Links
Aspects of the meaning of estimation and approximation should be tackled through discussion with the students. Exactness can also be introduced, and the nature of the number system, and decimals in particular should enhance levels of understanding.	Equations are used to model and predict the behaviour of avalanches. Scientists use equations that take account of the weather conditions, wind speed, temperature, precipitation and terrain to predict whether or not the snow is stable and whether an avalanche is likely. As information is updated, the scientists recalculate and refine their predictions to make them more accurate. More information about avalanche forecasts in Scotland can be found at http://www.sais.gov.uk/

Alternative approach

An open modelling approach to solving an exemplar equation may be used to discuss each section of a thought process, with students responding both verbally and using mini whiteboards. Initial questioning can focus on how one might solve such a problem, evolving to possible 'guesses' and trialling those guesses individually on whiteboards, thus also opening up efficient use of the calculator. This may well lead to simplified versions of trial table recording,

e.g.

Trial	$x^3 + x^2 =$	Comment

This better reflects efficient use of the calculator, and also helps students to focus on the aim of the activity, not that of the recording. Appropriate differentiation here will support those who may need to include extra steps. Use of a spreadsheet can be similarly simplified; perhaps also include a 'difference' column to highlight comments of too high or low and may replace a comments column. When consolidating this work, half the group may work with calculators and the other with computers, with a change over mid way

Checkpoint

A number plus its cube is 50. Find the number.   3.6 (1 dp) or 3.59 (2 dp)

Starter – The answer is minus one half

Write $x = -\frac{1}{2}$ on the board. Ask students to give an equation with this answer. Challenge students to include brackets, for example, $2(4x + 3) = 2$

Hint, work backwards, $2x = -1$, $8x = -4$, $8x + 6 = -4 + 6$ etc.

Teaching notes

Students should understand that some equations (such as Ben's $x^3 + x^2 = 576$) cannot be solved using algebra and a different approach must be used.

The logic of the process of trial-and-improvement can be an obstacle to some students, so the dynamic visualization of the process illustrated in the example, of 'narrowing the goalposts' by moving one in at a time until the solution is found (to any degree of accuracy), can be very helpful. A whole-class discussion can be generated around the idea that you can always just use the mid-interval value but you can probably do better by thinking about how close the target is to each of the current endpoints.

Once students have completed a few questions ask them to explain to a partner how they got their answer. Then as a class discuss an example where the solution is only approached from one side and an example where a mistake has been made deciding which decimal place the answer must round to.

Plenary

Sometimes students fret unduly over the choice of the next value. Work though an example using more than one sequence of intermediate values and use whole-class discussion to decide which was better. Take the opportunity to emphasise that, usually, there will be very little difference in the amount of effort required.

Exercise commentary

Questions 1 and 2 – These equations give integer answers. Question 1 provides a table of values which can be used as a model for question 2.

Questions 3 and 4 – Question 3 provides a lead-in to the equations in question 4. The example provides a model for the method to use. Some students may need help in choosing a suitable starting value from part **d** of question 4 onwards.

Question 5 – Part **a** gives an integer solution which provides a good starting value for part **b**, as 600 is only slightly greater than 584.

Questions 6 and 7 – These provide contexts in which this type of equation can arise.

Question 8 – The expression being explored is $n(n + 2)(n + 4)$. A computer spreadsheet is a powerful tool to see the product approaching the required value.

Answers

1 7

2 a 17 **b** 9 **c** 12 **d** 11
  e 7 **f** 6 **g** 17.1 **h** 23
  i 169 **j** 14

3 5.4

4 a 4.6 **b** 7.6 **c** 8.5 **d** 5.5
  e 3.1 **f** 6.6 **g** 5.1 **h** 6.3
  i 20.5 **j** 4.7

5 a 8 **b** 8.1

6 6.6 cm

7 a 10 cm **b** 8.3 cm

8 a $n + 4$ **b** 47, 49, 51

Trial and improvement

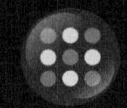

10 Equations – MySummary

Key outcomes	Quick check
Solve equations, including with brackets and fractions. L6	Solve **a** $3x - 16 = 20$ (12) **b** $2(x - 6) = 14$ (13) **c** $2x - 5 = 5x - 2$ (-1)
Create your own equations and solve them. L6	**a** I think of a number and multiply it by 7 before adding 2. The answer is 58. What is my number? (8) **b** The length of a rectangle is four times the width. If the perimeter is 45cm, what is the width of the rectangle? (4.5cm)
Use trial and improvement to solve equations. L6	Solve (accurate to 1 decimal place) **a** $x^3 - x = 40$ (3.5) **b** $2x^2 - 3x = 17$ (3.8)

MyMaths extra support

Lesson/online homework	Description
Rules and formulae 1158 L5	Using letters to represent unknown numbers in simple formulae

MyReview

10 MySummary

Check out
You should now be able to ...

	Test it → Questions
✓ Solve equations, including with brackets and fractions.	1 – 3
✓ Create your own equations and solve them.	4 – 5
✓ Use trial and improvement to solve equations.	6 – 7

Language	Meaning	Example
Equation	A statement using letters and numbers that contains an equals symbol and an unknown.	$6x - 2 = 28$
Unknown	The letter in the equation that you are trying to find the value of.	In the equation $6x - 2 = 28$ x is the unknown.
Inverse operation	The mathematical operation that undoes an operation.	Multiplying and dividing are inverse operations. When you multiply by 5, you can undo this by dividing by 5.
Expand brackets	Remove brackets by multiplying by the value outside the bracket.	Expand the brackets: $6(4x - 3)$ becomes $24x - 18$.
Trial and improvement	A method for solving complex equations by making a guess, then improving on that guess until you are very close to the correct answer.	The equation $x^3 + x = 245$ can be solved by trial and improvement.

Algebra Equations

10 MyReview

1 Solve these equations.
   a $7x - 5 = 58$
   b $4x + 9 = 11$
   c $8x + 20 = 4$
   d $-25 = 14x - 4$
   e $\frac{3x - 1}{4} = 2$
   f $\frac{x}{2} + 13 = 19$
   g $14 - 2x = -6$

2 Solve these equations.
   a $24 = 6(3x + 16)$
   b $6(3b - 4) + 8(2b - 5) = 140$
   c $3(5c + 7) - 2(9c - 3) = -6$
   d $2(4x - 1) + 3x = -13$

3 Solve these equations.
   a $6g + 14 = 28 - g$
   b $21 - 3h = 69 \div h$
   c $8(6i - 15) = 12(38 - 2i)$
   d $12 - 5j = -66 - 11j$
   e $\frac{1}{2}(11x - 3) = 8x + 6$
   f $\frac{12x - 7}{5} = 2x + 5$

4 Find the value of x in each diagram.
   a

   b Area = $98\,cm^2$, $3x + 2$, $7\,cm$

   c Perimeter = $37\,cm$, $x + 4$, $3x - 1$

5 Copy and complete this table to find a solution of $x^3 + x = 200$.

x	x^3	$x^3 + x$	Result
5	125	130	low

6 Use a trial and improvement method to find a positive solution of the following equations. Give your answers correct to 1 dp.
   a $x^4 = 35$
   b $3^x = 18$
   c $x^3 + x^2 = 100$

7 A cuboid has side lengths p, p and $p + 2$. The volume of the cuboid is $70\,cm^3$. Find p correct to 1 dp.

What next?

Score	
0 – 2	Your knowledge of this topic is still developing. To improve look at Formative test: 3B-10; MyMaths: 1057, 1154, 1157 and 1182
3 – 5	You are gaining a secure knowledge of this topic. To improve look at InvisiPen: 214, 231, 234, 235, 236, 237, 238 and 242
6	You have mastered this topic. Well done, you are ready to progress!

MyMaths.co.uk

Question commentary

Question 1 – Students should be aware that answers could be fractions or negatives.

Question 2 – Students should expand brackets and collect like terms first in **b** and **c**. In **c** a common error is with the double negative in the second bracket leading to an incorrect answer of 7.

Question 3 – Students should aim to subtract the lowest algebraic term. In these cases where one or both of them are negative they will be subtracting a negative from both sides of the equation and errors can easily occur here.

Question 4 – Students should start by forming equations to solve: **a** $4x - 44 = 180$, **b** $7(3x + 2) = 98$, **c** $7x + 2 = 37$.

Question 5 – Once they know it is between 5.7 and 5.8 they must check 5.75. This is too low so the answer is between 5.75 and 5.8, i.e. 5.8 to 1 dp.

Question 6 – Students should draw tables as in question **5**. The final check for each part is **a** 2.45, **b** 2.65 **c** 4.35.

Question 7 – Students should first form an equation and expand the brackets: $p^3 + 2p^2 = 70$ and then solve using trial and improvement as in question **6**. The final check is $p = 3.55$.

Answers

1 a 9   b ½   c -2   d $-\frac{3}{2}$
   e 3   f 12   g 10

2 a -4   b 6   c 11   d -1

3 a 2   b -12   c 24   d 13
   e -1   f 16

4 a 56   b 4   c 5

5 5.8

6 a 2.4   b 2.6   c 4.3

7 3.6

10 MyPractice

1 Use inverse operations to solve these equations.
  a $x + 5 = 7$ **b** $x - 8 = 2$ **c** $3x = 18$ **d** $\dfrac{x}{2} = 5$

2 Solve these equations. Each solution takes two steps.
  a $2x + 3 = 11$ **b** $2x - 3 = 11$ **c** $6x + 1 = 19$
  d $\dfrac{x}{2} + 1 = 4$ **e** $\dfrac{x}{2} - 1 = 4$ **f** $\dfrac{x}{3} + 2 = 7$

3 Solve these equations. Take care with the signs and fractions.
  a $2x + 7 = 3$ **b** $3x - 8 = -2$ **c** $2x + 1 = 6$
  d $4x - 2 = 7$ **e** $-1 = 5x + 8$ **f** $4 = \dfrac{x}{4} - 1$

4 Solve these equations.
  a $2(3x + 5) = 22$ **b** $5(2x + 4) = 30$ **c** $7(3x - 2) = 28$
  d $3(2x - 1) = 12$ **e** $16 = 2(4x + 3)$ **f** $18 = 6(2 + 3x)$

5 Solve these equations. You will need to collect like terms.
  a $2(3x + 1) + 3(4x + 2) = 44$ **b** $5(3x - 2) + 2(x + 7) = 55$
  c $4(4x + 1) + 3(5 - x) = 32$ **d** $2(x + 3) + 3(4 - 2x) = 16$
  e $2(x - 1) + 8(x + 3) = 2$ **f** $5(2x + 7) + 6(2 - x) = 43$

6 Solve these equations. Remember how to multiply positive and negative numbers.
  a $5(2x + 3) - 3(2x + 4) = 15$ **b** $3(6x + 1) - 2(7x - 4) = 43$
  c $3(3x + 4) - 2(2x + 1) = 30$ **d** $9(2x + 1) - 3(5x - 3) = 18$
  e $3(2 + 4x) + 3(5 - x) = 30$ **f** $7(2 + 5x) + 4(8 - 7x) = 60$

7 Solve these equations which have unknowns on both sides.
  a $5x + 7 = 3x + 15$ **b** $4x - 1 = 2x + 13$ **c** $2(3x + 2) = 5(x + 3)$
  d $3(3x + 2) = 8x + 5$ **e** $4(2x - 1) = 6x + 8$ **f** $4(2x - 1) = 6x - 8$
  g $x + 4 = 13 - 2x$ **h** $2x + 6 = 9 - x$ **i** $2x - 6 = 9 - x$
  j $8x - 4 = 6x + 1$ **k** $x + 5 = 12 - x$ **l** $2(2x - 1) = 3x - 7$

8 Solve these equations.
  a $\dfrac{5x + 1}{2} = 2x + 3$ **b** $\dfrac{5x - 1}{2} = 2x + 3$ **c** $\dfrac{7x + 2}{4} = x + 2$
  d $2x - 3 = \dfrac{8x + 2}{5}$ **e** $3x - 1 = \dfrac{7x - 2}{3}$ **f** $\dfrac{1}{2}(3x - 1) = 2x - 1$

9 Cerys thinks of a number.
She doubles it, subtracts 5 and then trebles the result.
Her final answer is four times her original number.
What number did Cerys think of?

10 a The triangle has a perimeter of $6x$.
   Find the value of x.
  b For this rectangle
   i find the value of x
   ii work out the perimeter.

11 a Ethan has £x. He earns £30.
   He now has three times his original sum.
   How much did Ethan have to start with?
  b April has £x and June has £20.
   They add what they have and then share it out equally.
   April now has £4 more than she started with.
   How much did April have to start with?

12 A rectangular sheet of metal has a rectangular hole cut in it.
This diagram gives the dimensions in metres.
The area which is left is $11x\text{m}^2$.
Find the value of x and the area of the original sheet.

13 Use this table to solve $x^2 + x = 48$.
Give your answer correct to 1dp.
Try $x = 6$ as your first trial.

Try	x^2	x	$x^2 + x$	Comment
$x = 6$				

14 Use your own table to solve $2x + \sqrt{x} = 100$.
Give your answer correct to 1dp.
Try $x = 49$ as your first trial.

Question commentary

Questions 1, 2 and 3 – These equations should be reasonably straightforward to solve but ensure students take care with negative numbers.

Questions 4, 5 and 6 – Students must ensure that they take care when expanding brackets, particularly in question **6** parts **b** and **d** where there is a double negative.

Questions 7 and 8 – Encourage students to collect the xs on the side where there are most of them and to take care with negative numbers.

Questions 9 to 12 – In each question, students will need to form the equation first before solving. Encourage them to check their answer by substituting it into to original context.

Questions 13 and 14 – Ensure students are using a check value before confirming their answer correct to one decimal place.

Answers

1	a	2	b	10	c	6	d	10
2	a	4	b	7	c	3	d	6
	e	10	f	15				
3	a	-2	b	2	c	2½	d	2¼
	e	$-1\frac{4}{5}$	f	20				
4	a	2	b	1	c	2	d	2½
	e	1¼	f	$\frac{1}{3}$				
5	a	2	b	3	c	1	d	½
	e	-2	f	-1				
6	a	3	b	8	c	4	d	0
	e	1	f	2				
7	a	4	b	7	c	11	d	-1
	e	6	f	-2	g	3	h	1
	i	5	j	2½	k	3½	l	-5
8	a	5	b	7	c	2	d	8½
	e	½	f	1				

9 7½

10 a 2   b i 2   ii 20

11 a £15   b £12

12 $x = 5$m, area = 70 m^2

13 6.4

14 46.6

MyPractice **195**

11 Powers and roots

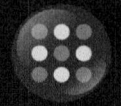

Learning outcomes	
N5	Use conventional notation for the priority of operations, including brackets, powers, roots and reciprocals (L6)
N7	Use integer powers and associated real roots (square, cube and higher), recognise powers of 2, 3, 4, 5 and distinguish between exact representations of roots and their decimal approximations (L6/7)
N8	Interpret and compare numbers in standard form $a \times 10^n$ $1 \le a < 10$, where n is a positive or negative integer or 0 (L7)

Introduction	Prior knowledge
The chapter starts by looking at square and cube roots, both exact and found using a calculator. Some of the rules of indices are looked at from an algebraic point of view before this is linked to work on (simple) surds and fractional indexes. The final two sections cover standard index form for large and small numbers. The introduction discusses how standard index form can be used to represent the large number 24,000,000,000,000,000,000 more efficiently (as 2.4×10^{19}). The 'need' for scientists and astronomers to use this kind of notation arises not from any absolute necessity, but to simplify the written calculations and the way the numbers are written. There is an excellent website which shows how the sizes of things in our universe *really* relate to each other. This website is called 'The Scale of the Universe' and can be found at http://htwins.net/scale/ or http://htwins.net/scale2/. Thinking about massive numbers or minute numbers is really quite difficult and something like this interactive 'zooming' universe can help us to relate to these quantities. Alternatively, consider things like football stadiums: How many people is 'one million people'? Well a crowd that size would fill Wembley Stadium 11 times over!	Students should already know how to… • Identify square and cube numbers • Evaluate using simple rules of indices
	Starter problem
	The starter problem requires students to carry out calculations with large numbers. There is also an element of unit conversion as well since the distance to the moon is given in kilometres and the stride length in centimetres. Converting the distance to the moon into centimetres gives a very large number which can naturally lead into a discussion of standard index form. 384,000 kilometres is equivalent to 38,400,000,000 centimetres so it would take us 480,000,000 strides to walk to the moon. If we walked four strides a second, it would take 120,000,000 seconds to walk there… This is equivalent to over 198 weeks or nearly four years! The problem also poses alternative questions such as 'what if you had to walk to the sun?' This gives rise to an opportunity for some research on behalf of the students since they could go and investigate these cosmological distances on the internet.

Resources

MyMaths

Indices 1	1033	Standard form small	1049	Standard form large	1051
Squares and cubes	1053	Surds 1	1064		

Online assessment   **InvisiPen solutions**

Chapter test	3B–11	Squares and square roots	181	Powers of 10	182
Formative test	3B–11	Standard form	183	Indices	184
Summative test	3B–11	Negative and fractional indices			185
		Surds	186		

Topic scheme

Teaching time = 5 lessons/2 weeks

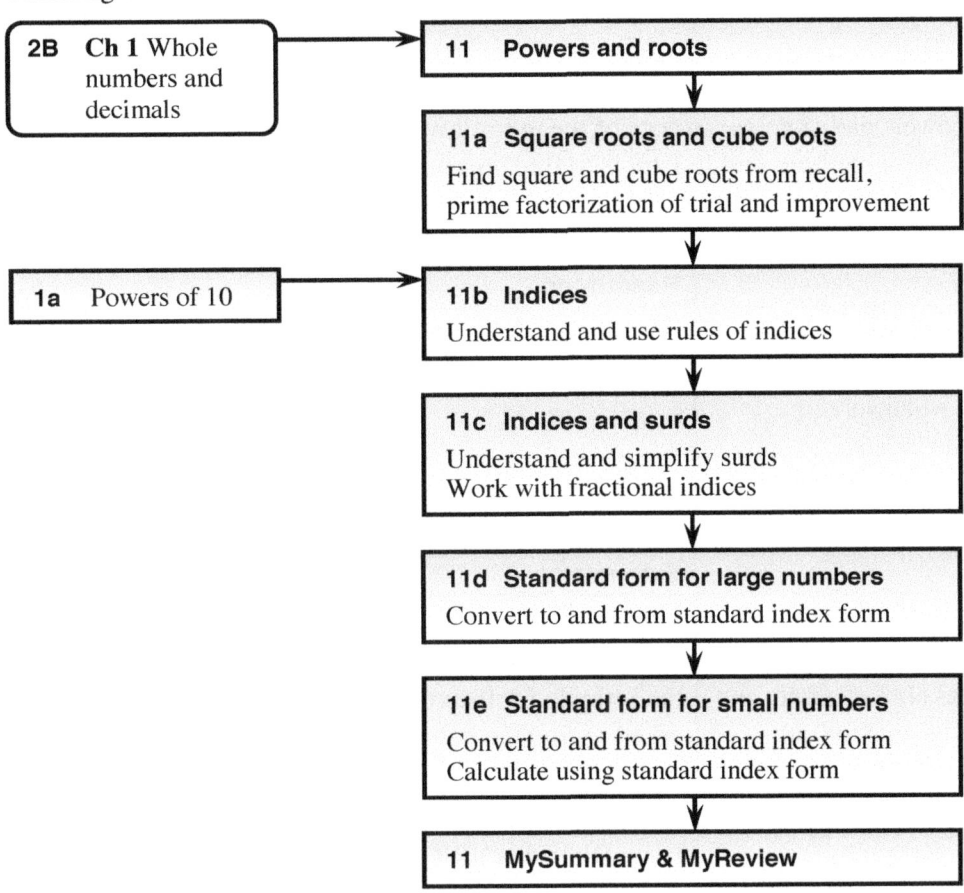

```
2B  Ch 1 Whole numbers and decimals  →  11   Powers and roots
                                              ↓
                                         11a  Square roots and cube roots
                                              Find square and cube roots from recall,
                                              prime factorization of trial and improvement
                                              ↓
1a  Powers of 10                     →   11b  Indices
                                              Understand and use rules of indices
                                              ↓
                                         11c  Indices and surds
                                              Understand and simplify surds
                                              Work with fractional indices
                                              ↓
                                         11d  Standard form for large numbers
                                              Convert to and from standard index form
                                              ↓
                                         11e  Standard form for small numbers
                                              Convert to and from standard index form
                                              Calculate using standard index form
                                              ↓
                                         11   MySummary & MyReview
```

Differentiation

Student book 3A 200 – 213

Understand and use square numbers and square roots
Understand basic rules of indices
Understand standard index form

Student book 3B 196 – 211

Find square and cube roots using a variety of methods
Work with rules of indices including fractional indexes
Simplify using indices and surds
Work with standard index form for large and small numbers
Calculate using standard index form

Student book 3C 196 – 209

Work with standard index form for large and small numbers
Calculate using standard index form
Understand powers and operations
Work with rules for indices and surds

Introduction

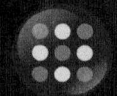

11a Square roots and cube roots

Objectives

- Use squares, positive and negative square roots, cubes and cube roots, and index notation for small positive integer powers (L6)
- Use index notation for integer powers (L6)
- Use ICT to estimate square roots and cube roots (L6)
- Use index notation for integer powers and simple instances of the index laws (L6)
- Use systematic trial and improvement methods and ICT tools to find approximate solutions to equations such as $x^2 + x = 20$ (L6)
- Explain how to find, calculate and use the interior and exterior angles of regular polygons (L7)

Key ideas	Resources
1 Familiarity with the process of finding power and its inverse 2 Applying a variety of strategies when solving problems involving power and its inverse. 3 Confidently apply trial and improvement strategies to finding square or cube roots.	Squares and cubes (1053) Dice Calculators

Simplification	Extension
Mini whiteboards can be used for students to write down squares, square roots, cubes and cube roots of numbers given by the teacher; found both mentally and using a calculator. Students should be able to find mentally the squares and square roots of the numbers 4 and 9 as a final check on their understanding.	Those students who are successful with finding the radius of the football in question **8** can be introduced to the formula for the volume of a sphere, $V = \frac{4}{3}\pi r^3$ and asked to find the radius of a sphere with a volume of 1 litre. Finding square roots before calculators....Unusual Long Division (NRICH): http://nrich.maths.org/5955

Literacy	Links
Establish clearly the difference between square and square root; cube and cube root – students will be aware of this but frequently confuse the two terms. Remind students of the notation, particularly of the convention of accepting a root sign without the index 2 as a square root.	The Ancient Babylonians used square numbers in their calculations and could also calculate square roots. A picture of a clay tablet dating from between 1800 B.C. and 1600 B.C. showing the calculation of the square root of two can be found at http://www.math.ubc.ca/~cass/Euclid/ybc/ybc.html

Alternative approach

Ask students to record the as many square numbers as they can in sequence starting from 1 in a given limited time – say 30 secs. Check and verbally see how many further are known. Repeat with the sequence of cube numbers. Follow up with requesting estimates of roots – both square and cube roots – where students may use their lists to help. Students may then use calculators to see whose estimates are the closest.. Apply calculator use to problems, reminding students by asking them what the difference is between πr^2 and $(\pi r)^2$. Finally, ask students to consider their approaches should they only have a basic calculator to hand in order to refresh work on trial and improvement. Concentrate on the level of accuracy, reflecting back to the early estimation task. Why is it necessary to work to two decimals places when we require an answer correct to one only decimal place?

Checkpoint

Write down the square root of 2025. (45)

Find, by trial and improvement, the cube root of 70, correct to one decimal place. (4.1)

Number Powers and roots

Starter – Dice factors

Ask students to draw a 3 × 3 table,
label the rows 9, 12, 30
label the columns 7, 15, 24.

Throw a dice nine times and after each throw ask students to place the score in one of the nine cells. Students get points if the score is a factor of either the column label or the row label or both.

Teaching notes

Encourage students to develop strategies to know the order of magnitude for square roots and cube roots so that they can find approximations for calculations which involve these functions. Emphasise the importance of having an idea of the approximate size of a calculation before entering it into a calculator.

Many students do not see the need for testing the mid-interval value using one decimal place more than a trial-and-improvement solution requires. They simply take the value for which *f(x)* is closer to the target value. While this often gives the right solution, it is not a guarantee (since *f(x)* is non-linear) and students need to get into the habit of always completing this last step explicitly.

Plenary

Ask students to work in pairs to discuss what happens with square roots and cube roots of negative numbers. Take whole class feedback to ensure everyone grasps the reasons why cube roots of negative numbers exist but square roots do not exist in the real number system.

Exercise commentary

Question 1 – Once students separate out the 100s, the answers are easily found.

Question 2 – Students should realise that the same correct answer can come from different factor trees.

Question 3 – The worked example on the previous page provides a good model. Students should take special care in the final step to find the answer to one decimal place.

Question 4 – Provides repeated practice. Students can follow the worked-example on the previous page as a model.

Questions 5 and **6** – These use the method of question 4 in various contexts. Students should note the different units involved.

Question 7 – This provides a modern-day context from science.

Question 8 – The first stage of this task is a development of the method above used with $A = \pi r^2$. The Internet puts the calculations in context.

Answers

1. a 20   b 40   c 50   d 100
   e $\frac{3}{10}$ f $\frac{2}{10}$

2. a 14   b 15   c 33   d 55
   e 42

3. a 5.5   b 6.8   c 7.9   d 9.2
   e 10.2   f 3.1   g 2.2   h 3.8
   i 4.6   j 4.9

4. a 2.76   b 3.99   c 4.89   d 6.18
   e 8.74

5. 1.4 cm

6. a 15 m   b 30 m

7. a 0.25   b 0.05

8. a Radius = 11.1 cm
   b Size 5, circumference = 27–28" (radius 11 cm)
      Size 4, circumference = 25–26" (radius 10 cm)
   c Size 3, circumference = 23–24" (radius 9 cm)
      Used by children under 8 or for team handball.

Square roots and cube roots

11b Indices

Objectives

- Use squares, positive and negative square roots, cubes and cube roots, and index notation for small positive integer powers (L6)
- Know and use the index laws for multiplication and division of positive integer powers (L6)
- Use index notation for integer powers and simple instances of the index laws (L6)

Key ideas	Resources
1 Familiarity with indices and their meaning 2 Apply indices knowledge to simplify both number and algebraic expressions.	Indices 1 (1033) Mini whiteboards Power Mad (NRICH): http://nrich.maths.org/6401

Simplification	Extension
Simplifications of the kind offered in questions **1** to **4** can initially be undertaken by students writing their answers on mini whiteboards. This use of whiteboards, prior to attempting the exercise, allows assessment of students' understanding early in the activity.	There are many words, other than *million* and *billion*, for large numbers. Students could draw up a list of them. Alternatively students could compare $2^4 \times 2^{-1}$ and $2^4 \times \frac{1}{2}$ to give meaning to the index -1

Literacy	Links
Check the notation and how to read these values. Include the notation used on calculators and also on computers, including ^ for raising to a power.	In recent years, Britain has adopted the American system for naming large numbers. Traditionally, one billion referred to 10^{12}, but the term is now used to refer to 10^9, that is, one thousand million instead of one million million. However, in science, confusion is avoided by using SI prefixes. The prefix giga- always means 10^9 and tera- always means 10^{12}, so 2 gigajoules means 2×10^9 joules. For a table listing other SI prefixes see http://www.unc.edu/~rowlett/units/prefixes.html

Alternative approach

Begin by asking the students if 3^4 is the same as 4^3. Mini whiteboards should be used here. Examine the responses and elaborate if and where necessary. Continue with 5^6 and 6^5; then ask students to consider 2^4 and 4^2 – why is this a special case? Continue with encouraging students to use mini whiteboards when extending to generalisation of indices, asking both for simplification of expressions and also for possible questions resulting in a simplified term. Encourage students to work in pairs to investigate possible rules for multiplying and dividing with same-base powers. Further investigatory work of powers can be be found at NRICH as referenced, either exploring further properties of powers of two, or extending for the more able to other interesting power sequences.

Checkpoint

Write these values as a term with one index number:

$3^6 \times 3^4 \div 3^5$ (3^5)

$(4^3)^2 \div 4^5$ (4 or 4^1)

$\dfrac{3a^3 \times 2a^5}{a^4}$ ($6a^4$)

Starter – Four in a line

Ask students to draw a 5 × 5 grid and enter the numbers 1 to 25 in any order. Give questions involving primes, factors and multiples. For example,

What is the highest common factor of 12 and 20?
An even prime number?
A prime number between 8 and 12?
The lowest common multiple of 6 and 8?
A prime factor of 27?
An odd factor of 34?

The winner is the first student to cross out four in a line.

Teaching notes

Review the notation carefully to ensure students do not confuse, for example, 3^5 with 3×5. Ask students to write out a small number of cases similar to the first two examples as this may help them to learn why the rules work as they do, however, the correct application of these rules tends to be a persistent problem for some students.

Plenary

Ask students to work in pairs to compare the values of $2x^3$ and $(2x)^3$ when $x = 5$ and to explain why they are different.
Algebraically, what would be equivalent to $(2x)^3$?

Exercise commentary

Question 1 – The numerical elements of parts **e** and **f** should be worked out and not left in index form.

Question 2 – Students still unsure of the rule can write out the terms in full and then count the total number of symbols.

Question 3 – As in question **2**, insecure students can write out the terms in full, cancel as far as possible and then give their final answer.

Question 4 – Students should be confident in the earlier rules before extending into the more complicated examples in this question.

Question 5 – Students should write down intermediate stages before finding their final answers for many of the parts of this question.

Question 6 – It should be pointed out that, even in the UK, the US meanings of these words are increasingly more often used than the original UK meanings.

Question 7 – Two alternative ways of calculating fractional and zero indices are compared. Meanings can then be given to the indices.

Answers

1. a a^4 b y^5 c a^4z^3 d r^4s^3
   e $8p^3$ f $9a^3y^2$

2. a x^9 b y^{10} c z^8 d p^6
   e k^6 f a^9 g b^7y^5 h q^6r^9
   i m^7t^5 j a^3b^7 k x^6y^4 l a^6b^9

3. a x^4 b y^6 c z d a^2
   e m^5 f a^6b^3 g p^2q^5 h x^2y
   i st j z

4. a x^6 b y^6 c z^{15} d m^{15}
   e n^8 f x^6y^8 g $a^{12}b^6$ h $m^{10}n^5$
   i s^6t^{12} j $p^{15}q^{20}$

5. a $8x^8$ b $18y^9$ c $2z^4$ d p^3
   e q^5 f r g $4a^4$ h $2c^3$
   i $2x$ j $2x^{10}$ k $3y^5$ l $15y^{10}$

6. US billion = 10^9 UK billion = 10^{12}
   US trillion = 10^{12} UK trillion = 10^{18}

7. a $2^0 = 1, x^0 = 1$
   b $9^{\frac{1}{2}} = \sqrt{9}, x^{\frac{1}{2}} = \sqrt{x}$

Indices

11c Indices and surds

Objectives
- Know that $n^{\frac{1}{2}} = \sqrt{n}$ and $n^{\frac{1}{3}} = \sqrt[3]{n}$ for any positive number n (L6)
- Use surds and π in exact calculations, without a calculator (L8)

Key ideas	Resources
1 Begin to understand indices other than positive whole numbers 2 Recognise that a surd is the most accurate and efficient way of representing some values.	Surds 1 (1064) Mini whiteboards Calculators Indices and Surds (NRICH): http://nrich.maths.org/8587+ SU Box: N11 Manipulating Surds: http://www.nationalstemcentre.org.uk/elibrary/collection/282/improving-learning-in-mathematics

Simplification	Extension
The weaker students may need to spend more time on the square roots of numbers which are perfect squares until they grasp that $\sqrt{ab} = \sqrt{a} \times \sqrt{b}$ and vice versa. For example in question **2b**, $\sqrt{4} \times \sqrt{4} = \sqrt{16}$ can be seen to be $\quad 2 \times 2 \quad = 4$	The more able students could investigate negative fractional powers and see if all the rules for multiplying, dividing and raising to a power still work.

Literacy	Links
The word surd is likely to be new for most of the students. Refer to its origins with the Pythagoreans and also the conflict that arose when it was found that numbers such as $\sqrt{2}$ were not rational. (Note that the idea of a surd can be further developed in the next chapter relating it to work of Pythagoras.) http://www.mathsisgoodforyou.com/AS/surds.htm Draw out why the term $2\sqrt{3}$ is not written as $\sqrt{3} \times 2$ to emphasise the importnace of accurate communication.	The Ancient Babylonians used square numbers in their calculations and could also calculate square roots. A picture of a clay tablet dating from between 1800 BC and 1600 BC showing the calculation of the square root of two can be found at http://www.math.ubc.ca/~cass/Euclid/ybc/ybc.html

Alternative approach

Sequencing with indices using a base number of 2 and/or 3 makes a good introductory activity in order to explore what a fractional index number might mean. Suggest students then examine powers of 9 with a calculator, asking them to see if they can find out what a value to the power of a half actually means. This can include or be extended to include zero and negative indices as appropriate. Ask students to consider the statement: $\sqrt{6} = \sqrt{2} \times \sqrt{3}$ in pairs. Is it true? Why? Then explore equivalent spider diagrams with a centre of say $\sqrt{30}$ with the whole class offering suggestions using mini whiteboards. The students may want to use calculators here to check themselves. Repeat with a value such as $\sqrt{45}$. What is different about $\sqrt{2}, \sqrt{3}, \sqrt{5}$, and so on? Establish the principles here relating to the numerical values and exactness. Further activities using surds and indices can be found at NRICH and in the SU Box as referenced in Resources.

Checkpoint

Simplify: $\quad (a^2 \times a^4)^{1/3}$ $\hfill (a^2)$
$\quad\quad\quad\quad\quad \sqrt{x} \times 3\sqrt{x}$ $\hfill (3x)$
$\quad\quad\quad\quad\quad \sqrt{75}$ $\hfill (5\sqrt{3})$

Starter – Estimate

Write decimal numbers on the board, for example 3.2, 14.81, 5.9, 7.06, 27.9, 79.4, 69.4, 11.8.
Ask questions
- Which two numbers have a product close to 90? (3.2, 27.9)
- Which number has a square root close to 9? (79.4)
- What calculation has an answer close to 2? (14.81 ÷ 7.06)
- Which two numbers have a product close to 4.9×10^2? (69.4, 7.06)

Teaching notes

What happens when a square root is multiplied by itself? Discuss the fact that square root and square are inverse operations. What about multiplying two square roots that are not the same? For example, $\sqrt{25} \times \sqrt{4}$. This is just 5×2 or 10 or $\sqrt{100}$. Is there a way to squeeze the two roots together as a single root? Write the rule $\sqrt{a} \times \sqrt{b} = \sqrt{ab}$. Is it possible to use this last rule in reverse; can a single root be split into two smaller roots? For example, $\sqrt{60}$. Look at all five possible pairs or roots that 60 can be split into. Are any of them any better than $\sqrt{60}$?

Show how the pair $\sqrt{4} \times \sqrt{15}$ can be simplified to leave the root of a smaller number. Look at an example like $2\sqrt{6} \times 3\sqrt{3}$ and show how it can simplified by drawing an analogy with multiplication in algebra $2x \times 3x$. Examine the sequence of powers of 9 from 9^3 to 9^0. Where does $9^{\frac{1}{2}}$ fit into the sequence? Agree that it means square root. Discuss the meaning of other fractional powers.

Plenary

Solve linear equations that involve surds, leaving the answers in their simplest form.

$x\sqrt{5} + 3\sqrt{5} = 7\sqrt{5}$ $x = 4$

$2(x + \sqrt{3}) = 6\sqrt{3}$ $x = 2\sqrt{3}$

Can students make up their own examples of linear equations that involve surds? This may lead to division by a surd. Explain that this is generally avoided in maths. Is there a way round this?

Exercise commentary

Question 1 – Calculator practice that will allow a discussion on the effects of rounding.

Questions 2 to 4 – These questions all draw on the examples from the previous page and provide lots of basic practice of the skills.

Question 5 – Simplification is not required, but students could be asked to extend their answers to do this, for example in part **b**, the value (= 2) can be worked out.

Question 6 – These can be worked out using observation rather than more complicated calculation methods. Calculators should not be allowed.

Question 7 – A good question for discussion. Ask the students what formulas they will need to use for the area and missing side of this right-angled triangle.

Answers

1. a i 2.99   ii 1.73
   b i 5.01   ii 2.24
   c i 7.02   ii 2.65

Square roots of non-squares are irrational, the values in part i are approximations.

2. a 3   b 4   c $\sqrt{15}$ d $2\sqrt{3}$
   e $\sqrt{21}$ f 6   g 8   h 10
   i 9   j 12   k $2\sqrt{14}$ 8   l 20
   m 30   n 12   o $2\sqrt{15}$ p 15

3. a $2\sqrt{3}$ b $2\sqrt{2}$ c $3\sqrt{2}$ d $2\sqrt{6}$
   e $2\sqrt{10}$ f $4\sqrt{3}$ g $4\sqrt{2}$ h $5\sqrt{2}$
   i $6\sqrt{2}$ j $7\sqrt{2}$

4. a 18   b 6   c $8\sqrt{15}$ d $8\sqrt{3}$
   e $8\sqrt{21}$ f $12\sqrt{10}$ g $2\sqrt{6}$ h 30
   i 60   j 36   k 16   l 144

5. a $8^{\frac{1}{2}}$ b $8^{\frac{1}{3}}$ c $18^{\frac{1}{2}}$ d $24^{\frac{1}{3}}$
   e $40^{\frac{1}{3}}$

6. a 9   b 3   c 2   d 4
   e 4   f 3   g 5   h 5
   i 12   j 8   k 10   l 9

7. a 12 units²   b $5\sqrt{2}$

Indices and surds

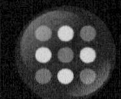

11d Standard form for large numbers

Objectives

- Extend knowledge of integer powers of 10 (L6)
- Recognise the equivalence of $0.1, \frac{1}{10}$ and 10^{-1} (L6)
- Convert between ordinary and standard index form representations (L7)
- Express numbers in standard index form, both in conventional notation and on a calculator display (L8)

Key ideas	Resources
1 Familiarity with the meaning of powers of 10 when expressing both large and small numbers 2 Ability to express values in both ordinary form and standard form	Standard form large (1051) Mini whiteboards Calculator Big and Small numbers in contexts (NRICH): http://nrich.maths.org/public/leg.php?code=18 Estimating length Using St.form - SU Box unit N4: http://www.nationalstemcentre.org.uk/elibrary/collection/282/improving-learning-in-mathematics

Simplification	Extension
It might be worth revising multiplying and dividing by 10, 100 and 1000 with the weaker students. The students will often latch on to the use of standard form very quickly but make sure they check that their answers are of the right order of magnitude and that they are moving the digits not the decimal point.	The students could begin to look at the more formal rules for multiplying and dividing numbers written in standard form.

Literacy	Links
Students may be unfamiliar with or lack confidence with the term standard form, though many will have come across numbers expressed in this way in contexts across the curriculum. The convention will need to be explained. Remind students of common prefixes: centi, milli, kilo and so on with their power equivalents.	In recent years, Britain has adopted the American system for naming large numbers. Traditionally, one billion meant 10^{12} but it is now used for 10^9, that is, one thousand million instead of one million million. However, in science, confusion is avoided by using SI prefixes. The prefix giga- always means 10^9 and tera- always means 10^{12}, so 2 gigajoules means 2×10^9 joules. For a table listing other SI prefixes see http://www.unc.edu/~rowlett/units/prefixes.html

Alternative approach

It may be more appropriate here to deal with both large and small numbers together, though expecting less able pupils to concentrate of large numbers only. Begin by examining the power sequence of the base 10, similar to previous work relating to other base sequences. Students may remember some of the key prefixes linked with some of the powers such as kilo for 10^3. Activities relating to contexts will help to establish the concepts. Liaise with other curricular areas and/or use some of the materials from NRICH or the Standards Unit Box as referenced.

Checkpoint

Write in standard form: 48 000 000. (4.8×10^7)

Write as a normal number: 5.6×10^5 (560 000)

Starter – Order!

Write the following list of fractions on the board. $\frac{13}{40}, \frac{1}{3}, \frac{7}{20}, \frac{5}{16}, \frac{3}{10}, \frac{3}{8}, \frac{17}{50}, \frac{8}{25}$

Ask students to put them in order from the lowest value to the highest value.

Correct order. $\frac{3}{10}, \frac{5}{16}, \frac{8}{25}, \frac{13}{40}, \frac{1}{3}, \frac{17}{50}, \frac{7}{20}, \frac{3}{8}$

Can be differentiated by the choice of fractions. Can be extended by challenging students to give fractions in-between the ordered values

Teaching notes

Is there a quick way to write large number like 100 000 000 000 or 1 000 000? How are they said in words? Why could this become confusing? Look at these large number as powers of 10. Consider introducing a few new terms like trillion (10^{12}) and quintillion (10^{18}). How can a large number that does not start with a one be written as two different numbers multiplied together? Consider different possibilities, involving a power of ten, for example, 3 000 000 equals 3 × 1 000 000 or 30 × 100 000 or 300 × 10 000. Use index form for the powers of ten. One of these ways is the 'standard' way of writing large numbers around the world, known as 'standard form' or 'standard index form'. Ask students to suggest which they think it is and why. Establish that the first number must be between one and ten, not including ten. Look at a few examples of conversions in both directions. Does the power of ten give the number of zeros in the number? No, but this is a common misconception.

Plenary

Look at examples of linear equations that involve standard form. Avoid examples that include division by a standard form number or the multiplication of two standard form numbers. Include examples like

$$x + 3 \times 10^8 = 4.2 \times 10^9 \qquad x = 3.9 \times 10^9$$

$$2(x - 1.2 \times 10^5) = 3 \times 10^5 \qquad x = 2.7 \times 10^5$$

$$3 \times 10^4 \times x + 10^3 = 2.9999 \times 10^4 \times x + 10^4$$

$$x = 9 \times 10^3$$

Exercise commentary

Question 1 – Ask the students to give a quick rule for working out the answer, that is, something that uses the power to tell you how many places the digits need to move.

Question 2 – Encourage students to check their answers by multiplying them out. For example, in part **a**, an answer of 2.3×10^2 could be checked by doing 2.3×100.

Question 3 – Students may be more comfortable converting the numbers from standard form before performing the operation and converting back again.

Question 4 – Students will need to adjust the digits first and then work out the effect on the index. Ensure they are increasing or decreasing the index correctly.

Question 5 – Ask the students which is the key digit in each number to be rounded. Encourage them to answer the question without first rewriting the number as an ordinary number.

Question 6 – Standard form in context.

Question 7 – Numbers should all be converted either to standard form or to normal numbers to enable comparison.

Question 8 – Standard form in context again, this time with a calculation to do. In part **b**, students may well work in normal numbers.

Answers

1. a 370 b 4 700
   c 1 230 000 d 40 200 000
   e 3 010 000 f 4 900 000 000
   g 737 000 000 000 h 1 004 000
2. a 2.3×10^2 b 4.87×10^3
   c 3.4×10^5 d 7.8×10^7
   e 4.1×10^9 f 2.38×10^6
   g 2.383×10^2 h 3.8788×10^3
3. a 5.8×10^4 b 2.6×10^4
4. a 2.7×10^2 b 5.73×10^4
   c 5.3×10^3 d 3.42×10^4
   e 3.01×10^7 f 4.92×10^5
   g 4.8×10^3 h 3.78×10^4
5. a 5×10^3 b 2.9×10^4
   c 4.14×10^5 d 3.5×10^4
6. a 3.56×10^4 b 5.9×10^7
   c 1.86×10^5 miles/s d 2.479×10^{13} miles
7. a 270, 2.58×10^3, 2.6×10^3, 2.5×10^4, 2.55×10^4
   b 3×10^{12}, 2.9×10^{13}, 2.8×10^{14}, 2 980 000 000 000 000
8. a 600 mph
   b €12 582 500
9. b $n - 4$ c $n + 2$ d $n + 4$

Standard form for large numbers **205**

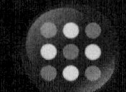

11e Standard form for small numbers

Objectives

- Multiply and divide by any integer power of 10 (L6)
- Convert between ordinary and standard index form representations (L7)
- Express numbers in standard index form, both in conventional notation and on a calculator display (L8)
- Know how to enter numbers in standard index form (L8)

Key ideas

1. Familiarity with the meaning of powers of 10 when expressing both large and small numbers
2. Ability to express values in both ordinary form and standard form

Resources

Standard form small (1049)

Calculator

Mini whiteboards

Big and Small numbers in contexts (NRICH): http://nrich.maths.org/public/leg.php?code=18

Estimating length Using St.form - SU Box unit N4: http://www.nationalstemcentre.org.uk/elibrary/collection/282/improving-learning-in-mathematics

Simplification

It might be worth revising multiplying and dividing by 0.1, 0.01 *etc*. with the weaker students.

By repeated practice with numbers multiplied by negative powers of 10, students will quickly catch on to the idea of moving the digits in the opposite direction to multiplying by positive powers of 10.

Extension

The students could extend the work of question **8b** to look at the population densities of other countries. Thi wosuld make a good computer-based homework task.

Literacy

Check accuracy of standard form convention both in writing and in interpreting calculator display

Links

Micrometres (μm or microns) are used to measure the thickness or diameter of microscopic objects. One micrometre is a thousandth of a millimetre or 1×10^{-6} meters. Human hair is about 100 μm wide and red blood cells are 7 μm in diameter. There is a picture of human eye tissue in clusters of 50-200 μm at http://www.sciencedaily.com/releases/2007/06/070624121236.htm

Alternative approach

Following the introductory activities of standard form with both large and small numbers continue to extend familiarity with their use in contexts. The referenced resources from NRICH and/or the Standards Unit may be utilised here. Include the use of the calculator ensuring that students are familiar with both entering a number in standard form, recognising and intepreting the display, as well as carrying out simple calulations with standard form. Students can respond to questions here using mini whiteboards, in order to expose any misconceptions.

Checkpoint

Write in standard form: 0.00045. (4.5×10^{-4})

Write as a normal number: 3.78×10^{-3} (0.00378)

Starter – Matching form

Ask students to find equivalent pairs in the following numbers.

3.1×10^3, 30100, 3.1×10^5, 3.1, 310, 3.01×10^4, 3.01×10^2, 30.1, 3100, 3.01×10^0, 310000, 3.01, 3.1×10^2, 3.01×10^1

Ask students to complete the pairs for any not matched up. (3.01×10^2 and 3.1)

Teaching notes

Examine the sequence of numbers produced by the integer powers of ten. Ask, what is 10^0 and 10^{-1}? Encourage students to look for a pattern that will back up their suggestions. Establish that negative powers of ten represent decimals between zero and one. What happens if you multiply a number by a negative power of ten? By comparing previous work with large numbers, show that negative powers of ten are equivalent to repeated division by ten. Look at examples that convert in both directions for small numbers. Emphasise the importance of checking the number of places that the digits are moving. Look at the different ways in which calculators input numbers in standard form. Insist students to use the '$\times 10^x$' or 'EXP' button rather than using the power button when using the calculator. Be aware that some calculators will automatically put some answers into standard form.

Plenary

Look at question **5a** and **5c** again. Is there a way to solve them without a calculator? Set students the challenge of trying to solve them without a calculator. Is there a way to tackle the multiplication without having to write out lots of zeros? Is there a way to tackle the division using an equivalent fraction? Look at an example of a standard form multiplication and division that can be very easily tackled using a non calculator short cut method.

Exercise commentary

Question 1 – Encourage students to rewrite each negative power of ten as a fraction, and then as a division using a whole number power of 10, as in the example.

Question 2 – It is useful to first work through these calculations by rewriting them as divisions by the corresponding positive powers of 10. Then ask students for a quick rule for working out the answer, that is, something that uses the negative power to tell you how many places the digits need to move.

Question 3 – Encourage students to check their answers by carrying out a division as in question **2**.

Question 4 – Students may want to convert the standard form numbers before comparing.

Question 5 – A good starting point for finding out about how to perform calculations written in standard form. The more able students should be able to identify rules for adding, subtracting, multiplying and dividing such numbers.

Question 6 – Standard form for small numbers in context.

Question 7 – A good activity for paired work and discussion.

Question 8 – Part **b** offers a natural link to geography and investigating the population density of other countries.

Answers

1 a 0.47   b 2.9   c 0.0123   d 0.000 04
   e 0.00318   f 390   g 0.0003   h 0.024

2 a 0.028   b 0.0036   c 0.000 934   d 0.005 13
   e 0.0000492   f 0.0000038
   g 0.000 000 062 5   h 0.000 000 000 123 4

3 a 3×10^{-1} b 4.8×10^{-1}
   c 3.4×10^{-2} d 7.8×10^{-4}
   e 3×10^{-6} f 6.7×10^{-3}
   g 4.56×10^{-6} h 2.4×10^{-11}

4 2×10^{-8}, 2.3×10^{-8}, 1.8×10^{-7}, 2.2×10^{-7}

5 a 1.56×10^9 b 2.465×10^5
   c 2.70833×10^2 d 6.476×10^{-3}

6 a 9.4×10^{-2} b 6.8×10^{-7}

7 a 1×10^{-2} km   b 3×10^{-3} g
   c 5×10^{-6} l   d 1.1×10^{-2} m

8 a 1.17×10^{14} km   b 3.18×10^2 people/km^2

Standard form for small numbers

11 Powers and roots – MySummary

Key outcomes		Quick check
Find square roots.	L6	a Find the square root of 289 (17) b Find, correct to one decimal place, the square root of 71 (8.4)
Find cube roots.	L6	a Find the cube root of 125 (5) b Find, correct to one decimal place, the cube root of 85 (4.4)
Use the rules of indices.	L7	a Write as a single index: $3^8 \times 3^{11} \div 3^4$ (3^{15}) b Simplify $x^3 \times (x^2)^4$ (x^{11})
Simplify surds.	L8	a Simplify $\sqrt{24}$ ($2\sqrt{6}$) b Write as a single number $3\sqrt{2} \times 2\sqrt{3}$ ($6\sqrt{6}$ or $\sqrt{216}$)
Convert to and from standard index form.	L7	a Write in standard form 4 320 000 (4.32×10^6) b Write as a normal number 2.4×10^{-2} (0.024)

MyMaths extra support

Lesson/online homework			Description
Factors and primes	1032	L4	Finding factors of whole numbers, and identifying prime numbers.
Squares and Cubes	1053	L4	How to find square numbers, square roots, cubes and cube roots.

MyReview

11 MySummary

Check out
You should now be able to ... **Test it ➡ Questions**

- ✓ Find square roots. — 1
- ✓ Find cube roots. — 2
- ✓ Use the rules of indices. — 3
- ✓ Simplify surds. — 4 – 8
- ✓ Convert to and from standard index form. — 9 – 10

Language	Meaning	Example
Square root	The square root of any number is the number which, when multiplied by itself, gives the starting number.	The square root of 81 is 9 because 9 × 9 is 81.
Cube root	The cube root of any number is the number which, when multiplied by itself and then multiplied by itself again, gives the starting number.	The cube root of 27 is 3 because 3 × 3 × 3 is 27.
Index / power	The index or power tells you how many times to multiply a number by itself.	In 4^3, the index or power is 3. This represents 4 × 4 × 4.
Surds	A root that cannot be written as a fraction, or as a terminating or recurring decimal.	$\sqrt{2}$ is in surd form – the decimal value cannot be given completely.
Standard index form	A short way of writing very large or very small numbers. A standard index form number is a number between 1 and 10 multiplied by a power of 10: $A \times 10^n$	42000 can be written as 4.2×10^4 in standard form. 0.00042 can be written as 4.2×10^{-4} in standard form.

11 MyReview

1. Use prime factors to find these square roots.
   a $\sqrt{576}$ b $\sqrt{1225}$

2. Use trial and improvement to find these roots to 1 dp.
   a $\sqrt{700}$ b $\sqrt[3]{200}$

3. Simplify these expressions, using indices in your answers.
   a $a \times a \times 3$
   b $b \times 2 \times b \times 3 \times c \times c \times b$
   c $d^2 \times 4 \times d^3 \times d$
   d $e^2 \times e^6 \times f^3 \times f$
   e $g^3h^2 \times h^4g$
   f $\dfrac{j^6}{j^5}$
   g $\dfrac{j^5k^7}{j^2k}$
   h $(m^2)^4$
   i $(n^3p^2)^5$
   j $\dfrac{4q^3 \times 7q^6}{14q^4}$
   k $\dfrac{8(sr^3)^2}{2r^4s}$

4. Calculate the following.
   a $\sqrt{5} \times \sqrt{5}$ b $\sqrt{9} \times \sqrt{4}$
   c $\sqrt{6} \times \sqrt{24}$ d $\sqrt{8} \times \sqrt{50}$

5. Write these numbers in their simplest form.
   a $\sqrt{28}$ b $\sqrt{72}$
   c $\sqrt{125}$ d $\sqrt{363}$

6. Calculate the following leaving your answers in surd form.
   a $\sqrt{3} \times \sqrt{6}$ b $2\sqrt{5} \times \sqrt{3}$
   c $3\sqrt{7} \times 2\sqrt{21}$ d $5\sqrt{2} \times 3\sqrt{24}$

7. Write these numbers using index notation.
   a $\sqrt{3}$ b $\sqrt[4]{4}$
   c $\sqrt{7}$ d $\sqrt[3]{10}$

8. Work out the value of each of these expressions.
   a $25^{\frac{1}{2}}$ b $1000^{\frac{1}{3}}$
   c $121^{\frac{1}{2}}$ d $64^{\frac{1}{3}}$

9. Write each of the numbers out in full.
   a 8.2×10^7 b 5.42×10^3
   c 3.1×10^{-4} d 6.09×10^{-6}

10. Write each number in standard form.
    a 5600   b 873000
    c 0.062   d 0.000107
    e 24.5×10^5 f 0.42×10^{-1}

What next?

Score	
0 – 4	Your knowledge of this topic is still developing. To improve look at Formative test: 3B-11; MyMaths: 1033, 1049, 1051, 1053 and 1064
5 – 8	You are gaining a secure knowledge of this topic. To improve look at InvisiPen: 181, 182, 183, 184, 185, and 186
9, 10	You have mastered this topic. Well done, you are ready to progress!

Question commentary

Question 1 – (Students should first find all the prime factors then pair them up **a** $576 = 2^2 \times 2^2 \times 2^2 \times 3^2$ so the square root is $2 \times 2 \times 2 \times 3$, **b** $1225 = 5^2 \times 7^2$ so the square root is 5×7.

Question 2 – (Students should show their working. They should be choosing values to check in a logical manner. Once they have found the two values with 1dp the solution lies between they must check the number in the middle to verify which is correct to 1 dp, so for **a** check 26.45 and for **b** check 5.85.

Question 3 – In part **i**, students must remember the raise both n^3 and p^2 to the power 5; similarly with s and r^3 to the power 2 in **k**. Fractions must be fully simplified.

Questions 4 to 6 – Students should split the number in each surd into factors first where possible.

Questions 7 and 8 – Students need to understand the meaning of fractional powers for square roots and cube roots. A calculator should not be used.

Questions 9 and 10 – Students may think **10e** and **f** are already in standard form but they do not use a number between 1 and 10 so they need to be rewritten. This is likely to cause confusion.

Answers

1. a 24   b 35
2. a 26.5   b 5.8
3. a $3a^2$ b $6b^3c^2$ c $4d^6$
   d $e^{10}f^3$ e g^4h^6 f i
   g j^2k^6 h m^8 i $n^{15}p^{10}$
   j $2q^5$ k $4r^2s$
4. a 5   b 6   c 12
   d 20
5. a $2\sqrt{7}$ b $6\sqrt{2}$ c $5\sqrt{5}$
   d $11\sqrt{3}$
6. a $3\sqrt{2}$ b $2\sqrt{15}$ c $42\sqrt{3}$
   d $60\sqrt{3}$
7. a $3^{\frac{1}{2}}$ b $4^{\frac{1}{3}}$ c $7^{\frac{1}{2}}$
   d $10^{\frac{1}{3}}$
8. a 5   b 10   c 11
   d 4
9. a 82 000 000   b 5420   c 0.000 31
   d 0.000 006 09
10. a 5.6×10^3 b 8.73×10^5
    c 6.2×10^{-2} d 1.07×10^{-4}
    e 2.45×10^6 f 4.2×10^{-2}

11 MyPractice

1 Work out these square roots.
  a $\sqrt{1600}$
  b $\sqrt{4900}$
  c $\sqrt{14400}$
  d $\sqrt{\frac{81}{100}}$

2 Use trial and improvement to find these roots to 1 dp.
  You could use tables like the ones on the right.
  a $\sqrt{38}$
  b $\sqrt{62}$
  c $\sqrt[3]{38}$
  d $\sqrt[3]{250}$

Check your answers by finding squares or cubes.

x	x^2	Comment

x	x^3	Comment

3 A circle of radius r has an area $A = \pi r^2$.
  a Find A to 1 decimal place when $r = 6$ cm.
  b Find r to 1 decimal place when $A = 240$ cm^2.

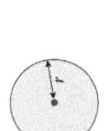

4 An ice cube has a volume of 10 cm^3.
  Find the length x of its edges, to 1 dp.

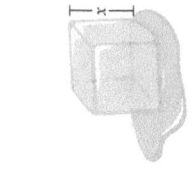

5 Simplify these expressions using indices in your answers.
  a $y \times y \times y \times y \times y$
  b $a \times a \times a \times a \times a \times a$
  c $x \times x \times x \times z \times z \times x$
  d $m \times n \times m \times m \times n \times n$
  e $n \times 4 \times n \times n \times 4$
  f $3 \times c \times c \times 3 \times c$

6 Use the rules of indices to simplify these expressions.
  a $x^6 \times x^7$
  b $3a^3 \times a^5$
  c $2x^6 \times 4x^7$
  d $a^2 \times b^4 \times a^3 \times b^2$
  e $s^3 t^2 \times s^4 t$
  f $x^3 y^4 \times x^2 y^3$
  g $\frac{x^8}{x^2}$
  h $\frac{m^6 n^2}{m^3}$
  i $\frac{x^8 y^5}{x^2 y^3}$
  j $(x^4)^2$
  k $(2y^5)^3$
  l $(m^3 n^4)^4$

7 Use the x^2 and $\sqrt{}$ keys on your calculator to work out these amounts.
  Give answers to 2 dp where appropriate.
  a 2.25^2
  b 3.14^2
  c 6.01^2
  d $\sqrt{10}$
  e $\sqrt{20}$
  f $\sqrt{62}$

8 Calculate the following, leaving your answers in surd form.
  a $\sqrt{3} \times \sqrt{4}$
  b $\sqrt{5} \times \sqrt{2}$
  c $\sqrt{6} \times \sqrt{3}$
  d $2\sqrt{3} \times \sqrt{8}$
  e $\sqrt{7} \times 3\sqrt{3}$
  f $2\sqrt{7} \times \sqrt{4}$

9 Write these amounts using index notation.
  a $\sqrt{10}$
  b $\sqrt{12}$
  c $\sqrt[3]{5}$
  d $\sqrt[3]{50}$

10 Each of these numbers is in standard index form.
  Write out each number in full.
  a 4.2×10^2
  b 5.1×10^3
  c 4.38×10^5
  d 3.09×10^6
  e 2.001×10^7
  f 7.281×10^8

11 Write each number in standard index form.
  a 270
  b 3190
  c 42875
  d 38291
  e 491500
  f 2810000

12 Each of these numbers is in standard index form.
  Write each number as a decimal.
  a 3.1×10^{-1}
  b 2.9×10^{-2}
  c 9.25×10^{-4}
  d 6.19×10^{-6}
  e 3.25×10^{-8}
  f 1.9871×10^{-9}

13 Write each number in standard index form.
  a 0.2
  b 0.58
  c 0.075
  d 0.00089
  e 0.000009
  f 0.0078
  g 0.00000567
  h 0.000000000037

Question commentary

Questions 1 to 4 – Successively, these questions use recognition, trial and improvement and then context to provide examples in increasing order of difficulty.

Questions 5 and 6 – In question **6** part **k**, students must remember to raise the 2 to the power of 3 as well as the *y* term. In part **l**, they must raise both the *m* and the *n* term to the power.

Questions 7 to 9 – Basic practice of the skills covered in **11c**.

Questions 10 and 11 – Basic practice of the skills covered in **11d**.

Questions 12 and 13 – Basic practice of the skills covered in **11e**.

Answers

1. **a** 40 **b** 70 **c** 120 **d** $\frac{9}{10}$

2. **a** 6.2 **b** 7.9 **c** 3.4 **d** 6.3

3. **a** 113.1 cm² **b** 8.7 cm

4. 2.2

5. **a** y^5 **b** a^6 **c** x^3z^2 **d** m^3n^3
   e $16n^3$ **f** $27c^3$

6. **a** x^{13} **b** $3a^8$ **c** $8x^{13}$ **d** a^5b^6
   e s^7t^3 **f** x^5y^7 **g** x^6 **h** m^3n^2
   i x^6y^2 **j** x^8 **k** $8y^{15}$ **l** $m^{12}n^{16}$

7. **a** 5.06 **b** 9.86 **c** 36.12 **d** 3.16
   e 4.47 **f** 7.87

8. **a** $2\sqrt{3}$ **b** $\sqrt{10}$ **c** $3\sqrt{2}$ **d** $4\sqrt{6}$
   e $3\sqrt{21}$ **f** $4\sqrt{7}$

9. **a** $10^{\frac{1}{2}}$ **b** $12^{\frac{1}{2}}$ **c** $5^{\frac{1}{3}}$ **d** $50^{\frac{1}{3}}$

10. **a** 420 **b** 5100 **c** 438 000 **d** 3 090 000
    e 20 010 000 **f** 728 100 000

11. **a** 2.7×10^2 **b** 3.19×10^3
    c 4.2875×10^4 **d** 3.8291×10^4
    e 4.915×10^5 **f** 2.81×10^6

12. **a** 0.31 **b** 0.029
    c 0.000925 **d** 0.00000619
    e 0.000 000 032 5 **f** 0.000 000 001 987 1

13. **a** 2×10^{-1} **b** 5.8×10^{-1}
    c 7.5×10^{-2} **d** 8.9×10^{-4}
    e 9×10^{-6} **f** 7.8×10^{-3}
    g 5.67×10^{-6} **h** 3.7×10^{-11}

MyPractice

12 Constructions and Pythagoras

Learning outcomes

G4 Derive and use the standard ruler and compass constructions (perpendicular bisector of a line segment, constructing a perpendicular to a given line from/at a given point, bisecting a given angle); recognise and use the perpendicular distance from a point to a line as the shortest distance to the line (L6)

G13 Apply angle facts, triangle congruence, similarity and properties of quadrilaterals to derive results about angles and sides, including Pythagoras' Theorem, and use known results to obtain simple proofs (L7)

G14 Use Pythagoras' Theorem and trigonometric ratios in similar triangles to solve problems involving right-angled triangles (L7)

Introduction

The chapter starts by looking at constructing triangles using a ruler and protractor and a ruler and pair of compasses before moving on the consider constructions and loci. Pythagoras' Theorem is introduced along with the application of Pythagoras' Theorem to solve problems in two dimensions.

The introduction discusses the Great Pyramid of Giza which was completed in 2560 BC. The height of the pyramid is 146.5 metres and its base is 230.4 metres along each side. The amount of blocks used has been estimated at two million and each block is thought to weigh about 2 tonnes. This makes the total weight of the pyramid 4 million tonnes. Its volume is over 2.5 million cubic metres and while there are large parts of the inside that are empty space, we could still estimate the density of the stones at approximately 1.6-1.7 tonnes per cubic metre.

The pyramid was constructed using right-angled corners and these were measured using a knotted rope arranged into a triangle of dimensions 3 cubits, 4 cubits and 5 cubits. This is the first recorded *use* of Pythagoras' Theorem and predates Pythagoras himself by over 2000 years!

Prior knowledge

Students should already know how to…
- Draw angles
- Work out squares of numbers
- Plot coordinate points on a Cartesian grid

Starter problem

The starter problem asks the students to create an accurate scale model of the Great Pyramid of Giza. They will need to choose a suitable scale (perhaps 1 centimetre representing 20 metres on the actual pyramid) and create a net of the pyramid. Accurate construction of the four triangular faces could be emphasised at this point. The problem obviously comes from knowing the height of the pyramid, rather than the slope length of the triangles.

Applying Pythagoras' Theorem in three dimensions will enable us to work out the slope length of the triangular faces but this is beyond the scope of the chapter, and certainly before they even begin. In order to overcome this problem, students could draw an accurate scale diagram of the cross-section of the pyramid and measure the slope length before using this distance to construct their triangles for the net.

Resources

MyMaths

Constructing shapes	1089	Constructing triangles	1090	Pythagoras' Theorem	1112
Drawing loci	1147				

Online assessment

Chapter test	3B–12
Formative test	3B–12
Summative test	3B–12

InvisiPen solutions

Constructing a triangle	371	Constructing bisectors	373
Loci	375	Pythagoras	381

Topic scheme

Teaching time = 5 lessons/2 weeks

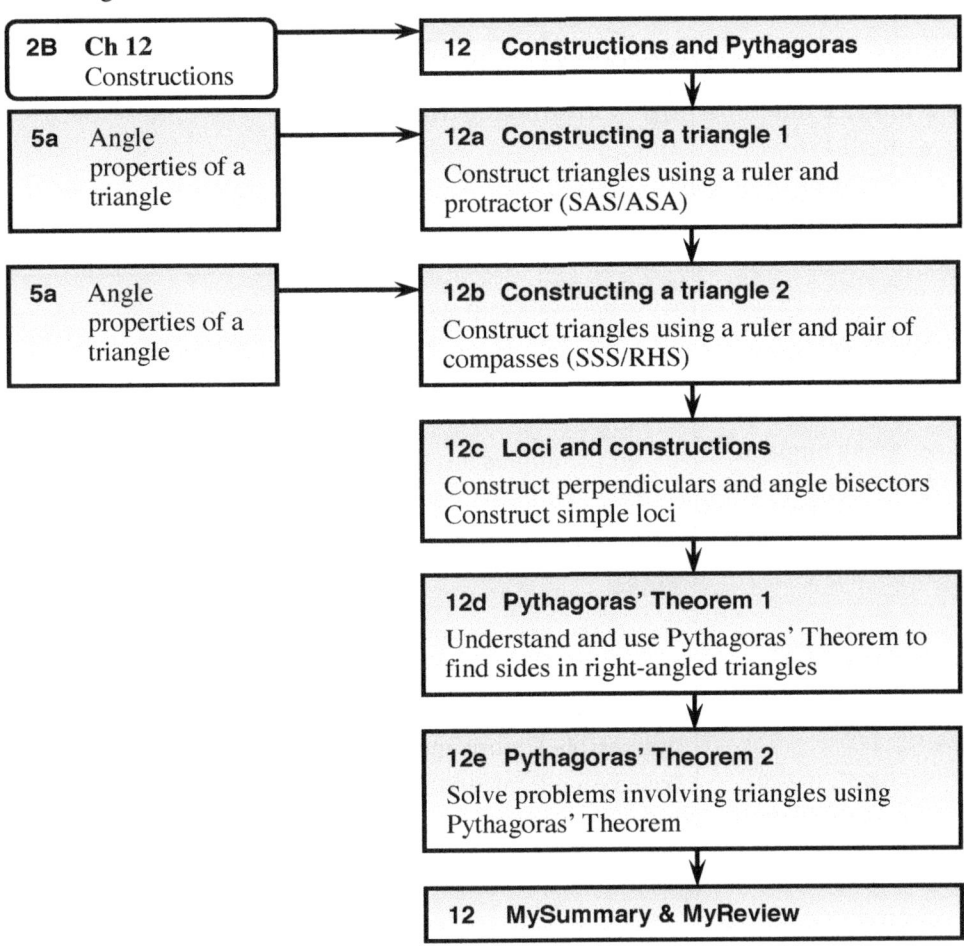

```
2B  Ch 12
    Constructions
```
→ **12 Constructions and Pythagoras**

```
5a  Angle properties of a triangle
```
→ **12a Constructing a triangle 1**
Construct triangles using a ruler and protractor (SAS/ASA)

```
5a  Angle properties of a triangle
```
→ **12b Constructing a triangle 2**
Construct triangles using a ruler and pair of compasses (SSS/RHS)

12c Loci and constructions
Construct perpendiculars and angle bisectors
Construct simple loci

12d Pythagoras' Theorem 1
Understand and use Pythagoras' Theorem to find sides in right-angled triangles

12e Pythagoras' Theorem 2
Solve problems involving triangles using Pythagoras' Theorem

12 MySummary & MyReview

Differentiation

Student book 3A   214 – 231
Constructing perpendicular lines, bisectors and angle bisectors
Constructing triangles
Bearings

Student book 3B   212 – 227
Constructing triangles using a ruler and protractor or ruler and pair of compasses.
Constructing perpendiculars, bisectors and simple loci
Understand and use Pythagoras' Theorem

Student book 3C   210 – 223
Understand and use Pythagoras' Theorem
Constructing triangles
Loci

Introduction

12a Constructing a triangle 1

Objectives

- Construct a triangle, given two sides and the included angle (SAS) or two angles and the included side (ASA) (L6)

Key ideas	Resources
1 Construct to an accurate level of within ±1 mm 2 Construct to an accurate level of within ±1°	Constructing triangles (1090) Rulers Protractors Geometry package, such as Geogebra

Simplification	Extension

As preparation for the exercise, ask students to measure and draw angles using a protractor and to measure and draw lines using a ruler. Emphasise the importance of first estimating the size of any angle at least to the level of acute, obtuse or reflex as an aide to correctly using a protractor.	Ask students to construct a triangle where,
	    one angle is the same as the sum of the other two angles.
	    all the angles are equal.
	    two angles are equal.
	This task is suitable for paired work.

Literacy	Links
Remind students of the difference between the instruction CONSTRUCT and SKETCH. Encourage students to to sketch as a preliminary task before constructing. Draw attention to the 'included' requirement, in the short forms ASA and SAS. Involve the term congruent when requiring exact copies to be constructed.	Roger Penrose created the Penrose triangle after attending a lecture by the Dutch artist MC Escher. Escher went on to produce many works of art based on impossible figures including Waterfall (1961), which is based on a Penrose triangle. There is a gallery of Escher's work at http://www.mcescher.com

Alternative approach

For a given set of information, ask the students to sketch using a mini whiteboard then discuss in pairs how they would construct accurately. This should both rehearse and remind the students of work covered previously. Share the key points, modelling the construction using a geometry software package such as Geogebra. Follow with the students carrying out the construction, measuring, sharing and comparing the missing detail. Ask students to explore if other sets of information would be sufficient to draw specific traingles, such as 2 angles or three angles; 2 or three sides, and so on.

Checkpoint

Construct a triangle with base 6cm and base angles 32° and 68°. (Answers can be checked by students comparing work, by a template, or by measuring the lengths of the other two sides or the third angle, 80°)

Starter – Four in a line

Ask students to draw a 5 × 5 grid and enter the numbers 1 to 25 in any order. Ask questions, for example,

> A polygon has an angle sum of 720°. How many sides does it have? (6)
> How many lines of symmetry does an isosceles triangle have? (1)
> How many sides altogether in two squares, three kites and one pentagon? (25)

The winner is the first student to cross out four in a line.

Teaching notes

Before starting, make sure that all students have a ruler and protractor and a sharp pencil.

Draw a line (as a base for a triangle) and discuss with students what other information would be needed to draw a unique triangle. Highlight the SAS and ASA cases, and discuss whether where you draw the angle(s) makes a difference to the triangle produced.

Review how to use the protractor correctly, and the benefit of being able to estimate angles reasonably well by eye. Using the wrong scale on the protractor should be avoided if students consider whether their answer makes sense, or whether the triangle they draw looks right.

To encourage accurate constructions a points system could be used awarding 10 points for an unknown angle/side accurate to ±1°/±1 mm or 5 points of accuracies of ±3°/±2 mm.

Plenary

Ask students how many different triangles they can construct which have an angle of 30° and sides of 8 cm and 6 cm. (there are four: one as SAS, one with the 30° angle at one end of the 6 cm side and the 8 cm side coming from the other end, and then two where the 30° angle is at one end of the 8 cm side and the 6 cm side comes from the other end).

Exercise commentary

A sharp pencil, ruler and protractor are needed for this exercise.

Question 1 – Parts **a** and **c** are SAS constructions. The other parts are ASA constructions.

Question 2 – A labelled sketch of each triangle is essential before beginning the constructions. Parts **a** and **c** are ASA constructions while part **b** is SAS.

Question 3 – Encourage students to construct each triangle separately to create the quadrilaterals.

Question 4 – This is an ASA construction. The angles are 45° as the lawn is a square.

Question 5 – Students may need to draw and cut out the four congruent right-angled triangles to find the required configurations. This is suitable for paired work.

Answers

1. a Students' construction, scalene
   b Students' construction, right-angled
   c Students' construction, equilateral
   d Students' constructions, scalene
   e Students' constructions, scalene
   f Students' constructions, scalene
2. Check students' constructions
   a 15.3 cm   b 15.7 cm   c 12.0 cm
3. a Kite, 3 cm   b Rhombus, 14.9 cm
   c Isosceles trapezium, 6 cm
4. a Students' constructions b 22.6 m
5. a Students' constructions
   b 16 cm, 20 cm, 20.9 cm, 16.5 cm, 24.5 cm

Constructing a triangle 1

12b Constructing a triangle 2

Objectives		
• Use straight edge and compasses to construct a triangle, given three sides (SSS)		(L6)
• Use straight edge and compasses to construct triangles, given right angle, hypotenuse and side (RHS)		(L6)

Key ideas	Resources	
1 Using a compass effectively for length markers 2 Exploring the special case of RHS triangle information	Constructing shapes Spare drawing equipment Stiff card Scissors and glue	(1089)

Simplification	Extension
To build up confidence in doing SSS constructions, ask students to use a ruler and compasses to construct equilateral triangles given the three side lengths. Then extend to isosceles triangles and finally to scalene triangles.	On stiff card ask students to construct the nets of a regular tetrahedron, a regular octahedron and a square-based pyramid and then construct the 3D shapes using their nets. Students should be reminded to leave some tabs when they cut out their shapes. These models can be used as the basis of a classroom display.

Literacy	Links
Maintain reference to congruent shapes. Introduce the short form RHS, the terms and their meanings. Hypoteneuse may be a word unfamiliar to students. Check spelling with them. Remind students that construction lines and arcs should be left on construction diagrams as they can provide useful guides and checking points.	Roof trusses always employ one or more triangles in their construction to give them strength. Roof trusses are pre-built in a factory, usually from wood, and are lifted into place at the construction site. Each truss is designed to carry its own weight together with the extra weight of the roofing material. There are design drawings of roof trusses at www.raftertales.com/home-remodeling/roof-truss and a photograph showing the trusses in place at http://www.rtcts.co.uk/timber-systems/roof-trusses

Alternative approach
Begin by asking students to sketch triangles to a given set of information, SSA, where A is not 90°. Students should use a mini whiteboard and be challenged but reassured as this is not easy. The activity should have the result of reminding the students of the problems involved where an angle is not included. A few students may be able to establish or be reminded that a compass might help in this type of construction, but that it may result in two possible triangles. If this does not arise, bring this point to the attention of the group. Ask them to try sketching SSA with a 90°, suggesting that they use a horizontal line upon which to work with their sketching. Draw student attention to the fact that the hypoteneuse must be opposite the 90° angle – why? Sketches should be congruent, though some will be reflections/rotations of others.

Checkpoint
Construct a triangle with sides 5cm, 3cm and 4cm. (Answers can be checked by students comparing work, use of a template, or by measuring the angles (90°, 37° and 53°))

Starter – Symmetrical equality

Challenge students to sketch quadrilaterals where the order of rotational symmetry equals the number of lines of symmetry. (Possible solution: 1 isosceles trapezium, 2 rectangle, 3 impossible, 4 square)

Can be extended to triangles and other polygons.

Teaching notes

Before starting, make sure that all students have a ruler, compasses, protractor and a sharp pencil; preferably two pencils, one in the compasses and another to do any other drawing.

Review basic strategies of measuring angles using a protractor. Emphasise using the correct scale and extending lines where necessary so that the lines reach the scale on the protractor.

When drawing, emphasis that it is important not to erase any construction lines and arcs as these show how the construction was actually done. Instead show them as fainter lines.

As in the previous spread, to encourage accurate constructions a points system could be used awarding 10 points for an unknown angle/side accurate to ±1°/±1 mm or 5 points of accuracies of ±3°/±2 mm.

Plenary

Ask students whether they can construct triangles with sides 4 cm, 5 cm and 10 cm; if not, can they explain why it is not possible? What happens with sides of 4 cm, 5 cm and 9 cm?

Can they construct a general rule to decide whether a triangle can be drawn from 3 given sides?

Exercise commentary

A sharp pencil, ruler, protractor and pair of compasses are needed for this exercise.

Question 1 – All SSS constructions and based on the first example.

Question 2 – All RHS constructions and based on the second example.

Question 3 – The triangles need to be constructed in turn using SSS.

Question 4 – Ask students if this an SSS or an RHS construction. It is an RHS construction with a simple scale.

Question 5 – The tessellation should consist of three sets of parallel lines. Ask students to explain why the lines are parallel.

Question 6 – Useful for class discussion, or can be set as a 'red herring' challenge during the initial phase of the lesson.

Answers

1. a 39°, 71.5°, 71.5°   b 37°, 37°, 106°
   c 54°, 54°, 72°   d 77°, 77°, 26°

2. a 14.2 cm   b 156.9 mm   c 19.1 cm

3. a Students' constructions b 6.9 cm
   c Two checks: 90° and bisect

4. a Students' constructions b 66.4°

5. Student's construction of a tessellation with the equal angles coloured.

6. No, the two 3 cm sides will not meet as they are each less than half the length of the longest side (9 cm)

Constructing a triangle 2

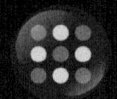

12c Loci and constructions

Objectives

- Use straight edge and compasses to construct the midpoint and perpendicular bisector of a line segment, the bisector of an angle, the perpendicular from a point to a line, the perpendicular from a point on a line (L6)
- Find simple loci, both by reasoning and by using ICT, to produce shapes and paths, e.g. an equilateral triangle (L6)
- Use ICT to explore constructions of triangles and other 2D shapes (L6)
- Find the locus of a point that moves according to a simple rule, both by reasoning and by using ICT (L7)

Key ideas	Resources
1 Understand the principles of loci, and recognise some simple examples of loci 2 Recognsie and reproduce accurately simple loci from given conditions.	Constructing shapes (1089) Drawing loci (1147) Spare drawing equipment Pieces of paper/markers Loci problems & demos, with Geogebra: http://www.tes.co.uk/teaching-resource/Loci-6082780/

Simplification	Extension
To prepare for this exercise, give students questions asking for simple loci that do not involve constructions, for example, the saddle of a bicycle travelling along a level road (parallel line). In question 7 it may help some students to cut out an equilateral triangle and a square and to roll these along the edge of a ruler, in order to answer this question.	Students can use LOGO, or similar software, to generate shapes. This task is suitable for paired work.

Literacy	Links
Students will have met the terms here before, but it is unlikely that they will be familiar with them, let alone confident. Check the singular and plural versions: locus and loci, the pronunciation and the spelling. Again be explicit between sketching and constructing, encouraging sketching to help the construction process.	When a photograph is taken using a long shutter speed of several seconds or more, a moving light leaves a light trail on the photograph, often resulting in dramatic effects. The trail is the locus of the moving light. The camera must be held completely still while the shutter is open, so a tripod is generally used. There are examples of light trail photography at http://digital-photography-school.com/long-exposure-photography and at http://www.digitalpicturezone.com/digital-pictures/25-awesome-light-trails/

Alternative approach

Begin with some visualisations such as those in Teaching Mental Maths (Shape & Space). Encourage students to work in pairs with mini whiteboard sketches to discuss and compare results and thoughts. Angle bisector and perpendicular bisector may be demonstrated using resources from TES, or alternatively using a visualiser with a recording of each stage. Both constructions will have been met before, but students are unlikley to remeber the finer detail. Consolidate thoroughly, working with student pairs so that they can act as critical friends for each other through the processes.

Checkpoint

Describe the construction that gives the locus of all points equidistant from two fixed points. (Perpendicular bisector)

Describe the construction that gives the locus of all points equidistant from two (non-parallel) lines. (Angle bisector)

Starter – Impossible triangles?

Ask students which of the following triangles cannot be constructed and why?

A triangle with sides 3 cm, 7 cm, 10 cm. (Impossible, flat)

A triangle containing angles of 43°, 111° and a side of 9.5 cm. (Possible)

A triangle containing angles of 103°, 89° and a side of 6 cm. (Impossible, 103 + 89 > 180)

A triangle with sides 6 cm, 8 cm, 10 cm. (Possible)

Ask students what is special about the last triangle.

Teaching notes

It is important for students to know that a locus of points is a mathematical way to describe a path by specifying conditions that the points satisfy. So they need to learn the conditions and the constructions to be used. It may be useful to have students explore 'equidistant from a point', 'equidistant from two points' or 'equidistant from two lines' practically by moving around in the classroom – leaving pieces of paper at points the class agree satisfy the condition – and then discussing what geometrical property the locus (the line of paper) has in relation to the reference objects.

Students should be encouraged to draw sketches of loci before beginning the accurate construction. Construction lines and arcs should not be erased.

Plenary

Show a number of loci similar to those constructed in the exercise and ask the students to work in pairs to describe the locus for each.

Exercise commentary

A sharp pencil, ruler, protractor and pair of compasses are needed for this exercise.

Questions 1 and **3** – The constructions for the perpendicular bisector and angle bisector are shown in the initial text on the previous page.

Question 4 – Students should recognise the need for a circle in this question.

Question 5 – Part **a** uses an SSS construction for an equilateral triangle to construct an angle of 60°. Part **b** uses the example method to bisect the angle of 60°. Parts **c** and **d** can be constructed using combined constructions of angles of 30° and 60°.

Question 6 – These constructions are in the initial text on the previous page. Can students explain why the lines are parallel?

Question 7 – The lines from the centre of rotation to P and Q forms the radius of a circle.

Question 8 – Part **e** shows that the diagonals of a rhombus are perpendicular and bisect each other.

Answers

1   The perpendicular bisector of AB.

2   A line 2 cm from each parallel line.

3   **a, b** Angle bisectors: check constructions

4   A circle centre O, of radius 30 mm.

5   Students' angle constructions

6   **a i** Students' constructions
      ii Students' constructions
     b They are parallel to each other.

7   **a** An arc of a circle.   **b** An arc of a circle.

8   **a-c** Check students' constructions.
     d Yes, triangles ABX and CBX are congruent.
     e angle AXB = angle CXB as triangles ABX and CBX are congruent.
        Therefore angle AXB = 90° by angles on a straight line adding up to 180°.
        Therefore BD is perpendicular to AC.
        AX = XC as triangles ABX and CBX are congruent.
        Therefore BD is perpendicular bisector of AC.

Loci and constructions   219

12d Pythagoras' theorem 1

Objectives

- Understand and apply Pythagoras' theorem when solving problems in 2D (L7)

Key ideas	Resources
1 Understand that Pythagoras' rule is a special case of right angled triangles 2 Use the theorem in order solve 2D probems	Pythagoras' Theorem (1112) Pre-drawn Perigal's dissection Square dotty paper Tiltted Squares (NRICH): http://nrich.maths.org/2293

Simplification	Extension
For question **4** provide students with large squares with Perigal's dissection pre-drawn on them.	Students can construct various right-angled triangles, measure the side measurements and then check Pythagoras' theorem for each triangle. Alternatively students can also try to find other dissections that show Pythagoras' theorem.

Literacy	Links
Students will often have heard of Pythagoras' theorem, but may not know the details. Check the spelling and the necessity of an upper case letter for the name. Revisit the term hypotenuse as well, indicating the side opposite the 90° angle.	Pythagoras is also commemorated on coins. In 2000, Uganda issued a silver coin to commemorate the Millennium showing a portrait of Pythagoras. The shape of the coin was a right-angled triangle. There is a picture of the Uganda Millennium coin at http://www.dig4coins.com/articles/other-coins/triangular-coins

Alternative approach

Use square dotty paper with students and encourage them to find suqares with areas of 1, 2, 3, and so on if possible up to 30; which are impossible? Why? See Tilted Squares for further details. Alternatively you may have these sheets pre-prepared with the squares and ask students to find and label the area of each. Cut outs of these squares may then be arranged by students to form triangles. Students may then classify these triangles into acute, right-angled and obtuse. As this is by observation, noting the area relationships of each of these categories helps with the grouping, so assist and prompt as required towards the $a^2 + b^2$ link to c^2 using $<, =, >$ signs. In terms of remembering the theorem it is better to describe it as 'the square of the longest side is equal to the sum of the squares of the other two sides'. Students find this of more help when solving problems relating to right angled triangles, as identifying the longest side or hypotenuse is key.

Checkpoint

A right-angled triangle has shorter sides equal to 4cm and 5cm. Work out the length of the hypotenuse. ($\sqrt{41}$ or 6.4cm to one decimal place)

Geometry and measures Constructions and Pythagoras

Starter – Jumble

Write a list of anagrams on the board and ask students to unscramble them and then make up their own. Possible anagrams are
ROADWHARE, EQUARTIALLARD, RICCIMDECBURS, GOATPENN, GANNETT, MERYMYST, RETOXIER, LAPOLMARGERAL, RECCIL
(arrowhead, quadrilateral, circumscribed, pentagon, tangent, symmetry, exterior, parallelogram, circle)

Teaching notes

Ask, is there a connection between the lengths of the sides of a right-angled triangle? Draw two examples and ask students to consider possible links. Use 6, 8, 10 and 5, 12, 13. After a short period of time, advise students to square the side lengths and look for a connection between these squared lengths. Establish that the square of the longest side is equal to the sum of the squares of the two shorter sides. This can be expressed as a formula. Consider using one of the following with the class, $a^2 = b^2 + c^2$ or $c^2 = a^2 + b^2$ or $h^2 = a^2 + b^2$. Define the longest side as the hypotenuse. Where is the hypotenuse in relation to the right angle? (Always opposite) Show that the formula works by considering the area of squares built on the sides of the triangle. Look at two examples of the application of Pythagoras to find the hypotenuse and then a shorter side. Include the use of the square root function on calculator. Emphasise the importance of the following procedure: diagram, formula, substitute numbers, solve in steps, answer and units.

Plenary

Is it possible to find the other sides of a right-angled triangle if you know only one side? Consider a right-angled isosceles triangle where the hypotenuse is known. Can Pythagoras' theorem be applied here? Encourage students to try an approach and check their solution by testing it against the theorem. Some students may manage to get as far as $h^2 = 2 \times a^2$ but then think that this leads to $h = 2a$. Apply this problem to finding the area of a square from its diagonal length. Use an example or find a general formula.
Area = $\frac{1}{2}$(hypotenuse)^2.

Exercise commentary.

Encourage students to check that their answers are realistic. The hypotenuse is the longest side of a right-angled triangle. This will help students to decide whether to add or subtract the areas of the squares.

Question 1 – This question provides a neat step-by-step guide for checking whether the triangles are right-angled.

Question 2 – This question is based on example **a** on the previous page when the areas are added.

Question 3 – This question is a mixture of adding and subtracting areas.

Question 4 – This task is suitable for a display poster to illustrate Pythagoras' theorem.

Answers

1.   a No, $4^2 + 5^2 \neq 6^2$ b Yes, $6^2 + 8^2 = 10^2$
    b No, $5^2 + 10^2 \neq 12^2$ d Yes, $5^2 + 12^2 = 13^2$

2.   a 17 cm   b 25 m

3.   a 15 cm   b 6 cm   c 35 cm   d 41 cm
    e 2 cm   f 14 cm

4. The pieces fit exactly into the 5 cm by 5 cm square

Pythagoras' theorem 1

12e Pythagoras' theorem 2

Objectives

- Understand and apply Pythagoras' theorem when solving problems in 2D (L7)
- Calculate the length AB, given the coordinates of points A and B (L7)

Key ideas	Resources
1 Know and apply Pythagoras' theorem in a variety of 2D contexts including coordinate geometry	Pythagoras' Theorem (1112) Pre-drawn axes for the Simplification task Pythagoras Theorem challenges (NRICH): http://nrich.maths.org/8479 Problems involving surds (TES): http://www.tes.co.uk/teaching-resource/Pythagoras-Thinking-Questions-including-Surds-6341879

Simplification	Extension
Question 2 – Students can be given coordinate axes with the points and the right-angled triangles pre-drawn.	Challenge students to find the 16 basic Pythagorean triples (a, b, c) with $c \leq 100$. This task is suitable for group work.

Literacy	Links
Encourage students to check that maths sentencing used in presenting solutions are accurate. For example, "$3^2 + 4^2 = 25 = 5$" is a common but inaccurate recording of correct thinking. Units and approximates need to be considered in order to raise the standard of communication.	Egyptian land surveyors used Pythagorean triples when re-establishing the field boundaries along the River Nile after the annual flooding. They divided a rope into twelve equal parts using knots or paint and used this to create a 3 : 4 : 5 right-angled triangle, even though they did not know Pythagoras' theorem. The surveyors were called harpedonaptai or rope-stretchers. There is a small picture of harpenedonaptai using a knotted rope at http://plsurvey.com/surveyinghistory.html

Alternative approach

Paired problem solving with thorough presentation of a solution for display will encourage students to raise their standards. Construction challenges can be included such as draw successive right-angled triangles, where each following triangle is built on the hypotenuse of the previous, resulting in attractive spirals. How accurate is the work after ten such drawings? Students can use Pythagoras to calculate a final length and compare. This can also be a challenge for plotting on a graphic calculator, geometry software or by hand on a grid. Other problems may be found at the Nrich site referenced. Also, TES resources provide an opportunity for students to work with surds through application of Pythagoras.

Checkpoint

A 6m ladder leans against a wall with its foot 1.8m away from the wall.

How far up the wall does the ladder reach? (5.72 m)

Starter – Name the shape

Ask students to take the following letters and rearrange them to spell a shape. The first from arrowhead, the last from square, sixth from pentagon, first from rhombus, sixth from parallelogram, first from trapezium, second from kite, sixth from scalene. (Triangle)

Can be extended by giving clues to each shape, for example, the first letter from a quadrilateral with a reflex angle.

Teaching notes

Ask, how can you check if a triangle has a right angle if you know only the lengths of the sides? Remind students of Pythagoras' theorem and ask them to explain in words what the theorem tells us about the connection between the lengths of the sides. Show how the theorem proves or disproves a triangle is right-angled using two examples. Look at a coordinate grid. Ask the class to estimate how far apart two particular points are. Is there a way to measure this distance exactly? Show how a right-angled triangle can be formed from the two points. How can the base and height be counted? Encourage students to include both counting the squares and looking at the difference between both the *x* and *y* coordinates. Show how Pythagoras can be used with non-right-angled triangles. For example, find the area of an isosceles triangle with known sides. Challenge students to spot where the right-angled triangle could be placed. Describe the process of drawing in the height as 'dropping the perpendicular to the base'.

Plenary

Engineers sometimes make use of a special right-angled triangle. It has interior angles of 30° and 60°. If the side between the 90° and 30° angle measures exactly $\sqrt{3}$, can the other two sides be found by trying to construct the triangle accurately? Ask students to be as accurate as possible when using rulers and angle-measurers. Most students are likely to use $\sqrt{3}$ cm, does it make a difference what units are used? (No) Once solutions are suggested, check them using Pythagoras' theorem.

Exercise commentary

Encourage students to check that their answers are realistic. The hypotenuse is the longest side of a right-angled triangle. This will help students to decide whether to add or subtract the areas of the squares.

Question 1 – Remind students that $c^2 = a^2 + b^2$ only if the triangle is right-angled.

Question 2 – This question is based on the first example. Encourage students to plot the points on coordinate axes and to draw the appropriate right-angled triangle.

Question 3 – A practical application of Pythagoras' theorem.

Question 4 – Students will need a protractor to construct the rectangle. Ensure students apply Pythagoras' theorem to a right-angled triangle.

Question 5 – This is based on the second example. Students must use a right-angled triangle when calculating the perpendicular height.

Questions 6 and **7** – These are multi-step questions. Encourage students to set out their working logically and clearly. This task is suitable for paired or group work.

Answers

1	a Yes	b Yes	c No	d Yes
2	a 5	b 3.16	c 5.66	d 2.83

3 3.71 m

4 a Student's constructions b 7.21 cm

5 a i 16 cm   ii 192 cm^2
   b i 12 cm   ii 192 cm^2

6 a PR = 16.12 cm   b PS = 16.25 cm

7 a AC = 19.36 cm   b AB = 19.13 cm

Pythagoras' theorem 2

12 Constructions and Pythagoras – MySummary

Key outcomes	Quick check
Know how to construct ASA, SAS, SSS and RHS triangles, bisectors and perpendiculars. **L6**	Construct a triangle with side lengths 4cm, 6cm and 5cm. (Students can check their working with a partner or measure the angles to check the accuracy of their constructions (83°, 56°, 41°))
Find and describe loci. **L7**	**a** Describe the locus of points 1cm from a fixed point A. (A circle, centred on A, radius 1cm) **b** In triangle ABC, describe the locus of points equidistant from sides AB and BC. (The angle bisector of angle B)
Use Pythagoras' theorem to solve problems involving right-angled triangles. **L7**	**a** Triangle PQR is right-angled at Q. If PQ = 6cm and QR = 7cm, find PR. ($\sqrt{85}$ or 9.2cm) **b** Triangle XYZ is right-angled at Y. If XY = 13cm and XZ = 18cm, find YZ. ($\sqrt{155}$ or 12.4cm)

MyMaths extra support

Lesson/online homework	Description
Measuring angles 1081 L5	Learn how to use a protractor. Measure acute and obtuse angles. Also, estimating angles.
Bearings 1086 L5	Plotting and measuring three figure bearings.

MyReview

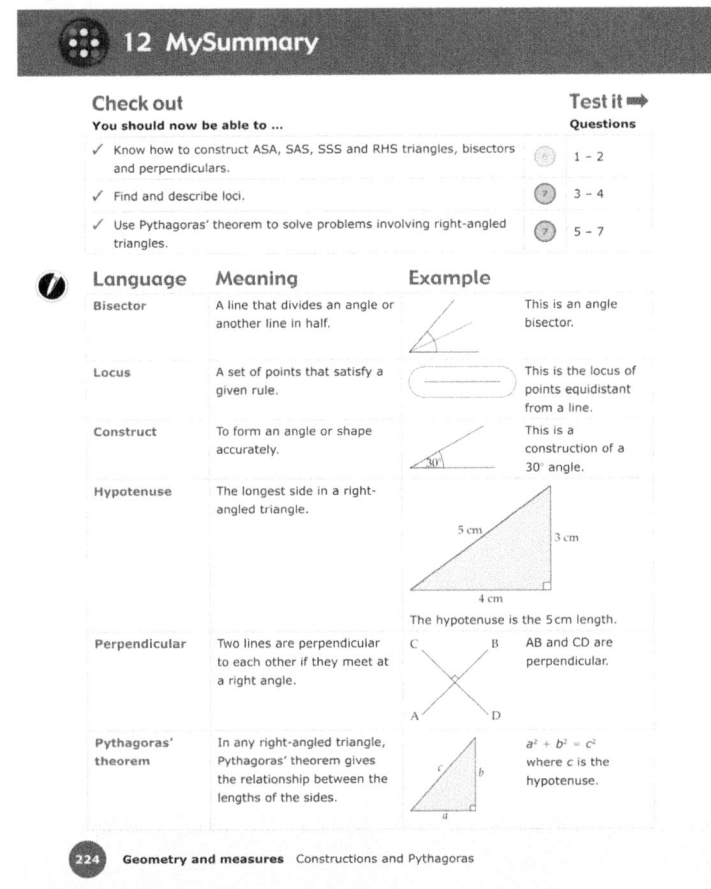

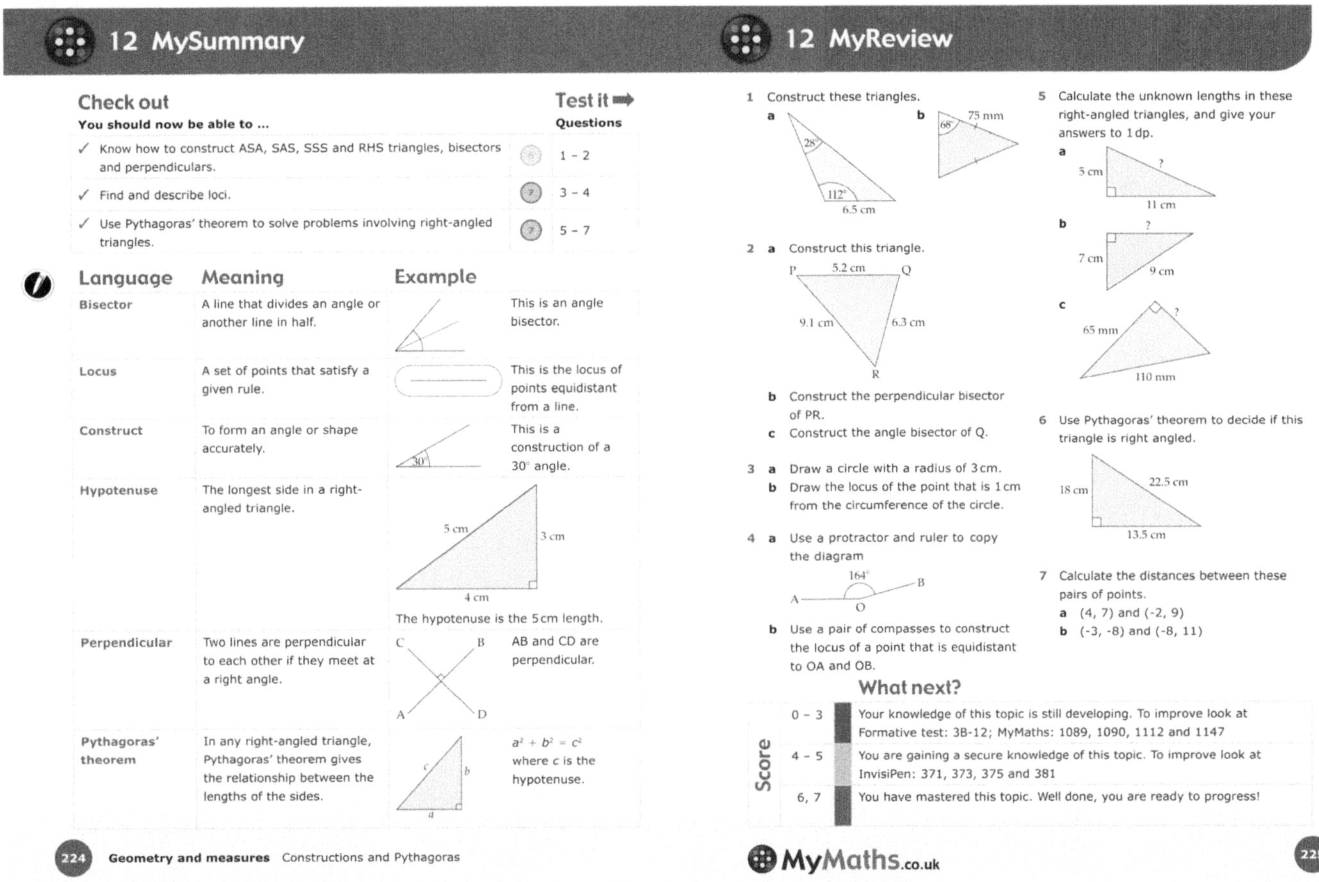

12 MySummary

Check out
You should now be able to ...

	Test it → Questions
✓ Know how to construct ASA, SAS, SSS and RHS triangles, bisectors and perpendiculars.	1 – 2
✓ Find and describe loci.	3 – 4
✓ Use Pythagoras' theorem to solve problems involving right-angled triangles.	5 – 7

Language	Meaning	Example
Bisector	A line that divides an angle or another line in half.	This is an angle bisector.
Locus	A set of points that satisfy a given rule.	This is the locus of points equidistant from a line.
Construct	To form an angle or shape accurately.	This is a construction of a 30° angle.
Hypotenuse	The longest side in a right-angled triangle.	The hypotenuse is the 5 cm length.
Perpendicular	Two lines are perpendicular to each other if they meet at a right angle.	AB and CD are perpendicular.
Pythagoras' theorem	In any right-angled triangle, Pythagoras' theorem gives the relationship between the lengths of the sides.	$a^2 + b^2 = c^2$ where c is the hypotenuse.

Geometry and measures — Constructions and Pythagoras

12 MyReview

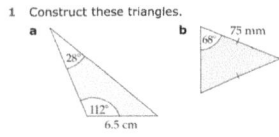

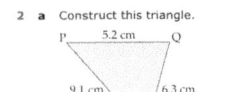

1. Construct these triangles.
   a. (28°, 112°, 6.5 cm)
   b. (68°, 75 mm)

2. a. Construct this triangle. P, 5.2 cm, Q, 9.1 cm, 6.3 cm, R
   b. Construct the perpendicular bisector of PR.
   c. Construct the angle bisector of Q.

3. a. Draw a circle with a radius of 3 cm.
   b. Draw the locus of the point that is 1 cm from the circumference of the circle.

4. a. Use a protractor and ruler to copy the diagram (164° at O, A to B)
   b. Use a pair of compasses to construct the locus of a point that is equidistant to OA and OB.

5. Calculate the unknown lengths in these right-angled triangles, and give your answers to 1 dp.
   a. 5 cm, 11 cm
   b. 7 cm, 9 cm
   c. 65 mm, 110 mm

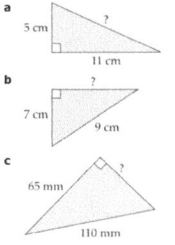

6. Use Pythagoras' theorem to decide if this triangle is right angled. (18 cm, 22.5 cm, 13.5 cm)

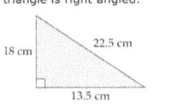

7. Calculate the distances between these pairs of points.
   a. (4, 7) and (-2, 9)
   b. (-3, -8) and (-8, 11)

What next?

Score	
0 – 3	Your knowledge of this topic is still developing. To improve look at Formative test: 3B-12; MyMaths: 1089, 1090, 1112 and 1147
4 – 5	You are gaining a secure knowledge of this topic. To improve look at InvisiPen: 371, 373, 375 and 381
6, 7	You have mastered this topic. Well done, you are ready to progress!

MyMaths.co.uk

Question commentary

Ensure students have a protractor, a ruler, a pair of compasses and a sharp pencil that fits in them. Allow ±1° and ±1 mm on all constructions.

Question 1 – Students will need to find the missing angles before they can construct the triangles. They should know that they require SAS or ASA.

Question 2 – Students should be using a ruler and pair of compasses for this construction; their construction lines should be clearly visible.

Question 3 – The diameter of the outer circle is 8 cm. Students will often forget the inner circle which should have diameter of 6 cm.

Question 4 – Students should be using a ruler and pair of compasses for this construction; their construction lines should be clearly visible.

Question 5 – Students need to decide whether they are finding the hypotenuse (part **a**) or one of the shorter sides (parts **b** and **c**), choosing incorrectly will give **a** 9.8, **b** 11.4, **c** 127.8.

Question 6 – Students need to check if $18^2 + 13.5^2 = 22.5^2$

Question 7 – Students should take care with the negatives: they may need to draw the points on coordinate axes to understand how to find the length. The calculations are **a** $\sqrt{(6^2 + 2^2)}$, **b** $\sqrt{(5^2 + 19^2)}$.

Answers

1. a. Check ASA: 112°, 6.5 cm, 40°
   b. Check SAS: 75 mm, 44°, 75 mm
      or ASA: 68°, 75 mm, 44°

2. a. Check SSS: 5.2 cm, 6.3 cm, 9.1 cm
   b, c. Check students' constructions

3. Concentric circles; one with 3 cm radius, one with 2 cm radius and one with 4 cm radius.

4. Check angle of 164° bisected to two 82° angles

5. a. 12.1 cm   b. 5.7 cm   c. 88.7 mm

6. Yes

7. a. 6.32   b. 19.6

MySummary/MyReview 225

12 MyPractice

12 MyPractice

1 Calculate the unknown angles in these triangles.
Then use a ruler and protractor to construct the triangles.

a Triangle ABC with angle B = 36°, angle C = 25°, side AC = 5 cm

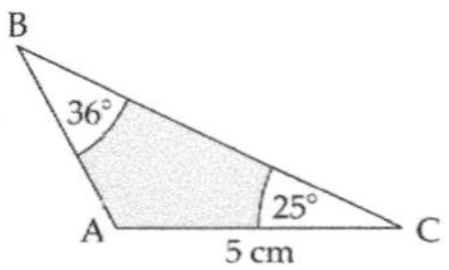

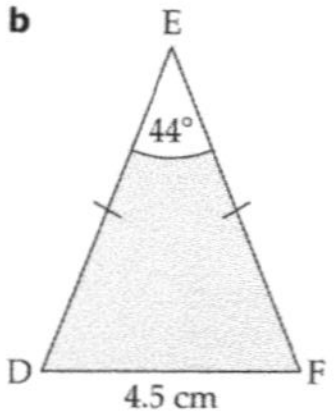

b Triangle DEF with angle E = 44°, DE = EF (marked equal), DF = 4.5 cm

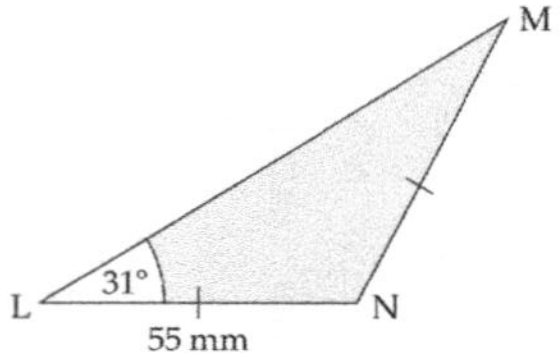

c Triangle LMN with angle L = 31°, LN = 55 mm, LM = MN (marked equal)

12a

2 Construct these triangles accurately.
Calculate the perimeter of each triangle.

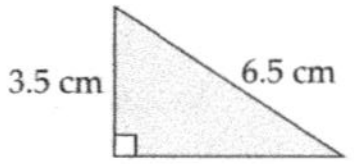

a Right-angled triangle with legs 4 cm and 7 cm, hypotenuse 7.5 cm

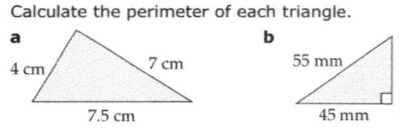

b Right-angled triangle with 55 mm and 45 mm

c Right-angled triangle with 3.5 cm and 6.5 cm

12b

3 You can use these instructions to draw a square.
REPEAT 4
[FORWARD 10 TURN RIGHT 90°]
Devise similar instructions to draw
a an equilateral triangle
b a regular hexagon
c a regular octagon.

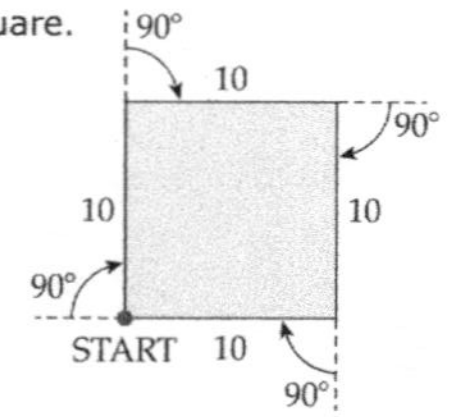

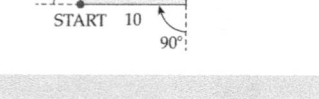

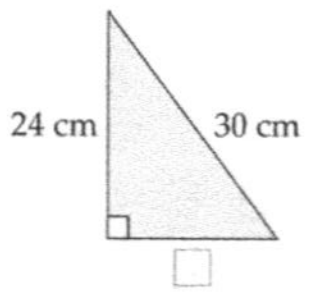

12c

4 Use Pythagoras' theorem to calculate the unknown lengths.

a Right triangle with legs 20 m and 15 m

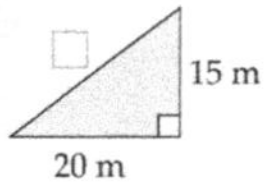

b Right triangle with 24 cm and 30 cm

c Right triangle with 8.5 cm and 7.5 cm

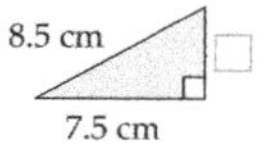

Each answer is an integer.

12d

5 A square is drawn inside a 4 by 4 square. Calculate 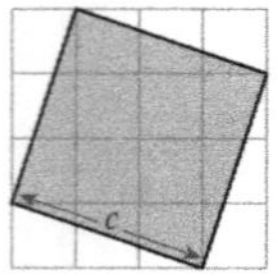
a the length c
b the area of the shaded square.

6 There are two right-angled triangles in the diagram. 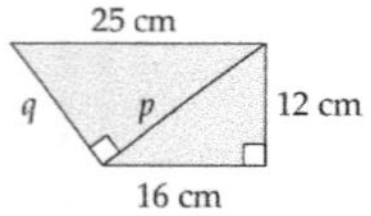
(25 cm, 12 cm, 16 cm, with p and q)
Calculate the value of p and q.

7 Calculate the distance between each pair of points.
Give your answer to 1 dp where appropriate.
a (1, 2) and (5, 6) **b** (2, 2) and (6, 5)
c (1, 2) and (2, 5) **d** (0, 5) and (4, 1)
e (3, 6) and (6, 0) **f** (−2, −1) and (1, 0)

8 A telegraph pole 6 metres tall is held in place by a sloping wire as shown.
Calculate the length, x, of the wire.
(6 m pole, 3.2 m base)

12e

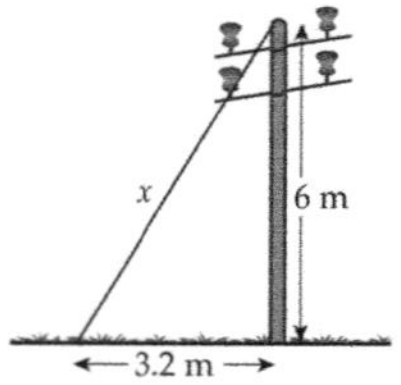

226 **Geometry and measures** Constructions and Pythagoras

Question commentary

Question 1 – Students will need to work out the missing angles in the triangles before constructing them. They are all ASA constructions.

Question 2 – Students could construct the triangles but part **a** is best worked out directly while parts **b** and **c** can be worked out by calculating the length of the third side using Pythagoras' theorem.

Question 3 – This is an example of a LOGO programme and students could be asked to work with the programme itself if computer facilities exist.

Question 4 – Students should take care to identify if they are finding the hypotenuse or one of the shorter sides.

Questions 5 to 8 – These questions are all applications of Pythagoras' theorem and students will need to recognise this.

Answers

1. a 119° and construction   b 68°, 68° and construction
   c 31°, 118° and construction

2. a Students' construction, 18.5 cm
   b Students' construction, 132 mm
   c Students' construction, 15.5 cm

3. a REPEAT 3
      [FORWARD 10 TURN RIGHT 120°]
   b REPEAT 6
      [FORWARD 10 TURN RIGHT 60°]
   c REPEAT 8
      [FORWARD 10 TURN RIGHT 45°]

4. a 25 cm   b 18 cm   c 4 cm

5. a 3.16 units   b 10 units^2

6. $p = 20$ cm, $q = 15$ cm

7. a 5.7   b 5   c 3.2   d 5.7
   e 6.7   f 3.2

8. 6.8 m

MyPractice 227

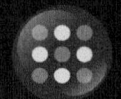

Case Study 4: Garden design

Related lessons		Resources	
Rounding	1b	Decimal places	(1001)
Area of a 2D shape	2c	Area of a parallelogram	(1108)
Circumference of a circle	2d	Area of a trapezium	(1128)
Area of a circle	2e	Circumference of a circle	(1088)
Compound measures	2f	Area of circles	(1083)
Interpreting the calculator display	7e	Scale drawing	(1117)
Maps and scale drawings	9d	Volume of cuboids	(1137)
Volume of a prism	14e	Books and catalogues with information about plants	

Simplification	Extension
Encourage students to focus on a single task. Task 4, only requires areas to be calculated; suggest finding the total area of the garden then the areas of shapes A, B, D and then C. Ensure students are reading the correct dimensions from the plan. Working in pairs may help them to clarify their ideas.	Students could design their own sensory garden, working out quantities of materials needed for any hard landscaping included. They could research plants to use to give different sensory experiences throughout the year and maybe work out an approximate cost for the whole project, finding the cost of building materials and plants from catalogues and the internet.

Links

There are a number of websites that discuss the design of sensory gardens; see, for example
http://www.schoolplaygrounddesigners.co.uk/Sensory-Gardens.html

The UK requirements for disabled access are contained in: The Building Regulations 2010, Part M, Access to and use of buildings. Section 1 covers ramped access, p.21, with the constraints on gradients in 1.26
http://www.planningportal.gov.uk/uploads/br/BR_PDF_ADM_2004.pdf

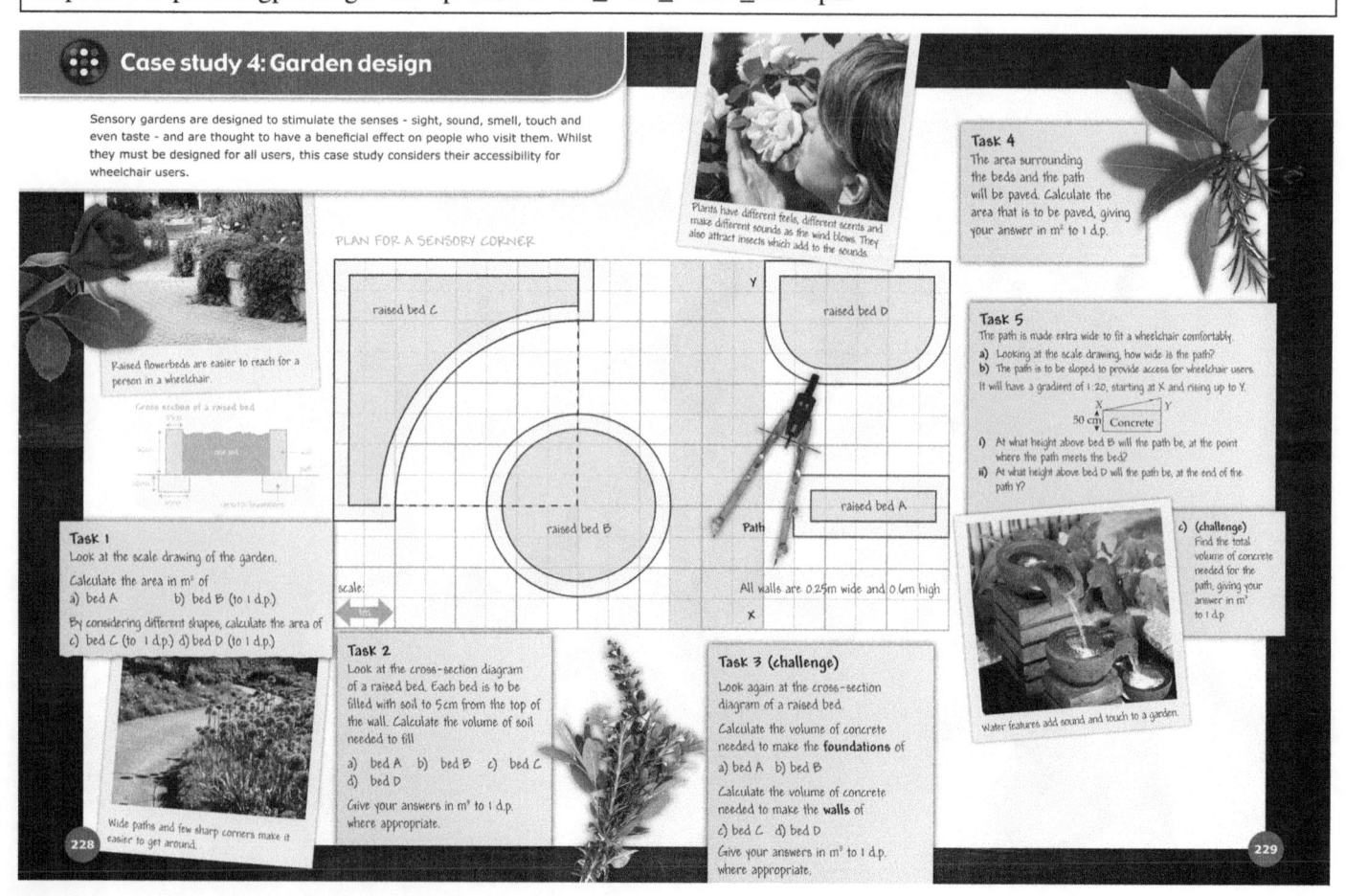

Case study 4: Garden design

Sensory gardens are designed to stimulate the senses - sight, sound, smell, touch and even taste - and are thought to have a beneficial effect on people who visit them. Whilst they must be designed for all users, this case study considers their accessibility for wheelchair users.

Plants have different feels, different scents and make different sounds as the wind blows. They also attract insects which add to the sounds.

PLAN FOR A SENSORY CORNER

raised bed C
raised bed D
raised bed B
raised bed A
Path
Y
X
scale:
1 m
All walls are 0.25m wide and 0.6m high

Raised flowerbeds are easier to reach for a person in a wheelchair.

Cross section of a raised bed

Task 1
Look at the scale drawing of the garden.
Calculate the area in m² of
a) bed A   b) bed B (to 1 d.p.)
By considering different shapes, calculate the area of
c) bed C (to 1 d.p.)   d) bed D (to 1 d.p.)

Wide paths and few sharp corners make it easier to get around.

Task 2
Look at the cross-section diagram of a raised bed. Each bed is to be filled with soil to 5cm from the top of the wall. Calculate the volume of soil needed to fill
a) bed A   b) bed B   c) bed C
d) bed D
Give your answers in m³ to 1 d.p. where appropriate.

Task 3 (challenge)
Look again at the cross-section diagram of a raised bed.
Calculate the volume of concrete needed to make the **foundations** of
a) bed A   b) bed B
Calculate the volume of concrete needed to make the **walls** of
c) bed C   d) bed D
Give your answers in m³ to 1 d.p. where appropriate.

Task 4
The area surrounding the beds and the path will be paved. Calculate the area that is to be paved, giving your answer in m² to 1 d.p.

Task 5
The path is made extra wide to fit a wheelchair comfortably.
a) Looking at the scale drawing, how wide is the path?
b) The path is to be sloped to provide access for wheelchair users. It will have a gradient of 1:20, starting at X and rising up to Y.

50 cm | Concrete

i) At what height above bed B will the path be, at the point where the path meets the bed?
ii) At what height above bed D will the path be, at the end of the path Y?

c) (challenge)
Find the total volume of concrete needed for the path, giving your answer in m³ to 1 d.p.

Water features add sound and touch to a garden.

Case Study

Teaching notes

Look at the case study and discuss the purpose of a sensory area in a public garden. Talk about some of the features that such an area could have, using the information around the outside of the plan. Then look at the plan itself, noting that it is drawn to scale. Ask a few questions about the sizes of the flowerbeds to check that the students are using the scale correctly.

Tasks 1, 2 and 3

Look at the information about the dimensions of the raised flowerbeds. Ask, how deep is the soil in the flowerbeds? How would you work out the volume of soil needed for flowerbed A?

Hear ideas and establish that the soil is 55 cm deep and that, to find the volume needed, you would first need to find the dimensions of the inner shaded part of the flowerbed and then work out the volume from those and the depth. As it is a cuboid (assuming level soil), multiplying the dimensions will give the volume needed. Then look at flowerbed B and ask, how would you work out the volume of soil needed for this flowerbed? Discuss how, if you can find the surface area of the soil, multiplying that by the depth of soil will give you the volume needed.

Then discuss how you could find the surface areas for the other two flowerbeds which are more complex shapes. Talk about methods such as splitting the shape into smaller parts, which might be a good way of tackling flowerbed D, and the idea of finding the area of a shape and taking away the bits that aren't there, which might be a better method for flowerbed C where the soil area could be found by removing a quarter of a circle from a square. Give the students time to tackle the questions about the volume of soil.

Ask, how will you find the volume of concrete needed for the foundations? Discuss how they will need to determine the dimensions of the foundations from the dimensions of the walls, noting that the foundations extend by equal amounts either side of the wall. Also discuss how, to get the surface area of the foundations. For flowerbed A you could break the shape into four rectangles and find the areas of those, but for flowerbed B that will not be possible. Ask, how could you find the surface area of the foundations for flowerbed B? Discuss ideas and establish that you can find the area of the outer and inner circles (foundations, not walls) and then subtract the inner from the outer. Mention that this might also be a quicker way of find the surface area of the foundations for flowerbed A. Give students time to tackle these questions.

Task 4

Discuss how the work that students have already tackled might contain useful information that will help them with this and give them some time to work out the area. When they have, discuss the methods they used, which are likely to include finding the overall area and taking away the parts that do not need to be paved.

Task 5

Look at the information about gradients of paths. Ask, What is meant by a gradient of 1 : 20? Establish that it means that there is a vertical rise of 1 unit for every 20 units of horizontal distance.

If the ground that the slope is built on is flat, what shape will the slope be and how will you find the volume of concrete needed for it? Hear the students' thoughts and discuss how to find the volume of a triangular prism. Give the students time to answer all the questions relating to the slope and then discuss their solutions.

Answers

1. A 1 m^2 B 4.5 m^2
   C 5.8 m^2 D 3.5 m^2
2. A 0.55 m^3 B 2.5 m^3
   C 3.2 m^3 D 1.9 m^3
3. a 0.5 m^3 b 0.8 m^3
   c 4.5 m^3 d 1.3 m^3
4. 29.0 m^2
5. a 1.5 m
   b i 0 ii 20 cm
   c 5.9 m^3

Garden design

MyAssessment 3

These questions will test you on your knowledge of the topics in chapters 9 to 12.
They give you practice in the questions that you may see in your GCSE exams.
There are 100 marks in total.

1. a Copy this diagram on square grid paper. (2 marks)
   b Reflect the shape about the y-axis as a mirror line. (2 marks)
   c Translate this reflection four squares down. (1 mark)
   d Rotate this translated shape 180° anticlockwise about the point X. (3 marks)
   e What is the name of the quadrilateral formed at the centre of the pattern? (1 mark)

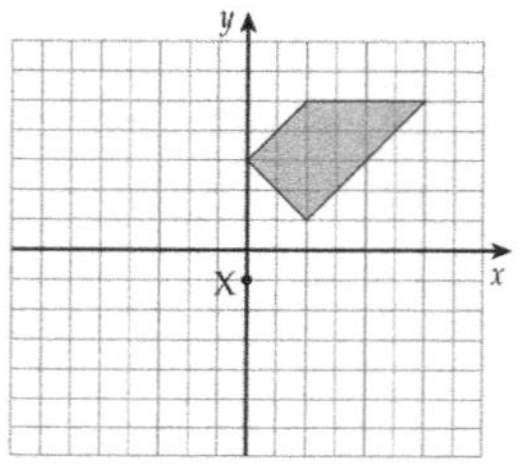

2. a Draw the triangle ABC on a coordinate grid. (2 marks)
   b Enlarge the triangle by scale factor 2 using (0, 0) as the centre of enlargement. (3 marks)
   c What are the coordinates of the vertices of the enlarged triangle? (2 marks)
   d What do you notice about the coordinates of the object and the image? (1 mark)

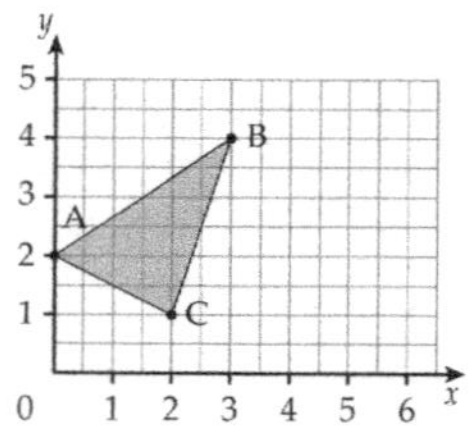

3. The city of Leeds is 58km away from Manchester on a bearing of 050°.
   The city of Sheffield is 52km away from Manchester on a bearing of 103°.
   a Draw a scale drawing showing these three cities (use 1cm = 10km). (3 marks)
   b What is the distance between Leeds and Sheffield? (1 mark)
   c What is the bearing of Sheffield from Leeds? (2 marks)

4. Solve these equations. Some answers are negative.
   a $5x - 7 = 13$ (1 mark)
   b $\frac{4x}{3} - 2 = 2$ (2 marks)
   c $3(5x - 22) = 24$ (2 marks)
   d $6(2x + 13) = 54$ (2 marks)
   e $4(2x + 2) = 2(5x + 7)$ (3 marks)
   f $\frac{5x-4}{3} = \frac{10+4x}{9}$ (3 marks)

5. Find the value of x in each diagram.
   a   b Perimeter = 23 (4 marks)

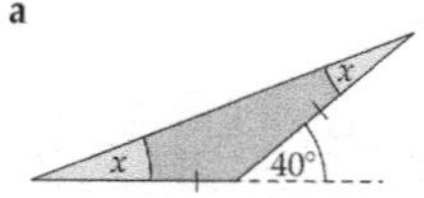

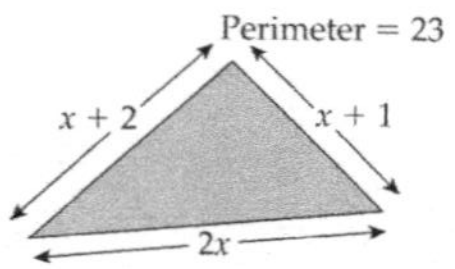

6. A rectangular playing field has an area of 3000m². It is 20m longer than it is wide.
   If its width is w, solve the equation $w(w + 20) = 3000$ to find the length and width of the field to 1dp. Initially try $w = 40$. (4 marks)

7. Solve these equations giving your answer correct to 2dp.
   a $x^3 + 3x = 200$ (4 marks)
   b $2x + \sqrt{x} = 24$ (4 marks)

8. a The velocity of an object is related to its energy by $v = \sqrt{\frac{2E}{m}}$.
     Calculate v when $E = 2000$ and $m = 12$ to 2dp. (2 marks)
   b The time period for a simple pendulum is $T = 2\pi\sqrt{\frac{L}{g}}$.
     Calculate the time period when $L = 0.6$ and $g = 10$. (2 marks)
   c The volume of a sphere is $V = \frac{4}{3}\pi r^3$.
     Rearrange the equation to find the value of r when $V = 125$. (4 marks)

9. Simplify these expressions
   a $\frac{4(m^3)^2 \times 6m^4}{8m^5}$ (3 marks)
   b $(10^8 \times 10^2)^2$ (2 marks)

10. Give these numbers in standard index form.
    a 0.034×10^4 (1 mark)
    b 300 million km per second (2 marks)
    c $6.3 \times 10^5 - 2.7 \times 10^4$ (2 marks)
    d 2980000000000000 (2 marks)
    e $7.2 \times 10^{-8} - 5.8 \times 10^{-7}$ (2 marks)
    f 0.00000000000000035 (2 marks)

11. Write these numbers in their simplest form.
    a $\sqrt{72}$ (2 marks)
    b $3\sqrt{2} \times 2\sqrt{8}$ (2 marks)

12. a Construct a triangle PQR with side lengths PR = 5cm, PQ = 7cm and RQ = 8cm using a ruler and compasses as accurately as possible. (4 marks)
    b Measure the angle PQR with a protractor. (1 mark)

13. Two mobile phone masts A and B are 20km apart. Mast A has a radius of 15km and mast B has a radius of 9km.
    a Draw the locus of points covered by these two masts. (3 marks)
    b Label the points where the two circles meet as C and D and draw lines AC, BC, AD and BD. (2 marks)
    c What is the name given to the quadrilateral ACBD? (1 mark)
    d Shade in the locus of points that is covered by both masts. (1 mark)

14. PQRS is a right-angled trapezium with PQ = 5.5cm, SR = 10.5cm and PS = 7.5cm. Angles at Q and R are right angles.
    a Draw the right-angled trapezium. (2 marks)
    b Work out the length of QR. (3 marks)
    c Work out the length of PR. (3 marks)

Mark scheme

Question 1 – 9 marks

a 2 Correct shape copied onto square grid paper; -1 mark for error

b 2 Coordinates: (0, 3), (-2, 5), (-6, 5), (-2, 1)

c 1 Coordinates: (0, -1), (-2, 1), (-6, 1), (-2, -3)

d 3 Coordinates: (0, -1), (2, -3), (6, -3), (2, 1)

e 1 Square

Question 2 – 8 marks

a 2 Correct triangle copied; -1 mark for error

b 3 correct enlargement from (0, 0); correct scale factor used; labeled A'B'C';

c 2 A(4, 0) B(6, 8) C(4, 2)

d 1 Coordinate values are doubled; accept × 2

Question 3 – 6 marks

a 3 Correct drawing of lengths and angles; correct scale used

b 1 49 km ± 2 km   **c** 2 bearing 173° ± 2°

Question 4 – 13 marks

a 1 $x = 4$ **b** 2 $x = 3$

c 2 $x = 6$ **d** 2 $x = -2$

e 3 $x = -3$ **f** 3 $x = 2$

Question 5 – 4 marks

a 2 $x = 20°$; 1 mark if $2x = 40$ seen; 1 mark if $2x + 140 = 180$ seen;

b 2 $x = 5$; 1 mark if $4x + 3$ seen; 1 mark if $4x = 20$ seen;

Question 6 – 4 marks

4 Width 45.7m, length 65.7m; correct trial and improvement method shown (2 marks); correct rounding

Question 7 – 8 marks

a 4 5.68; correct trial and improvement method;

b 4 10.39; correct trial and improvement method;

Question 8 – 8 marks

a 2 18.26; correct substitution; correct rounding

b 2 1.54; correct substitution; correct rounding

c 4 3.10; 2 marks correct formula used; correct substitution; correct rounding

Question 9 – 5 marks

a 3 $3m^5$; 1 mark for $4m^6$; 1 mark for $24m^{10}$

b 2 10^{20}; 1 mark for 10^{10};

Question 10 – 11 marks

a 1 3.4×10^2 **b** 2 3×10^8

c 2 6.03×10^5 **d** 2 2.98×10^{16}

e 2 -5.08×10^{-7} **f** 2 3.5×10^{-14}

Question 11 – 4 marks

a 2 $6\sqrt{2}$ **b** 2 24

Question 12 – 5 marks

a 4 Correct triangle constructed; lengths and angles correct; construction lines visible

b 1 38.2° ± 1°

Question 13 – 7 marks

a 3 Correct circles drawn; correct radii; correct distance apart

b 2 Correct labeling and lines drawn

c 1 Kite

d 1 Correct shading/cross hatched area

Question 14 – 8 marks

a 2 Correct trapezium drawn; lengths and angles correct

b 3 5.6cm; accept 5.59cm; $7.5^2 - 5^2$ seen for 1 mark

c 3 7.9cm; accept 7.85cm; $5.5^2 + 5^2$ seen for 1 mark

13 Sequences

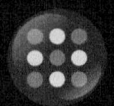

Learning outcomes

A14 Generate terms of a sequence from either a term-to-term or a position-to-term rule (L5/6)
A15 Recognise arithmetic sequences and find the *n*th term (L6)
A16 Recognise geometric sequences and appreciate other sequences that arise (L7)

Introduction

The chapter starts by looking at term-to-term rules for number sequences and then position-to-term rules. Finding the general, or *n*th term rule of a sequence is covered in the third section before sequences which occur in real –life are examined. The final section looks at recursive sequences of the form $T(n + 1) = f(T(n))$.

The introduction discusses the famous puzzle of rice on a chessboard. The pattern looks simple enough to continue since on the first square is one grain, the second square two grains, the third square four grains, etc. The pattern is obviously doubling each time so the sequence will continue:

1, 2, 4, 8, 16, 32, 64, 128,…

The formula for the number of grains on each square is two to the power of one less than the number of the square (or 2^{n-1}) so on the 64th square there will be 2^{63} grains of rice.

Abstracting from the practicalities of this, or the value of the rice, we can still look at the magnitude of such a number: 2^{63} is a number in excess of 9 quintillion (9 followed by 18 zeros!)

It is fair to say that the king has probably made a mistake agreeing to this prize!

Prior knowledge

Students should already know how to…
- Substitute numbers into formulae
- Recognise simple patterns in sequences of numbers

Starter problem

The starter problem considers how a specific sequence in context grows. The girl is asking for just 50 pence in the first week but then 20 pence more each week thereafter. At first it seems like she is taking a significant cut in pocket money but if you watch the sequence grow, you can see how long it takes her to get more than the original £3:

50p, 70p, 90p, £1.10, £1.30, £1.50, £1.70, £1.90, £2.10, £2.30, £2.50, £2.70, £2.90, £3.10

After 14 weeks, she gets more than the original, but remember that this will keep growing by 20 pence per week thereafter.

The father is clearly getting a good deal at the start, but it will not take him long after this period of time to be 'out of pocket'. Questions could be posed to the students such as:

How much does the girl lose out on in the first 13 weeks?

How long will it take her after her pocket money exceeds £3 to get this back?

How much pocket money would she get in one year?

How much *more* pocket money would she get in one year?

Resources

MyMaths
*n*th term   1165

Online assessment   **InvisiPen solutions**

Chapter test	3B–13	Next terms in a sequence	281	Term-to-term rules	282
Formative test	3B–13	Position-to-term rules	283	Sequences in context	285
Summative test	3B–13	*n*th term	286		

Topic scheme

Teaching time = 5 lessons/2 weeks

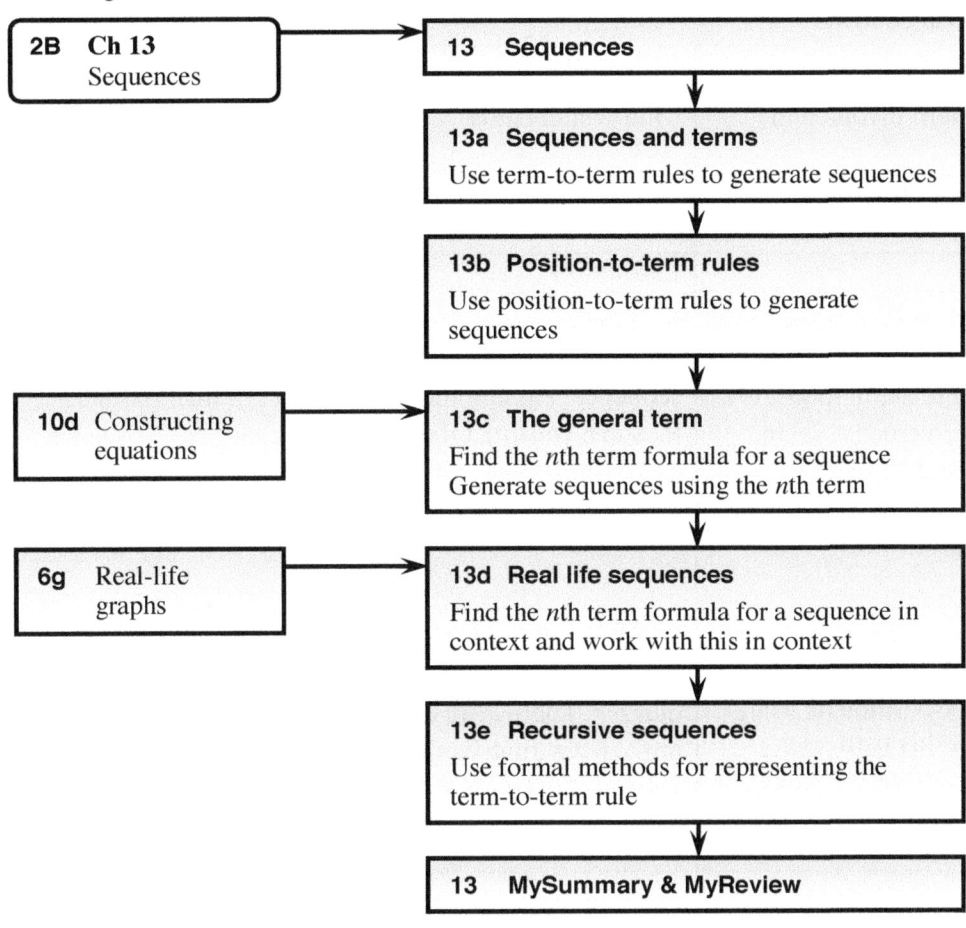

- **2B Ch 13** Sequences → **13 Sequences**
  - **13a Sequences and terms** — Use term-to-term rules to generate sequences
  - **13b Position-to-term rules** — Use position-to-term rules to generate sequences
  - **10d Constructing equations** → **13c The general term** — Find the nth term formula for a sequence; Generate sequences using the nth term
  - **6g Real-life graphs** → **13d Real life sequences** — Find the nth term formula for a sequence in context and work with this in context
  - **13e Recursive sequences** — Use formal methods for representing the term-to-term rule
  - **13 MySummary & MyReview**

Differentiation

Student book 3A   236 – 249
Term-to-term rules and position-to-term rules for generating sequences
Finding the general term of a sequence
Recursive sequences

Student book 3B   232 – 247
Term-to-term rules and position-to-term rules for generating sequences
Finding the general term of a sequence
Understanding sequences in context
Recursive sequences

Student book 3C   228 – 241
Position-to-term rules for generating sequences
Patterns and sequences
Quadratic sequences
General behaviour of a sequence

Introduction

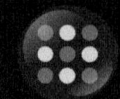

13a Sequences and terms

Objectives		
• Generate terms of a sequence using term-to-term rules, on paper and using ICT		(L6)
• Generate sequences from practical contexts		(L6)

Key ideas	Resources
1 Recognition of the repeated pattern involved in sequences 2 Describing and using the term-to-term rule or pattern.	Mini whiteboards

Simplification	Extension
Use physical objects to build up the sequence as a class demonstration, asking students at each stage how many have been added and how many there are in total. As a development, build up the sequence verbally, saying (for example) 'I'm starting with 5 and I add 3'. Students write the next term on their mini whiteboards and show it, thereby providing an assessment opportunity for the teacher.	Students, working in pairs, can each use a spreadsheet and enter formulae (as in question **6**) for the terms of a sequence. Passing their spreadsheet to their partner, they can construct the terms of each other's sequence and, with access to a computer, check that it works.

Literacy	Links
Revise sequence terminology, met in previous work. Be prepared to include the notion of position as well, though it may not be a key focus of this particular lesson. Encourage clarity in verbal descriptions and wherever appropriate, encourage algebraic/general representation of these descriptions.	Sequences are often found in puzzle books and online quizzes. There is an example of a sequence quiz at http://www.funtrivia.com/quizzes/general/thematic_fun/sequences.html

Alternative approach
Show a sample of about three or four different sequences and ask pupils to work in pairs identifying any key vocabulary, including 'sequence'. Share and clarify as required. Extend requesting next terms in each sequence, with explanations. Student pairs or individuals can be requested to come up with term-to-term rules of about four sequences, for swapping in order to generate these sequences. Use a group of different sequences which share the same term-to-term rule, with about two further, different sequences, and request that student pairs sort them into two or more groups, or find the 'odd ones out'. This can be set up as a card sort activity.

Checkpoint
Find the next three terms in these sequences:

a 4, 7, 10, 13, ... (16, 19, 22)

b 17, 11, 5, -1 , ... (-7, -13, -19)

c 1, 3, 7, 13, ... (21, 31, 43)

Starter – What comes next?

Give students two starting numbers, for example, 2 and -4. Ask students what comes next and why, for example,

2, -4, -10, -16, ...   (subtract 6)

2, -4, 8, -16, ... (multiply previous term by -2)

2, -4, -2, -6, ... (add previous two terms together)

Teaching notes

To make sure that students recall the terminology required for this unit, ask the students to write down definitions of 'term,' 'rule' and 'sequence'. Discuss what 'term-to-term rule' means and ask how else sequences are sometimes defined (position-to-term rule).

Review the use of function machines to define relationships. Here, students will meet the use of a function machine iteratively. The starting term is the input, and the function machine generates the second term as the output but this is then used as the input to the function machine to find the third term, *etc*. Showing this iterative process diagrammatically with the output looping back as the next input may help students to grasp the process.

Identifying a term-to-term rule from a sequence requires some imagination and perseverance. Students need to realise that there may be more than one rule which will give the same start to a sequence, so checking it works for all given terms is important.

Plenary

Ask students to work in pairs, one writing a rule and using it to generate the start of a sequence. The other student tries to use the generated terms to find the rule.

Exercise commentary

Question 1 – Students see a sequence derived from a geometric pattern. The related numeric pattern is then extended. The term-to-term rule can be explained both geometrically and numerically.

Question 2 – The sequence derives from a function machine rather than a geometric pattern. The term-to-term rule is defined by the function machine.

Question 3 – The sequence is now derived from a written rule (rather than geometric pattern or function machine).

Question 4 – A further way of deriving a sequence using a flow diagram.

Question 5 – Students should be encouraged to look at the differences between consecutive terms and to try a simple one-step strategy first using addition or subtraction. If this fails, then they should try a two-step strategy of multiplying/dividing and adding/subtracting.

Question 6 – Students need only a little ICT skill to set up these formulae. If they know how to copy a formula, then they can find many more terms very quickly.

Answers

1   **a**   Check students' drawings
    b   8, 11, 14, 17
    c   Start with 8 and add 3 each time   **d**   20, 23, 26

2   **a**   11, 19, 35, 67, 131   **b**   8, 10, 14, 22, 38

3   **a**   4, 6, 10, 18, 34   **b**   600, 280, 120, 40, 0
    c   0, 1, 4, 13, 40   **d**   0, 3, 12, 39, 120
    e   ¼, 1½, 4, 9, 19   **f**   4, 4, 4, 4, 4, 4

4   **a**   2, 6, 8, 9, 9½   **b**   50, 30, 20, 15, 12½
    c   -30, -10, 0, 5, 7½

5   **a**   Start with 7 and add 3 each time; 19, 22, 25
    b   Start with 20 and subtract 3 each time; 8, 5, 2
    c   Start with 3 and double and add 1 each time; 63, 127, 255
    d   Start with 3, double and subtract 1 each time; 33, 65, 129
    e   Start with 1, treble and add 1 each time; 121, 364, 1093
    f   Start with 1, treble and subtract 1 each time; 41, 122, 365
    g   Start with 200 and halve each time; $12\frac{1}{2}, 6\frac{1}{4}, 3\frac{1}{8}$
    h   Start with $\frac{1}{2}$ and double and add 2; 38, 78, 158
    i   Start with 3 and subtract 1 then double; 18, 34, 66

6   Students' sequences

13b Position-to-term rules

Objectives
• Generate terms of a sequence using term-to-term and position-to-term rules, on paper and using ICT   (L6)

Key ideas	Resources
1 Recognising and interpreting patterns in sequences 2 Finding and using 'function machines' for the *n*th term	Mini whiteboards Graphic calculators or online version (iteration)

Simplification	Extension
Initially, use position-to-term rules which are only a single multiplication (for example, 4, 8, 12, 16, …), so that students can see that a simple multiplication can predict, say, the hundredth term. Then, add 1 to the sequence (for example, 5, 9, 11, 17, …) so that students are introduced to a rule with a two-stage relationship. Recording the outcomes in tabular form builds up their understanding of the table.	Simple non-linear sequences are a natural development. Use position-to-term rules involving squares, such as $T(n) = n^2 + 1$. Avoid more complicated quadratic rules such as $T(n) = n^2 + 2n - 3$ as these are more appropriate for abler students and require different techniques.

Literacy	Links
Continue to refresh correct use of sequence vocabulary. Encourage students to use the correct terms in any responses and verbal descriptions. In recording position and term, use both vertical tables as well as horizontal versions.	Fibonacci numbers can be found in the structure of a piano keyboard. There are eight notes in an octave. In the scale between middle C and the next C there are eight white keys and five black keys, thirteen keys in all. The black keys are arranged in groups of two and three. There is more information about Fibonacci and music at http://goldennumber.net/music.htm

Alternative approach
Use the examples selected for the 'card sort' activity in the previous section for a closer analysis using both function machine versions of term-to-term rules and versions for position-to-term rules. The nature of term to term rules can be illustrated by the use of ANS button on any graphical calculator, and can then be compared with the use of position to term rules in terms of the advantages and limitations of each. The similarities and differences between the sequences chosen can be used to illustrate and strengthen these concepts. Students may be sufficiently confident to generalise these terms during this session, allowing further consolidation and possible extension in the next session.

Checkpoint
Find the position-to-term rules for these sequences: a 6, 9, 12, 15,…   (Multiply the position by 3 and add 3) b 3, 5, 7, 9,…   (Multiply the position by 2 and add 1) c 7, 4, 1, -2,…   (Multiply the position by -3 and add 10)

Starter – Expressions

Write expressions, for example $3n + 5, 6n - 1, 13 - 4n$, on the board and ask students for values for each expression when $n = 1, n = 2, n = 3$.

($3n + 5$ gives values of 8, 11, 14; $6n - 1$ gives values of 5, 11, 17; $13 - 4n$ gives values of 9, 5, 1)

Can be differentiated by choice of expressions and number of terms requested.

Teaching notes

The key process in finding the position-to-term rule for a linear sequence is identifying the common difference between terms and constructing the beginning of the times table for that number to compare with the sequence. Students need to be able to work confidently and accurately on these basic arithmetical operations, so consider whether the students need a short review before starting this lesson.

The worked examples show the process that students can use to provide a clear pathway to finding the position-to-term rule for a linear sequence. The use of the table to organise thinking is especially important.

Plenary

Ask students to work in pairs, one writing a position-to-term rule and using it to generate the start of a sequence. The other student then tries to use the generated terms to find the rule.

Exercise commentary

Question 1 – As in exercise **13a**, the sequence derives from a geometric pattern. In part **e**, students need to realise that the term-to-term rule is very inefficient and slow in finding the fiftieth position and hence the need for a different rule.

Question 2 – This question reinforces the methods of question **1**. Students may need explicit help to realise that the difference of consecutive terms tells them which 'times table' they must use.

Question 3 – This question provides more practice.

Question 4 – Students should use the term-to-term rule to find the missing numbers and the position-to-term rule to find the fiftieth terms.

Question 5 – Students should realise that not all sequences respond successfully to the above treatment. This historical sequence (and its discoverer) can be explored on the Internet.

Answers

1   a   3
      b   Check students' drawings
      c   Start with 4 and add 3 each time
      d

Position	1	2	3	4	5
3× table	3	6	9	12	15
Term	4	7	10	13	16

         Multiply the position by 3 and add 1
      e   151

2   a   i   Check students' drawings
         ii

Position	1	2	3	4
4× table	4	8	12	16
Term	7	11	15	19

         iii   Multiply position by 4 and add 3
         iv   403
      b   i   Check students' drawings
         ii

Position	1	2	3	4
2 × table	2	4	6	8
Term	6	8	10	12

         iii   Multiply position by 2 and add 4
         iv   204

3   see master Answers file

4   a   17, 35; 299   b   5, 9½; 77

5   a   13, 21, 34   b   Students' answers

13c The general term

Objectives
- Write and justify an expression to describe the nth term of an arithmetic sequence (L6)

Key ideas
1. Finding and using expressions for the nth term
2. Confidently using algebra in order to express properties of a sequence.

Resources
- nth Term (1165)
- Equilateral triangles, squares, pentagons, hexagons and octagons
- Copies of table in question **1**
- Mini whiteboards

Simplification
As in the previous exercise, introduce the general term for position-to-term rules requiring only a single multiplication. Students will find it straightforward to generalise the nth term, for example, for the sequence 4, 8, 12, 16, ... The progression would then be to 5, 9, 13, 17, ... where an extra 1 is also added to the nth term.

Extension
Working in pairs, students can write down a general term T(n) and ask their partner to decide if the sequence will be linear or not and to explain their choice by generating and discussing the first six terms of the sequence.

Literacy
Continue to refresh correct use of sequence vocabulary. Encourage students to use the correct terms in any responses and verbal descriptions.

In recording position and term, use both vertical tables as well as horizontal versions.

The notation for nth term, T(n), will need to be included and used fully.

Links
Time-lapse photography uses a sequence of photographs taken from the same view point at regular intervals. The resulting images are edited together to form a video. There is an example of time-lapse photography of a plant growing at http://www.teachertube.com/view_video.php?viewkey=0920782586a9843ee078

Alternative approach
Follow and extend the comparative work on term-to term rules with position-to-term rules encouraging students to use algebra to simplify the recording of these rules, evolving expressions to writing a formula for the nth term of a sequence. Students should record their versions of expressions using mini whiteboards. Students will need to discuss those sequences that involve regular subtraction in order to increase confidence fully. Further consolidation work can involve students in writing their own sequences and asking another student to give an expression for its nth term and vice versa.

Checkpoint
Find the nth term of each of these sequences: 7, 12, 17, 22, 27,...   (T(n) = 5n + 2)

                                                 10, 4, -2, -8, -14,...   (T(n) = 16 – 6n)

Starter – Missing values

Write sequences on the board and ask students to fill in the gaps, for example,

107, 99,   , 83, 75,   ,   (91, 67, 59)
31, 28, 31, 30,   ,   ,   (31, 30, 31)
(number of days in months in non leap year)

Teaching notes

Review basic work in algebra of substituting values into linear expressions, using different variables. Students are likely to be familiar with the use of x and y but perhaps less so with other letters such as n.

The use of standard notation, such as n rather than $1n$ and the meaning of $2n$ (and not $n2$) etc. is an important tool in this spread and may need review.

Plenary

Students work in pairs, one writing an expression for the nth term and using it to generate the start of a sequence, which the other student tries to use to find the formula for the nth term.

Exercise commentary

Question 1 – This question follows the same approach as in the previous exercise but with one extra step. The numeric pattern of the table is generalised by adding the nth term. The arrows on the RHS of the table help in writing the nth term.

Question 2 – The question instructions set out the series of steps required. In step **iv**, the sixth term can be found using the term-to-term rule as well as the position-to-term rule.

Question 3 – This question is the reverse of questions 1 and 2. Students are given the general term and asked to find the sequence.

Question 4 – The missing terms and next terms can be found from either the term-to-term rule or the position-to-term rule. The hundredth term requires only the position-to-term rule.

Question 5 – This task reinforces the original links with geometric patterns. No intermediate steps are provided. The challenge is to know how to progress without structured support.

Answers

3	a	7, 9, 11, 13, 15, 17	b	1, 4, 7, 10, 13, 16
	c	5, 9, 13, 17, 21, 25	d	3, 13, 23, 33, 43, 53
	e	9, 15, 21, 27, 33, 39	f	-3, -1, 1, 3, 5, 7
	g	4, 6, 8, 10, 12, 14	h	0, 3, 6, 9, 12, 15
	i	4, 12, 20, 28, 36, 44	j	$2\frac{1}{2}, 3, 3\frac{1}{2}, 4, 4\frac{1}{2}, 5$
	k	28, 26, 24, 22, 20, 18	l	2, -2, -6, -10, -14, -18
4	a	$5n + 1$; 21; 31; 501	b	$10n + 2$; 32; 62; 1002
	c	$4n - 1$; 15; 23; 399	d	$8n - 3$; 29; 45; 797

All other questions, see master Answers file

The general term

13d Real-life sequences

Objectives	
• Generate sequences from practical contexts	(L6)

Key ideas	Resources
1 Find, identify and record sequences in different contexts 2 Express findings algebraically and test them	Matchsticks Mini whiteboards Number sequences in a variety of contexts (NRICH): http://nrich.maths.org/6029 Sequence Activites (TES): http://www.tes.co.uk/teaching-resource/Sequence-activities-and-investigations-6172166/

Simplification	Extension
Whatever the context in which the sequence is generated, much initial discussion is needed to explore why a sequence occurs. Students can then use their mini whiteboards to write and show the first few terms of the sequence. For a given sequence, they will find it easier to 'spot' a term-to-term rule than a position-to-term rule.	Working in pairs, students should each make notes on a context of their own creation where a sequence might occur.

Literacy	Links
Continue to encourage the correct use of sequence vocabulary. Check that students record any algebraic expressions and formula accurately, including defining any variables if necessary. Written reasoning or explanations should be encouraged and can be checked by partner students for sense.	There are many types of savings account. Regular savings accounts are designed for people who want to save a regular amount of money each month. Other types of account include notice accounts where cash can be withdrawn only after giving an agreed period of notice, instant access savings accounts where no notice is required and Individual Savings Accounts (ISAs) where interest earned is tax-free. There is more information about savings accounts at http://www.bankingandsavings.co.uk/bs1142954971.html

Alternative approach

A number of alternative investigational activities that result in sequences can be used in this section, and may also be used for some extended maths work. Sources of such activities may be found at NRICH or TES as referenced

Checkpoint

Water (in litres) flows from a barrel in such a way that the amount of water left after each hour is given by the sequence $T(n) = 700 - 4n$. How much water is left in the barrel after 2, 4, 6 and 8 hours? How long will it take the barrel to completely empty? (692, 684, 676 and 668 litres, 175 hours)

Starter – Sequences

Write the first term of a sequence, for example 5, on the board. Ask students for the next five terms if the rule is double the previous term and subtract three (7, 11, 19, 35, 67).

Ask students to find a first term that will lead to a decreasing sequence (a number less than three).

Teaching notes

A focus in this lesson is to illustrate the occurrence of linear sequences in real life. Use visual examples such as a farmer creating square sheep pens with lengths of fences (which can be illustrated using matches), generating the sequence

| 1 | 2 | 3 | ... | n | 3n + 1 |

Three edges are needed for each new square plus one edge to complete the first square.

Students can be encouraged to describe other contexts they think would produce a linear sequence.

There is an opportunity to encourage collaboration between students to develop confidence and to promote mathematical discussion about contexts where more complex non-linear sequences occur. Examples are the number of blocks required to build a triangular tower n blocks high (the triangular numbers, a quadratic sequence), or the chessboard problem – one grain of rice on the first square, two on the second, four on the third *etc.* – how many on the last (64th) square? (powers of 2), total number of grains of rice ($2^n - 1$ for sum up to n^{th} square).

Plenary

Ask students to work in pairs to produce other examples of linear sequences they can think of in real life. Feed back to the whole class one example from each pair, explaining the context and what they think the relationship would be (approximately).

Exercise commentary

This exercise provides more practice without introducing new methods.

Question 1 – The link with geometric patterns is explored once again.

Questions 2 and **3** – These questions require the student to understand the contexts in which sequences arise.

Questions 4 and **5** – These questions provide the general terms and ask students to generate sequences from T(n) (rather than asking students to find the general terms). Part **b** in both questions requires students to interpret the contextual situations.

Question 6 – Simple keyboard skills are sufficient to make the point that computers can generate sequences. A more powerful approach requires students to know how to copy a formula.

Answers

1   a   Start with 2 and add 4 each time
    b

position	1	2	3	4	5
4 × table	4	8	12	16	20
Tiles	2	6	10	14	18

      Multiply the position by 4 and subtract 2
    c $4n - 2$ d   78

2   a   100, 115, 130, 145, 160
    b   Start with 100 and add 15 each time
    c

Day	1	2	3	4	5
Number of miles	100	115	130	145	160

      Multiply the position by 15 and add 85
    d $15n + 85$ e   295 miles

3   a   10, 14, 18, 22, 26
    b   Start with 10 and add 4 each time
        Multiply the position by 4 and add 6
    c   i $4n + 6$ ii   246

4   a   50, 52, 54, 56, 58   b   2 ml

5   a   995, 990, 985, 980, 975, 970, 965
    b   895 l

6   8, 13, 18, 23, 28, ...
      Students' answers

Real-life sequences

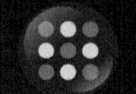

13e Recursive sequences

Objectives

- Understand that a linear sequence always has a constant difference between successive terms (L7)
- Geometric sequences have a common multiplier (L7)

Key ideas	Resources
1 Algebraic representations of term-to-term rules 2 Applying term-to-term rules in context	Calculators

Simplification	Extension
More examples of simple linear sequences can be given such as those in question **1**. Similarly, further examples of simple geometric sequences can be given such as that in question **2a**. Two-step recursive formulae could be omitted. Students may need guidance on how to write the recursive formulae for questions **3** and **4**, particularly when there are gaps in the sequences.	Students can investigate other types of recursive formulae such as the Fibonacci sequence (see **13b** question **5**). How can this sequence be written in recursive form? What about if we allow our recursive formulae to involve squaring or cubing? For example $T(n + 1) = [T(n)]^2$ with $T(1) = 2$ gives 2, 4, 16, 256,... What is we start with $T(1) = 1$? Or $T(1) = 0.5$?

Literacy	Links
Linear sequence Geometric sequence Recursion/recursive formula	Recursive sequences occur in many areas of real life whenever there is a clear progression of a sequence of numbers over time. The exercise illustrates three examples such as bank account interest, population growth and 'viral' hits on the Internet. Students could investigate other real-life sequences that exhibit patterns such as exponential growth and/or decay in biology or physics.

Alternative approach

Students could be provided with two sets of cards (or two jumbled lists), one set with recursive formulae on and one set with the terms of sequences on. They can then try to work out, in pairs or threes, how the two sets link together and match them. This will encourage discussion about the structure of the algebraic formulae and how they link to the generation of recursive sequences.

Checkpoint

Write the first five terms of this sequence: $T(n + 1) = 3T(n) + 1, T(1) = 1$ (1, 4, 13, 40, 121)

Describe this sequence using a recursive formula: 4, 9, 19, 39, 79,...   ($T(n + 1) = 2T(n) + 1, T(1) = 4$)

Starter – Number Jumble

These numbers belong to two different arithmetic sequences but have been jumbled up. Sort them into two sets and write down the two sequences:

1, 17, 4, 13, 7, 10, 8, 11, 5, 14, 16, 2

(1, 4, 7, 10, 13, 16 and 2, 5, 8, 11, 14, 17)

Teaching notes

Since the recursive formula is basically a formal algebraic way of writing the term-to-term rule, students could be asked to look back at **13a** where term-to-term sequences are introduced first of all. Can they think of a way of writing the 'wordy' rule using symbols? Describe the structure of the algebraic statements and show, using a few simple examples, the way that a recursive formula works. Show the difference between a linear sequence and a geometric sequence. Students can then complete selected questions from the exercise and work through the practical problems in questions **5** to **7**. There is scope for students to 'invent' their own sequences and challenge a partner to find the recursive formula, or to generate terms with their own formula.

Plenary

Are the following sequences linear, geometric, or neither?

$T(n + 1) = T(n) + 4$, $T(1) = 7$ (arithmetic)

$T(n + 1) = 3T(n) - 1$, $T(1) = 1$ (neither)

$T(n + 1) = 4T(n)$, $T(1) = 4$ (geometric)

$T(n + 1) = -T(n)$, $T(1) = 5$ (geometric)

$T(n + 1) = T(n) - ½$, $T(1) = 7$ (arithmetic)

Exercise commentary

Question 1 – Basic practice at writing out the terms of a linear sequence using a recursive formula.

Question 2 – The first question is geometric while the rest of them are neither geometric nor arithmetic. Students will need to check their arithmetic, particularly with negative operations.

Questions 3 and **4** – Writing the recursive formulae correctly may be a challenge for some students so check their notation early on. Where there are gaps in the sequences in question **4**, encourage them to fill these in before proceeding to write the recursive formulae.

Questions 5 to **7** – Real life problems which illustrate that sequences may occur in many different contexts. Encourage students to write out the terms of the sequences and look for patterns.

Answers

1　a　2, 3, 4, 5, 6　　b　0, 2, 4, 6, 8
　　c　3, 7, 11, 13, 17　d　-1, -3, -5, -7, -9
　　e　1, ½, 0, -½, -1　f　0.5, -0.25, -1, -1.75, -2.5

2　a　2, 4, 8, 16, 32　　b　0, 1, 3, 7, 15
　　c　3, 5, 9, 17, 33　　d　1, 2, 5, 14, 41
　　e　1, 2, 0, 4, -4　　f　1, 1, 1, 1, 1

3　a　$T(n + 1) = T(n) + 2$　$T(1) = 2$
　　b　$T(n + 1) = T(n) + 4$　$T(1) = 3$
　　c　$T(n + 1) = T(n) + 6$　$T(1) = -2$
　　d　$T(n + 1) = T(n) - 3$　$T(1) = 4$
　　e　$T(n + 1) = T(n) - 4$　$T(1) = -5$
　　f　$T(n + 1) = T(n) + ¾$　$T(1) = ½$

4　a　$T(n + 1) = T(n) + 6$　$T(1) = 5$
　　b　$T(n + 1) = T(n) + 8$　$T(1) = 7$
　　c　$T(n + 1) = T(n) + 17$　$T(1) = 13$
　　d　$T(n + 1) = 3T(n)$　　$T(1) = 1$
　　e　$T(n + 1) = 4T(n)$　　$T(1) = 1$
　　f　$T(n + 1) = 2T(n)$　　$T(1) = 5$

5　a　$T(n + 1) = T(n) + 3$　$T(1) = 303$
　　c　303, 306.03, 309.09, 312.18, 315.30
　　d　Zadie

6　a　54　　　　b　30 714

7　Yes, after 9 months

Recursive sequences　243

13 Sequences – MySummary

Key outcomes	Quick check
Find the term-to-term rule for a sequence. **L5**	Find the term-to-term rules for these sequences **a** 1, 6, 11, 16,… (add 5) **b** 5, 3, 1, -1,… (subtract 2)
Find the position-to-term rule for a sequence, and write it as the nth term. **L6**	Find the position-to-term rules for these sequences **a** 4, 9, 14, 19,… ($T(n) = 5n - 1$) **b** 6, 4, 2, 0,… ($T(n) = -2n + 8$)
Use sequences to solve problems in practical situations. **L6**	Oil flows into a reservoir at a rate of 600 litres per hour. If there are 1000 litres of oil in the reservoir at the start, write down a rule for the number of litres after n hours. ($T(n) = 1000 + 600n$)
Generate sequences using a recursive formula. **L7**	Generate the first five terms of the following sequences **a** $T(n+1) = T(n) + 7$, $T(1) = 3$ (3, 10, 17, 24, 31) **b** $T(n+1) = 3T(n) + 1$, $T(1) = 2$ (2, 7, 22, 67, 202)

MyMaths extra support

Lesson/online homework	Description
Sequences 1173 L4	Creating simple sequences and discovering sequences in picture patterns.

MyReview

13 MySummary

Check out
You should now be able to ...

	Test it ➡ Questions
✓ Find the term-to-term rule for a sequence.	1
✓ Find the position-to-term rule for a sequence, and write it as the *n*th term.	2 – 5
✓ Use sequences to solve problems in practical situations.	6
✓ Generate sequences using a recursive formula.	7

Language	Meaning	Example
Sequence	A set of numbers that follow a rule.	4, 7, 10, 13, ... is a sequence.
Term	A number in a sequence.	10 is the third term of the sequence 4, 7, 10, 13, ...
Position	The place that a term has in a sequence.	10 is in the third position in the sequence 4, 7, 10, 13, ...
Term-to-term rule	A rule that explains how to get from one term to the next term.	In the sequence 4, 7, 10, 13, ... the rule is 'add 3 each time'.
Position-to-term rule	A rule that uses the position to work out the term.	In this sequence Position: 1, 2, 3, 4 Term: 4, 7, 10, 13 the position to term rule is 'Multiply the position by 3 and then add 1'.
*n*th term	A shorter way to write the position-to-term rule that uses the letter *n*.	The position-to-term rule 'multiply the position by 3 and then add 1' can be written $3n + 1$.

Algebra Sequences

13 MyReview

1. Write the term-to-term rule and the next two terms in each case.
   a 1, 2, 4, 8, ...
   b 80, 40, 20, 10, ...
   c 2, 5, 11, 23, ...

2. This sequences is made using short sticks.

   Position 1   2   3

   a Write the term-to-term rule in words.
   b How many sticks are needed to make position 4?
   c Copy and complete the table.

Position	1	2	3	4	5
...× table					
Term	4	7			

   d Use the table to find the position-to-term rule.
   e How many sticks are needed to make the 20th position?

3. Find the position-to-term rule for each of these sequences.
   a 5, 9, 13, 17, ...
   b 18, 25, 32, 39, ...
   c 3.5, 4, 4.5, 5, ...
   d 9, 8, 7, 6, ...

4. Generate the first 5 terms of the sequences with these position-to-term rules.
   a $T(n) = 6n - 2$
   b $T(n) = \frac{1}{2}n - 1$
   c $T(n) = 2(n + 3)$
   d $T(n) = 12 - 2n$

5. Find the *n*th term for each of these sequences.
   a 3, 5, 7, 9, ...   b 8, 18, 28, 38, ...
   c -5, 0, 5, 10, ...   d 10, 7, 4, 1, ...

6. The volume of diesel (in litres) left in a fuel tank at the end of each day is given by $T(n) = 78 - 5n$.
   a Write a sequence for the volume of diesel in the tank at the end of each day for a week.
   b How many litres of diesel will be left in the tank after two weeks?
   c Day one was a Monday. On which day of the third week will it run out of diesel completely?

7. Describe each sequence using a recursive formula.
   a 5, 8, 11, 14, 17, ...
   b 16, 11, 6, 1, -4, ...
   c 3, 6, 12, 24, 48, ...
   d 324, 108, 36, 12, 4, ...

What next?

Score	
0 – 3	Your knowledge of this topic is still developing. To improve look at Formative test: 3B-13; MyMaths: 1165
4, 5	You are gaining a secure knowledge of this topic. To improve look at InvisiPen: 281, 282, 283, 285, 286 and 293
6, 7	You have mastered this topic. Well done, you are ready to progress!

MyMaths.co.uk

Question commentary

Question 1 – Part **c** is most tricky. You could give students a hint by telling them to try doubling each number first.

Question 2 – The position-to-term rule could also be expressed algebraically as $3n + 1$

Question 3 – The position-to-term rules could also be expressed algebraically as **a** $4n + 1$, **b** $7n + 11$, **c** $0.5n + 3$, **d** $10 - n$.

Question 4 – Students must take care with the brackets in **c**. Failure to multiply the 3 by 2 would result in sequence 5, 7, 9, 11, 13.

Question 5 – Students could draw out tables of values as in question **2** if needed.

Question 6 – There is still 3 litres at the end of the 15th day which is a Monday so it will run out during the Tuesday.

Question 7 – Students need to examine the term-to-term rules for each sequence to deduce the recursive formula.

Answers

1. a Double (the previous term); 16, 32
   b Halve; 5, 2.5
   c Double then add 1; 47, 95

2. a Add 3   b 13
   d Multiply (the position) by 3 then add 1
   e 61

3. a Multiply (the position) by 4 then add 1
   b Multiply by 7 then add 11
   c Multiply by 0.5 then add 3
   d Subtract the position from 10

4. a 4, 10, 16, 22, 28   b -0.5, 0, 0.5, 1, 1.5
   c 8, 10, 12, 14, 16   d 10, 8, 6, 4, 2

5. a $2n + 1$ b $10n - 2$ c $5n - 10$ d $13 - 3n$

6. a 73, 68, 63, 58, 53, 48, 43
   b 8   c Tuesday

7. a $T(n + 1) = T(n) + 3$ $T(1) = 5$
   b $T(n + 1) = T(n) - 5$ $T(1) = 16$
   c $T(n + 1) = 2T(n)$ $T(1) = 3$
   d $T(n + 1) = T(n) \div 3$ $T(1) = 324$

13 MyPractice

1 You can use matches to make this sequence of patterns. 
   a Draw the next pattern of the sequence.
   b Write the first four terms of the sequence that gives the numbers of matches.
   c Find the term-to-term rule.
   d Write the next three consecutive terms of the sequence.

2 Use this flow diagram to generate the terms of a sequence.

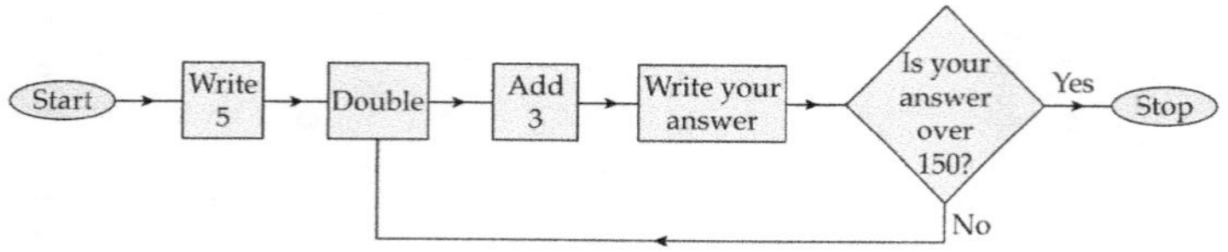

Start → Write 5 → Double → Add 3 → Write your answer → Is your answer over 150? — Yes → Stop / No → (loop back)

3 For each of these sequences, describe the term-to-term rule in words and find the next three consecutive terms.
   a 3, 7, 15, 31, ...
   b 4, 7, 13, 25, ...
   c 30, 27, 24, 21, ...
   d $\frac{1}{2}$, 2, 8, 32, ...
   e 400, 200, 100, 50, ...
   f 1, 11, 111, 1111, ...

4 This sequence of crosses is made using square tiles. 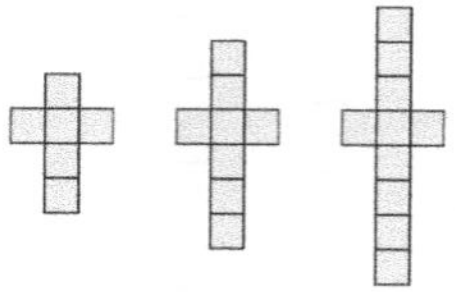
   a How many extra tiles are added to make the next term in the sequence?
   b Draw the diagram for position 4.
   c Copy and complete this table and use it to find the position-to-term rule.

Position	1	2	3	4	5	...	n
...× table							
Term							

   d How many tiles are needed to make the 20th position?

5 For each of these sequences,
   i use a table of values to find the position-to-term rule
   ii find the next two terms and the 50th term.
   a 4, 7, 10, 13, 16, ...
   b 6, 11, 16, 21, 26, ...
   c 2, 5, 8, 11, 14, ...
   d 98, 96, 94, 92, 90, ...

6 Find the missing terms and the 100th terms of each of these sequences.
   a 5, 8, 11, ☐, 17, 20
   b 1, 4, 7, 10, ☐, 16, ...

7 For each of these sequences,
   i construct a table of values
   ii write the position-to-term rule in words
   iii find the nth term
   iv find the value of the 6th term and the 100th term.
   a 5, 7, 9, 11, 13, ...
   b 13, 16, 19, 22, 25, ...
   c 2, 7, 12, 17, 22, ...
   d 1, 5, 9, 13, 17, ...

8 Generate the first six terms of the sequences with these general terms.
   a $T(n) = 2n + 10$
   b $T(n) = 5n - 5$
   c $T(n) = 4n + 6$
   d $T(n) = 50 - 2n$
   e $T(n) = 15 - 5n$
   f $T(n) = 2(3n - 2)$

9 Here is part of a spreadsheet.
   Column A gives the position of each term.
   Column B gives the actual terms of a sequence.

	A	B
1	Position	Term
2	1	=3*A2−1
3	=A2+1	=3*A3−1
4	=A3+1	=3*A4−1

   a Write the position-to-term rule in words.
   b Write the nth term.
   c Write the first six terms of the sequence.

10 A kitchen wall has three rows of tiles.
   The two end columns have tiles with floral patterns.
   There are n central columns of plain white tiles. 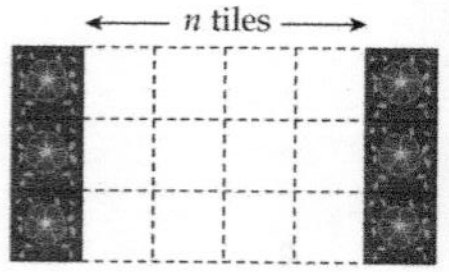
   a Find the total number of tiles used when $n = 3$.
   b Find an expression $T(n)$ for the total number of tiles.
   c Write the sequence of the values of $T(n)$ for $n = 40$ to $n = 45$.

11 David is saving for his summer holiday.
   He starts with £20 and then he saves £8 each week.
   a How much has he saved after
      i 2 weeks   **ii** 5 weeks?
   b Find an expression for $T(n)$, the amount, in pounds, he has saved after n weeks.
   c How much has he saved after 20 weeks?

12 Describe each sequence using a recursive formula.
   a 4, 7, 10, 13, 16, ...
   b 3, 0, −3, −6, −9, ...
   c 2, 8, 32, 128, 512, ...
   d 3, 9, 27, 81, 243, ...

Question commentary

Questions 1 to 3 – Students are presented with sequences in different forms. Being able to describe sequences in these different forms is important for understanding when they might arise in real-life situations.

Questions 4 to 6 – In all questions, students can tabulate the sequence to find the position-to-term rules.

Questions 7 to 9 – Students are first asked to work out the nth term formula and then use it to generate terms.

Questions 10 and 11 – Two real-life examples where nth term formulae are required.

Question 12 – (14e) Students should look for the term-to-term progression in each case.

Answers

1.   a Check students' drawings
    b 5, 9, 13, 17
    c Start with 5 and add 4 each time
    d 21, 25, 29

2.   5, 13, 29, 61, 125, 253

3.   a Start with 3, then double and add 1 each time; 63, 127, 255
    b Start with 4 then double and subtract 1 each time; 49, 97, 193
    c Start with 30, then subtract 3 each time; 18, 15, 12
    d Start with $\frac{1}{2}$, then multiply by 4 each time; 128, 512, 2048
    e Start with 400, halve each time; 25, $12\frac{1}{2}$, $6\frac{1}{4}$
    f Start with 1, then multiply by 10 and add 1 each time; 11111, 111111, 1111111

5.   a i Multiply the position by 3 and add 1
       ii 19, 22; 151
    b i Multiply the position by 5 and add 1
       ii 31, 36; 251
    c i Multiply the position by 3 and subtract 1
       ii 17, 20; 149
    d i Multiply the position by -2 and add 100
       ii 88, 86; 0

6.   a 14, 302   b 13, 298

8.   a 12, 14, 16, 18, 20, 22   b 0, 5, 10, 15, 20, 25
    c 10, 14, 18, 22, 26, 30   d 48, 46, 44, 42, 40, 38
    e 10, 5, 0, -5, -10, -15   f 2, 8, 14, 20, 26, 32

9.   a Multiply the position by 3 and subtract 1 each time.
    b $3n - 1$ c 2, 5, 8, 11, 14, 17

10. a 15   b $3n + 6$
    c 126, 129, 132, 135, 138, 141

11. a i £36   ii £60   b $8n + 20$ c £180

12. a $T(n + 1) = T(n) + 3$ $T(1) = 4$
    b $T(n + 1) = T(n) - 3$ $T(1) = 3$
    c $T(n + 1) = 4T(n)$ $T(1) = 2$
    d $T(n + 1) = 3T(n)$ $T(1) = 3$

For all other questions, see master Answers file

MyPractice

14 3D shapes

Learning outcomes

G1 Derive and apply formulae to calculate and solve problems involving: perimeter and area of triangles, parallelograms, trapezia, volume of cuboids (including cubes) and other prisms (including cylinders) (L7)

G15 Use the properties of faces, surfaces, edges and vertices of cubes, cuboids, prisms, cylinders, pyramids, cones and spheres to solve problems in 3-D (L6)

Introduction

The chapter starts by reviewing a range of facts about 3D shapes such as naming, describing and drawing them. Plans and elevations are covered in the second section while planes of symmetry and nets are covered in the third. The chapter finishes with work on the surface area and volume of a prism.

The introduction discusses the relative masses and surface areas of meerkats and humans in relation to how much they eat. Since the meerkat has the larger surface area relative to body mass, the more heat is lost through the skin and the more the meerkat must eat to replace this, relative to its mass.

It is interesting to consider other mammals and birds in this context. Mice, for example, weight between 20 and 35 grams and eat on average 4 to 5 grams of food per day. This is means that they would eat their own body weight in food in 5 to 7 days, very similar to the meerkat.

Birds typically eat between one half and one quarter of their body weight per day while bats eat the equivalent amount of insects in a single night as a person eating 20 pizzas!

Prior knowledge

Students should already know how to…
- Identify and name simple 2D and 3D shapes
- Calculate the surface and area and volume of cuboids
- Calculate the area of simple 2D shapes

Starter problem

The starter problem is a cube animal. The students are asked to work out the surface area and volume of the animal before considering the same facts about an enlarged version. Cubes could be used to physically build the animal to enable easier counting, but otherwise the students should be able to 'see' that the volume is 16 cubes and the surface area is 64 squares.

If the shape is enlarged by scale factor two, each original cube is now made up of eight cubes and each original square is now made up of four squares.

Hence the volume of the enlarged animal is 128 cubes and the surface area is 256 squares.

Students could be asked to consider alternative scale factors of enlargement such as three or one half.

Resources

MyMaths

3D shapes	1078	Plans elevations	1098	Nets, surface area	1107
Volume of cuboids	1137	Volume of prisms	1139		

Online assessment

Chapter test	3B–14
Formative test	3B–14
Summative test	3B–14

InvisiPen solutions

Properties of 3D shapes	321	Surface area of cuboid	322
Volume of shapes made from cuboids			323
Isometric grids	324	Nets of simple 3D shapes	325
2D representations of 3D solids			326
Volume of a prism	327	Surface area of a prism	328

Topic scheme

Teaching time = 5 lessons/2 weeks

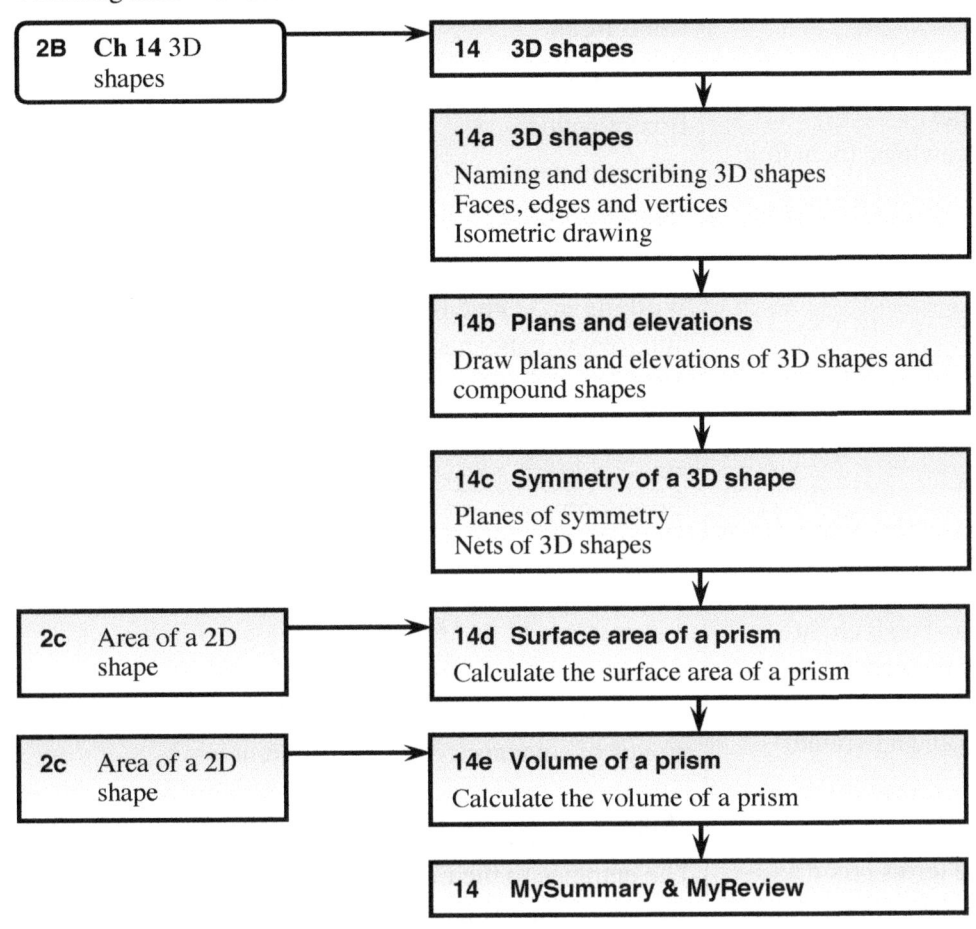

```
2B  Ch 14 3D shapes  →  14   3D shapes
                            ↓
                         14a  3D shapes
                         Naming and describing 3D shapes
                         Faces, edges and vertices
                         Isometric drawing
                            ↓
                         14b  Plans and elevations
                         Draw plans and elevations of 3D shapes and
                         compound shapes
                            ↓
                         14c  Symmetry of a 3D shape
                         Planes of symmetry
                         Nets of 3D shapes
                            ↓
2c  Area of a 2D shape  →  14d  Surface area of a prism
                         Calculate the surface area of a prism
                            ↓
2c  Area of a 2D shape  →  14e  Volume of a prism
                         Calculate the volume of a prism
                            ↓
                         14   MySummary & MyReview
```

Differentiation

Student book 3A   250 – 267
Properties of 3D shapes
Nets
Plans and elevations
Volume of a cuboid and shapes made from cuboids
Surface area of a cuboid

Student book 3B   248 – 263
Properties of 3D shapes including faces, edges and vertices
Isometric drawing, plans and elevations
Planes of symmetry and nets of 3D shapes
Surface area and volume of a cuboid and other prisms

Student book 3C   242 – 257
3D shapes and 3D geometry
Introduction to trigonometry
Bearings

Introduction

14a 3D shapes

Objectives	
• Use geometric properties of cuboids, and shapes made from cuboids	(L6)

Key ideas	Resources	
1 Visualise, recognise and describe the groups of prisms, pyramids and other shapes 2 Represent 3D shapes with 2D drawings, including with isometric paper.	3D shapes Box of solids Isometric paper Multilink cubes Photographs of solids Working in 3 Dimensions (TMM – Shape & Space): http://www.nationalstemcentre.org.uk/elibrary/resource/4628/teaching-mental-maths-from-level-five-geometry	(1078)

Simplification	Extension
Visualising 2D representations of 3D shapes can be difficult for some students and so a box of solids may be useful. In question **2**, students can be given three Multilink cubes to make the solids. In question **3**, students need to know the names of polygons and be able to distinguish between a prism and a pyramid before completing the question.	Extend question **4** to six points, one at the centre of each face. What shape is formed by these six points? Ask students to justify the answer. In question **5**, there are several ways that the seven solids can be fitted together to form the cube. Ask groups of students to find the different ways.

Literacy	Links
Establish clear understanding of the terms prism and pyramid. Other specific names or group names should also be encouraged from the students, rehearsing prefixes of both -gons and – hedra.	The entrance to the Louvre museum in Paris is a large metal and glass square-based pyramid that was designed by the American architect Leoh Ming Pei. It stands about 20.6 metres tall and was completed in 1989. The pyramid is covered by almost 700 glass panes and is surrounded by three smaller pyramids. There are pictures of the Louvre Pyramid at http://www.e-architect.co.uk/paris/louvre-pyramid-building

Alternative approach
Working with a class set of solids makes a good introduction to this work while also revising previous language and related facts. Students may work in pairs or threes with one or two labeled shapes, classify each into prsim, pyramid or other, name if appropriate and record the number of faces, edges and vertices. The shapes can be circulated around to ensure every student sees and handles each one. Share results and establish any key points, inlcuding Euler's Rule. For isometric drawing practice, students may continue to work in twos or threes with the task of drawing all the possible shapes made from four mulitlink cubes. Ask how many each group has found intermittently in order to maintain the pace. Further ideas and work with 3D shape can be found in the chapter TMM-Shape & Space, referenced.

Checkpoint	
How many faces does a square-based pyramid have?	(5)
How many vertices are there on a cube?	(8)
How many edges are there on a triangular prism?	(9)

Starter – Growing triangles

Ask students to plot (or imagine) a triangle with vertices at (1, 1), (4, 1) and (1, 3). Then ask students to multiply the coordinates by two. What does the new shape look like? What has happened to the area? What is the scale factor of enlargement? What happens if the coordinates are multiplied by three?

Teaching notes

This work is often difficult for students to do in the abstract. Working with some physical objects such as a cube, cuboid, pyramid and triangular prism (some chocolate bars come in this shape), will give students a mental schema. They can then use this when working with other objects that are not so easy to bring in to the classroom as examples, such as an octagonal-based pyramid.

Looking at photographs of solids will help students to understand the structure of perspective on isometric paper. For example, that the vertical must stay vertical.

Plenary

Ask students to work in pairs to extend question **2** to working with four cubes, matching face to face exactly. Do the numbers of faces, vertices and edges satisfy the rule in question **3**?

Exercise commentary

Question 1 – Students may not count the back triangular face since they cannot 'see' it.

Question 2 and **5** – Ensure that students orientate the isometric paper correctly.

Question 3 – The formula $e + v = f + 2$ was first published by Leonhard Euler in 1758 but was known to Rene Descartes 100 years earlier.

Question 4 – Ask students to slice the cube in a plane containing A, B, C and D and to draw this plane. Suggest to students that they need to look at the side lengths and the angles to decide the type of quadrilateral.

Question 5 – Multilink cubes are necessary for this activity. Ensure that students realise that shape **v** and shape **vi** are not the same, but are mirror images of each other. The total number of cubes used to make the seven solids is 27. Hence the dimensions of the cube must be $3 \times 3 \times 3$.

Answers

1   **a**   3 edges   **b**   6 edges   **c**   0 edges

2   **a**   Check students' drawings: One a 'line of three', the other an 'L' shape.
    b   6 faces, 12 edges, 8 vertices; 8 faces, 18 edges, 12 vertices.

3   **a**

Name	f	v	e
Cube	6	8	12
Cuboid	6	8	12
Square-based pyramid	5	5	8
Tetrahedron	4	4	6
Triangular prism	5	6	9
Hexagon-based pyramid	7	7	12
Hexagonal prism	8	12	18
Octagon-based pyramid	9	9	16
Octahedron	8	6	12

    b $f + v = e + 2$

4   **a**   Square
    b   ABCD has four equal sides and four right angles

5   **a**   Check students' drawings
    b   27 cubes   **c**   Student activity
    d   3 by 3 by 3

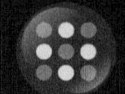

14b Plans and elevations

Objectives	
• Visualise and use 2D representations of 3D objects	(L6)
• Analyse 3D shapes through 2D projections, including plans and elevations	(L6)

Key ideas	Resources
1 Visualise, recognise and represent 3D shapes 2 Understanding the aspects of elevations and plans	Plans elevations (1098) CAD software Architectural plans Multilink cubes Square grid paper Representing 3D Shapes (SS6 Improving Learning in Mathematics, Standards Unit): http://www.nationalstemcentre.org.uk/elibrary/collection/492/mostly-shape-and-space-materials

Simplification	Extension
For question **1**, give students exactly 12 Multilink cubes (6 of one colour and 6 of another colour) to make the solids. Similarly for question **3**, give students exactly 10 cubes.	This is suitable for pairs of students using square grid paper and Multilink cubes. Ask students to devise problems of their own similar to question **3**. Students then challenge their partner to build and then draw the solid given the plan and elevations.

Literacy	Links
Remind students that the word elevation is linked to the height or rise (elevators, and so on); plan is either the top or bottom view, sometimes 'bird's eye view'.	From the mid-nineteenth to mid-twentieth century, drawings were copied using a low-cost process called the cyanotype process. The resulting copies were composed of either white lines on a blue background or blue lines on a white background and so were called blueprints. The term blueprint later came to mean any technical drawing or design plan. There are examples of architectural drawings and engineering blueprints at http://www.sanalco.com/plan_design_elevation.htm and at http://www.armchairgeneral.com/rkkaww2/galleries/T-26/T-26M31_bp.htm

Alternative approach
The Standards Unit resources, including the software Build, provide an active approach to this section. Another approach is to set up pairs of students to build with multilink cubes, draw plans and elevations, then challenge another pair to recreate the shape from the plans. This can also be set up as a team 'collective memory' game, where one student from the group is allowed to view the shape for a short amount of time, and then reports back to the group. The group challenge is to produce a set of plans and elevations for the 'hidden' shape based on the team's observatons and feedback.

Checkpoint
Create a shape made from 4 cubes (either using multilink cubes or drawn on isometric paper). Draw the front and side elevations and the plan view.   (Students' own answers, can be checked by a partner)

Starter – Name the shape

Give students a clue to a shape. Continue with clues until students guess the shape. For example

My shape has six vertices ... has five faces... has an odd number of edges... is a prism. (Triangular prism)

Can be differentiated by the choice of shape and complexity of clues.

Teaching notes

Students may be familiar with computer-aided design in technology and the T&D department may let you use their software to display figures in three-dimensions. Show the relationship between plan, front and side elevations and the (apparently) solid figure seen when the views are manipulated on screen.

Concrete examples, for example made from Multilink cubes, will allow students to move round an object physically and to compare the diagrammatic representations of plan, front and side elevations with the view of the object from these positions. This will help students to construct mental processes for relating the three-dimensional object with the two-dimensional representation.

Plenary

The school may have some architect's plans which could be borrowed for students to see real-life examples of the use of this topic. It is not just the architect who uses the plans; the structural engineers, construction workers, client *etc*. all need to have a common view of the building and most students can imagine themselves in one or more of these roles at some stage in the future.

Exercise commentary

Questions 1 and **3** – Students should have access to multilink cubes, although the questions can be attempted first without cubes.

Question 2 – Encourage students to draw the plans and elevations accurately. For example, in part **a**, the height of the rectangle in the side elevation should be the same as the perpendicular height of the triangle. Similarly, the width of the rectangle in the plan view should be the same length as the base of the triangle.

Question 4 – This question is suitable for discussion between pairs of students.

Question 5 – This question is open-ended and depending on the complexity of the chosen object, could be omitted or used as a homework task.

Answers

1   a   View B   b   View D   c   View A   d   View C

2   a   Check students' drawings
     b   Check students' drawings
     c   Check students' drawings

3   a   A 3 by 2 by 2 cuboid with the middle row cut out the top
     b   10 cubes

4   These are possible answers
     a   Square-based cuboid   b   Cuboid
     c   Cylinder   d   Hexagonal prism

5   Students' answers

Plans and elevations

14c Symmetry of a 3D shape

Objectives

- Identify reflection symmetry in 3D shapes (L5)
- Visualise 3D shapes from their nets (L6)

Key ideas	Resources
1 Begin to visualise plane symmetry of 3D shapes	Mini whiteboards Box of solids Skeletons of solids (straws; pipe cleaners; Geomag; etc) Mirror boards Planes of symmetry of a cube: http://www.youtube.com/watch?v=nmr46D5Cy9E

Simplification	Extension

Visualising 2D representations of 3D shapes can be difficult for some students and so a box of solids may be useful.
 	
 Students must be familiar with reflection symmetry for 2D shapes before attempting 3D symmetry. Ask students to find lines of symmetry for 2D shapes.
	Extend the problem in question **4** by asking, can a cube be sliced to reveal a cross-section of
	    an equilateral triangle an octagon
	    a parallelogram a circle
	    an isosceles trapezium?
	 Then ask students to explain and illustrate their answer to question **6**.

Literacy	Links
The word plane is not likely to familiar to students, and will need explicit introduction, particularly in terms of its infinite nature. It may help to liken the term to a sheet of glass, also floor, ceiling, walls and so on.	Molecules are often shaped liked polyhedra. Buckminsterfullerene contains molecules made up of 60 carbon atoms arranged in a shape similar to a soccer ball with hexagonal and pentagonal faces. The correct name for the shape is a truncated icosahedron but it has been nicknamed a buckyball. There is a net for a buckyball at http://www.korthalsaltes.com/pdf/truncated_icosahedron.pdf and at http://mathforum.org/alejandre/workshops/bucky.net.html

Alternative approach

Begin by asking students to visualise a cuboid – not a cube. Then ask them how many planes of symmetry can they picture the cuboid having. Mini whiteboards for sketching may help them with this task, and should stimulate discussion about symmetry of 3D shapes. Skeleton models and mirror boards will also help. Try some of the solids such as a square-based pyramid. Extend to a cube, which will be a real challenge. Support students here by providing, say, a skeleton cube and encourage paired working. Use the referenced Youtube clip to help show the 9 planes.

Checkpoint

How many planes of symmetry does an equilateral triangular prism have? (4)

Starter – Reflect

Give students coordinates of points or shapes and ask them to give the transformed coordinates after reflection. For example

    (4, 7) reflected in the line $y = 0$ (4, -7)
    (-3, 5.5) reflected in the y-axis   (3, 5.5)
    (4, 6) reflected in the line $y = 1$.   (4, -4)

Can be differentiated by the choice of mirror line.

Teaching notes

Many students need practical experience with using nets to construct 3D figures in order to build a mental process to imagine what happens when a net is folded. For example, why some configurations of six squares will build a cube and others will not.

For a cuboid where all three dimensions are different, it can be a challenge for students to identify which lengths need to be the same in the net.

Plenary

A cuboid with three different dimensions (as in the example) has exactly three planes of symmetry. How many planes of symmetry are there if two of the dimensions are equal? How many in a cube? How many in a sphere? Ask students to discuss this in small groups before taking whole-class feedback.

Exercise commentary

Question 1 – Emphasise that reflection symmetry in 3D is similar to reflection symmetry in 2D. This should ensure that part **b** is answered correctly, as some students will think that the diagonal plane is a plane of symmetry.

Question 2 – Ask students to consider the lines of symmetry for part **a** a square, part **b** a triangle, and part **c** a hexagon.

Questions 3, 5 and **6** – Ask students to construct the solid before finding the planes of symmetry.

Question 5 – In part **c**, each plane of symmetry passes through an edge of the regular tetrahedron.

Question 6 – The nine planes of symmetry can be split into four groups:
    3 planes as if the cube was a cuboid
    2 planes forming an X on one face
    2 planes forming an X on another face
    2 planes forming an X on another face.

This activity is suitable for students to work in pairs.

Answers

1   a   Yes, as each half is a mirror image of the other.
    b   No, as each half is not a mirror image of the other.
    c   Yes, as each half is a mirror image of the other.

2   a   Four planes running from the top to the bottom (two through opposite vertices, two through opposite sides) plus the 'half-way' cut across the cuboid
    b   Four planes running from the top to the bottom (two through opposite vertices, two through opposite sides)
    c   One cutting the prism into two vertically, one cutting it through the interior vertex to the opposite corner

3   a   Triangular-based pyramid or tetrahedron.
    b   3 planes of symmetry.

4   a   Across the diagonals of two opposite faces
    b   Across the diagonals of three adjacent faces
    c   Through any five faces (irregular pentagon)

5   a   Students' constructions
    b   6 edges   c   6 planes of symmetry

6   a   Students' constructions   b   9 planes of symmetry

14d Surface area of a prism

Objectives	
• Calculate surface areas of cuboids, and shapes made from cuboids	(L6)
• Calculate the surface area of right prisms	(L7)

Key ideas	Resources	
1 Understand the nature of surface area as a measurement 2 Find surface area of a variety of prisms.	Nets, surface area Mini whiteboards Empty food packaging Rulers, tapes Cuboids (NRICH): http://nrich.maths.org/2383	(1107)

Simplification	Extension
Students should be able to calculate the surface area of cuboids, before attempting this exercise. Provide several examples before moving on to more complex shapes.	Ask pairs of students to find the surface area of a cylinder; drawing a net should clarify the basic shapes involved when the cylinder is unrolled. Can the idea of unrolling a prism to obtain a central rectangle plus two end shapes be used to streamline the calculation of the surface area?

Literacy	Links
Remind students of the importance of including correct units.	Bring in some empty food or other packaging for the class to use or look at the unusual designs at http://dezignus.com/packaging-design/. Which of the packets are prisms? Can the class name the different prisms? What other products do the class know that are packaged in prisms other than cuboids?

Alternative approach

Begin with the Cuboids problem from (NRICH) referenced. Working in pairs will help them progress, and supporting the group with reminders about surface area points may be needed. Weaker students may find it easier to work with an area of 60 cm^2. Consolidate using either questions from the exercise, or by finding surface area of the empty package samples. By way of a plenary, challenge students about whether a particular surface area of a box always results in the same capacity – keeping cuboid packaging may help focus most students towards considering the effects of dimensions.

Checkpoint

Find the surface area of a triangular prism of length 12cm if the triangular cross-section has base 6cm and height 4cm.

(NOTE: Students will have to use Pythagoras' theorem to work out the slope length (= 5cm) before working out the area of all the faces: two triangles = 24cm^2, one rectangle 12 × 6 and two rectangles 12 × 5 = 192cm^2. Total SA = 216 cm^2)

Starter – 3D

Draw a 2D shape on the board representing the plan or elevation of a 3D shape and ask students to guess the 3D shape. For example

    Circle   (sphere, cone or cylinder)
    Triangle   (triangular prism, square-based pyramid or tetrahedron)

Encourage students to think of the different possibilities for each plan or elevation, remembering that the shape can be orientated in different ways!

Teaching notes

Draw the net of a triangular prism, separate out the composite shape into component parts, and ask students what these parts are in the solid. Develop the idea that there is not a 'formula' for the surface area of prisms generally, but it is a matter of working methodically to find the surface area of each of the faces, bearing in mind that often a number of these will be the same.

Emphasise the need to communicate what is being worked out at each stage, so that they know which sides they have considered and which they still have to calculate.

Plenary

Ask students to work in pairs to devise problems similar to question **4** (starting with the dimensions, they can calculate the three surface areas to give to their partner).

Exercise commentary

Emphasise that area is measured in square units, for example, cm^2.

Question 1 – Students could find the surface area of the prism as if each square measures 1 m by 1m (28 m^2). Then multiply this answer by 25.

Question 2 – Students should systematically find the area of the ten faces of the prism.

Question 3 – Students should find the area of the five faces of each prism.

Question 4 – In part **b**, encourage a systematic approach to find the length, width and height. Students should find the factors of 48, 84 and 112 and put them in pairs, for example, 4 × 12 = 48.

Question 5 – This is based on the second example.

Question 6 – Some students may find this question difficult. Ask them to first find the surface area of a cube for different numerical values of a.

Question 7 – This question is a nice, multi-stage problem which encourages the students to solve a practical problem using the skills developed in this section.

Answers

1   700 m^2

2   190 cm^2

3 a 1020 cm^2 b 1380 cm^2

4 a 488 cm^2 b 14 cm, 8 cm, 6 cm

5 a 10 cm b 15 cm c 2.5 cm d 4.5 cm

6 $6a^2$

7 a 72 × 9 × 9, 36 × 18 × 9, 18 × 18 × 18
    b Check students' drawings
    c 2754 cm^2, 2268 cm^2, 1944 cm^2
    d Largest surface area occurs for a long and thin box, the smallest surface area occurs for the most symmetrical box – a cube.
       The cubic box would be the cheapest to make.
    e Students' answers.

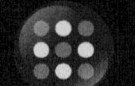

14e Volume of a prism

Objectives	
• Know and use the formula for the volume of a cuboid	(L6)
• Calculate volumes of cuboids, and shapes made from cuboids	(L6)
• Calculate the volume of right prisms	(L7)

Key ideas	Resources	
1 Appreciate that volume is a measure of capacity 2 Find and use the volume of a right prism to solve problems	Volume of cuboids Volume of prisms Boxes or equivalent in the form of cubes & cuboids Examples of other prisms that can be passed around 2D visual images of a range of prisms in different orientations. Mini whiteboards	(1137) (1139)

Simplification	Extension
As preparation for this exercise, ask students to calculate the areas of rectangles, triangles and trapeziums. Also ask students to verify that they can calculate the volume of cuboids using the area of cross-section × length formula.	Extend problem **7** for other scale factors until a generalisation is found.

Literacy	Links
Make sure that the units are stated clearly by students, particularly the 'cubic' or 'cubed', emphasising the nature of volume. Check this both in written and verbal form. Check also that students have an understanding of the term cross-section, relating it to everyday items such as sliced bread.	When white light is passed through a prism, the different colours are refracted or bent at different angles to create a rainbow. Sir Isaac Newton was the first person to realise that the prism separates the white light into its constituent colours. The traditional shape of an optical prism is a triangular prism. There is a demonstration of refraction by a prism at http://mistupid.com/science/prism.htm

Alternative approach

Students can struggle with associating the dimensions of length, width and height to a diagram, particularly when there is no diagram given. It is worth encouraging them that order does not matter as multiplication is commutative, and that a cuboid can be stood or arranged in (how many) different ways. It may help students to recognise that the dimensions radiate out from any vertex of the cuboid. Trace these dimensions with students using a model, and encourage them to do this as well. If the formula for cuboid volume was developed in Y8 with students in terms of 'base area' multiplied by height, build on this concept in order to draw all prisms together with the one formula. Encourage students to identify the cross-section physically, using actual solid examples as well as visual images. Students may be encouraged to record how to find each cross-sectional area using mini whiteboards, providing instant feedback in terms of area knowledge. This can then be extended to displaying solids and requesting how to find the volume using mini whiteboards, before consolidating and applying to problems.

Checkpoint

Find the volume of a cuboid measuring 6cm by 7cm by 8cm. (336 cm^3)

Find the volume of a triangular prism of length 9cm if the triangular cross section has base 4cm and perpendicular height 5cm. (90 cm^3)

Geometry and measures   3D shapes

Starter – Find the cuboid

Ask students to find a cuboid where the number of cm^3 in its volume is half the number of cm^2 in its surface area.

Hint, volume = 36 cm^3. (2 × 3 × 6)

Can be extended by asking for a cuboid where the number of cm^3 in its volume is equal to the number of cm^2 in its surface area. (4 × 6 × 12)

Teaching notes

Students often want to have formulae to cover every individual case, so emphasise the simplicity of finding the area of the cross-section as the first step which will lead directly to the volume calculation. The cross-section is often relatively simple: a rectangle, triangle or circle, where the area can be calculated very easily.

Emphasise the importance of including the units in any answers, and of making sure that all lengths in a problem are stated in the same units.

Plenary

Ask students to calculate the surface area for the three cuboids in **q7** and the corresponding ratios. Show the length, area and volume ratios (in their lowest forms) for the three cuboids and ask students to comment why they are in this form.

Exercise commentary

Emphasise that volume is measured in cubic units, for example, cm^3.

Question 1 – Suggest to students that a cuboid is a prism and so the formula for the volume of a prism can be used.

Question 2 – You could ask students if it would be easy to first add the three areas and then multiply by 5m or to add three separate volumes.

Question 3 – This is based on the first example.

Question 4 – In part **a**, students need to find the area of a trapezium: see section **2c** if necessary. In part **b**, ensure that students realise that the cross-section is a trapezium.

Question 5 – This asks students to reverse the process in preparation for question **6**.

Question 6 – This is based on the second example.

Question 7 – This question is an investigation into volume scale factors. Students could repeat the question with different cuboids to reinforce the relationship.

Question 8 – This question is open-ended and students could work in pairs to generate as many examples as they can in a fixed time.

Answers

1 16 m^3

2 **a** 42.5 m^3 **b** 27.5 m^3

3 **a** 31.5 cm^2 **b** 378 cm^3

4 **a** 1 m^2 **b** 1.5 m^3

5 8.5 cm

6 **a** 36 m^2 **b** 6 cm

7 **a** 24 cm^3 **b** 192 cm^3 **c** 27 times bigger

8 **a** 1000 cm^3 **b** Students' answers

Volume of a prism

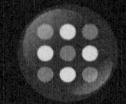

14 3D shapes – MySummary

Key outcomes		Quick check
Recognise 3D shapes.	L6	How many faces, edges and vertices are there on **a** a cuboid (6, 12, 8) **b** a triangular prism (5, 9, 6)
Draw the plan and elevation of a 3D solid.	L6	Draw the plan and elevations of the prism in question 8
Identify planes of symmetry.	L6	How many planes of symmetry does a square-based pyramid have? (2)
Calculate the surface area of a prism, and draw its net.	L7	A cuboid measures 7cm by 5cm by 3cm. Calculate the surface area. (142 cm^2)
Calculate the volume of a prism.	L7	A triangular prism has length 15cm. If the triangular cross-section has base 5cm and height 3cm, what is the volume? (112.5 cm^3)

MyMaths extra support

Lesson/online homework			Description
Nets of 3D shapes	1106	L4	Looking at the nets of cuboids and prisms

MyReview

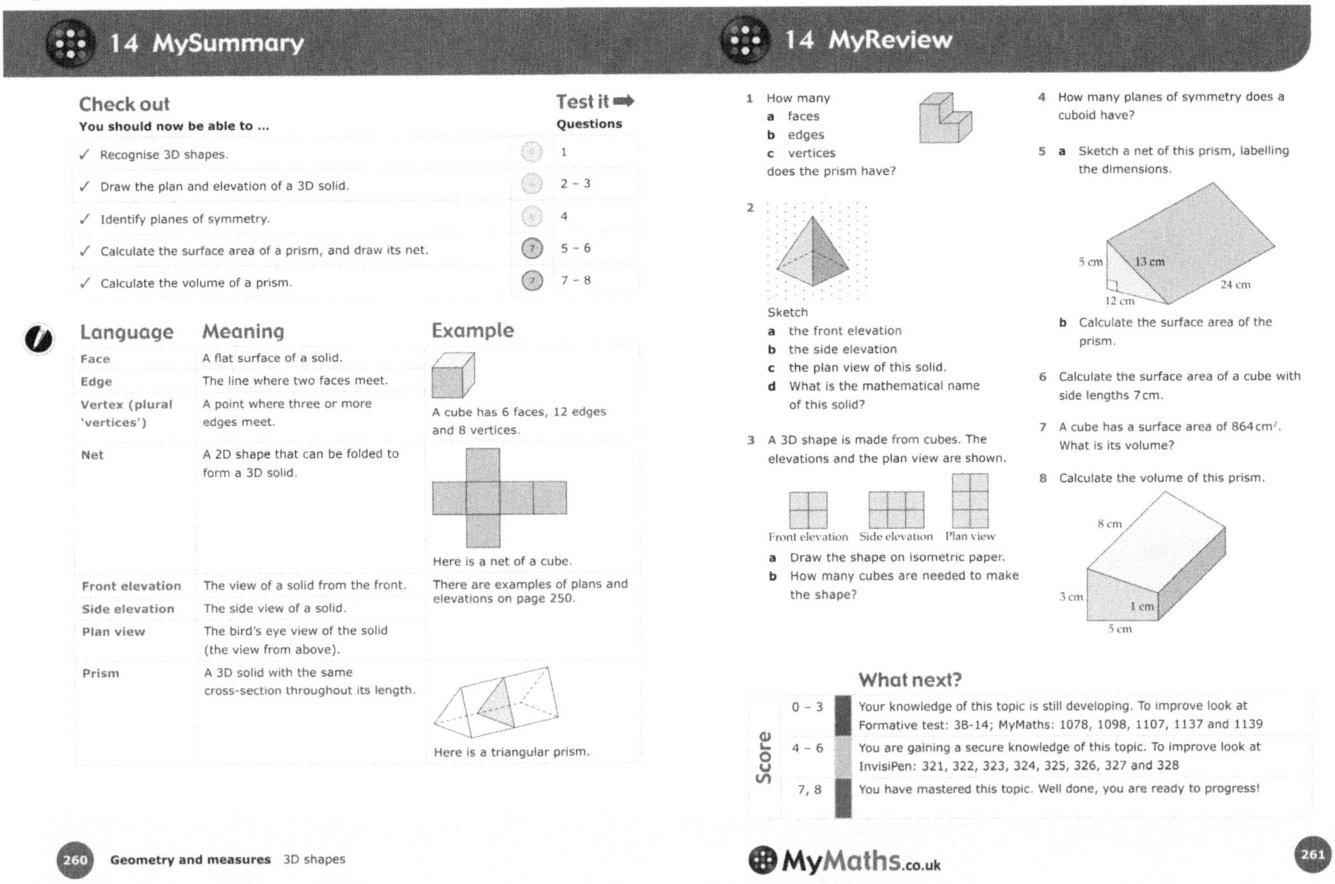

14 MySummary

Check out
You should now be able to ...

	Test it ➡ Questions
✓ Recognise 3D shapes.	1
✓ Draw the plan and elevation of a 3D solid.	2 – 3
✓ Identify planes of symmetry.	4
✓ Calculate the surface area of a prism, and draw its net.	5 – 6
✓ Calculate the volume of a prism.	7 – 8

Language	Meaning	Example
Face	A flat surface of a solid.	
Edge	The line where two faces meet.	
Vertex (plural 'vertices')	A point where three or more edges meet.	A cube has 6 faces, 12 edges and 8 vertices.
Net	A 2D shape that can be folded to form a 3D solid.	Here is a net of a cube.
Front elevation	The view of a solid from the front.	There are examples of plans and elevations on page 250.
Side elevation	The side view of a solid.	
Plan view	The bird's eye view of the solid (the view from above).	
Prism	A 3D solid with the same cross-section throughout its length.	Here is a triangular prism.

Geometry and measures   3D shapes

14 MyReview

1. How many
   a   faces
   b   edges
   c   vertices
   does the prism have?

2. Sketch
   a   the front elevation
   b   the side elevation
   c   the plan view of this solid.
   d   What is the mathematical name of this solid?

3. A 3D shape is made from cubes. The elevations and the plan view are shown.

   Front elevation   Side elevation   Plan view
   a   Draw the shape on isometric paper.
   b   How many cubes are needed to make the shape?

4. How many planes of symmetry does a cuboid have?

5. a   Sketch a net of this prism, labelling the dimensions.
   b   Calculate the surface area of the prism.

6. Calculate the surface area of a cube with side lengths 7 cm.

7. A cube has a surface area of 864 cm². What is its volume?

8. Calculate the volume of this prism.

What next?

Score	
0 – 3	Your knowledge of this topic is still developing. To improve look at Formative test: 3B-14; MyMaths: 1078, 1098, 1107, 1137 and 1139
4 – 6	You are gaining a secure knowledge of this topic. To improve look at InvisiPen: 321, 322, 323, 324, 325, 326, 327 and 328
7, 8	You have mastered this topic. Well done, you are ready to progress!

MyMaths.co.uk

Question commentary

Question 1 – This is an observational question. Ensure the students are also counting the faces, edges and vertices that they cannot 'see'.

Questions 2 and 3 – In question 2 students should not attempt to make their drawings look 3D.

Question 4 – Discuss how cuboids can have more lines of symmetry if they are a cube or have a square face, but always have at least 3.

Question 5 – Students sometime miss out faces or get confused with volume. The areas of the faces are: 312, 288, 120, 30 and 30. If they forget to halve the base × height for the triangles they will get 840.

Question 6 – Students may mistakenly calculate the volume giving 343.

Question 7 – First they should find the area of each face (864 ÷ 6 = 144), then square root this to get the side length (12).

Question 8 – Students need to identify the cross-section as a trapezium and use the formula for the area of a trapezium. They can look back at section **2c** for this. The area of the trapezium is 10 cm².

Answers

1   a   8   b   18   c   12

2   a,b (triangle)   c   (square)

    d   Square-based pyramid

3   a   Students' drawing (3 by 2 cuboid)   b   12

4   3

5   780 cm²

6   294 cm²

7   1728 cm³

8   80 cm³

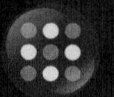

14 MyPractice

14a

1 A regular tetrahedron is made from four equilateral triangles.
How many faces, edges and vertices does this solid have?

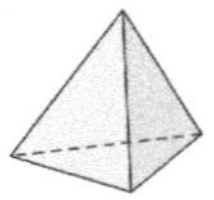

2 A cube is made from 27 identical small cubes.
 a Draw the solid on isometric paper.
 The centre cube on each face of the solid is now removed.
 b Draw the new solid on isometric paper.

14b

3 A square-based pyramid is joined to a cube.
Sketch the front elevation (F), the side elevation (S) and the plan (P) of this solid.

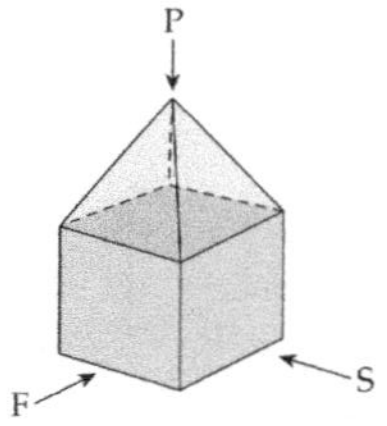

4 The diagram shows the plan of a solid made from cubes.
The number in each square represents the number of cubes in that column.
 a Draw the solid on isometric paper. 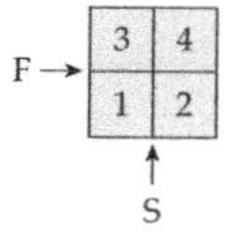
 b Draw the front elevation (F) and the side elevation (S) of the solid.

14c

5 A square-based pyramid is sliced horizontally.
Describe the shapes of the cross-section at different heights.

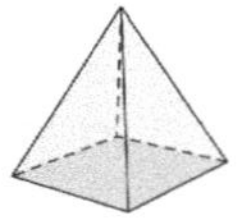

6 A regular octahedron is made from eight equilateral triangles.
Draw diagrams to show all the planes of symmetry of a regular octahedron.

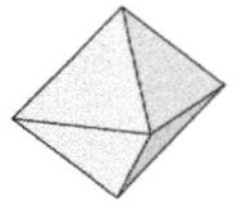

14d

7 Calculate the surface area of this prism.

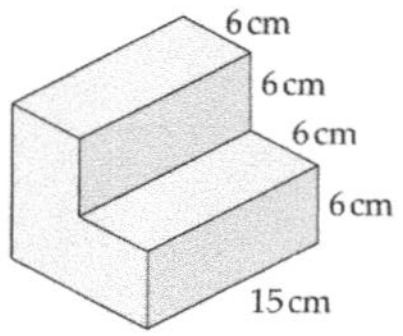

14e

8 A box is made in the shape of a hexagonal prism.
The length of the box is 10cm and the dimensions of the hexagon are shown in the diagram. 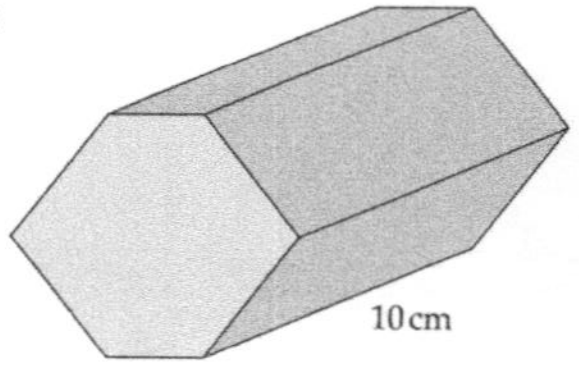 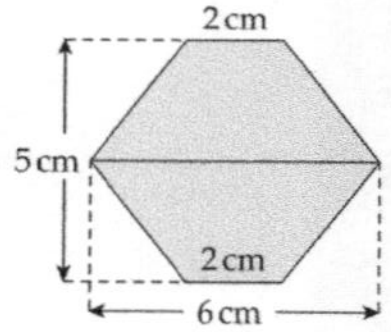
 a Calculate the area of the hexagon.
 b Hence find the volume of the prism.

9 A tent is in the shape of a triangular prism.
The length of the tent is 5 metres.
 a Calculate the area of the triangle.
 b Hence find the volume of the tent.
State the units of your answers.

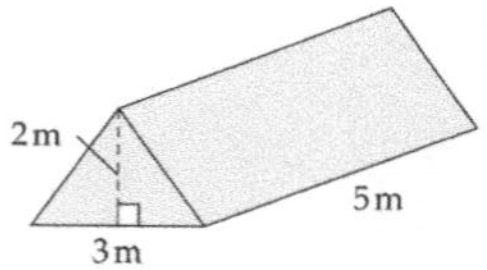

10 A cuboid is made from a rectangular sheet of card 30cm long and 25cm wide.
The cuboid is 9cm high.
The diagram shows the net of the cuboid.
Calculate the volume of the cuboid.

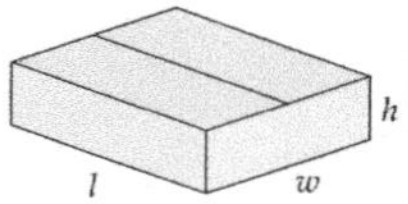

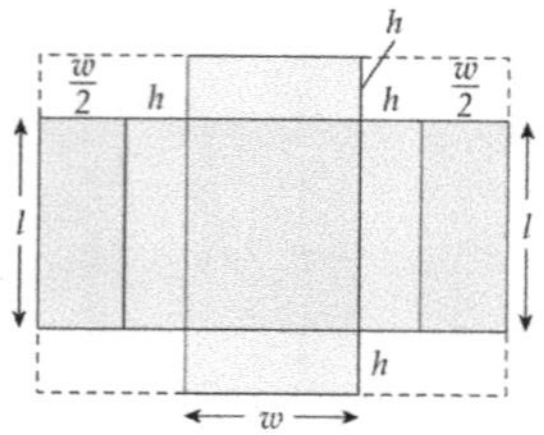

Question commentary

Question 1 – Students should be able to 'see' all of the faces, edges and vertices on the tetrahedron.

Question 2 – Ensure the students have the isometric paper in the correct orientation before proceeding.

Questions 3 and **4** – Students first need to sketch, and then draw accurately, the elevations. In question **4**, they could make the model from cubes first.

Questions 5 and **6** – Students should be able to visualise the shapes, but physical objects might also be useful.

Question 7 – Students can often miss faces out so ensure that they are adding together eight different areas.

Questions 8 to **10** – Mixed problem-solving questions involving the volume of prisms. These questions are challenging but in questions **8** and **9** the students are guided through the process.

Answers

1   4 faces; 6 edges; 4 vertices

2   **a**   A 3 by 3 by 3 cube   **b**   Like a 3D donut

3   F and S: square with a triangle on top, P: a square

4   **a**   1, 2, 3 and 4 cube stacked towers
    b   4 squares in the first column, two in the second; 3 squares in the first column, four in the second

5   Different sized squares

6   Students' diagrams (5 lines of symmetry)

7   936 cm^2

8   **a**   20 cm^2 **b**   200 cm^3

9   **a**   3 m^2 **b**   15 m^3

10 l = 7 cm; w = 6 cm; h = 9 cm; 378 cm^3

Case Study 5: The Golden Rectangle

Related lessons		Resources	
Rounding	1b	Decimal places	(1001)
Area of a 2D shape	2c	Order of operations	(1167)
Using a calculator	7d	Ratio dividing	(1039)
Real life sequences	13d	Map scales	(1103)
Recursive sequences	13e	Credit cards or business cards to measure	
Ratio	15c		
Uses of ratio	15d		

Simplification

Students may need reminding what it means to say that shapes are mathematically 'similar'.

Students occasionally struggle with the accurate construction of geometric shapes. Hence task **3** part **bi** and task **5** could be omitted.

Calculators will help students to work out the required ratios quickly throughout.

Extension

Students could use algebra to find the value of the golden ratio.

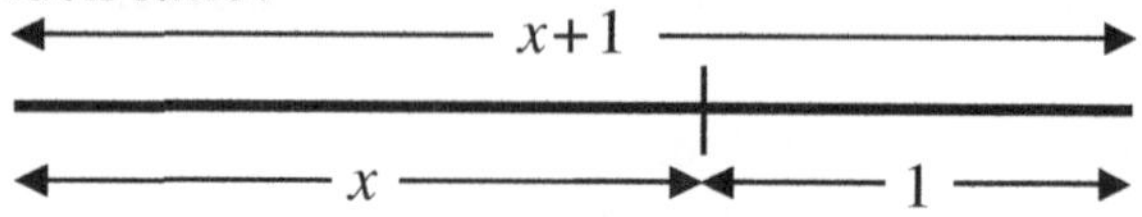

According to its definition the golden ratio is $\dfrac{x+1}{x} = \dfrac{x}{1}$ and so $\varphi = x$.

Solving the equation for the positive value of x gives the value for φ.

Links

The golden 'number' Phi has its own website which contains lots of useful information and articles: www.goldennumber.net

Another good website for students to explore is http://www.mathsisfun.com/numbers/golden-ratio.html

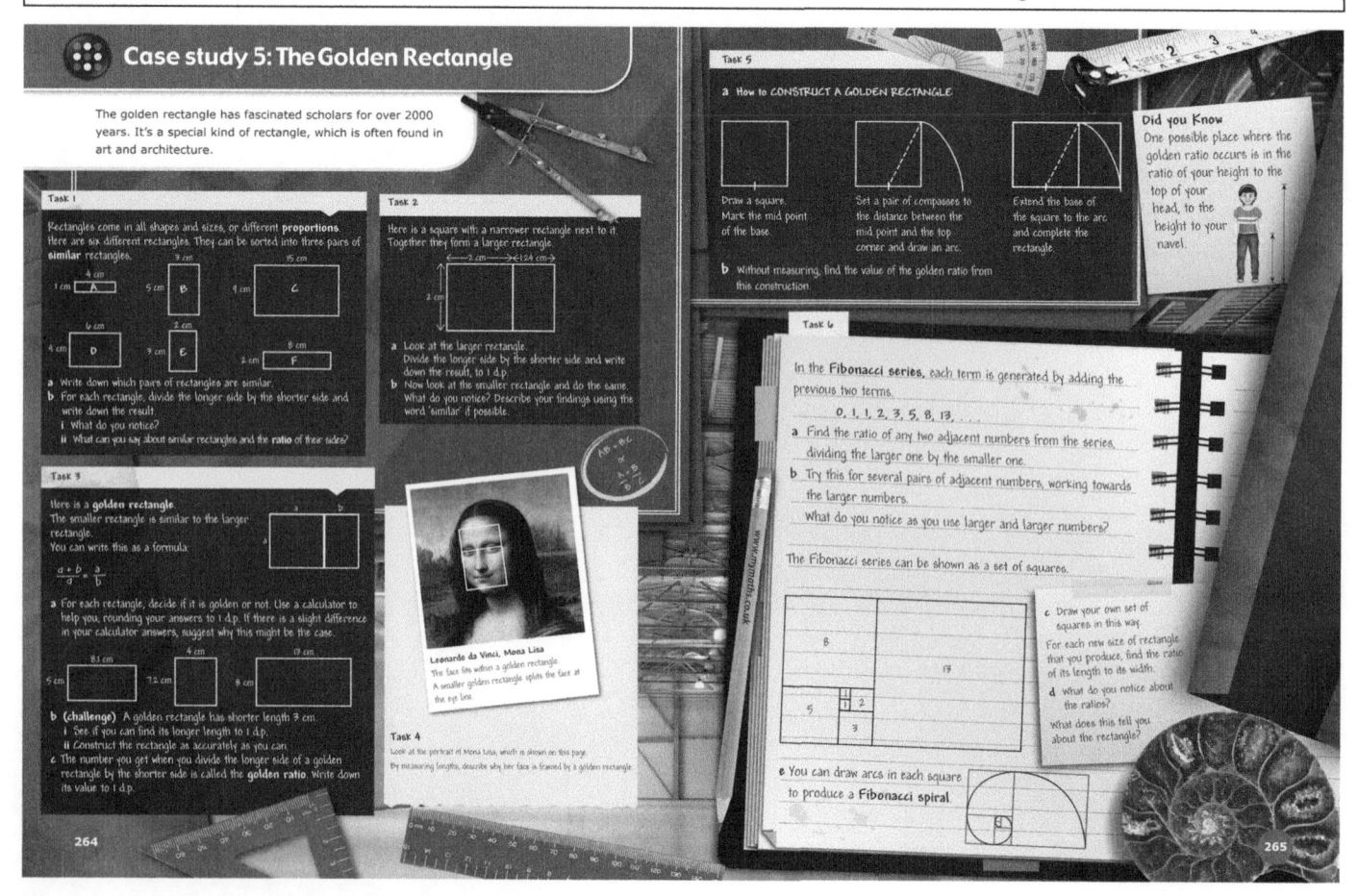

Teaching notes

Phi (φ) is an irrational number defined by the geometric relationship: 'when line A is split at a particular point, the ratio of the whole line A to the larger segment B is the same as the ratio of the larger segment B to the smaller segment C or A : B = B : C'. This happens only when the line is split in one particular ratio now known as the golden ratio and gives a value for phi of approximately 1.618.

Explain that the golden rectangle is widely believed to have a balance and proportion that is pleasing to the eye, as are things that are divided into sections according to the golden ratio. Because of this, it is often suggested that the golden ratio has been used in art and architecture.

Look at the examples shown and claim that both the ancient Greeks and, later, Renaissance artists knew about φ. Discuss the possibility that, as the ratio is pleasing to the eye, artists and architects could produce work with features close to the ratio simply because they want their work to have pleasing visual balance.

Task 5

Using the instructions at the top of the right hand page, give students a few minutes to construct a golden rectangle, suggesting that different groups use different sizes for the initial square. Once completed, remind students that the golden ratio is the ratio of the longer side to the shorter side. Ask them how they could find its value without actually measuring the rectangle. Establish that you need to know the size of the original square; ask them to assume that it is 2. Give them a few minutes to work with a partner and then hear their ideas. Elicit that you can use Pythagoras' theorem to find the radius of the arc (assuming a square of side 2, this will be $\sqrt{5}$) and, knowing that, you can find the length of the longer side $(1 + \sqrt{5})$. Once they have the longer side, the golden ratio can be found by diving this by the length of the shorter side (2). Students could then measure their rectangles divide the longer side by the shorter side to see if they give approximately the same ratio, regardless of the original size of their square.

Task 6

Look at the section on the Fibonacci series. Ask them to copy the series and continue it until they reach a number greater than 300. Then ask them to find the ratios of adjacent numbers, starting with the smaller ones and working towards the larger ones. Ask, what do you notice about the ratios of the numbers? Establish that, as the numbers get larger, the ratio settles around φ. You could ask students to set up a spreadsheet to explore this.

Now look at the diagram showing how the Fibonacci series can be represented as a set of squares, explaining that the diagram has been built up in a clockwise spiral starting with a square of side 1 and then adding another square of side 1 and then squares of sides 2, 3, 5, etc. Note how each time a square is added it results in a larger rectangle than before. Give the students some time to draw their own set of squares in this way. Each time they add a new square, they should note down the ratio of the longer side to the shorter side of the rectangle created. Ask, what do you notice? What happens with the ratios of the sides? What does this tell you about the rectangle that you are creating?

Establish that the sides of the rectangles are always adjacent terms from the Fibonacci series, so the ratios of these numbers will get closer to the golden ratio as the numbers used become larger, in just the same way as the terms of the Fibonacci series did before. So, having started as a square, the rectangle must be becoming closer to a golden rectangle.

Answers

1. **a** A & F, B & C, D & E
   b i 4, 1.67, 1.67, 1.5, 1.5, 4
   ii Ratios are the same
2. **a** 1.6   **b** 1.6
   The two rectangles are similar
3. **a** Yes, no, yes
   b i 4.9 cm   ii Check constructions
   c 1.6
4. The ratio of side lengths is approximately 1.6
5. **a** Students' constructions
   b $\varphi = \frac{\text{longer side}}{\text{shorter side}} = \frac{1+\sqrt{5}}{2} \approx 1.618...$
6. **a** 1, 2, 1.5, 1.6, 1.625, 1.615, 1.619, 1.618, 1.618,...
   b The ratio tends to the golden ratio
   c Students' constructions
   d Length of rectangle = preceding rectangle's width, give the Fibonacci numbers: 1, 1, 2, 3, 5, 8, 13, 21, 34, 55, 89, 144, 233, 277,... so that the ratio tends to the golden ratio. The rectangle is a golden rectangle.
   e Students' own drawings

The Golden Rectangle

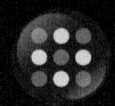

15 Ratio and proportion

Learning outcomes

SP2 Develop their use of formal mathematical knowledge to interpret and solve problems, including in financial mathematics (L6)

R3 Express one quantity as a fraction of another, where the fraction is less than 1 and greater than 1 (L6)

R4 Use ratio notation, including reduction to simplest form (L6)

R5 Divide a given quantity in two parts in a given part : part or part : whole ratio; express the division of a quantity into two parts as a ratio (L6)

R7 Understand that a multiplicative relationship between two quantities can be expressed as a ratio or a fraction (L6)

R8 Solve problems involving percentage change, including: percentage increase, decrease and original value problems and simple interest in financial mathematics (L7)

Introduction

The chapter starts by looking at the unitary and scaling methods for dealing with direct proportion before looking at comparing proportions using percentages. It moves onto simplifying and dividing into ratios and ratios of the form 1: n. Ratio and proportion problems and proportional reasoning are covered before the final section which looks at financial mathematics from the point of view of budgeting.

The introduction discusses the relationship between the amount of exercise we do and the amount of kilocalories we 'burn off'. The amount of kilocalories burnt off is directly proportional to both doing more exercise and the rate at which we do it. An example is given in the starter activity of 243 kilocalories burnt off walking three miles. Some other examples that you might give the students are:

- 30 minutes of jogging will burn on average 300 kilocalories;
- 8 hours sleep will burn off approximately 720 kilocalories;
- Watching TV for an hour will burn off 100 kilocalories;
- Sitting quietly and still for an hour will burn off approximately 80 kilocalories.

Prior knowledge

Students should already know how to…
- Simplify fractions
- Convert from fractions to percentages
- Simplify basic ratios including mixed units

Starter problem

The starter problem looks at how much exercise you would need to do to burn off the kilocalories in what you eat. At 243 kilocalories for a three mile walk, we can divide the amount of kilocalories in our food by this to find the equivalences.

Students could be asked to investigate the amount of kilocalories in the food they typically eat. The examples given are a chocolate bar and 'lunch'. All chocolate will vary in calorific value and it entirely depends what you have for lunch, but websites such as this one will give some guidelines:

http://www.nutracheck.co.uk/calories/calories_in_snacks_and_confectionary/calories_in_chocolate.html

Students could be asked to keep a diary of what they eat and the kilocalories contained within for a day or a week so that they can perform the kind of analysis suggested in the starter problem.

Resources

MyMaths

Proportion unitary method	1036	Ratio dividing 2	1039	Map scales	1103
Budgeting	1245	Change as a percentage	1302		

Online assessment

Chapter test	3B–15
Formative test	3B–15
Summative test	3B–15

InvisiPen solutions

Calculating a percentage change			153
Reverse percentages	154	Simplify and use ratio	191
Simple ratio and proportion	192	Ratio and proportion	193
Comparing proportions	194	Direct proportion	195

Topic scheme

Teaching time = 7 lessons/3 weeks

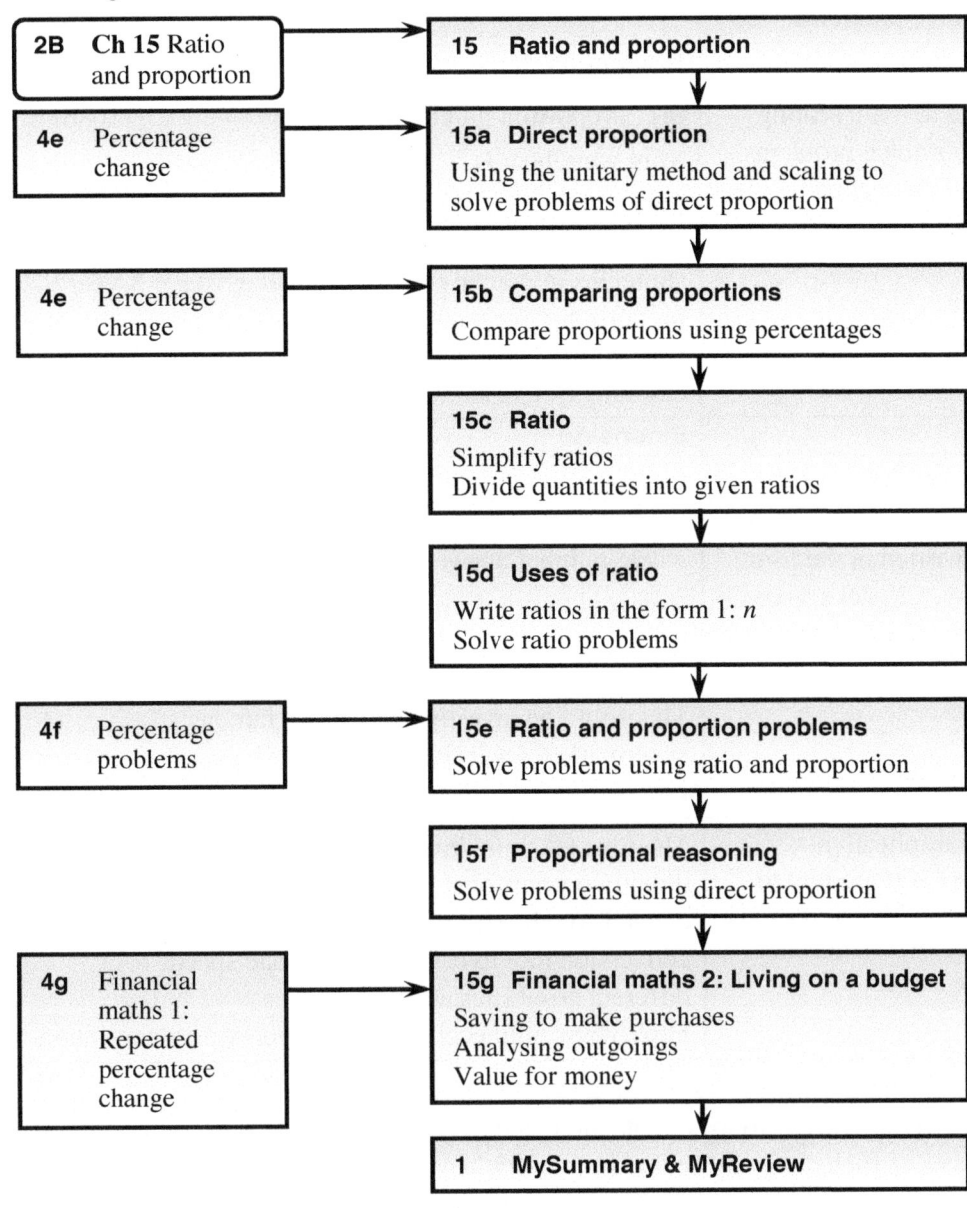

```
2B  Ch 15 Ratio          →   15   Ratio and proportion
    and proportion

4e  Percentage           →   15a  Direct proportion
    change                        Using the unitary method and scaling to
                                  solve problems of direct proportion

4e  Percentage           →   15b  Comparing proportions
    change                        Compare proportions using percentages

                             15c  Ratio
                                  Simplify ratios
                                  Divide quantities into given ratios

                             15d  Uses of ratio
                                  Write ratios in the form 1: n
                                  Solve ratio problems

4f  Percentage           →   15e  Ratio and proportion problems
    problems                      Solve problems using ratio and proportion

                             15f  Proportional reasoning
                                  Solve problems using direct proportion

4g  Financial            →   15g  Financial maths 2: Living on a budget
    maths 1:                      Saving to make purchases
    Repeated                      Analysing outgoings
    percentage                    Value for money
    change

                             1    MySummary & MyReview
```

Differentiation

Student book 3A 270 – 287	Student book 3B 266 – 285	Student book 3C 260 – 277
Ratio, dividing into a given ratio Ratio and proportion Percentages and proportion Proportional reasoning Financial mathematics: budgeting	Direct proportion Comparing proportions Ratio Using ratio and proportion to solve problems Financial mathematics: budgeting	Fractions and proportion Ratio and proportion Proportionality, scale and proportional reasoning Financial mathematics: budgeting

Introduction

15a Direct proportion

Objectives
- Use the unitary method to solve simple problems involving ratio and direct proportion (L6)
- Use proportional reasoning to solve problems (L6)

Key ideas	Resources
1 Recognise when it is appropriate to use a scaling strategy when dealing with proportional problems 2 Recognise that a unitary approach is a staged scaling strategy	Proportion unitary method (1036) Mini whiteboards Enhancing proportional reasoning Y8 & Y9: (Nat.Strat.): http://teachfind.com/national-strategies/interacting-mathematics-key-stage-3-year-9-proportional-reasoning-mini-pack?current_search=enhancing%20proportional%20reasoning%20y8%20%2526%20y9
Simplification	**Extension**
Students should be given lots of practice at solving problems which involve simple multiplication/division by a whole number. This could be written in the form of a spider diagram starting with say '12 packets cost £3, so how much do six packets cost, three packets cost etc.?'	Students should be given questions which involve use of a calculator and decimal answers, rather than just whole number answers. You could use information from supermarkets giving a comparison of the price of 100g of different products to illustrate a real life example of the unitary method. This could be investigated using a famous supermarket's website.
Literacy	**Links**
The sense of unitary method and multiplicative relationship method being equivalent is important to communicate here, with students realising that they are actually the 'same', but one involves two stages and the other combines the two into one stage.	The time taken to download a file onto a computer is directly proportional to the size of the file but also depends on the speed of the modem. There is a conversion tool to estimate download speeds for different sized files at http://www.onlineconversion.com/downloadspeed.htm

Alternative approach

Begin with a paired or small group activity where groups of data tabulated may be sorted into those in proportion and those not in proportion. Resources of such data may be found in the Enhancing proportional reasoning Y8 & Y9 pack. PR1 and/or PR2. Encourage students to think of contexts themselves resulting in values which are in direct proportion. Encourage students by using simple problems relying on intuitive scaling strategies mentally, responding with mini whiteboards. Use a visual image of the unitary method using vertical bar lengths thus:

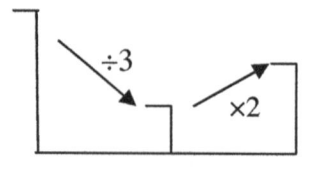

$\div 3$, $\times 2$ and compare to a scaling or multiplicative relationship: $\times 2/3$

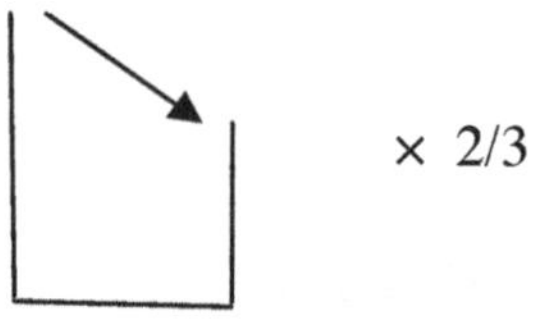

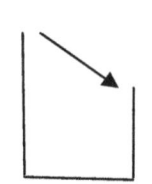

Compare and use with less familiar values and a calculator. Establish the similarities and the differences with the students by asking them to discuss and compare for themselves.

Checkpoint
a 5 litres of milk costs £2.40. How much would 8 litres cost? (£3.84)
b 18 little oranges cost 90 pence. How much would 20 little oranges cost? (£1.00)

Starter – One-third

Write the following equations on the board:

$$\frac{1}{x} + \frac{1}{x} + \frac{1}{x} = \frac{1}{3}$$

Ask students to find the value of x. Discuss strategies, reminding students that the calculation is the same as

$$\frac{1}{3} \div 3 \quad \text{or} \quad \frac{1}{3} \times \frac{1}{3}.$$

Can be extended by asking for three different unit fractions that add up to one-third.

Teaching notes

Some students find it difficult having alternative methods available, and having to decide which to use. However, in some cases, for example knowing the cost of 7 litres and wanting to know the cost of 21 litres, the scaling method is very simple, where in others the unitary method gives very simple calculations, for example knowing the cost of 10 or 100 of anything. Class discussion of a range of examples of both types (and examples where neither method is particularly simple) will help students to appreciate the benefits of being able to use both approaches.

Plenary

Ask students to work in pairs to identify real life situations where direct proportion occurs, and others where quantities do not vary in direct proportion. Opportunities for class discussion are why shops put on special offers such as 3 for 2, buy 1 get 1 half-price etc., and which offers are better value.

Exercise commentary

Question 1 – Encourage students to explain the methods they are using for these simple problems.

Question 2 – Students should either look for the cost of a single text or find a common multiplier.

Question 3 – Students will need to use a calculator for some parts of this question.

Question 4 – This question provides an opportunity to show that a graph of quantities in direct proportion must pass through the origin, and has obvious links to conversion graphs.

Answers

1. a £2.40   b 180 calories
   c 300 ml   d £5.70

2. Offer A because one text message costs 1.2 pence

3. a £2.19   b 300 g
   c i 56 km   ii 47.5 miles
   d 171.9 g   e 500 g

4. a i 333.3 km   ii 12 litres

Direct proportion

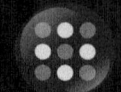

15b Comparing proportions

Objectives	
• Use proportional reasoning to solve problems	(L6)
• Recognise when fractions or percentages are needed to compare proportions	(L6)
• Use the equivalence of fractions, decimals and percentages to compare proportions	(L6)

Key ideas	Resources
1 Recognise and describe proportion accurately 2 Use proportional reasoning and language in order to compare proportion	Empty food packages Blank 100 square grids Mini whiteboards

Simplification	Extension
Students need plenty of practice at converting between fractions, decimals and percentages. This should focus upon fractions whose denominators are factors of 100. Simple diagrams such as blank 100 squares might be useful here to support understanding. Use of a calculator to convert a fraction into a decimal and then into a percentage should be reinforced by confirming the answers to the previous examples.	Students could examine situations where the answers are proportions which may differ by only a fraction of 1%, for example, the interest rate of money invested in different bank accounts, the shooting accuracy of two different footballers, the salt content of different foods, the reliability of two printers *etc*. The need to work out the proportion as a percentage to say three decimal places should be emphasised.

Literacy	Links
Encourage students to use the full variety of proportional language: fractions, decimals, percentage and ratio. Encourage them to construct sentences when communicating information about proportion.	Bring in some empty food packages. In addition to the nutrition information on the reverse of the packet there may be a panel on the front showing the Guideline Daily Amounts (GDAs). The panel gives the calorie, fat and salt content of a typical serving, expressed as a percentage of the guideline daily amounts for an average adult. The GDA panel is a recent initiative to help consumers make informed choices about their diet. There is more information about GDA labelling at http://www.whatsinsideguide.com/Home.aspx

Alternative approach

In order to refresh students' knowledge of proportional vocabulary use one of the parts from Qu.3, say 3ii, and ask them to devise sentences describing the diagram using proportional language in pairs using mini whiteboards. Record sentences as given,9 for instance the ratio of white to yellow is 2 to 6; three quarters of the rod is yellow; the amount of yellow is 3 times that of the white; and so on. Extend these to be written as mathematical sentences, so $w : y = 2 : 6 = 1 : 3$; $y = 3w$; where w represents number of white blocks, and so on. Draw out the difference between comparing, e.g. yellow to white versus yellow to whole rod. Students may find that block diagram representations of worded questions may help them towards giving clear comparisons.

Checkpoint

A brand of squash recommends a mix of one part squash to five parts water. A different brand suggests mixing one part squash to eight parts water. If the first brand is squash A and the second brand squash B, what is the proportion of water in each drink? (A would be $\frac{5}{6}$ water, while B would be $\frac{8}{9}$ water)

Starter – Four in a line

Ask students to draw a 5 × 5 grid and enter the numbers 1 to 25 in any order.

Give fractions or decimals, for example,

$\frac{1}{50}$, $\frac{13}{100}$, 0.17, $\frac{1}{25}$, $\frac{1}{5}$, ...

Students cross out the equivalent percentage in their grid. The winner is the first student to cross out four in a line.

Teaching notes

Discuss how percentages, fractions and decimals can be used to make comparisons between proportions of quantities.

For fractions, finding a common denominator may be easy in some cases but is often difficult. For percentages, the use of a standard denominator of 100 makes the process easy to understand although the equivalence is not always easy numerically. Decimals are very similar to percentages but the numbers in percentages are easier to make comparisons with, especially where decimals are not always shown with the same number of digits (0.1 may feel smaller than 0.06 to many students).

There are opportunities to develop collaborative working in considering the best approach to particular problems.

Plenary

Ask students to work in pairs to ask questions involving comparing proportions in real life situations for their partner to solve. Students can compare the method they used for each problem and discuss any different approaches.

Exercise commentary

Question 1 – Students should be able to check their answers to parts **a** and **b** using a mental method.

Question 2 – This question will challenge some students' understanding of a percentage. Expressing the percentage as a fraction and cancelling down may need to be made explicit.

Question 3 – Students will need to use a calculator to convert the proportions to percentages, so a simple checking strategy could be employed. For example, looking at their answer and calculating that percentage of the original amount.

Question 4 – A nice collection of problem-solving questions which use proportional reasoning. Calculators are likely to be required.

Question 5 – Look at labels from packets, tins, etc. or make use of the many 'slimming' websites which often give very precise figures for fat content, sugar content, etc.

Answers

1   a   85%   b   52%   c   70%   d   71.43%
    e   84.44%

2   a   50   b   Any fraction equivalent to $\frac{3}{20}$

3   a   i $\frac{5}{6}$ ii $\frac{6}{8}$ iii $\frac{7}{9}$

    b   i $\frac{5}{6}$, 83.3%   ii   ¾, 75%

       iii $\frac{7}{9}$, 77.8%

    c   The rectangle in **i**

4   a   Geoff
      John 46.7%
      Geoff 48%

    b   English
      History 31.3%
      English 31.7%

    c   i   14.6% of women   ii   10.4% of people

5   a   Crisps   33.14%
      Olives   11.07%
      Cereal bar   7.08%
      Chocolate bar 24.03%
      French fries   11.54%

    b   The Crisps have the highest fat content at 33.14%

    c   Students' answers

Comparing proportions

15c Ratio

Objectives

- Use the unitary method to solve simple problems involving ratio and direct proportion (L6)
- Use proportional reasoning to solve problems (L6)
- Simplify ratios, including those expressed in different units, recognising links with fraction notation (L6)
- Divide a quantity into two or more parts in a given ratio (L6)

Key ideas	Resources
1 Understand ratio notation and its links to other proportional vocabulary 2 Divide quantities into given ratios.	Ratio dividing 2 (1039) Mini whiteboards Tarsia puzzles on simplifying & dividing ratios (NUMBER, Section 4): http://www.mrbartonmaths.com/jigsaw.htm

Simplification	Extension
Students will need to see the connection between cancelling down an equivalent fraction and cancelling down a ratio; that is, doing the same division to both parts. They should be shown a method of dividing in smaller steps. Start by dividing by the smallest prime number (2) and then continue dividing using the same divisor or moving onto the next prime number until the two parts of the ratio have no more common factors.	Students should attempt more questions that require rounding of the answers to a certain degree of accuracy. More able students should be shown how to express each part of the ratio as a proportion of the whole. This could then be used as the basis of an alternative method for calculating a division in a given ratio (see lesson **15e**).

Literacy	Links
Encourage students to use the full variety of proportional language: fractions, decimals, percentage and ratio. Check that students understand and use contexts of any problem when conveying a solution, by using the correct units or terms.	Artists mix paints together to produce different colours and shades. The colour produced depends on the ratio of the component colours used in the mixture. Online colour mixing palettes can be found at http://painting.about.com/library/blpaint/blcolormixingpalette1.htm and at http://colorblender.com/ which also produces a palette of matching colours

Alternative approach

Begin with an equivalent spider diagram adding a centre of, say, 18cm : 60mm, in order to revise the basic concepts previously met. Ask students to suggest any equivalent ratio to add to the diagram using mini whiteboards. Add appropriate values, addressing any misconceptions if they arise. Encourage versions which include decimals or fractions if possible, then extend to which value would be considered the simplest version. Consolidate both simplifying and dividing into given ratios using equivalent matching activities or similar. Tarsia jigsaw problems on ratio are referenced in Resources.

Checkpoint

The angles of a triangle are in the ratio of 3 : 4 : 5. Find all the angles of this triangle. (45°, 60°, 75°)

Starter – Heads and tails

I have some coins on the table. Half of them show heads. I turn over four of the coins showing a head and now one-third of them show heads. How many coins do I have? (24 coins)

Can be extended by challenging students to make up their own coin problems.

Teaching notes

Fluency in converting between units of length, mass (weight), time and volume is an important component skill in working with ratios, so some review and practice of these conversions will be helpful.

Explicitly linking the ideas of cancelling in fractions and ratios to simplify working should be encouraged.

A class activity using mini whiteboards with some simple examples of the different component skills will facilitate assessment of students' prior competencies.

The second worked example emphasises the value of a simple checking strategy and students should be encouraged to use this for themselves.

Plenary

Ask students to work in pairs to ask questions involving ratios in real life situations for their partner to solve.

Exercise commentary

Question 1 – Students should be encouraged to show the division (by common factor) which they have used to simplify each ratio.

Question 2 – Remind students that ratios can be simplified only when quantities are written in the same units.

Question 3 – A useful discussion point is to explain how we can divide quantities using different methods, not just division in a given ratio.

Question 4 – Students should need a calculator only for part **f**. It may be worth discussing rounding here.

Question 5 – Two real life problems to be solved using the methods covered in this section.

Question 6 – Students could be asked to find all the possible ways of dividing the square into squares and rectangles and expressing each of these as a ratio in its simplest form.

Question 7 – Students should solve this problem the same as the other questions but may need reminding of the angle sum in a quadrilateral.

Answers

1. **a** 3 : 5   **b** 2 : 3   **c** 5 : 8   **d** 5 : 3
   e 2 : 3 : 5   **f** 3 : 6 : 8

2. **a** 1 : 3   **b** 5 : 1   **c** 5 : 4   **d** 5 : 16
   e 4 : 1   **f** 6 : 1

3. **a** 22 boys and 11 girls   **b** 16 boys and 13 girls
   c 16 boys and 20 girls

4. **a** 15 apples and 25 apples   **b** £100 and £20
   c 8 kg and 28 kg   **d** 4 km, 8 km and 12 km
   e £42, £18 and £12   **f** £36.11 and £28.89

5. **a** 62 teachers   **b** 225 g of butter

6. **a** Red area = 104 cm^2 and blue area = 40 cm^2
   b A red 9 × 9 square and a red 3 × 3 square

7. 36°, 72°, 108°, 144°
   Students' sketch

Ratio

15d Uses of ratio

Objectives	
• Use the unitary method to solve simple problems involving ratio and direct proportion	(L6)
• Compare two ratios	(L6)
• Interpret and use ratio in a range of contexts	(L6)

Key ideas	Resources
1 Solve problems involving ratio and proportion 2 Become familiar with expressing ratio in the form $1 : n$, to support comparison work	Map scales (1103) Tarsia puzzles on ratios (NUMBER, Section 4): http://www.mrbartonmaths.com/jigsaw.htm

Simplification	Extension
Begin with ratios written in the form $1 : n$, such as scales, and solve related problems. Students should be able to see that the ratio $1 : n$ gives them a scale factor by which to multiply or divide as appropriate. Further work on writing ratios in the form $1 : n$ will then make more sense to the students if it is interpreted as the relative size of the two parts of the ratio, that is, a ratio of $1 : 2.5$ tells us that the second part is two and a half times bigger than the first part.	Students should be encouraged to write ratios in the form $1 : n$ and then in the ratio $n : 1$. They should be asked to explain why this might be useful. Students could be given questions on related topics and asked to look for the connection with the ratio $1 : n$ such as converting between units and converting between currencies.

Literacy	Links
Relate the use of $1 : n$ with the concept of multiplicative relationships, building on previous work. Revise strategies for interpreting word problems, where students highlight or underline key information. Liaise with other curricular areas such as geography, and involve contexts familiar to studentsd through these connections.	Scale is usually shown on a map both in terms of a ratio and as a graphic or bar scale. A graphic scale is a bar drawn on the map showing the actual corresponding distance on the ground. The scale of the map will change if it is copied and reduced or enlarged, however, the bar scale is also enlarged and so will remain accurate. There are instructions for using a graphic scale at http://www.map-reading.com/ch5-2.php

Alternative approach
Use visual representations such as those of bars, rods or lines to demonstrate reduction of a numerical ratio from $a : b$ into $1 : b/a$. Students will tend to maintain intuitive and informal approaches when comparing ratios, and often find the jump to difficult values a very challenging one, so relating to a multiplicative relationship or scale factor will be assisted through the use of visual aids such as diagrams such as those given in **15a**. Students may not be sufficiently confident to move from a unitary approach to a scale factor or multiplicative approach, but encourage both, and encourage discussion about which of the approaches is more effficient.

Checkpoint	
5 miles is roughly equivalent to 8 km. How many miles are equivalent to 100 km? How may kilometres are equivalent to 12 miles?	(62.5miles) (19.2km)

Ratio and proportion Ratio and proportion

Starter – Square ratios

Ask students to find pairs of square numbers that are in the ratio of 8 : 50.

Possible solutions are 4 : 25, 16 : 100, 64 : 400.

Can be differentiated by the choice of ratio.

Teaching notes

Comparing ratios in which neither part is the same can be very difficult (especially if the ratios are similar). Using 1 : n where n can be a decimal allows a simple comparison to be made between two or more ratios.

Accurate reading of text material is essential in working with ratios to identify whether the whole quantity has been given, or the size of one of the component parts. Communicating this orally and on paper, to both the teacher and to other students, should be encouraged.

Plenary

Working with ratios is an important skill in becoming functional in mathematics. Ask students to suggest examples where this skill is needed.

Exercise commentary

Question 1 – The first three examples result in whole number answers while the remainder may require the use of a calculator.

Question 2 – A common misconception is for students to divide the quantity in the given ratio.

Question 3 – Practical examples of maps, particularly of your own local area, are very powerful ways of conveying the idea of scale to the students. Emphasise the need to change units.

Question 4 – For most students you will need to clarify the interpretation of the answer (1: n) in the context of the question.

Question 5 – A good plenary question for students to explain the strategies they would use. Diagrams of the tile may improve understanding.

Question 6 – Students could investigate estimating and measuring lengths of different objects in the classroom and then working out accuracy ratios.

Answers

1 a 1 : 3   b 1 : 4   c 1 : 5   d 1 : 1.5
   e 1 : 2.25 f 1 : 2.4 g 1 : 3.33 h 1 : 1.78

2 a 208   b 92 kg

3 a i 84 000 cm = 840 m   ii 7.5 cm
   b 45 cm

4 a 1st t-shirt is 1 : 12.5, 2nd t-shirt is 1 : 13.3.
       First t-shirt has highest proportion of nylon
   b Oxford School 1: 13.7, Melville 1 : 14.5
       Oxford has the highest proportion of teachers

5 a 9 cm   b 7.5 cm   c 1.5 cm

6 a Bottle of pop 1 : 0.86; Can of pop 1: 0.83;
       Loaf of bread 1 : 1.07; Cake 1 : 1.20
   b Loaf of bread (closest to 1:1)
   c Students' answers

Uses of ratio

15e Ratio and proportion problems

Objectives
- Use proportional reasoning to solve problems (L6)
- Solve problems involving percentage changes, choosing the correct numbers to take as 100%, or as a whole (L6)
- Calculate an original amount when given the transformed amount after a percentage change (L7)

Key ideas	Resources
1 Recognising and allocating wholeness appropriately when working with proportional problems 2 Confidently apply strategies to solve proportional problems	Change as a percentage (1302) Mini whiteboards Ratio & Proportion (NRICH): http://nrich.maths.org/9003

Simplification	Extension
The use of simple diagrams to illustrate the ratio in each question will help students to visualise what fraction (proportion) of the whole each part of the ratio represents, for example, the ratio 2 : 3 can be drawn as a rectangle divided into five parts. Students could then be asked to illustrate each of the ratios in question **2** themselves.	More able students could be shown an alternative method (using decimal multipliers) to find the original amount after a percentage change. This would link with work completed in lesson **4e**.

Literacy	Links
Continue to encourage flexibility in use of all versions of proportional vocabulary, prompting equivalent statements and so on. Rehearse strategies of identification of key information and relating this to equivalent proportionality sentences. Include where appropriate references to multiplicative relationships including the term reciprocal.	An alloy is a mixture of two or more metals and perhaps a non-metal. The alloy is usually harder or more malleable than its component metals. The first alloy was bronze which was used throughout Europe in about 2000 BC and contains copper and tin. Today the most common alloys are steel and brass. There is more information about alloys at http://www.explainthatstuff.com/alloys.html

Alternative approach
Begin with oral prompts such as those given in Phase 3 of the Y9 minipack referenced. Students may respond with mini whiteboards. Model a problem such as **q4** with the whole group making use of a variety of visual prompts such number lines linking percentage scale with for instance sale values, as well as block and/or stick diagrams supporting unitary and scaling methods. Further problems can be found on the NRICH refereced link.

Checkpoint
a After a reduction of 15% a jacket cost £42.50. What was the original cost of this jacket? (£50)

b By using a comparision website, a saving of 22% was made when purchasing a television. If the saving was £66, what price was actually paid? (£234)

Starter – How many?

Give students the following clues.
- The ratio of boys to girls is 3 : 2.
- The number of girls is a multiple of 3.
- The total number of children is more than 5^2 but less than 6^2.
- How many boys are there? (18)

Can be extended by asking students to make up their own ratio puzzles.

Teaching notes

The English language is rich in the number of different ways to describe ratios and proportions and it is important that students are able to read the information in problems and extract the relevant ratio or proportion accurately. The worked examples show good practice in setting out the given information and showing the calculation processes clearly. Students should be encouraged to use these as models for their own working.

Again, emphasise connections with real life problems and becoming functional in mathematics.

Plenary

Ask students to work in pairs to pose ratio and proportion problems in real life situations for their partner to solve.

Exercise commentary

Question 1 – Each part of the ratio can be expressed as a fraction, but students should be encouraged to convert the fraction into a percentage.

Question 2 – Remind students to express the proportion as a percentage. All but parts **d** and **f** produce whole number percentages. Ask students to explain why.

Question 3 – Encourage students to show the scaling factor to turn the given percentage into 100%.

Question 4 – Students could use a simple scaling method as in question **3**.

Questions 5 and **6** – Remind the students to first calculate the reduction or increase before expressing it as a fraction. Students may need help in identifying which amount is the whole (original amount).

Question 7 – A mixture of problem-solving questions involving ratio and proportion. Encourage students to use methods with which they are confident and to explain all of their reasoning. This would make a good group work activity.

Answers

1. **a** 2 : 3   **b** 0.4 = 40%

2. **a** 40%   **b** 25%   **c** 30%   **d** 62.5%
   e 35%   **f** 43.75%   **g** 20%   **h** 44%

3. **a** £120   **b** £80   **c** £240   **d** £22.50

4. **a** £20   **b** 20 biscuits

5. Jacket — 30% reduction
   Suit — 20% reduction
   Tie — 5% increase
   Trousers — 12% reduction

6. **a** 15%   **b** 37.5%

7. **a** 180 g of fat   **b** 60p
   c 33 chocolates   **d** 26 kg

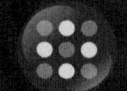

15f Proportional reasoning

Objectives

- Use proportional reasoning to solve problems (L6)
- Interpret and use ratio in a range of contexts (L6)

Key ideas	Resources
1 Recognising and allocating wholeness appropriately when working with proportional problems 2 Confidently apply strategies to solve proportional problems	Proportion unitary method (1036) Y9 Proportional reasoning mini pack (Nat.Strat.): http://teachfind.com/national-strategies/interacting-mathematics-key-stage-3-year-9-proportional-reasoning-mini-pack?current_search=enhancing%20proportional%20reasoning%20y8%20%2526%20y9

Simplification	Extension
Students will need to revise previous work on direct proportion (lesson **15a**). They should be referred to this lesson if they are having difficulties.	Students could investigate multiplying by a fraction and then multiplying the result by the reciprocal.

Literacy	Links
Maintain and encourage equivalent vocabulary, as well as strategies for re-reading and interpreting word problems.	Wedding cake recipes often give scaling information for cakes of different sizes and shapes. The quantity of mixture required depends on the volume of the tin rather than its diameter. There is an example of a recipe at http://www.deliaonline.com/cookery-school/scaling-up-cake-recipes,1002,AR.html Which quantities are in direct proportion?

Alternative approach

Repeat the acvtivity of oral prompts as in the last section's alternative approach before extending and continuing to work with worded problems. Encourage students to work on problems in pairs, differentaiting as appropriate. Pairs may share and discuss with another pair, and better more rigoropus solutions encouraged from the four.
A variety of mixed ratio and proportion questions with advice can be found in the Y9 minipack referenced in the Phase 3 Main sections.

Checkpoint

One 30g packet of crisps contains 9 g of fat and 0.3 g of salt.
How much fat and salt would be contained in a 50 g packet? (15g of fat and 0.5g of salt)

Starter – Discount

A jacket, normally selling at £35 + 15% VAT, is in a sale. It is advertised as 15% off the selling price. How much does the jacket cost now?
Hint not £35! (£34.21)

This can be extended by asking students to make up their own percentage problems.

Teaching notes

The material in this lesson is related to real life applications of mathematics. To embed functional skills, discuss when proportional reasoning does (unit conversions of length *etc.*, recipes, map scales, *etc.*) and does not (world record times for races of different lengths, mass of cubes with different side lengths using the same material, costs of packets of the same product of different sizes) apply in different contexts.

Emphasise the benefits of being able to use both the unitary method (when it is easy to do, or a calculator is available) and the use of the multiplier.

Plenary

Give students a number of contexts, some of which are directly proportional and some which are not. Ask students to discuss in pairs which are directly proportional, and to find at least two further examples of each for themselves. Then take whole-class feedback.

Exercise commentary

Questions 1 and **2** – Students could be encouraged to set up these problems on a spreadsheet to help them understand the role of the single multiplier. Emphasise the idea of dividing two corresponding values to find the multiplier.

Question 3 – In part **a**, for example, students could use the unitary method to find how many kilometres are equal to 1 mile and compare this answer with the single multiplier. They will need to use a calculator.

Question 4 – Students can compare their methods by working in pairs. This is an excellent opportunity for class discussion to look at the different methods being used by the students.

Question 5 – An opportunity to look at the multiplier to convert from inches to cm and from cm to inches. Once the multiplier is written as the fraction $\frac{5}{2}$ then the inverse multiplier $\frac{2}{5}$ becomes apparent.

Answers

1 B is in direct proportion, that is, each GB costs £4.50

2 **a** Yes   **b** number of packets × 0.65 = cost
   c =A3*0.65

3 **a** miles × 1.6 = km   **b** pizzas × 2.5 = cost
   c cm × 10 = mm
   d number of people × 70 = grams of rice

4 **a** 360 calories   **b** 675 ml   **c** £17

5

inches	cm	inches / cm	cm / inches
1	2.5	0.4	2.5
8	20	0.4	2.5
12	30	0.4	2.5
20	50	0.4	2.5

The two fractions (conversion factors) are constant.

Proportional reasoning

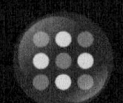

15g Financial maths 2: Living on a budget

Objectives	
• Interpret and solve problems in financial mathematics	(L7)

Key ideas	Resources	
1 Solve problems involving budgeting 2 Solve problems involving value for money	Budgeting Calculators	(1245)

Simplification	Extension
The amount of different types of expenditure can be reduced in order to simplify the calculations required of the students. Value for money problems can be simplified to be just about comparisons, rather than adding in complexity to do with special offers and 'buy 1 get 1 free' deals.	Students could be asked to look at how prices change over time due to inflation. The consumer price index is made up of a 'basket of goods' (and services). The cost of these goods and services changes each month and it is this that dictates the rate of inflation. Internet research can be carried out to see what is in the 'basket', how this itself changes over time, and how the prices fluctuate on a monthly or yearly basis.

Literacy	Links
Budget Salary Inflation Value for money Financial literacy	The work in this section links into two key areas: the idea of running household accounts and the concept of value for money. Understanding both of these areas is an important life skill. Encourage students to think about their own circumstances such as how they save and spend their pocket money, or whether they take advantage of special offers and bulk purchases in supermarkets and other shops. An investigation into real life offers and deals in supermarkets can be carried out using information from websites such as www.tesco.com, www.sainsburys.com.uk and www.waitrose.com.

Alternative approach
There are lots of different ways of introducing the concept of value for money to students. Real life examples of offers from the supermarket could be used – perhaps photos taken of price labels during the weekly shop can be used to provide specific and real examples. Comparisons of prices in different supermarkets could also be used to stimulate discussion. Are the claims of supermarkets really true when they say things like '35% cheaper than supermarket A!'?

Checkpoint
Joseph earns £1300 per month and spends £600 on rent. He spends a further £120 on food, £85 on bills and £60 on transport. How much does Joseph have left over? (£435) Two jars on jam are available: 180 grams for £1.50 or 250 grams for £2.20. Which represents the best value for money?   (The smaller jar)

Starter – Speed division

Divide these amounts up into the given number of equal parts as quickly as possible:

320 into 8 parts (40)

120 into 5 parts (24)

650 into 13 parts (50)

440 into 11 parts (40)

7.2 into 2 parts (3.6)

6.9 into 3 parts (2.3)

4.84 into 4 parts (1.21)

6.45 into 3 parts (2.15)

Teaching notes

The first two ideas are about budgeting to save and budgeting to live. The first two examples cover these ideas and students could be asked to work through them to check they understand the principles involved. Guide students to read the scenarios carefully and extract the useful information from the text. Questions 1 and 2 can then be attempted.

The focus then changes to 'value for money' and some simple examples of direct comparisons can be given before turning to the example in the book where special offers are built into the problem. Students will need to be careful to take the special offers into account before drawing a conclusion.

Plenary

Which is better value?

a) A 300 gram packet of sweets with 20% extra free for £1.50, or

b) A 500 gram packet of sweets with 15% extra free for £2.35?

(a: 2.4 grams per penny, b: 2.44 grams per penny, so b)

Exercise commentary

Question 1 – Each of these questions can be worked out by dividing the cost of the item by the monthly amount (and carefully rounding *up*).

Question 2 – Part **a** requires simple subtraction before linking into previous work on fractions and percentages in part **b** and pie charts in part **c**. Students may been reminding how to calculate the angles in a pie chart.

Questions 3 and **4** – Ensure students take account of the special offers before trying to compare the value for money.

Question 5 – This question can be used to stimulate discussion about price changes due to inflation, the more general concept of budgeting when salaries, costs and prices are changing and about prioritising spending.

Answers

1. a 7 months   b 8 months
   c 4 months   d 16 weeks

2. a £300
   b Accommodation: $\frac{5}{12}$
   Food Shopping: $\frac{1}{6}$
   Household bills: $\frac{1}{24}$
   Transport: $\frac{1}{20}$
   Other essentials: $\frac{3}{40}$
   Left Over: $\frac{1}{4}$
   c Angles 200°, 80°, 20°, 24°, 36°
   d Only an estimate as there is only approximately 4 weeks in a month as most months have a couple of extra days, making the weekly wage an estimate. Therefore, Laura's weekly wage is slightly less than this.

3. He should by Mountain Brand, as with the offer it is £1.20 per 100g whereas Club Coffee is £1.33 per 100g.

4. 50% off: £0.38 per 100g
   50% extra: £0.50 per 100 g
   Therefore, 50% off is a better deal

5. Students' answers, referring to non-essentials such as entertainment

Financial maths 2: Living on a budget

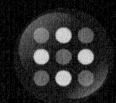

15 Ratio and proportion – MySummary

Key outcomes	Quick check
Solve problems involving direct proportion. L6	a 7 pencils cost 84 pence. What would 9 pencils cost? (£1.08) b 5 litres of diesel fuel costs £6.00. What would 8 litres cost? (£9.60)
Use percentages to compare proportions. L6	John scores 18 out of 20 in a maths test and Jemima scores 22 out of 25 in a chemistry test. Who got the best mark? (John: 90%, Jemima 88%)
Calculate with ratios, including dividing quantities in a given ratio. L6	a Divide £35 in the ratio 3: 4. (£15: £20) b A map has the scale 1: 20 000. If a road on the map measures 2.5cm, how far is it in real life? (500 m)
Solve problems involving ratio. L7	The ratio of boys to girls in a particular school is 2 : 3. If there are 375 girls, how many students are there all together? (625)
Calculate a percentage increase or decrease. L6	a Increase £450 by 15%. (£517.50) b Decrease 384kg by 12%. (337.92kg)

MyMaths extra support

Lesson/online homework	Description
Porportion 1037 L5	An introduction to simple proportion problems
Ratio dividing 1 1038 L5	Dividing amounts in a given ratio from the basics
Ratio introduction 1052 L4	Dividing patterns and simplifying ratios

MyReview

15 MySummary

Check out
You should now be able to ...

	Test it Questions
✓ Solve problems involving direct proportion.	1 – 2
✓ Use percentages to compare proportions.	3
✓ Calculate with ratios, including dividing quantities in a given ratio.	4 – 6
✓ Solve problems involving ratio.	7 – 8
✓ Calculate a percentage increase or decrease.	9 – 11

Language	Meaning	Example
Direct proportion	Two quantities that are related so that when one is multiplied by a number, the other is multiplied by the same number.	If text messages cost 5 pence each, then the number of text messages is proportional to the cost of the text messages.
Divide in a ratio	To share out a quantity into a number of (usually) unequal parts.	£60 divided in the ratio 2 : 1 is £40 : £20.
Simplify a ratio	To write a ratio in its simplest form by dividing by common factors.	28 : 14 can be simplified to 2 : 1 by dividing both parts by the common factor 14.
1 : n	A ratio that has been simplified so that the first number is 1.	4 : 10 can be divided by 4 to give the equivalent ratio 1 : 2.5
Percentage change	The percentage increase or decrease that changes an original amount to a new amount.	A car that cost £20 000 is now worth £15 000. This is a percentage reduction of 25%.

15 MyReview

1. 200 g of butter costs £1.28. What is the cost of 250 g of the same butter?

2. A 150 g sharing pack of crisps contains 1.35 g of salt. How much salt is in a single 35 g bag of the same crisps?

3. 67 out of 98 students passed test A and 268 out of 400 students passed test B. Which test had the higher percentage of students passing?

4. Write each of these ratios in its simplest form.
   a. 16 : 32 : 24
   b. 40 seconds : 3 minutes

5. a. Divide 600 m in the ratio 7 : 5.
   b. Divide £117 in the ratio 2 : 8 : 3.

6. Write each of these ratios in the form 1 : n.
   a. 5 : 12
   b. 150 cm : 2.25 m

7. A map has a scale of 1 : 15000.
   a. What distance does 4 cm on the map represent in real life?
   b. What length on the map represents a real-life measurements of 1.2 km?

8. The ratio of strawberry to raspberry yoghurts is 3 : 4. What proportion of the yoghurts are strawberry?

9. 20% of a quantity is £19. Calculate the whole amount.

10. A pair of trainers is reduced from £60 to £45. What was the percentage reduction in price?

11. 5 lb is approximately the same is 2.27 kg.
    a. Calculate the single multiplier that converts pounds (lb) to kg.
    b. Calculate the single multiplier that converts kg to pounds (lb).

What next?

Score	
0 – 4	Your knowledge of this topic is still developing. To improve look at Formative test: 3B-15; MyMaths: 1036, 1039, 1103, 1245 and 1302
5 – 9	You are gaining a secure knowledge of this topic. To improve look at InvisiPen: 136, 153, 154, 191, 192, 193, 194 and 195
10, 11	You have mastered this topic. Well done, you are ready to progress!

Question commentary

Question 1 – Students may calculate the cost of 1 g (0.64p) or 50 g (32p) of butter first.

Question 2 – Students could be advised to use the unitary method: ÷150 and then × 35.

Question 3 – A: 68%, B: 67%.

Question 4 – Students must take care with the units in part **b**: first convert to 40 : 180 (seconds). Ensure answers are fully simplified.

Question 5 – Part **a**: 12 parts, each worth 600 ÷ 12 (50m), part **b** 13 parts, each worth 117 ÷ 13 (£9). Students should check their answers add up to the original amount.

Question 6 – Students need to divide both sides by the number on the left. For part **b**, convert both sides to either cm or m first.

Question 7 – Students should convert final answers to sensible units.

Question 8 – Students sometimes think this is $\frac{3}{4}$.

Question 9 – You may need to explain to students that this means they need to find 100% of the amount, so they could × 5.

Question 10 – A common mistake is to divide the difference by the new price (£45) instead of the original price (£60), giving 33%.

Question 11 – Students could write these as a ratio and convert to the form 1 : n or n : 1.

Answers

1. £1.60
2. 0.315 g
3. A
4. a. 2 : 4 : 3   b. 2 : 9
5. a. 350 m, 250 m   b. £18, £72, £27
6. a. 1 : 2.4   b. 1 : 1.5
7. a. 600 m   b. 8 cm
8. $\frac{3}{7}$ or 42.9%
9. £95
10. 25%
11. a. 0.454   b. 2.20 (2dp)

15 MyPractice

1 Use direct proportion to solve these problems.
  a 3 litres of lemonade cost £2.13.
  What is the cost of 5 litres of lemonade?
  b There are 21 sweets in a packet.
  The mass of the packet is 336g.
  What is the mass of a packet of 30 sweets?
  c 12 inches is approximately 30 cm.
  i How many centimetres are equal to 20 inches?
  ii How many inches are equal to 100 cm?

15a

2 Statistics are given for three strikers over the course of a football season.
Write the number of goals scored as a proportion of the number of shots taken for each of these strikers.
  a Andrews   12 goals   48 shots
  b Roland   15 goals   40 shots
  c Tonaldo   22 goals   55 shots
Who is the best striker? Explain your answer.

15b

3 At the pony club there are 23 girls and 7 boys.
At the dance club there are 14 girls and 5 boys.
Which club has the higher proportion of boys?
Write your answer as a percentage (rounded to 1dp where appropriate).

4 Write these ratios in their simplest form.
First change the quantities into the same units.
  a £5 : 350p   **b** 4kg : 2500g
  c 12cm : 50mm   **d** 250ml : 30cl

5 Work out these quantities, giving your answers to 2dp where appropriate.
  a Divide 60 pears in the ratio 7 : 5.
  b Divide £300 in the ratio 2 : 3.

15c

6 At a school the ratio of boys to girls is 4 : 5.
There are 572 boys at the school. How many children are there at the school?

7 A model of a yacht is built to a scale of 1 : 24.
The length of the yacht is 15.6m.
What is the length of the model yacht?

15d

8 a John bought a CD in a sale and saved £5.20.
The label said that it was a 40% reduction.
What was the original price of the CD?
  b A mobile phone costs £240. In a sale the price is reduced to £204.
What is the percentage reduction?

15e

9 a Kelvin is choosing between two different offers for firewood.
In which of these offers are the numbers in direct proportion?
In each case explain and justify your answers.

Offer A

Mass of wood (kg)	Cost
3	£7.68
5	£12.80
10	£25.60

Offer B

Mass of wood (kg)	Cost
10	£28
50	£135
100	£260

  b Kelvin decides to buy 50kg of firewood.
How much cheaper is offer A?

10 For each of these problems
  i find the single multiplier that connects the quantities
  ii solve the problem.
  a 75g of cheese contains 30g of fat.
How many grams of fat are there in 120g of cheese?
  b A recipe for six people uses 420g of flour.
How much flour is needed for the same recipe for 11 people?
In part **b** assume the cost is in direct proportion.
  c 1.5 litres of fruit drink cost 87p.
What is the cost of 5 litres of fruit drink?

15f

284 Number Ratio and proportion

Question commentary

Question 1 – Students will likely use the unitary method (or a variation thereof) to solve these problems.

Questions 2 and **3** – Students should be encouraged to work in percentages to provide direct comparisons.

Questions 4 and **5** – Remind students to work in consistent units (question **4**).

Questions 6 and **7** – Students may divide the value given in question **6** by 9 instead of 4.

Question 8 – Encourage students to use a general approach to percentage change problems and think about a formula: Percentage change = change/original amount.

Questions 9 and **10** – Working with single multipliers links back to the work on the unitary method and percentage change.

Answers

1.   a   £3.55   b   480 g
     c   i   50 cm   ii   40"

2. Andrews 25%, Roland 38%, Tonaldo 45%
Tonaldo has the highest proportion of goals

3. Pony club 23.3%, Dance club 26.3%
Dance club

4.   a   10 : 7   b   8 : 5   c   12 : 5   d   5 : 6

5.   a   35, 25   b   £120, £180

6. 1287 children

7. 65 cm

8.   a   £13   b   15%

9.   a   Offer A is in direct proportion, cost is constant at £2.56/kg
     Offer B is not, cost per kg varies
     b   £4

10. a   i   0.4   ii   48 g
     b   i   70   ii   770 g
     c   i   58   ii   £2.90

MyPractice

16 Probability

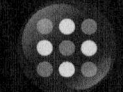

Learning outcomes

P1 Record, describe and analyse the frequency of outcomes of simple probability experiments involving randomness, fairness, equally and unequally likely outcomes, using appropriate language and the 0-1 probability scale (L6)

P2 Understand that the probabilities of all possible outcomes sum to 1 (L6)

P3 Enumerate sets and unions/intersections of sets systematically, using tables, grids and Venn diagrams (L7)

P4 Generate theoretical sample spaces for single and combined events with equally likely, mutually exclusive outcomes and use these to calculate theoretical probabilities (L6/7)

Introduction

The chapter starts by reviewing the language of probability and chance. Mutually exclusive events are looked at along with calculating probabilities from single events. Outcomes from two trials are then covered along with sections on experimental probability and comparing theoretical and experimental probabilities. The final section looks at Venn diagrams and sets.

The introduction discusses how manufacturers test products in order to find out the probability of them breaking, etc. The focus is on cars but nearly all consumer products are tested in a similar way using small samples across the production range. Manufacturers will set limits as to the acceptable failure rate (2%, or 5% for example) before a batch is thrown out or tested more extensively. This kind of probability analysis is covered in much more detail at A level but there is enough scope to discuss the general strategies with Key Stage 3 students.

It might also be interesting to discuss the ethical implications of allowing faulty goods to make it into the market place, linking to cross-curricular issues with, for example, Religious Studies.

Prior knowledge

Students should already know how to...
- Draw a probability scale and use the language of probability
- Calculate simple probabilities for single events
- Convert between fractions, decimals and percentages

Starter problem

The starter problem looks at the probability of picking numbered cards from a bag. The problem is a two-event situation where you pick one card, replace it and pick a second card. For the first card you pick, there is a 1/3 chance you will get each number. This probability is repeated for the second card and therefore we have three options which will give the desired result: 1 followed by 1, 2 followed by 2 and 3 followed by 3. The probability of 1 followed by 1 is 1/3 × 1/3 = 1/9 and this is the same for each of the other two successful results. So our overall probability is 1/9 + 1/9 + 1/9 = 3/9 = 1/3.

This problem could be solved using a sample space diagram or a tree diagram and students could be invited to solve alternative problems using a similar approach. What if there were four cards in the bag, for example?

Resources

MyMaths
Listing outcomes	1199	Probability intro	1209	Relative frequency	1211
The OR rule	1262	Experimental probability	1264		

Online assessment
Chapter test	3B–16
Formative test	3B–16
Summative test	3B–16

InvisiPen solutions
Probability scale	451	Finding probabilities	452
Probability rules	453	Mutually exclusive events	454
Experimental and theoretical probability			461
Outcomes	462	Tree diagrams	463
Further experimental probability			464

286 **Statistics and probability** Probability

Topic scheme

Teaching time = 7 lessons/3 weeks

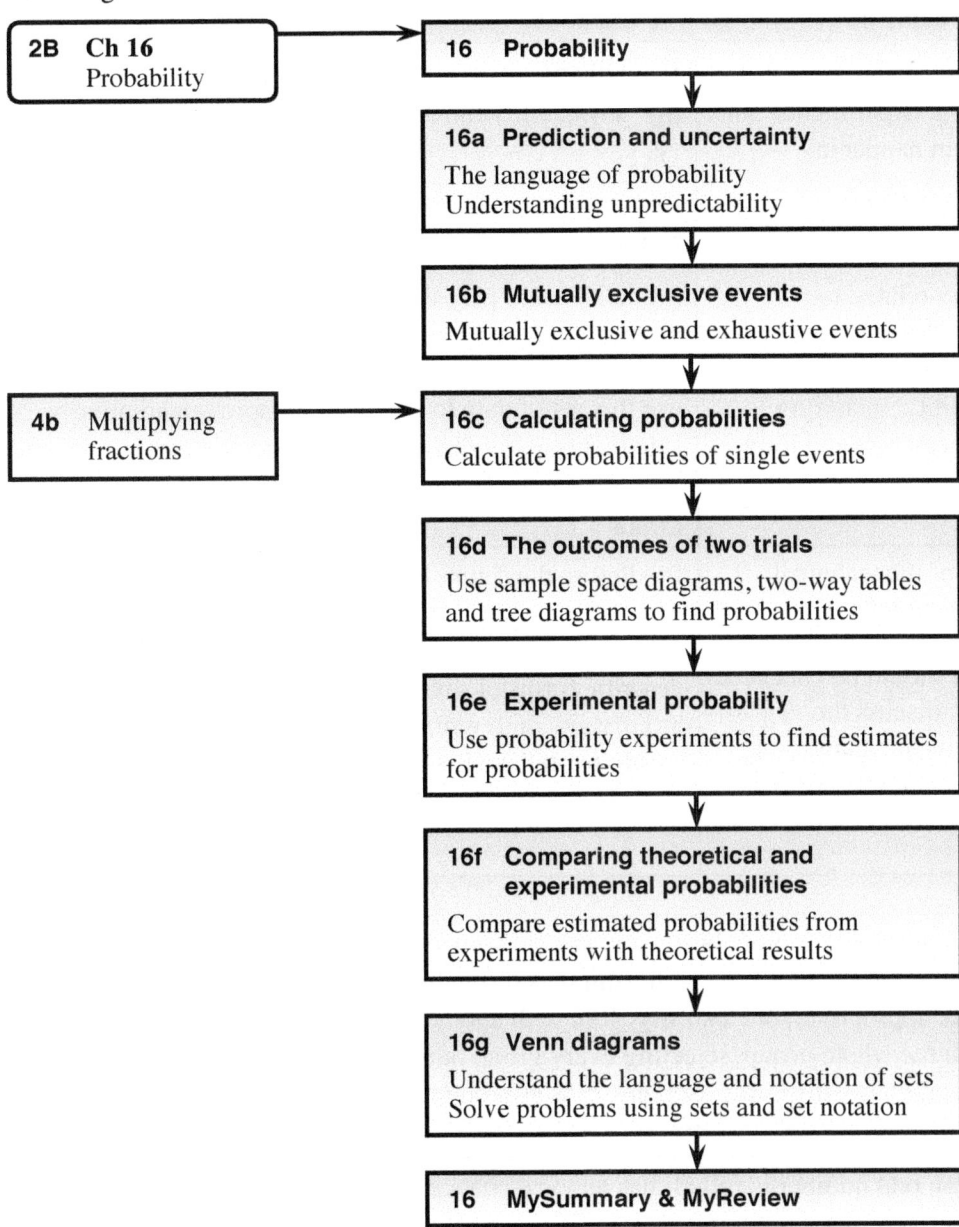

```
2B  Ch 16
    Probability
```
→
16 Probability

↓

16a Prediction and uncertainty
The language of probability
Understanding unpredictability

↓

16b Mutually exclusive events
Mutually exclusive and exhaustive events

↓

```
4b  Multiplying
    fractions
```
→
16c Calculating probabilities
Calculate probabilities of single events

↓

16d The outcomes of two trials
Use sample space diagrams, two-way tables and tree diagrams to find probabilities

↓

16e Experimental probability
Use probability experiments to find estimates for probabilities

↓

16f Comparing theoretical and experimental probabilities
Compare estimated probabilities from experiments with theoretical results

↓

16g Venn diagrams
Understand the language and notation of sets
Solve problems using sets and set notation

↓

16 MySummary & MyReview

Differentiation

Student book 3A   288 – 307
The language of probability
Mutually exclusive events
Calculating probabilities from single events and two events; counting outcomes
Experimental probability
Venn diagrams and sets

Student book 3B   286 – 305
The language of probability
Mutually exclusive events
Calculating probabilities from single events and two events
Experimental probability and its comparison to theoretical outcomes
Venn diagrams, sets and set notation

Student book 3C   278 – 297
The language of probability
Independent events
Tree diagrams and the probability of combined events
Experimental probability
Simulation
Venn diagrams and sets

16a Prediction and uncertainty

Objectives	
• Appreciate that random processes are unpredictable	(L5)
• Interpret results involving uncertainty and prediction	(L5)

Key ideas	Resources	
1 Results may be unpredictable, but experiments can help show the probability of them happening	Probability intro Dice Counters	(1209)

Simplification	Extension
Use question **1** to review vocabulary related to probability. What other words could be used and how do they compare to the terms given? Use questions **2** to **4** to discuss key ideas about probability, including variability ('the apparatus has no memory') and long-term predictability.	Students could play the game shown in question **5** several times and record their results (or pool their results with those from other groups). They could then use this set of data to make some more quantitative statements about the likely results of the game.

Literacy	Links
Involve students fully with the use of the technical vocabulary and also encourage reflection on equivalent descriptions of values (fraction, decimal or percentage) Spoken explanations and reasoning should be checked for its sense and logic, for example: discuss the meaning of the comment about sports and games on the first page of the lesson. Does it communicate fully the reasoning behind the statement? Could you provide a clearer statement?	Predicting the future by the use of supernatural means is called divination, one of Harry Potter's curriculum subjects at Hogwarts. There is a list of words used to describe forms of divination at http://www.dailywritingtips.com/words-for-telling-the-future/

Alternative approach
Select key vocabulary, used in previous work on probability, and ask students to work in pairs on two or three of these in order to provide an explanation of what each is, with examples if it helps. Differentiate by allocating the words to pairs as appropriate. Where appropriate, one pair may join with another pair to share and discuss. Use the students' final explanations with the whole group, selecting every group but each word only once. Again, this may be differentiated by selecting certain questions for each group as appropriate.

Checkpoint	
A fair dice is rolled. The outcome 'an odd number is rolled' has an even chance, true or false?	(True)
The same dice is rolled. The outcome 'a prime number is rolled' has an even chance, true or false?	(True)
(Good opportunity to dispel any misconception that 1 is a prime number)	

Starter – Four in a line

Ask students to draw a 5 × 5 grid and enter numbers between 2 and 12 inclusive. Numbers can be used more than once but not more than three times. Throw two dice. Students cross out one occurrence of the total. The winner is the first student to cross out four in a line.

Teaching notes

Many students are uncomfortable with probability because they regard mathematics as something where there are 'correct answers' and uncertainty does not sit well with that view. The presence of randomness does not mean you know nothing about what is going on, even though it obviously means that you do not know exactly what will happen. Encourage students to take the view that the study of probability will help them to have a realistic view of the likely outcomes in uncertain situations.

Ask each student to write a whole number between 1 and 6 and say that you are going to play a game. You will throw a fair dice, and they score a point if the dice does not show their number and lose a point if it does.

Throw the dice and then ask students who lost a point if they want to change their number.

Discuss whether it makes any difference which number they choose. Would they prefer the points to be awarded the other way round? Does it help to change the number?

Plenary

Eric was asked to toss a coin four times and said he got TTTT. Heather was asked to throw a dice four times and said she threw 3333. Should the teacher be suspicious that either student did not do the experiment for themselves? Can the teacher be certain in either case? Should he be equally suspicious? (Four the same in a coin toss occurs with probability $\frac{1}{8}$ but for a dice it is $\frac{1}{216}$.)

Exercise commentary

Question 1 – The range of values is inclusive of 1 and 100.

Question 2, 3 and **4** – These questions allow discussion of some important common misconceptions. In question **2**, can anyone estimate the probability of landing on green, either from the size of the sector or from Becky's results? In question **4**, could any of the coins be biased?

Question 5 – This simple game illustrates some key points about variability and predictability. Seven is the most likely 'winner', but other scores can win, especially in a shorter race.

Answers

1. **a** Certain (the computer only chooses whole numbers).
   b Evens chance (that leaves half of the possible outcomes)
   c Very unlikely (there is only one three-digit number that could be chosen).
2. It is likely that the other students' results will be similar to Becky's, but you should not expect them to be identical.
3. The dice have no memory, so the probability of Alesha getting doubles again remains the same as it was the first two times – $\frac{1}{6}$.
4. Andy's results look suspicious - it is highly unlikely that a real coin would alternate in this way. Similarly, Dean's results look very unlikely - a real coin would be very unlikely to produce a set of results like this.
5. In the long run, you should find that numbers in the middle do best, with a score of 7 being the favourite. However, especially over a short 'race', other scores could do better.

Prediction and uncertainty

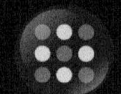

16b Mutually exclusive events

Objectives	
• Identify all the mutually exclusive outcomes of an experiment	(L6)

Key ideas	Resources
1 Understand and recognise events that are mutually exclusive 2 Be able to list all these outcomes	The OR rule (1262) Mutually Exclusive Events Card Sort (TES): http://www.tes.co.uk/teaching-resource/Mutually-Exclusive-Events-Cardsort-6295745/

Simplification	Extension
This lesson formalises some of the vocabulary of probability: events, outcomes, exclusive and exhaustive. Some students will benefit from working in pairs or small groups to develop their own definitions of these terms, perhaps comparing and improving their definitions after working on the exercise.	The whole numbers 1 to 10 are the possible outcomes of an experiment. Ask students to define two events that **are** collectively exhaustive but **are not** mutually exclusive. Now define events for the other possible combinations: exclusive but not exhaustive, *etc*.

Literacy	Links
The key words mutually exclusive and exhaustive may be familiar to the pupils but they are unlikely to be comfortable with them, and less likely to use them themselves. Consequently spend sufficient time to establish and cement this vocabulary through the activities.	Roulette is a game of chance which originated in France in the eighteenth century. Players bet on where they think a ball will come to rest when it is spun inside a numbered horizontal wheel and can choose to bet on either individual numbers or groups of numbers. The amount won depends on the probability of the ball landing on that particular choice, however the odds are always in favour of the bank. There is a picture of a roulette wheel at http://en.wikipedia.org/wiki/File:Rwheel.jpg

Alternative approach

Use a card sort such as that referenced from the TES, where pairs of students can divide events into two groups – mutually exclusive events or not. They may not recognise the names for each group as yet, but through discussion will be able to identify the differences in the nature of the events. This activity can then be used as a clear introduction to the terms, with the students themselves describing the reasoning. Extend the activity by asking students to find some more events that would fit clearly into either group. This activity may be a time for students to consider finding the probability of an event NOT happening, as it may occur naturally. If so, go with it and use this opportunity. This can lead towards examination of exhaustive outcomes, and listing them. Further listing activities can also be found on TES resources.

Checkpoint

Cards showing the numbers from 1 to 8 inclusive are placed in a bag. **a** List the outcomes belonging to the event 'a prime number'. **b** Are the events 'a prime number' and 'an even number' mutually exclusive?

(**a** 2, 3, 5, 7 and **b** NO)

Starter – Make one

Give students fractions or decimals between 0 and 1. Ask students to give the fraction or decimal that would add to make one. For example,

$\frac{5}{8}$, 0.65, $\frac{17}{24}$, ... ($\frac{3}{8}$, 0.35, $\frac{7}{24}$)

Can be extended by giving two numbers and asking for the third number needed to make 1 or can be varied by including percentages.

Teaching notes

Students often think very abstractly about this material and need to be encouraged to think explicitly about the basic outcomes. (To see if there are any common outcomes, rather than try to decide abstractly.)

Ask students to construct as many pairs of mutually exclusive events that they can think of when throwing an ordinary dice. Which of these pairs are also exhaustive? Ask students to construct exhaustive pairs of events which are not mutually exclusive.

Plenary

Ask students to construct as many pairs of mutually exclusive events that they can think of for the cards in question **4**. Which of these pairs are also exhaustive? Ask students to construct exhaustive pairs of events which are not mutually exclusive.

Exercise commentary

Question 1 – These events are also exhaustive.

Question 2 – Encourage students to give detailed reasons for their answers here.

Question 3 – Each card is a separate outcome and there are 11 altogether.

Question 4 – Remind students that the number 1 is not prime but that 2 is prime. These questions allow discussion of some important common misconceptions.

Question 5 – This question allows discussion between students or as a class.

Answers

1. **a** **i** 2, 4 and 6   **ii** 1, 3, 5
   b These events are mutually exclusive because there is no outcome that belongs to both of them.
2. **a** The three results are mutually exclusive because only one of them can happen; it is impossible for more than one of these results to happen at the same time.
   b The three results are collectively exhaustive because between them they cover all of the possibilities.
3. **a** There are 11 possible outcomes - the chosen card can be P, R, O, B, A, B, I, L, I, T, or Y.
   (Note that although there are only 9 different letters, there are 11 different cards that could be chosen, so the experiment has 11 possible outcomes.)
   b There are 4 cards with vowels - O, A, I, I.
   c There are 7 cards with consonants - P, R, B, B, L, T and Y.
   d The events A and B are mutually exclusive: they have no outcomes in common.
   e The events A and B are collectively exhaustive: between them they include all of the possible outcomes.
4. **a** A = {2, 3, 5, 7}   B = {1, 3, 5, 7, 9}
   C = {2, 4, 6, 8, 10}   D = {1, 2, 3, 4, 6, 12}
   b **i** True: no outcomes in common.
   ii True: every number is either odd or even.
   iii False: the number 2 belongs to both events.
   iv False: there are outcomes that belong to neither event.
5. **a** This is true – because the events are collectively exhaustive, and between them they include all of the possible outcomes.
   b This is also true – because the events are mutually exclusive, and there is no possible outcome that belongs to both events.

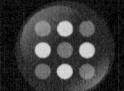

16c Calculating probabilities

Objectives

- Know that if the probability of an event occurring is p then the probability of it not occurring is $1 - p$ (L6)
- Know that the sum of probabilities of all mutually exclusive outcomes is 1 and use this when solving problems (L6)

Key ideas	Resources
1 Know and apply the rule for finding the probability of an event not happening 2 Refreshing finding theoretical probabilities.	The OR rule (1262)

Simplification	Extension
Some students may benefit from a very structured approach to calculating theoretical probabilities. For example, listing and counting the outcomes belonging to particular events. The distinction between an outcome (each of the possible results of a trial) and an event (a subset of the possible outcomes) is important, and worth reviewing here. The exercise also provides an opportunity to revisit techniques for converting between fractions, decimals and percentages.	Ask students to plot the probabilities P(A) and P(not A) on a probability scale, for a variety of events A, and to note any patterns arising. Since P(not A) = 1 − P(A), the pairs of probabilities are arranged symmetrically around the probability value of 0.5.

Literacy	Links
Continue to stress equivalence of responses using fractions, decimals and percentage. Encourage discussion about which is best or easiest to use in various contexts. Check or recap on the notation associated with probability. Encourage students to use the correct notation themselves. Include the notation P'(A) relating to probability of event A not occurring.	From 1711 until 1960, decks of playing cards printed and sold in the UK were subject to tax and were sealed with a special wrapper. Until 1862, the Ace of spades was used to show that the tax had been paid. An official version was printed with an ornate design bearing the maker's name. Even today the Ace of Spades is usually very ornate and shows the name of the manufacturer. There is more about the history of playing cards at http://www.wopc.co.uk/cards/collecting.html

Alternative approach

Question 7 should be tackled in pairs and given sufficient thinking and discussion time. It can act as a model for similar situations such as those found in the Standards Unit Box S2, referenced. Select a small number of the situations, differentiated appropriately, for each student pair. Student pairs may share their findings and reasoning with the whole group after sufficient time.

Checkpoint

A 5p coin and a 1p coin are flipped together. What is the probability of getting two heads? What is the probability of *not* getting two heads? Explain your reasoning. (P(HH) = ¼, P'(HH) = ¾, reasoning indicates an understanding of the total number of outcomes, and also that 1 − ¼ = ¾)

Statistics and probability   Probability

Starter – Events

Ask students whether pairs of events obtained by rolling a six-sided dice are mutually exclusive, collectively exhaustive, both or neither. For example

An odd number, a factor of 12   (Collectively exhaustive)
A prime number, a factor of 6   (Neither)
A multiple of 2, a factor of 15   (Both) *etc.*

Teaching notes

Probabilities can be expressed as fractions, decimals or percentages (but not as ratios, or in 'odds form' – the way betting odds are given). Review working with different types of numbers and converting between them.

For weaker students, reviewing subtraction of fractions and decimals from 1 may be helpful before starting to calculate probabilities of an event not happening. Also, discussing what to do if the probability is given as a percentage.

Encourage students to write down the probabilities as fractions in their most immediate form before cancelling to an equivalent simplest form or converting into a decimal or percentage. Emphasise that the probability work finishes at the point of identifying the number of 'successes' and the total number of outcomes but accuracy and confidence in working with numbers is important.

Plenary

Students can work in pairs to ask their partner to calculate more probabilities for the contexts in questions **6** and **7**.

Exercise commentary

Question 1 and **2** – An opportunity to review the connections between fractions, decimals and percentages.

Question 3 – A basic question about complementary probability.

Question 4 and **5** – Some students may need to be reminded that 1 is not prime but that 2 is.

Question 6 – Note the difference between parts **c** and **d** and parts **e** and **f**. In parts **e** and **f**, eight is not included in either list.

Question 7 – Students may need reminding that there are 26 letters of the alphabet.

Question 8 – This question explores the distinction between 'outcomes' and 'equally likely outcomes'.

Answers

1 **a** P(2) = $\frac{1}{6}$ = 0.167 = 16.7%

   b P(3 or 4) = $\frac{1}{3}$ = 0.333 = 33.3%

   c P(a prime number) = ½ = 0.5 = 50%

2 **a** P(not 2) = $\frac{5}{6}$ = 0.833 = 83.3%

   b P(neither 3 nor 4) = $\frac{2}{3}$ = 0.667 = 66.7%

   c P(not a prime number) = ½ = 0.5 = 50%

3 P(not A) = $\frac{13}{16}$, P(not B) = 0.08, P(not C) = 87.5%

4 **a** P(even number) = ½ = 0.5 = 50%

   b P(multiple of 3) = $\frac{3}{10}$ = 0.3 = 30%

   c P(factor of 18) = $\frac{3}{10}$ = 0.3 = 30%

   d P(prime number) = $\frac{2}{5}$ = 0.4 = 40%

5 P(not an even) = ½ = 0.5 = 50%

   P(not a multiple of 3) = $\frac{7}{10}$ = 0.7 = 70%

   P(not a factor of 18) = $\frac{7}{10}$ = 0.7 = 70%

   P(not a prime number) = $\frac{3}{5}$ = 0.6 = 60%

6 **a** 0.01   **b** 0.5   **c** 0.25   **d** 0.75
   e 0.07   **f** 0.92

7 **a** P(a vowel) = $\frac{5}{26}$ = 0.192 = 19.2%

   b P(not a vowel) = $\frac{21}{26}$ = 0.808 = 80.8%

   c P(after 'T') = $\frac{3}{13}$ = 0.231 = 23.1%

   d P(not in the word 'dog') = $\frac{23}{26}$ = 0.885 = 88.5%

8 Phil's calculation is incorrect, because he cannot assume that all three outcomes are equally likely.

Calculating probabilities

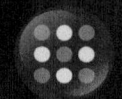

16d The outcomes of two trials

Objectives
• Use diagrams and tables to record in a systematic way all possible mutually exclusive outcomes for single events and for two successive events (L6) • Use tree diagrams to represent outcomes of two or more events and to calculate probabilities of combinations of independent events (L7)

Key ideas	Resources
1 Both use and interpret two-way tables recording the outcomes of two trials 2 Use and interpret tree diagrams for recording the outcomes of two or more events.	Listing outcomes (1199)

Simplification	Extension
One difficulty for some students is that two very different-looking diagrams (a two-way table or a tree diagram) are used to represent exactly the same set of information. It may be worth making the connections between the two representations explicit. For example, by asking students to trace out the route through a tree diagram that results in the outcome shown in a particular cell in a table.	Students who are confident with the use of these diagrams can be asked to indicate the sets of outcomes that correspond to particular events. For example, shade the cells in a table that correspond to the event 'a total score greater than 8'.

Literacy	Links
Both two-way tables and tree diagrams should have been met before, but students may not be comfortable with them yet. Note that tree diagrams may be representing event outcomes either from left to right or from top to bottom. It will be worth discussing the advantages and disadvantages of tables or tree diagrams within any given context with the students.	Quantum mechanics is a branch of physics which is concerned with the behaviour of atoms and even smaller sub-atomic particles. Tiny particles sometimes behave like particles and sometimes like waves. They are so small that the traditional laws of physics do not apply and their behaviour can only be described in terms of the probability that something will happen. There is a brief introduction to quantum mechanics at http://library.thinkquest.org/3487/qp.html

Alternative approach
The students met the idea of recording outcomes in a table in earlier work on probability, and as such they can be encouraged to consider ways of recording the outcomes from a number of situations for themselves. Present the students with a small number of events, such as the results of multiplying the scores of 2 dice together, finding the difference betwween the scores of 2 dice; throwing 2, 3 or even four coins to examine the head/tail combinations; and so on. Request that they examine all the outcomes posssbile as a pair, examining ways in which to record their results. After sufficient thinking and discussion time, pairs can share with each other and further results shared with the whole group. Tree diagrams *may* not arise naturally, so if they do not occur be prepared to model these in addition. Select two contrasting situations in order to encourage the students to review and discuss the advantages and disadvantages of each strategy.

Checkpoint
Two fair dice are rolled. What is the probability of: a rolling a total of 3? $\quad(\frac{2}{36}$ or $\frac{1}{18})$ b rolling a total of 7? $\quad(\frac{6}{36}$ or $\frac{1}{6})$ c rolling a total of 1? $\quad(0)$

Statistics and probability   Probability

Starter – Dice bingo

Ask students to draw a 3 × 3 grid and enter nine numbers from the following list.

1 2 3 4 5 6 8 9
10 12 15 16 18
20 24 25 30 36

Roll two dice. Students cross out the product of the scores if it is in their grid. The winner is the first student to cross out all nine of their numbers.

Teaching notes

Sample-space diagrams are ways of showing possible outcomes for two trials methodically. The outcomes can also be written in a list, and with small numbers of outcomes this is relatively easy to do. Writing a list for the second example (36 outcomes) would be difficult unless it was done methodically. Writing all the cases where one appeared on the first throw, then the twos, *etc.* which is the structure of the table form reading across the rows.

The table structure shows the outcomes of the two trials by the row and column headings, allowing the cell either to contain the 'outcome' written as (2, 5) or to contain some function of it, such as the sum (shown) or the product (in question **6**).

Plenary

Ask students to compare the sample-space diagrams in the second example and for part **a** of question **6**. What is the most likely sum on two dice? What is most likely product? Can they explain why there is such a strong pattern to the outcomes for the sum but not for the product?

Exercise commentary

Questions 1, 2 and 3 – Simple examples of tree diagrams and two-way tables to represent the outcomes of multi-stage processes.

Question 4 – Requires students to make an appropriate choice of representation.

Question 5 – Works backwards from a list of outcomes to a sample-space diagram.

Question 6 – Part **a** is revisited in the **plenary**. In part **b** a 'four-way' table cannot sensibly be drawn.

Answers

1   a   Two levels, two outcomes at each level. W/L on each set of branches
    b

	Win	Lose
Win	(Win, Win)	(Win, Lose)
Lose	(Lose, Win)	(Lose, Lose)

    c   {(win, win), (win, lose), (lose, win), (lose, lose)}

2   a

	Red	Amber	Green
Red	(Red, Red)	(Red, Amber)	(Red, Green)
Amber	(Amber, Red)	(Amber, Amber)	(Amber, Green)
Green	(Green, Red)	(Green, Amber)	(Green, Green)

    b   Two levels, three outcomes at each level. R/A/G on each set of branches
    c   {(red, red), (red, amber), (red, green), (amber, red), (amber, amber), (amber, green), (green, red), (green, amber), (green, green)}

3   a   Two levels, two outcomes at each level. P/F on each set of branches.
    b   {(pass, pass), (pass, fail), (fail, pass), (fail, fail)}

4   See master Answers file

5   a   Two levels, two outcomes on the first, three on the second. First level P/F, second level C/P/F.
    b

	Credit	Pass	Fail
Pass	(Pass, credit)	(Pass, pass)	(Pass, fail)
Fail	(Fail, credit)	(Fail, pass)	(Fail, fail)

    c   Various answers

6   a   A two-way table is a good choice here - there are too many combinations to show on a tree diagram.

    b   A tree diagram should be used here – it would not be possible to show all four stages of the experiment on a two-way table.

The outcomes of two trials

16e Experimental probability

Objectives	
• Compare experimental and theoretical probabilities in a range of contexts	(L7)
• Understand relative frequency as an estimate of probability and use this to compare outcomes of experiments	(L7)

Key ideas	Resources	
1 Understanding the links between experimental and theoretical probability 2 Using and interpreting relative frequency in order to estimate probability	Relative frequency Experimental probability	(1211) (1264)
	Coins Simulations of exp. probability: Spinners, dice: http://www.shodor.org/interactivate/activities/ExpProbability/ Coin tossing: http://nlvm.usu.edu/en/nav/frames_asid_305_g_3_t_5.html	

Simplification	Extension
Some students may benefit from being given further examples using manageable numbers, before moving on to consider the effect of larger sample sizes in improving estimates of experimental probability. For example, question 1 could be extended to the results of aiming at different sectors of the dart board: Tim hit the treble twenty 4 times out of 20, the double sixteen 6 times out of 12, and so on.	Students who are confident with these techniques can be asked to apply them to further experiments. For example, by examining a sample of text to estimate the probability that an English word chosen at random contains the letter 'e'. Students could be asked to compare the estimated probabilities obtained as the sample of text used increases in length.

Literacy	Links
The key word in this section is estimation. Students should be encouraged to discuss fully what this means in the context of probability. This also needs linking to an understanding that where we know a theoretical probability, any experiment may not replicate the result exactly.	The planet Neptune was the first planet to be found using mathematical prediction instead of observation. Astronomers noted that the orbit of the planet Uranus did not follow Newton's laws and predicted that there must be another planet exerting a gravitational pull that was affecting the orbit. Neptune was discovered on September 23rd 1846, within one degree of the predicted location. There is more information about Neptune at http://www.nmm.ac.uk/explore/astronomy-and-time/astronomy-facts/solar-system/neptune

Alternative approach
Simple simulations such as those given in the first two referenced resources, can be used to introduce and rehearse the notion of experimental probability with students. In these situations the theoretical probability can be easily deduced and compared. Invite the students to speculate how an experiment may help to analyse a situation where theoretical results are unknown. Use a simulation of such a situation for demonstration – a more complex version of that used in 2B, 16d, for example where a closed 'bag' contains three colours of counters or cubes, say twenty in all. Students will need to use the results of the experiment in order to suggest possible numbers of each colour. A more challenging situation – Cereal Boxes – may be used with some of the pupils.

Checkpoint	
A coin is tossed 120 times. If the coin lands on heads 88 times, what is the experimental probability of 'landing on heads'?	($\frac{88}{120}$ or $\frac{11}{15}$)
Do you think the coin is biased towards heads?	(impossible to tell)

Starter – Money, money, money!

Ask students to imagine a regular pentagonal spinner, labelled 2p, 5p, 10p, 20p and 50p, being spun twice. Ask questions, for example

    What is the probability of the total amount being an even number? ($\frac{17}{25}$)
    Being greater than 50p? ($\frac{9}{25}$)

    Being a prime number? ($\frac{2}{25}$) *etc*.

Can be differentiated by the choice of questions.

Teaching notes

Students need some practical experience of the variability of outcomes in order to appreciate the difficulty of using relative frequencies to estimate probabilities.

Give students, working in pairs, three coins. Ask each pair of students to toss the coins 20 times and record how often they get two heads and one tail in a row showing. Collect all the results on the board so that students can see the range of values and which come up most often.

Discuss how best to use all this information to estimate the probability of getting two heads and one tail in a row and whether they think they could calculate an exact probability (using the tree diagrams from the previous lesson).

Plenary

Students need to realise that experimental probabilities should not be used where an exact probability can be calculated. Toss an ordinary coin nine times (or any odd number of times) and calculate the relative frequency of heads which appear. Discuss with the class whether this should be used in place of 0.5 as an estimate of the probability that the next toss will be a head. Would it make a difference if the experiment had an even number of trials?

Exercise commentary

Question 1 – This question provides the framework for working with experimental probability.

Question 2 – This question involves improving estimates of experimental probability by increasing the number of trials in the experiment.

Question 3 – This question acts as a reminder that it cannot always be assumed that outcomes are equally likely.

Question 4 – This question should stimulate discussion about avoiding making predictions from past results.

Answers

1   a   60   b   13   c $\frac{13}{60} = 0.217 = 21.7\%$

2   a   Dan: 0.37
          Caz: 0.32
          Charlie: 0.325

    b   Charlie's results should be most reliable as his experiment had the greatest number of trials.

    c $\frac{118}{350} = 0.337$

3   a   Because the pieces of paper were not all the same size and shape.
    b   M = 0.24, A = 0.04, T = 0.08, H = 0.46, S = 0.18

4   The statement might be reasonable but there are a number of factors that should be taken into account. For example, have the players in the team changed significantly since last season? Are the other teams comparable? And so on.

Experimental probability

16f Comparing theoretical and experimental probabilities

Objectives		
• Compare experimental and theoretical probabilities in a range of contexts		(L7)
• Appreciate the difference between mathematical explanation and experimental evidence		(L7)

Key ideas	Resources	
1 Using a knowledge of experimental and theoretical probability in order to make informed decisions about bias or fairness.	Experimental probability	(1264)

Simplification	Extension
Some students may need to be reminded of the formulae for theoretical and experimental probabilities; these are sufficiently similar to cause some confusion and the distinction between them should be made clear.	Students who can confidently apply the techniques of this exercise can be encouraged to identify significant differences between theoretical and experimental probabilities. Even quite large departures from theoretical probabilities are little evidence for bias with a small number of trials. However, when differences persist as the number of trials increases, bias should be suspected. For example, students could be asked to calculate the experimental probability of a Club using just the first row of data in question **3**; then using the first two rows, three rows, *etc.*, comparing the results to the theoretical probability each time.

Literacy	Links
The notion of estimation needs to be referred to often. Check that students also have a clear concept of the meaning of both fairness and bias. This section relies heavily on the speaking and listening skills of the students and their ability to reason convincingly. As such, it also offer plenty of opportunities for such argument building to be rehearsed.	To eliminate any possible bias in the UK National lottery, the numbers are drawn by one of eleven machines. The machine to be used each particular week is chosen at random. http://www.lottery.co.uk/statistics/ lists the number of times that each ball has been drawn as a winning number in the National Lottery. Which number has been drawn the most number of times and which has been drawn the least?

Alternative approach
Prepare a range of results from some simple situations in table form, clearly showing the source of the experiment such as a diagram of a spinner, or dice. Ask students to decide whether the results seen are likely to reflect the expected results. The two areas to concentrate on with the students in terms of discussion are: how close any results are compared to those 'expected' and to raise questions either of the accuracy of the results or the fairness of the situation represented. In each area, students need to realise that they may not be fully convinced of a final answer, but may have a leaning towards their answer based on the evidence.

Checkpoint
A fair dice is rolled. What is the theoretical probability of rolling a factor of 6?   ($\frac{4}{6}$ or $\frac{2}{3}$) If I roll the dice 100 times, and I roll 17 '4s' and 23 '5s', what is the experimental probability of rolling 'a factor of 6'?   (0.6, $\frac{6}{10}$ or 60%)

Starter – Jumble

Write a list of anagrams on the board and ask students to unscramble them and then make up their own. Possible anagrams are

TRIPMEXENE, CYNQUERFE, VEXSHUTIAE, HAIRCLOTTEE, VEXICULES, TRAVONIIA, PRIDETALCEBUN, BOTIRYPALIB

(experiment, frequency, exhaustive, theoretical, exclusive, variation, unpredictable, probability)

Teaching notes

Students are often surprised at how much variability there is when experiments are repeated. They are often very happy in principle that different outcomes may occur but still expect the observations to be much closer to the average than it will actually be. For example, when tossing ten fair coins there is a greater than one in three chance that you will get a difference of at least four between the numbers of heads and tails.

Part of the difficulty is that if the number of heads is lower than expected, then the number of tails must be higher than expected so the difference appears very large.

Plenary

The language that students use to make comparisons between theoretical and experimental probabilities is important. Ask for volunteer feedback of the explanations and comparisons students made in the exercise to allow weaker students to hear how others have articulated their reasoning.

Exercise commentary

Question 1 – A useful opportunity to discuss how big a departure from 50% should be expected.

Question 2 – Another useful opportunity to review the effect of sample size.

Question 3 – Check that students know what cards are included in a British pack of playing cards.

Question 4 – See **16d** for a reminder of how to draw the sample-space diagram if necessary.

Answers

1. a P(Head) = 0.585
   b P(Tail) = 0.415
2. a 0.1, 0.12, 0.14, 0.16   b $\frac{1}{6} = 0.167$
   c The experimental probability approaches the theoretical probability as the number of trials increases.
3. a i   P(♣) = 16/60 = 0.267
      ii P(red card) = 30/60 = 0.5
      iii P(2, 3, 4) = 12/60 = 0.2
   b Theoretical probabilities are 0.25, 0.5 and 0.231 respectively. The experimental results are close to the theoretical values.
4. a, b

	First dice					
	1	2	3	4	5	6
1	2	3	4	5	6	7
2	3	4	5	6	7	8
3	4	5	6	7	8	9
4	5	6	7	8	9	10
5	6	7	8	9	10	11
6	7	8	9	10	11	12

(Second dice on vertical axis)

Total	2	3	4	5	6	
Theoretical probability	0.03	0.06	0.08	0.11	0.14	
Relative Frequency	0.01	0.06	0.07	0.17	0.13	
Total	7	8	9	10	11	12
Theoretical probability	0.17	0.14	0.11	0.08	0.06	0.03
Relative Frequency	0.21	0.09	0.07	0.08	0.08	0.03

  c Yes, the experimental and theoretical probabilities are similar; you would not expect them to be exactly equal.

Comparing theoretical and experimental probabilities

16g Venn diagrams

Objectives
- Enumerate sets and unions/intersections of sets systematically using Venn diagrams (L7)

Key ideas	Resources
1 Understand sets and subsets 2 Use Venn diagrams to work out probabilities 3 Derive the OR rule	The OR rule (1262)

Simplification	Extension
Problems involving algebra such as question **4** can be avoided. The notation associated with the Venn diagrams could be explained in words rather than symbols to help the students visualise the regions of the Venn diagram they are to consider.	Students could be encouraged to explore the idea of conditional probability. Using the example in question **3**, what is the probability that a member chosen at random does kickboxing *given that* they do aerobics? ($\frac{10}{18}$ or 0.556). Similar problems to this could be given to the students and they could also be asked to try to develop an understanding of independence of events and formalise more of the algebra of probability. Three region Venn diagrams can also be explored.

Literacy	Links
The language of sets, for example 'universal set', 'subset' and 'proper subset'. The mathematical notation associated with sets.	This is a nice topic to link to aspects of the history of mathematics. John Venn, the inventor of Venn diagrams, was born in 1834 and was a contemporary of another famous mathematician called Charles Dodgson. Dodgson also went on to develop techniques for analyzing probability using diagrams. His diagrams are called Carroll diagrams since Charles Dodgson is better known as Lewis Carroll, the author of the Alice in Wonderland books! http://lewiscarrollsociety.org.uk/index.html

Alternative approach
Students could be given a set of probabilties and the associated Venn diagram and asked to work out what the question was. For example, in a Venn diagram with numbers 3, 5 and 2 across the three regions in the circles and 2 outside, the probability $\frac{3}{12}$ represents the probability of A and not B.

Checkpoint
A set comprises the first 15 whole numbers. Are the following proper subsets?

a The factors of 15. (Yes)

b Prime numbers under 20. (No)

c {1, 2, 4, 8, 16}. (No)

d Integers less than 16. (No)

Statistics and probability   Probability

Starter – Factors Game

Ask students to choose three two-digit numbers (e.g. 12, 15 and 17). 'Randomly' generate one- and two-digit numbers and ask students to tick off each time they get a factor of one of their three numbers (each generated number can be used for more than one of theirs). The winner is the person who collects all their factors first.

Teaching notes

The concept of sets and subsets are covered first of all. Students need to be able to define the universal set, the empty set and what it means to be a proper subset. You can check understanding of these concepts by providing examples such as those given in the exercise.

Work on Venn diagrams follows and there are two main things to think about: Firstly, how can probabilities be worked out from the Venn diagram, and secondly, the shading of specific regions. Students may have trouble visualizing the regions indicated by the notation so further practice on this could be provided, or word descriptions instead of notation.

Plenary

Identify the region. By taking a standard '2-circle' Venn diagram, ask students to write down, either using notation or in words, the regions indicated by, for example, the 'moon-shaped' section of B plus the 'moon-shaped' section of A (A or B but not both). This can be tailored for ability and regions combined as appropriate.

Exercise commentary

Question 1 – Reiterate the definition of mutually exclusive and encourage further examples of elements from the intersection if they exist.

Question 2 – Make sure the full definition of proper subset is understood before proceeding.

Question 3 – Students may need help identifying the correct region(s) for parts **b** to **e**. Word descriptions could be used to simplify this.

Question 4 – By introducing an unknown into the problem, students will have to think more carefully about what each region in the Venn diagram represents

Question 5 – Students may need to refer to the first Venn diagram on the previous page for part **a**. In part **b**, they need to recognise that the intersection is 'double counted'.

Answers

1 a Not mutually exclusive, 2
   b Mutually exclusive
   c Not mutually exclusive, 1
   d Not mutually exclusive, 35

2 a No, 4 is in A but not in Z
   b Yes, B is contained in Z but not equal to it
   c Yes, C is contained in Z but not equal to it
   d No, 4 is in D but not in Z

3 a $\frac{1}{3}$
   b The 'moon-shaped' part of A
   c $\frac{4}{15}$
   d The whole region apart from the overlapping circles
   e $\frac{2}{3}$

4 a As the sum of all the areas of the Venn diagram is 40
   b i   0.5
      ii 0.6
      iii 0.8
      iv 0.1
   c $x = 6$, $P(A' \cup B) = 0.6$
   d If you are in set A you are also in set B.

5 a Circles do not overlap
   b $P(A \cup B) = P(A) + P(B) - P(A \cap B)$

Venn diagrams

16 Probability – MySummary

Key outcomes	Quick check
Generate sample spaces for events and use these to calculate probabilities. L6	By using a sample space diagram or otherwise, calculate the probability of rolling a total score of 8 when two fair dice are rolled. ($\frac{5}{36}$)
Understand that the probabilities of all possible outcomes sum to 1. L6	A biased coin is such that the probability of tossing a head is 0.6. What is the probability of tossing a tail? (0.4)
Analyse the frequency of outcomes of simple probability experiments. L7	A scientist decides to test the hypothesis that toast usually lands butter side down. He carries out 100 experiments and the toast lands butter side down on 72 of these occasions. Estimate the probability of toast landing butter side down. ($\frac{72}{100}$ or $\frac{18}{25}$ or 0.72)
Enumerate sets using Venn diagrams. L7	X = {1, 2, 4, 8, 16, 32}. Is the set Y = {factors of 16} a proper subset of X? (Yes)

MyMaths extra support

Lesson/online homework	Description
Simple probability 1210 L5	Using the probability scale from 0 to 1, and fractions to describe probabilities
Probability revision 1263 L7	Basic revision of all the probability learnt so far, including listing outcomes in a table and using two-way tables

MyReview

16 MySummary

Check out
You should now be able to ...

	Test it → Questions
✓ Generate sample spaces for events and use these to calculate probabilities.	1 – 4
✓ Understand that the probabilities of all possible outcomes sum to 1.	5
✓ Analyse the frequency of outcomes of simple probability experiments.	6 – 7
✓ Enumerate sets using Venn diagrams.	8

Language	Meaning	Example
Experiment	A series of trials.	Tossing a dice 100 times is an experiment.
Trial	An activity that you can record the result of.	Rolling a dice is a trial.
Outcome	Possible result of a trial.	The possible outcomes of rolling a dice are 1, 2, 3, 4, 5, 6.
Event	A set of outcomes.	'Rolling an even number' on a dice is an event.
Mutually exclusive	Events that cannot both happen together.	Raining and not raining are mutually exclusive events.
Exhaustive	All the possible outcomes of a trial.	'An even score' and 'an odd score' on a dice.
Relative frequency	An estimate of probability from experimental data.	Weather forecasters use patterns to estimate the probability of rain.
Probability	A measure of how likely an event is to occur.	'The probability of rain tomorrow is $\frac{3}{10}$.'

16 MyReview

1. Two dice are thrown. State if these pairs of events are mutually exclusive
   a 'one of the dice shows a 3' and 'the sum of both dice is 7'
   b 'one of the dice shows and even number' and 'the product of the two dice is even'
   c 'one of the dice shows a 4' and 'the difference between the dice is 5'

2. A card is chosen at random from a set of digit cards from 1 to 20. Find the probability of each of these events.
   a P(even number) b P(odd number)
   c P(multiple of 3) d P(prime number)

3. A letter from the word SUMMER is chosen at random. Find the probability of each of these events.
   a P(R)   b P(M)
   c P(a vowel)   d P(P)

4. Two fair dice are thrown and the numbers multiplied together.
   a Construct a two-way table which shows the sample space.
   b Calculate the probability of getting a product of more than 12.

5. A fair dice is thrown twice and each time it is recorded whether it is a 6 or not a 6. Record the outcomes on a tree diagram.

6. Aidan is practising on a putting green. He records how many shots per hole in the table.

Shots	1	2	3+
Frequency	3	11	4

   Estimate the probability Aidan take 3 or more shots.

7. A five-sided spinner is spun 20 times and the results recorded.

   1 4 5 3 5
   2 4 3 4 3
   3 5 4 2 3
   4 3 5 1 4

   a Calculate the relative frequency of each number.
   b Calculate the theoretical probability of each number.
   c Do you think the spinner is fair?

8. Ω = {the integers 1 to 10}
   A = {multiples of 2}
   B = {factors of 18}
   a Draw a Venn diagram to show this information.
   b Shade the region A' ∩ B.
   c Find P(A' ∩ B).
   C = {multiples of 4}
   d What can you say about the sets A and C?
   e What can you say about the sets B and C?

What next?

Score		
	0 – 3	Your knowledge of this topic is still developing. To improve look at Formative test: 3B-16; MyMaths: 1199, 1209, 1211, 1262 and 1264
	4 – 6	You are gaining a secure knowledge of this topic. To improve look at InvisiPen: 451, 452, 453, 454, 461, 462, 463, 464, 472, 474, 475 and 476
	7, 8	You have mastered this topic. Well done, you are ready to progress!

Question commentary

In general, theoretical probabilities are given as fractions and experimental probabilities are given as decimals. Fractions need not always be fully simplified.

Question 1 – Students could list the possible outcomes and identify which are used for each event.
Question 2 – Answers need not be fully simplified.
Question 3 – Answers need not be fully simplified.
Question 4 – 'More than 12' should not include 12.
Question 5 – Check for students drawing tree diagram with 6 branches instead of 2 - this would be very time consuming and probably untidy. Discuss why a sample space diagram would not be suitable for this.
Question 6 – The answer should be a decimal (4÷18).
Question 7 – The frequency of each number in brackets: 1(2), 2(2), 3(6), 4(6), 5(4). Discuss how you could investigate further e.g. more trials.
Question 8 – The Venn diagram should have the two circles labelled as A and B. Ensure students are also drawing a box around the circles to represent the universal set.

Answers

1. a No   b No   c Yes
2. a 0.5   b 0.5   c 0.3   d 0.4
3. a $\frac{1}{6}$ b $\frac{1}{3}$ c $\frac{1}{3}$ d 0
4. b $\frac{13}{36}$
5. Tree diagram with 4 branches, correctly labelled
6. 0.22
7. a 0.1, 0.1, 0.3, 0.3, 0.2   b All 0.2
   c Could be fair, results not unreasonable, not enough evidence.
8. a,b

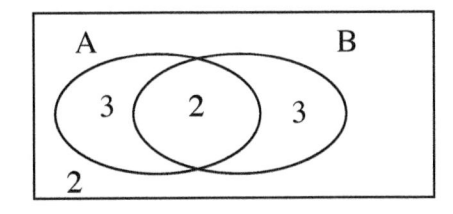

   Venn diagram: Universal set box with circles A and B overlapping. A contains 3, intersection contains 2, B contains 3, outside contains 2.

   b The 'moon-shaped' part of B
   c 0.3
   d C is a proper subset of A
   e B and C are mutually exclusive

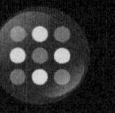

16 MyPractice

16a

1 Kate puts cards marked with each whole number from 1 to 100 into a box and then picks a card at random.
   Give an example of an outcome that is
   a Certain
   b Impossible
   c Very unlikely
   d An even chance.

16b

2 A computer is used to choose a number between 1 and 1000.
   Give examples of
   a a set of three events that are exhaustive
   b a set of four events that are mutually exclusive.

3 Peter rolls a red dice and a blue dice.
   The event X is 'The product of the scores on the two dice is odd'.
   The event Y is 'The score on the red dice is 4'.
   a Explain why the events X and Y are mutually exclusive.
   b Explain why the events X and Y are not exhaustive.

16c

4 Two 'Jokers' are added to an ordinary pack of 52 playing cards. A card is picked at random.
   a Find the probability that the card chosen is a Joker.
   Give your answer as a fraction in its simplest terms, a decimal and a percentage.
   b Use your answers to part a to find the probability that the chosen card is not a Joker.
   Give your answer in all three forms.

5 James deals these four cards from a pack of 20 cards labelled 1 to 20.

   3   16   5   1

   What is the probability that the next card dealt from the remaining pack is a prime number?
   Give your answer as a percentage.

16d

6 A brown bag contains three cards marked A, B and C.
   A white bag contains two cards marked X and Y.
   Shayla picks a card at random from each bag.
   Show all the possible outcomes using
   a a two-way table
   b a tree diagram.

7 This two-way table shows the possible outcomes when Ben chooses cards from two boxes.

	1	2	3
A	(A, 1)	(A, 2)	(A, 3)
B	(B, 1)	(B, 2)	(B, 3)

   Draw a tree diagram to show this set of outcomes.

16e

8 Steve was practising his basketball shooting and scored 9 times out of 32 attempts.
   Estimate the probability of Steve scoring with his next shot.

9 A radio show played 24 songs one morning.
   Nine of these songs were by solo female artists.
   Use this information to estimate the probability of the first song played in the next day's programme being by a female solo artist.

10 A technician checked the maintenance records for a computer network.
   He found that the server had crashed on 43 days over the past year.
   a Use this data to estimate the probability that the server crashes on any day chosen at random.
   b He was not told whether the data was for a leap year.
   Explain why this does not make much difference.

16f

11 Carol tested a dice and got three 6s out of six rolls.
   a Is there enough evidence to suggest that the dice is biased?
   Explain your answer.
   b Carol carried on testing the dice and ended up with 18 sixes in 60 rolls.
   Is there now enough evidence to suggest that the dice is biased?
   Explain your answer.

16g

12 Decide whether each set is a proper subset of Ω = {1, 2, 3, 4, 5, 6, 7, 8, 9, 10}
   a A = {4, 7, 9}   b B = {0, 3, 8}   c C = {factors of 10}   d D = {multiples of 3}

Question commentary

Question 1 – Students can make up whatever outcomes they like. There is an opportunity for 'creativity' in some of the parts.

Questions 2 and **3** – Again, encourage (sensible) creativity in question **2**. Emphasise the need for clear explanations in question **3**.

Questions 4 and **5** – Students may need reminding of the basic structure of a pack of playing cards. The link between fractions, decimals and percentages can also be explored.

Questions 5 and **7** – Both questions allow students to compare the two representations.

Question 8 to **10** – Experimental probabilities should be given as decimals.

Question 11 – This question allows discussion about the weight of evidence in favour of claims such as bias. Discourage students from jumping to too many conclusions and discuss how further evidence might be obtained.

Question 12 – Students may find listing the elements of the sets in parts **c** and **d** useful.

Answers

1 Students' answers.
2 Students' answers.
3   a   Events X and Y cannot happen together.
    b   There are outcomes that are contained in neither event X nor event Y.
4   a   P(Joker) = $\frac{1}{27}$ = 0.037 = 3.7%
    b   P(not Joker) = $\frac{26}{27}$ = 0.963 = 96.3%
5   37.5%
6   a

	A	B	C
X	(X,A)	(X, B)	(X, C)
Y	(Y, A)	(Y, B)	(Y, C)

    b   Two levels, three outcomes at level 1, two outcomes at level 2
7   Two levels, three outcomes at level 1, two outcomes at level 2
8   P(score) ≈ $\frac{9}{32}$ = 0.281 = 28.1%
9   P(solo female) = $\frac{3}{8}$ = 0.375 = 37.5%
10 a $\frac{43}{365}$ = 0.118
    b   If it was a leap year, we should divide by 366 instead of 365, giving $\frac{43}{366}$ = 0.117
11 a   This is suggestive of bias but not conclusive
       P(six) ≈ $\frac{3}{6}$ = 0.5
       P(6|fair) = $\frac{1}{6}$ = 0.167, and P(666|fair) = $\frac{1}{216}$
       = 0.0046
    b   P(six) ≈ $\frac{18}{60}$ = 0.3 but with more certainty
       In 60 rolls expect 6 to occur 60 × $\frac{1}{6}$ =10 times.
       P(18 sixes out of 60|fair) = 0.008.
12 a   Yes   b   No
    c   Yes   d   Yes

Case Study 6: Crime scene investigation

Related lessons		Resources	
Deriving and graphing formulae	3e	Conversion graphs	(1059)
Real life graphs	6g	Distance time graphs	(1132)
Distance-time graphs	6h	Scatter graphs	(1213)
Correlation	8h	Trial and improvement	(1057)
Constructing equations	10d	Standard form large/small	(1051, 1049)
Trial and improvement	10e	Soft pencils, clear sticky tape	
Standard form for large/small numbers	11d, 11e	Magnifying glasses	

Simplification	Extension
Students could think about the scenario in task **1** with fewer windows to begin with to try to build up a pattern of how the combinations work. In task **2**, students could be given guidance that the solution lies between 14 and 15 before narrowing the solution down to one decimal place. Students may need help graphing the data in task **4**. Prepared axes with scales marked will help to ensure they have enough room to extend their graph to answer part **g**.	Braking efficiency has not been included in the tyre marks equation; the equation that is given assumes 100% efficiency. Discuss how that might not be the case in reality and show a revised equation that takes into account efficiency: $s = \sqrt{90 \times L \times F \times E}$, where E = braking efficiency. Students could research information on braking efficiency, maybe including the minimum braking efficiency required by the MoT test and find the effect that different efficiencies would have on the results.

Links
An interesting website on DNA matching can be found at: http://science.howstuffworks.com/life/genetic/dna-evidence4.htm How to remember stopping distances in your driver theory test: http://tips.drivingtestsuccess.com/learner-car/stopping-distances-theory-test-uk/

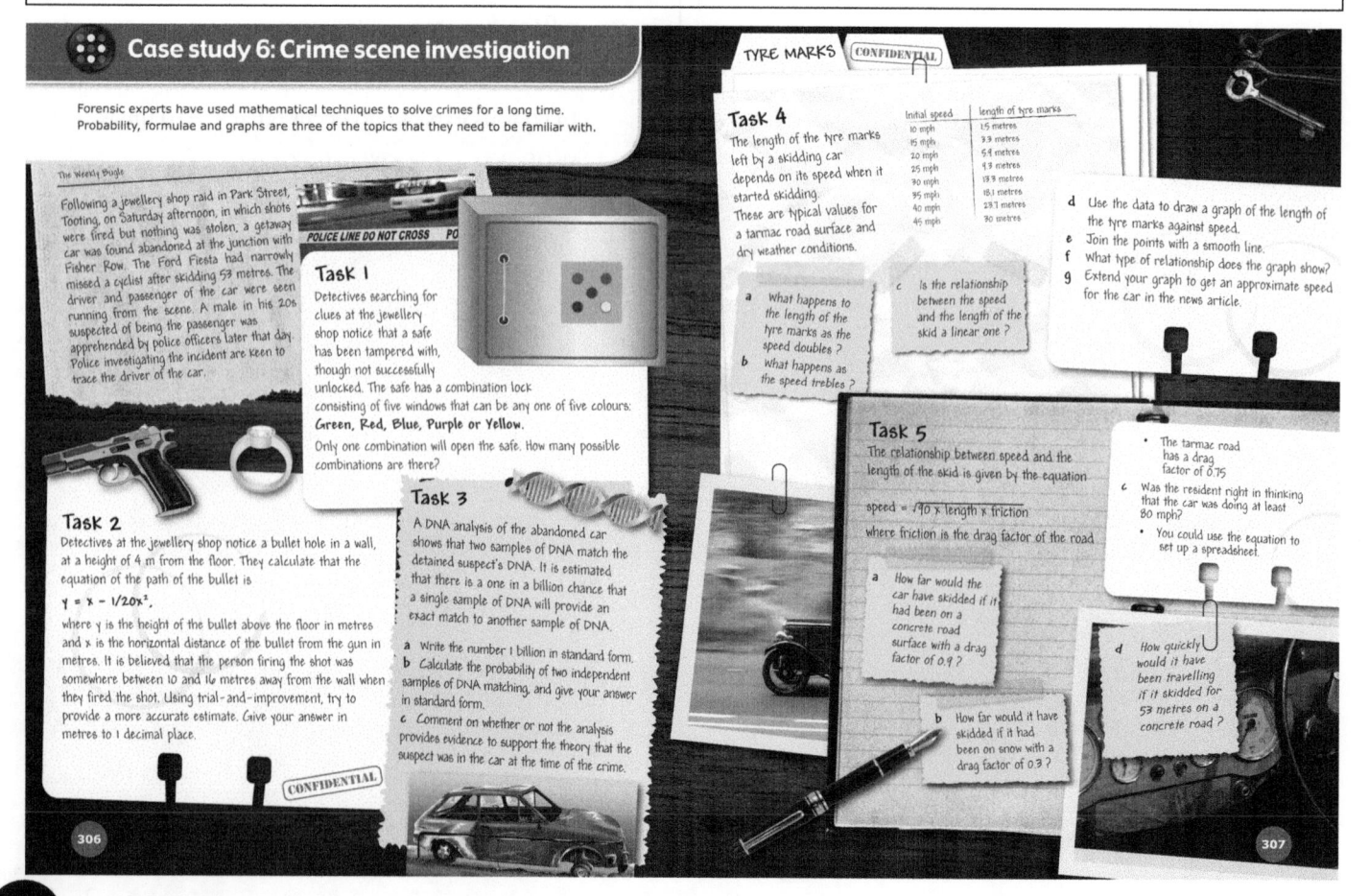

Case study 6: Crime scene investigation

Forensic experts have used mathematical techniques to solve crimes for a long time. Probability, formulae and graphs are three of the topics that they need to be familiar with.

The Weekly Bugle

Following a jewellery shop raid in Park Street, Tooting, on Saturday afternoon, in which shots were fired but nothing was stolen, a getaway car was found abandoned at the junction with Fisher Row. The Ford Fiesta had narrowly missed a cyclist after skidding 53 metres. The driver and passenger of the car were seen running from the scene. A male in his 20s suspected of being the passenger was apprehended by police officers later that day. Police investigating the incident are keen to trace the driver of the car.

Task 1
Detectives searching for clues at the jewellery shop notice that a safe has been tampered with, though not successfully unlocked. The safe has a combination lock consisting of five windows that can be any one of five colours: Green, Red, Blue, Purple or Yellow.

Only one combination will open the safe. How many possible combinations are there?

Task 2
Detectives at the jewellery shop notice a bullet hole in a wall, at a height of 4 m from the floor. They calculate that the equation of the path of the bullet is

$y = x - \frac{1}{20}x^2$,

where y is the height of the bullet above the floor in metres and x is the horizontal distance of the bullet from the gun in metres. It is believed that the person firing the shot was somewhere between 10 and 16 metres away from the wall when they fired the shot. Using trial-and-improvement, try to provide a more accurate estimate. Give your answer in metres to 1 decimal place.

CONFIDENTIAL

Task 3
A DNA analysis of the abandoned car shows that two samples of DNA match the detained suspect's DNA. It is estimated that there is a one in a billion chance that a single sample of DNA will provide an exact match to another sample of DNA.

a Write the number 1 billion in standard form.
b Calculate the probability of two independent samples of DNA matching, and give your answer in standard form.
c Comment on whether or not the analysis provides evidence to support the theory that the suspect was in the car at the time of the crime.

Task 4
The length of the tyre marks left by a skidding car depends on its speed when it started skidding. These are typical values for a tarmac road surface and dry weather conditions.

Initial speed	length of tyre marks
10 mph	1.5 metres
15 mph	3.3 metres
20 mph	5.9 metres
25 mph	9.3 metres
30 mph	13.3 metres
35 mph	18.1 metres
40 mph	23.7 metres
45 mph	30 metres

a What happens to the length of the tyre marks as the speed doubles?
b What happens as the speed trebles?
c Is the relationship between the speed and the length of the skid a linear one?
d Use the data to draw a graph of the length of the tyre marks against speed.
e Join the points with a smooth line.
f What type of relationship does the graph show?
g Extend your graph to get an approximate speed for the car in the news article.

Task 5
The relationship between speed and the length of the skid is given by the equation

$speed = \sqrt{90 \times length \times friction}$

where friction is the drag factor of the road.

a How far would the car have skidded if it had been on a concrete road surface with a drag factor of 0.9?
b How far would it have skidded if it had been on snow with a drag factor of 0.3?
c Was the resident right in thinking that the car was doing at least 80 mph?
• You could use the equation to set up a spreadsheet.
d How quickly would it have been travelling if it skidded for 53 metres on a concrete road?

• The tarmac road has a drag factor of 0.75

Teaching notes

Read The weekly Bugle article together and ask students to identify all the actual information that it contains and any speculation, such as the speed that the car was travelling at.

Ask, how might the police be able to identify the driver and passenger?

They could get descriptions from any witnesses and they could take fingerprints from the car.

Task 1

Initially it might seem like there will be many, many combinations, but only 3125 different combinations doesn't seem enough, or does it? What would the number of combinations jump to if numbers 0 to 9 were used instead of colours? Is a safe's combination any more or less secure using colours than numbers? Do the students think that a colour-coded combination would be easier to remember than a number-coded one? Ask students to write down as many phone numbers for people that they know. It is likely that this number will be very small, given that we all programme numbers into our phones and then don't need to memorise them. Not so with passwords. How many passwords do students use for all the websites and services that they use? Is it safe to make them all the same password?

Task 2

Students could be asked to graph the equation on paper, or by using a digital geometry software package. How would such a graph help them with this problem? (Plot the graphs of $y = x - \frac{1}{20}x^2$ and $y = 4$)

Task 4

For the second part of the case study, look together at the table of speeds and lengths of tyre marks. Give students a few minutes to consider the questions on the grey notes before discussing their ideas.

Ask, does the length of the skid double when the speed doubles? How did you find out?

Hear their thoughts and elicit that the length does not double but that it is approximately quadrupled. Discuss how you can find out by comparing the lengths for any two speeds where one speed was double the other. As the lengths in the table are rounded to 1 decimal place, rounding errors will be magnified when the smaller length is multiplied by 4.

Then discuss what happens if the speed is trebled before asking, what do you think will happen if the speed is quadrupled? Hear ideas and establish that the length will be 16 times longer. Check that this is about right by looking at the data for 10 mph and 40 mph.

Discuss how rounding errors have been magnified even more this time.

Task 5

Finally, look at the equation that relates length of skid to speed. Discuss how the friction of the road surface needs to be included as a car will stop more quickly on a dry road than on a wet or icy road.

Using the information by the equation, give the students a few minutes to find out what speed the car in the article was travelling at. Check that students can use the equation (the speed is 59.8 mph) and then give them time to try the questions on the notes. They could work in groups to set up two spreadsheets: one that finds skid lengths from given speeds and drag factors and the other that finds initial speeds from given skid lengths and drag factors.

Answers

1. $5^5 = 3125$
2. 14 gives 4.2, 15 gives 3.75. 14.4 gives 4.032, 14.5 gives 3.9875. To one decimal place, $x = 14.5$ m
3. a 1×10^9 b 1×10^{18}
   c It is extremely strong evidence
4. a 4 times as long
   b 9 times as long
   c non-linear
   d Students' graphs
   e Quadratic relationship
   f 60 mph
5. a 44.4 m b 133.3 m
   c Wrong, the formula gives 59.8 mph
   d 65.5 mph

Crime scene investigation

MyAssessment 4

These questions will test you on your knowledge of the topics in chapters 13 to 16.
They give you practice in questions that you may see in your GCSE exams.
There are 95 marks in total.

1 a Find the term-to-term rule of each of these linear sequences.
      i 27, 31, 35, 39, 43, …   ii 77, 67, 57, 47, 37, …   (4 marks)
   b For each sequence in **a**, find the position-to-term rule in words and hence
      give the equation for the general term.   (6 marks)
   c Use the general term to find the value of the 20th term of each sequence. (2 marks)

2 The amount of fuel left (in litres) in a car after n days $T(n) = 45 - 4n$.
   a Write a sequence for the amount of fuel during the first week. (2 marks)
   b How much fuel is left after 11 days?   (2 marks)

3 A group of walkers are dropped off 50 km from their home base and walk back
   at an average pace of 5 km per hour.
   a Generate a sequence for the number of km they are from their home base. (2 marks)
   b Write a term-to-term rule and hence find the position-to-term rule. (3 marks)
   c Find an expression for $T(n)$, the total number of km travelled after n hours. (3 marks)
   d How long does it take the group to reach the home base?   (1 mark)

4 a For each of these shapes determine the number of faces, vertices and edges. (3 marks)
      i   ii   iii 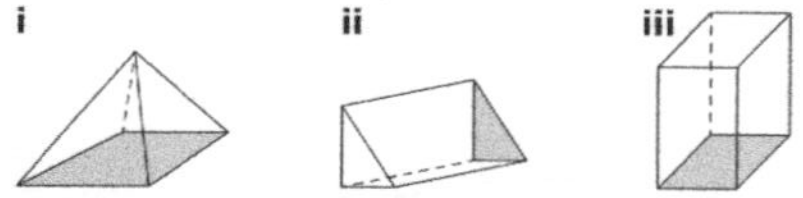
   b What names are associated with each of these shapes?   (3 marks)

5 a Copy this 8-cube shape onto squared grid paper.   (2 marks)
   b Draw the elevations and plan views of
      this solid on squared grid paper.   (6 marks)

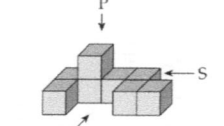

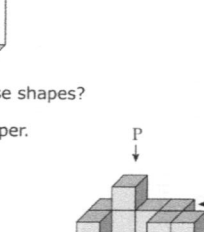

6 a For the shapes shown in question 4 give the number of planes of
      reflection symmetry.   (3 marks)
   b For the shapes in question 4 draw the net of each shape.   (6 marks)

7 For each of these triangular prisms calculate
   a the surface area   (8 marks)   b the volume.   (4 marks)
      i   ii

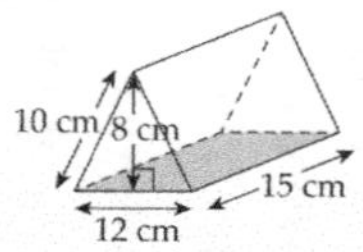

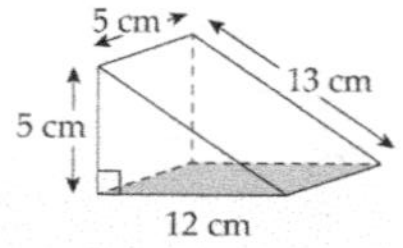

8 a 250 g of butter is used to make a Queen Victoria Sponge.
      How much butter is needed to make 5 sponges?   (2 marks)
   b 18 litres of diesel costs £25.00.
      How much diesel can you get for £40?   (2 marks)

9 The World's land area is about 150 million km². Europe's land area
   is approximately 10 million km². What proportion of the World's land
   area is occupied by Europe? Give your answer to 1 dp.   (6 marks)

10 The area occupied by the World's oceans is 360 million km² and that of the
   land is 150 million km². Write this as a ratio in its simplest form. (2 marks)

11 a A map has a scale of 1 : 10000.
      What distance does 4.6 cm on the map represent?   (2 marks)
   b A model plane has a wingspan of 22 cm.
      If the scale is 1 : 32 what is the actual length of the wing?   (2 marks)
   c In a bag there are 10 red sweets and 16 yellow sweets.
      i   Write the ratio of yellow to red sweets.   (1 mark)
      ii What proportion of sweets are red?   (2 marks)

12 a An ordinary dice is rolled. List all the outcomes.   (1 mark)
   b Calculate the probability of these events.
      Give your answer as a fraction and as a percentage (1dp).
      i   'a prime number is rolled'   (2 marks)
      ii 'a score more than 3 but less than 5 is rolled'.   (2 marks)

13 A three-sided coloured spinner, with equal colour areas of red, blue and green
   is spun twice.
   a Record all the possible outcomes in a two-way table and a tree diagram. (6 marks)
   b Calculate the probability of the event 'red–green' in that order. (2 marks)
   c What is the probability of 'red–green' or 'green–red'?   (3 marks)

14 An ordinary drawing pin is tossed 100 times and the results for pin-up and
   pin-down are recorded, as shown; the experiment is repeated.

	Pin-up	Pin-down
Experiment A	65	35
Experiment B	71	29

   a Find the relative frequency for 'pin-up' in both experiments (to 1 dp). (2 marks)
   b Find the relative frequency for both experiments combined.   (1 mark)
   c What would you do to provide a better value for the relative frequency? (1 mark)

Mark scheme

Question 1 – 12 marks
- **a i** 2   start with 27 and + 4
- **ii** 2   start with 77 and − 10
- **b i** 2   multiply by 4 and + 23; $4n + 23$
- **ii** 2   multiply by -10 and + 87; $-10n + 87$
- **c i** 1   103
- **ii** 1   -113

Question 2 – 4 marks
- **a** 2   41, 37, 33, 29, 25, 21, 17
- **b** 2   1 litre; $T(11) = 45 − 44 = 1$

Question 3 – 9 marks
- **a** 2   45, 40, 35, 30, 25, 20, 15, 10, 5, 0
- **b** 3   start at 50 and − 5; multiply by -5 and + 50
- **c** 3 $T(n) = -5n + 50$ or $50 − 5n$; 1 mark for seeing $-5n$; 2 marks for $T(n) = 45 − 5n$;
- **d** 1   10 hours; accept when $n = 10$

Question 4 – 6 marks
- **a i** 1   5 faces, 5 vertices, 8 edges
- **ii** 1   5 faces, 6 vertices, 9 edges
- **iii** 1   6 faces, 8 vertices, 12 edges
- **b i** 1   square-based pyramid
- **ii** 1   (right-angled) triangular prism
- **iii** 1   cuboid (rectangular prism)

Question 5 – 8 marks
- **a** 2   Correct copy made of object; -1 mark for each error
- **b** 6   2 marks correct plan; 2 marks correct side elevation; 2 marks correct front elevation; accept follow through error in part 'a'

Question 6 – 9 marks
- **a i** 1   4 planes of reflection symmetry
- **ii** 1   1 plane of reflection symmetry
- **iii** 1   3 planes of reflection symmetry
- **b i** 2   correct net showing 5 faces
- **ii** 2   correct net showing 5 faces
- **iii** 2   correct net showing 6 faces

Question 7 – 12 marks
- **a i** 4   576cm^2 ; marks for 300, 180 or 96 seen
- **ii** 4   210cm^2 ; marks for 65, 25 or 60 seen
- **b i** 2   720cm^3 ; 1 mark for 48 × 15 seen
- **ii** 2   150cm^3 ; 1 mark for 30 × 15 seen

Question 8 – 4 marks
- **a** 2   1250g; 1 mark for 5 × 250g
- **b** 2   28.8 litres; 1 mark for 18/25 seen

Question 9 – 2 marks
- 2   0.1; 1 mark for 10/150 seen

Question 10 – 2 marks
- 2   12 : 5; 1 mark for 360 : 150

Question 11 – 7 marks
- **a** 2   0.46km; 1 mark for 46 000cm seen
- **b** 2   7.04m; 1 mark for 704cm seen
- **c i** 1   8 : 5; accept 16 : 10
- **ii** 2 $\frac{5}{13}$ or 0.38 or 38% ; mark for 10/26 seen

Question 12 – 5 marks
- **a** 1   1, 2, 3, 4, 5, 6
- **b i** 2 $\frac{1}{2}$, 50.0%
- **ii** 2 $\frac{1}{6}$, 16.7%

Question 13 – 11 marks
- **a** 6   3 marks for correct two-way table; 3 marks for correctly drawn tree-diagram
- **b** 2 $\frac{1}{9}$ or 0.11 or 11%;
- **c** 3 $\frac{2}{9}$ or 0.22 or 22%; 1 mark for evidence of $\frac{1}{9} + \frac{1}{9}$;

Question 14 – 4 marks
- **a** 2   65% Exp A; 71% Exp B; accept decimals and fractions
- **b** 1   68% or 0.68 or 136/200; accept 17/25
- **c** 1   carry out more experiments

17 Everyday maths

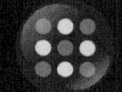

Learning outcomes

DF2 Select and use appropriate calculation strategies to solve increasingly complex problems (L6/7)

DF3 Use algebra to generalise the structure of arithmetic, including to formulate mathematical relationships (L6/7)

DF5 Move freely between different numerical, algebraic, graphical and diagrammatic representations [for example, equivalent fractions, fractions and decimals, and equations and graphs] (L6/7)

DF7 Use language and properties precisely to analyse numbers, algebraic expressions, 2D and 3D shapes, probability and statistics (L6/7)

RM2 Extend and formalise their knowledge of ratio and proportion in working with measures and geometry, and in formulating proportional relations algebraically (L6/7)

RM6 Interpret when the structure of a numerical problem requires additive, multiplicative or proportional reasoning (L6/7)

RM7 Explore what can and cannot be inferred in statistical and probabilistic settings, and begin to express their arguments formally (L6/7)

SP1 Develop their mathematical knowledge, in part through solving problems and evaluating the outcomes, including multi-step problems (L6/7)

SP2 Develop their use of formal mathematical knowledge to interpret and solve problems, including in financial mathematics (L6/7)

SP4 Select appropriate concepts, methods and techniques to apply to unfamiliar and non-routine problems (L6/7)

Introduction	Prior knowledge
The chapter consists of a sequence of five spreads based on the theme of a group of six British students travelling to Africa to help rebuild a school. This allows questions to cover a wide range of topics taken from algebra, statistics, geometry and number. The questions are word-based and often do not directly indicate what type of mathematics is involved. Therefore students will need to work to identify the relevant mathematics and in several instances which of a variety of methods to apply before commencing. This approach is rather different from the previous topic-based spreads and students may require additional support in this aspect of functional maths.	The chapter covers many topics, including lessons on rounding, charts, tabular data, bearings, scale drawings, mental and written multiplication and division, calculator skills, angles, measures, ratio and proportion, sequences, circle properties and formulae, tessellations, area, perimeter, combinations, probability and statistics, averages, metric measurements and conversions, problem solving.

Using mathematics

The student book start of chapter suggests three areas of everyday life where aspects of the ability to apply mathematical ideas prove highly valuable.

Fluency: Scale drawings based on careful measurements and 3D reasoning are used throughout building and engineering to plan projects. Many of the same ideas are used to produce graphics in computer games.

Mathematical reasoning: In the information age we are bombarded with statistics. Making sense of them requires understanding of the mathematics and the ability to reflect on what the statements might mean. Perhaps you will be asked to produce a report explaining some statistics.

Problem solving: Scientists use mathematics to describe and reason about the world around us.
By understanding how forces change on a scale model engineers can investigate the drag on a real car and using their real and mathematical models design it to be more fuel efficient.

Topic scheme

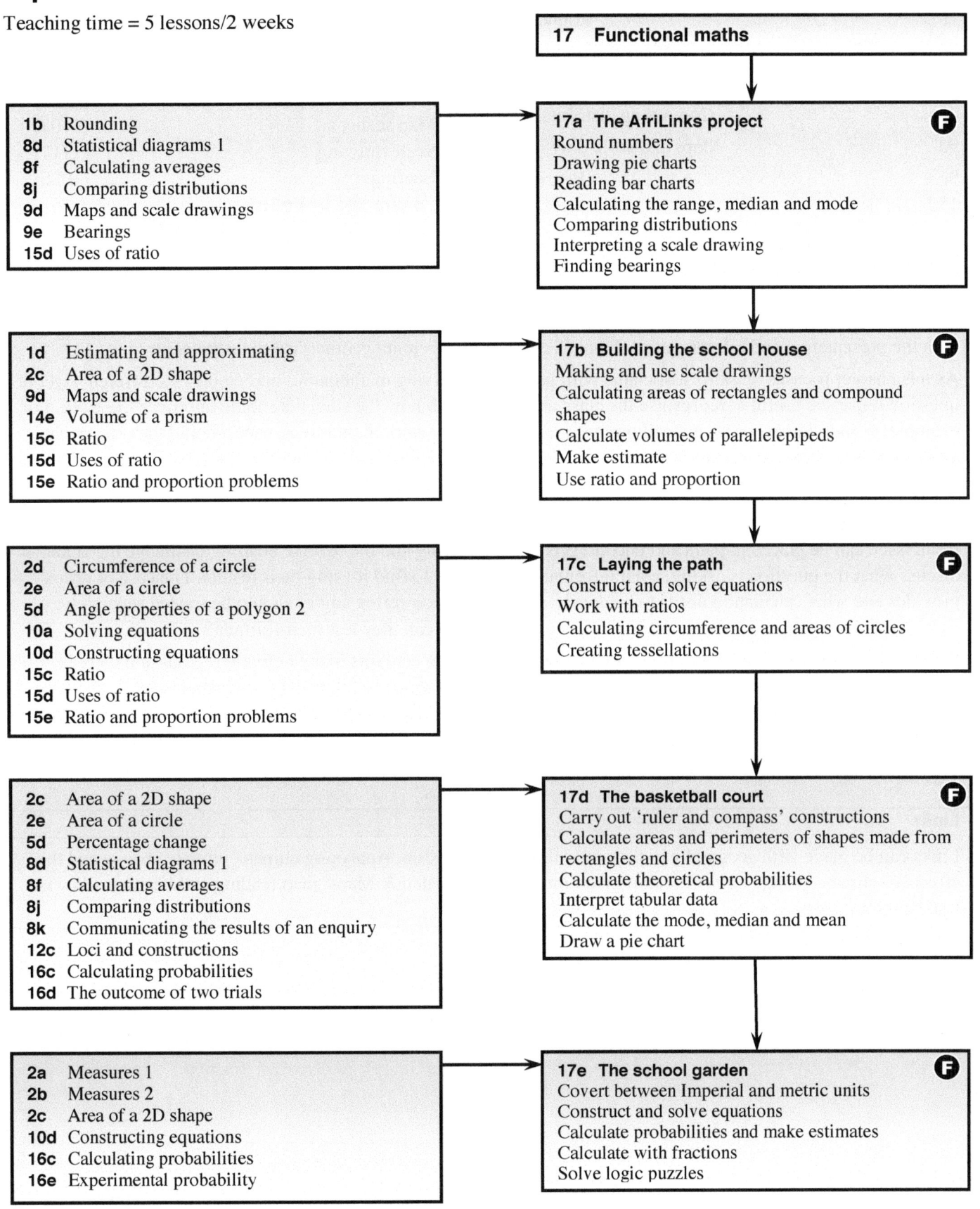

Teaching time = 5 lessons/2 weeks

17 Functional maths

1b Rounding **8d** Statistical diagrams 1 **8f** Calculating averages **8j** Comparing distributions **9d** Maps and scale drawings **9e** Bearings **15d** Uses of ratio	**17a The AfriLinks project** ⓕ Round numbers Drawing pie charts Reading bar charts Calculating the range, median and mode Comparing distributions Interpreting a scale drawing Finding bearings
1d Estimating and approximating **2c** Area of a 2D shape **9d** Maps and scale drawings **14e** Volume of a prism **15c** Ratio **15d** Uses of ratio **15e** Ratio and proportion problems	**17b Building the school house** ⓕ Making and use scale drawings Calculating areas of rectangles and compound shapes Calculate volumes of parallelepipeds Make estimate Use ratio and proportion
2d Circumference of a circle **2e** Area of a circle **5d** Angle properties of a polygon 2 **10a** Solving equations **10d** Constructing equations **15c** Ratio **15d** Uses of ratio **15e** Ratio and proportion problems	**17c Laying the path** ⓕ Construct and solve equations Work with ratios Calculating circumference and areas of circles Creating tessellations
2c Area of a 2D shape **2e** Area of a circle **5d** Percentage change **8d** Statistical diagrams 1 **8f** Calculating averages **8j** Comparing distributions **8k** Communicating the results of an enquiry **12c** Loci and constructions **16c** Calculating probabilities **16d** The outcome of two trials	**17d The basketball court** ⓕ Carry out 'ruler and compass' constructions Calculate areas and perimeters of shapes made from rectangles and circles Calculate theoretical probabilities Interpret tabular data Calculate the mode, median and mean Draw a pie chart
2a Measures 1 **2b** Measures 2 **2c** Area of a 2D shape **10d** Constructing equations **16c** Calculating probabilities **16e** Experimental probability	**17e The school garden** ⓕ Covert between Imperial and metric units Construct and solve equations Calculate probabilities and make estimates Calculate with fractions Solve logic puzzles

Introduction

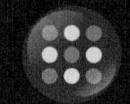

17a The AfriLinks project

Related lessons		Resources	
1b	Rounding	Decimal places	(1001)
8d	Statistical diagrams 1	Drawing pie charts	(1207)
8f	Calculating averages	Mean and mode	(1200)
8j	Comparing distributions	Median and range	(1203)
9d	Maps and scale drawings	Map scales	(1103)
9e	Bearings	Scale drawing	(1117)
15d	Uses of ratio	Bearings	(1086)
		Spare protractors and rulers	
		Local area map(s)	

Background

This lesson sets the scene for the chapter and is concerned with aspects of the 'Kangera' region's population, climate and geography (loosely based on the Kagera region of NW Tanzania). The mathematics is concerned with the presentation and interpretation of statistical data and accurate geometrical measurement.

As this chapter focuses on skills associated with using and applying mathematics and employs a different style of question it may be useful to reorganise the class and to establish how the students should approach the work. For example, as individuals, pairs or small groups, *etc.*, should they work at their own pace, should they start right away or will an introduction be given, *etc.*

Simplification	Extension
Weaker students or those for whom the language may be an issue can be placed in pairs and encouraged to discuss what the question is asking, what information it provides and what calculation needs to be done. The calculation of the angles in a pie chart can be treated as an exercise in dividing 360 in a given ratio. Provide simpler numbers so that students can focus on the method rather than the calculation.	In question **4** there is a relationship between the bearing and the reverse bearing; challenge the students to try to find it using their results. The case of reflex and non-reflex angles should be treated separately. How can they test their formula? Africa contains many climatic regions and there is great scope for carrying out comparative investigations. For example, how do the yearly patterns of rainfall compare across different regions of Africa, what are typical temperatures and temperatures ranges?

Links

Links can be made with geography in particular through this lesson. Analysing climate, climate change and the effects of climate change link particularly well into questions **2** and **3**. Maps, map reading and bearings likewise link well into question **4**.

Teaching notes

To set the context, put students into small groups and ask them to discuss how life might be different if they lived in equatorial Africa. What would the climate be like? How many young people versus old people would there be? How would they get to school? What would they eat and where would they get their food? Take feedback and explain how this lesson provides them with some of the information they need to answer these questions.

To make bearings and interpreting scales more real, have available a large map of your school and local area, perhaps projected on an IWB. Ask students to measure distances on the map and convert them into real life distances. Ask if the answers match with their expectations based on experience of the real distance. Review and revise their calculations as necessary.

Pick a point on the map and ask students to describe the journey to school in terms of approximate distances and directions, first using compass points and then using three-figure bearings. Check that students measure clockwise from North and quote three digits, adding leading zeros as required. Include examples where a protractor will need to be correctly used to measure the acute/obtuse/reflex angles.

Pose a question: given the bearing of A from B, what is the reverse bearing of B from A? Emphasise drawing a sketch with parallel north lines at A and B to encourage reasoning based on alternate angles. Encourage students to explain their approaches.

Exercise commentary

Question 1 – Ask, what is the total population? What fraction of the total population is aged 0 – 20 and what fraction of 360 is this? As a check of accurate drawing, test if the last sector is the size calculated.

Question 2 – Parts **a** and **b** can be done by eye whilst to do parts **c** and **d** it is advisable to make a list of the rainfalls and temperatures. In part **d**, the arithmetic is made easier by focusing on the temperatures above 20, that is, the mean = 20 + (3 + 2 + … + 2) ÷ 12.

Question 3 – It may help to plot the average rainfall and this year's rainfall on the same graph. Ask, how much more rain fell in the rainy season than on average? (As an absolute number and as a percentage).

Question 4 – Distance should be measured to ± 1 mm and angles to ± 1°. It is easiest to start by calculating the bearings of school from the various homes. For Michael, ask: why are bearings quoted using three digits? For Mary and Frieda, does subtracting the non-reflex angle from 360° give the same result as adding the acute/obtuse angle onto 180°? The reverse bearings should be done by calculation based on parallel lines; it is easiest to work through the people in reverse order.

Answers

1 a

Age group	0 – 20	21 – 40	41 – 60	60+
Rounded number	3500	3000	2500	1000
Angle	126°	108°	90°	36°

b Angles as per table

2 a 26 – 21 = 5° C **b** 279 – 37 = 242 mm
c 135 mm **d** $\frac{270}{12}$ = 22.5° C

3 a January had below average rainfall but March, April and May had significantly higher rainfall that the 30 year average.

b A lot of rain would saturate the ground causing it to become soft and unable to absorb more water. Further rain would then wash over the ground, possibly washing it away.

4

Name	Distance (km)	Bearing in ° from school to home	Bearing in ° from home to school
Albert	2.25	330°	150°
Constance	3.75	286°	106°
Michael	1.85	200°	020°
Mary	2.80	141°	321°
Frieda	3.20	045°	235°

The AfriLinks project

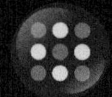

17b Building the schoolhouse

Related lessons		Resources	
1d	Estimating and approximating	Significant figures	(1005)
2c	Area of a 2D shape	Area of a parallelogram	(1108)
9d	Maps and scale drawings	Area of a trapezium	(1128)
14e	Volume of a prism	Map scales	(1103)
15c	Ratio	Scale drawing	(1117)
15d	Uses of ratio	Volume of cuboids	(1137)
15e	Ratio and proportion problems	Volume of prisms	(1139)
		Change as a percentage	(1302)
		Ratio dividing 2	(1039)
		Mini whiteboards	
		Squared paper	

Background

This lesson takes up the theme of rebuilding the school house. The mathematics involves drawing and interpreting scale drawings, calculating perimeters, areas and volumes and working with ratios.

It is possible that some students might have direct knowledge of aspects of building work, and their knowledge can be used to enliven discussion and provide alternative real life scenarios to discuss.

Simplification	Extension
Several of these questions are multifaceted and it may be appropriate to focus attention on fewer aspects. For example, in question **2** only part **a**, in question **3** only part **a** and in question **4** only parts **a** to **c**. Once these parts are succesfully completed students can go back to complete the remaining parts. Pairing students will allow them to discuss approaches and clarify what needs to be calculated.	In question **3** ask students to investigate the assumption of whether the trench lies inside, outside or centred on the perimeter of the school. How should corners be treated? Question **4** uses Pythagoras' theorem; ask students to investigate what this is and present their findings to the class.

Links

This lesson requires students to employ skills in visualization. It links well to Design and Technology among other subjects where working with scales is important in producing accurate drawings and models before producing full-sized products.

Students could also investigate the various techniques that architects and builders use to accurately estimate the amount of materials they will need for constructing their buildings.

314 Everyday maths AfriLinks

Teaching notes

One of the themes of this lesson is perimeters, areas and volumes. To test understanding, provide students with an L-shaped hexagon and ask them to calculate its perimeter and area.

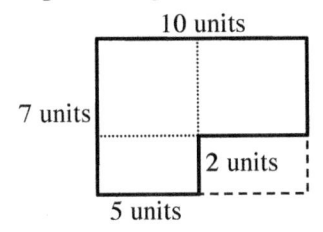

```
        10 units
       ┌─────────┐
7 units│         │
       │   ┌─────┘
       └───┤ 2 units
        5 units
```

Ask students to explain how they did the calculations and what alternative methods were used. Which missing sides need calculating? Is it better to divide the shape into two sub-areas or three? Are the two sub-areas unique? Can the calculation be done using a subtraction? Is the perimeter the same as for the 'bounding' dashed rectangle? If so why?

Discuss which methods the students found 'best'. Which method is easier to remember? Which is less likely to result in an error?

If the L-shape were the plan of a building 4 units high what would be its volume? Check for appropriate units.

Repeat the question but now give the L-shape 'awkward' dimensions and ask the students to estimate the perimeter and area. Discuss the strategies used to do the estimation.

Question 5 revolves around ratios. Test understanding using mini whiteboards. Ask students to simplify some ratios. Pose the questions like the following, if $a : 3 = 2 : 1$, what is a? (6) If $2 : b = 4 : 6$, what is b? (3) If $a : b = 1 : 2$ and $a + b = 9$, what are a and b?

Exercise commentary

Question 1 – Using squared paper will help with accuracy. Ask students how big the scale drawing will be before starting (14 cm × 7 cm).

Question 2 – In part **a** there are several ways to dissect the compound shape. Can students see more than one way? Does any method involve a subtraction? Which is the most efficient method? Does your answer change once you have read part **b**? In part **b** is it easier to subtract the area of the hall and corridor from the total or add up the areas of the classrooms?

Question 3 – This requires the perimeter of the school to be calculated. Does it make a difference if the trench lies inside, outside or centred on the boundary? How are corners treated?

Question 4 – Again using squared paper is likely to result in more accurate drawings. In part **b** suggest that $s^2 = h^2 + 4^2$ (Pythagoras' theorem). Do their measurements agree with this claim? How accurately can the students measure the lengths of the lines? How accurately does this mean they know the lengths in real life? (1 mm : 10 cm).

Question 5 – This exercises various aspects of ratio and proportion. In part **aiii** beware the reversed order of sand and cement.

Answers

1. Check students' drawing: should be 14 cm × 7 cm

2. a 320 m²   b Yes, area rooms 1 – 4 = 216 m²
   c $\frac{216}{320} = 67.5\% \approx 70\%$

3. a Perimeter = 96 m
      Volume = 96 × 0.8 × 0.4 = 30.72 m³ ≈ 31 m³
   b $1410

4. a Check students' drawings
   b i 2.8 m   ii 4.9 m
   c 8 × 3.5 + 0.5 × 8 × 2.8 = 39.2 m²
   d Assuming whole blocks 0.5 × 0.2 = 0.1 m²
      392 blocks required.
      Overestimated by 108 blocks.

5. a i Medium   ii Strong   iii Weak
   b 6 parts   c 300 kg sand, 60 kg cement

Building the schoolhouse

17c Laying the path

Related lessons		Resources	
2d	Circumference of a circle	Circumference of a circle	(1088)
2e	Area of a circle	Area of circles	(1083)
5d	Angle properties of a polygon 2	Sum of angles in a polygon	(1320)
10a	Solving equations	Simple equations	(1154)
10d	Constructing equations	Change as a percentage	(1302)
15c	Ratio	Map scales	(1103)
15d	Uses of ratio	Ratio dividing 2	(1039)
15e	Ratio and proportion problems		

Background

This lesson continues the building theme with an investigation of some of the issues associated with laying paving. The mathematics involved covers ratio and proportion, simple linear equations, areas and circumferences of circles and tessellations.

It is possible that your school grounds provides examples of tiling patterns or circular 'flower beds' The details of these could be substituted for those in the lesson to make the questions seem more real.

Simplification	Extension
Question **4** can be simplified by replacing the circular flower bed by a rectangular flower bed and posing the same questions. Pairing students will allow them to discuss approaches and clarify what needs to be calculated.	Tessellations provide many opportunities for further work. Students could investigate wall paper patterns and try to identify their various symmetries. The work of artists like MC Escher could provide the inspiration for interlocking tessellations based on adding and subtracting regions on a simple base shape. Students could also investigate which regular polygons will tessellate either singly in pairs or in triples.

Links

Practical applications of planning designs and calculating areas occur in both Art and Design. Students could be asked to investigate 'famous' tiling patterns such as those that occur in the Alhambra Palace in Spain. The website for the palace can be found at http://www.alhambradegranada.org/en/.

Everyday maths AfriLinks

Teaching notes

Question **1** provides a realistic scenario where the need for basic mathematics arises naturally. Use this as an opportunity to discuss other everyday situations where mathematics is used. Examples can be taken from this chapter, the students own lives, the work that their parents/guardians do *etc*. Try to impress upon them the idea that mathematics is all around and not just confined to the classroom.

Question **2** provides an opportunity to revise the construction and solution of linear equations. Pair students and ask one of them to pose a question of the form 'I think of a number, perform two operations (say, multiply by 3 and subtract 6) and the answer is X (say, 3). What is my original number?' The second student should then formulate this as an equation, $3n - 6 = 3$, and solve it. Once the solution is agreed, the students should then reverse roles. As a class, students should explain what they needed to do to write down their equation and how they went about solving it.

Question **5** and the **Extension** both relate to tessellations. This is a rich topic from which to initiate further investigations and a potential source of student generated display material for the classroom. Tessellations naturally involve symmetries and it can be a challenge to identify these. There are examples and a discussion of the symmetries of wall paper groups at http://en.wikipedia.org/wiki/Wallpaper_group

An alternative avenue of investigation is tessellations using regular polygons, where the key is the observation that the sum of the angles at a vertex must add to 360°. This limits the possibilities to those involving equilateral triangles, squares, hexagons, octagons and dodecagons (12 sides)

Exercise commentary

Question 1 – The question can be repeated using different ratios of yellow to red tiles to reinforce the underlying calculations. Can students find a formula for the number of red tiles?

Question 2 – In part **b** the equation is straightforward to solve using an informal balancing approach. The size of the numbers however may prove unsettling and a similar example with smaller numbers may prove reassuring. Part **c** can also be set up as an equation, $75t + 14 = 126.5$, but is more likely to be solved informally. Can the division $112.5 \div 75$ be done without a calculator? Try first doubling to $225 \div 150 = 9 \div 6 = 1.5$

Question 3 – If the path used 10, 20, n green slabs, how many red blocks would be needed?

Question 4 – Remind students that for a circle, $C = 2\pi r$ and $A = \pi r^2$. Check that they are correctly using these formulae and using the radius.

Question 5 – Part **a** should generate many possible solutions. Encourage a discussion of which patterns the students think are the same and why. Are there any patterns which stay the same under particular reflections, rotations or translations? For example, the famous herringbone pattern is symmetric under both horizontal and vertical translations and under 180° rotations

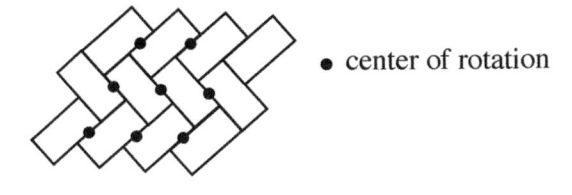

• center of rotation

Answers

1. **a** $1 : 6$
   b **i** No, $6 \times 24 = 144 > 142$ **ii** 2
2. **a** $3p + 16 = p + 166$ **b** $p = 75$
   c 1.5 kg
3. **a** 4   **b** $1 : 9$
4. **a** Total perimeter 35.80 m
      8 rolls
   b 4.2 m   **c** 59.09 m^2
5. **a** Many possibilities
   b **i** One row/diagonal can be slid past another to create infinitely many different patterns.
      ii Check students' diagrams
      iii Check students' diagrams
   c $n : m = 1 : 2$ **d** 128 cm

17d The basketball court

Related lessons		Resources	
2c	Area of a 2D shape	Area of a parallelogram	(1108)
2e	Area of a circle	Area of a trapezium	(1128)
5d	Percentage change	Area of circles	(1083)
8d	Statistical diagrams 1	Mean and mode	(1200)
8f	Calculating averages	Median and range	(1203)
8j	Comparing distributions	Drawing pie charts	(1207)
8k	Communicating the results of an enquiry	Listing outcomes	(1199)
12c	Loci and constructions	The OR rule	(1262)
16c	Calculating probabilities	Rope, sticks, a tape measure and chalk	
16d	The outcome of two trials	A bag and coloured cards	
		Spare drawing instruments	
		Table of results with scaffolding	

Background

This lesson has a loose focus around a game of basketball. The mathematics covered includes geometry, two-way tables and probabilities, understanding mathematical data and calculating and interpreting the three types of average and constructing a pie chart.

For added realism the school grounds may provide examples of sports pitches marked out in a similar fashion to the basketball court in question **1**. It may also be possible to use actual results for question **5** to **8**.

Simplification	Extension
For questions **5** and **6** provide a table of results but with extra scaffolding to aid in the calculations. For example, add an extra column at the end of the table to show the total number of games in which a particular number of baskets was scored. Add an extra row to show the total number of games scored. Show a calculation of how the mean number of baskets per game is calculated for Isaac. $$\text{mean} = \frac{1\times1+6\times3+3\times4+1\times5+4\times6}{1+6+3+1+4} = \frac{60}{15} = 4$$	Invite students to find statistics on, for example, the number of goals scored by various football teams during a season. Using this data, calculate the mode, median and mean number of goals scored by each team. Ask which average is most representative. How would you rank the teams based on the averages? Do the averages reflect the positions that the teams finished in their league? If not what other factors do they think might be important?

Links

There are some clear links in this spread to sports pitches and court dimensions. Students could investigate whether there are fixed dimensions for various pitches, e.g. a football pitch (no, but there are limits between what the length and width must be, and the internal markings are all standard) or a hockey pitch (yes).

http://en.wikipedia.org/wiki/Association_football_pitch

http://www.realbuzz.com/articles/hockey-pitch-dimensions/

Teaching notes

Question **1** provides an opportunity for practical geometry that has echoes of the fabled rope stretchers of ancient Egypt. Groups of students could be challenged to do various standard constructions – triangles, bisectors, circles *etc*. – using a taut rope as a ruler or as a pair of compasses. If this was done on the school playground, chalk could be used to mark out the diagrams.

The mathematics involved in question **4** can be illustrated using a bag containing coloured cards of two basic shapes. By varying the colours and types of cards in the bag, students' intuition about how likely various combinations are can be developed before it is formalized by counting combinations in a two-way table.

Questions **5** and **6** involve interpreting a table of raw results. This may prove a little overwhelming and it may be advisable to discuss the questions as a whole class, calculating partial results together before leaving the students, perhaps in groups, to complete the analysis.

After the students have calculated one further mode and mean, discuss the results that students have found and identify any mistakes before encouraging students to complete the calculations.

Exercise commentary

Question 1 – Ask students how they would mark out the whole basketball court using the rope, sticks and tape measure. Remind students that a taut rope provides a ruler and if one end is fixed a pair of compasses.

Question 2 – Given π = 3.14 would it make sense to give the answer to more than 3 significant figures? Is accuracy to 2 decimal places sensible?

Question 3 – Remind students to add the 10%. This could be extended to include the 'D' shaped arcs.

Question 4 – If ten shirts and ten pairs of shorts of each colour were placed in a bag, what is the probability of picking out a green shirt? And for a green shirt and blue or green shorts?

Question 5 – Encourage students to work in pairs and to agree what needs to be found and how before starting this question and the next.

Question 6 – Can students construct data sets where one or more of the mode, median or mean is not representative of the data?

Question 7 – Remind students that the mean is the total number of baskets scored over the total number of games played.

Question 8 – A similar graph for Veronica or Maxine will involve awkward angles.

Answers

1. **a** To draw a (semi)circle: tie two pegs to the ends of a piece of rope of length the desired radius, fix one peg at the centre of the circle and pulling the rope taut use the other peg to mark out the circumference.

2. **a** 401.625 m^2 = 402 m^2 (3 sf)
   b 12 + 18π = 68.52 = 68.5 m^2 (3 sf)

3. perimeter = 82.5 m, + 10% = 90.75 m, 5 rolls

4. **a** 4 × 3 = 12 combinations

	Shirt colour			
	Green	Blue	Red	Brown
Shorts colour — Blue	Green + blue	Blue + blue	Red + blue	Brown + blue
Shorts colour — Green	Green + green	Blue + green	Red + green	Brown + green
Shorts colour — Red	Green + red	Blue + red	Red + red	Brown + red

   b ¼ = 0.25

5. **a** Imran **b** 4

6. **a**

	Isaac	Imran	Veronica	Jacob	Oilolay	Maxine
Mode	3	4	2, 4	4	4	7
Median	4	4	3	4	3.5	7
Mean	4	5	3	4.5	2.5	6

   The mean gives the best idea of a students' performance. The mode and median identify the best player but are not good at separating the other players.

   b Maxine, Imran, Jacob, Isaac, Veronica, Oilolay

7. 60 + 3 × 4 = 72

8. Check students' pie charts.

The basketball court 319

17e The school garden

Related lessons		Resources	
2a	Measures 1	Imperial measures	(1191)
2b	Measures 2	The OR rule	(1262)
2c	Area of a 2D shape	Relative frequency	(1211)
10d	Constructing equations	Experimental probability	(1264)
16c	Calculating probabilities	Metric conversion	(1061)
16e	Experimental probability	Converting measures	(1091)

Background

This lesson uses activities associated with gardening to allow a diverse variety of mathematics to be covered. This includes: metric–imperial conversions, constructing and solving simultaneous equations, probability, area and perimeter and using systematic approaches to problem solving.

Simplification	Extension
There is a large varietey of material in this lesson, some of which is quite challenging. Initially encourage students to choose those questions that they are most confident about in order to build up their confidence before tackling the questions that they see as harder. Working in pairs or small groups is also likely to be beneficial in terms of generating ideas and sharing the work load.	Ask pairs of students to make their own balance problem like that in question **2** which they must be able to solve. Then swap problems with another pair and see who gets the correct answer first. Alternatively ask pairs of students to create a conundrum like question **5**, which can be solved by temporarily adding in an extra goat.

Links

Question **1** links well with Food Technology where there is an emphasis on mixing ingredients together in the correct ratios in order for recipes to be made (and so the food tastes good!) There are also links to gardening and practical outdoor mathematics. If your school is fortunate to have good outdoor facilities, these tasks can be linked to the projects run by the school to take advantage of the facilities (e.g. a kitchen garden, or an area for animals to live).

Everyday maths   AfriLinks

Teaching notes

Students may need reminding why knowing about metric-imperial conversions is useful. Ask them for examples of when non-metric units are commonly encountered. For example, British roads use miles, people often quote heights in feet and inches and weights in stones and pounds, pints and gallons are still commonly encountered units of capacity, newspapers often quote temperatures in Fahrenheit rather than Centigrade (for impact), *etc*.

The simultaneous equations required to solve question **2** is new material and will require whole class discussion. Various approaches are possible: a version of trial-and-improvement, elimination of a variable by 'subtraction' or direct substitution, finding the crossing point of the straight-line graphs. Pose a simpler two-variable problem involving smaller numbers and invite students to suggest ways of solving the equations. Guide them towards a correct method that will work in the case of the question. Test their understanding on a second straightforward pair of equations. Finally ask how they would solve a third equation involving a third variable; agree that this can be done by substituting in the known values of two of the variables and solving the resulting one-variable equation. A fuller discussion and examples can be found in *MyMaths for Keys Stage 3* book **9C** lessons **10b-e**.

Question **3** part **c** reverses the estimation of probabilities that the students have previously encountered. Ask, if you tossed a coin 100 times how often would you expect it to come up heads? Suppose the coin was biased so that P(heads) = 0.75, how many heads would you now expect?

Exercise commentary

Question 1 – The conversions require divisions. Ask how you can check the answers: convert back using multiplication.

Question 2 – This is a difficult multistep question and it may help to discuss as a class possible strategies. Algebraically,
(1) $3s + 2c = 79$, (2) $s + 3c = 52$ and
(3) $2s + 4c + I = 79$. Solving for s and c would allow I to be found from (3). Recommend eliminating s via, $3(2) - (1)$: $7c = 77$. Check by back substitution.

Question 3 – Ask what does 'at random' mean? In part **b**, how is P(not chilli) related to P(chilli)? For part **c**, prompt by asking how many times 6 would come up if a regular dice were rolled 60 times. Are the ratios of the expected number of plants equal to the ratios of the number of seeds? (yes)

Question 4 – Suggest students begin by calculating the perimeter of the pen and experiment with various lengths of side to see which rectangle gives the largest area (a square, side 5 m). Which panel has to be put with the 4 m panel? Must the 0.5/1.5/2.5 m panels occur in pairs?

Question 5 – Part **c** is likely to cause most difficulty. Ensure that students know what would happen if there were only 11 goats and why this is a problem.

Answers

1   **a** $15\frac{5}{9}$ lbs   **b** $6\frac{2}{3}$ lbs   **c**   20 oz
    d   3.5 pints = 3.5 × 0.6 litres = 2.1 litres
    e   Yes   **f**   28"
2   **a**   soil 19 kg   **b**   compost 11 kg   **c**   Imran 53 kg
3   **a** $\frac{6}{36} = \frac{1}{6}$ **b** $\frac{24}{36} = \frac{2}{3}$
    c   20 onions, 25 tomatoes, 15 peppers, 30 chillies
4   Biggest area = 25 m²; 4 + 1, 3 + 2, 2 + 1.5 + 1.5, 2.5 + 2 + 0.5
5   **a**   6, 4, 1   **b**   12 − (6 + 4 + 1) = 1
    c   The original allocation is in the ratio 6 : 4 : 1 : 1 where the last amount is a remainder. Using the trick the allocation is 6 : 4 : 1 : 0 with no remainder. In effect the remainder 11/12 is divided as 6/12, 4/12 and 1/12 to give integer allocations.

The school garden

Notes

Notes